W9-CDI-721

Mastering the SAP® Business Information Warehouse

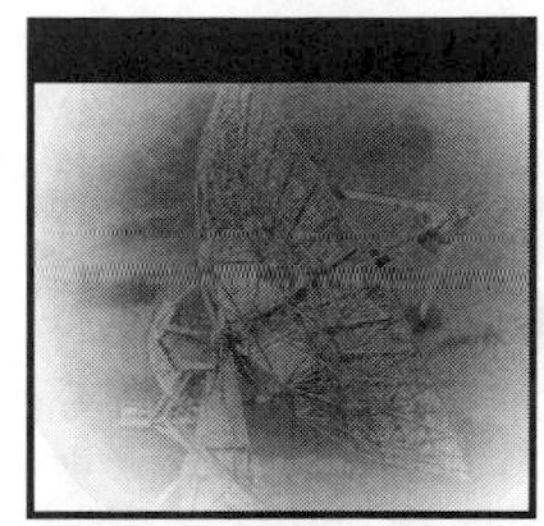

Mastering the SAP® Business Information Warehouse

Kevin McDonald
Andreas Wilmsmeier
David C. Dixon
W.H. Inmon

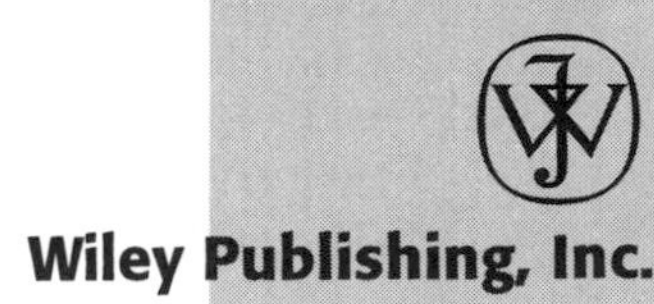

Wiley Publishing, Inc.

Publisher: Robert Ipsen
Executive Editor: Robert M. Elliott
Assistant Editor: Emilie Herman
Managing Editor: John Atkins
New Media Editor: Brian Snapp
Text Design & Composition: John Wiley Composition Services

This book is printed on acid-free paper. ♾

Published by Wiley Publishing, Inc.

Published simultaneously in Canada.

Wiley also publishes its books in a variety of electronic formats. Some content that appears in print may not be available in electronic books.

Library of Congress Cataloging-in-Publication Data:

Mastering the SAP business information warehouse / Kevin McDonald ...
[et al.].
p. cm.
Includes bibliographical references and index.
ISBN 0-471-21971-1
1. SAP Business information warehouse. 2. Data warehousing. 3.
Management information systems. 4. Business—Computer programs. I.
McDonald, Kevin, 1969-
HF5548.4.B875 M37 2002
650'.0285'5785—dc21

2002008736

Printed in the United States of America.

10 9 8 7 6 5 4 3 2 1

Advance Praise for *Mastering the SAP Business Information Warehouse*

"This book is insightful, educational, and thought provoking for even the most seasoned SAP BI individual. The authors did an excellent job of incorporating historical business warehousing into an up-to-date guide to SAP BW and business intelligence that will be very valuable to readers for years to come."

Richard M. Dunning
Chair, American SAP Users Group and BW-BI & Analytics Interest Group

"Kevin McDonald and his team of experts know more about SAP's Business Intelligence offerings than anyone else—including SAP. This book demonstrates their expertise clearly and precisely. It is a must-have for anyone initiating a BW implementation."

Claudia Imhoff
Co-author of Corporate Information Factory, 2nd Edition; Building the Customer-Centric Enterprise; *and* Exploration Warehousing *(Wiley)*
President, Intelligent Solutions, Inc.

"SAP BW is today an essential part of any SAP implementation, as it is becoming the leading Business Intelligence suite in the world. *Mastering the SAP Business Information Warehouse* provides a deep understanding of BW's core capabilities, and serves as a great head start in the development of new collaborative and predictive solutions for your enterprise."

Shai Agassi
Executive Board Member, Collaborative Solutions Group, SAP AG

"This book is an excellent guide to traversing SAP terminology and provides comprehensive coverage of the Business Intelligence solution, which is critical for every SAP customer."

Mark A. Smith
President, Full Circle Strategies and x-CMO of SAP Portals

"*Mastering the SAP Business Information Warehouse* provides a comprehensive, cradle-to-grave review of the most important aspects of the design, development, and implementation of the SAP BW. The authors have combined years of data warehousing and SAP BW experience into an effective mix of theory and practical applications. This is an excellent handbook for project members involved in the implementation of SAP business intelligence solutions such as SAP BW or mySAP."

Catherine M. Roze
Author of SAP BW Certification: A Business Information Warehouse Study Guide *(Wiley)*
IBM and SAP BW Certified Consultant

"It would be hard to imagine a more complete guide to SAP BW for administrators, programmers, and users. The authors know the territory well, and have produced a valuable reference work. But more than this, the authors are able to weave in the story of the history and evolution of BW from Hasso Plattner's mandate to create a 'reporting server' to BW's current state as a platform for business intelligence and analytic applications."

Henry Morris
VP for Applications and Information Access, IDC

"Along the lines of the information supply chain, this book lays out the options the SAP Business Information Warehouse provides to build collaborative, closed-loop Analytic Applications based upon the Business Content building blocks."

Dr. Wolfgang Martin
META Group Research Fellow

For

Julia

Rita, Theresa, and Arne

Karl, Noriko, and Danjiro

Contents

Foreword

Today's challenging business environment calls for an enterprise data warehouse approach that integrates and standardizes information from within the enterprise and from outside the enterprise, and it serves as an information hub for internal and external information consumers. In 1997 SAP started developing its own enterprise data warehouse solution, the SAP Business Information Warehouse. Five years later, the 3.0B release of the SAP BW™ software not only provides a mature, end-to-end data warehouse technology, it also serves as a cornerstone of the mySAP™ Business Intelligence solution.

SAP Business Information Warehouse now plays a central role in nearly every solution brought to market by SAP. SAP BW enables customers to accurately forecast and strategically analyze information for better customer service, optimized business operations, and improved corporate performance. By applying analytics solutions and innovative technologies such as Enterprise Portal ™ across the enterprise, SAP customers may realize maximum benefits as quickly as possible. Whether the software component is CRM, APO, or SEM, they rely on SAP BW as an information hub and platform for analytics.

The writing and publishing of this book reflects the success of and the growing interest in the SAP Business Information Warehouse. Thousands of customers are already using the software in productive applications—sourcing data from SAP R/3™ and non SAP R/3 systems, some with thousands of users and terabyte-sized databases.

With the release of SAP BW 3.0™, there was a vacuum for an independent guide to understanding the SAP Business Information Warehouse. *Mastering the SAP Business Information Warehouse* links theoretical data warehouse concepts to customer requirements, and offers a guide for implementing the solutions. It speaks to data warehousing specialists as well as those that have implemented ERP. The authors of this book all have longterm experience in data warehousing, reporting, and analytic applications.

Their perspective on SAP BW comes from years of implementing the product and working with our development teams on enhancing the offering.

Integral to the success of any data warehouse is the availability of resources and guides that describe how to successfully deploy professional solutions. You need this information from people who have been in the trenches, who have implemented successful data warehouses, and who can speak from experience, not simply theory. This book provides you with the best of three worlds: an understanding of data warehousing, application of these concepts to the SAP BW, and the authors' own expertise in deploying the solutions.

So sit back, enjoy this book from cover to cover, and use it as a reference guide for your SAP BW implementation.

Dr. Heinz Haefner
Vice President SAP BW Development
SAP AG, Walldorf

Acknowledgments

First, we would like to thank Bob Elliott and Emilie Herman of Wiley for their guidance and patience through the authoring process and for providing us the opportunity to share what we have learned about SAP® in this book. The copyediting team at Wiley has helped create a common voice and a consistency throughout the chapters that we may not have been able to accomplish on our own. We would also like to thank our coauthor Bill Inmon, who joined the authoring team shortly after the project started. He provided the needed stimulus to take the project through to completion.

Writing a book about a software component that has hundreds of people dedicated to evolving the product as quickly as possible presented an interesting challenge. There were many individuals and teams at SAP AG, SAP Portals, SAP America, and SAP International that provided invaluable feedback and support without which this book may never have happened. The list below does not come close to acknowledging all the people who supported us in our lives, careers, and on this project.

A special thank you goes to Klaus Kreplin, Dr. Werner Sinzig, and Lothar Kallweit for their guidance and mentoring through the years. The SAP BW™ development and product management teams, namely Heinz Häfner, Lothar Henkes, Claudia Weller, Gunther Rothermel, and from the marketing department, Sabine Eggl, provided great support in straightening out the SAP BW architecture sections in the book. We'd also like to thank Mark A. Smith for his eleventh-hour briefing on the SAP Business Intelligence Solution and his insight over the years as we have often debated the future of the industry. Naeem Hashmi and Claudia Imhoff both lent an empathetic ear and helped contemplate key decisions, notably to write or not to write a book.

Countless discussions on information modeling, data extraction, and staging with Rainer Höltke and Christian Dressler from the SAP BW development team as well as Jürgen Habermeier have evolved our thinking on these subjects. The SAP BW Regional Implementation Groups (RIGs) have rounded out our thoughts in several areas related to system administration. Much appreciation goes specifically to Joachim Mette and his keen scrutiny during review and Rudolph Hennecke for his meaningful ideas and insightful thoughts. They have somehow found the time to discuss product plans, review our outline, and provide invaluable feedback. Thanks to Lonnie Luehmann of Nike for his meticulous attention to detail and helpful comments.

Many thanks go to Jürgen Hagedorn for his advice and candid commentary on the future of analytic applications, Marcus Dill for his feedback and enthusiastic support, and Armin Elbert for his contributions to our book discussions. Also, thank you to Albrecht Ricken of Quandian and Colin Bailey for lending their expertise and suggestions for improving the analytic applications chapter in the book. Stefan Sigg, Guido Schröder, Falko Schneider, and Andreas Wesselmann, thank you all for your input, candid feedback, and understanding. Your development on the Business Explorer is deserving of a book of its own.

Since the release of SAP BW in 1998, Klaus Majenz has always provided invaluable insight into planning for and managing performance. He, Thomas Zurek, Alex Peter, Thomas Becker, and Uwe Heinz supported us throughout the authoring process.

A very special thank you to Julia McDonald for her patience and understanding throughout yet another project, to a good friend and colleague, Bryan Katis, for the many years of knowledge sharing, collaboration, and valued support, and to Rita, Theresa, and Arne Holverscheid for their support and patience throughout the authoring process. The COMPENDIT team, specifically Stefan Krauskopf, Mohammad Mazhar, Bahram Assadollahzadeh, Jens Koerner, Rob Valcich, and those team members who help us research 3.0 topics, thank you all.

A final thanks to you the readers and organizations that have opted to implement SAP BW as part of a business intelligence solution.

About the Authors

Kevin McDonald is a cofounder and the CEO of COMPENDIT, Inc., a leading business intelligence consulting services firm that was named in *Entrepreneur* magazine's "Hot 100" listing of America's fastest-growing new businesses. He has instructed, implemented, and designed mission-critical client/server transaction processing systems and enterprise decision-support systems for dozens of clients. Prior to cofounding COMPENDIT in 1999, Kevin was the Director of New Dimension Technology and a corporate spokesperson for SAP, where he had worked since 1993 in both America and Germany. He was Program Manager during the successful market launch of SAP Business Information Warehouse (SAP BW), and he authored the SAP BW product map that was first used to define the scope and development direction for the software component.

Kevin started his career at Baxter Healthcare, where he held positions in both IT and Finance functions. He has authored numerous articles about SAP's Business Intelligence Solution for The Data Warehouse Institute's newsletter, and he has made presentations on business intelligence at DCI's Data Warehouse World, HP World, ERP World, TDWI conferences, ASUG, SAP TechEd, SAP Sapphire, Informix User Conference, Decision Processing 98 and 99, and Informatica World. Kevin may be contacted at kevin.mcdonald@compendit.com.

Andreas Wilmsmeier is a managing director of COMPENDIT Deutschland. Andreas has been a member of the initial SAP BW core development team, where he has been responsible for designing and implementing parts of the Staging Engine (e.g., the Staging BAPI). Andreas has been consulting SAP BW clients since the initial first customer shipment of SAP BW 1.2A in early 1998 and has continued to contribute to the development of SAP BW by providing feedback from the field.

After receiving his diploma in computer science and business economics, Andreas started his career in developing data warehouse and Internet solutions. Prior to joining COMPENDIT, Andreas developed and managed the Business Intelligence line of business at a German consulting company.

His knowledge of data warehousing, data mining, and knowledge management has been showcased at numerous international conferences, including SAP Sapphire, SAP TechEd, ASUG, Cebit in Hanover, Germany, and Systems in Munich, Germany. Andreas has authored articles in the SAP Technical Journal, now featured on intelligentERP.com and the German language *E/3 Magazine*. Andreas may be contacted at andreas.wilmsmeier@compendit.com.

David C. Dixon is a Director of Business Intelligence at COMPENDIT, Inc. David started his career in 1995 as a financials and controlling (FI/CO) consultant with SAP, specializing in all of the SAP reporting and analysis applications and tools. Prior to joining COMPENDIT as a founding team member, David was a Platinum Consultant with SAP.

David has worked with SAP's SEM development team on numerous occasions in support of Business Consolidations and Business Planning and Simulation. He has extensive project experience in implementing complicated global solutions for Fortune 100 companies. David has presented at various SAP BW forums such as SAP TechEd and ASUG. He may be contacted at david.dixon@compendit.com.

Bill Inmon is thought of as the "father of the data warehouse" and is co-creator of the "corporate information factory." He has over 28 years of experience in database technology management and data warehouse design. He is known globally for his seminars on developing data warehouses and has been a keynote speaker for every major computing association and many industry conferences, seminars, and trade shows. As an author, Bill has written about a variety of topics on building, usage, and maintenance of the data warehouse and the corporate information factory. More than 500 of his articles have been published in major computer journals such as *Datamation*, *ComputerWorld*, and *Byte* magazine. Bill is currently a columnist with *Data Management Review*, and has been since its inception. He has published 39 books.

Bill founded and took public a Silicon Valley company, Prism Solutions, in 1991. Prism Solutions became Ardent Software, which was recently acquired by Informix, and subsequently renamed Ascential Software. Most recently (1999) Bill decided to publish his vast data warehousing information resources on his Web site at www.billinmon.com. The Web site has now grown to support millions of visitors a month. Bill consults with a large number of Fortune 1000 clients, offering data warehouse design and database management services. Recently Bill collaborated with Claudia Imhoff and others to develop the corporate information factory.

Introduction

The enterprise resource planning (ERP) and data warehousing industries have evolved in parallel over the past decade. Now these two trends are finally converging. More and more corporations have successfully implemented SAP® or another ERP package as a transaction-processing solution. These organizations may have started their projects in isolated divisions, but over the past several years, larger portions of the business are being run on ERP software.

While we have seen only a few IT shops that rely exclusively on SAP software, the percentage of online transaction processing that is conducted via SAP software has steadily increased. We see many organizations adopting IT philosophies that have SAP software as the default solution. It is not uncommon to hear a CFO comment, "You better have a very good reason not to use the SAP software we already paid for." These organizations have moved beyond automating and integrating business processes and now wish to optimize their business performance, reduce the slack in their supply chains, and realize the potential value of their customer relationships.

Parallel to the ERP and business process reengineering evolution was the evolution of informational processing, now commonly referred to as business intelligence. The explosive growth in data captured by organizations, in part due to the rapid adoption of the Internet, has made available an increasing amount of business information. This, combined with the increased pace in the way business is conducted, has created significant demand for efficient decision-making processes. The data warehouse was conceived to enable such processes.

SAP has brought to market software that has created a tremendous opportunity for organizations to lay a common foundation for both the transaction-processing application and the decision-processing applications. Organizations that have implemented SAP as an ERP solution may find themselves able to bypass their competition by quickly deploying closed-loop analytic applications and Enterprise Portals that are not only technically integrated with their transaction processing systems but also integrated from a business perspective. The SAP Business Intelligence Solution, which includes an Enterprise Portal™ with Knowledge Management and SAP Business Information Warehouse (SAP BW™), not only establishes a new benchmark for business intelligence solutions but also creates, when implemented in conjunction with the mySAP® solutions, a new benchmark for enterprise computing.

We have often stated that the decision to use SAP BW is less a matter of volume of data that is found in SAP software versus that found in non-SAP systems than of the volume and potency of the meta data found in an organization. Regardless of the role SAP BW is to play in your organization, there are several steps you may take to ensure that you are getting the most out of your SAP data while leveraging the processes, people, and products you already employ.

Why did we write this book? First, many books on SAP focus on step-by-step instructions for accomplishing a given configuration task and spoon-feed readers with checklists, transaction codes, and code samples. Our goal was to bridge the gap between these low-level books and the high-level books that focus on data warehousing architecture but do not necessarily explain how the SAP BW software may be used to realize such architecture. Furthermore, a goal was to expose the various implementation options available in the SAP BW component and to explore the fundamental architecture and concepts in order to enable readers to understand and use these options. We have included how-to guides on the accompanying Web site that address some of the options in a step-by-step manner.

Our hope is that this book will inspire readers to implement these options in order to strategically analyze information and accurately forecast optimized operations, better customer service, and improved bottom-line performance. Much like the SAP R/3® product, the SAP BW 3.0 version is approaching a richness in functionality that will soon extend beyond the capacity of any one person in the world, not even among its creators, to know in detail every option available in the software and the potential consequences that implementing one option may have on another. The product's maturity, combined with the fact that the SAP BW component is now part of nearly every solution sold by SAP, compelled us to share our knowledge from years of developing and implementing the SAP BW and put our experience in writing for the data warehousing industry.

We have taken the approach that technology is there to serve business and have attempted to counterbalance technical sections with commentary on how a particular option may be used to drive business value.

As the lines between transaction processing and decision processing blur and the unification of these system and Web services becomes dynamic, and with the adoption of Enterprise Portals, organizations implementing SAP will search for ways to get the most out of their SAP data. *Mastering SAP Business Information Warehouse* looks at options for designing, building, deploying, populating, accessing, analyzing, presenting, and administering the data and information in the SAP BW component. This book is our contribution to accelerating the search actionable information.

Who Should Read This Book

In our experience, most SAP BW implementations are deployed in organizations that have implemented SAP as an ERP solution. As such, we assume that you, the SAP BW project team member, are familiar with SAP, although you may not be as familiar with data warehousing and business intelligence. We have included a list of other resources that offer more in-depth background on these subjects on the accompanying Web site for this book (www.wiley.com/compbooks/mcdonald).

Business and IT professionals of large organizations who are considering implementing any of the mySAP Solutions will also find this book useful, as SAP BW is included as a component in nearly every SAP business solution that is sold.

How This Book Is Organized

This book may be thought of as consisting of four parts, meant to reflect the process an organization goes through during an implementation of the software.

We begin with an introduction to business intelligence and the SAP BW architecture, which is meant to provide a backdrop for readers that may come from more of an SAP ERP implementation background than a data warehousing background. Chapter 1 is an introduction to business intelligence and how enterprises tackled challenges such as:

- Extracting data form online transaction processing systems
- Eliminating poor data quality
- Structuring data in such a way that history may be recorded and recalled

From these needs arose the idea of combining both traditional data with documents to offer organizations a collaborative platform for analyzing information and optimizing business performance. Today this is called business intelligence.

While data warehousing and analytic applications are not new, the toolsets available to realize them are—relatively speaking. We have entered into a time where technical integration is a worry of the past and semantic integration is at the forefront. The recent introduction of Enterprise Portals has enabled dynamic closed-loop analytical processing. In Chapter 1, we examine SAP's flagship enterprise resource planning package. You will quickly see what SAP realized around 1996: ERP systems are not designed for analytical processing. We explain the challenges of reporting and analyzing data in the ERP system.

Readers who are familiar with data warehousing, the evolution of SAP, and information processing may wish to start reading the book at Chapter 2, where we discuss the SAP BW component and how it fits into the SAP Business Intelligence Solution that includes Enterprise Portal. There we define the major architectural components of the SAP BI Solution and set the stage for the services found in SAP BW. From the SAP production data extractors to the analysis of information via a Web browser, readers will start to understand the breadth and depth of functionality in the SAP BW in Chapter 3. We also map the SAP BW to the corporate information factory (CIF). You will quickly see the characteristics SAP BW has in common with non-SAP data warehousing platforms, as well as the unique features found in SAP BW.

The second part focuses on the business content and the options available to information modelers as they work to deliver value from the data stored in SAP BW. Chapter 4 explains the information model and how this collection of meta data objects, which describes business processes, business objects, information containers, and their mutual relationships, as well as the scope, granularity, and semantics of the information available in the data warehouse system, is an important part of a proper deployment of SAP BW. We also comment on the design of an information flow model, or the flow of information from the originating systems through a possibly multistaged data warehouse system landscape to an information consumer that might be an end user, an analyst, or another system utilizing the information provided to control a specific decision or business process (closed-loop approach).

Chapter 5 defines business content and its application. We use the analogy of building blocks to help describe Business Content, in the sense that Business Content includes the extraction for data sources, transformation of that data, storage in a schema, and the queries and applications that access and present the information. These building blocks are foundational to analytic applications. Business Content meta data can also be mapped to architectural components of the CIF. You will see how Business Content has grown horizontally and vertically in scope. The usability of Business Content is assessed and the challenges to its growth critiqued. We end the chapter by presenting three subject area scenarios in Business Content linking the information models to information modeling concepts introduced in Chapter 4.

The third section focuses on the services available in the SAP BW used to realize such an information model (Chapters 6 to 8). These include:

- Extraction, transfer, and loading (ETL) services
- Data storage services
- Information access, analysis, and presentation services

Chapter 6 leads readers through identifying the SAP sources of data, extracting data from these sources, applying the transformations required, and storing the transformed data in a way that best supports reporting and analysis. In other words, this chapter presents the functionality provided by the ETL services layer of the SAP BW architecture. This is often the most time-consuming part of building a data warehouse solution. In the CIF framework this is referred to as *sourcing* and *manufacturing* of data and information. The options described in Chapter 6 will enable readers to take an information model and instantiate it in the SAP BW software.

In Chapter 6, we describe how to integrate and transform data so it may be stored in the various SAP BW storage constructs such as ODS Objects, InfoCubes, and Master Data. Chapter 7 picks up the information logistics process where Chapter 6 left off and highlights the main services provided in SAP BW that retrieve data, turn it into meaningful business information, and deliver it to an information consumer. The chapter has been organized in two main sections: SAP BW Information access and analysis services and SAP BW presentation services. The Business Explorer suite of tools, including BEx Designer, BEx Analyzer, BEx Formatted Reporting, BEx Mobile, and BEx Web Application Designer, are described. We also have included a section on the application programming interfaces (APIs) options, with which custom applications or third-party tools may interface.

The SAP BW is a platform for building analytic applications. The architecture of an analytic application is detailed in Chapter 8. Readers will see three different examples of analytic applications and how they each interact with SAP BW. The three analytic applications covered are customer relationship analytics supported by mySAP Customer Relationship Management (mySAP CRM), supply chain analytics supported by mySAP Supply Chain Management (mySAP SCM), and Corporate Performance Measurement supported by mySAP Financials.

The last section focuses on the administration and performance options for the software component (Chapters 9 and 10). In this section of the book, SAP BW administration tasks—both process-oriented tasks and system-oriented tasks—are described. Process-oriented tasks consist of application processes such as scheduling, monitoring, and troubleshooting of data loads, as well as archiving. System-oriented tasks consist of security measures, transports, and upgrades. There are many different application processes besides data loading, such as index maintenance, building aggregates, and batch scheduling of reporting jobs. All these application processes can have complex dependencies. The SAP BW technology process chains are covered in detail.

SAP BW security is explained from a design perspective, detailing the decisions to make when building authorizations, such as making them user-based versus role-based or object-centric versus data-centric. We continue the administration section by describing the options in the SAP BW transport system with specific attention on the transportation of meta data from a development system to quality assurance and production. We end Chapter 9 looking at the considerations for a multilayered application environment when performing an upgrade.

From an end user's perspective, the data warehouse is only as good as the last query. Performance should be carefully planned and given constant attention. However, because of the discontinuous, unpredictable user behavior characteristic of an information consumer, this may prove to be a challenging task. In Chapter 10 we describe the performance management process. We have divided this discussion into two parts: performance planning and performance management.

During the system development process, performance planning is essential. Performance planning lays the foundation for overall system performance. It involves reviewing information models; designing an appropriate information logistics model and system landscape; implementing efficient transformations; defining parallel, collision-free data loads and data maintenance process chains; and managing user expectations.

Performance management, on the other hand, is part of production system administration. It entails monitoring all processes and resources in the system. We describe how the system may be tuned by defining aggregates, adjusting operating system parameters, determining database management system settings, and configuring hardware. Like many of the options that we describe in the book, performance planning and performance management deal with trade-offs. The trade-offs in this case are between disk and memory space, flexibility, loading time, and retrieval time.

Throughout the book we have included images, lists, notes, and tips to you to help you implement your own solutions. This book is not a step-by-step list of configuration settings, and it is not intended to be a substitute for hands-on learning. You do not become a black belt in karate by reading a book. The same is the case with SAP BW. We encourage our readers to log in to a test system, configure the services described in this book, and assess the trade-offs.

What's on the Web Site

The accompanying Web site for this book can be found at www.wiley.com/compbooks/mcdonald. It contains:

- Guides with the steps for configuring your system in order to make the SAP BW system behave in a particular manner.
- Industry case studies based on the project implementation experience of the authors and the business drivers that lead to the use of SAP BW. The case studies are intended to be an executive overview of how the SAP BW is used to solve specific business issues.
- Updates to the technology and the book.

From Here

In the third century B.C., Greek writer Plutarch may have put it best when he wrote, "The mind is not a vessel to be filled, yet a spark to be lighted." It is our hope that readers of this book will discover the options that are available in the SAP BW software component and uncover a new means to drive business performance through the implementation of the SAP Business Intelligence Solution. We hope you enjoy the book as we open with Chapter 1 and an introduction to business intelligence.

CHAPTER 1 The Origins of Business Intelligence

The origins of business intelligence may be traced back to the first data processing applications, which were simple applications such as accounts payable and receivable. These applications ran on sequential technology, such as magnetic and paper tapes. Using sequential media for storage meant the entire file had to be accessed, even if only a fraction of the file was needed. Oxide often stripped off of magnetic tapes, and entire files were lost. These issues led to the need for a new way to analyze information.

In this chapter we discuss how enterprises tackled the challenges of extracting data from online transaction processing systems, dealing with poor data quality, and structuring the data. We describe what a data warehouse is from its data model, table structure, granularity, and support of historical data, and how it fits into a broader intellectual concept called the corporate information factory, discussed later in the chapter.

Early Data Processing Applications

With sequential storage, data was organized onto what was called a master file, which held central information that was useful to many applications. Punch cards, magnetic tapes, and reports were generated from the applications, but were soon replaced by disk storage. With disk storage, data could be accessed directly and efficiently. Processors grew more powerful and versatile, and the speed and costs of processing dropped dramatically. As data was stored onto disk, master files mutated into databases. A *database* is a centralized collection of data that resides on disk storage and is available for processing by any application that needs it.

With disk storage, transactions could be processed directly and online against the central databases that were built. This meant that the transaction could execute in a short amount of time—from 2 to 3 seconds. Soon, online transaction processing resulted in online applications. Online applications were tied together by the central online databases that they ran against.

Online applications focused on high availability and good response time. The online transaction application soon became central to running the business, as the online transaction became an essential part of direct interaction with the customer. However, the custom development of online transaction applications led to several challenges:

- Aging of applications as soon as they were put online
- Sheer number of applications
- No documentation
- New requirements
- Inability to change the system once developed
- Fragility of the system
- Sensitivity to response time

An additional problem with many online applications was lack of integration among them. Each online application was developed according to its own specification, and a different set of requirements shaped each one. There was no common understanding of what was:

- A customer
- A product
- A transaction
- A vendor
- A shipment

Because each application was so difficult to change, no significant reinterpretation could be accomplished. The result was that even the largest and most sophisticated corporation did not know who its customers were. A corporation would spend a huge amount of money each month on technology without knowing the most basic information, such as who are the best customers, what products are selling, and how much revenue was made last quarter.

Enter Extract Files

The first reaction to the challenge of not having corporate data was to create what was called an *extract file*. An extract file would be created by a database from one application and shipped to another application, so it seemed that data could be shared and corporate data could be created. Extracts became very popular, and soon there were a lot of them. Every new extraction exacerbated the problems of the spiderweb. Adding extractions made matters worse, not better. The problems of the spiderweb included:

Data integrity. The same element of data appeared in many places. In one place the element had a value of 25. In another place the element had a value of 67. In still another place the element had a value of 135. No one really knew what the right value was.

Data redundancy. The sheer redundancy of data was enormous. The same data was being shuffled from one place to the next, and in doing so, the burden of massive amounts of data being repeated over and over began to add up to significant amounts of storage and processing power.

Timeliness of data. While being shuffled around the system, data was aging. In one day, the value of a unit of data may change five or six times. The extract processing simply was not capable of keeping up with the speed with which data changed.

Multiple *silo* of data were created. Each silo was its own operating domain with no coordination or integration with outside silos. The organization found itself making decisions that were contrary to the interest of other parts of the organization.

The extract processing froze an already moribund system. Online transaction applications were difficult to change in any case. But wrapping lines of extraction around the online applications glued those applications into a permanent position.

Data became much more inaccessible. The extract processing placed coordination requirements on the environment, which ensured that accurate data was impossible to obtain, and so forth.

Of particular interest is the lack of historical data. Online applications value current data. How much is a bank account balance right now? Where is a shipment right now? What is the status of an insurance claim right now? Online applications optimize the "right now" aspect of information processing. As soon as data became dated, it was discarded. Lots of historical data clogged the arteries of efficient online processing. Therefore, online data and processing required that older data be jettisoned as soon as possible.

But there is real value in historical data. With historical data, organizations can start to see the forest *and* the trees. With historical data, organizations can start to understand their customer base, because customers are creatures of habit.

Because there was no corporate integrated data or historical data, data was difficult to access. Even if accessed, data was not trustworthy, so it is no wonder organizations began to grow frustrated with their ability to find and process information. Department after department would say, "I know the data is somewhere in my corporation; if I could only get at it."

The frustrations of the end user with data locked in the spiderweb environment resulted in the realization that there were different kinds of data. There was an essential difference between *operational data* and *informational data*. Table 1.1 outlines those differences.

Table 1.1 Characteristics of Operational versus Informational Systems

OPERATIONAL	INFORMATIONAL/DSS
Detailed	Summarized
Can be updated	Snapshot records; no updates allowed
Accurate up to the second	Timestamp on each record
Used for clerical purposes	Used by management
Built based on requirements	Built without knowing requirements
Supports small uniform transactions	Supports mixed workload
Yields 2- to 3-second response time	Yields 30- to 24-hour response time
Data designed for optimal storage	Data designed for optimal access
Very current data	Mainly historical data
Data is application oriented	Data is integrated
Data designed around functional usage	Data designed around subject areas
Referential integrity is useful	Referential integrity is not useful
High availability is normal	High availability is nice to have

A fundamental split exists between *operational information* and *informational information*. Operational information is used to support the daily operations of a business. Informational information is commonly called *decision support systems* (DSS) information. The foundation for DSS processing became an architectural structure known as the data warehouse. A *data warehouse* is a physically distinct place from the online operational application. In the following sections we describe the data warehouse and how it enables informational information.

What Is a Data Warehouse?

Since the beginning of movement toward data warehousing, data warehouses have been defined as being:

Subject-oriented. Data is organized around a major object or process of an organization. Classic examples include subject area databases for customer, material, vendor, and transaction.

Integrated. The data from various subject areas should be rationalized with one another.

Nonvolatile. Data in a data warehouse is not updated. Once a record is properly placed in the warehouse, it is not subject to change. This contrasts with a record of data in an online environment, which is indeed very much subject to change.

Time-variant. A record is accurate only as of some moment in time. In some cases the moment in time is a single moment. In other cases it is a span of time. But in any case, the values of data found in a data warehouse are accurate and relevant only to some moment in time.

Created for the purpose of management decisions.

The preceding definition has remained unchanged since the inception of the data warehouse. In addition, the data warehouse provides:

- Detailed or granular data
- Integrated data
- Historical data
- Easy-access data

The data warehouse is at the center of the business intelligence environment. The data warehouse represents the single version of truth for the corporation and holds data at a granular level. In addition, the data warehouse contains a robust amount of historical data. The need for a data warehouse is as true within the confines of SAP as it is outside of SAP. And the elements of a data warehouse are as valid for SAP as for the non-SAP environment.

The data warehouse evolves from these requirements and supports the process of moving data from source systems, transforming, and cleansing the data so that it may be stored in an integrated data model at an atomic level of granularity. There are many factors that influence the design of a data warehouse and the structure that data records are stored. We discuss some of these factors in the next sections.

The Data Model

The design of the data warehouse begins with a data model. At the highest level, the data model is known as an *entity relationship diagram* (ERD). The ERD represents the abstraction of the granular data found in the data warehouse. Note that for the purposes of data warehouse design the ERD represents only granular data, not derived data. This distinction is important because it greatly limits the size and complexity of the data model. There are, of course, other data models outside of the data warehouse environment that do attempt to take into account derived data and atomic data.

The ERD consists of entities and relationships. Each entity represents a major subject area of the corporation. Typical subject areas are customer, product, transaction, and vendor. Each entity is further defined at a lower level of data modeling called the *data item set* (DIS). The DIS specifies a lower level of detail than the entity does, encompassing such things as keys and attributes, as well as the structure of those things. The DIS is further broken down into a low level of design called the *physical design*. At the physical level of design the physical characteristics of the data are created.

NOTE For a more detailed description of the methodology required to build a data warehouse, visit the Web site www.billinmon.com.

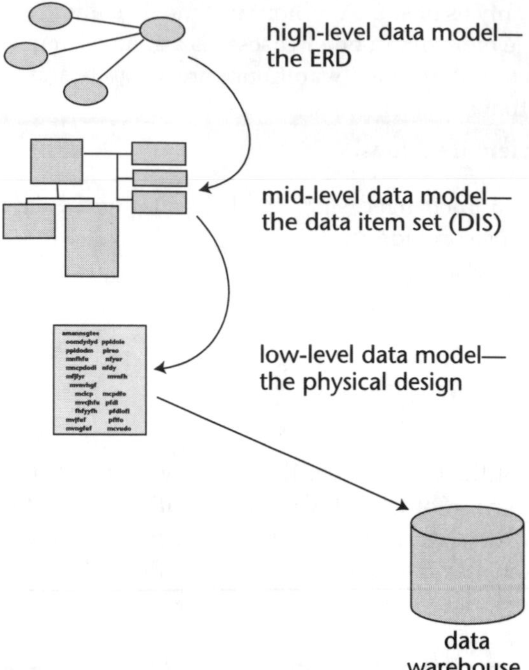

Figure 1.1 The data warehouse is designed from the data model.

The data warehouse is now specified and defined to the database management system that will house it. Other physical aspects of database design such as partitioning, loading, indexing, storage media, and timestamping are determined here as well. Figure 1.1 shows the design of the data warehouse from the different components of the data model.

Different Physical Tables

The data warehouse is made up of interrelated tables or physical databases. Within the data warehouse, there are different physical tables that represent different subject areas or even subsets of subject areas. One table relates to another by means of a shared key or foreign key relationship. The data warehouse has five subject areas:

- Customer
- Product
- Shipment
- Vendor
- Order

Each subject area resides on a separate physical table or database. Collectively the different tables along with their relationships form a data warehouse.

Integration and Transformation Processing

One of the most important and most difficult aspects of data warehouse development and population is that the movement and conversion of data from the operational/legacy source environment. It is estimated that for the first iteration of development, at least 75 percent of the resources required for development will be expended here. During extraction, data is pulled from the legacy environment and moved into the data warehouse environment. This data is pulled from a variety of sources, such as mainframe order entry systems, proprietary shop flow control systems, and custom-built payroll systems.

But data is not merely moved from the legacy environment to the data warehouse environment. Instead, data undergoes a thorough transformation as it is moved, including:

- Converting data into a common format
- Reformatting data
- Realigning encoded values
- Restructuring data
- Assigning default values
- Summarizing
- Resequencing
- Converting keys
- Converting from one database management system (DBMS) to another
- Converting from one operating system to another
- Converting from one hardware architecture to another
- Merging different record types
- Creating meta data that describes the activities of conversion
- Editing data
- Adding a timestamp

In the early days of data warehousing there was no way to create the interface programs between the legacy environment and the data warehouse other than to write them by hand. But with recent technology, extract/transfer/load (ETL) software automatically creates the interfaces needed to bring the data into the world of data warehouse. Figure 1.2 shows the place of ETL between the source systems and the data warehouse.

One of the real benefits of ETL processing is that data enters the ETL process in an application mode and exits in an integrated corporate mode. The processing that occurs inside ETL software allows the data to be integrated.

SAP BW addresses the ETL process by including a so-called Staging Engine to perform simple transformations and conversions. In Chapter 6 we detail the function delivered within the SAP BW related to ETL, as well as discuss the usage of specialized ETL tools that are certified with SAP BW.

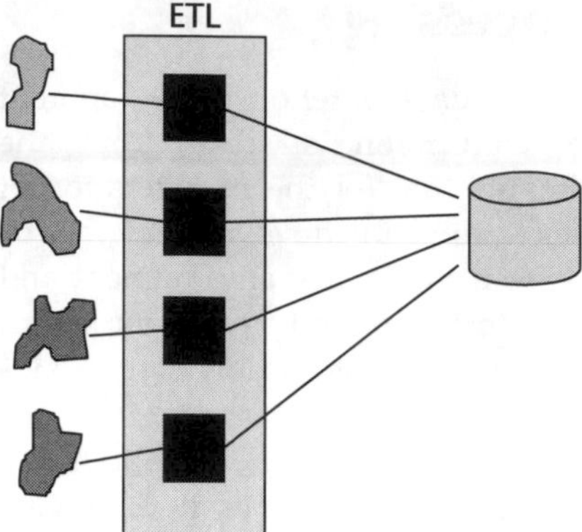

Figure 1.2 Integration and conversion is performed by ETL processing.

Granular Data

The data found in a data warehouse is very granular. This means that the data is placed in the data warehouse at a very low level of detail. The data may then be reshaped by an application so that it can be viewed in a distinct manner.

Sometimes called the atomic data of the corporation, granular data makes up the "single version of truth" that is at the basis of reconciliation for informational processing. Having the granular data at the core of the data warehouse provides many benefits. A primary advantage is the same data can be viewed in different ways. Figure 1.3 shows that marketing looks at data one way, sales looks at it another way, and finance yet another way. But all three departments have a single source of reconcilability.

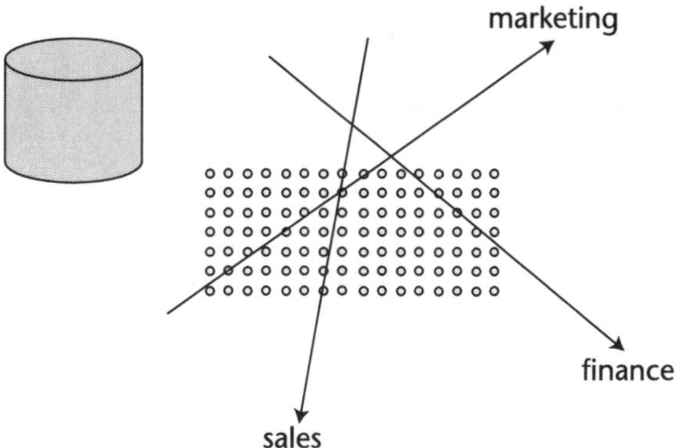

Figure 1.3 Granular data allows the same data to be examined in different ways.

Usually each grain of information in the data warehouse represents some finite unit of measure or business activity for the corporation. For instance, a grain of information might represent details of the following:

A sale. The amount, the date, the item sold, the location of the sale, or the customer

An order. The date of the order, the product ordered, or the amount of the order

A telephone call. The time of the call, the length of the call, the calling party, or the person called

A delivery of a product. The date of the delivery, the location of the delivery, or the person making the delivery

Each grain of information can be combined with other grains to provide a different perspective of data.

In addition to allowing data to be viewed differently by different parties, another benefit is that the granular data may lie in wait in the data warehouse for unknown and future requirements. Then when a requirement becomes known, the granular data can be shaped immediately to suit the new requirements. There is no need to go to the operational/legacy environment and pull data out. This means that the data warehouse puts the corporation in a proactive rather than reactive position for new needs for information.

Historical Data

One of the most important characteristics of a data warehouse is that it contains a robust amount of historical data. Figure 1.4 shows a data warehouse that contains 5 years of history. Such an amount of history is typical. However, some warehouses may contain even more historical data and other data warehouses may contain less data, depending on the business needs of the corporation.

Although historical data has many applications, perhaps the most potent is the ability to step backward in time and do what-if analysis. Doing so allows you to gain insights that cannot be achieved any other way.

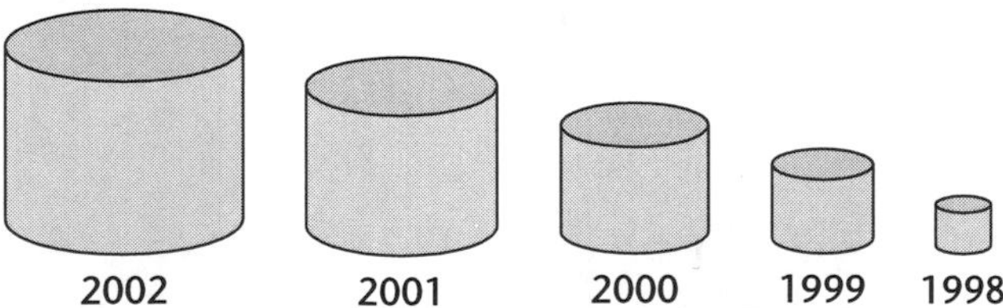

Figure 1.4 The data warehouse contains robust amounts of historical data.

Timestamping

The units of data stored inside the data warehouse are timestamped so that each unit of data in the data warehouse has some element of time associated with the record. The timestamping of data warehouse data signifies that the unit of data is accurate as of the timestamp.

In general, there are two ways that a record is stored in the data warehouse: discretely or continuously (see Figure 1.5). In a discrete record there is one instant in time for which the record is accurate. In a continuous record, there is a span of time for which the record is accurate. These records form a larger definition of information over time.

Usually discrete records are used for a large number of fast-changing variables. Continuous timestamps are used for a small number of variables that change slowly and for which there is value in knowing information over time.

The records in a data warehouse have a distinctive structure, including:

- A timestamp
- A key
- Primary data
- Secondary data

Data Relationships

The different types of data found in the data warehouse relate to each other by means of foreign keys pointing to actual keys. As an example, suppose customer ABC places an order. There would be a customer record for customer ABC, as well as a separate order record for the order. The order record, in its body, would have a foreign key reference to customer ABC.

The data relationships found in the data warehouse are special in that they are delimited by time. When a relationship is indicated in the data warehouse, the relationship is intended to only be valid for the moment in time indicated by the timestamps found on the participating records. This interpretation of a relationship is quite different from that of referential integrity found in the online environment.

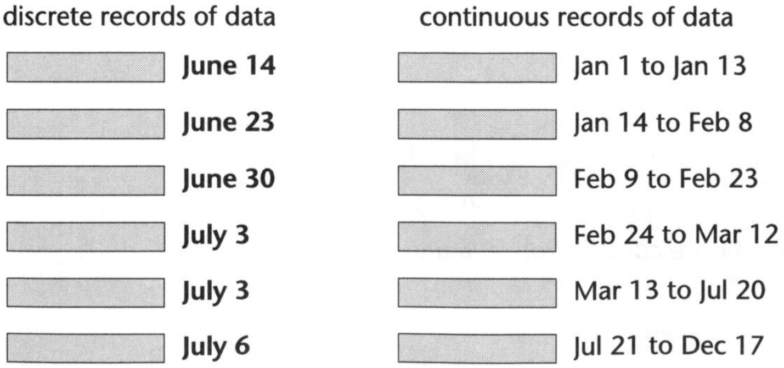

discrete records of data	continuous records of data
June 14	Jan 1 to Jan 13
June 23	Jan 14 to Feb 8
June 30	Feb 9 to Feb 23
July 3	Feb 24 to Mar 12
July 3	Mar 13 to Jul 20
July 6	Jul 21 to Dec 17

Figure 1.5 Timestamped records are either continuous or discrete.

Generic Data versus Specific Data

One design issue that arises in every data warehouse is how to account for generic data and specific data at the same time. Generic data applies to all instances of a subject area. Specific data applies to only certain occurrences of a subject area.

The generic database stores customer information, along with related tables, including a wholesale customer table, a European customer table, a long-term customer table, and a preferred customer table. Each of the outlying tables contains information specific to only the class of tables that meet the criteria. For example, a preferred wholesale customer would have data in the generic customer table, in the preferred customer table, and in the wholesale customer table.

In such a manner, data of different types can be represented efficiently in a data warehouse.

Data Quality

Data quality is an important issue for the data warehouse environment. As shown in Figure 1.6, there are three places where data quality is addressed:

- At the point of data entry to the legacy/operational environment
- At the point of ETL processing
- Once the data resides inside the data warehouse itself

For instance, raw data entry is addressed inside the legacy/operational environment. The problem is that the budget for doing tasks such as maintenance here has long gone away. In addition, no shop is anxious to go poking around old, fragile, undocumented legacy applications lest something untoward and unexpected happen. Therefore, not much data quality activity occurs in the legacy/operational environment.

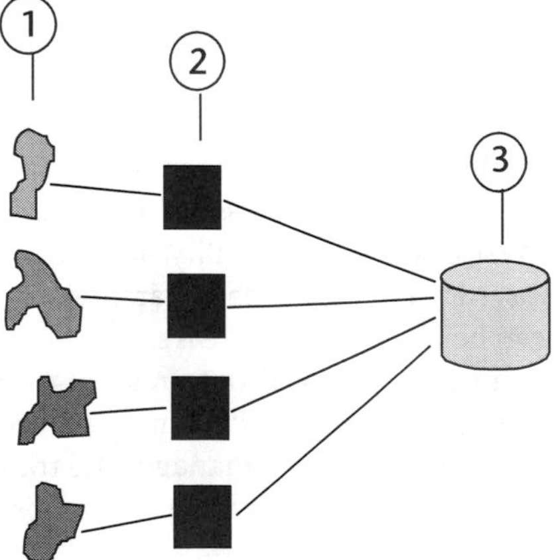

Figure 1.6 Base data for all customers is kept in one table; specific data for different types of customers is kept in separate, unique tables.

Most data quality activity occurs at the moment of ETL. ETL does not require that older applications be manipulated or touched in any way. The data that comes out of the legacy application can be isolated. And data coming from different applications can be integrated. The data is in transit in any case, so this becomes an ideal place in which to examine and audit data, and to make changes if needed.

The third place where data quality can be applied is once the data has arrived in the data warehouse. Over time data changes, and what was accurate and proper one year is not accurate and proper the next. So even if the data is loaded perfectly into the data warehouse, there still is a need for periodic adjustment of data based on changes in business conditions that have occurred over time.

Volumes of Data

The volume of data grows beyond any expectations in a data warehouse. Once terabyte data warehouses were a dream; today they are a reality. In fact, it is not unheard of to build petabyte data warehouses.

As data volumes grow large, the techniques and approaches to their management change. One of the most important characteristics of a data warehouse growing is the appearance of dormant data that just sits there taking up space and costing money. When the data warehouse was small, all or nearly all of the data that resides inside of it was used. But as the data warehouse grows large, increasingly large amounts of data reside in the warehouse in an unused state.

When a data warehouse is around the 100-GB range, there may be only 10 to 20 percent dormant data. But as a data warehouse approaches a terabyte, it is not unusual for the dormancy ratio to go to 50 to 75 percent. And as a data warehouse goes beyond several terabytes, the amount of dormant data frequently approaches 90 to 99 percent.

It is wasteful for the corporation to continue to increase the size of a data warehouse when the proportion of data that is dormant increases as well. In addition, increasing the size of a data warehouse when there is much dormant data grossly hurts performance.

Removing Dormant Data

Dormant data needs to be periodically removed from disk storage and placed on another media. Active data is placed on disk storage and is managed and accessed in a normal manner, while data that is inactive is placed in a physically separate facility, sometimes called alternate storage or near-line storage. This causes the cost of the data warehouse to drop dramatically and the speed with which data can be accessed to increase.

To make the marriage between dormant data and actively used data residing on disk work well, a technology called a *cross-media storage manager* (CMSM) may be utilized. The CMSM sits between disk storage and alternate storage and manages the traffic between the two environments so that the end user is presented with a seamless view of the data residing in the data warehouse.

Meta Data

One of the essential aspects of the data warehouse is meta data. *Meta data* is the information about the contents of what has come to be termed the corporate information factory, or CIF. (The evolution of the CIF is discussed in detail in the next section.) Every application has its own meta data, which is distributed across the entire landscape of architectural components. The meta data has two functions: to describe the data that is found in the architectural component and to exchange meta data with other components.

Meta data in the data warehouse plays several roles. One role is describing what data resides where for normal usage. It also acts as a coordinator between different services from ETL to information access. The different services of the architecture have very different foundations and functions. Some serve under one database management system, others under another database management system. Some services operate under one type of multidimensional technology, and other services operate under other multidimensional technologies. And there is a very different function for all of the services. For the services to operate in unison with each other, there must be coordination from one service to the next. The coordination is achieved through meta data being passed from one architectural layer to another.

There are distinctly different kinds of meta data, including technical meta data, operating meta data, and business meta data. *Technical meta data* describes the structure and content of the different types of data. This type of data has been housed in data dictionaries and repositories for a long time. Operational meta data is the metrics that are generated by the day-to-day operation of the data warehouse. Metrics such as records passed from one software component to another, length of operation of a program, number of records in a database, and so forth make up operating meta data. *Business meta data* is couched in terms the business person understands. Business definitions, business formulae, and business conditions all make up business meta data. All three types of meta data are needed for controlling the operation of a data warehouse.

One concern is the integrity of the meta data. To maintain control and believability of meta data when it is distributed across many different components, a certain protocol for the meta data is necessary. To maintain integrity of meta data across a distributed environment, each unit of meta data must be unique and each unit of meta data must have one owner. The owner of the meta data is the only person or organization that has the right of update, creation, and deletion of the unit of meta data. Everyone else becomes a sharer of the meta data. As meta data is passed from one node to the next, careful track of ownership of the meta data must be kept.

Evolution of Information Processing

For a variety of reasons information was once nearly impossible to get out of applications. Corporate applications were not integrated, applications did not contain historical data, and applications were housed in technology that was not easy to access. The result was frustration for the end user.

This frustration led to the notion of a data warehouse. The data warehouse was a radical departure from the database theory of the day that mandated all data be gathered into a single database. The data warehouse concept focused on different kinds of databases for different purposes. Operational transaction processing was served by one type of database, and informational processing was served by another. The data warehouse called for data to be integrated and stored over time in a physically separate database technology that was optimal for access and analysis of information.

Data marts grew from the data warehouse, DSS applications appeared, and the data warehouses grew in size to a point where the volumes of data in a warehouse easily exceeded the size of earlier databases by several orders of magnitude. Early online databases were considered large at 10 GB. Today, 10-TB data warehouses are considered large, and 10 TB is three orders of magnitude larger than 10 GB. Even with the data warehouse, other forms of informational technology were needed.

As the different architectural structures appeared in conjunction with the data warehouse, even more architectural structures were spawned. Soon there were operational data stores (ODSs), data mining and exploration facilities, alternative forms of storage, and so forth. The data warehouse gave birth to different forms of environments that accomplished very different types of informational processing. At the center of these structures was the data warehouse. The data warehouse provided the granular data that was reshaped into many different forms in order to feed the many different forms of decision support processing. The architectural framework that blossomed was called the *corporate information factory* (CIF). Figure 1.7 shows the progression of the world of informational processing and data warehouse. At the forefront of informational processing is the data warehouse and the larger architecture that centers around the data warehouse—the CIF.

Often the architecture that resulted was called *hub-and-spoke architecture*. Similar to the flight plans and strategies used by the commercial airline industry where a city acts as the hub and enables connection to various destinations through routes, the data warehouse sits at the hub and various analytical applications and data marts act as destinations. The process of delivering information to the destinations is then analogous to the routes or spokes.

The CIF represents the progression of thought and development that occurred with informational processing. This progression occurred in the same timeframe that SAP and Enterprise Resource Planning (ERP) were developing and maturing. It was inevitable that the worlds of SAP/ERP and data warehouse/corporate information factory would merge.

From the standpoint of timing, the CIF was intellectually articulated before SAP BW became available. However, this fact hardly means that the business world went out and built the CIF immediately. Yet that SAP BW followed the intellectual establishment of the CIF in no way diminishes or tarnishes the value of the SAP BW product. Indeed, SAP BW provides an easy path to the actualization of the CIF for many organizations.

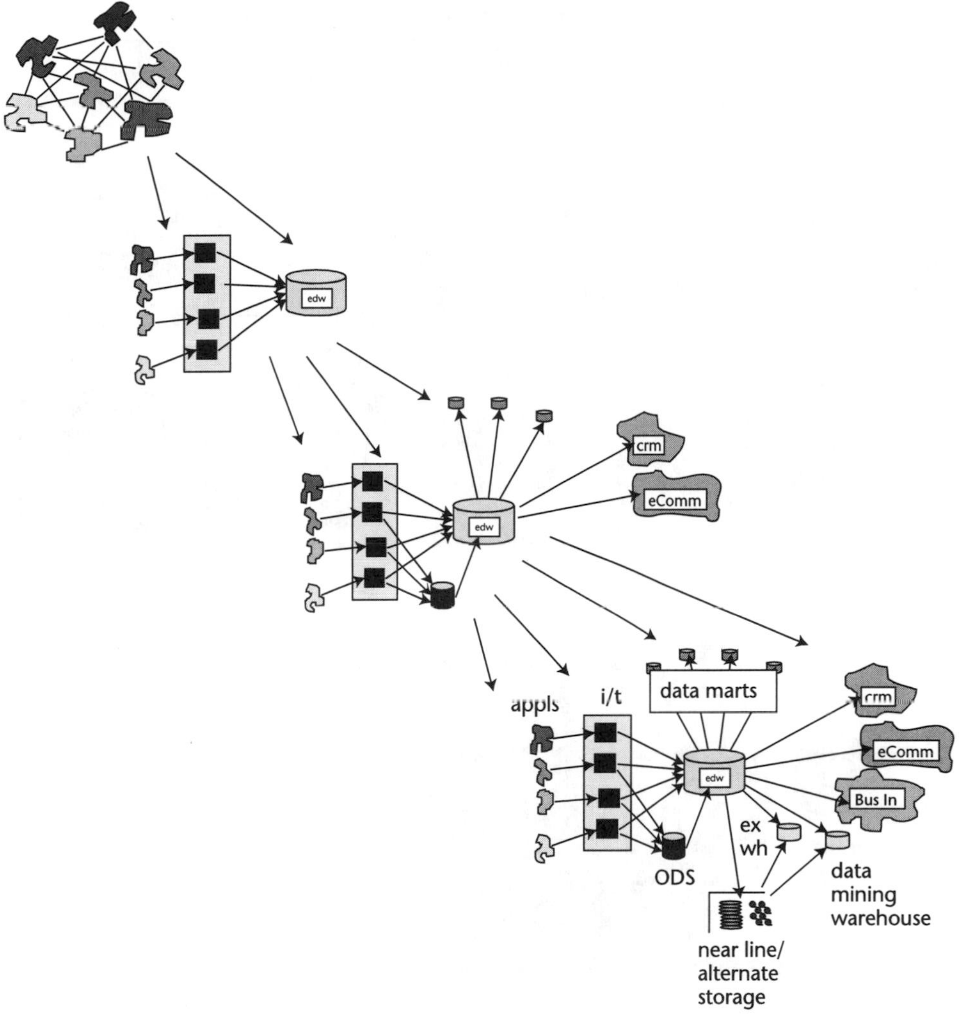

Figure 1.7 The evolution of the CIF.

In many ways the CIF is like a city plan. A city plan takes years and decades to develop. In the case of grand cities built from a plan (such as Washington, DC), it may take decades for the city plan to be realized. And thus it is with the CIF. The CIF is a blueprint and as such may require many years for implementation. The CIF in a robust state is pictured in Figure 1.8.

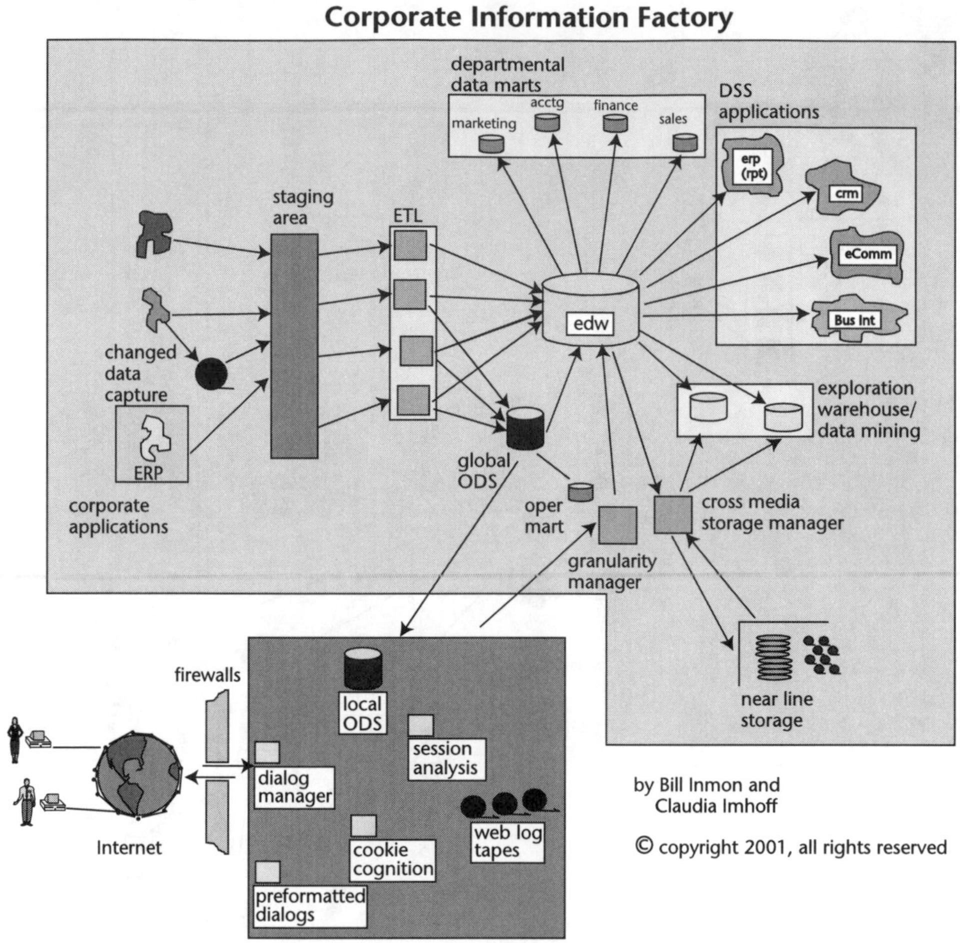

Figure 1.8 The CIF and the Web-based e-business environment.

Setting the Stage for Business Intelligence

Once the data warehouse has been constructed, the stage is set for effective business intelligence. There are many different forms of business intelligence. As shown in Figure 1.9, business intelligence is found in exploration and data mining, data marts, e-business support, and decision support system (DSS).

In a sense, a data warehouse becomes the support infrastructure for business intelligence. Once the data warehouse is built, it becomes very easy and natural to build business intelligence on top of the foundation.

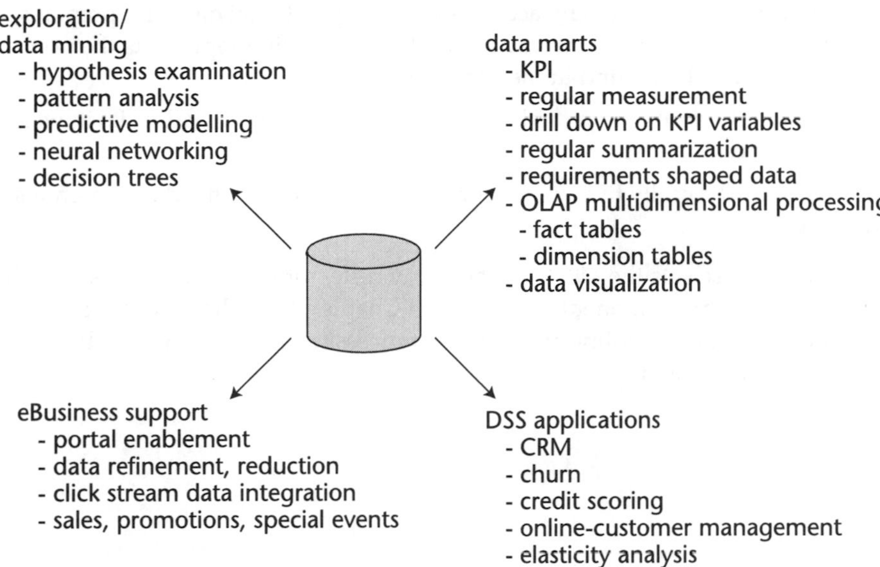

Figure 1.9 Forms of business intelligence.

Summary

In the beginning were simple applications, followed by online applications. Soon a spiderweb of systems and data was created. With the spiderweb came many difficulties, such as redundancy of data, lack of integrity, and the inability to make changes. In parallel it was recognized that there was a fundamental difference between operational data and informational or DSS data, requiring a change in architecture. The spiderweb environment needed to be split into two kinds of processing: operational processing and informational processing. Operational processing was done out of an ERP system like SAP, and informational processing was done out of a data warehouse, which became the "single version of truth" for the corporation at the most granular level.

Data warehouses—whether from SAP environments or non-SAP environments—share some common elements:

Data model. The ERD determines what the major subject areas are. The data item set determines what the attribution and keys will be.

Different physical tables or databases linked by a common key structure. The different tables are built in an iterative manner. It is patently a mistake to build the data warehouse in an all-at-once manner, or a "big bang" approach.

ETL processing. ETL processing accesses legacy/operational data and prepares the data for entry into the data warehouse. ETL processing represents the point of integration for data found in the data warehouse.

Granular data. Granular data can be examined in many ways, and it sits in wait for unknown requirements.

Robust history. Typically five years' worth of data is found in the data warehouse environment.

The data warehouse sets the stage for the many different forms of business intelligence and is the central component in the CIF. In Chapter 2, we discuss how SAP has evolved from a provider of online transactions processing applications to a business intelligence solutions provider.

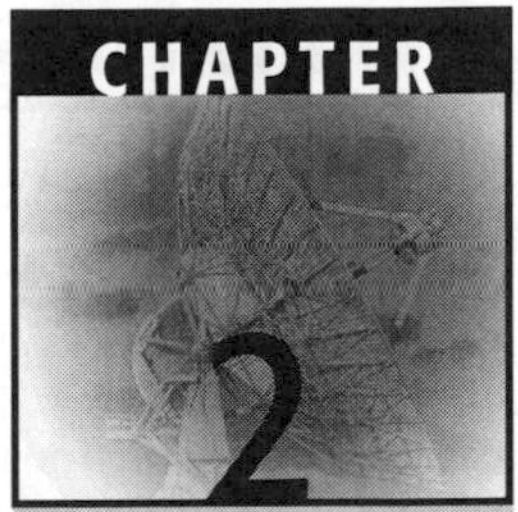

CHAPTER 2

The SAP Business Intelligence Solution

SAP has been developing software according to its city plan, or as they refer to it, *solution map*, for the past five years. Unlike a city plan, SAP's solution maps do not span decades but the maps do provide the general direction SAP is heading with the software releases they are providing. More or less according to plan, SAP has evolved from its Enterprise Resource Planning (ERP) origins into an e-business software solutions company covering areas such as customer relationship management, supply chain optimization, and business intelligence.

SAP did not invent the software components of the mySAP Business Intelligence solution (mySAP BI™) overnight. The business intelligence capabilities found in SAP software have evolved in parallel to the CIF and other informational processing frameworks. The SAP BI solution evolution has been quite rapid since the first generally available release of the SAP BW software in 1998. In fact organizations interested in implementing the SAP BW software component to realize a CIF will find themselves licensing the SAP Business Intelligence Solution rather than the SAP BW component.

We'll open this chapter with a short explanation of the development path SAP has taken over the years and how it has led to today's SAP BI solution. The focus will then turn to the two main components of the solution. The two main components are Enterprise Portal (EP) and SAP BW. The Enterprise Portal and its Knowledge Management capabilities, along with the SAP BW software components, create a broad foundation for organizations on which to build analytical applications and collaborative business intelligence solutions. The remainder of this book focuses on the options available to those implementing the SAP BW component. However, first we need to place the SAP BW into the SAP BI solution and set the context for the subsequent chapters.

Evolution of SAP

The progression of SAP started with the early vestiges of R/2®, the mainframe predecessor to its client/server brother SAP R/3®. What made SAP so enormously successful and set it on the road to dominating the ERP market? Was it the support of complex business processes without writing specific application code for each variation of a business process? The technological advancements of so-called lock objects? SAP's heavy investment into its proprietary Advanced Business Application Programming (ABAP™) language? The partnering with the big consulting firms? Business process reengineering? Y2K? Perhaps it was the elimination of the cap on the commissions SAP sales people could earn. Whatever the reason, today the letters SAP are synonymous with ERP, and there are many indications that SAP will also become synonymous with business intelligence (BI).

SAP and ERP have developed from early applications that ran financial transactions to a complete solutions set that serves the needs of entire vertical markets. More recently, SAP extended the product line to e-business, customer relationship management, supply chain management, and enterprise portals.

NOTE SAP markets solutions that contain components. For example, the mySAP.com Financials solution consists of the SAP R/3, SAP BW, and among others, the SAP Strategic Enterprise Management (SAP SEM) components.

The advent of SAP occurred over a two-decade period. The progression shown in Figure 2.1 encompasses many submarket places, many pieces of software, and many systems.

Movement was afoot for organizations to build a solid applications base well before the year 2000, but there is no question that the challenges to the world of information technology posed by the turn of the century gave impetus to the need for revamping the enterprise software applications. Many organizations decided to completely replace their legacy applications rather than go back into those older applications and refurbish the applications to handle the year 2000 problem. But there were other problems with the older applications other than those posed by the year 2000 dilemma. Some of the problems included:

Older applications had long ago ceased to be documented. No one knew what the application really did or how it worked.

The applications were brittle and fragile. Corporations were afraid to go into an application and make changes unless something completely unexpected and unrelated happened.

The applications were written in older technology. Applications were designed to store data efficiently rather than in an easily accessible way. Consequently, data was hard to get to.

They were not integrated. Often acquired by merger, purchase, or other means, older legacy applications were never designed to run in an integrated manner.

The staff that built the older legacy applications left. This means that no one has the knowledge or skills to update older legacy applications.

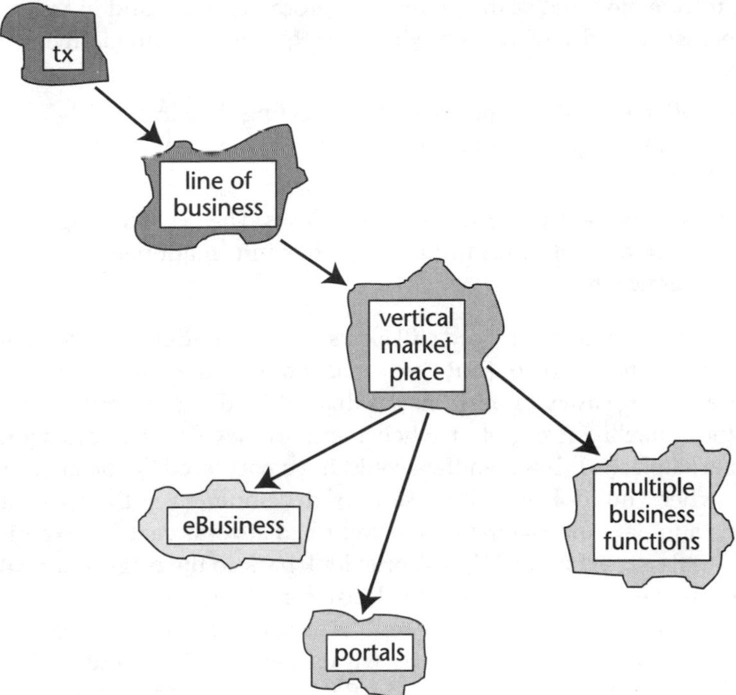

Figure 2.1 The progression of SAP.

Enterprise Resource Planning (ERP) applications promised not only to be the panacea for Y2K and business process reengineering, but they also promised to provide an integrated view of a corporation's information. Once the ERP solution was implemented, however, organizations discovered that solving the problems of transaction processing was different from solving the problems of informational processing. In truth, this was the same discovery that had been made previously by the non-ERP community, the result of which was the advent of data warehousing.

There still was the need for information in the face of a successful ERP implementation. Once the ERP environment was created, the corporation asked, "Where's my information?" It simply wasn't there or could not be accessed.

Why is there a need for information in the ERP environment even when there is a solid application foundation? There are several reasons:

- ERP applications were not designed to store history. Applications store current information, and many powerful forms of analysis need history.
- ERP applications create an integrated environment when *all* of the applications are under the ERP umbrella. But often only some of the applications are ERP based. In this case there is still a need for integration.
- The technology that is optimal for running ERP processing is optimized on the efficient running of transactions. Informational processing does not run well

on this kind of technology; that is, the predictable processes are found in the transaction-processing world, while unpredictable requests are made in the analysis world.

- ERP applications often have thousands of tables collecting data in a highly normalized schema that may be difficult to access and to make available to the informational analyst.
- ERP applications require their own processing windows. These processing requirements are often for real-time information, while informational processing may tolerate latency.

There are then a host of reasons why a need still exists for informational processing even after a successful implementation of ERP. One of the more common questions we are asked by data warehousing savvy professionals is this: "Why did SAP *create* a data warehouse and business intelligence toolset when there are several vendors with mature tools in the marketplace with whom they could have partnered?" The answer is really quite simple when you look at SAP's history of development in the areas of reporting and analysis and data management. It already had several years of experience developing such tools as part of SAP R/3. A brief look back to the origins of SAP reporting and analysis may shed some light on the decision making process.

The first approach taken by SAP was to make reports easier to obtain. SAP accomplished this by creating an *information systems layer* within the SAP R/3 product. The information systems layer was built directly in the SAP R/3 in releases as early as 2.0. The information systems layer differed throughout the different application areas in the SAP R/3 product. For example, the Logistics Information System (LIS) had its own set of information access tools called *standard and flexible analysis*, whereas the Human Resources Information System (HRIS) had its own set of query tools. Each of these tools was developed by their respective development teams. While this leveraged the deep domain expertise of the application developers, it did create challenges for implementing organizations.

The first challenge was that the different information systems needed to be configured in totally different ways. Where the LIS utilized InfoStructures, Communication Structures, and Copy Methods, the HRIS utilized Infotypes, Logical Databases, and ABAP Queries. These configuration and administration differences created a need for specialists to configure the information systems, because the data structures and update mechanisms varied widely. The second challenge was for the information consumers, or end users. The end users were forced to learn different tools for accessing information depending on the application area the information was originally processed in. In many cases, seemingly simple cross-application reporting requirements were only satisfied by creating multiple reports or custom-written ABAP programs. These differences caused a tremendous amount of frustration and waste as end users were requesting information that crossed modules. A seemingly simple request to view purchase orders' line items with accounts payable to a vendor would more than likely be satisfied with two different reporting tools.

The original development work that had been done in SAP R/3 in the online analytic processing (OLAP) area was originally called a *research processor.* In the early 1990s the tool was used initially by the Controlling Profitability Analysis (CO-PA) development team as a means of reporting profitability across numerous dimensions by allowing the end user to interactively navigate through a virtual cube of aggregated data. Today this tool is found in SAP R/3 and is referred to as *Drill-Down Reporting*. It was the customer demand for multidimensional analysis that caused the different development departments to start to adopt the Drill-Down Reporting tool in recent versions of SAP R/3.

SAP found itself with a handful of very powerful analytical tools developed in the SAP R/3 application, a dissatisfied customer base hungry for information processing, a thriving partner ecosystem consisting of vendors of maturing business intelligence tools, and a fair amount of knowledge on how to architect a proper separate data warehousing solution. This combination led to SAP cofounder Hasso Platner's mandate that SAP create a reporting server. Thus, the SAP Business Information Warehouse (SAP BW) was conceived.

When SAP BW was designed, it may never have been a consideration to use a third-party OLAP engine. More than likely it was a very quick decision to port the concepts from SAP R/3 to SAP BW and leverage its past development experience. Two examples of tools developed years ago as a core part of SAP R/3 that have found their way into SAP BW (not the code but the concepts) are the Early Warning System and the Report-to-Report Interface (RRI). In highlighting the reuse of R/3 tools, we are not saying that specific code was ported from one product to the next, only that SAP has had many years of experience in business intelligence and OLAP.

Readers familiar with the Report-to-Report Interface in R/3 will quickly realize the power of information surfing in SAP BW. In R/3 a single developer who was satisfying a customer's need to jump from a report with summarized financial information to a report with detailed line items originally developed the RRI. Although the RRI recognizes the context of an end user's analysis and passes the characteristic values of that analysis to a receiver object, the receiver object may be one of several queries or transactions. For example, a financial controller may be analyzing the costs for the marketing department for the past reporting period of the current year. The context of the analysis path in this case would be the department number, the period, and the current year. Upon recognizing a significant negative cost variance from the planned cost, the controller may be interested in analyzing the revenue generated in this or a subsequent period to determine if the marketing costs were contributing to an increase in revenue. In this example, the RRI would enable the end user to jump from the current query reporting cost information to a query reporting sales information and pass the current period and fiscal year as parameters into the data selection variables of the receiving query.

NOTE Information surfing occurs when an analysis path crosses from one InfoMart to another. The Report-to-Report Interface enables information surfing.

The Early Warning System, developed as part of the LIS in SAP R/3, has also found its functionality, not its code, in SAP BW as the reporting agent. Setting thresholds for conditions and exceptions and announcing the findings to a user or group of users is by no means a development revelation but an evolution from R/3. A common use of the reporting agent is monitoring vendor-managed inventory. The quantity of inventory at a customer's location may be the vendor's responsibility to restock. This process may be managed with the assistance of the reporting agent. The vendor in this case would set an alert in SAP BW that is to be evaluated at regular intervals to make certain that when inventory levels of the product reach a reorder amount the category manager is automatically notified so a replenishment order is shipped.

The RRI and the reporting agent are just two examples of many functions that were originally developed in R/3. SAP BW is built on the same base technology as SAP R/3: the SAP Web Application Server. (We discuss this technology further in Chapter 3.) SAP has significant experience gained over many years solving business problems with OLAP and data management technologies that predate SAP BW. When evaluating the credibility of SAP as a data warehousing and business intelligence vendor, you should consider this experience.

Some authors and gurus may claim SAP BW is not SAP's first attempt at creating a data warehouse solution; they point to the Open Information Warehouse, R/3-based Data Warehouse, or ALE-based Data Warehouse as examples. Organizations and consultants have tried more or less unsuccessfully to use these tools to create data warehouses. We believe that until the release of SAP BW 3.0, SAP had not created a complete solution to address components of a CIF.

The SAP Business Intelligence Solution

SAP has bundled and rebundled its software several times during the past 2 years to maximize revenue and market share. SAP's solution approach to selling simply means that when a solution is purchased, the necessary software components to realize the solution are delivered by SAP. For example, SAP now sells the mySAP.com® Financials Solutions. In this solution customers would receive several software components—in this case the SAP BW, the financial applications found in SAP R/3, SAP SEM, and so forth. The SAP BW software component is delivered with nearly every solution sold by SAP. In fact, at this writing, the SAP BW software component is no longer sold independent from a solution.

The SAP BI solution contains the Enterprise Portal and the SAP BW components. The architecture of the Enterprise Portal and its Knowledge Management capabilities, along with the SAP BW is illustrated in Figure 2.2. Together these components create a broad foundation for organizations on which to build collaborative analytic applications.

SAP BW

The early requirements for the SAP BW were well known, as customer after customer had asked for better, if not simple, access to the information that was locked away in SAP R/3. The product development teams from the logistics area as well as the EIS and profitability analysis areas were assembled, the product requirements planning team conducted customer surveys and focus groups, and before long the first SAP BW product map was defined.

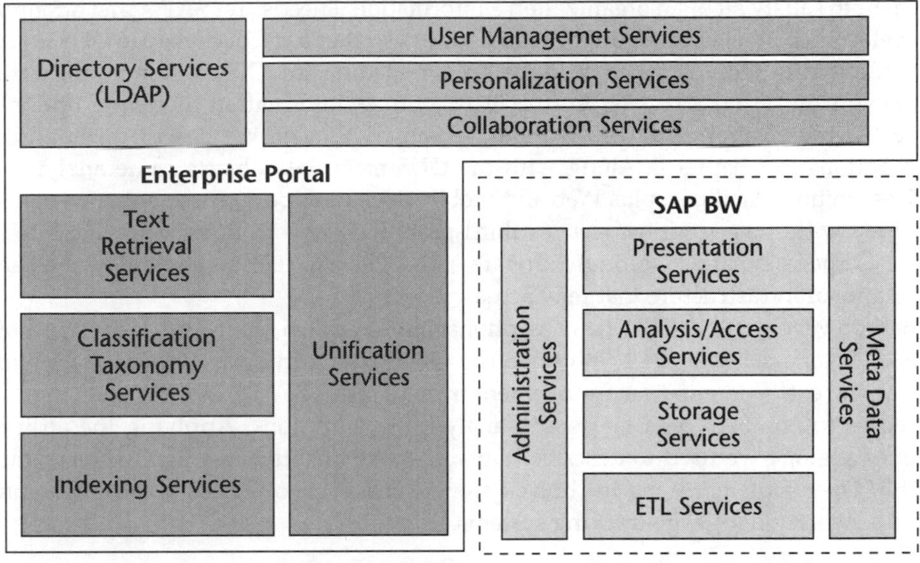

Figure 2.2 SAP BI architecture.

Like all software releases, the SAP BW faced the classic time-to-market, scope-of-functionality, quality-of-software dilemma. While the product map and strategy had been complete, the desire to release a new product and recognize a new revenue stream pushed forward the first release of SAP BW (version 1.2a) a bit ahead of its time.

The SAP BW in its first versions merely set a first step in the path to information. The creation of *InfoCubes* as a foundation for the OLAP engine enabled end users to access and analyze data. This was the cornerstone of the product release. In traditional SAP fashion, the SAP BW was marketed to the information consumers in an organization and not to the information technology departments. Business Content was the leading differentiator for the product as it entered an already maturing data warehousing market. Business Content, as we discuss in great detail in Chapter 5, is the preconfigured extraction of data from the SAP R/3 system, the transformation routines to integrate various data sources, the InfoCubes or enhanced star schema, and queries and reports. Business Content from extraction to query put SAP BW on a short list of products that could address an organization's information processing needs from end to end. While the InfoCubes, as we further define in Chapter 3, represented a step toward actualizing a CIF, it may be argued that it was Business Content that opened the wallets of SAP's installed base.

However, missing from the 1.2 versions of SAP BW were mechanisms for creating a data warehouse and operational data store (ODS) layers. InfoCubes alone was not sufficient to satisfy all of an organization's informational needs. Yet SAP's first attempt to develop such an ODS layer did not satisfy the customer base, because the ODS layer was little more than a place to store data for reloading InfoCubes. It was not until the 3.0 version of the SAP BW product that complex information modeling options supported the creation of a data warehouse and ODS layer. We describe several of these options in Chapter 4. Along with the ODS meta data objects came analytical services, archival facilities, plus Web and mobile device support. These enhancements combined with the open interfaces for third-party ETL tools from vendors like Informatica Corporation and Ascential Software enable the SAP BW to be deployed as an informational infrastructure that may actualize a CIF.

The 3.0b version of SAP BW has on optional add-on called Open Hub that is part of the SAP Business Intelligence Solution. The Open Hub add-on provides services to manage the extraction and data movement from the SAP BW to SAP BW data marts, as well as to non-SAP data marts and analytical applications. Applying the airline industry analogy we used to describe hub-and-spoke architectures in Chapter 1, the SAP BW Open Hub represents the hub city for an airline, the routes between cities, and the passenger- and luggage-tracking systems.

Enterprise Portal

The second main component in the mySAP Business Intelligence solution is the Enterprise Portal (SAP EP), shown in Figure 2.3. The goal of the Enterprise Portal is to create a common entryway into corporate applications and information, as well as into applications and information that may exist outside of the enterprise. Enterprise Portals are generally described as Yahoo! for corporate information. While this description is valid, it is incomplete. The SAP EP includes services for security and single sign-on; personalization of content and applications; indexing, categorizing, and retrieving documents; workflow approvals; and online collaboration; as well as the ability to execute applications.

The SAP EP component takes these information and application services one step further. The SAP EP contains an optional business unification layer that enables the dynamic integration of both applications and information from various sources. This is often referred to as *drag and relate technology*. We will describe unification in greater detail in a moment, but first note that Business Unification runs on a separate server from the SAP EP and is tightly integrated; but only works in conjunction with the SAP EP. One way to think about the relationship between Business Unification and the Enterprise Portal is to compare it with a VCR and a television. The television enables you to watch programming without a VCR, but the VCR provides little value without being attached to a television.

The unification services expose the relationships between objects and tables and allow the portal end user to dynamically link information and applications with a few clicks. Not unlike a data warehouse implementation, Enterprise Portal projects define meta data repositories and spend a fair amount of time on data integration work in order for end users to make only a few clicks.

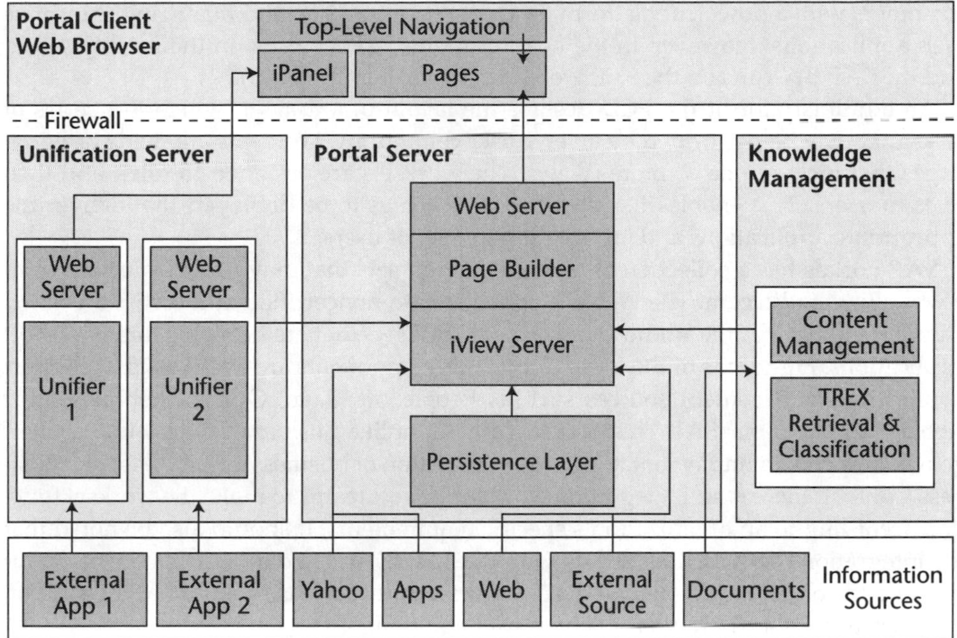

Figure 2.3 Enterprise Portal architecture.
Copyright © SAP AG

Portal Server

The Portal Content Directory (PCD) is the heart of the SAP EP, and at the center of the PDC are iViews, which are frames within the portal that may be customized on a per-user basis for a given applications or information source. These iViews are analogous to Portlets (Viador), Gadgets (Plumtree), or Web Parts (Microsoft) that are delivered by competing portal vendors. A portal user may drag information from an iView to any number of components on the portal work area. These components are not limited to SAP systems but include other systems from other enterprise application vendors or custom systems. External Web services such as FedEx for shipment tracking may be launched and passed context-sensitive information about a business object.

The PCD is a file-based directory that includes not only iViews but roles and the systems with which the portal is to interact. The PCD runs on a Java 2 Enterprise Edition-compliant application server. SAP delivers the InQMy Web Application Server with the EP. InQMy was quietly acquired by SAP over a year ago and is at the center of SAP's Java strategy. SAP has indicated that it plans to merge the traditional SAP Basis technical infrastructure and its recently added Web services (renamed the SAP Web Application Server) with the InQMy Application Server. The combination will provide customers with a powerful platform for creating, deploying, and managing enterprise Web applications. However, in the near term, the SAP EP runs on the InQMy server and the SAP BW runs on the SAP Web Application Server (WAS).

An administrator of the PCD designs the layout of a *workset,* which is a series of tasks that may be performed by an end-user community. Worksets are made of portal pages that include one or more iViews. The worksets are assigned to roles, and then roles to users. This enables flexible security schemes to be deployed that deliver the appropriate applications and information to a set of users.

SAP Portals has a collection of predefined worksets that may be downloaded from www.iViewStudio.com. The Web site contains both noncertified and certified iViews. Figure 2.4 illustrates the studio and a few of the iViews that are available for PeopleSoft applications. Hundreds of Business Unification components are available that support applications and content sources such as PeopleSoft, Baan, Oracle, WebEx, FedEx, Siebel, and of course, SAP. The worksets are not unlike Business Content in that their goal is to speed an implementation to the realization of business value. Also, like Business Content, there is still integration work for project teams to make the workset function according to an organization's specific requirements. It should also be noted that the integration of SAP EP meta data with the SAP BW meta data is in a state of evolution and the object models may indeed change in future releases of the SAP BI solution in order to support tighter out-of-the-box integration.

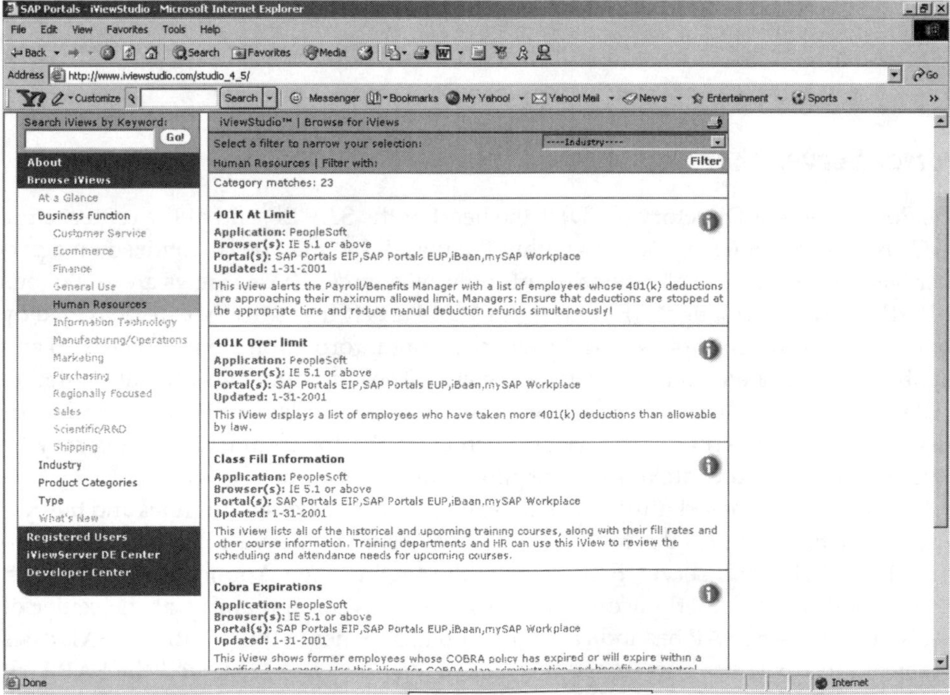

Figure 2.4 The iView studio.

The Enterprise Portal utilizes the Lightweight Directory Access Protocol (LDAP) to retrieve user entries and attributes stored in the directory. Several vendors including Microsoft and Novell support the LDAP standard. The SAP EP requires an LDAP-compatible directory. The SAP EP may use any LDAP directory that is already in place within a corporation, or the Novell eDirectory delivered by SAP with the SAP BI solution may be implemented. LDAP is a standard method by which to access a user directory. The directory is similar to a database in many ways, but it is designed to support reading information more so than writing, and as such it lacks many of the rollback restore features of a conventional database.

The portal uses the directory to store users and their information, such as full name, password, and address. The mapping of each user to the various component systems is also stored in the directory. The directory may include passwords to each of these systems as well. Access is controlled by the directory server.

Many corporations already have some kind of directory deployed. It is possible to synchronize the LDAP-compliant directory that is delivered as part of the SAP EP with one or many existing corporate directories. In the end SAP customers have a choice of using the directory delivered by SAP, a non-SAP directory, or a combination of both. The end goal is to support a single sign-on to corporate applications and information sources. The SAP EP makes this possible by the use of a certificate that may be loaded into a corporate application, SAP BW, for example. Once the certificate is loaded into the SAP BW, a user in the portal may be granted access to the system.

Knowledge Management

SAP EP contains a set of services for managing knowledge and collaboration. The Knowledge Management (KM) aspect of the SAP EP provides efficient document management, automatic classification, check in/check out, subscription, feedback, versioning, and retrieval of documents and unstructured data.

The Knowledge Management functionality delivered with the SAP EP component is not a document management system or Web content management system like Vignette, Interwoven, or Documentum. The platform is designed to harmonize these tools under one enterprise knowledge management platform regardless of the data's physical location. The platform consists of five areas that work together on unstructured content: subscription and notification services, the repository framework, taxonomy and classification engines, communication and collaboration services, and index and search engines.

Repository Framework

The repository framework is at the center of Knowledge Management. The content of documents and the corresponding document attributes, are managed here. Content may physically reside in any number of places, including pure play document or Web content management subsystems. The repository framework is an integration layer used to communicate with the subsystems that physically hold the documents. The subsystem may be a filesystem, document management applications, or a database such as the one SAP BW runs on. In fact, the SAP Web Application Server has its own set of document management services. We will touch on this in Chapter 7 as we investigate attaching documents to query results in the Business Explorer suite of tools.

A Repository Manager is defined for each content source or subsystem. The Repository Manager's role is to integrate the repositories of each content source. The Repository Manager utilizes application programming interfaces (APIs) to access the functionality of the subsystems. So, if an SAP EP administrator would like to interface with Documentum and take advantage of Documentum's capability to lock documents, he or she may do so programmatically through the APIs.

Classification Systems

Two primary classification systems are available in the SAP EP: manual classification and automatic classification. The KM services organize content in folders, or tree structures, analogous to the folder structure found in the Microsoft Windows Explorer. This allows, for example, folders for Wine to have subfolders for Varietals, Regions, Glassware, and so on. In addition, the subfolder Varietals may have subfolders of its own such as Cabernet, Zinfandel, Malbec, Viognier, and Pinotage. The platform supports the automatic generation of taxonomies as well as traditional manual classification. A folder structure may be automatically generated after the classification engine is "trained." The training process weighs different subjects according to an organization's preferences and is similar to the training of a data mining method (a concept we discuss in Chapter 8).

Once content is classified, it is made available to the portal user in a few different ways. Documents have a *home folder* that may be navigated to by expanding and collapsing the folder tree or each document may be access by a Uniform Resource Locator (URL). The URL enables documents to be linked to other documents that may be categorized in different logical folders. This provides end users the option of navigating the treelike structure to find information, as well as the ability to jump to associated information based on the links.

Communication and Collaboration Services

The Enterprise Portal supports the entry of personal notes for any given document. A collection of feedback and rating forms is also delivered with the SAP EP. The feedback and polling information is then used during the automatic classification as a preference for categorizing new documents or reclassifying existing documents. The collaboration services allow, for example, a document to be published to a specific business workflow process for approval.

The integration points between the SAP BW and the Enterprise Portal components are quickly increasing in breadth. The SAP BI solution with SAP BW version 3.0 supports the publishing of Web-based analytics to the portal and the ability to attach documents to query results. These features alone provide a solid platform for collaborative business intelligence. We are optimistic that SAP will integrate instant messaging and *aware routing* features that send real-time alerts to online and available individuals or services that may take corrective action into the mySAP Business Intelligence solution and take collaborative business intelligence to a new level.

Index, Search, and Retrieval

Until recent years, SAP's attitude has been "if it was not invented here, it does not exist." The acquisition of TopTier Software and InQMy may have helped SAP shake the perception that all technology must be created in its labs for it to be brought to market. However, in the area of text indexing and retrieval, SAP has stuck to the built-versus-buy heritage and created an indexing service called TRex. TRex can index Web sites, corporate directories, local directories, and other file management systems. TRex creates an index for both structured and unstructured information and supports Java and .NET services. Three primary search features are available: basic, linguistic, and fuzzy. The basic search is a standard boolean search. A linguistic search retrieves words of the same family; for example, a search for *grapes* may return documents about wine, raisins, farming, and so on. A fuzzy search is best applied when the spelling of a word is unknown.

Business Unification

The SAP Business Intelligence Solution includes an optional Enterprise Portal component call Business Unification. Business Unification enables the creation of a unified object model so that a portal user may dynamically integrate applications and information from various sources.

This functionality may best be described with an example. Imagine that a manager logs on to her intranet. Navigating to the iView she then displays a list of sales orders that have been entered for her division. She sees a unification icon next to each sales order, which lets her know that a relationship exists between this sales order and another object in this or another system. In this case, there is an object defined that represents customer master data in a separate CRM system. The manager can drag any part of the sales order to the object representing the customer, and the unification technology will relate the sales order to the details of the corresponding customer.

The unification concept was perhaps the primary benefit of SAP AG acquiring TopTier Software in the spring of 2001, aside from the talented human capital. Unification uses logical business objects from component systems to create a unification object model of sorts. This object model is stored in the repository, and a mapping links objects to one another. Through the use of the unification server portal, users are able to dynamically pass content from one information source or application to another.

Unification within mySAP.com components is reasonably straightforward, as SAP has developed its application components, for the most part, on a consistent business object model. These logical business objects represent such things as purchase orders, vendors, even users of a system. Let's look at the aforementioned sales order example. The sales order has different attributes such as the customer's PO number, document date, the product ordered, the quantities that are being purchased, customer that is requesting the order, price, and so on. These attributes may be used as input for various transactions. The customer placing the sales order may only be displayed by perhaps a unique identifying number. Most users will not know which customer the number is associated with unless they go to the transaction to display the master data for the customer that placed a specific order.

Since the repository contains an object representing the customer and an object representing the purchase order along with the relationship between the two objects, unification is possible. The so-called unifier is stored in the Business Object Repository (BOR). This enables a portal user that may be picking products in order to fill the sales order to take the order and drag it to the customer master data display transaction within the portal page and release. The customer number, along with the other attributes of the sales order object, would be passed as input parameters to the receiver, in this case, the master data display transaction. This drag and relate utilizes the Hyper-relational Navigation Protocol (HRNP), which passes the information about the object, as well as the object key.

For example, a sales order object in the BOR may be referenced by BUS2012. An instantiation of the order object—that is, a specific sales order—may be given the number 12345. The Hyper-relational Navigation Protocol would enable the association of the specific sales order as it is displayed on the portal page. This is seen by the portal user as a dragable link displayed as a unification icon. The hypertext markup for this would look like the following considering this unifier is available through port 3500:

```
<href a="hrnp://mysystem.mydomain:3500/BUS2012/OBJECTKEY/12345">
```

All of the sales orders in a system will have the same dragable link as seen in the preceding code snippet. However, the last five digits would represent each unique purchase order. Since the object is dragged as a whole, it does not matter which attributes are specifically dragged to the master data display transaction. The object model and underlying relationships between the objects will take care to determine the appropriate values to pass. Therefore, you may drag the customer number, the sales order number, or perhaps even an item within the sales order to the display customer transaction and display the correct customer master data.

The business objects of a component system are mapped within their respective BOR. These relationships are defined with the Correlater Wizard. The wizard evaluates the business objects within the repository and finds potential objects that may be related. It is possible to manually establish relationships that are not picked up by the wizard.

It should be noted that a unifier project is necessary per component system. Each project is then defined within the portal as a data source. For example, SAP R/3 would be defined in the EP as a data source so the business objects found in SAP R/3 may be included in a Unifier Project. Within the data source definition users are mapped to their appropriate component user IDs. This can be done using either certificates or standard user mapping. Once this linkage is established, the unifier project is assigned to a role, and the role is assigned to a portal user.

An important aspect of unification is the *connector*. A connector provides an interface to communicate with component system whether that system is an SAP component or non-SAP component. A connector must be installed or activated for a unification project. In the case of unifying non-SAP systems, databases take the place of the SAP business objects.

Summary

SAP with ERP has long been a force in the information technology industry. SAP has evolved its offering beyond just ERP into e-business software solutions including customer relationship management, supply chain optimization, and business intelligence. This transformation has been driven by customer demand and technological innovation. The mySAP Business Intelligence Solution consists of two main components: Enterprise Portal and SAP BW. Together, the SAP EP and SAP BW create a significant opportunity for companies to lay the foundation for collaborative business intelligence and analytic applications that combine traditional structured data and content from the Web and document management systems.

Starting in Chapter 3 and throughout the remainder of this book, we will describe SAP BW software capabilities, its architecture, and the options available to those implementing the software to solve business challenges.

SAP Business Information Warehouse Architecture

SAP entered the data warehouse market when it started maturing and has been able to take advantage of the experience available and avoid many mistakes made by early adopters. To those familiar with other data warehouse solutions and custom data warehouse development, as well as anyone following discussions about data warehousing, the high-level SAP business warehouse (BW) architecture will look familiar.

Building SAP BW on top of the SAP Web Application Server (formerly known as SAP Basis), SAP has been able to inherit not only the multi-tier architecture implemented there but also a complete software development environment, a large amount of systems management tools, and a lot of additional functionality (e.g., currency conversion or security) and tools available there. Because SAP BW is implemented on top of the SAP Web Application Server, it is often considered a part of or an add-on to SAP R/3. This is not correct: SAP BW, though still closely related to SAP R/3, is a completely separate software package that can be used in any—SAP or non-SAP—environment. At the end of this chapter, we'll have a closer look at the common architecture of SAP systems and how it serves SAP BW.

In Chapter 3 we continue the discussion from Chapter 2 on the SAP Business Intelligence strategy and how SAP BW is embedded into this. We provide an overview of the SAP BW architecture and its meta data concept, and map the SAP BW features to the corporate information factory (CIF) concept developed by Bill Inmon. This chapter concludes with the architecture of the SAP Web Application Server.

SAP BW Architectural Components

Figure 3.1 shows a high-level view of the SAP BW architecture, with six main building blocks. It is no surprise to see that SAP BW is completely based on an integrated meta data concept, with meta data being managed by *meta data services*. SAP BW is one of the few data warehouse products that offer an integrated, one-stop-shopping user interface for administering and monitoring SAP BW: the administration services available through the Administrator Workbench.

Looking at the center of Figure 3.1, we find the usual layered architecture of an end-to-end data warehouse accompanied by two administrative architectural components:

- Extraction, loading, and transformation (ETL) services layer
- Storage services layer, including services for storing and archiving information
- Analysis and access services layer, providing access to the information stored in SAP BW
- Presentation services layer, offering different options for presenting information to end users
- Administration services
- Meta data services

Each layer will be discussed in more detail in the sections that follow.

Administration Services

The *administration services* include all services required to administer an SAP BW system. Administration services are available through the *Administrator Workbench* (AWB), a single point of entry for data warehouse development, administration, and maintenance tasks in SAP BW. Figure 3.2 shows a screenshot of the AWB.

As the most prominent architectural component, the AWB includes a *meta data modeling* component, a *scheduler,* and a *monitor*, as shown in Figure 3.2. Other components of the AWB include the following:

- The *transport connector* supports the information modeling and development process by collecting objects that have to be transported from the development system to a test or production system and assigning those objects to transport requests. The details of the transport connector are covered later in this chapter.
- The *reporting agent* allows scheduling query execution for batch printing or raising exception alerts. The reporting agent is covered in more detail in Chapters 7 and 9.
- The *document interface* allows managing documents of any type assigned to SAP BW meta data objects.
- The *translation component* supports the implementation of multilingual systems.

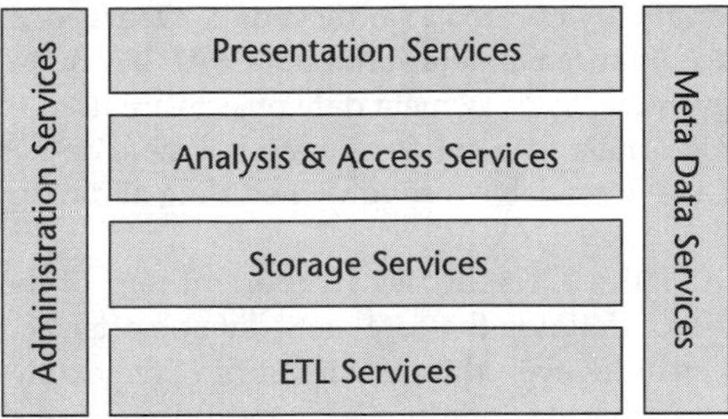

Figure 3.1 SAP BW architecture.

Meta Data Modeling

Like other data warehouse solutions, SAP BW is based on meta data, or data about data. Bill Inmon defines three classes of meta data:

- Technical meta data
- Business meta data
- Operational meta data

On the other hand, SAP BW distinguishes two basic classes of meta data: predefined meta data called Business Content and client-defined meta data. Both classes of meta data can be maintained using the same user interface. A detailed definition of the Business Content and a discussion of its role in SAP BW implementation projects can be found in Chapter 5.

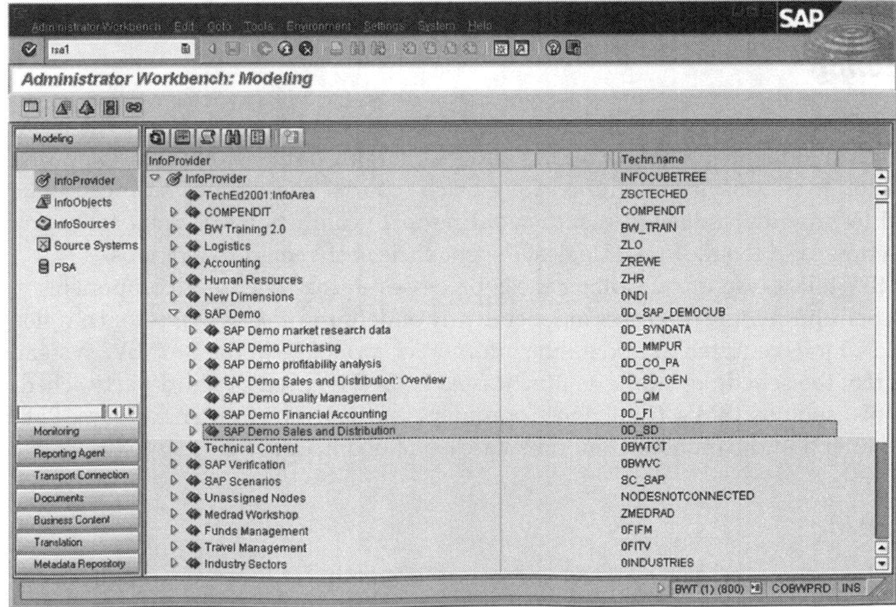

Figure 3.2 The Administrator Workbench.

Business and technical meta data is commonly referred to as meta data. Operational meta data refers to data about processes as opposed to data about data. SAP BW maintains all three types of meta data. However, the SAP BW meta data objects are used to model and maintain business and technical meta data, while operational meta data is generated by data warehouse processes and is available through scheduling and monitoring components.

The modeling functionality shown in Figure 3.2 is the most important part of the AWB, as it provides the main entry point for defining the core meta data objects used to support reporting and analysis. This includes everything from defining the extraction processes and implementing transformations to defining flat or multidimensional objects for information storage. The Business Content component allows you to browse through the predefined models available and activate them. Once activated, you can use these information models without further modification or extend them using the modeling component of the AWB.

The Meta Data Repository provides an online hypertext documentation of either activated meta data objects (the ones actually used in the BW system) and the meta data objects of the Business Content. You can export this hypertext documentation to a set of HTML files and publish it on a Web server, where it may also serve as an online and automatically updated project documentation.

An offline meta data modeling tool tentatively called *Repository Studio* is currently under development at SAP. The Repository Studio is designed to support offline meta data modeling for SAP BW meta data. SAP BW meta data is imported into the offline repository. There you can modify it using the modeling functionality of the Repository Studio and export it back into an SAP BW system. The Repository Studio is a completely Web-based, multi-user application that you can use in team environments without having to be connected to an SAP BW system. However, it still supports working offline (e.g., on laptops while traveling) by integrating a standalone Web server.

Scheduling

Data warehousing requires batch processing for loading and transforming data, creating and maintaining aggregates, creating and maintaining database indexes, exporting information to other systems, and creating batch reports. These processes need to be planned to provide results in time, to avoid resource conflicts by running too many jobs at a time, and to take care of logical dependencies between different jobs.

SAP BW takes care of controlling these processes in the scheduler component by either scheduling single processes independently or defining *process chains* for complex networks of jobs required to update the information available in the SAP BW system. In addition, the scheduler supports Business APIs (BAPIs) used by third-party scheduling tools, such as IBM's Tivoli and Computer Associate's Unicenter Autosys. Both the scheduler and the monitor component are explained in detail in Chapter 9.

Monitoring

Equally important as starting batch processes is monitoring and eventually troubleshooting them. This is what the SAP BW monitor is designed for. Figure 3.3 shows a screenshot of the Data Load Monitor.

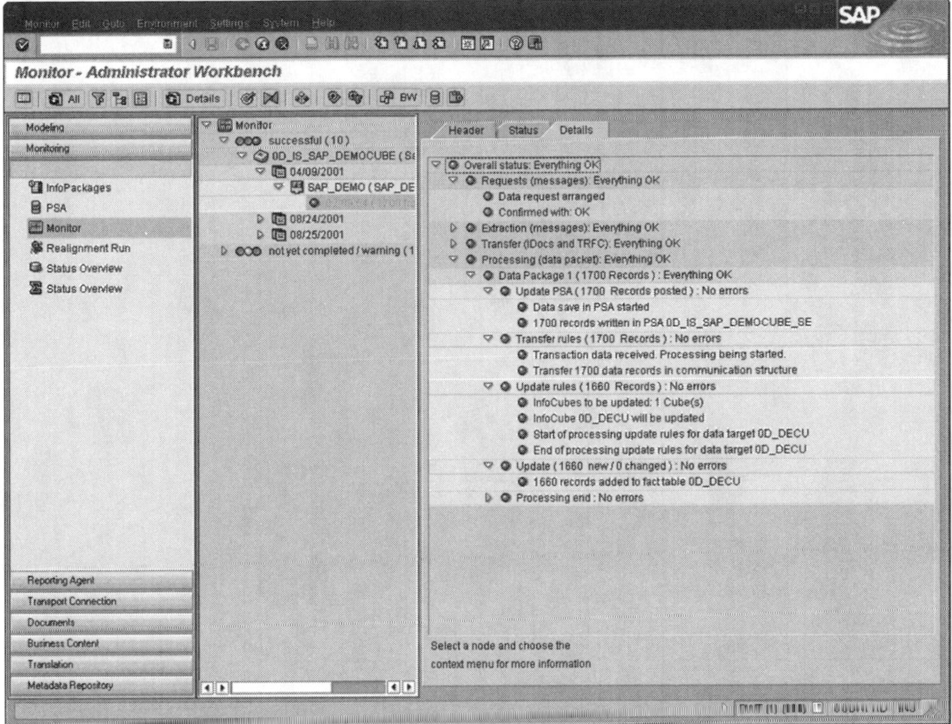

Figure 3.3 The Data Load Monitor.

The Data Load Monitor supports troubleshooting by providing access to detailed protocols of all activities related to loading, transforming, and storing data in SAP BW—allowing you to access single data records and to simulate and debug user-defined transformations. Other processes monitored are ODS object activation, master data attribute activation, hierarchy activation, aggregate rollup, realignment and readjustment jobs, InfoCube compression jobs, database index maintenance, database statistics maintenance, and data exports.

Reporting Agent

The *reporting agent* allows the execution of queries in batch mode. Batch mode query execution can be used to:

- Print reports.
- Automatically identify exception conditions and notify users responsible for taking appropriate action.
- Precompute query results for use in Web templates.
- Precompute value sets for use with value set variables (see the *Queries* section, later in the chapter, for a definition of variables).

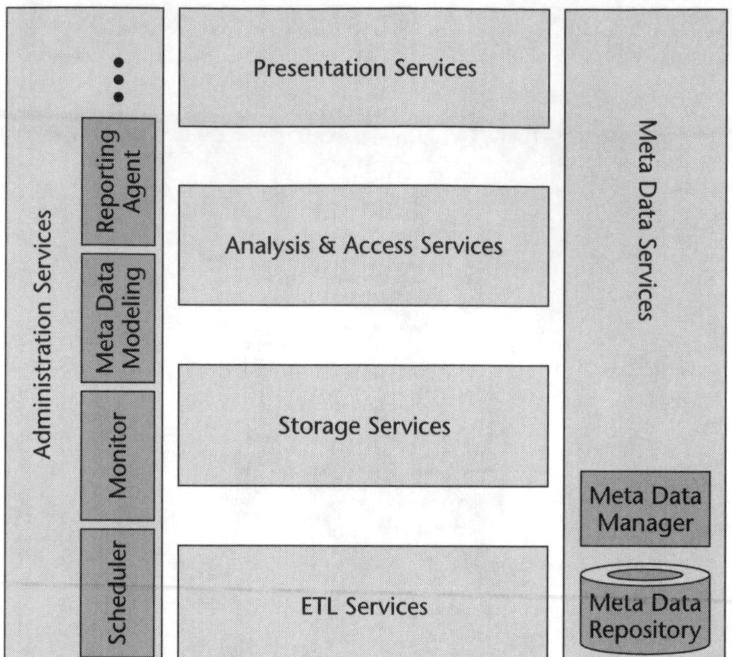

Figure 3.4 Meta data services architecture.

Meta Data Services

The SAP BW Meta Data Services components provide both an integrated *Meta Data Repository* where all meta data is stored and a *Meta Data Manager* that handles all requests for retrieving, adding, changing, or deleting meta data. The Meta Data Manager also allows the exchange of meta data with other systems compliant to the Common Warehouse Metamodel Initiative (CWMI) specified by the Object Management Group (www.omg.org). Figure 3.4 shows the meta data services layer architecture.

Figure 3.5 shows the Meta Data Repository integrated into the Administrator Workbench, with a list of all meta data objects available there. A detailed discussion of the meta data available in SAP BW can be found in the SAP BW Meta Data Objects section later in this chapter.

ETL Services

The extraction, transformation, and loading (ETL) services layer of the SAP BW architecture includes services for data extraction, data transformation, and loading of data and serves as a staging area for intermediate data storage for quality assurance purposes.

SAP BW has long been regarded as a proprietary solution, not allowing, or at least not very good at, loading data from non-SAP source systems. This is not true, and it has not been true right from the early days of the 1.2 release. With the Staging BAPI, SAP has provided an open interface for exchanging meta data with SAP BW and uploading data to SAP BW. This interface has been widely adopted by ETL vendors like Ascential Software, ETI, and Informatica. While it has been limited to downloading meta data from SAP BW and uploading data to SAP BW, the Staging BAPI today supports two-way meta data transfers.

It is true, however, that the extraction technology provided as an integral part of SAP BW is restricted to database management systems supported by mySAP technology and that it does not allow extracting data from other database systems like IBM IMS and Sybase. It also does not support proprietary file formats such as dBase file formats, Microsoft Access file formats, Microsoft Excel file formats, and others. On the other hand, the ETL services layer of SAP BW provides all the functionality required to load data from non-SAP systems in exactly the same way as it does for data from SAP systems. SAP BW does not in fact distinguish between different types of source systems after data has arrived in the staging area. The ETL services layer provides open interfaces for loading non-SAP data. Figure 3.6 shows the architecture of the ETL service layer.

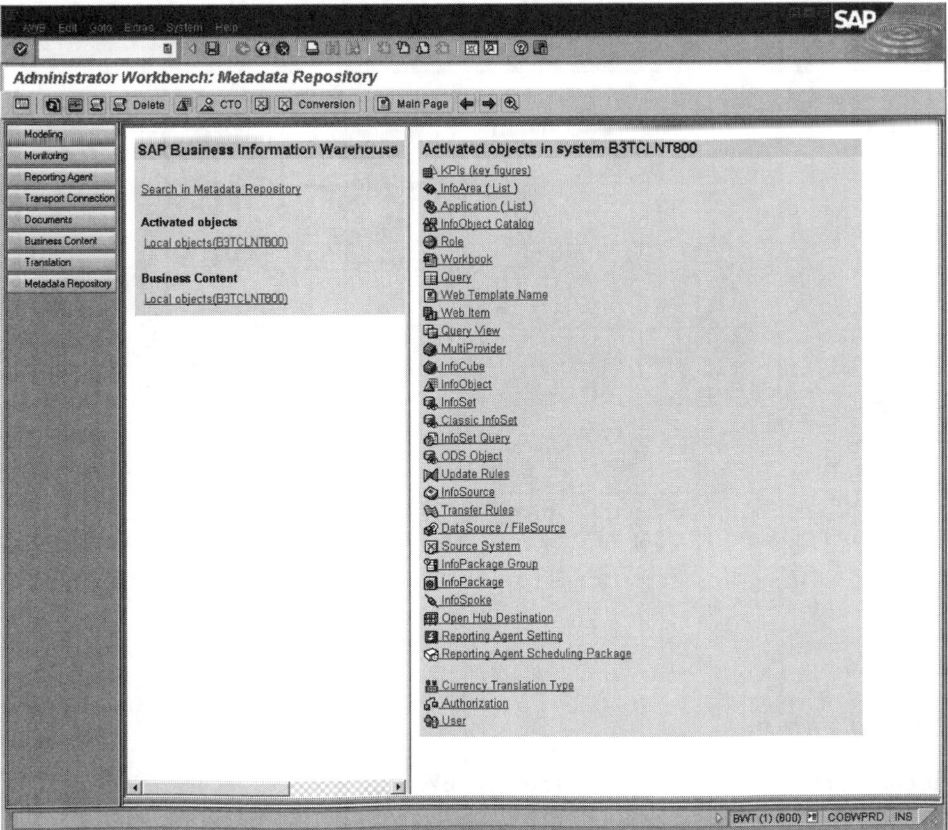

Figure 3.5 SAP BW Meta Data Repository.

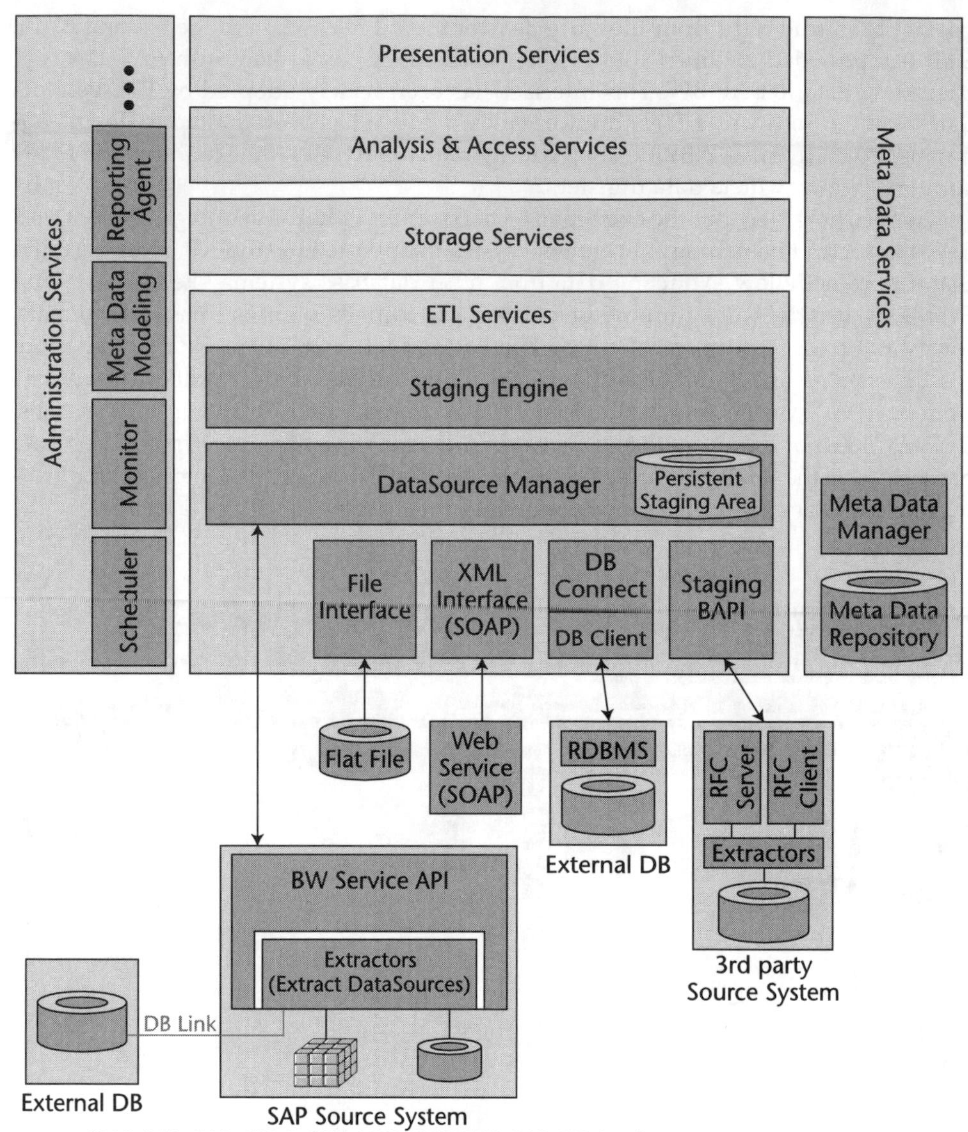

Figure 3.6 ETL services architecture.

Staging Engine

The core part of the ETL services layer of SAP BW is the *Staging Engine*, which manages the staging process for all data received from several types of source systems. The Staging Engine generates and executes transformation programs, performing the transfer and update rules defined in the AWB. It interfaces with the AWB scheduler and monitor for scheduling and monitoring data load processes. The Staging Engine does not care about the type of source system and applies the same staging process to non-SAP data as it does for SAP data.

However, the actual implementation of transformation rules will differ for different systems or different types of systems, simply because different systems may deliver data about the same business events (e.g., sales orders) using different record layouts, different data types, and different characteristics values for the same business semantics. In addition, different systems may provide different levels of data quality. A detailed discussion of the staging process can be found in Chapter 6.

DataSource Manager

The Staging Engine is supported by the *DataSource Manager*. The DataSource Manager manages the definitions of the different sources of data known to the SAP BW system and supports five different types of interfaces:

- BW Service API
- File interface
- XML interface
- DB Connect interface
- Staging BAPI

The DataSource Manager also allows capturing and intermediately storing uploaded data in the persistent staging area (PSA). Data stored in the PSA is used for several purposes:

Data quality. Complex check routines and correction routines can be implemented to make sure data in the PSA is consistent before it is integrated with other data sources or is uploaded to its final data target.

Repeated delta updates. Many extraction programs do not allow you to repeat uploads of *deltas,* which are sets of records in the data source that have been inserted or updated since the last upload. Repeated delta uploads are required in cases where the same delta data has to be updated into multiple data targets at different points of time.

Short-term backup data source. A short-term backup data source is required in cases where update processes fail for some technical reason (such as insufficient disk space or network availability) or where subtle errors in the transformations performed on the data warehouse side are only discovered at a later point in time. Once stored in the PSA, data may be read from the PSA and updated into the final data target at any point in time and as often as required.

Supporting development. Based on data in the PSA, SAP BW allows you to simulate transfer rules, and update rules, and to debug the implemented transformations.

BW Service API

The most important interface supported by the DataSource Manager in SAP environments is the *BW Service API*. The BW Service API is available for two basic types of SAP systems: SAP R/3-based systems, including SAP R/3 and SAP Customer Relationship Management (mySAP CRM™), and SAP BW-based systems, such as SAP BW itself; SAP Strategic Enterprise Management (mySAP SEM™); and SAP Advanced Planner and Optimizer (mySAP SCM™). SAP R/3-type systems usually provide operational data, while SAP BW-based systems allow the creation of complex information flow scenarios with cascading SAP BW instances (see Figure 3.7).

The BW Service API provides a framework for data replication from SAP systems, including generic data extraction, sophisticated delta handling, and online access to extraction programs via the remote InfoCube technology. It handles all communication between the source system and the requesting SAP BW system and makes a wide range of predefined extraction programs—encapsulating application know-how—available to SAP BW. It is included in most mySAP.com application components (such as SAP BW, SAP SEM, and SAP APO) and is available as part of the SAP R/3 plug-in, which also includes the actual extraction programs for SAP R/3.

Extraction programs either are part of the Business Content from where they may be enhanced according to client requirements or they are custom extraction programs defined by the client using the generic extraction technology. Generic extractors allow accessing any table or database view available in the SAP ABAP dictionary. Used in an SAP BW-based systems, the BW Service API provides access to the data stored in master data tables, ODS objects, and InfoCubes.

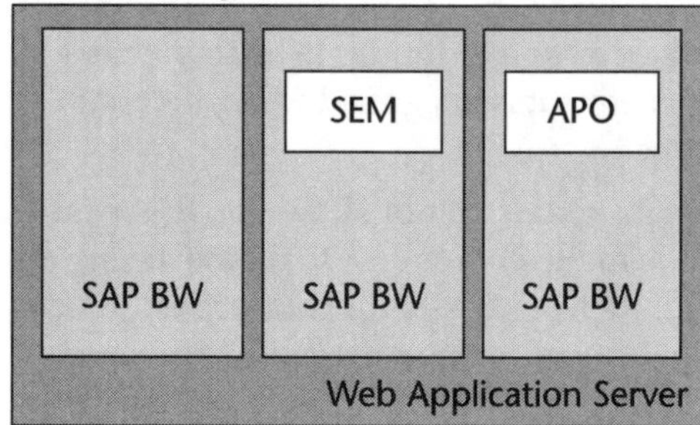

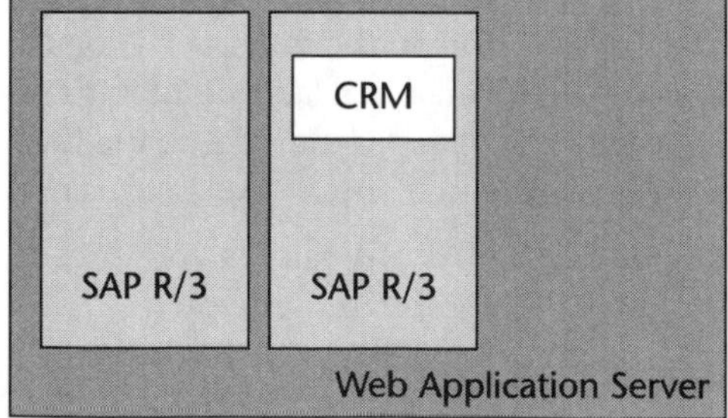

Figure 3.7 Types of SAP systems.

To provide access to external, non-SAP databases, SAP has developed the *DB Link* tool, which allows access to data stored in an external database through the BW Service API. The basic idea behind the DB Link tool is to connect to a remote database, to make the required remote table or view visible to the SAP ABAP Workbench dictionary, and to define a generic extractor for the remote table or view. The DB Link tool is supported for Oracle, Microsoft SQL Server, and IBM DB/2 databases.

With the DB Connect Interface a part of SAP BW release 3.0, the DB Link tool will lose relevance for new developments. We strongly recommend using the DB Connect interface instead.

DB Connect Interface

The *DB Connect interface* is pursuing the same goal as the DB Link interface in that it connects to a remote database and makes remote database tables available to an SAP BW system. The technical implementation, however, is completely different. The DB Connect interface uses core parts of the SAP database interface layer and the database client software (which needs to be installed separately if the remote database system differs from the local database system) to connect to the remote database. The DB Connect interface can read the remote data dictionary, replicate table, and view meta data into the local SAP BW Meta Data Repository, and it allows extraction of data from those tables and views. The DB Connect interface supports all database systems supported by SAP BW.

File Interface

The *File interface* allows loading flat files of three different types into SAP BW:

ASCII files. The file interface reads ASCII files with fixed field lengths and variable record lengths, filling missing fields with blanks and ignoring extra fields at the end of data records.

Comma-separated variables (CSV) files. CSV files are text files using a variable field delimiter (usually ";" or ",") and variable field and record length. They are commonly used to exchange data among different applications.

Binary files. The File interface can import binary files that comply with the physical data format used by ABAP programs writing data in binary format (documentation on the physical format used can be found at http://help.sap.com).

XML Interface

The *XML interface* introduced with the SAP BW 3.0 release accepts XML data streams compliant with the Simple Object Access Protocol (SOAP). While all other SAP BW interfaces follow the pull philosophy, meaning that SAP BW pulls data out of these systems by initiating data load requests, the XML interface follows a push philosophy where the actual data transfer is initiated by the source system.

Data loads through the XML interface are always triggered by an external Web service using SOAP to send XML format data to an SAP BW system, where the data is temporarily stored using the delta queue mechanism. SAP BW pulls data out of that delta queue using the same scheduling mechanisms as for other interfaces. The XML interface and the push and pull philosophies are discussed in more detail in Chapter 6.

Staging BAPI

The *Staging BAPI* is an open interface based on the BAPI technology. Available from the early days of SAP BW 1.2, the Staging BAPI allows third-party ETL tools as well as custom programs to connect to SAP BW, exchange meta data with SAP BW, and transfer data to SAP BW.

Systems using the Staging BAPI need to implement a simple RFC server program that waits for and schedules SAP BW data load requests, starts executing extraction programs accordingly, and sends the resulting data set back to SAP BW using Remote Function Call (RFC) client functionality. SAP has published detailed information about this open interface and has provided a sample extraction program implemented in Microsoft Visual Basic to showcase the use of the Staging BAPI.

As mentioned earlier in the chapter, the Staging BAPI has been widely adopted by third-party ETL tool vendors like Ascential Software, ETI, Informatica, and others. SAP has decided to strategically team up with Ascential Software to provide SAP BW clients with a low-cost, quality ETL solution for accessing arbitrary external database systems and file formats. A complete list of third-party ETL tools certified for use with SAP BW can be found on the SAP Web site (www.sap.com).

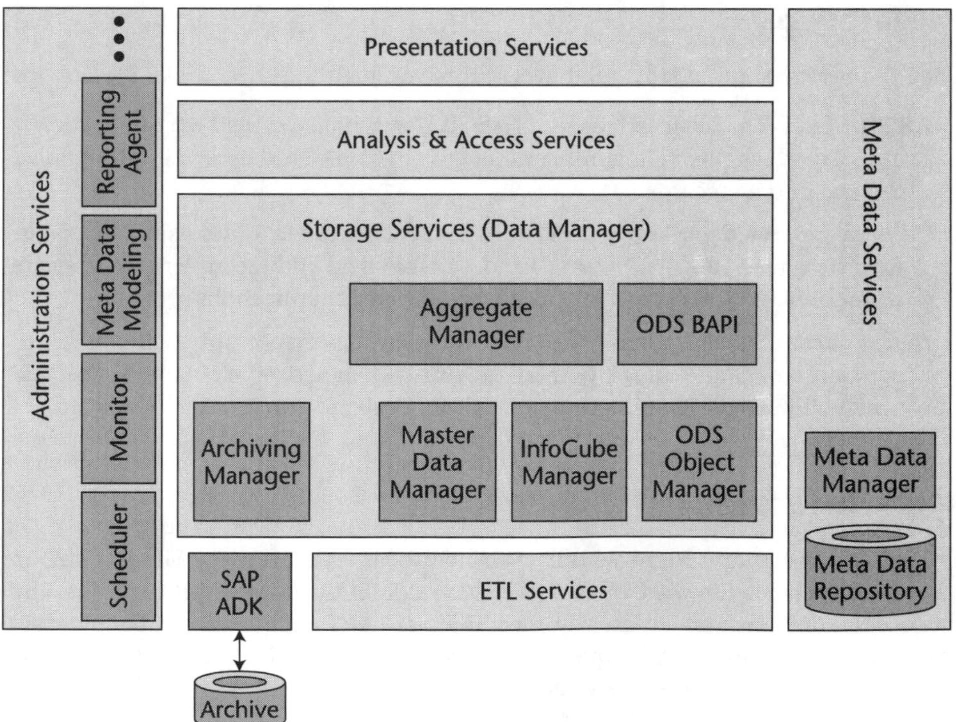

Figure 3.8 Storage services architecture.

Storage Services

The *storage services* layer (also known as the SAP BW Data Manager) manages and provides access to the different data targets available in SAP BW, as well as aggregates stored in relational or multidimensional database management systems. The storage services connect to the SAP archiving module for archiving dormant data (data that is used infrequently or no longer used at all). Figure 3.8 provides an overview of the components of the storage services layer.

Master Data Manager

The *Master Data Manager* generates the master data infrastructure consisting of master data tables as well as master data update and retrieval routines according to the definition stored in the Meta Data Repository. It maintains master data and provides access to master data for SAP BW reporting and analysis services. In Chapter 4 we'll take a closer look at the SAP BW master-data data model and discuss meta data that describes master data.

The task of maintaining master data includes:

- Handling master data uploads
- Finding or generating surrogate keys
- Handling time windows for time-dependent master data
- Ensuring the technical correctness of master data hierarchies
- Providing a generic user interface for interactive master data maintenance
- Activating master data, a process that copies modified data in the master data tables from a *modified* version, which is not visible in reporting and analysis, to an *active* version, which is visible in reporting and analysis

From an output point of view, the Master Data Manager provides access to the master data for use by SAP BW reporting components (e.g., the BEx Analyzer), as well as for exporting to other data warehouse systems via the analysis and access services.

ODS Object Manager

ODS objects are flat data structures used to support reporting, analysis, and data integration in SAP BW. The *ODS Object Manager* generates the ODS object infrastructure, which consists of an active data table, a change log, and an activation queue, as well as update and retrieval routines according to the definition stored in the Meta Data Repository. It maintains ODS object data, creates a change log for every update applied to the ODS object data as part of the activation process, and provides access to ODS object data for SAP BW reporting and analysis functionality.

The ODS Object Manager allows real-time updates to transactional ODS objects through the ODS API. Closely related to the ODS Object Manager, the ODS BAPI provides open read access to ODS objects. The details on the ODS object data model are discussed in Chapter 4, while more information about the ODS object meta data definition can be found later in this chapter.

NOTE While BAPIs are documented and supported from release to release, an API is not necessarily documented, or guaranteed to remain unchanged from release to release.

InfoCube Manager

The main structures used for multidimensional analysis in SAP BW are called InfoCubes. The *InfoCube Manager* generates the InfoCube infrastructure consisting of fact and dimension tables, as well as the update and retrieval routines according to the definition stored in the Meta Data Repository. It maintains InfoCube data, interfaces with the Aggregate Manager (discussed in the next section) and provides access to InfoCube data for SAP BW reporting and analysis services.

More details on the InfoCube data model can be found in Chapter 4; a discussion of the InfoCube meta data definition can be found later in this chapter.

Aggregate Manager

Aggregates are multidimensional data structures similar to InfoCubes containing an aggregated subset of information available through InfoCubes. Aggregates are used for optimizing reporting performance. The *Aggregate Manager* generates the aggregate infrastructure consisting of fact and dimension tables, along with the update and retrieval routines according to the definition stored in the Meta Data Repository. Maintenance of aggregates implies keeping track of updates applied to the underlying InfoCube and of updates to master data used in these aggregates, as well as applying those changes to the data stored in the aggregate.

Since SAP BW 3.0, aggregates can not only be stored in relational but also in multidimensional database systems, providing the best of both worlds to SAP BW users. Although SAP BW 3.0 was initially developed to support the multidimensional technology of Microsoft SQL Server, there are discussions about supporting other multidimensional database systems in future releases.

Archiving Manager

The *Archiving Manager* connects SAP BW to the *Archive Development Kit* (ADK). The Archiving Manager allows archiving unused, dormant data in a safe place, where it is still available if required. The Archiving Manager does not only store raw data, it also keeps track of relevant meta data—such as the layout of InfoCubes and ODS objects—which may change over time. Information archived using the ADK has to be restored in order to make it available for reporting again.

Another option available with the Archiving Manager in cooperation with FileTek's StorHouse solution allows transparent access to information archived from ODS objects without the need for explicitly restoring that information. For more information about this solution visit the FileTek Web site: www.filetek.com.

Analysis and Access Services

The *analysis and access services layer* provides access to analysis services and structured and unstructured information stored in the SAP Business Information Warehouse. Structured information is retrieved through so-named InfoProviders; unstructured information resides on a content server, which is accessed using the content management framework. Figure 3.9 provides an overview of the components of the analysis and access services layer.

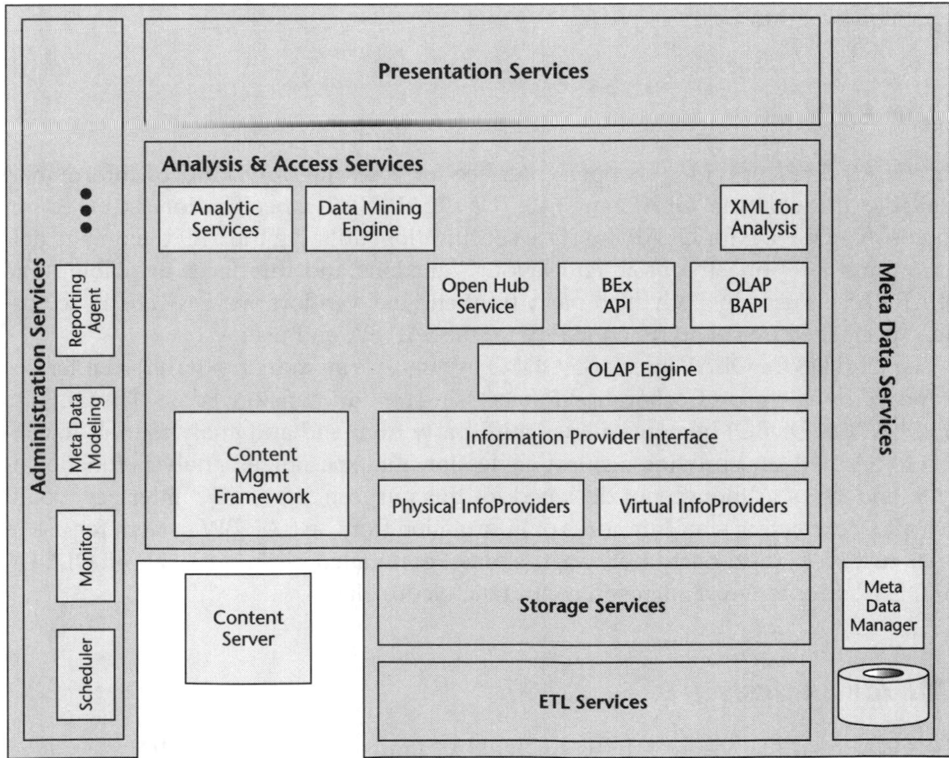

Figure 3.9 Analysis and access services architecture.

Information Provider Interface

With SAP BW 3.0 the *Information Provider interface* has been introduced to generalize access to data available in SAP BW. The Information Provider interface allows access to physical and virtual InfoProviders. Physical InfoProviders include basic InfoCubes, ODS objects, master data tables, and InfoSets physically available on the same system. Access to physical InfoProviders is handled by the storage services layer. Virtual InfoProviders include MultiProviders and remote InfoCubes. Access to virtual InfoProviders requires analyzing the request and routing the actual access to a remote system (in case of remote InfoCubes) or accessing several physical objects through the storage services layer (in case of MultiProviders).

OLAP Engine

All analysis and navigational functions—like filtering, runtime calculations, currency conversions, and authorization checks—are provided by the *OLAP engine*. The OLAP engine retrieves query definitions from the Meta Data Repository, eventually generates or updates query execution programs, and finally executes the queries by running the generated program.

OLAP BAPI

The *OLAP BAPI* provides an open interface for accessing any kind of information available through the OLAP engine. The OLAP BAPI specification is based on Microsoft's OLE DB for OLAP interface specification, utilizing the MDX language definition and adopting the basic API layout (functions and interfaces available). The OLAP BAPI is used by both third-party front-end tool vendors and SAP clients to provide specialized front-end functionality for the SAP BW end user.

The OLE DB for OLAP Interface (ODBO Interface) is an industry-standard interface proposed by Microsoft Corporation for accessing multidimensional data. The OLE DB for OLAP (or ODBO) Interface allows third-party front-end and analysis tools to connect to SAP BW and provide display, navigation, and specialized analysis functionality to end users. Although not designed for this purpose, the ODBO interface would also allow extracting small amounts of information from an SAP BW system for use in other custom or third-party software systems. For detailed information about OLE DB for OLAP, refer to www.microsoft.com/data/oledb/olap.

XML for Analysis

The OLAP BAPI serves as a basis for the SAP implementation of *XML for Analysis*. XML for Analysis is an XML API based on SOAP designed for standardized access to an analytical data provider (OLAP and data mining) over the Web.

Business Explorer API

The *Business Explorer API* connects the Business Explorer (BEx)—the SAP BW reporting and analysis front-end solution—to the OLAP engine, allowing access to all available queries. While the BEx API provides the most comprehensive set of functionality, it is not an officially published interface available for use by other applications.

Open Hub Service

The *Open Hub Service* allows controlled distribution of consistent data from any SAP BW InfoProvider to flat files, database tables. and other applications with full support for delta management, selections (filtering records), projections (selecting columns), and aggregation. All operations of the Open Hub Service are fully integrated into the scheduler and monitor.

Analytic Services and Data Mining Engine

As part of the Business Content and analytical application development, SAP has incorporated a number of analytical services, including a data mining engine, into SAP BW. While these services are integrated into the analytical applications (e.g., the data mining engine has originally been developed as part of the CRM analytics analytical application), they can still be used in custom applications.

Content Management Framework

The *content management framework* (CMF) allows you to link documents stored in the SAP Web Content Management Server or any other content server available through the HTTP-based content server interface to SAP BW meta data objects, such as InfoObjects, InfoCubes, and queries, to dynamic query result sets and even single cells of query result sets. This enables you to add additional comments, descriptions, and documentation to these objects. You can access these documents from the Administrator Workbench, the Business Explorer, and from the Web.

The SAP Web Content Management Server stores unstructured information and allows you to find and use this information efficiently. Integration with the SAP BW content management framework provides an integrated view on structured and unstructured information to the end user.

Presentation Services

The SAP BW *presentation services* layer includes all components required to present information available on the SAP BW server in the traditional Microsoft Excel-based Business Explorer Analyzer (BEx Analyzer), in the BEx Web environment, or in third-party applications. Figure 3.10 provides an overview of the components of the presentation services layer.

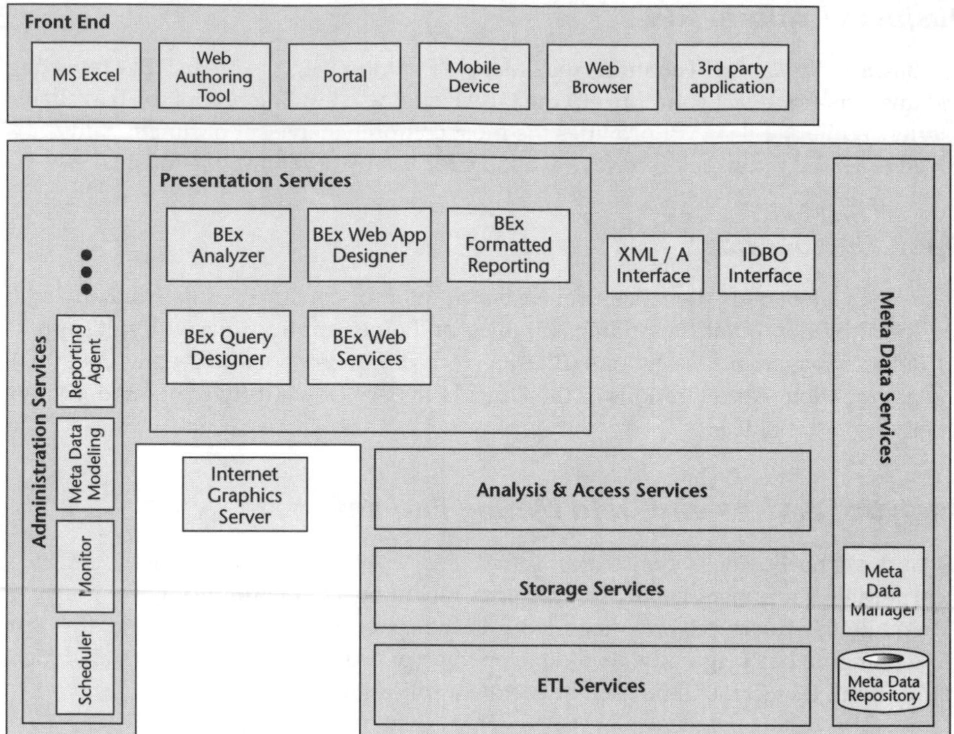

Figure 3.10 Presentation services architecture.

BEx Analyzer

The traditional SAP BW tool for actually invoking multidimensional reporting and analysis in SAP BW is the *BEx Analyzer*. The BEx Analyzer is implemented as an add-on to Microsoft Excel, combining the power of SAP BW OLAP analysis with all the features (e.g., charting) and the Visual Basic for Applications (VBA) development environment of Microsoft Excel. Storing query results in Microsoft Excel workbooks, for example, allows you to use information in offline mode, send offline information to other users, or implement complex VBA applications.

NOTE **You may note that the BEx Browser is missing in Figure 3.10. While the BEx Browser still is a part of the SAP BW offering and still is supported by SAP, many clients have chosen to either start with a Web-based approach or replace the BEx Browser by an intranet solution, making the BEx Browser obsolete.**

BEx Query Designer

All multidimensional reporting and analysis performed in SAP BW is based on query definitions stored in the Meta Data Repository. Queries provide access to multidimensional information providers (InfoCubes), as well as flat information providers (InfoSets, ODS objects, master data). The *BEx Query Designer* provides easy-to-use yet comprehensive functionality for defining queries in an interactive standalone application.

BEx Web Application Designer

The *BEx Web Application Designer* is one of the most important additions to SAP BW functionality in the 3.0 release. It allows you to quickly design complex Web pages, including not only the traditional query elements (such as query results and navigation blocks, business charts, and maps) but also interactive components like push buttons and drop-down boxes by simply dragging and dropping the required objects into the layout window, adding some additional text and graphics, adjusting the object properties, and publishing the new page to the integrated Web server. If required, users can also directly manipulate the generated HTML code. Web pages designed with the BEx Web Application Designer provide all functionality available in the traditional BEx Analyzer.

BEx Web Services

The *BEx Web Services* handle query navigation requests by converting URLs and parameters specified in these URLs into OLAP engine requests and by rendering the data sets returned into query result tables, business charts, maps, or controls supported by the Web application designer toolbox in a device-dependent way. SAP BW application developers no longer have to care about different display properties on different types of devices, such as computer screens, mobile phones, and handheld computers.

Formerly being implemented on top of the *SAP Internet Transaction Server* (ITS), the BEx Web Services have been enhanced significantly and are now integrated into the SAP Web Application Server, which is a core part of the SAP BW software.

BEx Formatted Reporting

Although much of the formatting functionality required can now be provided by the BEx Web Application Designer, there still are many applications where reports have to follow specific formatting rules—for instance, for legal reporting in many countries. SAP BW integrates with Crystal Reports by Crystal Decisions to provide comprehensive pixel-level formatted reporting functionality on a cell-by-cell basis. Details on formatted reporting can be found in Chapter 7.

Internet Graphics Server

The *Internet Graphics Server* (IGS) takes care of dynamically rendering graphics to a device-dependent format. The IGS is used to generate interactive business charts and maps based on dynamic SAP BW query for display by the Web services and the Microsoft Excel-based Business Explorer Analyzer.

Front-End Tools

SAP BW allows different types of OLAP front ends to be used. Microsoft Excel can be used in conjunction with the traditional BEx Analyzer discussed previously, while mobile devices and HTML-compliant Web browsers utilize the Web functionality of SAP BW. Web authoring tools can be used to further enhance the look and feel of Web applications—possibly in conjunction with optional Java applets, Java Server Pages, VBScripts, and other technologies supported by modern Web browsers.

Third-party applications either use the ODBO, OLAP BAPI, or XML for Analysis features. Examples of third-party tools optimized for use with SAP BW include Business Objects, Cognos PowerPlay, dynaSight by Arcplan, and others. A complete list of third-party ODBO consumers certified for use with SAP BW can be found on the SAP Service Marketplace (http://service.sap.com/bw).

Finally, SAP BW queries may be integrated into any kind of portal implementation, including, of course, the SAP Enterprise Portal offering.

SAP BW Meta Data Objects

This section provides a definition and a more detailed discussion of all relevant meta data objects available, including InfoObjects, InfoSources, InfoCubes, and queries. Figure 3.11 shows SAP BW meta data objects in the context of the SAP BW architecture.

Besides fundamental meta data needed by data extraction, staging, and analysis processes stored in SAP BW itself, any kind of documentation maintained in the content management framework—such as word processor documents, spreadsheets, and presentations—may be linked to relevant meta data objects (e.g., InfoObjects, InfoSources, InfoCubes, queries) and even dynamic query result sets.

InfoObjects

InfoObjects are the core building blocks for all other data warehouse-related meta data objects in SAP BW, for example, sources of data, analysis structures, and queries. InfoObjects implemented in SAP BW provide a powerful basis for setting up complex information models supporting multiple languages, multiple currencies with automated translations based on the same sophisticated currency conversion rules as in SAP R/3, multiple units of measure, multiple hierarchies, multiple versions of hierarchies of any type, and time-dependent master data.

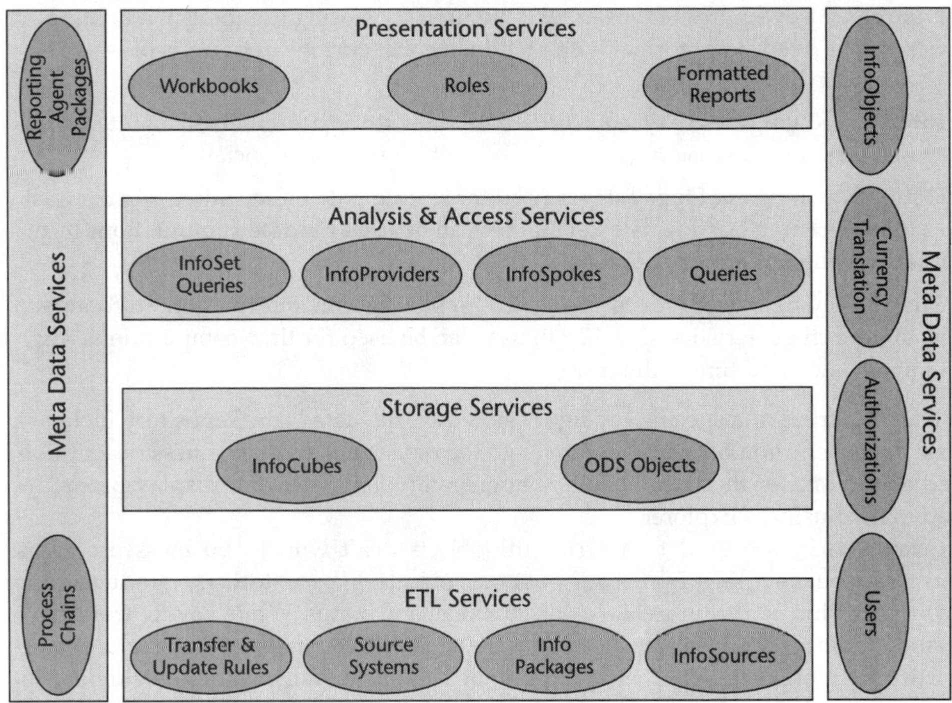

Figure 3.11 Meta data objects in context.

An *InfoObject* is the SAP BW representation of the lowest-level business object used to describe business processes and information requirements. There are four types of InfoObjects available in SAP BW: key figures, characteristics, unit characteristics, and time characteristics.

Key figures are used to describe any kind of numeric information from the business process level. Low-level numbers such as sales quantities or sales revenues and high-level key performance indicators such as customer lifetime value are all modeled using SAP BW key figures. SAP BW distinguishes six different types of key figures: amount, quantity, number, integer, date, and time key figures:

Money

Amount. Key figures of type *amount* are numeric values with an associated fixed or variable currency. SAP BW enforces a consistent representation consisting of both the key figure and the currency through the whole staging and reporting/analysis process. Variable currencies are specified by unit characteristics (see later in this section), whereas fixed currencies are specified by currency codes stored in the InfoObject description.

Quantity. Key figures of type *quantity* are numeric values with an associated fixed or variable unit of measure. As with amount key figures, SAP BW enforces a consistent representation of the key figure and the unit of measure. Variable units of measure are specified by unit characteristics (see later in this section), and fixed currencies are specified by codes for units of measure stored in the InfoObject description.

Number. Key figures of type *number* are used for storing numbers in a floating-point or fixed-point format with no dimensions (currencies or units of weight) associated.

Integer. Key figures of type *integer* are used for storing numbers in an integer format with no dimensions (currencies or units of weight) associated.

Date. Key figures of type *date* are used for storing date information. In contrast to time characteristics, date key figures can be used for date computations (e.g., actual date - planned date = delay).

Time. Key figures of type *time* are used for storing time information. In contrast to time characteristics, time key figures can be used for time computations (e.g., start time - end time = duration).

The properties of a specific key figure stored in the Meta Data Repository include a technical description of the key figure (e.g., the data type) and a business description, such as the unit of measure, currency, aggregation behavior, and display properties used in the Business Explorer.

Characteristics are used to describe the objects dealt with in business processes. These can be anything from core business objects like customers, products, and accounts to simple attributes like color, zip code, and status. While key figures from a database point of view simply describe a single field in a database base table, characteristics are more complex. The description of a characteristic includes a field description as it does for key figures, but it may also include the description of a complete set of master data tables storing attributes, texts, and hierarchies associated to that field. An InfoObject definition includes:

- Technical field descriptions such as data type, length, and conversion exits.
- Display properties such as display keys/texts, value help, relevance, and properties for geographical representations.
- Transfer routines that are executed whenever data records referencing this InfoObject are uploaded.
- Master data descriptions such as a list of attributes (which themselves are InfoObjects of any type), time dependency, and navigational properties of attributes, text properties (short, medium, long texts, time and language dependency), properties of hierarchies associated with the InfoObject (time and version dependency, among others), and finally a list of other characteristics used in a compound key for this InfoObject.

A more detailed description of the data model used for storing master data can be found in Chapter 4.

Unit characteristics are used to store either currencies or units of measure in conjunction with key figures of type *amount* and *quantity*. Unit characteristics have a reduced set of properties compared with regular characteristics.

Time characteristics are used in the obligatory time dimension of InfoCubes to express the time reference of business events. As time characteristics in SAP BW are internally treated in a special way, there is currently no way to create client-specific time characteristics. Time characteristics provided by SAP are shown in Table 3.1.

Table 3.1 Time Characteristics in SAP BW

TIME CHARACTERISTIC	DESCRIPTION
0CALDAY	Full date in YYYYMMDD format
0CALMONTH	Month in YYYYMM format
0CALMONTH2	Month in MM format
0CALQUART1	Quarter in Q format
0CALQUARTER	Quarter in YYYYQ format
0CALWEEK	Week in YYYYWW format
0CALYEAR	Year in YYYY format
0FISCPER	Fiscal period including fiscal year variant in YYYYMMM format
0FISCPER3	Fiscal period with fiscal year in YYYYMMM format
0FISCVARNT	Fiscal year variant in VV format
0FISCYEAR	Fiscal year in YYYY format
0HALFYEAR1	Half yearQuarter in H format
0WEEKDAY1	Day of week in D format

InfoObject Catalogs

An *InfoObject catalog* is a directory of InfoObjects used in the same business context. Separate types of InfoObject catalogs are used for key figures and characteristics. In addition, InfoObjects can be assigned to several InfoObject catalogs simultaneously.

InfoObject catalogs are very useful in organizing project work in large SAP BW implementations, as there are hundreds of different InfoObjects mostly used in several business contexts (e.g., an InfoObject for products would be used in production, sales, and marketing). There should be two InfoObject catalogs (one for key figures and one for characteristics assigned) defined for every business context, and every InfoObject used in this business context should be assigned to these InfoObject catalogs.

InfoCubes

An *InfoCube* is a multidimensional data container used as a basis for analysis and reporting processes in SAP BW. InfoCubes consist of key figures and characteristics, the latter being organized in dimensions. SAP BW supports two classes of InfoCubes: physical InfoCubes called *basic InfoCubes* and virtual InfoCubes called *remote InfoCubes*. While basic InfoCubes are physically stored in the same SAP BW system as their meta data description, remote InfoCube contents are physically stored on a remote SAP BW, SAP R/3, or third-party/custom system supporting the remote InfoCube BAPI.

Basic InfoCubes come in two flavors: standard and transactional. *Standard InfoCubes* are optimized for read access, allowing for scheduled uploads initiated by SAP BW. *Transactional InfoCubes* have been developed for use by applications that need to directly write data into the InfoCube, for example, planning applications such as SAP APO.

Three different types of remote InfoCubes are available in SAP BW as of today:

SAP remote InfoCubes. SAP remote InfoCubes refer to sources of data available in SAP R/3 systems through the BW Service API discussed in *the ETL Services* section at the beginning of this chapter.

General remote InfoCubes. General remote InfoCubes refer to data stored on a remote system available through the remote InfoCube BAPI. This BAPI is used for third-party and custom data providers.

Remote InfoCubes with services. Remote InfoCubes with services refer to data stored on a remote system available through a user-defined function module. This type of remote InfoCube allows flexible user-defined online access to data stored on an arbitrary remote system.

Regardless of which class they belong to, InfoCubes always consist of key figures and characteristics. SAP BW organizes characteristics used in the InfoCube in up to 16 dimensions. Three of these dimensions are predefined by SAP: the time dimension, the unit dimension, and the data packet dimension. You can customize the *time dimension* by assigning time characteristics. The unit characteristics associated to key figures included in the InfoCube definition are automatically added to the *unit dimension*. The *data packet dimension* uniquely identifies data packages loaded into the InfoCube, supporting the data quality efforts of SAP BW administrators.

The terminology SAP uses to describe InfoCubes has caused some confusion in the data warehouse community. In that community, *dimension* is commonly used for what SAP calls a *characteristic* and *dimension* is used by SAP to refer to a collection of characteristics. This explains why a maximum of 13 dimensions in SAP BW is not actually a serious restriction; one single dimension in SAP BW may be composed of more than 250 different characteristics.

InfoCubes can also include *navigational attributes*. Navigational attributes are not physically stored in the InfoCube; instead, they are available through characteristics used in the InfoCube definition. From an end user's perspective, characteristics and navigational attributes are used in exactly the same manner. However, navigational attributes differ from characteristics in two important ways: First, the use of navigational attributes results in slightly more expensive data access paths at query execution time, and second, characteristics and navigational have different semantics in reporting and analysis. For a more detailed discussion of both topics, refer to Chapter 4.

NOTE While you cannot define custom characteristics that are treated as time characteristics, you can define characteristics of an appropriate data type and use those to store time references of various kinds. These characteristics cannot be assigned to the standard time dimension but need to be assigned to a custom dimension. See Chapter 4 for a more detailed discussion of characteristics and dimensions.

Aggregates

Most of the result sets of reporting and analysis processes consist of aggregated data. An *aggregate* is a redundantly stored, usually aggregated view on a specific InfoCube. Without aggregates, the OLAP engine would have to read all relevant records at the lowest level stored in the InfoCube—which obviously takes some time for large InfoCubes. Aggregates allow you to physically store frequently used aggregated result sets in relational or multidimensional databases. Aggregates stored in relational databases essentially use the same data model as used for storing InfoCubes. Aggregates stored in multidimensional databases (Microsoft SQL Server 2000) have been introduced with SAP BW 3.0.

Aggregates are still the most powerful means SAP BW provides to optimize the performance of reporting and analysis processes. Not only can SAP BW automatically take care of updating aggregates whenever necessary (upload of master or transaction data), it also automatically determines the most efficient aggregate available at query execution time. Refer to Chapter 10 for a more detailed discussion of aggregates.

ODS Objects

An *ODS object* is a flat data container used for reporting and data cleansing/quality assurance purposes. An ODS object consists of key figures and characteristics being organized into key and data fields, where key figures cannot be used as key fields. As with InfoCubes, there are two flavors of ODS objects: standard ODS objects and transactional ODS objects, the latter again allowing for direct updates. Transactional ODS objects are used by planning applications such as SAP APO that need to directly write back forecasts and planning result data.

It is important not to confuse ODS objects with the operational data store (ODS) as defined by Bill Inmon. ODS objects are building blocks for the operational data store—they may be *objects in the ODS*. ODS objects play an important role in designing a data warehouse layer, and from an end-user point of view, ODS objects made available for reporting purposes behave just like ordinary InfoCubes.

A more detailed discussion of the role of ODS objects in the context of the corporate information factory and the differences between ODS objects and InfoCubes can be found later in this chapter. Modeling aspects of ODS objects are discussed in Chapter 4.

Data Target

A *data target* is a physical data container available in an SAP BW system. Data target is a generic term subsuming basic InfoCubes, ODS objects, and master data tables.

InfoProviders

An *InfoProvider* is a physical or virtual data object that is available in an SAP BW system and that provides information. InfoProvider is a generic term subsuming all data targets (InfoCubes, ODS objects, and master data tables), in addition to InfoSets, remote InfoCubes, and MultiProviders. InfoProviders are generally available for reporting and analysis purposes.

MultiProviders

A *MultiProvider* is a union of at least two physical or virtual InfoProviders available in an SAP BW system. A MultiProvider itself is a virtual InfoProvider.

MultiProviders actually succeed the MultiCube concept of the 2.0 release of SAP BW, which was restricted to defining a union of InfoCubes instead of a union of general InfoProviders. MultiProviders allow combining information from different subject areas on the fly at reporting/analysis execution time.

InfoAreas

An *InfoArea* is a directory of InfoProviders and InfoObject catalogs used in the same business context. Every InfoProvider or InfoObject catalog belongs to exactly one single InfoArea.

InfoAreas in the same way as InfoObject catalogs help organize project work in large SAP BW implementations.

Source Systems

A *source system* is a definition of a physical or logical system providing data to an SAP BW system. Six types of source systems are available:

- SAP R/3-based mySAP.com application components (e.g., SAP R/3, SAP CRM) equipped with the SAP BW extraction program add-n.
- SAP BW-based mySAP.com application components (e.g., SAP BW, SAP APO, SAP SEM) source systems, allowing the user to extract data from other SAP BW-based systems or to extract data from itself.
- Flat-file source systems, used for uploading flat files in ASCII, CSV (comma-separated variables), or binary format.
- DB Connect source systems providing access to external database systems.
- Third-party systems using the Staging BAPI interface; these can either be standard ETL tools supporting the Staging BAPI interface (like Ascential, ETI, or Informatica) or custom programs.
- XML source systems accepting XML data streams.

All types of source systems except the flat-file source system include references to some physical source system or service. The description of a flat-file source system just consists of a name and a short verbal description of the source system; requests for data loads are executed by the SAP BW server itself in this case.

The description of physical source systems includes network or service contact information (such as the RFC destination) to allow SAP BW to automatically connect to the source system and retrieve meta data or request data extractions.

InfoSources

An *InfoSource* describes a source of business information (business events or business object description) available in one or multiple source systems. The core part of an InfoSource definition is the *communication structure* that is composed of a set of InfoObjects.

An InfoSource is not used to store data. Instead, it is an intermediary between the technical details of the data transfer process and the specific business requirements modeled into the InfoCubes, ODS objects, and master data. Figure 3.12 shows an InfoSource and its communication structure.

SAP BW used to distinguish between transaction and master data InfoSources. Transaction data InfoSources were used for updating ODS objects and InfoCubes, whereas master data InfoSources were used for updating master data tables (attribute tables, texts, and hierarchies). In release 3.0 SAP replaced transaction data InfoSources with a more flexible type of InfoSource capable of staging transaction and master data to all kinds of data targets. For compatibility reasons, master data updates are still supported.

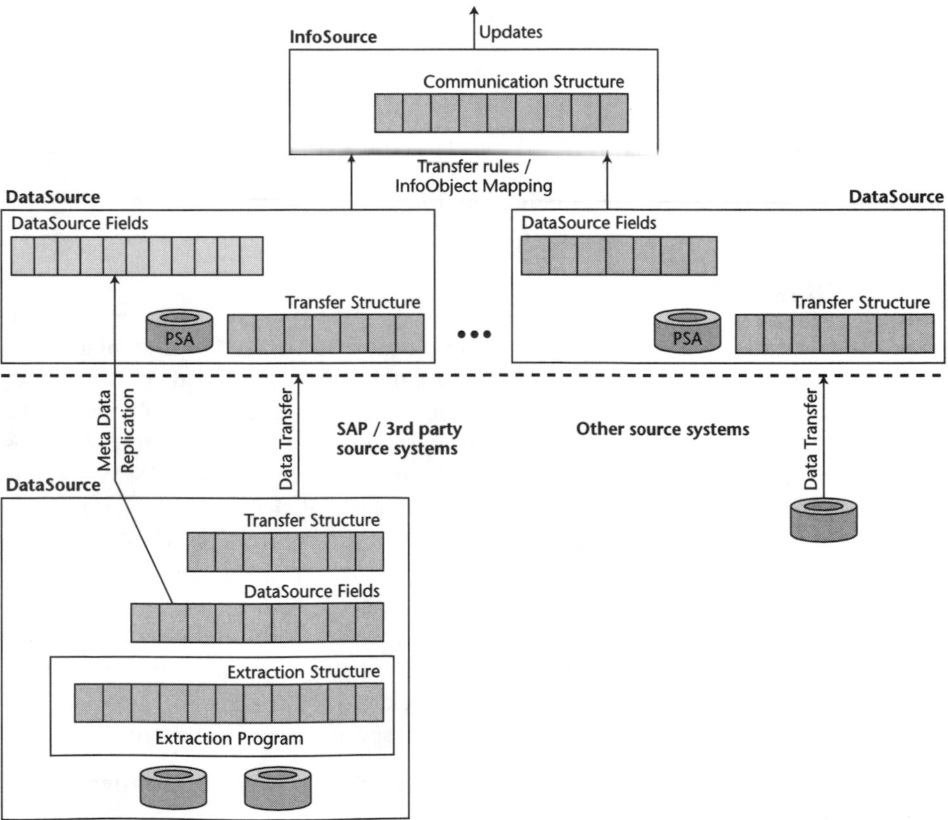

Figure 3.12 InfoSources and DataSources.

Application Hierarchy

The *application hierarchy* is used to group InfoSources available in SAP BW according to the applications they represent (e.g., SAP R/3 Sales and Distribution).

Just as InfoObject catalogs are useful for organizing InfoObjects, the application hierarchy helps to organize InfoSources. InfoSources cannot be assigned to more than one node in the application hierarchy.

DataSources

A *DataSource* describes a specific source of data on a specific source system from a technical point of view. The DataSource description includes information about the extraction process and the data transfer process, and it provides the option to store data transferred to SAP BW in the persistent staging area. SAP BW distinguishes between DataSources for transaction data, master data attributes, texts, and hierarchies.

DataSource descriptions are source-system-specific, as different source systems may provide the same data in different specifications, technical formats, or with a different level of detail. Source systems may provide a list of fields available for the DataSource, which may be replicated to the SAP BW Meta Data Repository, as shown on the lower left-hand side of Figure 3.12. Or DataSources may have to be maintained manually, as for DataSources for flat-file source systems (lower right-hand side of Figure 3.12).

Note that regardless of the type of source system, the DataSource definition itself is always controlled by SAP BW, while the extraction process and the technical specifications of the extraction program are defined by the source system.

Transfer Rules

Transfer rules are a set of transformations defining the mapping of fields available in a specific DataSource to the fields used in the InfoSource definition. You create transfer rules by assigning a DataSource to an InfoSource and assigning InfoObjects to the fields of the extract structure (InfoObject mapping). The main purpose of transfer rules is converting the source-system-specific representation of data into an SAP BW-specific view and eliminating technical or semantic differences between multiple source systems providing the same data. Typical transformations used for this purpose include data type conversions, key harmonization, and addition of missing data. Transfer rules allow you to check the data loaded for referential integrity—enforcing that all characteristics values sent by the source system are already available in the corresponding master data tables. In conjunction with the persistent staging area (more on the PSA coming up), you can also use transfer rules to check and ensure data integrity.

SAP BW offers several ways to actually define a specific transformation:

- Simple field assignments, where a field of the transfer structure is assigned to a field of the InfoSource
- Constant value assignment, where a constant value is assigned to a field of the InfoSource
- Formulas, where predefined transformation functions can be used to fill a field of the InfoSource

- Routines, which allow you to implement custom ABAP code for complex transformations

A *transfer structure* is data structure used to describe the technical data format used to transfer data from a source system to an SAP BW system. The transfer structure can be regarded as a contract or an agreement between the SAP BW system and its source system on how to transfer data and what data to transfer. Transfer structures effectively are a projection view upon the fields of the DataSource, as they usually are made up of a subset of those fields.

Multiple DataSources can be assigned to a single InfoSource, allowing you to extract the same kind of data from different source systems (e.g., sales orders from different operational systems used in different regions) or to extract different flavors of the same kind of data from one single source system (e.g., standard material master data and material classification data from an SAP R/3 system). A DataSource can only be assigned to one single InfoSource; assigning a DataSource implicitly assigns a source system to that InfoSource.

The *persistent staging area (PSA)* is a set of database tables for storing data uploaded to an SAP BW system prior to applying transformation rules. The main purpose of the persistent staging area is to store uploaded data for data quality and consistency maintenance purposes. Once stored in the PSA, data is available for multiple updates into multiple data targets at different points of time, avoiding multiple extraction runs for the same set of data.

The PSA can be accessed using a published API and supports error handling and simulation of data updates. A complete error-handling scenario based on the PSA includes identifying and tagging invalid records as part of the upload process, manually or automatically correcting the tagged records utilizing the PSA API, and restarting the upload for the corrected records. The simulation feature includes debugging options and has proved to be helpful in developing transfer and update rules.

Update Rules

Update rules connect an InfoSource to a data target (InfoCube, ODS object, or master data table), allowing it to specify additional transformations from a business point of view.

Update rules establish a many-to-many relationship between InfoSources and data targets. An InfoSource can be used to update multiple data targets, and a data target can be updated from multiple InfoSources. While transfer rules are used to eliminate technical differences, update rules are used to perform transformations required from a business point of view. For example:

- Perform additional data validity and integrity checks
- Perform data enrichment (e.g., adding fields read from master data tables)
- Skip unnecessary data records
- Aggregate data
- Dissociate data provided in a single data record into several records in the InfoCube (e.g., dissociate plan and actual data delivered in one record)
- Convert currency and unit of measure

Update rules support the same types of transformations as transfer rules, plus an automated lookup of master data attributes that, for example, allows you to assign a material group value read from the material master data table to the material group characteristic of an InfoCube. Update rules automatically take care of mapping the logical data flow to the physical implementation of the data target, including generation of surrogate keys. For more information, see Chapter 4.

InfoPackages

All scheduling and monitoring functions for data load processes in SAP BW are based on InfoPackages. InfoPackages are defined per DataSource. The following paragraphs present an overview of the properties of an InfoPackage:

Selection criteria. Selection criteria are similar to the standard ABAP select options. Fields available in the InfoSource and tagged as selection fields can be used to restrict the set of data extracted from the source system, provided that the source system supports field selections. Selection parameters can be specified as fixed or variable values. Hierarchies do not support selections based on field values; instead, the selection screen for hierarchies allows you to select one of the hierarchies available in the source system for the current InfoSource for upload.

External filename, location, and format. These options are available only for uploads from a file source system and specify the details about the file to be uploaded.

Third-party parameters. Third-party parameters are those required by the third-party extraction program (ETL tool or custom program). These parameters heavily depend on the actual source system and typically include usernames and passwords.

Processing options. Processing options depend on the definition of the transfer rules. If the transfer rules are PSA-enabled, the processing options allow you to specify if and how the PSA should be used during the upload process.

Data target selection. Data target selection allows you to select which of the data targets available for the InfoSource should be updated by the upload process and how to handle existing data in the data target (keep data, delete based on selection criteria, or delete all data).

Update parameters. Update parameters are used to request full or delta loads and for defining basic error handling parameters.

Scheduling. Scheduling parameters allow you to specify exactly when and at what frequency a specific data upload is supposed to be executed. Options for specifying the time of an upload include immediate upload, upload at a specific point of time, upload after completion of a specific job, and upload at a certain event.

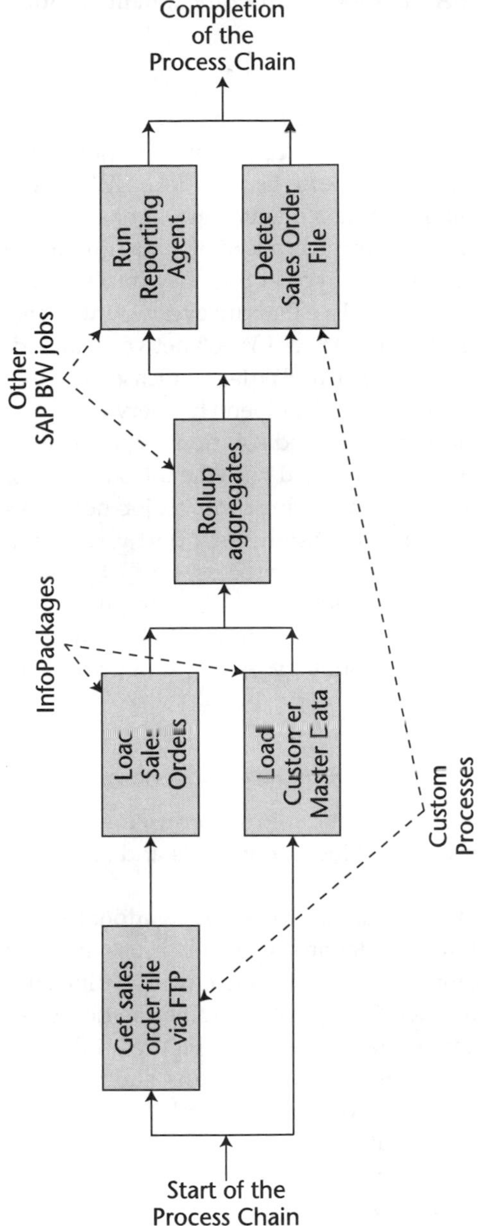

Figure 3.13 Sample process chain.

InfoPackages are fully integrated into the SAP BW job control functionality around process chains, discussed in the next section.

Process Chains

A *process chain* is a defined sequence of interdependent processes required to perform a complex task in an SAP BW environment. Data maintenance tasks in SAP BW are not restricted to uploading data. Aggregate rollups, index maintenance, master data and ODS activation, and a variety of other jobs are required to update data, guarantee best-possible performance, and maintain data integrity. Typical SAP BW implementations have complex interdependent networks of jobs in place that run every night, week, or month. Figure 3.13 shows a simple example of a typical SAP BW job network, including external custom processes, InfoPackages, and other SAP BW tasks. Please note that process chains may also include jobs exporting data using the Open Hub Service.

Previous releases of SAP BW did not provide an integrated solution for scheduling and monitoring those kinds of job networks. This has changed with the introduction of process chains in release 3.0. Process chains allow you to define complex job networks consisting of standard SAP BW jobs, as well as custom jobs; they support visualizing the job network and centrally controlling and monitoring the processes.

While SAP BW still supports the use of the old meta data objects for modeling process meta data (InfoPackage groups and event chains), it includes a tool for migrating those meta data objects to the process chain technology. All new development work should be done using process chains.

Queries

A *query* is a specification of a certain dynamic view on an InfoProvider used for multidimensional navigation. Queries are the basis for all kinds of analysis and reporting functionality available in SAP BW.

Queries are based on exactly one InfoProvider. All characteristics, navigational attributes, and key figures available through that InfoProvider are available for use in query definitions. Because queries are multidimensional objects, they effectively define subcubes called *query cubes* on top of the InfoProvider. Query cubes define the degree of freedom available for query navigation in the presentation layer (see Figure 3.14).

A query basically consists of query elements arranged in rows, columns, and free characteristics. While query elements assigned to rows and columns are displayed in the initial query view, free characteristics are not displayed but are available for navigation. Each individual navigational step (drill down, drill across, add or remove filters) in the analysis process provides a different query view. Following are all available query elements:

- A *reusable structure* is a particular commonly used collection of key figures or characteristics stored in the Meta Data Repository for reuse in multiple queries (e.g., a plan/actual variance).
- A *calculated key figure* is a formula consisting of basic, restricted, or other calculated key figures available in the InfoProvider. Calculated key figures are stored in the Meta Data Repository for reuse in multiple queries (e.g., an average discount rate).
- A *restricted key figure* is a key figure with an associated filter on certain characteristic values stored in the Meta Data Repository for reuse in multiple queries (e.g., year-to-date sales of previous year).

- A *variable* is a parameter of a query. Usually SAP BW determines values of variables at query execution time by running a user exit or requesting user input, but you may also choose to specify constant values as part of the variable definition. Variables are available for characteristic values, hierarchies, hierarchy nodes, texts, and formulas.
- A *condition* is a filter on key figure values with respect to a certain combination of characteristic values.
- An *exception* assigns an alert level from 1 to 9 (1 meaning lowest, 9 meaning highest) to a range of key figure values with respect to a certain combination of characteristic values. Alerts can be visualized in queries or in the alert monitor and can be used to automatically trigger a workflow (e.g., by sending an email).

As Figure 3.14 shows, queries are not device- or presentation-tool-dependent. The same query definition may be used by the BEx Analyzer, in a Web environment, on a mobile device, for batch and exception reporting in the reporting agent, in formatted reporting, and in a third-party presentation tool.

Query definitions are created and maintained in the graphical Query Designer by simply dragging the available query elements into the rows, columns, free characteristics, or filter area and eventually defining additional properties. The Query Designer also integrates all functionality required to define the query elements in the preceding list.

Query Workbooks

A *query workbook* is a standard Microsoft Excel workbook with embedded references to query views and optional application elements built using Microsoft Excel functionality (e.g., business charts or graphical elements such as push buttons and list boxes) and Visual Basic for Applications (VBA) code.

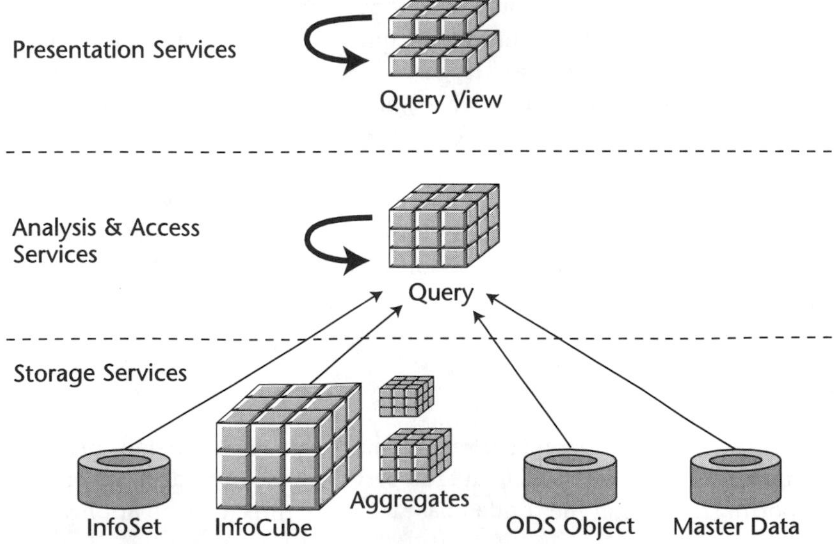

Figure 3.14 Queries and navigation.

Using Microsoft Excel as one of the query execution options in SAP BW allows you to combine the functionality of multidimensional analysis on top of a data warehouse solution with the functionality of the Microsoft Excel. In addition to the application development functionality mentioned in the preceding definition, workbooks allow for using query results (and the applications built on top of that) embedded in a query workbook offline or for distributing the query workbooks to a bigger audience via email or other file distribution mechanisms.

Reporting Agent

Reporting agent settings define the details of a particular activity performed by the reporting agent. Possible activities include printing query results in batch mode, identifying exception conditions and eventually triggering follow-up events, calculating Web templates, and calculating value sets for use with query variables. *Reporting agent scheduling packages* are used to schedule the execution of a specific reporting agent setting.

For batch printing of query results the reporting agent settings include selecting a query and designing the page layout (cover sheets, table and page headers, and footers) and query properties. Exception reporting requires selection of a query, an associated exception, and follow-up activities. Possible follow-up activities include sending email messages and adding entries to the alert monitor. Calculating Web templates requires specification of a Web template and a query. Calculating value sets requires specification of a characteristic and a query used to calculate the values for the value set.

InfoSets

An *InfoSet* is a virtual InfoProvider implementing an additional abstraction layer on top of the SAP BW Meta Data Repository. InfoSets allow defining joins of multiple ODS objects and master data tables using the InfoSet Builder. An SAP BW InfoSet differs from classical InfoSets known from other mySAP.com application components in that they are specially designed to support SAP BW meta data objects.

While SAP BW 2.0 only supported defining BEx queries for ODS objects, release 3.0 provides a lot more flexibility because it generalizes the different data targets (InfoCubes, ODS objects, and master data tables), introducing the InfoProvider concept and extending this concept by adding InfoSets to the list of meta data objects available for reporting purposes.

Keep in mind that InfoSets neither replace MultiProviders nor are MultiProviders designed to replace InfoSets. MultiProviders implement a union of several InfoProviders of all types, while InfoSets provide joins of ODS objects and master data tables but do not support InfoCubes.

Open Hub Destination

An *open hub destination* is a logical target system defining the technical details required to export data from SAP BW using the Open Hub Service. Open hub destinations are available for exporting data to flat files or database tables, or directly to an application.

The definition of an open hub destination includes a logical target system name and detail information about the data target, for example, name and format of the export or name of a database table.

InfoSpokes

InfoSpokes are the core meta data objects of the Open Hub Service. An InfoSpoke definition is composed of a data source definition that refers to an InfoProvider, a set of selection and projection (selection of columns) criteria, and a set of simple mapping rules. InfoSpokes are the outbound counterpart of (inbound) InfoSources, mapping a business view available as an InfoProvider back to the technical specification of an outbound data interface. An InfoSpoke may have multiple open hub destinations assigned, allowing for different physical data targets. This again resembles the InfoSource concept to some extent.

InfoSpokes are fully integrated into the scheduling and monitoring functionality of SAP BW. InfoSpokes have become generally available with release 3.0B of SAP BW. Further development is expected in this particular area, so watch for updates on the accompanying Web site.

Users

Users are individuals or automated processes that have a unique identifier allowing them to log on to and to use a specific SAP BW system. Automated processes in SAP BW are used to load data into an SAP BW system and to extract information from the SAP BW system for further processing.

Authorizations

An *authorization* warrants a specific user the right to perform a specific action or retrieve a certain bit of information from an SAP BW system. SAP BW utilizes the technical infrastructure known from SAP R/3 for implementing its own specific authorization concept. These technical foundations are discussed later in this chapter. A more detailed description of SAP BW authorizations can be found in Chapter 9.

Roles

As implemented in SAP BW, the *role* concept resembles the role or function individuals have in an organization. Role definitions in SAP BW are composed of a collection of menu items (referring to queries, transactions, and documents), authorizations, iViews, and a set of users assigned to this role.

Examples of such roles include a purchasing manager role, a sales representative role, and the CEO role. In the same way as in an organization, roles can be assigned to multiple individuals simultaneously (such as there may be multiple sales representatives), and the assignment of roles to individuals may change over time without affecting the definition of the role itself (a purchasing manager will always be expected to manage the purchasing process regardless of the individual filling that role).

Currency Translation Types

Currency translation types are used to define how to convert currencies from a source to a target currency and which currency exchange rates to use for this conversion in the update rules or in reporting and analysis processes. Many OLAP tools and data warehouse solutions currently available only provide poor or actually no support for handling multiple currencies, although for most companies running a data warehouse, multiple currencies are everyday business in many business processes. SAP BW again utilizes existing SAP technology for the provision of currency translation mechanism and even allows synchronizing currency conversion types as well as conversion rates with existing SAP R/3 systems.

Mapping the Corporate Information Factory to SAP BW components

Before we actually start laying out the options, methods, and tools available in SAP BW to implement the best-possible solution for analysis and reporting, let's first focus on the architectural layers of an SAP BW implementation along the lines of the CIF defined by Bill Inmon (see www.billinmon.com or *Corporate Information Factory,* 2nd Edition, Wiley). (See Figure 3.15.)

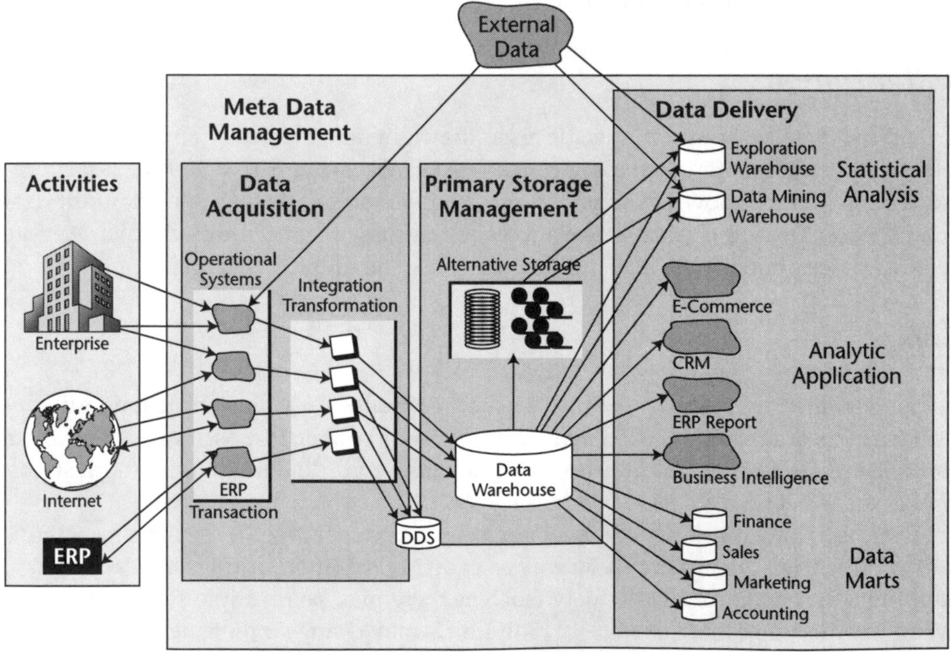

Figure 3.15 The corporate information factory.

Although SAP BW 3.0 provides meta data objects, tools, and methods allowing us to implement nearly all components of the CIF, the terminology used by SAP does not exactly match the terminology defined and used by Bill Inmon—especially in the primary storage management and data delivery layers.

The data acquisition layer is now completely covered by the SAP BW Staging Engine and by partnerships with ETL tool vendors like Ascential Software, Informatica, and others (the staging process is discussed in more detail in Chapter 6). Meta data management is handled by the Meta Data Repository, along with the Administrator Workbench, as a tool to view and modify SAP BW meta data.

One terminology mismatch is related to the ODS, which is defined by Bill Inmon as follows (see www.billinmon.com or *Building the Operational Data Store,* 2nd Edition, Wiley):

> *The Operational Data Store (ODS) is a hybrid structure that has characteristics of both the data warehouse and operational systems. Because the ODS is a hybrid structure, it is difficult to build and operate. The ODS allows the user to have OLTP response time (2-3 seconds), update capabilities, and decision support systems (DSS) capabilities.*

Bill Inmon distinguishes four types of operational data stores:

Class I. The time lag from execution in the operational environment until the moment that the update is reflected in the ODS is synchronous (i.e., less than a second)

Class II. The time lag from execution in the operational environment until the moment that the update is reflected in the ODS is in the 2- to 4-hour range (i.e., in a store-and-forward mode)

Class III. The time lag from execution in the operational environment until the moment that the update is reflected in the ODS is overnight (i.e., in a batch mode)

Class IV. Data is processed in the data warehouse and fed back to the ODS in an aggregated manner

SAP BW provides remote InfoCubes and ODS objects—nontransactional or transactional—to model the ODS layer of the CIF. Keep in mind that ODS objects are completely different concepts: ODS objects are meta data objects providing a certain functionality, whereas the ODS is an architectural layer in a data warehousing framework.

The data warehouse part of the corporate information factory is defined by Bill Inmon as follows (see www.billinmon.com or *Building the Data Warehouse,* 3rd Edition, Wiley).

> *The data warehouse is a subject-oriented, integrated, time-variant, non-volatile collection of data used to support the strategic decision-making process for the enterprise. It is the central point of data integration for business intelligence and is the source of data for the data marts, delivering a common view of enterprise data.*

The meta data object of choice for modeling the data warehouse layer in SAP BW is the ODS object, now equipped with complete archiving functionality.

Looking at the data delivery layer, we see there is an exploration warehouse, a data mining warehouse, analytical applications, and data marts. While exploration warehouses, data mining warehouses, and data marts can be built with SAP BW functionality using ODS objects, InfoCubes, and the data mining functionality/interfaces, analytical applications are usually built on top of the core functionality of SAP BW, utilizing open interfaces for data and meta data exchange and the integrated ABAP Workbench. To draw a line between the data delivery layer as defined in the CIF and the information modeling options in SAP BW that may be used to implement the data delivery layer, we use the term *InfoMart*.

An InfoMart has the following properties:

It is dynamic and disposable. InfoMarts may but do not have to be rebuilt dynamically or even disposed of, following adjustments driven by changing business environments. New or changed InfoMarts can be created very easily based on the data stored in the data warehouse layer.

It is volatile. Data in an InfoMart may or may not be updated depending on the analytical application. Pure reporting and analysis InfoMarts will be nonvolatile; InfoMarts used in other types of applications, such as planning (e.g., SAP SEM, SAP SCM) will be volatile.

It is a subset of information for a specific audience. InfoMarts focus on the reporting and analysis requirements of a specific, possibly cross-business-area audience inside or outside the organization and provide the subset of information required for this audience.

It is persistent or virtual, multidimensional, or flat. InfoMarts can be built using persistent (InfoCubes, ODS objects) or virtual InfoProviders (MultiProviders, remote InfoCubes) using multidimensional (InfoCubes) or flat (ODS objects) data models.

It focuses on reporting and analysis. InfoMarts are used primarily for reporting and analysis services, including analytical applications.

Table 3.2 summarizes the differences between InfoMarts and data marts.

Table 3.2 Characteristics of InfoMarts and Data Marts

CHARACTERISTIC	INFOMART	DATA MART
Dynamic	Yes	No
Disposable	Yes	Yes
Volatile	Yes	No
Nonvolatile	Yes	Yes
Flat	Yes	No
Dimensional	Yes	Yes
Virtual	Yes	No
Specific audience	Yes	Yes
Focus on reporting and analysis	Yes	Yes
Exploration/mining	Limited	Limited

Table 3.3 ODS Objects versus Remote Cubes for Building the ODS

CHARACTERISTIC ODS OBJECT	NONTRANSACTIONAL ODS OBJECT	TRANSACTIONAL CUBES	REMOTE
Redundancy	Yes	Yes	No
Class I ODS	No	Possible	Yes
Class II ODS	Yes	Possible	Possible
Class III ODS	Yes	Possible	Possible
Class IV ODS	Yes	Possible	Possible

The Operational Data Store

SAP BW offers two options when you are modeling the ODS layer of the CIF: ODS objects and remote InfoCubes. While ODS objects are physically stored copies of data in the SAP BW system, remote InfoCubes are references to data records stored on a separate system. Queries against ODS objects are executed on the data warehouse system; queries against remote cubes are executed on remote systems.

ODS objects come in two flavors: nontransactional and transactional. Because ODS objects provide OLTP response times for OLTP-type queries, allow updates, and provide DSS functionality, they are ideal candidates to build the operational data store. Nontransactional ODS objects (the traditional ODS objects) are updated in batch mode based on a schedule defined by an administrator. Transactional ODS objects (new with release 3.0) may be updated in real time.

Nontransactional ODS objects can be used to build operational data stores of classes II, III, and IV. You can use transactional ODS objects to build class I (as well as II, III, and IV) operational data stores, provided the OLTP system has a real-time change data capture queue and allows you to automatically propagate updates to OLTP tables to this ODS object in real-time.

Another option to simulate rather than implement class I operational data stores is using a remote InfoCube referencing to the OLTP table. Remote InfoCubes fulfill the class I ODS requirements by mimicking multidimensional analysis on operational data, avoiding redundant storage in the data warehouse system through the remote InfoCube interface. Table 3.3 provides a summary of the preceding discussion.

The Data Warehouse Layer

The main function of the data warehouse layer of the CIF is to provide an integrated history of data relevant for business decisions. The most important aspects of integration are:

Selection. Not all available data is relevant to information processing.

Harmonization. Data type conversions, calculations, and unification of technical values representing a property of an object, for example.

Data quality. Add missing information (default values or derived values) and plausibility checks.

Time. Add timestamps.

Aggregation. Aggregation of data where the level of detail provided by a source system is too high.

Looking at these characteristics of integrated data, we see that modeling the data warehouse layer means defining the foundations for the corporate information infrastructure—what data at what level of granularity is available to fulfill today's and future reporting and analysis requirements.

The main SAP BW meta data object available for modeling the data warehouse layer is the ODS object already discussed in the previous section on modeling the operational data store. In releases prior to 3.0, the ODS object, not being enabled for master data, did not fully cover the requirements of a data warehouse.

The InfoMart Layer

The final—and from an end user's point of view most important—layer of the CIF is the data delivery layer, which we refer to as the *InfoMart layer*. Most of the information available to end users is available on this level.

While InfoCubes still are the most important SAP BW meta data objects when it comes to delivering reporting and analysis functionality to end users, power users, and analytical applications, there are applications for ODS objects on this level, especially in multilevel staging scenarios where data from different applications areas need to be integrated into a single InfoProvider and for simple reporting applications. An overview of the differences between ODS objects and InfoCubes is shown in Table 3.4.

Table 3.4 Differences between ODS Objects and InfoCubes

PROPERTY	ODS OBJECT	INFOCUBE
Architecture	Flat database tables	Extended Star Schema (ESS)
Support for granular data	Yes	Yes
Staging for transactional data	Yes	Possible
Staging for master data	Yes	No
Update of key values	Not possible	Not possible
Update of characteristics	Possible	Not possible, due to ESS
Update of key figures	Possible	Only for additive key figures
Change log	Tracks every change	Tracks new records only
Support for BEx queries	Yes (medium performance)	Yes (good performance)
Support for InfoSets	Yes	No

Given the user and application requirements, there still is no silver bullet for identifying what InfoCubes or ODS objects are required or how exactly to lay out the InfoMart. The best advice we can give without knowing about specific requirements is to go for rapid, iterative development cycles as described in Chapter 2 when planning for an SAP BW implementation project. Besides mistakes possibly made in the initial requirements collection phase or the design phase, requirements tend to increase and change rapidly after going live, as new information retrieved from the system often changes the focus of business analysis and raises curiosity to look at business processes from a different angle or by a changing business environment. Having a sound data warehouse in place ensures that you can adjust InfoMarts within a reasonable amount of time and effort and be able to meet future requirements.

The Architectural Roots of SAP BW

SAP was among the first software development companies to fully adopt a multi-tier client/server model (see Figure 3.16) and move away from traditional host-based solutions for business software. This was the beginning of the SAP R/3 success story back in the early 1990s.

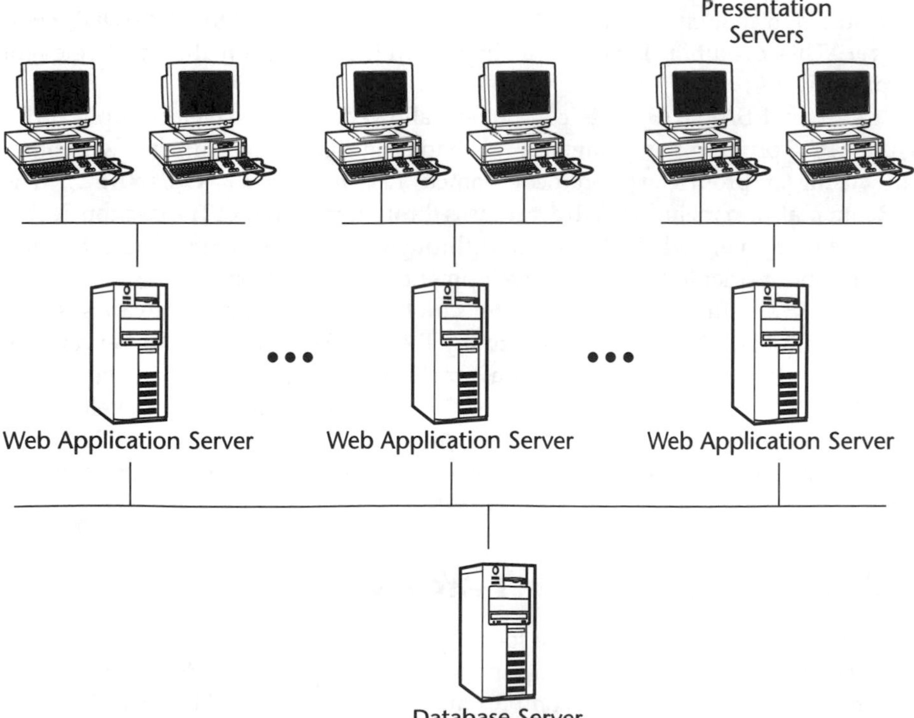

Figure 3.16 SAP multi-tier architecture.

To fully utilize the existing R/2 business applications—to a large extent implemented in the ABAP programming language—SAP had not only to implement a high-performance ABAP development and runtime environment but also a lot of tools that had been available on host computers at that time: transaction-based application server concept, job scheduling, and monitoring tools; a development environment; secure communication software; a business-driven authorization concept; a database abstraction layer; and so forth.

The result of this development process was the SAP Basis software, or Basis Component (BC). All SAP application modules—such as FI, CO, and SD—were originally developed using the BC functionality. Additional common functionality such as Application Link Enabling (ALE), Interchangeable Documents (IDocs), Business Application Programming Interfaces (BAPIs), handling of currencies and units of measure, documentation, and translation tools were developed separately and were distributed in a separate application component called Cross Application (CA).

There are some common misunderstandings about SAP BW being just another application module comparable to FI, CO, or SD, or about being able to install SAP BW as an add-on to SAP R/3 or SAP R/3-based systems like CRM. While SAP BW may be installed on the same physical server, it always has to be installed as a separate SAP instance and will always use its own separate database and its own separate application servers. SAP started developing the SAP Business Information Warehouse in late 1996 based on an SAP system with just the basis and cross-application components installed and with a completely separate architecture, optimized for reporting and analysis purposes, in mind.

Recent developments of the SAP Basis software toward Internet technologies finally resulted in changing the name from SAP Basis Component to *SAP Web Application Server*. This evolution is shown in Figure 3.17, focusing on the most relevant developments.

The traditional SAP R/3 Basis component allowed you to develop applications using the ABAP programming language and had been able to communicate with other systems using a proprietary protocol named *Remote Function Calls* (RFC). The mySAP.com platform included Web awareness through the Internet Transaction Server (ITS) for the first time, added XML support through the SAP Business Connector, and allowed for object-oriented software development using ABAP objects.

While the ITS and the SAP Business Connector have been separate software systems interfacing with core R/3 functionality, today the SAP Web Application Server provides an integrated server platform, fully aware of all relevant protocols and standards (such as HTTP, SMTP, XML, SOAP, and .NET) and allows application development using Java (including Enterprise JavaBeans; Java 2 Enterprise Edition, or J2EE; and Java Server Pages) and ABAP in all its flavors (ABAP, ABAP Objects, Business Server Pages).

SAP Web Application Server Architecture

The SAP Web Application Server is no longer just a platform for all SAP applications; it has now evolved into a serious multipurpose business application development and runtime environment with its own complex architecture, shown in Figure 3.18.

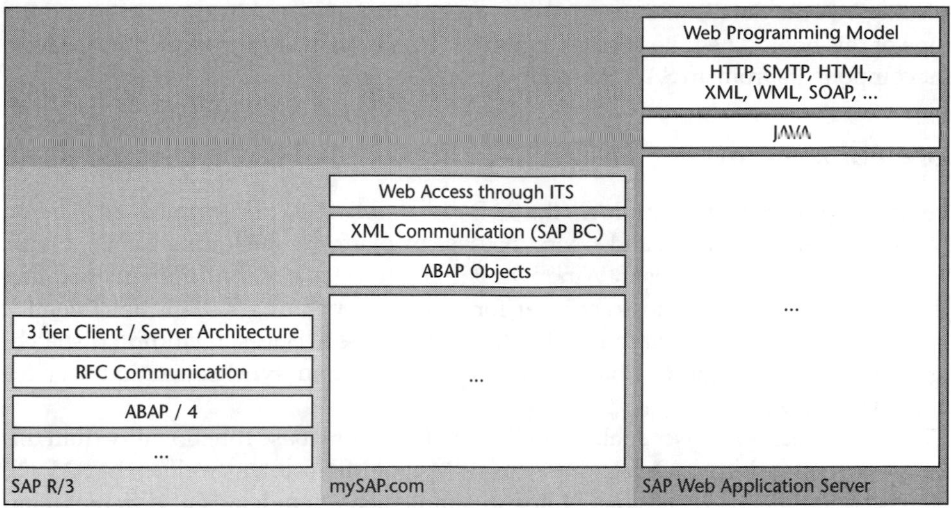

Figure 3.17 SAP application server evolution.

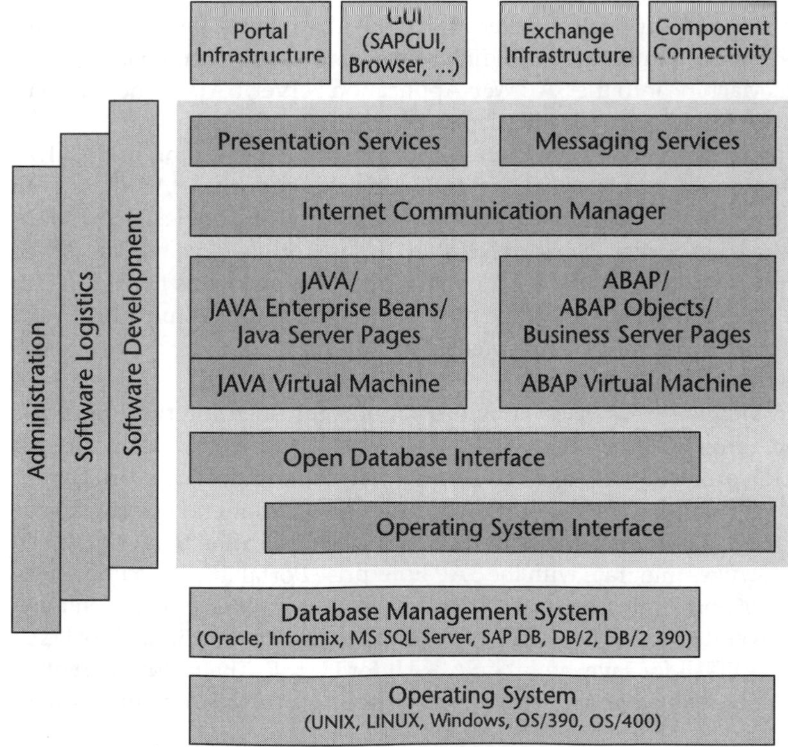

Figure 3.18 SAP Web Application Server architecture.

Going into the details of the SAP Web Application Server architecture is beyond the scope of this book. The following paragraphs provide an overview of the most important components from an SAP BW point of view.

Core Components

The *operating system interface* allows the SAP Web Application Server to be installed on several different hardware and operating system platforms including UNIX/Linux, OS/390, OS/400, and Microsoft Windows. It hides the details of the different operating systems and provides an abstract layer for access to operating system functionality. The operating system interface provides shared process services, including dispatching of application requests, shared memory services, and synchronization services (enqueue/dequeue).

The *open database interface* enables SAP BW to utilize database functionality from different vendors, including Oracle, Informix, IBM, and Microsoft, as well as the SAP DB database offered by SAP. Besides hiding the implementation details of different database systems, the open database interface allows application-specific caching of database requests and provides buffer synchronization between multiple application servers using the same database server. The special multidimensional requirements of SAP BW provoked some significant enhancements of the open database interface and forced the SAP BW development team to develop its own additional database abstraction layer on top of the open database interface.

The *Java Virtual Machine* supports the execution of Java programs, Java Server Pages (JSPs), and JavaScripts and integrates with Enterprise JavaBeans. With the integration of the Java Virtual Machine into the SAP Web Application Server, SAP opened its platform to a whole new world of application developers.

The *ABAP Virtual Machine* has been in place right from the beginning of SAP R/3 development. Originally a functional programming language, ABAP has been extended by object-oriented software development features (ABAP objects) and Web-enabled objects (Business Server Pages, or BSPs) in the last couple of years. The ABAP Virtual Machine precompiles the ABAP code into a byte code, which is then stored in the database and used for execution. While most of the core business functionality of SAP R/3 and SAP BW is and will be implemented in ABAP, a lot of the more front-end-related development will be done in Java.

The *Internet Communication Manager* provides support for open Internet standards and protocols, including HTTP, SOAP, HTML, XML, and WML, as well as traditional SAP communication protocols such as RFC. The Internet Communication Manager has an integrated Web server, allowing external applications and front-end systems to use the HTTP protocol for communicating with the SAP Web Application Server.

The *presentation services* integrate with the SAP Enterprise Portal infrastructure, offering iViews and other portal infrastructures from third-party vendors. The presentation services support several types of front-end systems, including the traditional SAPGUI for Windows, the SAPGUI for Java, and the SAPGUI for HTML. The *messaging services* allow exchanging data with other applications using the SAP protocols and open protocols like the SMTP and SOAP.

Software Development

One of the key success factors for SAP R/3 and SAP BW has been the integrated software development tools that allow customers to adapt the system to their specific requirements by implementing their own custom ABAP programs or by modifying programs delivered by SAP. The software development platform of SAP, called the ABAP Workbench, integrates various editors such as an ABAP editor, a screen designer, and a report designer with a data dictionary, allowing you to share common definitions of data types and table structures. Debugging functionality is available, allowing you to debug both custom and SAP code. Open interfaces—the BAPIs—allow access to SAP functionality by reading and writing data and meta data and by executing business processes.

SAP currently does not offer its own Java development environment; instead, it integrates with third-party development environments.

Software Logistics

The SAP Web Application Server includes sophisticated software logistics support for software development objects, meta data, and customization data based on the *Transport Management System (TMS).* The TMS performs the following major tasks around managing software development and distribution:

- It tracks all changes to development objects under its control, whether these are delivered by SAP or have been developed by the client. Objects under control of the TMS include programs, database tables, all BW meta data objects, and customizing data.
- The TMS provides sophisticated software distribution mechanisms to manage complex application development landscapes, including separate multistaged development, test, and production systems. More information about system development landscapes appears later in this chapter.
- It allows upgrading running systems and applying support packages; it automatically identifies modified objects and allows you to manually handle modifications during the upgrade or update process.

More information about the transport management system can be found at the end of this chapter.

Security

A key issue often neglected—or at least not implemented at a sufficient level of sophistication—in custom data warehouse solutions and sometimes even standard data warehousing tools is security. Protecting the information in the data warehouse is as important as protecting the data in your operational system against unauthorized access. SAP BW security relies on the SAP Web Application Server, which uses Secure Network Communications (SNC) to provide single sign-on and centrally managed LDAP-based user stores.

The SAP authorization does not simply rely on authorization concepts provided by operating systems and database systems. Instead, it comes with its own application authorization concept, allowing for very detailed adjustments of authorizations in operational and data warehouse systems to the policies of any organization. Authorization checks are executed and defined by the SAP application using application server functionality.

To ease the task of administering a large amount of users on that detail level, the whole authorization concept is role-based (see the subsection *Roles* in the *SAP BW Meta Data Objects* section earlier in this chapter for a definition of *roles*). Roles can consist of several profiles, which basically are collections of authorizations required to perform a specific task. Roles may be assigned to multiple users, and users may have different roles assigned. Profiles may include other profiles and normally do include a couple of authorizations. Each authorization is an instance of an authorization object, describing exactly which operations are allowed for a certain object. Figure 3.19 provides an overview of authorization.

NOTE Roles are not only used to collect all authorizations required to execute on a specific business role; they are also used to provide easy access to menus or complex personalized applications in a portal environment.

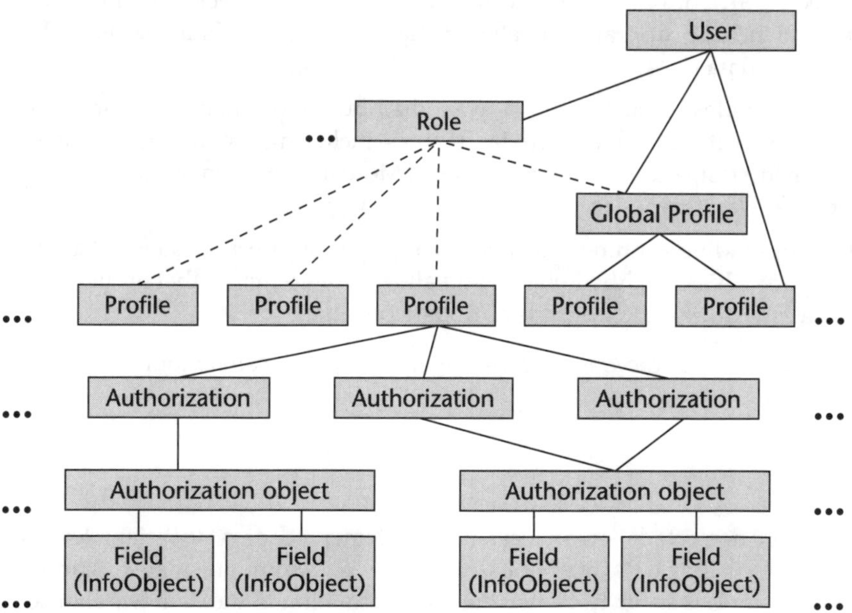

Figure 3.19 The SAP authorization concept.
Based on copyrighted material from SAP AG

While the authorization concept implemented in SAP BW allows you to define authorizations at a very granular level, we recommend keeping authorization models as simple as possible but as concise and restrictive as necessary. The more granular a model you choose, the more resources it will take to maintain the actual authorizations. Key to a simple authorization model is a proper set of naming conventions, as all objects that are effectively placed under control of the authorization concept have to be named. The more generic a name you can provide, the less effort you have to spend on ensuring the integrity of your authorization model.

The SAP authorization concept and strategies for implementing a customer authorization concept are discussed in more detail in Chapter 9.

Administration

SAP administration covers the whole range of functionality required to run complex online applications and batch processes—including job control and job monitoring, user and authorization management, performance monitoring and performance optimization, output management, and archiving.

Most of the functions related to the more technical aspects of administering an SAP system are integrated in the *computing center management system* (CCMS); frequently used functionality such as printing and job scheduling and monitoring are available from nearly all transactions.

Chapter 9 covers general administration strategies in greater detail, and Chapter 10 includes a discussion of the CCMS functionality for performance monitoring and optimizing an SAP system (especially an SAP BW system).

Additional Functionality

A lot of functionality for many different purposes has developed around the core of the SAP Web Application Server and is also available to SAP BW users. While there's not enough room in this book to describe all of these, we'll provide an overview of the most important functions.

Content management is generally available in SAP systems and has already been discussed briefly in the *SAP BW Architectural Components* section at the beginning of this chapter. SAP BW integrates access to the content management framework by linking meta data objects to documents available on the content server.

Workflow management functionality allows you to create and manage workflows in an SAP system. SAP BW currently uses workflow functionality in exception reporting to initialize workflows based on exceptional key figure values identified. It is also used in process monitoring where processes may kick off an alert workflow in case of failed processes or process chains to immediately notify administrators and keep track of the actions taken to recover from the problem.

The *Computer-Aided Test Tool* (CATT) supports testing applications of any kind by allowing you to define and—as far as possible—to automate tests of newly developed software, of customizing activities, and of other development results.

Development of multilingual applications is supported by *documentation and translation tools*, by a general distinction between master data and text data (the latter being language dependent), by integrated support for the Unicode standard, and by support for separate language imports by the transport management system.

Sophisticated *currency conversion services* allow manual and automated maintenance of currency translation rate tables and provide different currency conversion procedures that take different currency conversion regulations (such as euro conversion) into account. Currency conversions can be performed with respect to specific points or periods of time, allowing you to convert currencies according to current exchange rates, historical exchange rates, average exchange rates, and statistical exchange rates. SAP BW offers integrated support for currency conversions in the update rules and in reporting and analysis.

SAP systems come with predefined and customized tables defining *units of measure* and conversions between different units of measure.

Integrated country- and client-specific *calendar functionality* is available for defining work days, which then can be used as a basis for scheduling jobs and calculating days of work in HR applications.

System Landscape Considerations

It is good practice to keep separate instances of the system—especially for development, testing, and production purposes. SAP systems (including SAP BW) have always supported these activities with the Transport Management System introduced earlier this chapter. The TMS captures changes in many types of objects, including:

- All SAP BW meta data objects, including InfoObjects, InfoCubes, InfoSources, Data Sources, queries, Web applications, and process chains
- All programming objects, including ABAP programs, function groups, types, classes, includes, and messages
- All dictionary objects, including tables, views, data elements, and domains
- All customization tables, including currency translation types, application components, printer definitions, user profiles, authorizations, profiles, and calendars
- All meta data of other SAP systems such as SAP CRM, SAP SEM, and SAP APO

All development objects logically belonging together are assigned to *packages* (formerly known as development classes). These objects are stored in some table in the SAP database; the TMS now keeps track of changes by simply assigning the key values of such an object to a task, which itself is assigned to a transport request. Once all tasks are completed and released by the users assigned to the tasks, the request is released—effectively exporting the current versions (all table contents, not just the keys) of all objects tracked in that request into a flat file. Using the TMS, you can import this flat file into any SAP system (be careful not to import SAP R/3 requests into an SAP BW system and vice versa, unless you really know what you're doing), usually the test system, where special before- and after-import programs take care of additional actions after importing the objects. (Importing an InfoCube, for example, requires dynamically creating or modifying database tables and generating programs in the test system.) After testing is considered complete, you can import the same flat file into the production system for productive use.

Typical SAP BW transport requests are made up of a collection of different types of objects (e.g., an InfoCube consists of InfoObjects), making it difficult to manually ensure consistent transport requests. An SAP BW-specific transport connection tool allows you to select a specific object (e.g., an InfoCube) and collect all objects belonging to that object (e.g., InfoObjects from a definition perspective, InfoSources from a data sourcing perspective, or queries from an information delivery perspective).

The TMS not only keeps track of changes in development systems; it also keeps track of changes in the test or production system—or depending on global system settings, prevents users from changing anything in these systems at all.

This type of scenario is well known to SAP users and larger organizations for complex custom software development and maintenance. The same paradigm and the same technology are now being utilized by SAP BW to ensure stable and highly available software systems. The TMS allows you to define and maintain complex system landscapes for application development—the most popular one for combined SAP R/3 and SAP BW, shown in Figure 3.20.

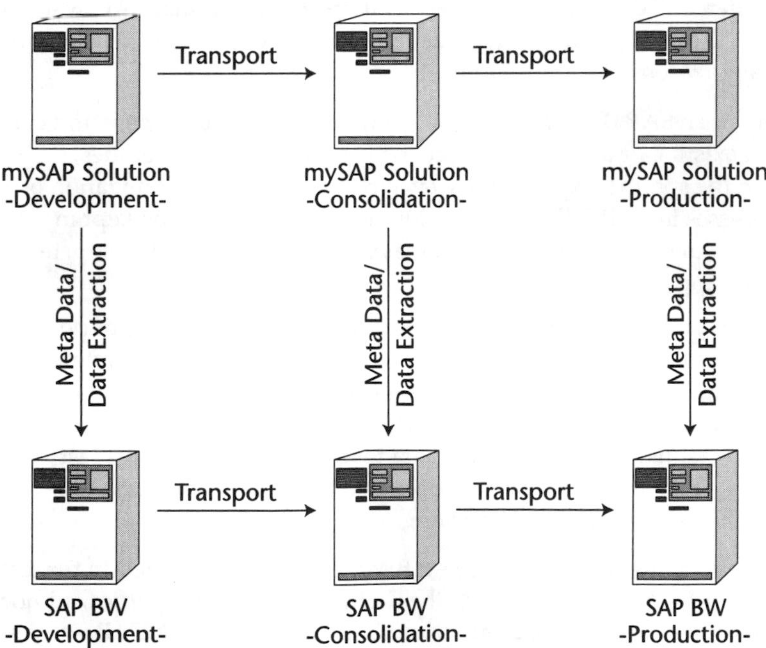

Figure 3.20 Standard SAP BW system landscape.

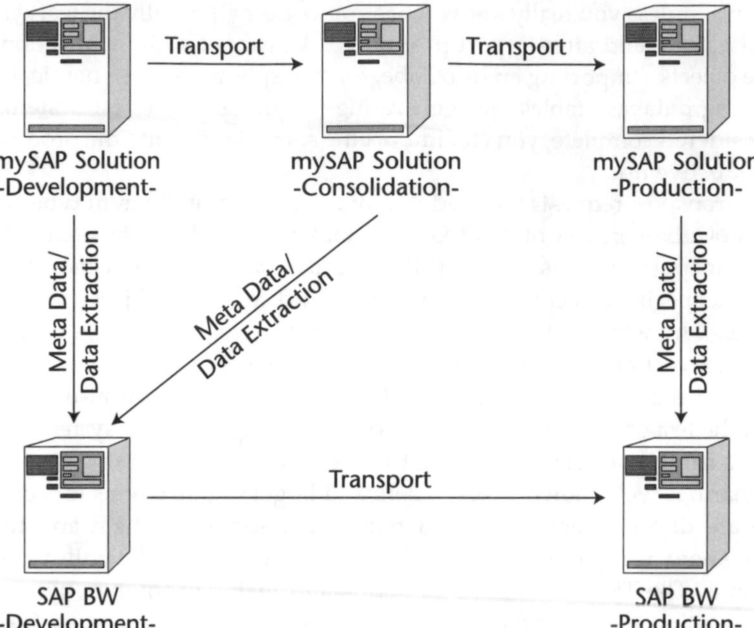

Figure 3.21 Poor man's SAP BW system landscape.

There are two complete system landscapes now: one for SAP R/3 and one for SAP BW. And possibly there are even more than two, if there are additional SAP systems like SAP CRM and SAP APO used in an organization. These systems need to be in sync as well, for two major reasons:

- Development of an SAP BW application usually requires development and customization of existing or additional extraction programs, and sometimes, depending on the specific requirements, even changes to the customization of business processes in SAP R/3. Both development paths need to be kept in sync over the whole system landscape so that you can efficiently develop, test, and deploy the application.
- In typical development systems, testing is nearly impossible because of poor data quality. Reasons for poor data quality are that (1) development systems are normally sized according to development needs and do not allow mass testing or just even storing mass data and (2) data in development systems are often modified manually to provide test data for specific development test cases. A separate SAP BW test instance connected to the corresponding SAP R/3 test system enables high-quality testing.

However, some development activities in SAP BW are usually conducted in the test or even the production system. These include the definition of ad hoc queries, ad hoc Web applications, definition of data load procedures, and others. The TMS allows you to define exceptions for these types of objects—but that also implies that the TMS no longer tracks changes to these objects.

Note that talking about system landscapes does not necessarily mean talking about multiple physical systems. Today's high-performance parallel servers with many CPUs, large amounts of main memory, and access to storage networks allow you to install multiple instances of SAP R/3 or SAP BW systems on one single physical system. Even smaller physical systems today allow you to run a development system and an integration test system on one physical server in smaller organizations where development and testing frequently are consecutive processes so that there are little testing activities in intense development phases and vice versa.

Keeping that in mind, there's actually no reason to go for a poor man's system landscape like the one shown in Figure 3.21. While it may be used in early stages of SAP BW prototype development or with very small implementation teams, it will lead to more complicated and costly test preparation phases. In a combined SAP BW development and test system, all data will have to be checked and eventually reloaded each time a new test phase is started. Many data warehouse projects fail because of a lack of data quality and data credibility. Don't let yours!

A more complex scenario has proven useful in global rollouts, where a central development team works on a global template system, which is then localized and tested locally. The global rollout system landscape is depicted in Figure 3.22. The point here is that objects from the global development system are first transported into a global test system where the system may be tested prior to being rolled out to several local development systems. The local development systems are used to adapt the global template to local needs to some extent (language, local legal requirements, local business requirements). Keeping track of local changes to global objects, the TMS supports identification and synchronization of global and local objects. Once the localization of the application is completed, it may be transported to the local test and production systems.

NOTE SAP is actually using a similar scenario to roll out support packages and new releases of its new software to customers. And the same or similar mechanisms for identifying and synchronizing changes to global (in this case SAP-defined) objects are used to maintain the system's integrity. The SAP software itself can be considered a template for a local (in this case local means customer-specific) rollout, developed by SAP. Although the system landscape at SAP is more complex than the one shown in Figure 3.22, the basic principles remain the same.

Other complex application development projects might also require using a software integration system landscape (as shown in Figure 3.23), where objects from several different development systems meet in a central development landscape for integration work, final testing, and productive use.

The actual system landscape chosen in a particular situation largely depends on the complexity of the development work and the complexity of the rollout; investments in hardware and system setup pay off in the long run, through ease of development, integration, and testing. Experience has proven the return on investment through achieved increase in information accessibility and quality.

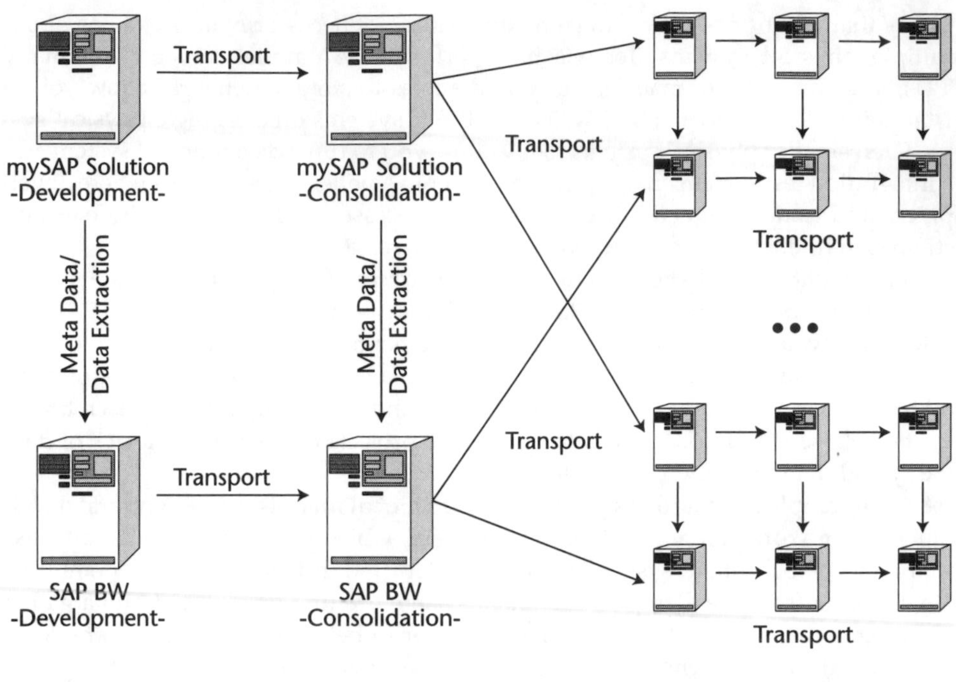

Figure 3.22 Global rollout system landscape.

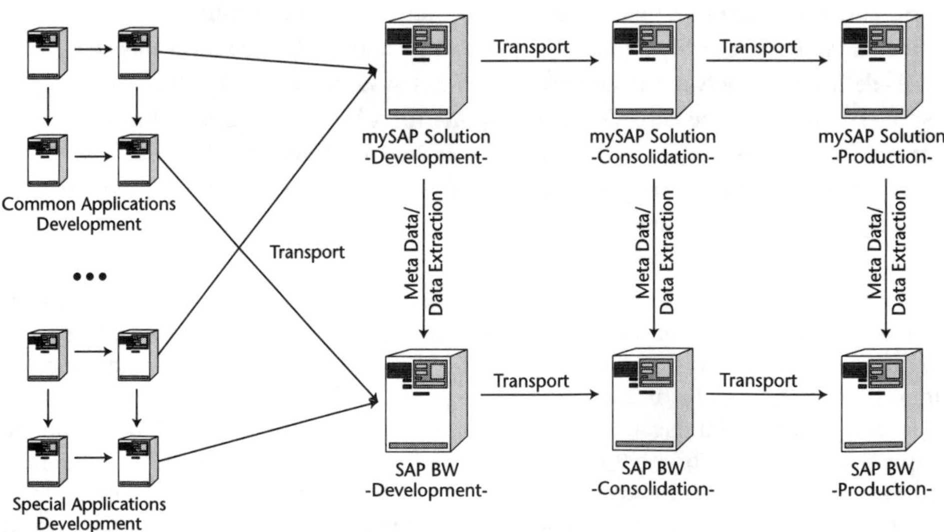

Figure 3.23 Software integration system landscape.

Summary

SAP BW uses the usual layered architecture with an ETL layer, a storage layer, an analysis and access layer, and a presentation layer. SAP BW is completely based on meta data managed by the meta data services, and it is centrally controlled by the Administrator Workbench utilizing the administration services.

SAP-specific open interfaces like the Staging BAPI and the OLAP BAPI allow you to exchange data and meta data with other systems and tools optimized for SAP BW; industry-standard interfaces like OLE DB for OLAP, XML, and XML for Analysis are supported, allowing easy access to data and meta data maintained in SAP BW for virtually every tool supporting those industry standards.

SAP BW now provides close to complete functionality for building the corporate information factory. Operational data stores, data warehouses, and InfoMarts (basically defined as an extended-functionality data mart) can be built using the meta data objects available in SAP BW. Analytical applications are contained in the system built on top of the predefined Business Content.

The SAP Web Application Server has been used as a basis for developing the SAP BW software, effectively inheriting a broad range of tools, functionality, and code that originally proved to be helpful in speeding up the development of data warehouse software from scratch and now proves at least as helpful in cost-effectively maintaining that software.

With the transport management system, the SAP BW architecture includes a separate component for managing the overall development and deployment process for data warehouse applications supporting complex system landscapes and scenarios.

Summary

CHAPTER 4

Information Modeling

In traditional data warehouse and database application software development, one of the most important tasks is developing a data model and a database design reflecting that data model. This keeps the focus of the development process on technical details rather than the information required. SAP BW comes with a predefined yet flexible data model, completely described and implicitly configured by business-level meta data stored in the Meta Data Repository. Using meta data to describe the contents of a data warehouse or any other database application is hardly new (see www.llnl.gov/liv_comp/metadata/index.html for early research). However, SAP BW was the first commercial, integrated data warehouse product to be completely based on business-level meta data describing the entities relevant to business and analysis processes from a business rather than a technical point of view. Examples of such meta data objects include:

- Business objects like customers, products, and sales organizations
- Business events like sales orders and purchase orders
- Status information like stock values and head counts
- Key performance indicators like customer profitability, product profitability, vendor service quality, and return on investment
- Providers of information, such as InfoCubes and ODS objects
- Queries like plan/actual comparisons and head count development

Business-level meta data has enabled data warehouse developers to evolve beyond data modeling and database design and focus on information and on the flow of information into and out of the data warehouse. Thus, the results of the data warehouse design process are an information model and an information flow model:

- An *information model* is a collection of meta data objects describing business processes, business objects, information containers and their mutual relationships, as well as the scope, granularity, and semantics of the information available in the data warehouse system. The process of developing an information model is called *information modeling*. Transformations performed during the extraction or staging process are not part of the information model; the information model defines the target of transformations.
- An *information flow model* is a description of the flow of information from the originating systems through a possibly multistaged data warehouse system landscape to an information consumer that might be an end user, an analyst, or another system utilizing the information provided to control a specific decision or business process (closed-loop approach). An example of automated control of a business process is a customer classification resulting from a data warehouse analysis process being propagated into the mySAP Financials application, causing the dunning process to use a more aggressive dunning policy for nonprofitable customers. The process of developing an information flow model is called *information flow modeling*.

Information modeling and information flow modeling are at the core of the overall SAP BW implementation process. Laying the foundations for the staging as well as reporting and analysis processes, they are crucial to the success of the SAP BW project.

We open this chapter with a discussion of the prerequisites for information modeling. In this context, we gain a basic understanding of relevant SAP BW concepts like the actual data model used by SAP BW and the SAP BW Business Content. Then we discuss in detail the options available for developing an information model. We conclude the chapter with the options for developing an information-flow model.

Information Modeling Prerequisites

The information model is the core deliverable of the technical design and architecture development phase of an SAP BW implementation project, which directly follows the business strategy development/validation and the requirements analysis steps in the overall project plan. The deliverables of those preceding steps are the most important prerequisites for the development of an information model for a successful SAP BW implementation:

Business processes and requirements. One of the deliverables of the business strategy definition phase is the set of business processes to focus on, including how to measure these business processes and a prioritization. This sets the pace for the overall data warehouse and analytical application development and defines the outer limits of the scope of the system.

Relevant entities. As a result of the requirements analysis phase, strong and weak entities relevant to the business processes are identified. *Strong entities* are persons, objects, or concepts directly related to a business event, such as customer, product, account, and time; *weak entities* are entities related to another entity that describe the business event in more detail. Examples of weak entities include customer groups and classification data. Entities of both kinds are candidates that can be modeled as characteristics, having master data attributes, texts, and hierarchies assigned to them.

Attributes of relevant entities. Strong and weak entities both may have attributes assigned in SAP BW. Attributes provide additional information about an entity, such as address information and customer group for a customer entity. Attributes may be made available for display and navigation in queries and are loaded in separate data load processes. This concept is important for the information modeling process, because using attributes allows handling the slowly changing dimension phenomenon in an elegant way (more on this later in this chapter).

Hierarchies of relevant entities. In a similar way as attributes, hierarchies provide a flexible way of handling slowly changing dimensions. In addition, hierarchies provide a flexible means of modeling unstable hierarchical relationships.

KPIs. The result of the requirements analysis phase includes a set of key performance indicators (KPIs) used to control anything from single business processes to the whole enterprise. In the SAP BW information modeling process, KPIs are modeled as key figures (InfoObjects of type *key figure*). Key figures may be anything from simple key figures describing a business event, such as a revenue in a sales transaction, to complex derived key figures, eventually based on restricted key figures and calculated key figures, such as a customer lifetime value.

External information. Measuring the performance of a company means comparing it to something else, such as internal information like budgets, plans, previous year results, and so on, as well as external information, like market shares and demographic data. External data sources (such as address databases and credibility databases) can also be used to verify and enrich information in the data warehouse. While the actual origin of information is not relevant for the information modeling process, information from outside the enterprise can be very valuable in terms of benchmarking the development of the enterprise against industry trends.

Granularity. As mentioned in Chapter 1, the granularity of information is the level of detail provided. It may range from a line-item or schedule line level in sales transactions to highly aggregated management information. There is, of course, a trade-off between performance and granularity: the higher the granularity, the larger the data volume and obviously the longer the query execution times and the time required to update aggregates.

Timeliness. The timeliness of transaction and master data basically is determined by the frequency in which updates on InfoCubes, ODS objects, and master data are performed. Usually, information in a data warehouse is updated on a daily, weekly, or monthly basis. Some applications, however, require more frequent updates or even synchronization with the operational system (e.g., Web log analysis).

Functional requirements. Functional requirements, as opposed to business requirements, include a description of user interfaces, systems to be available for extraction, Web servers for Web reporting, hardware, and software.

Nonfunctional requirements. Nonfunctional requirements include but are not restricted to system properties, such as environmental and implementation constraints, performance, platform dependencies, maintainability, extensibility, and availability.

Information delivery. Information delivery is not restricted to making reports available to end users. In many applications, information is also exported to external companies—for instance, market research transferred to ERP or legacy systems and planning results imported into SAP R/3 to manage production.

Usability. Although information modeling has little to do with designing front ends and front-end tools, it still has an impact on the usability of the information system. End users defining queries for a complex or hard-to-understand information model tend to produce inconsistent or incorrect results.

Table 4.1 shows the relevance of each of those deliverables to the information model and the information flow model.

Table 4.1 Information Modeling Relevance Matrix

REQUIREMENT	INFORMATION MODEL	INFORMATION FLOW MODEL
Business processes and requirements	High	High
Relevant entities	High	Low
Attributes of entities	High	Low
Hierarchies on entities	High	Low
KPIs	High	Low
External information	High	Medium
Granularity	High	High
Timeliness	Low	High
Functional requirements	Low	Low
Nonfunctional requirements	Low	High
Information delivery	Low	High
Usability	High	High

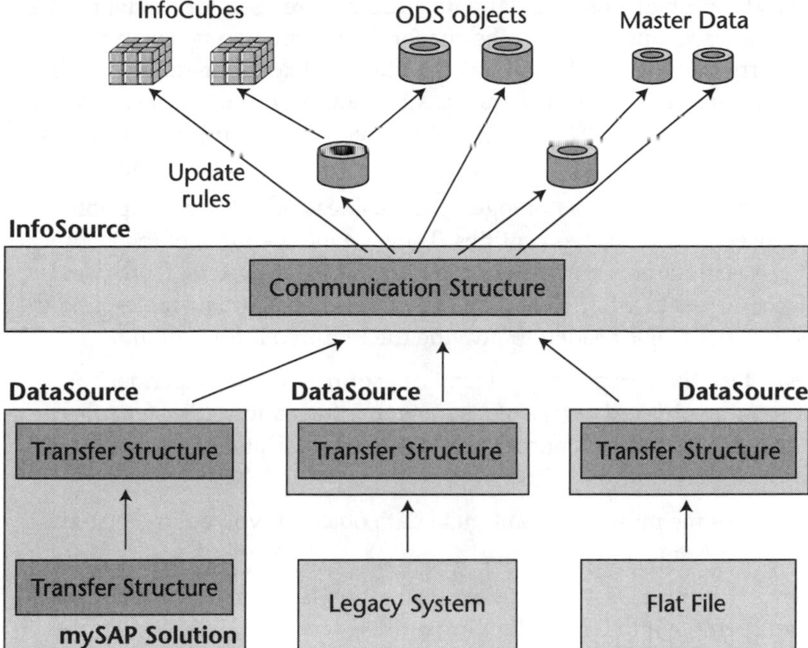

Figure 4.1 Meta data objects in the staging process.

Understanding the SAP BW Meta Data Model

Before we proceed with our discussion of information modeling, we need to put the SAP BW meta data objects into the context of information modeling and to sketch the data models used for storing information in InfoCubes, ODS objects, and master data. We begin with a list of the most important meta data objects involved in the staging process, as shown in Figure 4.1.

The objects are as follows:

InfoObjects. InfoObjects are the core building blocks of the information model; virtually everything is made of InfoObjects in the SAP BW world. InfoObjects are used for modeling business entities, attributes, hierarchies, key figures, or key performance indicators, as well as time, unit, and currency information. Master data tables are tied to InfoObjects of type *characteristic*.

InfoCubes. Multidimensional InfoCubes are the most important reporting structure available in SAP BW; much of the information modeling process—and our discussion in this chapter—focuses on InfoCubes. Different variants, such as basic and remote, transactional and nontransactional InfoCubes are available for different purposes. InfoCubes allow defining redundantly stored aggregates to support performance optimization.

ODS objects. ODS objects using a flat data structure are used for modeling the ODS and data warehouse layers of the corporate information factory and for creating information models for special applications like order-status tracking that require frequent updates of characteristics values or a complex staging logic involving multiple levels. ODS objects are also used to capture changes to operational data whenever the source system does not provide delta management.

InfoSources. InfoSources are a homogenized business-oriented description of business processes and business entities. They are independent of the technical details of a specific source system and the type of source system. Update rules connect InfoSources to InfoCubes, ODS objects, and master data tables, and they define the business logic needed to provide the required information.

DataSources. DataSources provide a technical, source-system-dependent description of the physical details of a source of information. Transfer rules define the technical transformations required to map a DataSource to the business view represented by an InfoSource.

Figure 4.2 shows the most important meta data objects involved in the analysis process.

InfoProviders. InfoProviders provide an abstraction layer on top of data targets, InfoSets, and remote InfoCubes, allowing unified access to all these different types of objects. InfoProviders are used as a basis for all reporting and analysis purposes, as well as for the Open Hub Service. MultiProviders are special types of InfoProviders, allowing you to create unions of arbitrary InfoProviders. This generalized concept of InfoProviders provides greater flexibility for information modelers.

Queries. Queries are the main reporting and analysis tool in SAP BW. Queries can be defined for all InfoProviders, multidimensional or flat, in a very similar way, and they can be displayed using the BEx Analyzer, the Web, or a third-party reporting tool. Queries are what the end user finally sees.

Workbooks. Workbooks are used to store query results, custom formatting, custom Excel VBA code, charts, and maps resulting from query execution. Workbooks can be used to provide specific user interfaces and to distribute offline information to other users.

InfoSpokes. InfoSpokes are the core meta data object of the Open Hub Service. The Open Hub Service allows controlled distribution of information to other SAP BW systems, third-party InfoMarts, and analytical applications based on InfoProviders. (We discuss the Open Hub Service further near the end of the chapter.)

Although the actual physical representation of meta data objects like master data tables, InfoCubes, and ODS objects on the database does not have to be in the focus of SAP BW information modelers, it is still helpful to have at least a basic notion of the data model used in order to understand the information modeling options and their impact on that data model. In the following paragraphs, we explain the basics of the data model used in SAP BW, providing details of the master-data data model, the InfoCube data model, and finally the ODS object data model.

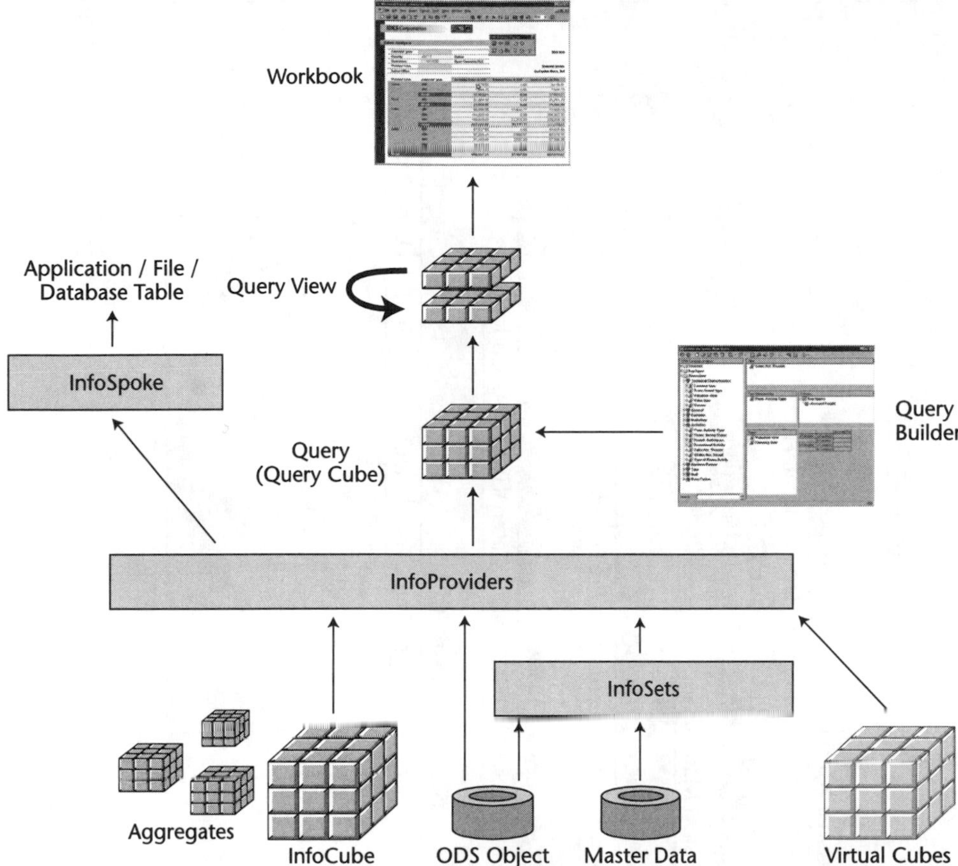

Figure 4.2 Meta data objects in the analysis process.

Master-Data Data Model

Master data in SAP BW is not just stored as a single table holding a couple of attributes assigned to an InfoObject (e.g., customers, products). Instead, SAP BW distinguishes three types of master data: attributes, texts, and hierarchies, each stored in different tables associated with the InfoObject. Figure 4.3 gives an overview of the tables involved in storing master data, using material master data as an example.

The SAP BW data model in general and the master-data data model in particular make extensive use of surrogate keys (SID = Surrogate ID). Surrogate keys are automatically generated uniform keys uniquely identifying specific real-world key values, such as a material number. SAP BW automatically creates and maintains entries in *SID tables* (Figure 4.3, #1), which map SIDs to real-world keys. In addition, SAP BW maintains information about SID usage—for instance, if a specific SID is used in an InfoCube—in a master data table or in a hierarchy.

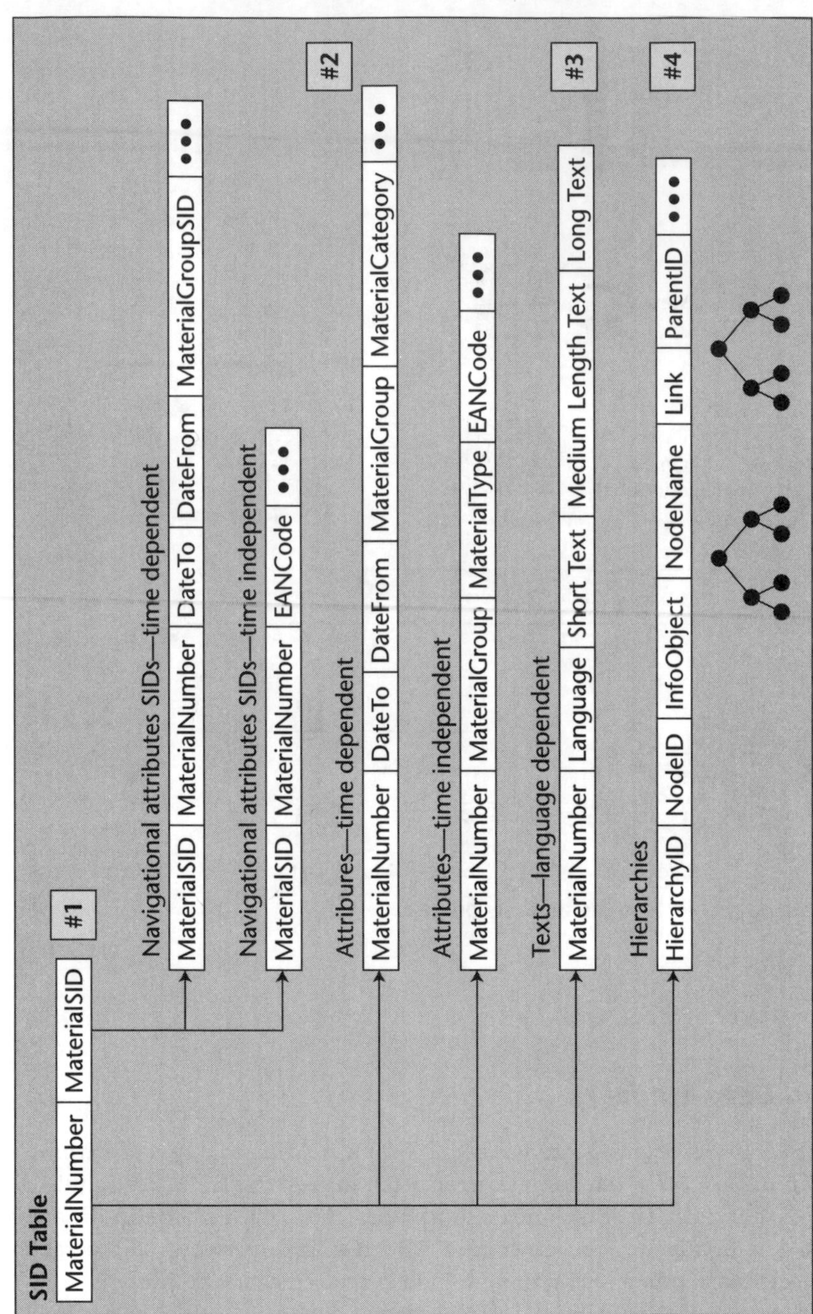

Figure 4.3 Master-data data model.

Attribute tables (Figure 4.3, #2) are used to store attribute values. SAP BW uses two tables to store time-independent and time-dependent attribute values, the latter using DateTo and DateFrom fields to identify the period of validity of a given combination of time-dependent attributes. Each attribute assigned to an InfoObject can independently be flagged as being time-dependent. The SAP BW data model uses two separate tables for time-dependent and time-independent master data to avoid redundant storage of the same unchanged time-independent attribute values for different periods of validity. Records in attribute tables carry automatically maintained version information (active and modified version) used to maintain data integrity (more on this in Chapter 6). For backward-compatibility reasons, SAP BW automatically generates a database view that holds all time-dependent and time-independent master data (see Table 4.2). Attributes that are supposed to be available for navigation in the Business Explorer may be flagged as *navigational attributes*.

NOTE It is important to recognize that a period of validity is always valid for the combination of all ti me-dependent attributes, not just for a single attribute.

Navigational attribute SID tables are semantically similar to attribute tables. Instead of using real-world keys to store attribute values, they use corresponding SID values to speed up access to navigational attributes at query run time. Navigational attribute SID tables are restricted to storing SIDs for navigational attributes.

Text tables (Figure 4.3, #3) are designed to store descriptions assigned to the key value (e.g., material names and descriptions). There are three reasons for separating textual and attribute information in the data model:

Ease of implementation. In most of the analysis and reporting requirements end users want to see texts instead of key values. Text tables provide a uniform way of retrieving text information at query run time, making it easier to generically implement access to text information.

Performance. Storing texts and attributes in the same tables would slow down text retrieval because database systems usually physically read complete data records (both texts and attributes), where just the texts are required.

Language dependency. In a global business environment you must be able to provide information in different languages. Both language dependency and time dependency (a feature that is rarely used for texts) are optional and can be turned on and off in the InfoObject maintenance dialogs. Defining texts as being time-dependent adds two additional fields to the text table: DateTo and DateFrom, identifying the period of validity for a specific text.

Hierarchy tables (Figure 4.3, #4) are used to store flexible *external* hierarchies—as opposed to *internal* hierarchies, which would be modeled as attributes. The basic layout of hierarchy tables is the same for every InfoObject, but it changes with the properties of those hierarchies. Options for modeling hierarchies include version and time dependency for the whole hierarchy tree, time dependency for the hierarchy structure, and the use of intervals instead of single values to assign a range of values to a specific hierarchy node. Figure 4.3 shows a simplistic picture of the hierarchy data model, including only the most important fields of one out of four different tables used for storing hierarchies. The hierarchy data model provides a very flexible means to store balanced and unbalanced hierarchies, with different types of hierarchy nodes on different hierarchy levels, and to store network structured hierarchies. More details on hierarchies are provided later in this chapter.

NOTE While the example in Figure 4.3 shows a simple master data table with only one key field (the material number), SAP BW allows you to define master data tables with more than one key field by defining compound InfoObjects. For compound InfoObjects SAP BW still uses a single SID field; however, the SID table and all other tables referring to the real-world key contain all key fields.

All master data tables are automatically created during InfoObject activation; there's no need to even think about how to model master data or what tables to create, or to maintain meta data about these tables in a separate meta data dictionary. SAP BW master data tables follow a specific naming convention:

/BI<C OR DIGIT>/<TABLE CODE><INFOOBJECT>

<C or digit>:	C = Customer-defined InfoObjects
	digit = SAP-defined InfoObjects
<table code>:	S = SID table
	T = Text table
	P = Time-independent master data attributes
	Q = Time-dependent master data attributes
	M = Union of time-dependent and time-independent master data attributes
	X = SID table for time-independent navigational attributes
	Y = SID table for time-dependent navigational attributes
	H = Hierarchy table
	K = Hierarchy SID table
	I = Hierarchy SID structure table
	J = Hierarchy interval table
<InfoObject>:	The name of the InfoObject without leading digits (if any)

Table 4.2 shows all possible master data tables for InfoObject 0MATERIAL. Table 4.3 lists all possible master data tables for a customer-defined InfoObject HOUSEHLD.

Table 4.2 Master Data Tables for SAP InfoObject 0MATERIAL

TABLE NAME	DESCRIPTION
/BI0/SMATERIAL	SID table
/BI0/TMATERIAL	Text table
/BI0/PMATERIAL	Time-independent master data attributes
/BI0/QMATERIAL	Time-dependent master data attributes
/BI0/MMATERIAL	Union of time-dependent and time-independent master data attributes
/BI0/XMATERIAL	SID table for time-independent navigational attributes
/BI0/YMATERIAL	SID table for time-dependent navigational attributes
/BI0/HMATERIAL	Hierarchy table
/BI0/KMATERIAL	Hierarchy SID table
/BI0/IMATERIAL	Hierarchy SID structure table
/BI0/JMATERIAL	Hierarchy interval table

NOTE **Depending on the InfoObject definition, some of these tables may or may not be created at InfoObject activation time.**

The InfoCube Data Model

InfoCubes are the relational SAP BW implementation of multidimensional data structures. The InfoCube data model basically is an extended star schema using surrogate keys (see definition earlier in the chapter) for referencing dimensions and characteristics (and through those also master data texts, attributes, and hierarchies). Figure 4.4 shows a slightly simplified representation of the InfoCube data model.

Table 4.3 Master Data Tables for Customer InfoObjects HOUSEHLD

TABLE NAME	DESCRIPTION
/BIC/SHOUSEHLD	SID table
...	...
/BIC/JHOUSEHLD	Hierarchy interval table

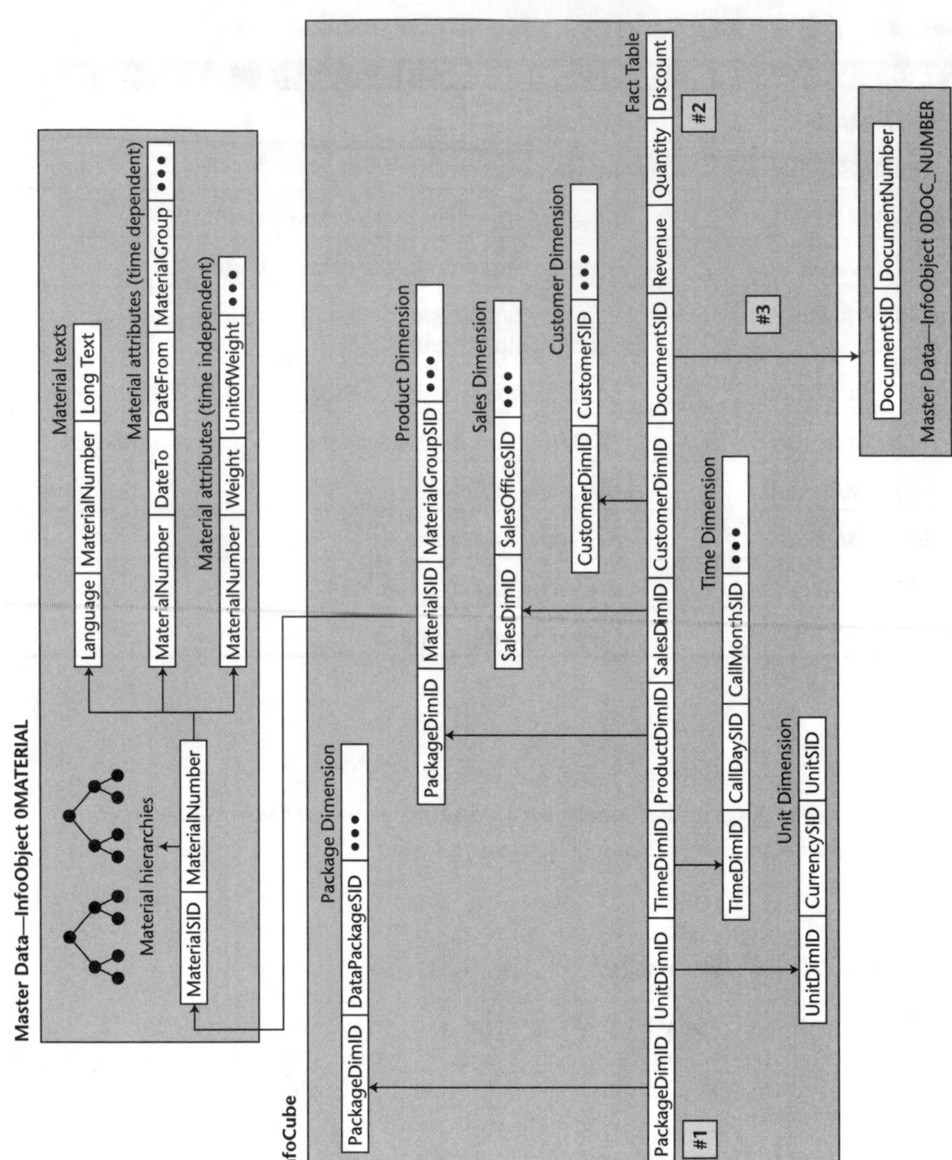

Figure 4.4 InfoCube data model.

An InfoCube is composed of two identical fact tables (an uncompressed and a compressed version), as shown in Figure 4.4, #1, and up to 13 dimension tables at the user's disposal. SAP BW automatically maintains three additional dimensions: the time dimension, the unit dimension, and the package dimension, all to be explained in more detail later in this chapter. Figure 4.4 only shows one of the two fact tables; both are technically identical and used for optimization and data administration purposes. A more detailed description of the roles both tables play is given in Chapter 9.

The fact tables store detailed or aggregated key figures also known as facts (e.g., revenue, quantity, discount), illustrated in Figure 4.4, #2, and references to dimension tables. Similar to the SID tables, the dimension tables are based on automatically generated and maintained surrogate key values known as dimension IDs, or DIMIDs. The role of dimension tables is to group associated characteristics to reduce the number of fields in the fact table and to reduce redundancies in storing frequent combinations of characteristics values in a table. Examples of characteristics typically grouped into one dimension include *Customer*, *Customer Group*, and *Zip Code* grouped into a *Customer* dimension, and *Material*, *Material Group*, *Color* grouped into a *Material* dimension. Dimension tables hold SID values that refer back to the associated characteristic value. This allows the master data to be shared across all InfoCubes.

A special case of a dimension is the *line-item dimension*, which is used for characteristics with a very high cardinality. A typical example is the document number in a line-item-level InfoCube; the document number may or may not have master data associated with it. Another example of a high-cardinality characteristic is the customer number in industries that deal with many end customers, such as telecommunications, banking, and insurance. For line-item dimensions SAP BW does not generate a DIMID or a dimension table but instead stores the characteristic's SID as a dimension ID in the fact table (see Figure 4.4, #3).

InfoCube tables are automatically created during InfoCube activation. The table names follow a specific naming convention. Table names for InfoCubes defined by SAP as part of the Business Content (discussed in Chapter 5) start with /BI<digit>/. Table names for customer-specific InfoCubes start with /BIC/. This prefix is followed by a one-character table code and the name of the InfoCube (without leading digits). This is then followed by the dimension code.

Following is a summary of the naming conventions:

/BI<C OR DIGIT>/<TABLE CODE><INFOCUBE><DIMENSION>

<C or digit>:	C = Customer-defined InfoCube
	Digit = SAP-defined InfoCube
<table code>:	D = Dimension table E = Compressed fact table F = Uncompressed fact table
<InfoCube>:	The name of the InfoCube without leading digits (if any)
<dimension>:	(only used for dimension tables)
	P = Package dimension
	U = Unit dimension
	T = Time dimension
	0-9, A, B, C = User-defined dimension tables

Table 4.4 lists tables for the Business Content InfoCube 0SD_C01.

Aggregates

SAP BW allows defining aggregates based on multidimensional (MOLAP) or relational OLAP (ROLAP) for query performance optimization purposes. While MOLAP aggregates are handled by a MOLAP database (Microsoft SQL Server), ROLAP aggregates are stored using the same relational data model used for InfoCubes, including both fact tables. In cases where all characteristics of a dimension of the InfoCube are also used in the aggregate definition, aggregates even share the existing dimension tables of the InfoCube, avoiding redundant data storage and maintenance.

The ODS Object Data Model

ODS objects are mostly used to keep a low-level, frequently changing history of data, for generating change logs where the source system is not capable of providing delta extraction facilities and for keeping track of deltas provided by the source system. ODS objects are frequently used to model the operational data store and the enterprise data warehouse layers of the CIF. A more detailed discussion of the role InfoCubes and ODS objects play in information modeling appears later in this chapter. Loading data into an ODS object is a two-step process In the first step, all uploaded data records are stored in an *activation queue*. The second step, called *activation of data*, compares the active records with those in the activation queue, identifies changes (inserts or updates) to existing data, writes those changes to a change log, and updates the active record table with data from the activation queue. The change log is stored in a PSA table for future processing.

Table 4.4 Tables for Business Content InfoCube 0SD_C01

TABLE NAME	DESCRIPTION
/BI0/D0SD_C011	Business Content-defined dimension table
/BI0/D0SD_C012	Business Content-defined dimension table
/BI0/D0SD_C013	Business Content-defined dimension table
/BI0/D0SD_C014	Business Content-defined dimension table
/BI0/D0SD_C015	Business Content-defined dimension table
/BI0/D0SD_C01P	Package dimension table
/BI0/D0SD_C01U	Unit dimension table
/BI0/D0SD_C01T	Time dimension table

Table 4.4 *(Continued)*

TABLE NAME	DESCRIPTION
/BIO/E0SD_C01	Compressed fact table
/BIO/F0SD_C01	Uncompressed fact table

The ODS object data model is based on a collection of flat database tables. All those tables are automatically created during activation, following a specific naming convention. Table names for ODS objects defined by SAP start with /BI<digit>/A. Table names for customer-specific ODS objects start with /BIC/A.

Following are the naming conventions for the ODS object data model:

/BI<C OR DIGIT>/A<ODS OBJECT><TABLE CODE>

<C or digit>:	C = Customer-defined InfoObjects
	Digit = SAP-defined InfoObjects
<ODS Object>:	The name of the ODS object without leading digits (if any)
<table code>:	00 = Active records (available for reporting)
	10 = New data records (prior to release 3.0, no longer used)
	40 = Activation queue (release 3.0)
	50 = Rollback queue (release 3.0)

Understanding the Business Content

One major advantage of SAP BW as compared to the competitors in the market of business intelligence market is the *Business Content.* Initially, the Business Content was composed of a large set of predefined information models and a set of extraction programs for mySAP.com application component data to populate the Business Content objects. The Business Content includes a comprehensive information model covering most of the business processes available today in mySAP.com applications. Whenever the source system is a mySAP.com application, even the extraction and staging process is already in place. SAP has constantly been increasing the coverage of the Business Content and started using it to implement closed-loop analytical applications—for instance, for customer relationship management and supply chain management.

In many cases substantial parts of an information model are already available from the Business Content. A thorough understanding of relevant parts of the Business Content helps to considerably cut down implementation time and costs. Possible uses of the Business Content include:

- Flatly installing and activating complete InfoCubes, with all required objects along the data flow (extraction programs, InfoSources, transfer/update rules, queries, workbooks), as shown in Figure 4.5
- Activating single useful meta data objects at various levels, such as InfoObjects, InfoSources, or transfer rules
- Activating and extending or modifying selected objects at various levels
- Using Business Content as a repository of industry-standard requirements and modeling ideas

SAP strongly encourages using the Business Content as a template for custom applications and modifying it wherever necessary. Changes made by SAP and imported into the system with a service package or during an upgrade do not affect activated Business Content objects. Active meta data and Business Content meta data are stored separately using different version keys. The activation process allows selectively applying changes and extensions made by SAP to active meta data objects.

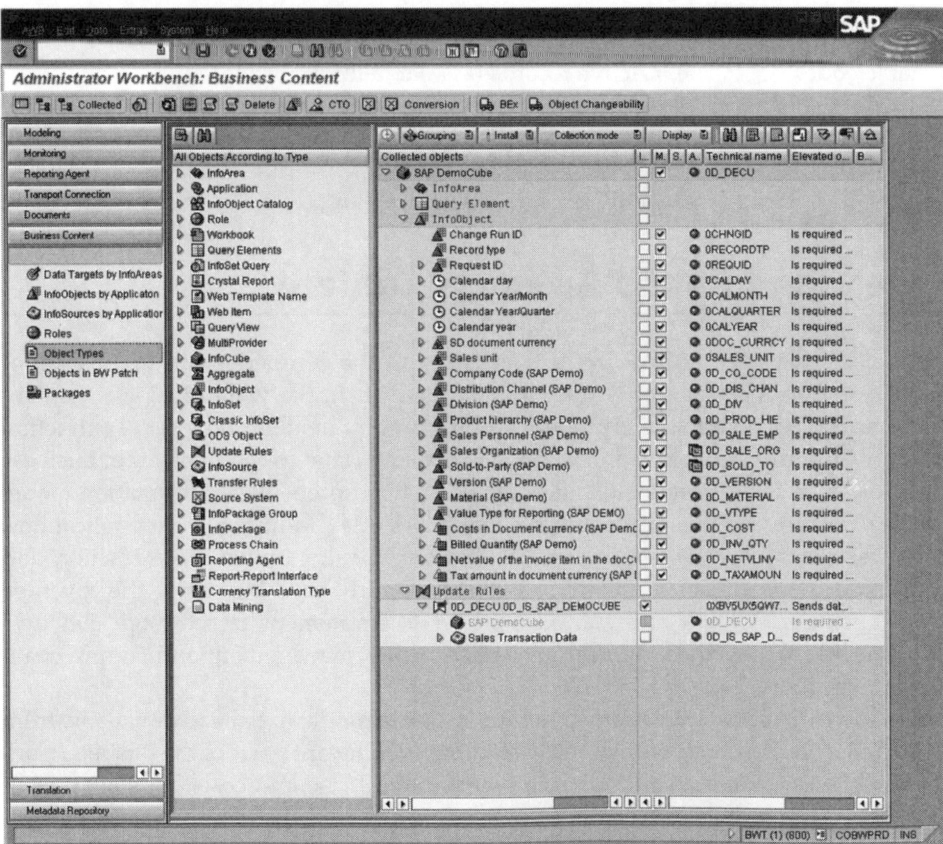

Figure 4.5 Activating Business Content.

Although originally designed for use with mySAP.com application components, the use of the Business Content does not end at the boundaries of the SAP system landscape. To a certain extent the actual business processes and their main characteristics are source-system agnostic. Apart from technical details, an accounting transaction, for example, is pretty much the same in SAP R/3, SAP R/2, Oracle, and probably many custom systems still in use; the Business Content, if used in heterogeneous (SAP and non-SAP) or homogeneous non-SAP environments still prove to be useful. The key in using the Business Content in such a situation is to map the business process data of the non-SAP systems to the corresponding InfoSource of the Business Content. While this step still may require some concept and programming work (which would, by the way, have to be done in any data warehouse project), the rest is nearly free.

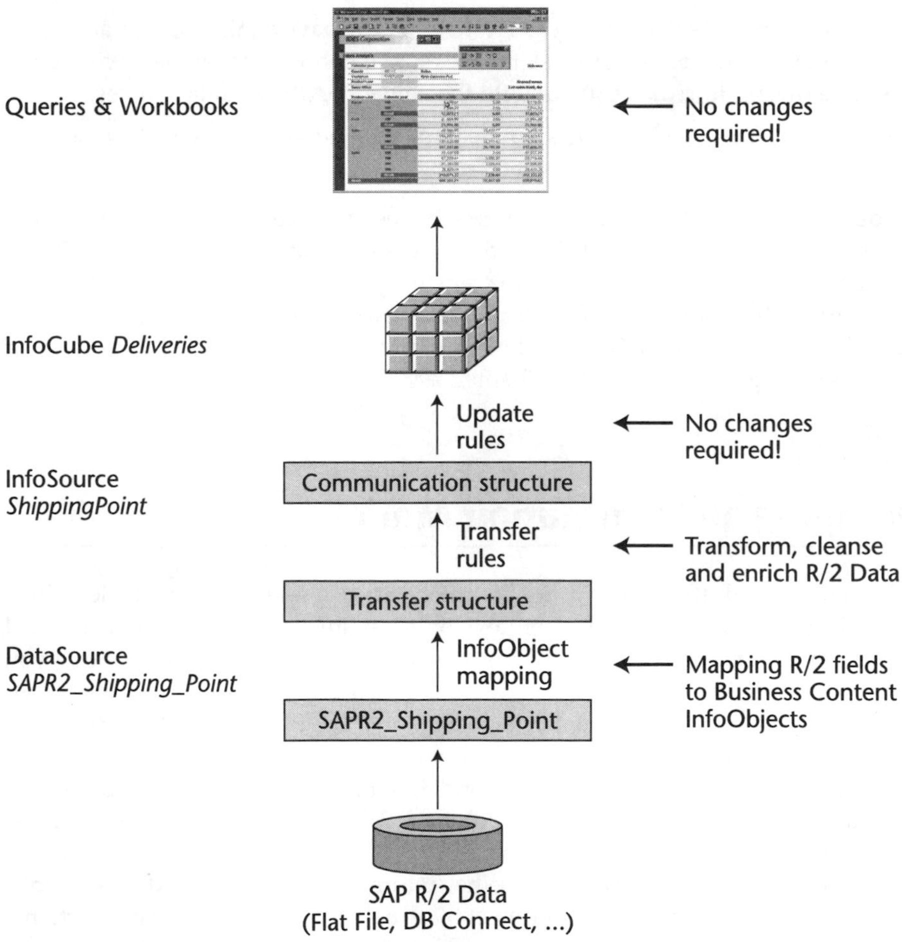

Figure 4.6 Sample use of the Business Content.

This approach is especially useful for SAP R/2 source systems. Because of some commonalities in their history, SAP R/2 and SAP R/3 have comparable core business processes. In particular, the financial and sales and distribution business processes are still fairly similar. Figure 4.6 illustrates how a flat file exported from an SAP R/2 system can be imported into an SAP BW system by mapping the R/2 fields to the fields of the Business Content InfoSource *ShippingPoints* using custom transfer rules. Analysis and reporting and the remainder of the staging process actually do not distinguish between different types of source systems.

There are three other advantages in implementing SAP BW in an SAP R/2 environment:

- As most of the existing SAP R/2 customers will most likely migrate to mySAP .com in the near future, the mapping process is a good preparation for the migration project. Many of the questions arising in the migration will already be discussed in the data warehouse implementation project, effectively implementing SAP BW before implementing SAP R/3.
- Migrating from SAP R/2 to mySAP.com will only have a minimal impact on the data warehouse; the core task for the data warehouse developers will be to replace the existing data sources with the new mySAP.com data sources.
- SAP's new dimension products can be implemented very quickly after the migration of the ERP system is completed.

The idea of providing Business Content has, by the way, been carried forward to the SAP Enterprise Portal software, where predefined portal content integrates functionality from a variety of systems: content management systems (like the SAP Web Content Management), ERP systems (like SAP R/3), data warehouse systems (e.g., SAP BW), and planning and simulation (SAP SEM BPS), to name a few. A detailed discussion of the Business Content can be found in Chapter 5.

Developing an Information Model

Now that we have all the prerequisites for information modeling in place, let's look more closely at the options available for developing an information model. In an ideal world, information modeling would be easy—just add every kind of information you need to the InfoProviders, make those available to end users, and you're done. However, there is a fundamental dilemma in developing an information model: Every information model will always be a compromise of some sort between business requirements, performance requirements, and fundamental data warehouse design aspects, part of which are already given by the SAP BW software itself. Figure 4.7 illustrates the information-modeling dilemma.

Usually, the answer to the question "What information do you need?" is simple: "I need everything!" Business requirements usually conflict with nonfunctional requirements like performance and usability. There is always a trade-off between performance and the amount of information available, and the more complex the information model, the more complex it is to use and the more difficult it is for occasional end users to create and execute meaningful queries with consistent and complete result sets.

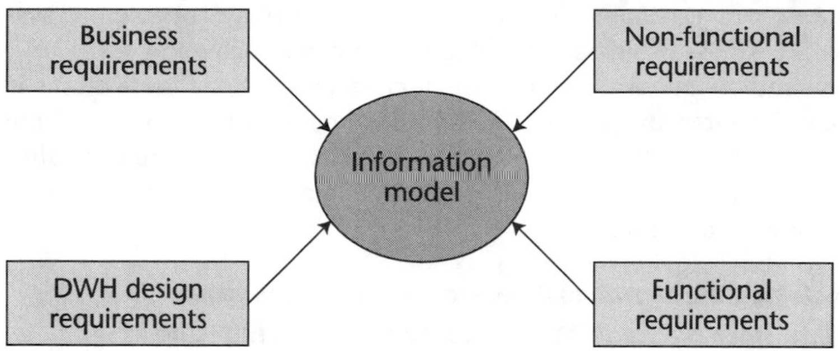

Figure 4.7 The information modeling dilemma.

In addition, there are general data warehouse design requirements conflicting with both of the preceding objectives, like the need for an enterprise data warehouse layer or the need for additional redundancies through the implementation of several InfoMarts providing correlated information. Sometimes, because of the predefined physical data model, the restrictions of standard software like SAP BW limit the degree of freedom in the information modeling process. Data warehouse design requirements are driven from the technical side of data warehouse development, as these people are responsible for actually developing and maintaining the data warehouse system. Though playing a minor role in the information modeling process, functional requirements may also be dragging the attention of the information modeler into their direction.

The art of information modeling is to define an information model that best suits all of these requirements without sacrificing too much of the business side of requirements; business requirements still are the most important requirements. Business users are the customers of the data warehouse development organization.

The remainder of this chapter lays out the options SAP BW provides for information modeling and shows examples of how to make use of these options.

Modeling the Operational Data Store

As discussed in Chapter 3, SAP BW offers two options when modeling the ODS layer of the CIF: ODS objects and remote InfoCubes. While ODS objects are physically stored copies of data in the SAP BW system, remote InfoCubes are references to data records stored on a separate system. Queries on ODS objects are executed by SAP BW itself; queries on a remote InfoCube are executed on the remote system.

ODS objects come in two flavors: nontransactional and transactional. Nontransactional ODS objects (the "standard" ODS objects) are updated in batch mode based on a schedule defined by an administrator. Nontransactional ODS objects can be used to model class II, class III, and class IV operational data stores.

Transactional ODS objects are potential candidates for modeling class I operational data stores, as these may be updated synchronously without involvement of the SAP BW scheduler. However, when using transactional ODS objects, keep in mind that synchronous updates into such an ODS object do not follow the regular SAP BW staging process but instead directly write records into the ODS object tables, bypassing all transfer and updates rules and all monitoring functionality. A prerequisite of implementing a class I operational data store is the ability to capture updates in the operational system and propagate those to the operational data store in real time—a feature rarely found in today's operational systems. At this writing the SAP BW Business Content did not include such a scenario.

Another option to simulate rather than implement class I operational data stores is using a remote InfoCube referencing to the OLTP source of data. This allows real-time access to transactional data, OLTP response times, updates, and DSS functionality mimicked through the remote InfoCube interface, which maps a flat data structure table to a multidimensional structure.

NOTE ODS objects and the operational data store are not the same. The operational data store is an architectural concept used in implementing information systems, while the ODS object is a technical object with a specific set of functions and properties—among other possible uses—appropriate for implementing an ODS. The actual design of the ODS objects in an operational data store is usually a denormalized variant of the data model used in the operational system.

Modeling the Data Warehouse

The main function of the data warehouse layer of the CIF is to provide an integrated history of data relevant for business decisions. The most important aspects of integration are:

Selection. Not all available data is relevant to information processing.

Harmonization. Perform data type conversions, calculations, and unification of technical values representing a property of an object.

Data quality. Add missing information (default values or derived values); perform plausibility checks.

Time. Add timestamps.

Aggregation. Aggregate data where the level of detail provided by a source system is too high.

Looking at these characteristics of integrated data, we see that modeling the data warehouse layer means defining the foundations for the corporate information infrastructure—what data at what level of granularity is available to fulfill today's and future reporting and analysis requirements.

The main SAP BW meta data object available for modeling the data warehouse layer is the ODS object already discussed in the previous section on modeling the operational data store. While in releases prior to 3.0 the ODS object did not fully cover the fundamental requirements for building a data warehouse layer, mainly because it was not enabled for master data; it now does. Figure 4.8 shows the evolution of the ODS object and the staging process in SAP BW.

The ODS object was originally introduced in the 2.0 release to provide operational data store functionality. The staging process for ODS objects (and InfoCubes, by the way) had been restricted to transactional data. SAP BW 3.0 has changed this significantly by adding flexible master data staging. Flexible master data staging effectively opens the same staging process that has been in place for transactional data for master data, including update rules, allowing for many-to-many relationships between master-data data sources and all kinds of data targets.

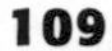

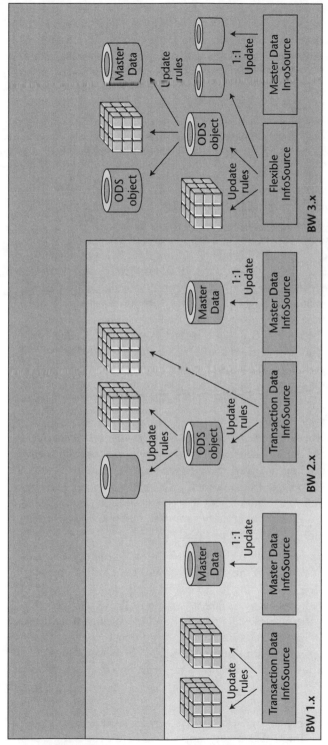

Figure 4.8 ODS object and staging process evolution.

Examples requiring flexible master data staging include tracking the history of master data changes in the data warehouse layer, and the use of hybrid data that may be considered master data as well as transaction data (e.g., loan contract data, which comprises attributes such as the customer number, sales organization, tariffs, or interest rates and transactional information).

From a technical point of view the ODS object is nothing more than a table, or, actually, a collection of tables (but that in fact is irrelevant to the information modeling discussion), holding key fields and data fields, allowing the tracking of changes, and allowing analysis and reporting. Going into more detail, there are three major application areas for ODS objects, all of which are key to modeling the data warehouse layer:

- *Keeping a history of granular data available for current and future requirements without having to go back to the source systems and extract the data again.* Usually, historical data is no longer available in the operational systems after a certain amount of time. At the least, it's being archived and is hard to get to at the extent required for data warehouse loads. Typically this means storing data fields that are currently not used or requested by any user or analytical application and are not at all useful in the average InfoCube. For instance, a complete sales order record may comprise more than a hundred data fields from different business areas, such as sales information, cost of production, or purchasing, and financial accounting information. While InfoCubes are perfectly suited to handle large granular data sets (InfoCubes with more than a billion data records are in productive use), it is not a good idea to overload InfoCubes with too many details not required for reporting and analysis purposes. Having an ODS object in place allows you to add information to InfoCubes as requested and load or reload the InfoCube from the ODS object.

- *Keeping track of changes not only of master data but also of transactional data records.* Looking, for example, at a typical sales order record, we notice that it is carrying certain status information that may change over time (e.g., from "sales order processed" to "delivered to the customer"). These changes may not be kept track of in the operational system. The ODS object allows you to do so for data warehousing purposes by making these changes available to other ODS objects and InfoCubes along the staging process.

  There are two options in modeling ODS objects for tracking history. The first option stores the current version of the sales record but keeps all changes available in the change log by defining the sales order number as the only key field. The second option stores every different version of the sales record by defining a combination of the sales order number and a timestamp as the key fields of the ODS object. Both options track the complete history of a sales order record. The first option requires more disk space (because of the change log storing before and after images) but allows reporting on the current status of the sales order.

- *Providing a harmonized database of all relevant business events and entities.* The breadth of information stored in the ODS object is key for actually using an ODS object as opposed to InfoCubes. Every single data field describing a business process or object must be harmonized to gain real value from the data warehouse layer.

Defining the information model of a data warehouse layer requires a thorough understanding of the business requirements and the technical details of the source systems. Here is a high-level method of defining the data warehouse layer information model:

1. Make sure the relevant information modeling prerequisites are there: business requirements, relevant entities and their attributes and hierarchies, KPIs.
2. Make sure the technical details of the relevant source applications are understood.
3. Identify relevant information about these processes and entities:
   a. *Projection:* Which fields
   b. *Selection:* Which records
   c. *Aggregation:* What level of detail
4. For each business process and entity, identify if keeping a history is required and how far this history is supposed to go back in time.
5. Define InfoObjects for each field describing those business processes and entities. This step includes defining technical details (such as data type), semantical details (such as representation of values, harmonization of key values, and aggregation rules), as well as reporting properties (such as default display formats).
6. Define ODS objects for each of these business processes and entities, based on the InfoObjects defined in Step 3.

We recommend that you conduct a Business Content gap analysis, although there are only a few ODS objects available in the Business Content for modeling the data warehouse level. The Business Content contains a large amount of predefined InfoObjects that can be used to implement the data warehouse layer.

Still, some open questions remain in defining the information model of the data warehouse layer, mostly related to the discussion of normalized versus denormalized modeling or, put differently, related to the question of how much redundancy should there be in a data warehouse. Although normalization is a term coined for data modeling, information modeling needs to cope with similar questions. Figure 4.9 shows two modeling options for ODS objects on the basis of a sales order. Similar examples could be given for master data, for example, material master data where there are generic attributes, attributes specific to the sales process, and attributes specific to the production process. The pros and cons of normalized and denormalized ODS objects are listed in Table 4.5.

Table 4.5 Normalized versus Denormalized ODS Objects

PROPERTY	NORMALIZED ODS OBJECT	DENORMALIZED ODS OBJECT
Redundancy	Low	High
Data volume	Low	High
Number of records	High	Low
Administration effort	High	Low
Support for realignment	Good	Poor
Delta handling	Easy	Difficult

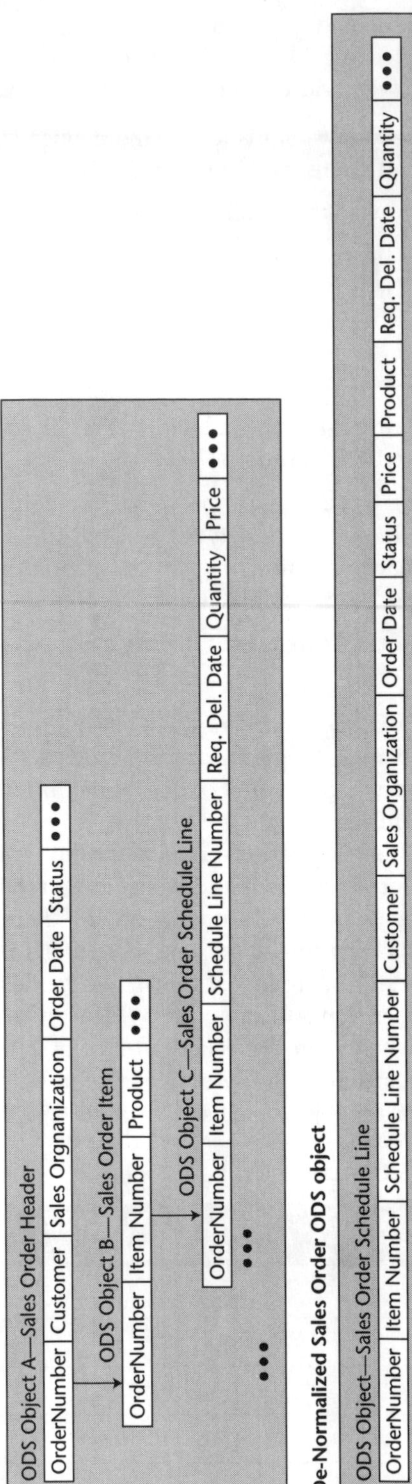

Figure 4.9 Different ODS object modeling approaches.

In general, we recommend going for an approach based on the normalized information model trading the total number of records for reduced redundancy, effectively leading to a lower overall data volume. The administration effort for normalized ODS objects is obviously higher, because multiple ODS objects have to be maintained instead of just one denormalized ODS object. However, for the same reasons, normalized ODS objects are better suited for capturing deltas and dealing with realignments. Assume the order status is changed in the operational system (which typically uses a normalized data model to store orders). For a normalized ODS object, just one data record on the order level needs to be updated; for a denormalized ODS object, all records relating to the updated order have to identified and changed. In many cases normalized ODS objects are enriched by aggregated information from dependent ODS objects, such as aggregated delivery quantity or aggregated revenue. This is because most of the mySAP.com extraction programs already provide this kind of information.

There's one important area of information modeling not yet covered in this chapter: modeling key figures and characteristics. We'll discuss this in the next section.

Modeling InfoMarts

Having introduced the InfoMart layer and its importance to end users in Chapter 3, and having clarified the major characteristics and uses of ODS objects and InfoCubes there already, it is no surprise that a major part of our information-modeling discussion concentrates on modeling InfoCubes, which still are the most important building blocks for InfoMart modeling.

One of the first questions to ask when starting the modeling process for an InfoMart is what should be the scope of each individual InfoCube in that InfoMart. In the early days of SAP BW, complex reporting or analysis requirements involving several types of events (e.g., sales orders and marketing campaigns for measuring the success of a campaign or sales orders and costs for calculating contribution margins) being reported and analyzed in a combined view compelled the definition of a complex InfoCube storing all required types of events, sometimes at different levels of granularity. Such InfoCubes tend to be more complex to manage and make it more difficult for occasional users to define their own consistent queries. Since MultiProviders have been available as an additional information modeling option in SAP BW, we now generally recommend not to define such composite InfoCubes to meet these kinds of requirements.

On the other hand, there are other applications—such as balanced scorecards—where there is a need for multibusiness area InfoCubes with highly aggregated or precomputed information merged from several data sources and several types of business events.

The truth for every SAP BW implementation lies somewhere in between those two extremes. The following sections describe the different modeling options available when defining InfoCubes and master data and get across a basic understanding of what option to choose for specific requirements. While modeling ODS objects has been covered in preceding sections, MultiProviders and multilevel staging scenarios are covered at the end of this chapter.

Dimensions

The starting point for modeling dimensions in SAP BW is to collect the characteristics required for reporting and analysis on top of the InfoCube. Modeling the dimensions of the InfoCube means to (1) define the dimensions and (2) assign all characteristics to one of these dimensions. SAP BW allows for a total of 16 dimensions, each holding up to 255 characteristics. Three of those dimensions are predefined by SAP:

The time dimension. All time characteristics included in the InfoCube definition are automatically assigned to the standard time dimension. Characteristics of any other type cannot be assigned to this dimension, nor can customers define their own time characteristics to be included in this dimension. It is, however, possible to define characteristics with a data type *date* or *time* and add these to any customer-defined dimension. This enables the use of additional time and date characteristics, as well as adding additional time information to the InfoCube.

The unit dimension. All unit characteristics (currencies and units of measure) assigned to the key figures included in the InfoCube definition are automatically assigned to the unit dimension. No unit dimension is available if there is no unit characteristic assigned to at least one key figure. The unit dimension cannot be maintained manually, whereas the assignment of units to a key figure is maintainable.

The package dimension. The package dimension is a technical dimension used by the data integrity maintenance functionality (see Chapter 9 on administering SAP BW) available in SAP BW. The main information contained in the package dimension is the request ID, uniquely identifying a request for data. The package dimension cannot be maintained manually.

Defining Dimensions

Let's look at an example of the dimension modeling process. A retailer implementing an InfoMart for point-of-sale detail information identifies the following characteristics and key figures as being available and important for analysis and reporting:

- Date
- Document number
- Product number
- Product group
- Outlet
- Region code
- Promotion number (if any)
- Promotion type
- Quantity sold
- Price

- VAT
- Discounts (if any)

He chooses to ignore additional information such as the time of sales and the cashier. A good starting point for the dimension design in SAP BW is to identify the strong entities (like product, outlet, and promotion), define a dimension for each of these, and assign all characteristics logically belonging to these strong entities to the same dimension, as shown in Figure 4.10 in the "good dimension design." Any characteristics left unassigned to a dimension after this process could be assigned to a dimension of their own (as shown for the document number in Figure 4.10) or could be assigned to a separate collector dimension.

This approach leads to an intuitively understandable design of dimensions. Every characteristic included in the InfoCube will be where it is expected to be even by the occasional end user. A clean dimension design for our retail example is shown in the upper left corner of Figure 4.10.

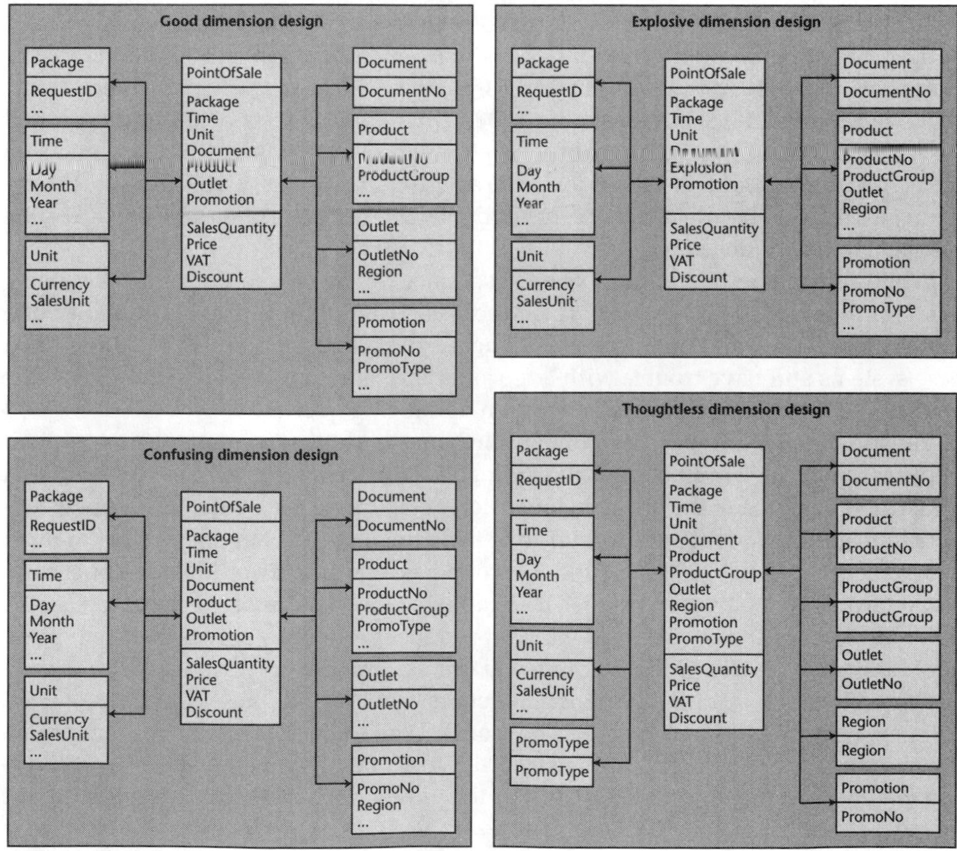

Figure 4.10 Dimension modeling examples.

The lower left and right dimension models show less intuitive dimension designs. The left one shows a less intuitive example that assigns the promotion number and the promotion type to two different dimensions, not even related to promotions at all in case of the promotion type. The lower right example shows a careless dimension that still is intuitive, because every characteristic is assigned to its own dimension, but it ends up in too many unnecessary key fields in the fact table of the InfoCube, increasing both the data volume of the fact table and the maintenance effort required to maintain indexes for these additional key fields.

Dimension Cardinality Considerations

In most of the cases both kinds of bad dimension design described in the preceding paragraph will not have too much of an impact from a technical point of view, as long as this does not lead to an effect called *explosion*. An example of an explosive dimension model is shown in the upper right corner of Figure 4.10. In this model the explosion dimension has a potential cardinality of:

```
# of product * # of outlets
```

Let's assume our retailer is offering a total of 150,000 different articles in a total of 2,000 outlets. The upper limit of the cardinality of this dimension then is 300 million records. Admitting that not every outlet offers and sells every single article, let's further assume an average outlet offers and sells some 20,000 different products (including assortment changes over time); we still end up with 40 million records stored in the dimension table. And these would have to be joined to a high cardinality fact table in almost every query, as two of the most frequently used characteristics—outlet and product—are assigned to this dimension.

While all this does not sound like rocket science, we have seen these mistakes being made in many of the projects we reviewed. As a rule of thumb, the cardinality of a dimension table should not exceed a number of 100,000 records, because today's database systems still have trouble with large joins and tend to ignore or even reverse the star schema character of an InfoCube when optimizing queries.

To estimate the cardinality of a dimension, you should first compute the upper limit of the cardinality by multiplying the cardinalities of all characteristics assigned to that dimension. Looking at the product dimension of our modeling example, we find product number and product group assigned to this dimension. Assuming product number has a cardinality of 150,000 and product group has a cardinality of 150, the upper limit of the cardinality of this dimension is 22.5 million. However, having a closer look at the relationship between product number and product group may reveal that each product is assigned a single product group, and this assignment only changes with a probability of 50 percent during the product lifetime. Considering this, we end up with an estimated cardinality of about 225,000 records. While 225,000 records in a dimension table exceeds the suggested limit of 100,000 records per dimension table, it is still reasonable to include both characteristics in this dimension; the product number alone already exceeds the 100,000 records limit, and adding the product group to the same dimension only adds a little to that cardinality.

Line-Item Dimensions

There are cases, however, where the cardinality of a single characteristic significantly exceeds this limit; examples include document numbers in granular InfoCubes and customer numbers in database marketing applications in consumer-centric businesses like telecommunications, banking, and insurance. This type of dimension is often called *degenerate dimension.*

Degenerate dimensions are implemented in SAP BW as line-item dimensions. The information modeling prerequisite to using line-item dimensions is to assign the high-cardinality characteristic (e.g., the customer number) and dependent lower cardinality characteristics (e.g., customer properties like zip code, date of birth, and customer group) to two separate dimensions. The high-cardinality dimension can then be defined as a line-item dimension as shown in Figure 4.11. The relationship between customer number and customer properties is maintained in the fact table rather than in the dimension tables.

The implementation of the line-item dimension concept to SAP BW release 2.0 has brought a significant enhancement for large-scale data warehouse applications, allowing you to store the surrogate key of the large-cardinality characteristic directly in the fact

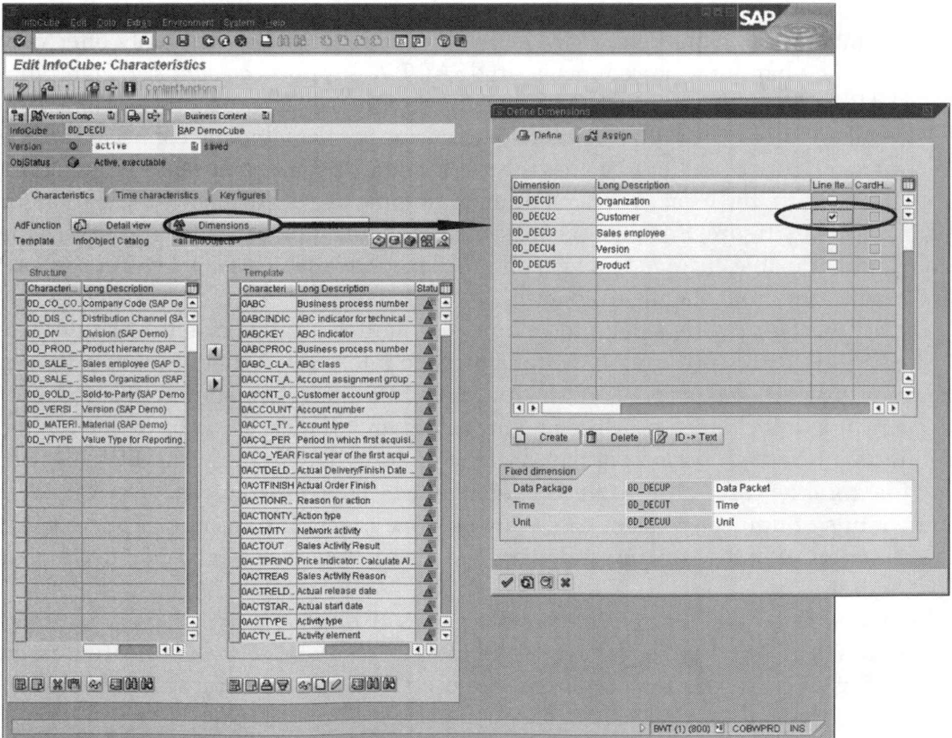

Figure 4.11 Defining a line-item dimension.

table instead of creating a dimension table with just a single key stored in it. Saving the dimension table does not only mean you save disk space; it also reduces a join of three very large tables (fact, dimension, and surrogate key tables) to a join of two very large tables (fact and surrogate key tables). The document dimension shown in the InfoCube data model in Figure 4.4 illustrates the implementation of line-item dimensions in SAP BW.

Granularity Mismatch

A granularity mismatch occurs whenever the lowest level of granularity in two different types of business events used in a single InfoCube is different—for example, if sales data is available on a daily basis and market research data is available on a monthly basis only. From a technical point of view, SAP BW does not force all business events to be on the same level of granularity—just leave the missing fields (e.g., the day) blank when updating the InfoCube with the less granular data set. However, in our little example, end users will obviously not be able to retrieve meaningful information for market research data when drilling down to the day level.

Key Figures

SAP BW provides five types of key figures for information modeling: amounts, quantities, numbers, date, and time. While many data warehouse products only offer very poor currency-handling procedures, if any, SAP BW supports *amount key figures* that are closely tied to either a fixed currency defined in the key figure meta data or a variable currency defined by the value of some currency characteristic connected to the amount key figure by either a business event (e.g., the document currency) or an entity relationship (e.g., the local currency). By enforcing the use of currency information for this kind of key figure, SAP BW ensures consistent currency handling and makes the same highly flexible currency conversion procedures available to any level of the SAP BW architecture from staging to analysis.

Quantity key figures are similar to amount key figures to some extent. Quantity key figures are used to store any type of quantitative information that requires a unit of measure. Instead of currency information, SAP BW enforces a specific fixed unit of measure or a unit characteristic holding the actual unit of measure to be defined in the key figure meta data. Because of the nature of quantity key figures, SAP BW does not provide complex unit-of-measure conversions as it does for currency conversions. These kinds of unit conversions can easily be done in either transfer or update rules. The data type of both—amount and quantity key figures—is either packed decimal or floating point.

Simple *numbers* are not connected to currencies or units as amounts and quantities are; numbers in SAP BW can be defined as integer, packed-decimal, or floating-point values. Typically, key figures of this type are used to store numerical values like counters, percentages, scores, rates, and deviations.

There are several ways to store date and time information in InfoCubes: predefined date and time characteristics in the system-defined time dimension, user-defined date and time characteristics in user-defined dimensions, and finally date or time key figures. While modeling date and time as characteristics allows for drill downs, time series analysis, or all kinds of navigation on date and time information, modeling date and time as key figures allows for arbitrary computations, such as the number of days between two dates.

Key figures can be used in InfoCubes, ODS objects, and master data attributes; they don't have attributes of their own, though. Key figures can represent the outcome of a business event (such as a sales revenue or a discount) or the current status of something—like weight and volume of a material, size of an outlet or a plant in square feet, or the number of children of an employee.

Aggregation Behavior

Besides the type of key figure described in the preceding section, there is another important categorization of key figures—additive, semi-additive, and nonadditive key figures:

Additive key figures. These may be aggregated by summing up all available values to a total value regardless of the dimension. Examples include sales revenues, discounts, and salary payments.

Semi-additive key figures. These may be aggregated by summing up all available values to a total value for some dimensions but not for others (mostly time dimensions). Examples include head counts, stock values, and number of customers (see *Counter Key Figures* coming up in this chapter.

Non-additive key figures. These cannot be aggregated at all. Examples include market share and growth rates.

Table 4.6 shows an example of semi-additive key figures based on head count data for several departments of a company. While adding up the head count values for December 1999 for all departments returns a meaningful number of employees for all three departments of 82, adding up the head count values for the accounting department of December and January would not return useful information. Defining the head count as being semi-additive would ensure that the head count for the accounting department returns the sum of only the last month regardless of the number of months returned by a query.

Table 4.6 Sample Head Count Data

DEPARTMENT	MONTH	HEAD COUNT
Accounting	12.1999	15
Sales	12.1999	45
Marketing	12.1999	22
Accounting	01.2000	17
Sales	01.2000	50
Marketing	01.2000	25

SAP BW supports additive, semi-additive, and nonadditive key figures in two ways:

- By allowing you to specify which aggregation algorithm to use in the meta data maintenance dialogs for key figures. Two types of aggregation are available there: standard aggregations and exception aggregations.
- By allowing you to specify a key figure as being a noncumulative key figure.

Figure 4.12 shows the key figure meta data maintenance dialog.

The standard aggregation function defined for a key figure is used whenever there's no exception aggregation defined for that key figure or whenever the exception aggregation does not apply. The exception aggregation function is applied whenever a query aggregates over the exception aggregation characteristic (e.g., day, month, year, customer number, document number). Put another way, the exception aggregation characteristic is not displayed or used as a filter in the query.

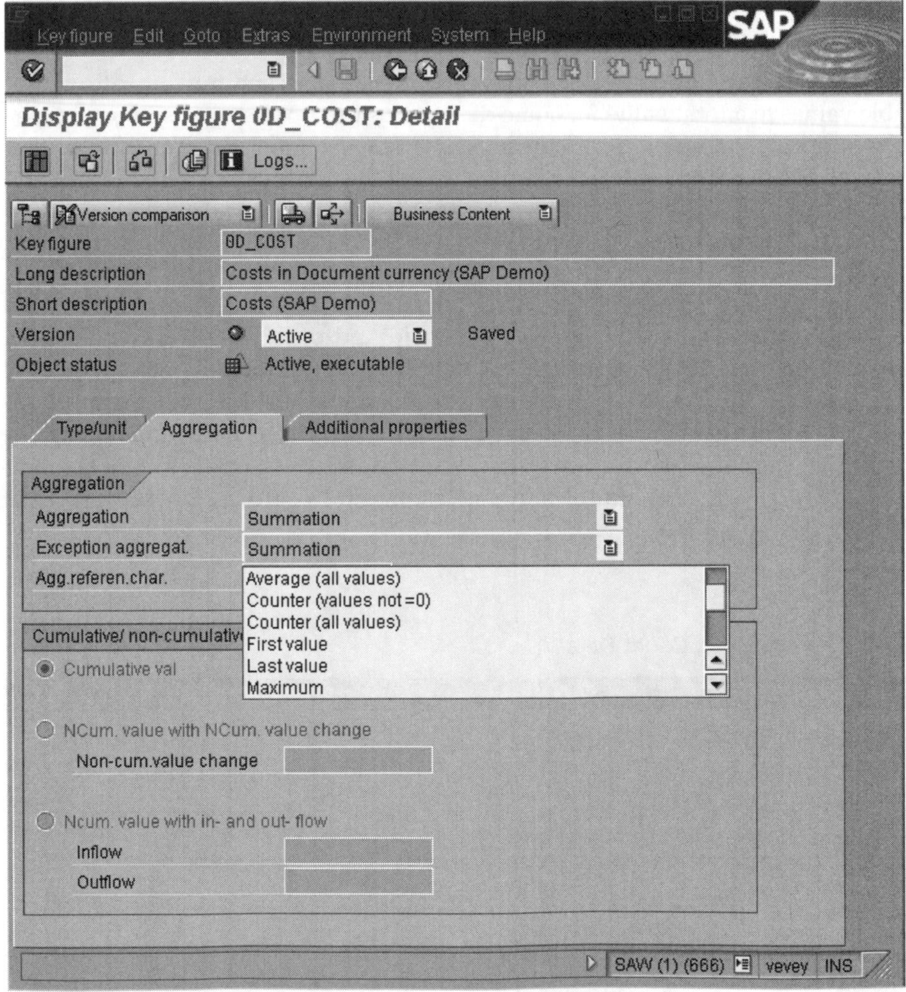

Figure 4.12 Key figure meta data maintenance.

SAP BW noncumulative key figures are used to model key figures that are semi-additive, or nonadditive with respect to time, such as head counts and stock values. Noncumulative key figures are discussed below.

Additive key figures have both the standard aggregation and the exception aggregation being set to "Summation," with no exception characteristic assigned. Semi-additive key figures are either defined as noncumulative or with the standard aggregation set to "Summation" but the exception aggregation set to something else. Nonadditive key figures are defined to have any other standard or exception aggregation but "Summation." Tables 4.7 and 4.8 show available standard and exception aggregation functions.

Table 4.7 Standard Aggregation Functions

FUNCTION	DESCRIPTION
Summation	The summation function is the default aggregation function in SAP BW. This function simply adds up all the values retrieved for the key figure according to the characteristics included in the query. The summation function is used to define additive key figures; for additive key figures there's no exception aggregation defined.
Maximum	The maximum function always returns the maximum values retrieved for the key figure according to the characteristics included in the query.
Minimum	The minimum function always returns the maximum values retrieved for the key figure according to the characteristics included in the query.
No aggregation	This function does not perform any aggregation at all, if an additional condition applies. Three variants of this function, with three different additional conditions, are currently available: ■ More than one record occurs for the characteristics included in the query. ■ More than one different value occurs for the characteristics included in the query. ■ More than one different value unequal to 0 occurs for the characteristics included in the query. The exception aggregation function is used whenever a query aggregates over the so-called exception aggregation characteristic; both are specified in the key figure meta data maintenance dialog. In the preceding example of the head count query, this would be the Month characteristic and the aggregation function used for exception aggregations would be the first variant of the "no aggregation" function.

Table 4.8 Exception Aggregation Functions

FUNCTION	DESCRIPTION
Average	The average function returns the average of the values retrieved for the key figure according to the characteristics included in the query. The average function comes in four different flavors: ■ Average of all values not equal to zero ■ Average of all values not equal to zero weighted with the number of calendar days ■ Average of all values not equal to zero weighted with the number of working days according to the SAP BW factory calendar ■ Average of all values
Count	The count function returns the number of values retrieved for the key figure according to the exception characteristic (which is not included in the query; the query aggregates over the exception characteristic). The count function comes in two different flavors: ■ Count all values unequal to 0 ■ Count all values
First value	The first value function returns the first value retrieved for the key figure according to the characteristics included in the query.
Last value	The last value function returns the first value retrieved for the key figure according to the characteristics included in the query.
Standard deviation	The standard deviation function returns the standard deviation of the values retrieved for the key figure according to the characteristics included in the query.
Variance	The variance function returns the variance of the values retrieved for the key figure according to the characteristics included in the query.

NOTE Aggregation functions for key figures are only relevant for reporting and analysis; they do not apply to the staging process. SAP BW does not prevent non- or semi-additive key figures from being aggregated during the staging process. Also, using exception aggregations reduces the degree of flexibility when defining aggregates. More on this in Chapter 10.

A noncumulative key figure always has one or two cumulative key figures assigned as counterparts (see Figure 4.13). While the noncumulative key figure stores the noncumulative values (like head counts and stocks) at a specific point of time, the cumulative key figures store changes to these noncumulative values within a period of time. Two scenarios are possible.

- If there is one single cumulative key figure associated with the noncumulative key figure, this key figure provides all changes (positive or negative) to the noncumulative value. If, for example, the noncumulative key figure is a head count, negative values of the associated cumulative key figure indicate employees leaving the company or department, while positive values indicate new employees in the company or assigned to the department.
- If there are two cumulative key figures associated with the noncumulative value, one is used for positive, the other is used for negative changes, and both values are specified as positive values (Figure 4.13).

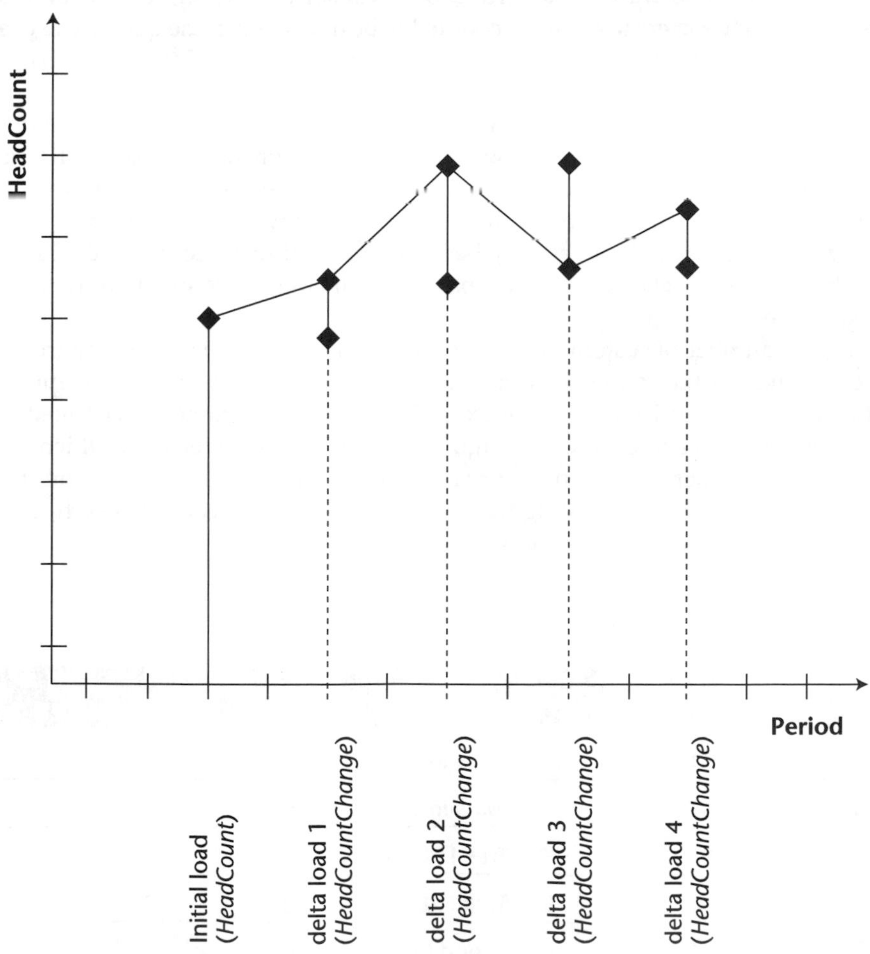

Figure 4.13 Use of noncumulative values.

NOTE SAP BW always physically stores the current values of noncumulative data and all historic changes to these values. A query requesting the current head counts by departments could directly read the results from the database. A query requesting historic head counts by departments from the beginning of last year reads the current values and all relevant changes to those current values back to beginning of last year.

Counter Key Figures

The SAP BW OLAP engine does not directly support counting the number of occurrences of a specific characteristic, although there are ways to implement counters using query formulas. The main reason for that is that support for counting arbitrary distinct values in the SQL language is poor (while it supports counting distinct occurrences of combinations of values using the *group by* clause).

Simple counters can be implemented in queries using formula variables for characteristics' values combined with the data functions available. However, these counters always require the characteristics' values counted to be displayed in the query. The use of counter key figure, as illustrated in Table 4.9, provides a more flexible means of counting.

Counting the number of line items can also be accomplished by adding a counter that is always set to a value of 1, as shown in Table 4.9. Aggregating this key figure using the standard aggregation function "Summation" provides the desired number of line items, as would the query formula discussed previously. However, counting the number of customers served is not as easy, because aggregating the counter key figure always yields a value of 5; however, in the example, something was sold to only three different customers.

Counting the number of customers requires using the "Count" exception aggregation to be assigned to the counter key figure, with "Customer" being the exception aggregation characteristic. Unfortunately, exception aggregation cannot be changed at run time, so we need to add counter key figures for every characteristic for which we need to count the number of different values in a query result set: a sales order counter key figure, a customer counter key figure, and finally a product counter key figure, each with a different exception characteristic.

Table 4.9 Sales Revenue Facts in the InfoCube

ORDER NUMBER	MATERIAL	CUSTOMER	REVENUE	COUNTER
100001	1234	Star Wars Inc.	110	1
100001	2345	Star Wars Inc.	80	1
100002	3456	Star Trek Ltd.	70	1
100002	1234	Star Trek Ltd.	150	1
100003	2345	Hollywood Inc.	300	1

Generic Key Figures

Some cases require a large number of key figures for analysis and reporting purposes. At one client there were two business areas having requirements for hundreds of key figures. The first was an InfoCube for sales analysis, where a consumer goods company had some 150 different types of discounts available for price calculation. The second was a highly aggregated InfoCube for management users, with some 250 different key figures to be reported. Often, many of these key figures are not used at all in most of the data records; the discount example given previously only used an average of five discounts on a single sales event. This leads to an effect called *key figure sparsity*, because many of the values stored in the database are actually empty.

As long as there are not too many sparse key figures, and as long as the number and semantics of key figures to report on are not changing too frequently, each of these key figures can be modeled as a separate key figure and included in the InfoCube definition. This is called the *specific key figure modeling approach* (sometimes also referred to as key-figure-based modeling).

However, in the scenarios described previously, there were not only many different key figures but there were new types of discounts being added, while other discounts were deleted. Using the specific key figure modeling approach, this would require periodically adapting the definition of the InfoCube by adding and removing key figures to cover new requirements. An approach to solving this modeling problem is what we call the *generic key figure modeling approach* (sometimes also referred to as account-based modeling).

The meaning of a generic key figure is not fully specified by the key figure value itself; instead, it is specified by an additional specification characteristic (e.g., a value type characteristic) that further specifies the actual meaning of the key figure value. The specification characteristic can either be assigned to another dimension available in the InfoCube or it can be assigned to a dimension of its own right, using the same dimension modeling considerations discussed previously.

Figure 4.14 shows two different layouts of a fact table: one using specific key figures, the other using a single generic key figure in combination with the value type characteristic. Tables 4.10 and 4.11 show the contents of those two fact tables for the same set of data.

Using the generic key figure approach provides a maximum of flexibility regarding the requirements mentioned previously. Additional key figures can be added by just defining another value for the value type characteristic and loading the data for this key figure. No space is wasted in the fact table by storing empty values for unused key figures; a record for a generic key figure only has to be stored if the key figure actually has a value unequal to 0.

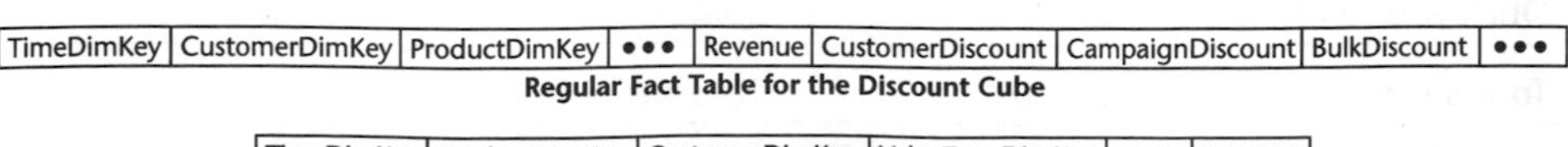

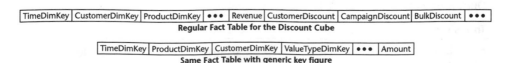

Figure 4.14 Generic key figures.

Table 4.10 Non-Generic Key Figures Example

CUSTOMER	MONTH	REVENUE	CUST. DISCNT	CAMP. DISCNT	BULK. DISCOUNT
Star Wars Inc.	12.2001	224	22	26	0
Duck Brothers	12.2001	459	68	0	30
Toons Inc.	12.2001	50	0	0	0
Star Trek Ltd.	12.2001	140	0	20	
...					

However, this flexibility comes at a cost. In InfoCubes based on generic key figures, the number of records (while being shorter) is significantly higher than in other InfoCubes. And end users can't just use the key figures stored in the InfoCubes, as they simply do not make sense at all without the associated characteristic. The BEx Analyzer supports the use of generic key figures by offering predefined restricted key figures, calculated key figures, and templates, allowing the data warehouse developers to provide predefined meaningful key figures.

There are other application scenarios where the generic key figure modeling approach should be considered, including planning and budgeting applications where actual values, different versions of plan values, budget values, and estimated budget values are required for reporting and analysis. In this case the value type would include values like *Actual*, *Plan*, *Plan Version 1*, and *Budget*. It is also possible to choose more than one characteristic to specify the actual meaning of a key figure, for instance, value type and version (which, in fact, is what you do anyway by including characteristics in an InfoCube—the more characteristics, the more specific an InfoCube is).

Table 4.11 Generic Key Figures Example

CUSTOMER	MONTH	VALUE TYPE	AMOUNT
Star Wars Inc.	12.2001	Revenue	224
Star Wars Inc.	12.2001	CustomerDiscount	22
Star Wars Inc.	12.2001	CampaignDiscount	26
Duck Brothers	12.2001	Revenue	459
Duck Brothers	12.2001	CustomerDiscount	68
Duck Brothers	12.2001	BulkDiscount	30
Toons Inc.	12.2001	Revenue	50
Star Trek Ltd.	12.2001	Revenue	140
Star Trek Ltd.	12.2001	CampaignDiscount	20

Please note that the generic key figure modeling approach is not new or unique to SAP BW. Some data warehouse products and custom data warehouse actually use the generic key figure approach as their primary method of storing information, calling the key figure a fact and having dimensions and attributes describe this fact.

Conversion of Currencies and Units of Measure

The basic principles of currency conversions and conversions of units of measure are discussed in more detail in Chapter 7. From an information modeling point of view, the question of conversion is a question of when and how to use the conversion mechanisms available.

Currency conversion during the staging process allows faster query execution but reduces the flexibility in choosing exchange rates at query execution time. Currency conversion at query execution time, on the other hand, takes some extra time to retrieve conversion rates and to actually convert the values, but it allows dynamically selecting the reporting currency. In the end, the choices made in a specific information model all depend on the degree of flexibility required at query execution time.

As opposed to currency conversions, unit conversion factors do not normally change over time. For this reason, unit conversions should in general be performed as part of the staging process to allow for faster query execution.

Master Data

The existence of master data has been widely ignored in the data warehouse industry. More precisely, master data has not been thought of as a separate class of data but instead as an integral part of the multidimensional model. This has led to a couple of problems for OLAP tools and data warehouse suites, including slowly changing dimensions, unbalanced modeling, and other irregular hierarchies.

Right from its early days, SAP BW has dealt with master data in a different way. The discussion of the master data model earlier in this chapter has already shown that there are completely different data models for master data, ODS objects, and the multidimensional InfoCubes linked together through surrogate keys, or in case of ODS objects, through real-world key values.

Modeling Text Information

There's not much to say about modeling text information in SAP BW. Master data texts are used to provide text information instead of or in addition to key values for characteristics. As already discussed in the data modeling part of this chapter, texts may be defined as being language-dependent and time-dependant. Language-dependent texts, along with the multilingual implementation of the SAP BW software, allow multinational companies to easily implement multilingual information systems. Time-dependent texts help keep track of renaming of products and organizational units, among other tasks. Figure 4.15 shows the InfoObject maintenance transaction related to modeling text information.

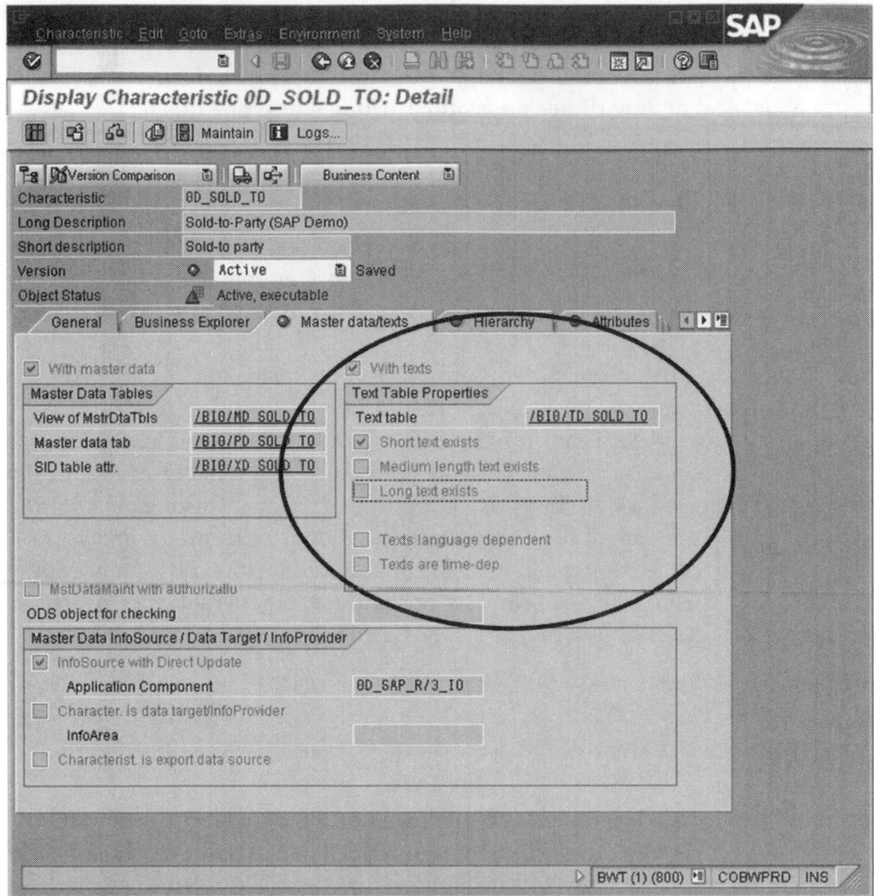

Figure 4.15 Options for modeling text information.

Different Kinds of Attributes

Attributes play a far more important role in information modeling. SAP BW distinguishes between two types of attributes (see Figure 4.16):

Display attributes. These can be used to display additional information in reports and queries. Examples include discrete information like street address, name of the city, customer phone number, name of contact person, and scalar information such as weight and volume of a product.

Navigational attributes. These can be used for display and for navigation and filtering in BEx queries. Use of navigational attributes, of course, is restricted to discrete information like zip code, customer group, and product category.

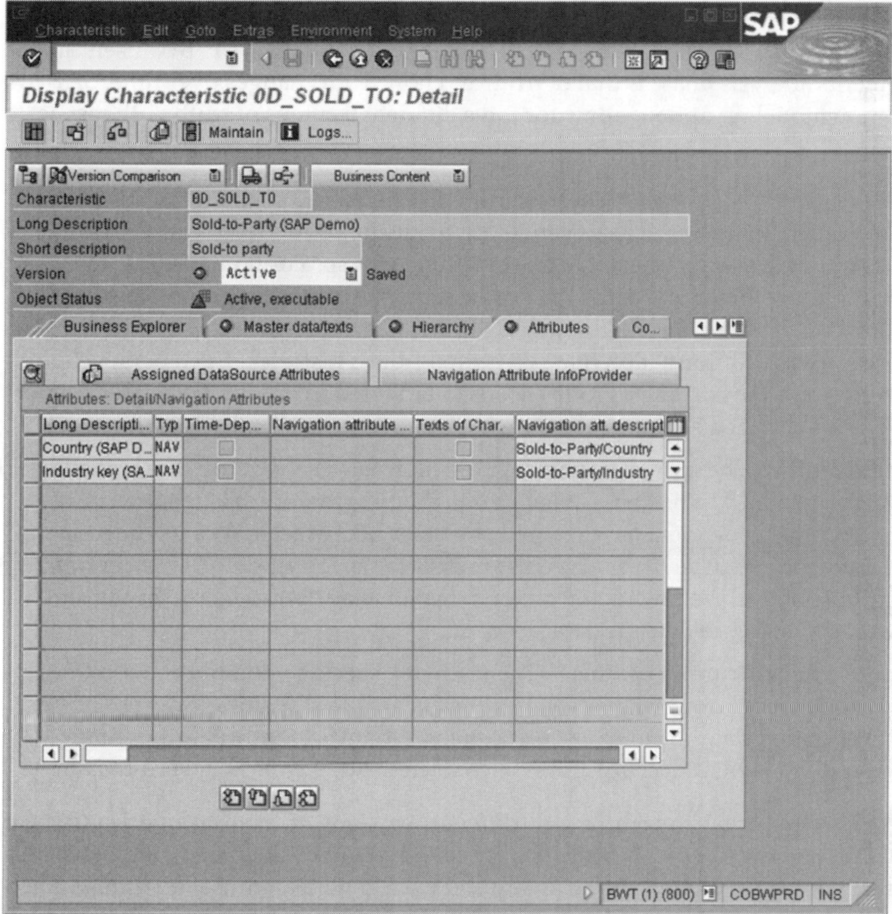

Figure 4.16 Options for modeling attributes.
Copyright © SAP AG

While display attributes play a minor role in information modeling, comparable to that of texts ("define, use, and don't think about it"), navigational attributes play a very important role with respect to realignment and covering different focuses on time. Both types of attributes may individually be flagged as being time-dependent. As described in the *master-data data model* section, time-dependent and non-time-dependent attributes are stored in two different database tables. Every distinct combination of attribute values of a characteristic has a distinct period of validity assigned, indicated by two database fields in the time-dependent attributes table: DateTo and DateFrom. Both dates are not automatically maintained by SAP BW, but either have to be extracted from the source system or have to be derived in the transformation or update rules. SAP BW, however, does take care of automatically adjusting validity periods of existing data records to avoid overlaps.

Different Versions of Truth in the Data Warehouse

One of the most important—and difficult—discussions with SAP BW users in the requirements analysis phase is that of truth and how truth changes over time. SAP BW information modeling options allow for three different versions of truth with respect to time:

Historical truth. The historical truth provides information about the status of all entities related to a business event (such as customers or products) at the time that business event occurred (e.g., something was sold or bought). Say, for example, customer Star Wars Inc. was assigned to customer group Science Fiction when he bought something in 2000. The historical truth is what we track in InfoCubes: All information that is required from a historical truth perspective (in this case the customer group) needs to be stored in the InfoCube and should never be changed again.

Current truth. The current truth provides information about the status of all entities related to a business event as of today. Current truth is what we find in non-time-dependent navigational attributes of characteristics included in an InfoCube ("current" in this context refers to the last update of master data attributes) or in the time-dependent navigational attributes using the current date as a reference date for data selection.

Truth of a specific point of time. The truth of a specific point of time provides information about the status of all entities related to a business event as of any specified date. Truth of a specific point of time is what we find in time-dependent navigational attributes of characteristics included in an InfoCube.

SAP BW allows you to compare all different versions of truth in queries (further information on how to use this functionality can be found in Chapter 7). However, this feature should be used with care, as many end users tend to confuse the different versions of truth presented in queries.

Storing and handling different versions of truth is also referred to as the *slowly changing dimensions* problem first described by Ralph Kimball (*The Data Warehouse Toolkit*, 2nd Edition, Wiley, 2002). Kimball initially defined three types of slowly changing dimensions:

Type 1. Storing current values with the facts. Slowly changing dimensions of type 1 are providing the current truth.

Type 2. Storing historic values with the facts. Slowly changing dimensions of type 2 are providing the historical truth.

Type 3. Storing current values and one previous value. Slowly changing dimensions of type 3 are providing the current truth and parts of the historical truth.

SAP does not use the term *slowly changing dimension* anywhere in the context of SAP BW. However, SAP BW does support all three types of slowly changing dimensions listed—and it goes beyond those by optionally storing all historical and current values using validity periods assigned to every specific combination of attributes. This option provides the current truth and all possible historical truths available in the database.

Table 4.12 Sales Facts in an InfoCube

CUSTOMER	CUSTOMER GROUP	DATE	REVENUE
Star Wars Inc.	Science Fiction	2000	100
Star Trek Ltd.	Science Fiction	2000	180
Poe Inc.	Mystery	2000	130
Duck Brothers	Crime	2000	150
Star Wars Inc.	Science Fiction	2001	90
Toons Inc.	Crime	2001	160
Star Trek Ltd.	Science Fiction	2001	170
Duck Brothers	Science Fiction	2001	150
Poe Inc.	Mystery	2001	210

To illustrate the effect of these different versions of truth, look at Table 4.12, which shows the sales data stored in an InfoCube. There is a customer/customer group assignment valid for 2000 and one for 2001. In the table a new customer, Toons Inc., was acquired in 2001 and assigned to customer group Crime. Also in 2001, Duck Brothers has been reclassified from customer group Crime to Science Fiction. The fact table of the InfoCube records the revenues achieved with these customers in the given period of time, as well as their customer group assignments at that point of time.

As stated, the InfoCube stores the historical truth about the sales facts—in this specific case, the historical truth about customer group to customer assignments, which involves an assignment of a weak entity to a strong entity. Queries asking for the historical truth about revenues per customer group would yield the results in Table 4.13.

Table 4.13 Reporting the Historical Truth

DATE	CUSTOMER GROUP	REVENUE
2000	Crime	150
	Mystery	130
	Science Fiction	280
Subtotals		**560**
2001	Crime	160
	Mystery	210
	Science Fiction	410
Subtotals		**780**
Totals		**1340**

Table 4.14 Sales Revenue Facts in the InfoCube (Revisited)

CUSTOMER	DATE	REVENUE
Star Wars Inc.	2000	100
Star Trek Ltd.	2000	180
Poe Inc.	2000	130
Duck Brothers	2000	150
Star Wars Inc.	2001	90
Toons Inc.	2001	160
Star Trek Ltd.	2001	170
Duck Brothers	2001	150
Poe Inc.	2001	210

In 2000 the total revenue of customers with customer group Science Fiction was 280. In 2000 the total revenue increased to 410 in this customer group, because Duck Brothers have been assigned to that group and removed from the Crime customer group. The Crime group revenue could only increase, because Toons Inc. instantly provided a total revenue of 160, covering the loss caused by regrouping Duck Brothers.

But what happens if the customer groups were not stored in the fact table but as an attribute of the customer characteristic? Table 4.14 shows our new fact table, without the customer group characteristic.

Because SAP BW now accesses current values of navigational attributes stored in master data tables (see Table 4.15), our query would yield a different result, shown in Table 4.16.

The results for 2000 would not show any revenue for the Crime customer group, as the only customer assigned to that group at that point of time (Duck Brothers) has been reassigned to Science Fiction and Toons Inc. has not been an active customer at that point of time. Science Fiction has profited from this reassignment, now showing a total revenue of 430.

Table 4.15 Customer Group as Navigational Attribute

CUSTOMER	CUSTOMER GROUP
Star Wars Inc.	Science Fiction
Toons Inc.	Crime
Star Trek Ltd.	Science Fiction
Duck Brothers	Science Fiction
Poe Inc.	Mystery

Table 4.16 Reporting the Current Truth

DATE	CUSTOMER GROUP	REVENUE
2000	Mystery	130
	Science Fiction	430
Subtotals		**560**
2001	Crime	160
	Mystery	210
	Science Fiction	410
Subtotals		**780**
Totals		**1340**

Because navigational attributes are not stored in the InfoCube tables (fact or dimension tables) but instead in the master data attribute tables, access to navigational attributes is slightly slower than to characteristics stored in the InfoCube. The OLAP engine has to join not only the SID table but also the attribute tables. However, our experience did not show serious impacts on performance for lower cardinality master data tables (< 100.000 records).

So far, we've been talking about characteristics in non-time-dependent master data tables. As mentioned, SAP BW also provides time-dependent master data attributes. What is the effect of using customer groups stored as a time-dependent attribute of the customer and using this in a query? Table 4.17 shows the results of a query with October 1, 2000, as a reference date for accessing time-dependent master data.

Table 4.17 Reporting the Truth as of October 1, 2000

DATE	CUSTOMER GROUP	REVENUE
2000	Crime	150
	Mystery	130
	Science Fiction	280
Subtotals		**560**
2001	Crime	150
	Mystery	210
	Science Fiction	260
	Not assigned	160
Subtotals		**780**
Totals		**1340**

Toons Inc. had not been a customer in 2000, and therefore it was not assigned to a customer group; this is why the revenue is shown as "Not assigned." Stated another way, since Toons Inc. was a customer in 2001, a query selecting all revenue for 2000 and 2001 must include Toons Inc.'s revenue. But this query is asking for the relationship of customer to customer group at some point in the past (in this case, October 1, 2000). Because there was no customer group for Toons Inc. prior to 2001, the revenue is reported in a customer group called "Not assigned."

The access path for this query is quite similar to that of non-time-dependent master data queries, except that the reference date specified is used to select the navigational attribute value valid for that point of time. Using the current date as a reference date would deliver the same results as for non-time-dependent master data.

Realignment

Having discussed the different versions of truth in data warehousing, we should also talk a bit about a problem closely related to the current truth and well known from SAP R/3 applications like CO-PA (Controlling-Profitability Analysis), from custom data warehouse systems, and from other standard data warehousing software. This problem is called *realignment*, the process of realigning reporting structures to changes applied to master data attributes and hierarchies.

Realignment usually is a very expensive process, not only in terms of process run time and use of resources. Realignment potentially destroys a wealth of historic data in traditional information systems. You can preserve the history by keeping the historic and the current truth separate in InfoCubes and navigational attributes. This way, SAP BW is able to realign information at query execution time without a significant performance impact and without throwing away the history.

However, there are realignment requirements in SAP BW, when navigational attributes are used in aggregate definitions (see Chapter 3 for a definition of aggregates). In these cases, affected aggregates have to be realigned. The difference here is that there is no information loss, because historic data still is available in the InfoCube and reporting would still be possible while the realignment is in progress, although you won't be able to use the affected aggregate (SAP BW would either read data from the InfoCube or from any other appropriate aggregate).

Master Data Key Figures

SAP BW allows the use of key figures as attributes of any characteristic; examples include the birth date of customers; price, weight, and volume of a material; and the size of a plant in square feet. As of SAP BW 2.0 you can use these *master data key figures* in query definitions for display and in calculations. Because master data key figures (or key figures in general) contain scalar information, they cannot be used as navigational attributes. In the same ways as navigational attributes, master data key figures can be used to model the current truth and the truth of a specific point of time.

Compound InfoObjects

Our discussion about the data model behind the SAP BW master data concept focused on single key field InfoObjects. In many cases, there is more than just one field required to fully qualify a business entity, for instance, cost centers, which are only unique within a controlling area or different aspects of a single product. Products have generic attributes like weight, volume, and color. But there may be different sales prices in different sales organizations, and there may also be different plants producing the product at different costs.

All of the preceding examples require additional key fields to be assigned to the product InfoObject. A typical SAP BW information model for this requirement would involve a generic product InfoObject, with all the generic attributes like weight and several specific InfoObjects that add the sales organization and the plant to the product InfoObject to form two additional compound InfoObjects: one for sales-organization-specific attributes and one for plant-specific attributes.

NOTE The example given here can be viewed in the Business Content: The product InfoObject is called 0MATERIAL, the sales-organization-specific InfoObject is called 0MAT_SALES, and the plant-related InfoObject is called 0MAT_PLANT.

There is not much to discuss here from a data model point of view; the data model discussed previously essentially stays the same, except that the SID table is composed of the SID and all real-world keys of all participating InfoObjects. The SID in these cases refers to a unique combination of key fields instead of just a single key field.

Compound InfoObjects are an important tool for integrating data from multiple, nonintegrated source systems, where master data cannot be easily integrated without a major impact on operative business process. Compounding, for example, the material number with the source system identifier allows keeping material master from different source systems separate in SAP BW. Using the source system identifier is not always appropriate, though. Some of the source systems may actually share the same material master, whereas others have their own material master. In these cases, a custom InfoObject such as *master data catalog* might be used in compounding to uniquely identify the origin of material master data records. In any case, it is an important task of information modeling to consider and take care of required and possible future integration scenarios; compounding plays an important role in accomplishing this task.

Multiple Use of Characteristics

SAP BW supports InfoObjects referring to other InfoObjects, effectively inheriting all properties of the referenced InfoObject except for the technical name and textual descriptions and linking to the master data tables of the referenced InfoObject instead of using master data tables of its own. Think of a sales transaction where several organizations or organizational units act in different roles: Organizational unit A orders some products to be delivered to organizational unit C, which are paid for by organizational unit B. In another sales transaction, A orders, products are delivered to A, and A also pays. While we want to know who ordered, who we delivered to, and who paid, we obviously do not want to keep separate customer master data in three different places: as an order customer, a shipment customer, and a paying customer.

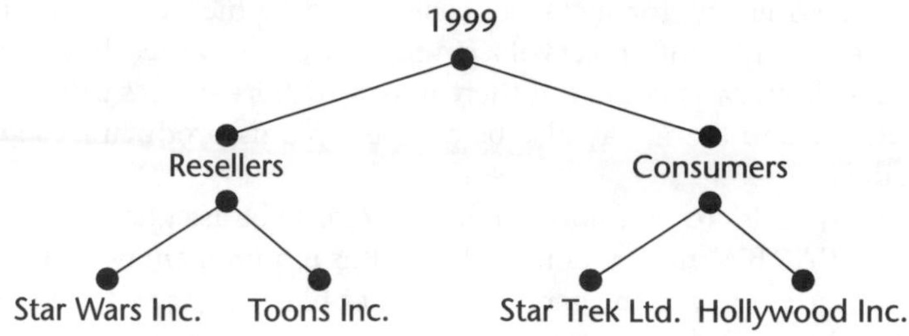

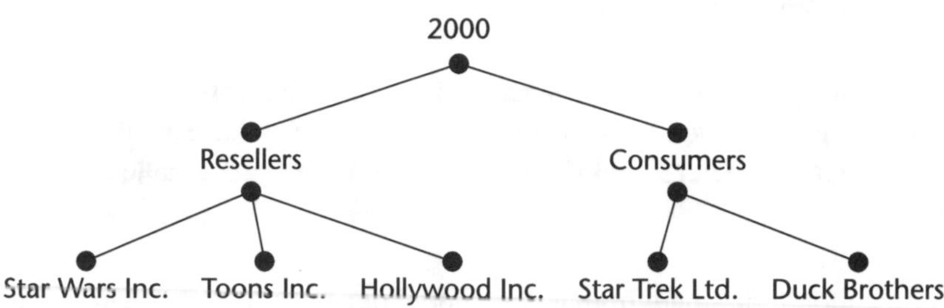

Figure 4.17 Two versions of a customer group hierarchy.

SAP BW allows defining InfoObjects referencing other InfoObjects to model these types of relationships. The Business Content, for example, provides multiple different *customer* InfoObjects: 0CUSTOMER to generically keep customer master data; 0SOLD_TO referring to 0CUSTOMER modeling the order customer role; 0SHIP_TO, also referring to 0CUSTOMER, modeling the shipment customer role; and finally 0PAYER, again referring to 0CUSTOMER, modeling the payment customer.

Hierarchies

In most reporting and analysis applications hierarchies are an important means of defining aggregation paths and visualizing KPIs in a convenient way. In SAP R/3, for example, there are hierarchies for cost centers, profit centers, accounts, customers, products, and many more. Figure 4.17 shows an example of two different versions for a hierarchy.

From an information modeling point of view, we distinguish several types of hierarchies:

Homogenous hierarchies. Every node of the hierarchy except the root node is of the same type. For example, in a customer hierarchy, every node of the hierarchy itself refers to a customer.

Heterogeneous hierarchies. Some nodes on a single level or on multiple levels of the hierarchy refer to different types of nodes, for example, hierarchy describing the assignment of customers to profit centers.

Balanced hierarchies. Every node of a single level of the hierarchy is of the same type and every branch of the hierarchy has the same number of levels, for example, a product hierarchy where product assignments to product groups are tracked.

Unbalanced hierarchies. There is a different number of hierarchy levels for the different branches of the hierarchy or where there are several types of InfoObjects referenced on a specific hierarchy level. Figure 4.18 shows an example of an unbalanced hierarchy. Unbalanced hierarchies are frequently used in human resources applications, in the consumer products industry, in project management, and other areas.

Network hierarchies. A node has more than one parent node, as shown in Figure 4.19. Network hierarchies are often used in sales organizations.

SAP BW provides two options for modeling hierarchies: *internal* and *external* hierarchies. Using internal hierarchies to model hierarchical relationships simply means adding one characteristic per level of the hierarchy to an InfoCube dimension or ODS object, or adding it as a navigational attribute. This way we can easily filter as well as drill down and across to navigate through the hierarchy. Whenever there is a homogeneous, balanced hierarchy where there are (1) no significant changes of the structure of the hierarchy anticipated (while there may well be changes to the actual relationships between hierarchy nodes) and (2) only a small number of hierarchy levels required, this is the method of choice. An example of this type of hierarchy is the product group hierarchy mentioned previously. In all other cases, use of external hierarchies should be considered.

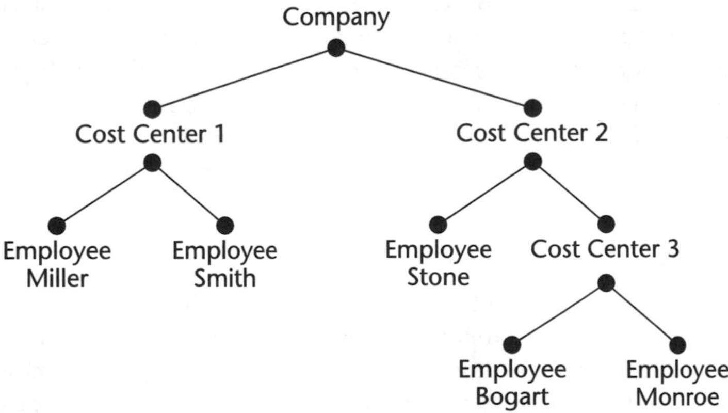

Figure 4.18 An unbalanced hierarchy.

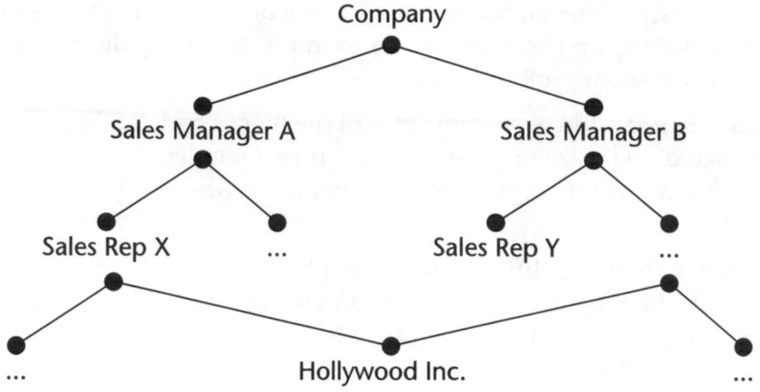

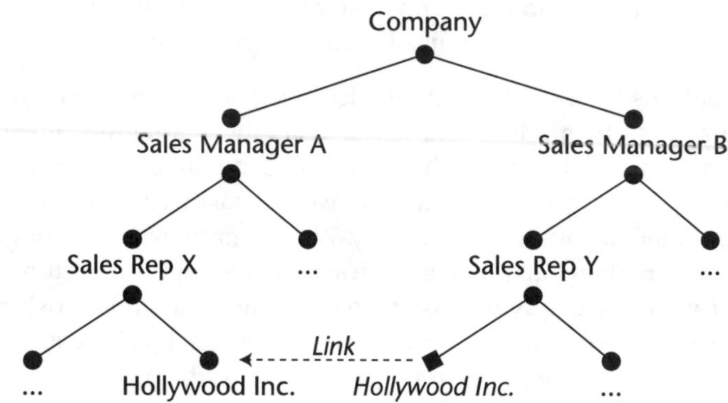

Figure 4.19 Network hierarchy.

External hierarchies in SAP BW are called external because they are neither stored in InfoCube dimensions nor in an ODS object nor as navigational attributes. Instead, they are stored in separate hierarchy tables associated to the base InfoObject (e.g., 0CUSTOMER for a customer hierarchy). Those hierarchy tables store a single record per hierarchy node that basically includes a unique node identifier and a reference to a parent node, as shown in Table 4.17, along with additional information. Table 4.18 shows the most important fields of a hierarchy table.

SAP BW external hierarchies allow for time-dependent hierarchy node assignments (time-dependent hierarchy structure) and for time- or version-dependent hierarchies. There are no restrictions to the type of truth that can be modeled with SAP BW external hierarchies. Additional features of hierarchies as implemented in SAP BW include *interval nodes*, allowing you to represent ranges of key values in a single hierarchy node, as well as *link nodes*, discussed a bit later. Attributes assigned to hierarchy nodes allow reversing the sign used for aggregation along the hierarchy: Aggregated values or values assigned to a node with the reverse flag set changes their sign from + to - and vice versa.

Table 4.18 Fields of Hierarchy Nodes Table

FIELD NAME	DESCRIPTION
HIEID	Unique hierarchy identifier
NODEID	Unique node identifier (unique within this hierarchy)
IOBJNM	Name of the InfoObject this hierarchy node refers to
NODENAME	Key value for the InfoObject this hierarchy node refers to
TLEVEL	Level of this hierarchy node
LINK	Link indicator for a hierarchy node (see the text that follows for more details)
PARENTID	Unique node identifier of the parent node of this hierarchy node
CHILDID	Unique node identifier of the first child node of this hierarchy node
NEXTID	Unique node identifier of the next node on the same level of this hierarchy node
DATEFROM	The starting date of the validity period of this hierarchy node record
DATETO	The end date of the validity period of this hierarchy node record
INTERVL	Flag: This hierarchy node is an interval node
SIGNCH	Flag: Reverse +/- sign

Table 4.19 shows how the sample hierarchy from Figure 4.17 is stored in the hierarchy table; Table 4.20 shows the same for our unbalanced hierarchy from Figure 4.18.

Looking at these two examples it becomes clear that external hierarchies provide a flexible means of modeling any type of hierarchy mentioned previously—except for the network hierarchy, which in fact is not exactly a hierarchy at all. SAP BW uses the link flag to allow for modeling network hierarchies. There is exactly one copy of the multiparent node for each of its parents. In one of these records the link flag (field LINK in the hierarchy table) is set to the initial value; the other records have the link flag set to X. The rest of the hierarchy remains unchanged compared to non-network hierarchies. When aggregating along the hierarchy, the OLAP processor takes into account that the values for the node flagged as a link must not be counted twice when computing the results for any node above the link node. Table 4.21 shows the network hierarchy stored in the database.

Table 4.19 The Customer Group Hierarchy 2000—Stored

NODEID	IOBJNM	NODENAME	TLEVEL	LINK	PARENTID	CHILDID	NEXTID
1	0HIER_NODE	2000	1	-	-	2	-
2	0CUST_GROUP	Resellers	2	-	1	3	6
3	0CUSTOMER	Star Wars Inc.	3	-	2	-	4
4	0CUSTOMER	Toons Inc.	3	-	2	-	5
5	0CUSTOMER	Hollywood Inc.	3	-	2	-	-
6	0CUST_GROUP	Consumers	2	-	1	7	-
7	0CUSTOMER	Star Trek Ltd.	3	-	6	-	8
8	0CUSTOMER	Duck Brothers	3	-	6	-	-

Table 4.20 The Unbalanced Hierarchy—Stored

NODEID	IOBJNM	NODENAME	TLEVEL	LINK	PARENTID	CHILDID	NEXTID
1	0HIER_NODE	Company	1	-	-	2	-
2	0COSTCENTER	Cost Center 1	2	-	1	3	5
3	0EMPLOYEE	Miller	3	-	2	-	4
4	0EMPLOYEE	Smith	3	-	2	-	-
5	0COSTCENTER	Cost Center 2	2	-	1	6	-
6	0EMPLOYEE	Stone	3	-	5	-	7
7	0COSTCENTER	Cost Center 3	3	-	5	8	-
8	0EMPLOYEE	Bogart	4	-	7	-	9
9	0EMPLOYEE	Monroe	4	-	7	-	-

Table 4.21 A Network Hierarchy—Stored

NODEID	IOBJNM	NODENAME	TLEVEL	LINK	PARENTID	CHILDID	NEXTID
1	0HIER_NODE	Company	1	-	-	2	-
2	0EMPLOYEE	Sales Mgr A	2	-	1	3	100
3	0EMPLOYEE	Sales Rep X	3	-	2	4	-
4	0CUSTOMER	Star Trek Ltd.	3	-	3	-	
...	...	...	...	...	...	...	...
100	0EMPLOYEE	Sales Mgr B	3	-	1	101	-
101	0EMPLOYEE	Sales Rep Y	3	-	100	...	-
102	0CUSTOMER	Star Trek Ltd.	4	X	101	-	-
...	...	...	...	...	...	...	...

From a query performance perspective, external hierarchies are, of course, slightly slower compared to navigational attributes. SAP BW maintains additional tables to speed up hierarchy access and utilizes recursive join support of modern database systems to provide the best-possible performance.

Another option to keep hierarchies small and effective is to create interval nodes specifying a range of key values instead of a single key value. Intervals are stored in a separate interval table not described here.

Virtual Key Figures and Characteristics

In SAP BW, values of key figures and characteristics do not necessarily have to be stored permanently in an InfoCube or in a master data attribute table. *Virtual key figures* and *virtual characteristics* allow the dynamic computation or derivation of values for key figures and characteristics at query execution time.

Examples of using virtual characteristics include dynamic categorization of key figure values such as age groups and price ranges, where the basis for calculating the categorical values is variable (as for the age). Another use of virtual characteristics is to compute complex compound values, combining information read from the InfoCube with current information retrieved from other sources (e.g., master data attributes).

Virtual key figures can be used to perform complex computations on the fly that are beyond the scope of the formulas available in the BEx Query Designer. Examples include the dynamic computation of the current age of a customer based on the current date and the birth date of the customer or the number of days on back order.

Both virtual key figures and virtual characteristics are rarely used, as they impact query performance and the degree of flexibility in defining aggregates significantly.

Additional Options for Information Modeling

Additional options in information modeling include the use of transactional data targets, the implications of multilevel staging of data on information modeling, and the use of the different types of virtual InfoProviders available in SAP BW.

Transactional Data Targets

SAP BW supports transactional InfoCubes and ODS objects that can be updated synchronously using a special API. This functionality is currently only used by SAP analytical applications such as SAP SEM, SAP APO, and SAP CRM. From an information modeling point of view, these objects are handled the same way as traditional InfoCubes and ODS objects. However, keep in mind the following restrictions when using transactional data targets:

- Transactional data targets are updated directly, without applying transfer and/or update rules.
- Updates to transactional data targets are not monitored by the SAP BW monitor.
- Updated data is not visible for standard reporting without making it visible explicitly or using special query variables.
- There is no synchronous rollup for aggregates on transactional InfoCubes.

Multilevel Staging Considerations

So far we've been discussing the data warehouse layer and the information delivery layer (e.g., how to model InfoCubes to deliver certain types of information). There are, however, scenarios where there's something in between those two layers. Such scenarios require a multilevel staging process with additional InfoCubes and/or ODS objects involved. Typical requirements that lead to these scenarios include status tracking and complex aggregations, as shown in Figure 4.20.

Applications that require the different statuses of a business process need to be able to update status values stored in the InfoMart. Given that InfoCubes do not allow direct updates, there are two ways to implement this functionality in SAP BW: (1) implement an ODS object that updates statuses as required and perform reporting and analysis using this ODS object and (2) implement an ODS object that updates status and creates a change log that can be propagated to an InfoCube. Option 1 would be used for small data volumes; option 2 would be used for large data volumes, taking advantage of the optimized data structure of the InfoCube.

Other applications, especially management information systems and balanced scorecards, mostly require highly aggregated key performance indicators that are calculated using complex formulas. While SAP BW does not provide complex aggregation algorithms to be defined for stored aggregates or online aggregations, it does allow you to populate InfoCubes with data extracted from other InfoCubes and ODS objects. Complex calculations can then be performed in the update rules.

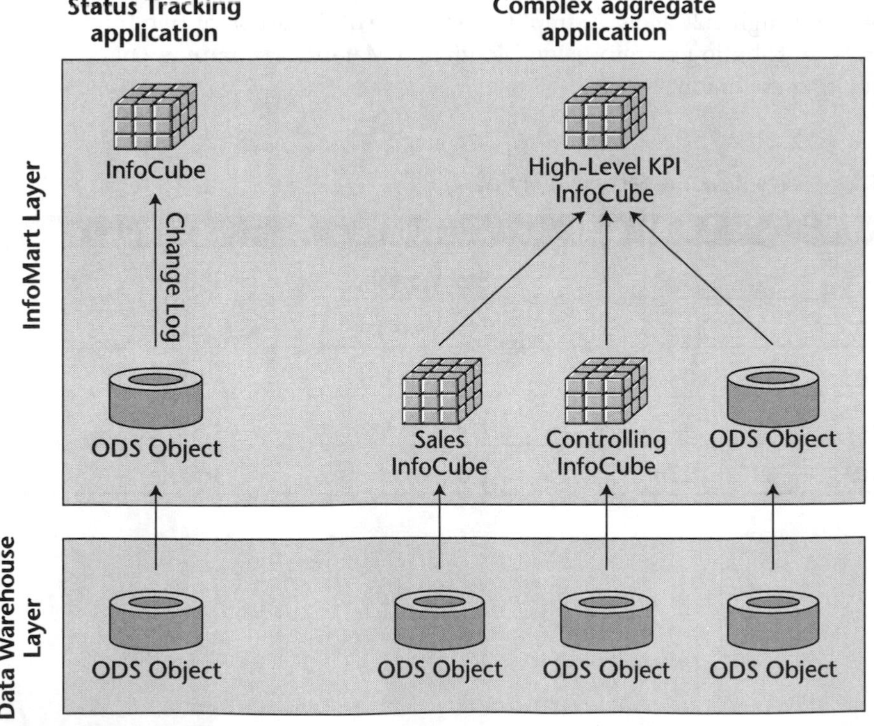

Figure 4.20 Multilevel staging scenarios.

In general, precalculated aggregates (discussed in more detail in Chapter 10) do not affect the information modeling process. However, from a reporting performance point of view, when you are modeling highly aggregated information from various sources, highly aggregated InfoCubes populated from more granular InfoProviders often are a better choice compared to a combination of MultiProviders and aggregates.

As Figure 4.20 also shows, SAP BW allows you to implement multiple stages of ODS objects. This is frequently used for merging data from different business processes into a single InfoCube or ODS object.

Modeling Virtual InfoProviders

SAP BW not only supports InfoProviders physically stored and managed directly on the SAP BW server, it also supports two types of *virtual* InfoProviders: *MultiProviders*, which are unions of other InfoProviders, and *remote InfoProviders*, which are InfoProviders available through BW Service API or from a non-SAP system.

MultiProviders

MultiProviders are typically used whenever there is information from different business processes or parts of a business process that needs to be displayed and available for navigation within a single query. MultiProviders are an alternative to modeling large (or, better, broad) physical InfoCubes or ODS objects holding all that information in a single place.

Keep in mind that MultiProviders are unions, not joins of InfoProviders—something that's been confused quite frequently in SAP BW implementation projects. Tables 4.22 through 4.24 show a simplified example of the union of two InfoCubes to compute a contribution margin using Month and Material as common characteristics for calculating the union.

Table 4.22 Sales Revenue Facts in an InfoCube

MONTH	MATERIAL	CUSTOMER	REVENUE
200101	1234	Star Wars Inc.	110
200101	2345	Star Wars Inc.	80
200102	3456	Star Trek Ltd.	70
200102	1234	Star Trek Ltd.	150
200103	2345	Duck Brothers	300

Table 4.23 Production Costs in an InfoCube

MONTH	MATERIAL	COST
200101	1234	97
200101	2345	80
200102	3456	80
200102	1234	110
200103	2345	200

Other uses of MultiProviders include handling of dormant data by implementing physically identical InfoProviders for separate periods of time and creating a MultiProvider for interperiod reporting and analysis. This approach allows you not only to delete dormant data by just dropping some of the physical providers, it also simulates database partitioning. With today's archiving functionality and the availability of data partitioning functionality within SAP BW, there's no need to use this approach any longer.

While SAP BW release 2.0 only supported MultiProviders composed of InfoCubes; release 3.0 now supports using all valid InfoProviders, including InfoCubes, ODS objects, InfoObjects, InfoSets, and remote InfoProviders. InfoSets are an important addition to the list, because they currently are the only means of defining a join of ODS objects and InfoObjects.

Table 4.24 Contribution margin retrieved from the MultiCube

MONTH	MATERIAL	REVENUE	COST	MARGIN
200101	1234	110	97	13
200101	2345	80	80	0
200102	3456	70	80	-10
200102	1234	150	110	40
200103	2345	300	200	100

Remote InfoCubes

Remote InfoCubes are useful whenever data residing on a remote system cannot or should not be copied to the local database. Sometimes external data cannot be copied to a local system for legal reasons, such as demographic or market research data; other times there is a design decision not to copy data from an operational system into the SAP BW database. This approach is frequently used to provide controlled instant access to live data on an operational system.

Remote InfoCubes can easily be defined for all SAP BW data sources available on mySAP.com applications, as SAP BW simply uses the BW Service API to directly access remote data on these types of systems. In addition, the remote cube BAPI enables custom-developed programs to act like a remote InfoProvider and provide online information to an SAP BW system.

Information Flow Modeling

Besides information modeling, the second major modeling task is information flow modeling, which deals with the flow of information from a source system to possible cascading data warehouse systems and eventually back into operational systems, establishing a closed-loop information flow. A simple information flow model has already been shown in Figure 4.6 (although we did not even call this an information flow model). Data from a source system (in this case SAP R/2) is processed and stored in SAP BW and delivered to end users as information. However, things are not that easy all the time. There are many business requirements, as well as functional and non-functional requirements, that might make it necessary to develop more complex information flow models, including:

- The physical allocation of users and systems to different locations, along with bandwidth considerations, data volume considerations in staging and reporting processes, and update frequencies.
- Heterogeneous source systems with different levels of data quality, detail, and availability of data and systems. You have to decide whether to integrate or deliberately not integrate data.
- Regional and organizational differences in the requirements for an SAP BW solution.
- Closed-loop analytical application requirements where information gathered needs to be fed from the data warehouse back into legacy systems, internal and external data providers, other data warehouses, and content management systems. Examples of these kinds of applications include but are not restricted to SAP CRM, SAP SCM, and SAP SEM.

Typical Information Flow Models

The enhanced ODS object technology now qualifies SAP BW as a platform for the implementation of the enterprise data warehouse building block of Bill Inmon's corporate information factory concept. Many SAP BW implementations, especially those in heterogeneous environments with different types of source systems, levels of data quality, and levels of detail now use ODS objects to create an enterprise data warehouse layer, feeding local or remote InfoMart and analytical applications of all kinds with harmonized and historical data (see Figure 4.21).

In an enterprise data warehouse model, all relevant data from different sources are staged into a single, integrated enterprise data warehouse. This enterprise data warehouse might not be one single physical machine but rather installed on some kind of

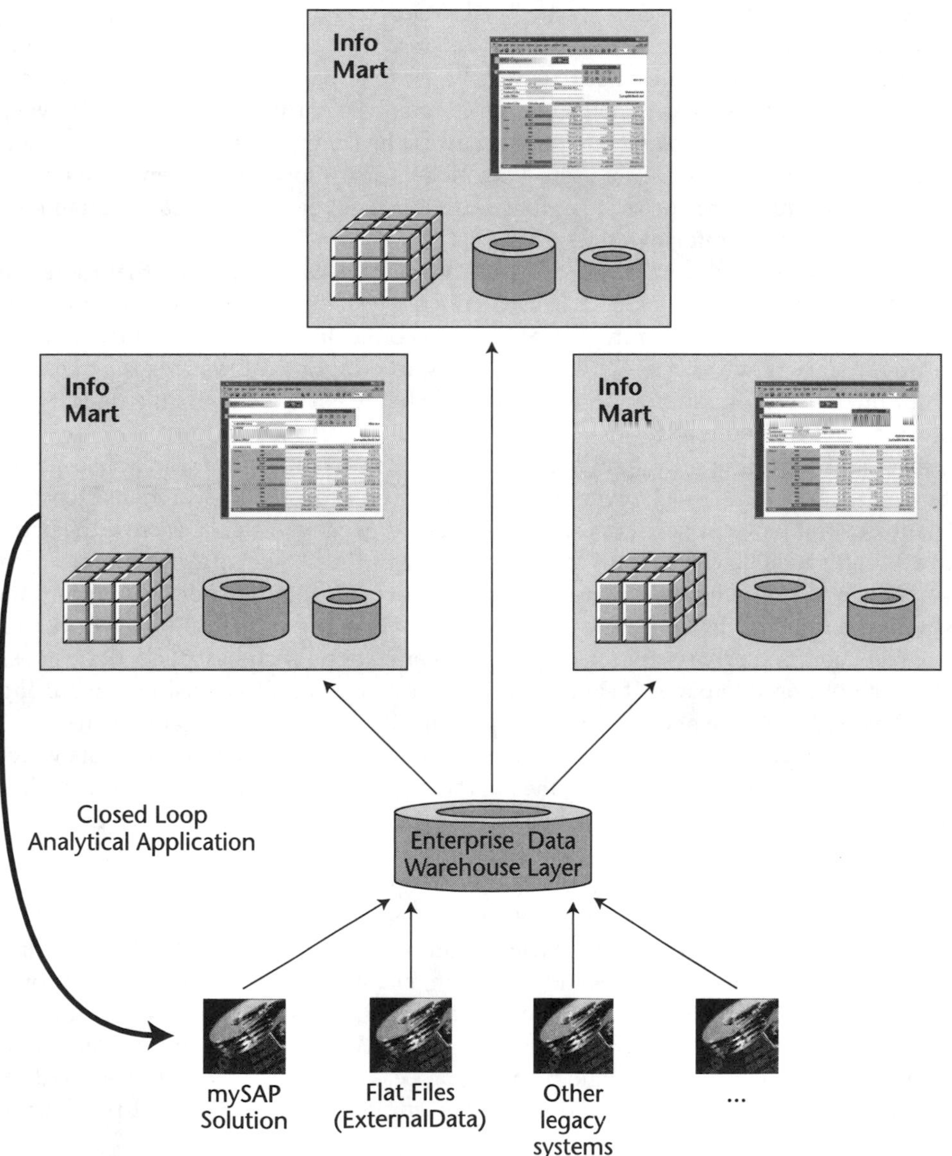

Figure 4.21 Enterprise data warehouse model.
Based on copyrighted material from SAP AG

server pool, or at least several physical machines connected in a multi-tier architecture for better performance. It still is a single logical enterprise data warehouse, however. Typically enterprise data warehouses store a large amount of data about different business processes, with many users accessing these data.

The InfoMarts shown in Figure 4.22 may be organized in different ways to help avoid or solve performance problems. The implementation of *regional InfoMarts* allows information required locally to be available on a local InfoMart. Because of network bandwidth limitations, user access to a local InfoMart is, of course, much faster than access to a remote data warehouse system, while data transfer from the enterprise data warehouse to the InfoMart can be scheduled for low-bandwidth utilization times.

Another concept is *functional InfoMarts*, where only a subset of the scope of information available in the enterprise data warehouse (e.g., sales information) is available in the InfoMart. This concept helps you avoid or solves performance issues with very large data warehouse implementation that covers the complete enterprise information needs and has a large number of users. Both models also allow for different local implementations of InfoMarts, providing more flexibility to cover specific local requirements (legal, functional, or information).

Our discussion of several InfoMarts here does not necessarily mean that these are residing on separate systems. SAP BW actually allows you to implement several InfoMarts on a single instance, run several instances on a single system, and run several instances on separate systems. Allocating InfoMarts to physical systems is a question of optimizing performance and minimizing hardware costs rather than a question of information flow modeling.

Another interesting information flow model is the corporate data warehouse model shown in Figure 4.23, which reverses the idea of an enterprise data warehouse to some extent. Several (enterprise) data warehouses spread geographically or across the organization are available for local, mostly detail reporting. A separate corporate data warehouse is populated with (usually) aggregated information from the local data warehouse systems. In these times of a constantly changing organizational world, this scenario is particularly useful for very large organizations with independent business units or holding companies heavily involved in mergers and acquisitions requiring high-level information about the most important KPIs of their suborganizations.

With increased functionality, performance, capacity, and tool support for data warehousing, closing the loop back from the data warehouse to the operational systems has become increasingly important in the last couple of years (see Figure 4.21). Examples of preconfigured *closed-loop analytical applications* include, but are of course not restricted to, customer analytics, demand planning, and business planning and simulation. SAP CRM, in fact, now is a closely integrated application utilizing the SAP R/3 functionality for operational CRM business processes and the SAP BW functionality for customer analytics purposes—for example, classifying customers based on purchasing and payment patterns and automatically feeding this back into the operational CRM system. In SAP SCM, which in fact uses an SAP BW core system for data management, the results of the demand planning process are fed back into the SAP R/3 PP (Production Planning) module and used as an input for production and purchasing processes.

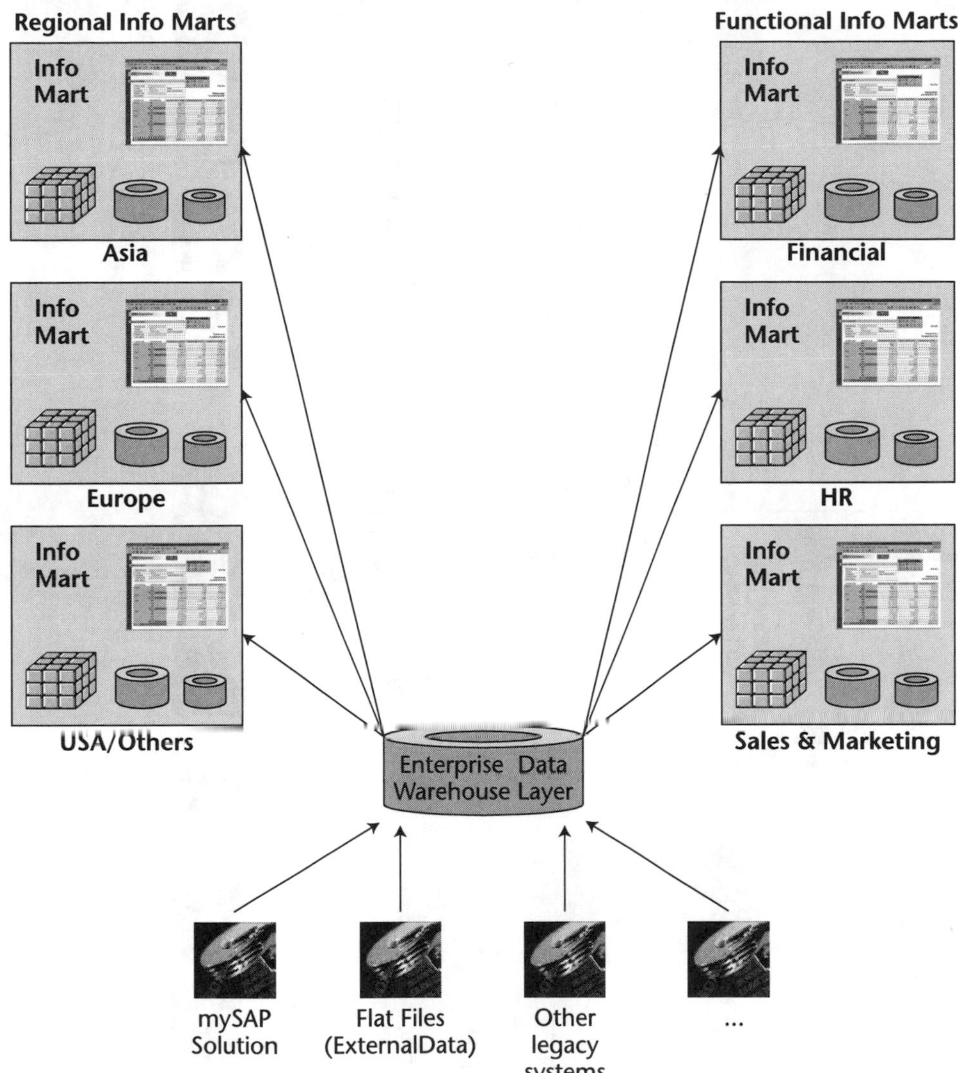

Figure 4.22 Functional and regional InfoMarts.
Based on copyrighted material from SAP AG

SAP recently has developed the first *retractors*—reverse extraction programs—available to extract data from SAP BW and write back to an ERP system. The first retractors have become available for closed-loop SAP CRM scenarios. The retractor concept has not yet grown into a mature retraction framework, such as the BW Service API for extractions has. However, we are anticipating further development in that area.

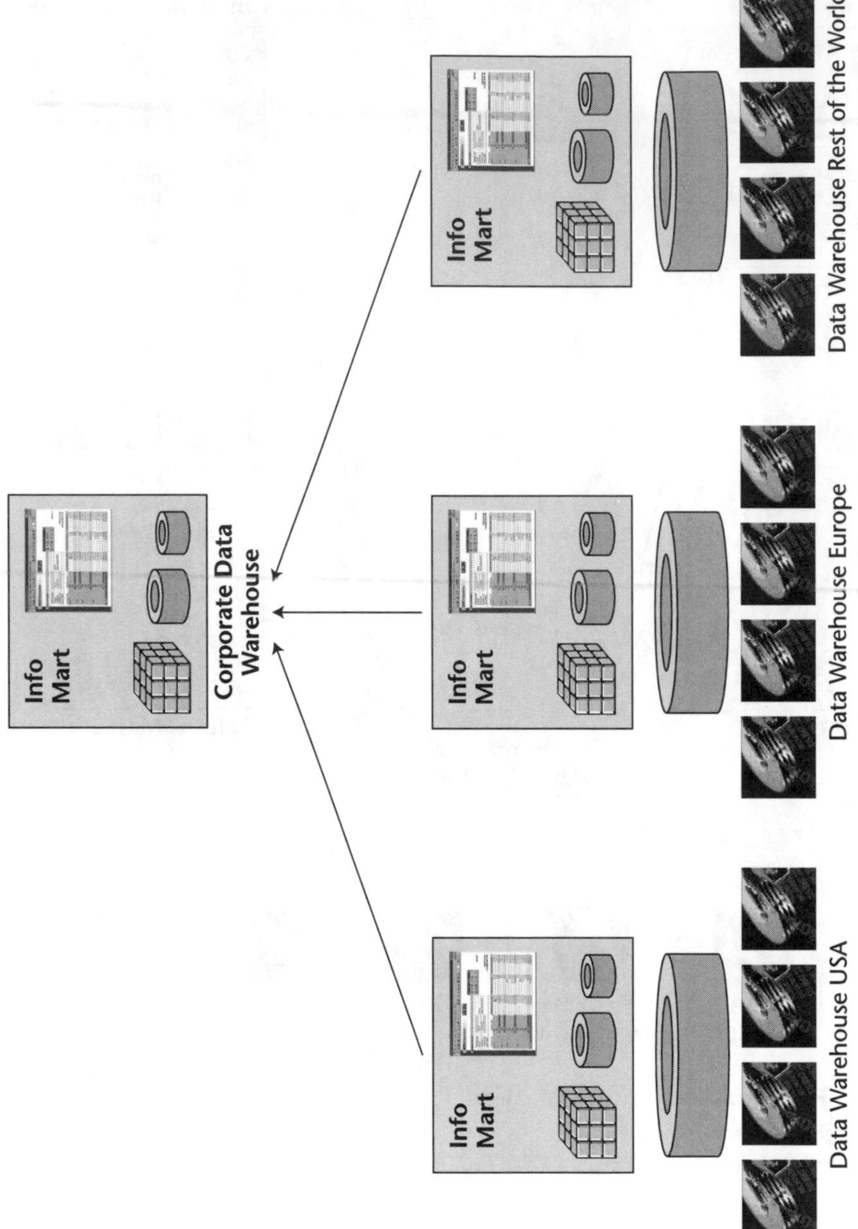

Figure 4.23 Corporate data warehouse model.
Based on copyrighted material from SAP AG

SAP BW Interfaces for Information Flow Modeling

The key to implementing complex information flow models are open interfaces allowing not only the extraction of data from operational systems but also the bidirectional exchange of data with ERP systems, different data warehouses, external information, and so forth. SAP BW release 3.0 has further extended the collection of interfaces on both ends of the information flow by the DB Connect interface, XML interfaces for staging, reporting and meta data exchange, and finally the Open Hub Service. Having discussed the SAP BW interfaces in Chapter 3 already, we'll now put them in context with our discussion of information flow modeling.

The *BW Service API* provides a flexible framework for data extraction, offering delta handling, generic data extraction, and online access via the remote cube technology for mySAP.com applications, including SAP BW itself. The BW Service API framework has been used by SAP developers to implement application-specific extraction programs for many application areas within the mySAP.com world. Integrated into the BW Service API, the generic extraction tool allows you to define custom extraction programs, extracting data from flat database tables or database views known to the ABAP dictionary and from InfoSet functional areas. In many SAP BW implementations, the BW Service API has become the backbone of the information flow model—not only because of its mySAP.com application support but also for its support for multiple cascading SAP BW systems. Additional staging interfaces such as the DB Connect interface, the file interface, and the XML interface extend the reach of SAP BW's onboard tools beyond the SAP world.

From the information flow modeling point of view, the Remote Cube interface provides an interesting means of avoiding data replication and providing access to real-time data. However, because of the performance implications of this kind of access, the Remote Cube interface needs to be used with care.

The *Staging BAPI*, supported by many third-party ETL tool vendors like Ascential Software, Informatica, and ETI, along with the strategic partnership of SAP and Ascential Software opens a whole world of applications outside of SAP for information flow modeling with SAP BW.

On the other end of the information flow through an SAP BW system, besides the BW Service API, a couple of interfaces and service are available to make information available to other applications. The SAP BW *Open Hub Service* provides controlled distribution of information to other applications with full support for delta management, selections, projection, and aggregation. The Open Hub Service is based on the InfoProvider concept and allows you to export data into flat files, database tables, and directly to other applications; it is fully integrated into the SAP BW scheduling and monitoring environment. We anticipate the Open Hub Service becoming the most important technology for information flow modeling, except for the BW Service API.

Mentioned earlier, the *OLAP BAPI* is a programming interface providing access to all available OLE DB for OLAP-enabled queries. External programs can call this interface to retrieve query meta data, execute a query, and retrieve the query result set. The OLAP BAPI can either be used through the SAP BAPI framework or by using the Microsoft Windows-based OLE DB for OLAP technology. The latter approach is used by most of the third-party reporting front-end tool vendors interfacing with SAP BW. From an information flow modeling point of view, the OLAP BAPI is useful whenever small bits of tailored information needs to be distributed to other applications and no delta management is required. In a similar way, the XML for Analysis interface allows to interface with Web services and portals.

It is not useful to make general recommendations on how to develop an information flow for a specific data warehouse project without knowing the business, functional and non-functional requirements, organizational details, user and system distribution, and details about the network, as well as the hardware and software environments in place. This is why the main focus of the preceding sections was on laying out different options used in real data warehouse projects and the options for information flow available with SAP BW. We also did not cover any of the information flow required to provide end users with appropriate information here; this discussion is reserved for Chapter 7, where we focus on the Business Explorer and Web reporting functionality of SAP BW.

Summary

Standard software solutions for data warehousing like SAP BW enable developers to turn their attention from data and technology to information and business. Modeling a data warehouse becomes more and more a task of modeling information and information flows instead of dealing with the technical details of a data warehouse implementation. Predefined information models contained in the Business Content add to that by taking some of the load of information modeling off the shoulders of the developers. The Business Content offers best-practice information models that can be extended and customized to specific needs.

The core part of an SAP BW implementation project, however, still remains information modeling based on a thorough understanding of the business strategy, the business processes, and user requirements. Information modeling options for the different layers of the CIF are laid out, explaining basic notions like the different versions of truth in a data warehouse, dimension modeling, and the role of master data, as well as different types of hierarchies. A discussion of typical examples of information flow models concluded this chapter.

This chapter provides the foundation for our discussion of the SAP BW Business Content (Chapter 5), which effectively is a predefined information model, covering large parts of the world of mySAP.com applications.

Understanding Business Content

Business Content has experienced significant growth and is continuing to progress in two directions: horizontally and vertically. Horizontal growth spans the processes, applications, and systems encompassed by the Business Content domain. Vertical growth segments Business Content into specialized industry sectors for more targeted and compelling Business Content information models. Business Content has also progressed with the growth of analytic applications, where its meta data objects can be used as building blocks to construct analytic applications. Analytic applications and Business Content fall within the corporate information factory (CIF) architecture. However, not all Business Content information models are aligned with the CIF design approach; these models take advantage of the integrated nature of SAP source systems and employ a data mart approach to design.

This chapter begins by offering a definition of Business Content, emphasizing its role-centric nature. The majority of this chapter is dedicated to using Business Content. In addition, we look at the Business Content value proposition and walk through the Business Content information models. After the Business Content value proposition is presented, we delve into the myths around, usability of, and challenges to Business Content. We also explore the Business Content information models, addressing how they relate to the information modeling challenges and concepts explained in Chapter 4.

By offering the attractive value proposition of accelerating the time it takes to implement SAP BW, Business Content is one of SAP's strongest selling points. With this in mind, we dispel the myths that belittle the significance of Business Content. At the same time, we also turn a critical eye on Business Content, exploring its limits and the ongoing challenges it will have in delivering usable information models.

The notion of using Business Content as templates for information modeling ideas is explored at length for three subject areas: procurement, financials, and human resources. A role and a business scenario are presented in each subject area, followed by information modeling questions Business Content addresses and how the information model is implemented.

The chapter concludes with a look at the future of Business Content, focusing on two trends: innovations in business intelligence technology and increasing segmentation in the business scenarios Business Content supports.

What Is Business Content?

Business Content is a roles-based, predelivered set of SAP BW information models. As a result, when Business Content information models are used out-of-the-box, SAP BW becomes a turnkey data warehouse solution.

When the prepackaged information models do not entirely meet business requirements, they can be flexibly extended via configuration and program enhancements. Additionally, Business Content information models consist of fundamental meta data elements that can be used as building blocks to quickly forge custom information models such as:

- InfoObjects (i.e., characteristics and key figures)
- InfoCubes
- Remote InfoCubes
- ODS objects
- InfoSets
- MultiProviders
- InfoSources
- DataSources (and their corresponding extractors)
- Transfer and update rules
- Queries (and their corresponding formulas, structures, calculated and restricted key figures, exceptions, conditions, etc.)
- Workbooks
- Web applications (and their corresponding Web templates, Web items, and data providers)
- Roles

See Chapter 3 to review the descriptions of the meta data object types.

Roles-based information models organize Business Content around delivering information needed to accomplish specific tasks. When used within analytic applications, Business Content enables business process support to accomplish the tasks necessary for analytic activities.

Tasks are the different physical or mental work assignments necessary to carry out a specific objective. A collection of tasks and information available for a group of users holding similar positions is called a *role*. From a portals perspective, a role can be further broken down into *worksets*, which are the tasks and information pertaining to specific activities. Worksets can be redundantly used across several roles that share similar tasks and activities. For example, a workset may consist of a series of tasks to perform a success analysis on a marketing campaign. The task-oriented workset Campaign Success Analysis could be simultaneously assigned to a campaign manager and a sales manager. Another example is the workset Cost Center Controlling, which can be assigned to all manager roles. Additionally, other applications can be integrated to the same manager roles, such as Human Resources worksets.

However, the impact of roles on Business Content is much more than on the organization of information deployment; it influences information modeling design and spawns analytic applications (more on analytic applications coming up in the chapter). There is an interrelationship between the processes being modeled, the key performance indicators (KPIs) that measure the processes, and the roles that evaluate the KPIs to plan, monitor, and control processes. The circular interrelationship forms a feedback-and-response system where roles not only monitor processes but also optimize them.

From a Business Content information modeling perspective, the impact of this interrelationship is such that:

- The processes drive what subject areas are being modeled; they determine the data sources and corresponding extractors needed.
- The KPIs dictate what queries and their InfoMarts should look like. Note that KPIs do not necessarily fall within a single process but can cross multiple processes for ratios such as inventory days of supply or cycle times like order to cash.
- Roles drive what KPIs are needed.

Because roles may need to plan, monitor, and control non-SAP processes, Business Content is being pushed outside the SAP domain. Heterogeneous system landscapes are a reality that a roles-based business intelligence solution must contend with. By necessity, SAP Business Content is strategically moving in this direction.

For example, a purchasing manager may need to measure supply chain processes sourced from i2 or Manugistics, such as inventory days supply or material cycle time. Figure 5.1 shows how the purchasing manager may need KPIs sourced from different processes like business-to-business e-procurement, materials management, quality control, human resources, cost management, and sales and marketing. These processes can potentially reside in differing non-SAP systems.

Similarly, KPIs can be used in more than one role. For example, a bottling facility measures the performance of its production process by monitoring the cost of scrap. Potential problems in the production line include running out of glue or labels in the labeling work center. Such a problem might not be identified until after bottles were put into cases and palletized. Mistakes in labeling meant bottles had to be scrapped. Because of the significant impact to product cost, many roles in the bottling organization (spanning production managers, production planners, quality control managers, and supply chain planners) evaluate the cost of scrap as a KPI to minimize. Figure 5.2 illustrates how a scrap KPI for measuring a production process can be used in several roles.

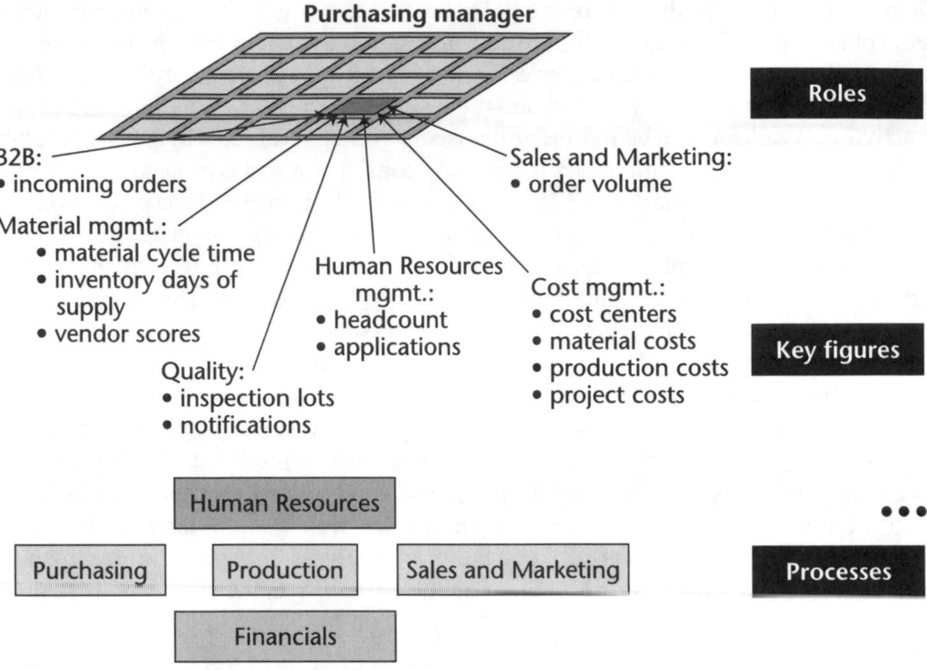

Figure 5.1 KPIs collect into roles.

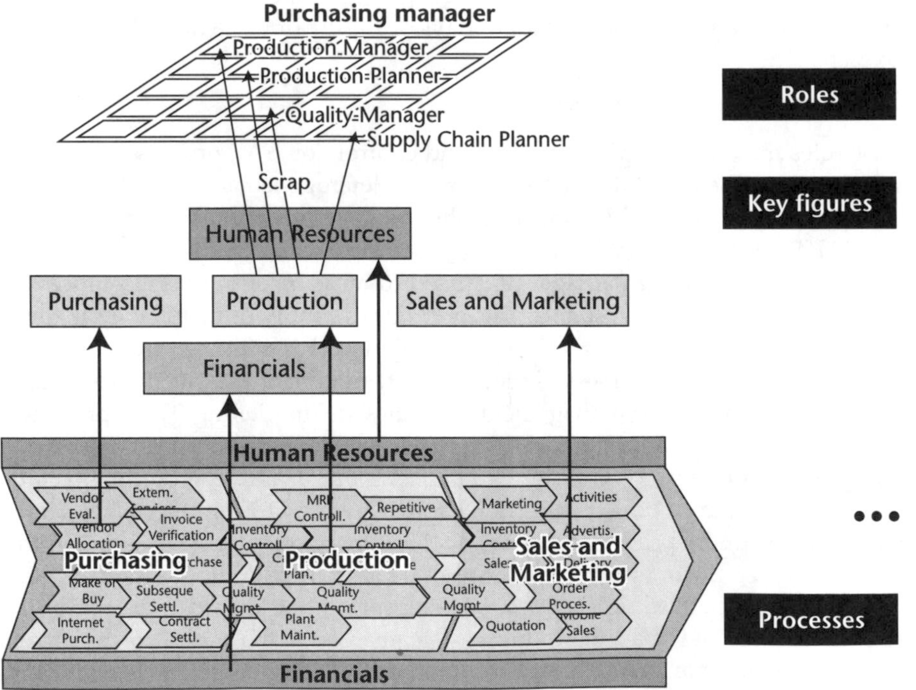

Figure 5.2 KPIs can feed multiple roles.

Besides the impact of roles-based information modeling, Business Content has grown horizontally across systems, applications, and processes, as well as vertically into different industry sectors.

Business Content Progression

From the beginning, SAP BW was meant to be a business intelligence platform that was source-system agnostic. In other words, there were native tools that supported the loading of non-SAP data into SAP BW. More explicitly, the file and BAPI interfaces were loading options present at the advent of the product. Furthermore, early Business Content scenarios included non-SAP data such as the information models for ACNielsen and Dun & Bradstreet information.

Nevertheless, before the recent proliferation of analytics and the incorporation of SAP BW into SAP's portal offering, Business Content had a distinctly SAP R/3 flavor. This propagated the myth that SAP BW is an SAP R/3-only reporting server.

Business Content has come a long way. In the earliest days of SAP BW, the most popular subject areas were sales and profitability analysis. Not only have these SAP R/3 application sources become less dominant, but SAP R/3 itself is not as central. New SAP and non-SAP applications are shrinking SAP R/3's share of the information in SAP BW. In addition to SAP R/3, Business Content supports SAP sources such as mySAP Supply Chain Management (mySAP SCM), mySAPCustomer Relationship Management (mySAP CRM), and SAP Markets Enterprise Buyer Professional Edition (SAPM EBP), as well as non-SAP sources through the use of tools from companies such as TeaLeaf and Ascential and support for XML. It is by no means a stretch of the imagination to envision all the major non-SAP applications (such as Siebel, i2, Oracle, PeopleSoft, and Manugistics) being supported by Business Content, especially through partnerships like Ascential's.

Additionally, Business Content has become more specialized, catering to the information needs of industry sectors. Because SAP industry solutions have their own unique processes, these systems are completely separate from mySAP solution offerings. These SAP industry-specific applications not only require separate information models but distinct new extractors.

Horizontal Growth

Before the emphasis on roles, Business Content was application-oriented. Business Content development took an *inside-out* approach; SAP R/3 applications were identified and corresponding extractors were written, passed to SAP BW InfoSources, and mapped to InfoCubes.

Business Content development then evolved into a more sophisticated *outside-in* approach. This approach focused on all the business processes available in SAP's solution map (SAP processes or a partner process). Using this approach, the interrelationships between roles, key figures, and processes were balanced.

The inside-out approach had limitations but created the foundation for an efficient implementation of the outside-in approach. Put differently, the inside-out approach provided what information was available, while the outside-in approach made that information more business-relevant and meaningful for supporting the tasks of a role.

With the outside-in approach, SAP Business Content encompasses processes that extend across applications and systems and encapsulates integrated information in order to deliver the relevant KPIs for specific roles. To reiterate, there is a circular and tight relationship between processes, roles, and KPIs. Examples of non-SAP Business Content include:

e-analytics. Clickstream analysis of Web logs

Market analytics. ACNielsen and Dun & Bradstreet InfoCubes

Benchmarking analytics. Benchmarking InfoCubes for the SEM Corporate Performance Monitor (SEM CPM)

SAP's partnership with TeaLeaf has accelerated the growth in e-analytics. Business Content now consists of specialized meta data with corresponding master data and transaction data. The Web content loads into ODS objects that make heavy use of transfer rules. The transfer rules parse the data into InfoObject values.

Third-party data provider information is accessed via InfoCubes that are loaded from flat files. As all master data must reside locally in BW, there are specialized flat files in Business Content that should be loaded prior to executing queries. ACNielsen examples align with industry solutions such as mySAP Consumer Products. Dun & Bradstreet scenarios have broader usage, being more geared toward customer relationship management and supplier relationship management.

For measures defined within SEM CPM, benchmark data (such as market research studies) can be loaded into a fixed SEM InfoCube by third-party benchmark providers. Whether benchmark data is available and who the benchmark provider is depends on the measure. Benchmark information can then be used for comparability purposes.

Business Content goes beyond providing non-SAP content; it also integrates it. For example, spend optimization analytics merges Dun & Bradstreet data with SAP Enterprise Buyer Pro (SAPM EBP) and SAP R/3 data across purchase orders, confirmations, goods movements, and invoices. In sales analytics Business Content for mySAP Pharmaceuticals, industry-specific content is merged with SAP CRM and external data from third-party data provider IMS Health.

Vertical Growth

Instead of developing Business Content as one-size-fits-all, SAP also develops industry-specific Business Content. More specifically, specialized Business Content can be found in the following verticals:

- mySAP Aerospace and Defense
- mySAP Automotive
- mySAP Banking
- mySAP Insurance
- mySAP Chemicals
- mySAP Consumer Products

- mySAP Retail
- mySAP Media
- mySAP Utilities
- mySAP Oil & Gas
- my SAP Pharmaceuticals
- mySAP Public Sector
- mySAP Healthcare

In some cases, industry-specific Business Content simply enhances the standard content rather than replaces it. For example, the Business Content for mySAP Media augments the standard extractors with media-specific extensions (or, more technically, appends the extraction structures).

In other cases, for instance, where there are no SAP R/3 counterparts, entirely new and separate BW meta data objects are introduced Two examples can be found in the mySAP Automotive and mySAP Healthcare Business Content. In the former there is a new InfoObject for vehicle, with requisite new master data extractors. For the latter, there is a new InfoObject and requisite extractors for diagnoses.

New industry-specific Business Content can take more advanced forms than simple augmentation of meta data. More specifically, some industry-specific requirements have birthed whole new techniques for extracting data out of SAP R/3 and using SAP BW. For example, SAP Apparel and Footwear (SAP AFS) solution of mySAP Consumer Products introduced a new concept for extraction transformation that breaks down data fields into *elementary fields*. Elementary fields, a term coined by SAP AFS Business Content, represent any piece of information that is contained in grids and categories of the SAP AFS solution (such as color, size, origin, and quality). Specialized function modules read information from SAP AFS tables and break down the fields for grid value and category into more elementary ones.

For mySAP Retail, SAP BW will be used to correctly derive the valuation of materials for the Retail Method of Accounting (RMA), functionality currently not available in SAP R/3. A specialized application called the RMA Engine must be configured in order to revalue the financial postings in SAP BW InfoCubes.

Lastly, more advanced industry-specific scenarios have integrated BW Business Content across several applications (examples include SAP SEM, SAP CRM, and SAP R/3). This is the case for mySAP Consumer Products' integrated sales planning application for key accounts. This particular solution also includes a specialized Excel component that allows offline planning and synchronization with online SAP applications for transferring plan and historical sales key figures. Analytic applications in mySAP Retail use Business Content for category management that also integrates with mySAP Enterprise Portals and SAP SEM.

Business Content and Analytic Applications

Business Content should be viewed as a collection of different types of building blocks that can be used to create analytic applications. The building blocks themselves are either individual meta data elements (like InfoObjects) or a preassembled set of meta data objects (such as a Web application). Business Content supports analytic applications by providing information models used for monitoring processes and the analysis paths to optimize processes in a feedback-and-response system (also referred to as a closed-loop application).

Henry Morris of IDC Research defines an analytic application as a packaged software application that performs the following tasks:[1]

Process support. This consists of organizing and automating tasks and activities oriented toward business process optimization and control. Process support can manifest itself in SAP BW in such ways as predefined analysis paths that lead to a decision, or any type of planning, simulation, and risks assessment. Process support should close the gap between analysis and execution.

Separation of function. The analytic application must be able to stand separate from any operational transaction system. Of course, any analytic application is heavily dependent on transactional systems for information and must have a closed-loop backflow to feed its results, but there must be a clear demarcation between the systems.

Time-oriented, integrated data. These are essential characteristics for any data warehouse or InfoMart that must always have a time dimension and the capability of integrating data from multiple internal and external sources.

Based on Henry Morris' definition, SAP BW is the ideal platform on which to build analytic applications, providing separation of function and time-oriented, integrated data. However, there are shades of gray as to what scenarios constitute enough process support to be considered an analytic application.

For example, does a Web application with drill-through to R/3 constitute a feature of an analytic application? Or is it part of Business Content or, more simply, Business Explorer functionality? As a guideline, if there is a feedback-and-response scenario along a predefined closed-loop analysis path—for example, a hiring freeze after a headcount assessment—then such a Web application has analytic application features. What about data mining? Data mining would be deemed a tool, not an analytic application. However, when used in conjunction with customer lifetime value (CLTV) analysis, data mining becomes a feature of an analytic customer relationship application. Again, the degree of process support is the deciding criteria.

Analytic applications themselves are divided along business processes such as:

Financial analytics. These include applications such as corporate investment management and customer credit management.

Human resource analytics. These include applications such as employee turnover analysis and retention management, headcount analysis, and overtime and illness analysis.

Customer relationship analytics (CRA). Probably one of the most advanced analytic areas, CRA spansCLTV analytics, customer segmentation analytics (with recency, frequency, and monetary analysis), market exploration, campaign monitoring, and campaign success analytics.

[1]Morris, Henry. 1997. "Analytic Applications and Market Forecast: Changing Structure of Information Access Markets." IDC # 14064 Vol. 1 (August). IDC Research. www.idc.com.

Supply chain analytics. This application has been most affected by the Supply Chain Council's SCOR model.[2] The Supply Chain Operations Reference (SCOR) model is a comprehensive set of key performance indicators for all the supply chain process.

- Analytic application examples are spending optimization, supplier performance analysis, production controlling, production lead-time analysis, and inventory analysis.
- The SCOR model is covered in more detail in Chapter 8.

E-analytics. Strengthened by the partnership with TeaLeaf and Ascential, this application includes e-selling analysis, marketplace analytics, and Web site monitoring, among others.

More-detailed examples of analytic applications in the technical components SAP Customer Relationship Management, SAP Advanced Planning and Optimization and SAP Strategic Enterprise Management are described in Chapter 8.

Business Content and Analytic Applications in the Corporate Information Factory

Analytic applications fall within the data delivery layer of the CIF, while Business Content and its building block components permeate throughout the CIF architecture. Chapter 3 discussed how SAP BW components map to the CIF. Examples of Business Content meta data objects that can be used within the CIF architecture are:

- Extractors for data acquisition
- ODS objects and InfoObjects for data warehouse management
- InfoCubes for data delivery
- Queries for information analysis
- Web applications and solution workbooks for presentation
- Roles for information deployment

Business content is moving in the direction of support for the CIF architecture. Examples of information models that have already adopted a CIF approach (by passing data to an integrated data warehouse layer before updating InfoMarts) can be found in financial accounting, e-procurement, and CRM.

However, the historical roots of the Business Content were not immersed in the concepts of CIF. Hence, there are terminology mismatches with the Inmon-defined ODS and the SAP BW-defined ODS objects, as well as a lack of Business Content scenarios for what Inmon would call an ODS, or the data warehouse layer. Business Content support for the ODS should manifest itself as remote InfoCubes or ODS objects (transactional and nontransactional); support for the data warehouse should manifest itself as ODS objects. Chapter 3 provided more details on how ODS objects map to ODS or a data warehouse in the CIF framework (noting the distinction between ODS object as an SAP BW meta data object and ODS as an architectural component).

[2]The SCOR model was developed by the Supply Chain Council. More can be read at www.supply-chain.org.

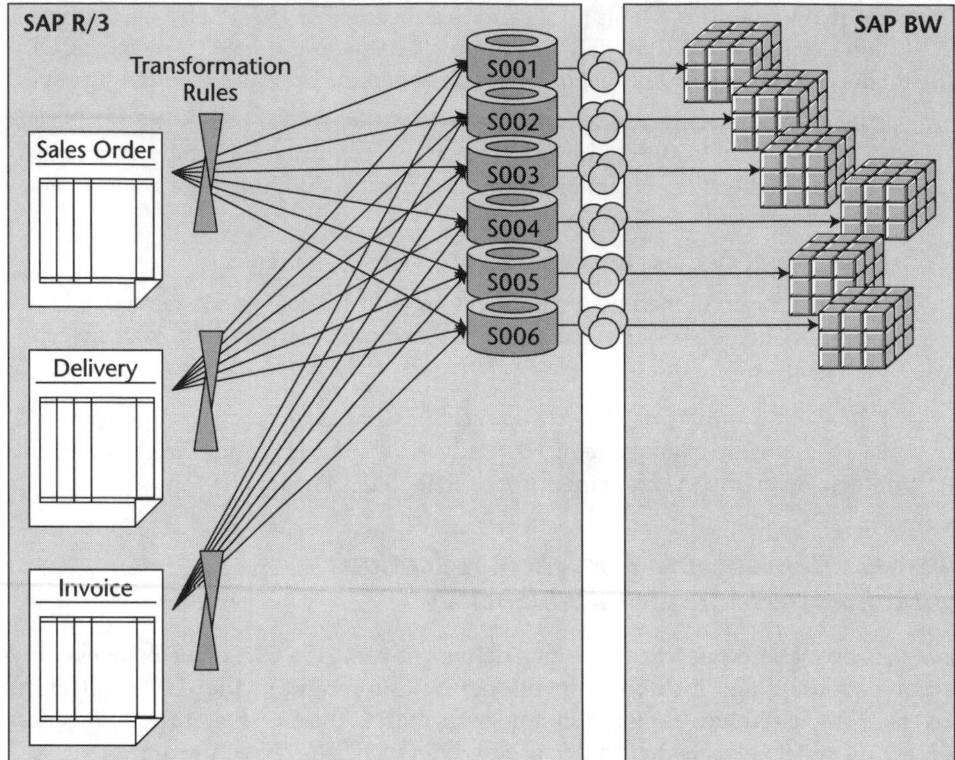

Figure 5.3 Data mart approach.

As a result, Business Content is InfoMart-driven; it currently contains many information models that are not built on a data warehouse layer. When SAP BW was first introduced, there were no ODS objects. The Business Content was modeled using a data mart approach. The Business Content information models leveraged the fact that its primary source of data was SAP R/3, which already contained integrated meta data. The need for an integration and transformation layer and a data warehouse layer as part of a CIF approach were not as great at this time. Consequently, the Business Content information models based on the data mart approach are still integrated even without the use of an Inmon-defined data warehouse.

The data mart approach consists of mapping SAP R/3 InfoSources directly to InfoCubes, skipping over what Inmon would call the real data warehouse. One added complication was that early Business Content extractors read from SAP dynamic summary tables rather than from OLTP tables. More recently, delta line-item extractors have replaced the summary-level extractors. Delta extraction only reads records that have changed in the source system. Line-item extraction reads OLTP-level information. Because OLTP extraction typically involves significant data volumes, delta extraction is a necessity for these extractors.

Among the disadvantages of the data mart approach is that as the environment grows, there is increasing extraction redundancy and decreasing reconcilability in support of the information delivery layer. Among the disadvantages of summary-level extractors was data redundancy and the lack of granular information (for specific analysis or for integrating information across application areas). Figure 5.3 illustrates the data mart approach using summary-level extractors.

Sales and Distribution Business Content extracted information from the Sales Information System, represented by the redundant reporting tables S001 through S006 in Figure 5.3. These tables represented different aggregations of orders, deliveries, and invoices. The Sales and Distribution Business Content has since replaced the summary-level extractors with OLTP extractors but continues to employ a data mart approach. Data redundancy is reduced and transformation rules have moved to SAP BW, but the disadvantages of the data mart approach persists.

In contrast, Business Content for mySAP E-Procurement takes an approach more in line with the CIF architecture. Figure 5.4 illustrates how this information model uses delta, line-item extractors to pull data into an ODS object before propagating the information to InfoMarts. The ODS object can serve as the data warehouse by providing integration (say, for e-procurement and standard procurement processes) and history of data. This information model is more aligned with the design of a CIF. Advantages of this approach are the use of consistent data basis on which InfoMarts can be built and improved performance through less data redundancy. The advantage of an integrated data warehouse grows as analytic scenarios incorporate increasing amounts of data from non-SAP R/3 systems with divergent meta data.

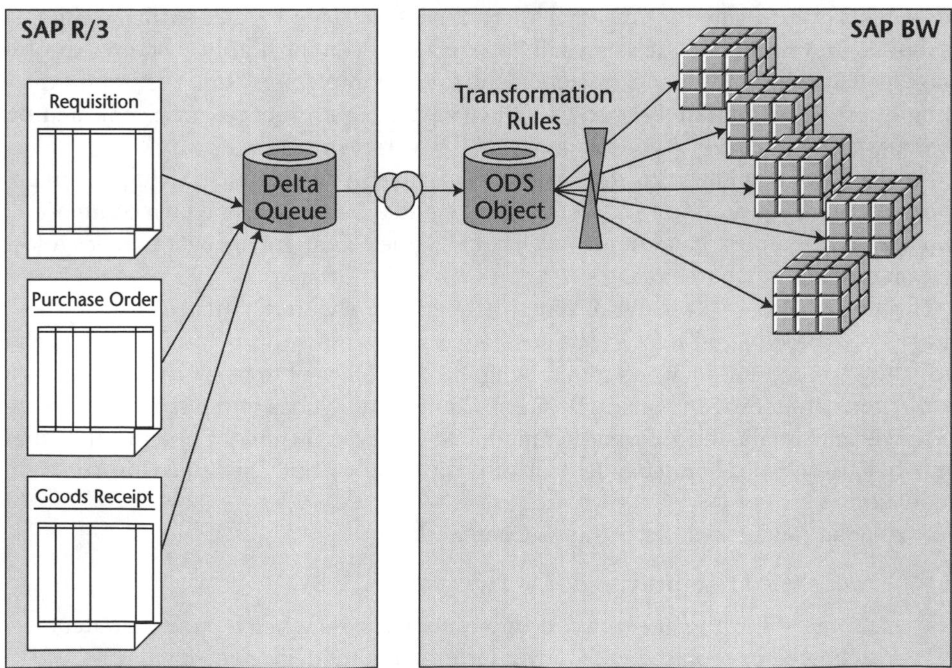

Figure 5.4 CIF approach.

If Business Content information models do not take a CIF approach, a CIF can be nonetheless constructed by reusing components of the model and assembling them into a custom development. The proliferation of delta, line-item extractors supports the construction of an ODS and data warehouse layer of the CIF where Business Content is missing. CIF construction consists of blueprinting the information and information flow models, and then activating and assembling all the relevant Business Content meta data objects.

Using Business Content

Business Content is a vital part of every SAP BW implementation. However, the degree to which you should use Business Content varies. To understand what to expect from Business Content, we'll discuss its value proposition. We will also evaluate its usability, postulate its challenges, and dispel some myths along the way.

Then we'll look at the Business Content information models, demonstrating how Business Content can be used as a repository for information modeling ideas and design approaches. Information modeling questions addressed by Business Content will be covered by different scenarios in three subject areas: procurement, financial accounting, and human resources.

Business Content Value Proposition

More usable Business Content translates into greater savings in design and implementation costs by reducing the time to delivery. Business Content is also easily extendable so that its information models can still be leveraged even for highly customized solutions. The Business Content extractors alone save an implementation costly programming efforts. SAP initiatives such as Quick Start or Best Practices are predicated on Business Content usage in order to make SAP BW implementations turnkey.

Business Content keeps the data warehouse in the SAP vernacular. Using the predelivered contents of the Meta Data Repository standardizes everyone on a common set of business semantics. In addition, implicit in Business Content are best-practice information models and extractors.

The end result of utilizing Business Content is ensured data consistency and integrity. SAP-delivered InfoObjects are shared across many of its InfoCubes, thereby reducing data redundancy and minimizing the possibility of mismatched values. As a result, you can iteratively deploy Business Content InfoCubes without too much concern over meta data and information modeling impacts. Business Content InfoCubes and their designs are independent of other InfoCubes but are linked by common InfoObjects.

Further advantages of BW Business Content are:

- Fewer skilled resources needed to implement SAP BW
- Automatic improvements to the information model when Business Content is reactivated or replaced with newer information modeling versions

- Easier environment for SAP to support
- Predocumented information models
- Tight integration with SAP applications (such as mySAP Enterprise Portal and SAP R/3)
- Ensured data quality, since the extractors revalidate the data before transmitting to SAP BW

Business Content has another impact on the nature of the BW project cycle: It enables BW to be implemented in reverse. Instead of implementing the BW data warehouse using the traditional software development life cycle (SDLC), the BW can be implemented via the iterative CLDS ("SDLC" in reverse) approach. In the CLDS approach, the data warehouse is implemented first and then backward-mapped to requirements.

There are a number of advantages to the CLDS approach:

- A "quick win" data warehouse can be immediately deployed (i.e., immediate progress can be demonstrated to the user community and project stakeholders, thereby increasing trust and confidence in the system and its implementation).
- If requirements are not met by Business Content, the process of gap analysis is accelerated, as users have an actual "live" system for evaluation. The real requirements can be deconstructed with concrete Business Content examples.
- Change management is accelerated, as users have a system they can touch and feel rather than having to conceptualize what may appear to them as a strawman system. Users get immediate exposure to the BW information analysis environment, and can more quickly shift them away from traditional operational reporting to adopt more analytical reporting.

Not surprisingly, Business Content has grown multiplicatively with each new release and is a cornerstone to any SAP BW implementation.

Myths

The technology industry is rife with jargon and exposure to catachresis, and Business Content is no exception. Some of the myths that belittle the value of Business Content are:

Business Content is merely a collection of pre-canned reports. Business Content's most valuable offering is information models made of ODS objects, InfoCubes, queries, extractors, and so on.

Business Content is SAP-specific. Many of the information models are generic enough to be source-system agnostic. For instance, the CRM information models can be used for Siebel data. Business Content for Web site monitoring can come from TeaLeaf or any other Web log. Then there is Business Content exclusively for non-SAP sources such as Dun & Bradstreet and ACNielsen data. Furthermore, the partnership with Ascential promises explicit Business Content for popular business applications such as PeopleSoft, Oracle, Siebel, Manugistics, and i2.

Business Content is just predelivered meta data. Business Content consists of not only meta data but complete information models and associated extraction programs. Furthermore, Business Content information models are not just designs but can be quickly implemented via a simple activation process.

Business Content is simply an example or a demonstration. Business Content should not be confused with demo content. Demo content is a very small subset of Business Content. In contrast to most standard Business Content, demo content is not to be used in production and usually comes with its own master data and transaction data for demonstration purposes only. Demo Business Content information models are exclusive of all other Business Content and are oversimplified versions of standard content. Standard Business Content is ready to run and is extensible. Business Content can be used in production systems for real business scenarios as is or enhanced. The extent to which Business Content is enhanced depends on requirements and source system customization. Business Content does not have to be used only as a template.

Usability

Business Content's usability can be organized into a pyramid (see Figure 5.5). Certain universal reporting needs, such as balance sheet and profit-and-loss reporting, are commonly found requirements that make up the foundation of Business Content and its usability pyramid. As reporting requirements become more specific, the usability of Business Content decreases. SAP does deliver industry-specific Business Content. If the needs become any more specific (such as a unique requirement for a specific corporation or even for an individual user), customization should be anticipated. In reality, your organization may be such that the Business Content usability pyramid is inverted. In such organizations, Business Content is only helpful as examples and templates.

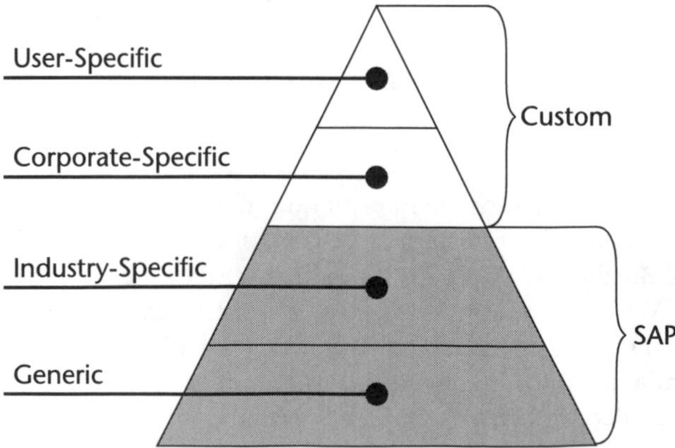

Figure 5.5 Business Content usability pyramid.

Business Content usability can also be alternatively viewed as a scale (see Figure 5.6). A relationship exists between where Business Content is situated in the SAP BW information flow and how usable it is. As data transforms into information (from source to provider), Business Content becomes less usable without customization. Standard-delivered workbook and queries are typically used as templates, since these BW meta data objects are often personalized and easy to develop. On the other hand, standard-delivered extractors are almost always adopted, because they can serve a gamut of information needs and are very difficult to custom-develop.

The popular adoption of Business Content extraction should not come as a surprise. Thousands of tables are relationally modeled in SAP R/3. The entity relationship diagrams are complex and hard to understand. Who else knows SAP like SAP? The SAP extractors are application-specific and can handle transforming the data in lots of tables into meaningful business information to SAP BW InfoSources.

Business Content extractors employ sophisticated delta change capture techniques as well. In many cases, SAP altered core SAP R/3 posting modules to effect a delta change management technique for extraction. Custom delta change capture is difficult to duplicate independently or with a third-party tool without modification. Often, change logs are read for custom delta extraction, which can be expensive from a performance perspective. As a result, you should unequivocally use Business Content extractors whenever available to spare an implementation the cost of development, the chance of poor performance, and the risk of poor data integrity. We cover extraction and delta change capture in more detail in Chapter 6.

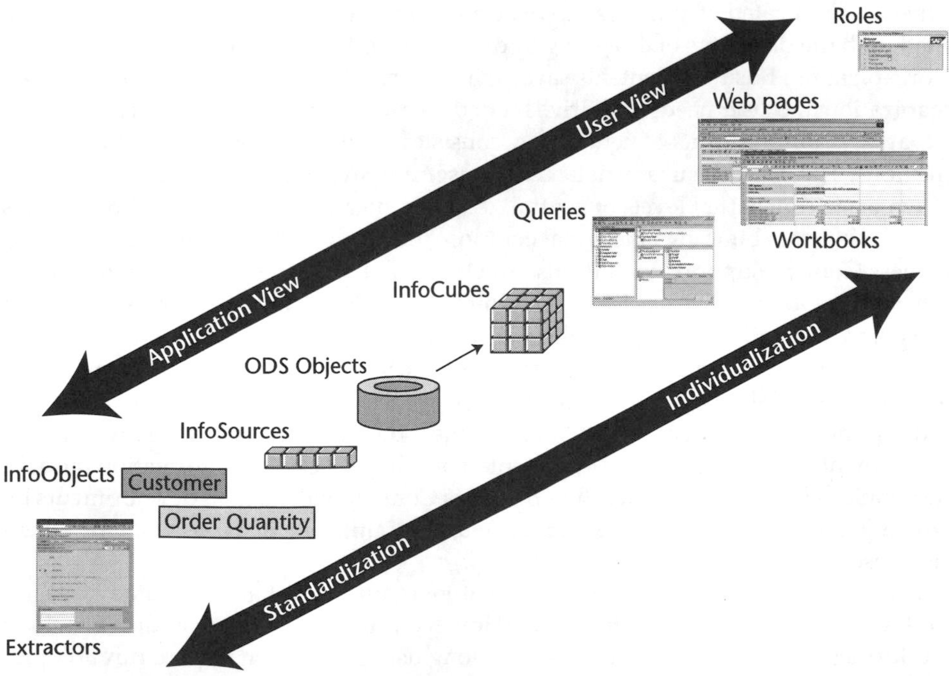

Figure 5.6 Business Content usability scale.
Based on copyrighted material from SAP AG

Business Content is biased by application area. Some applications have greater Business Content support than others. These tend to be the more popular SAP R/3 processes such as sales, distribution, or financials, or the more compelling scenarios such as analytics in mySAP CRM or mySAP SCM. The current trend is heavily tilted toward analytic applications, as this is where the current demand is.

Challenges

Business Content information models have been growing in sophistication with the increased capabilities of SAP BW. For example, the introduction of BW object types such as ODS objects and virtual InfoProviders has opened the gamut of information modeling options in SAP BW. The development trends have influenced Business Content design from both ends of the information flow spectrum. At the front end are the innovations in presentation and information deployment options; at the back end is the steady increase of more detailed and frequent data extraction.

Keep in mind not all Business Content is up-to-date. As SAP BW and SAP R/3 applications evolve, Business Content naturally becomes obsolete. Migration to improved information models is then required.

The two biggest challenges to managing Business Content result from SAP BW's fast-paced growth, namely maintaining conformity and controlling obsolescence.

Conformity

Business Content works best when meta data can be centralized and shared. Business Content is predicated on centralized, consistent meta data. Typically, a high cost is associated with the discipline of designing information models that get consistently used in an organization. Business Contents saves that expense. However, in reality, specialized organization and user needs will drive meta data away from Business Content (and, in fact, away from all forms of centralized consistency) into inconsistent and disparate directions. This happens in any data warehouse, and SAP BW is no exception.

Two basic conceptual levels of centralized meta data exist: the information models and the meta data building blocks that compose the preassembled information models. Business Content supports both forms. The building blocks are BW meta data objects, such as InfoObjects, ODS objects, and InfoCubes. Centralized information models incorporate the building blocks to ultimately deploy information delivery components such as queries, workbooks, and Web applications. Sharable meta data building blocks are more essential than conforming to a particular information model. However, undisciplined management of both levels of meta data will result in a data warehouse environment full of redundant or fragmented building blocks and information models. You should take care when extending Business Content with custom developments by enforcing consistent meta data governance and by utilizing Business Content whenever present.

Conceptually, sharable meta data and autonomous meta data are mutually exclusive forces that push at diametric odds. However, from this you shouldn't conclude that Business Content is more successful among user groups that require running precanned queries than among user groups that create ad hoc queries. This might be true for Business Content predelivered information models. However, it is not true for Business Content building blocks. Centralized, sharable meta data building blocks are necessary for any ad hoc analysis to ensure that information across applications and systems are easily combined.

Bill Inmon breaks the user community into groups, namely information tourists, farmers, explorers, and miners. The meta data needed for each user group is different. Predefined information models meet the information tourist's (who sporadically peruse what is available) and farmer's needs (who have a set repertoire of analysis they conduct). In contrast, predefined information models are a futile effort for information explorers (who may not know what they are looking for until they find it) and information miners (who depend on the explorers to determine what information to mine). Consequently, Business Content information models have a greater likelihood of success with tourists and farmers than with explorer and miner roles. However, all user groups benefit from the use of consistent, centralized meta data building blocks. Business Content at the very least provides this vital service.

There may always be a need for autonomous meta data outside of Business Content (or any centralized meta data for that matter)—for example, creating on-the-fly meta data while building ad hoc queries from unique user-specific data sources. More specifically, third-party OLAP tools are available that support scenarios where users want to merge data from files on their desktop. In essence, these tools bypass the centralized Meta Data Repository—a benefit that is debatable. Such scenarios do not leverage consistent and sharable centralized meta data that Business Content delivers.

Where the force for autonomy has had a divergent effect on Business Content is the specialized meta data needs of different applications for common business entities. For example, the Business Content for customer and material has spawned numerous InfoObjects that more or less represent the same thing. Not only is there separate customer and material InfoObjects for the different views of the same object (sales view, financial view), but each analytic application has its own version of the InfoObjects (the primary culprits being mySAP CRM and mySAP SCM). mySAP CRM alone has over two dozen InfoObjects that represent product, which are, in turn, different from mySAP CRM materials.

In these cases, delivering centralized meta data and information models is a double-edged sword. On the one hand, development could resign itself to only supporting generic information models. This would foster an easier-to-understand repository of centralized and shared meta data but would not address specialized needs.

On the other hand, Business Content creation could be opened up to partners and customers. creating a rich repository of information models at the expense of meta data chaos. The price of such chaos would be an overabundance of unneeded meta data, inconsistent information models, and decreased flexibility in data integration.

In reality, both options are being explored further. A project has already commenced to implement a more generic data model for central entities like product and customer. Also, the possibility of opening Business Content creation to third parties has always been a consideration.

Additionally, there are other techniques for handling meta data proliferation. For example, you can hide or unhide Business Content meta data depending on the components being used in SAP BW, and you can activate Business Content components to use its associated meta data. Currently this is not part of the general content activation mechanism and is only available for specific subject areas. To curtail the amount of meta data available in the system, the meta data for each component is hidden from the BW system until the component has been activated. Say, for example, the vendor master comes with over two dozen attributes as part of Business Content. When the Dun & Bradstreet Business Content component is activated, the number of attributes more than doubles; an undesirable effect for any implementation that is not using this Business Content.

Another way of handling the proliferation of attributes in InfoObjects is to allow more than one instance of the same InfoObject. For example, material could actually consist of several InfoObjects with different attributes (for CRM or for APO or for R/3) that all share the same surrogate id.

There is yet another dimension to our discussion about conformity. Some processes and related applications are less conformed to begin with. For example, logistics applications tend to be more divergent than accounting applications. Hence, a generalized information model for financials is more likely to be successful than a logistics information model. The more potentially divergent the process models, the harder it is for SAP to deliver generic content to meet specific information needs.

Similarly, processes configured in SAP R/2 and SAP R/3 may share enough resemblance for Business Content to serve both systems.

NOTE The SCOR model (explained further in Chapter 8) has taken on the challenge of standardizing the performance metrics for evaluating supply chains. Even in this area there is a convergence toward standardization.

Finally, there are practical limits to Business Content:

- Business Content cannot anticipate any customization or enhancement work in SAP R/3. Every SAP R/3 implementation we have been involved in has required significant customization and enhancement work.
- Business Content does not include custom dynamic summary structures in SAP R/3 (such as CO-PA, FI-SL, and custom Logistics Information System, or LIS). Although there are tools to generate extractors for these data sources, there is no delivered Business Content information models (it is possible, however, to generate all the requisite InfoObjects).
- Business Content is devoid of any logic based on organization-specific characteristic values or hierarchies. There are no predelivered organizational hierarchies or master data in SAP BW. Hence, no predelivered query can be hard-coded to any organizational hierarchies or master data values (although Business Content can work around this via variables in BEx queries). Similarly, there are no update rules that can take organizational or special characteristic values into consideration (although examples do exist where Business Content includes hierarchies for generic analysis such as age classifications in HR). For instance, financial profitability metrics are often predicated on the company's chart of accounts. SAP examples of calculated financial performance indicators must be based on a SAP-delivered chart of accounts and must be adapted to your own chart of accounts.

Fortunately, Business Content is easily extensible to accommodate such scenarios. After customizing Business Content, you must take special consideration before performing a functional upgrade of the Business Content. To take advantage of new Business Content, you need to reactivate the meta data with the new version of Business Content. When doing so, you have the option of merging the new version of Business Content with the older or customized version of Business Content or adopting the new Business Content entirely (effectively discarding the older version and any associated customizations). Business Content versioning is an ongoing maintenance consideration with each new SAP BW release.

Versioning

Not all Business Content stands the test of time. There are two drivers for versioning: new analytical tools and new information modeling options. The BEx Analyzer is constantly evolving. But it is no longer the only analytical tool. Now a host of Web-based presentation options are available in addition to the Excel add-in. Furthermore, the advent of data mining tools to SAP BW supports SAP CRM Business Content that utilizes decision trees, association analysis, and clustering. SEM introduces new planning tools that have specific information modeling impacts.

Along similar lines, since Business Content was introduced to SAP BW, numerous improvements have been made in the information modeling options available, including ODS objects, line-item dimensions, time-dependent aggregates, MultiProviders, and remote InfoCubes. These improvements have enabled more sophisticated and powerful Business Content scenarios. The downside is that some Business Content becomes obsolete or no longer best business practice. In such scenarios, you must upgrade Business Content to take advantage of the new features. Fortunately, SAP has proactively provided new information models in many cases. To do a functional upgrade, you must reactivate the Business Content with the new Business Content version or adopt a new information model.

For example, the first Business Content InfoCube delivered for costs and allocations in Cost Center Accounting of Controlling (CO-CCA) has been replaced with a new InfoCube for the same subject area. Both InfoCubes have the same text description and coexist, but the newer one should be used. The newer Business Content information model is mapped to the delta line-item extractor for actual costs, while the older Business Content information model is mapped to a summary-level extractor for actual data. In this case, migration is simply cutting over to the new information model.

Additionally, even delta line-item extractors can become outmoded. For example, there are two accounts receivables and accounts payable delta line-item extractors. One is an older version than the other. These extractors coexist, but only one extractor should be employed. The older version handled the deltas for accounts payable and accounts receivable in a decoupled and unsynchronized manner. Each could be loaded on separate schedules. The newer extractors are tightly coupled with a third delta line-item DataSource for general ledger accounts that guarantees that all three mySAP Financials extractors are in sync with each other.

LIS extractors have a similar versioning story: Newer delta extractors replaced the older summary-level LIS extractors. The migration path to new Business Content does not have to be immediate. At first glance, you might think that upgrading a SAP BW system entails the same level of effort for upgrading an SAP R/3 system. This is true to a certain extent, but note that there is a difference between a technical upgrade and a functional upgrade. When upgrading an R/3 system, you are typically doing both a technical upgrade and a functional upgrade at the same time. In a technical upgrade the system is upgraded to the next release. A functional upgrade, on the other hand, means that your design and implementation of the system must be changed to adopt the new functionality in the system.

When upgrading SAP BW systems, you do not have to change all existing information models, including Business Content. You can keep the existing Business Content information models without upgrading to the new Business Content. A technical upgrade can be performed with very little impact to the design and implementation of the system. To take advantage of any new functionality in the system, you must perform a functional upgrade that involves much more effort in evaluating the potential impact. However, you can perform this more or less separately by each business area. The considerations for functional upgrades are covered in more depth in Chapter 9.

How Business Content Models Information

You can use Business Content as a repository of industry-standard requirements and modeling ideas. Business Content is rich with information models that can be used as templates or examples for building custom information models. Before investing effort on the task of designing custom information models, you should investigate Business Content for SAP best business practices.

In addition, if you know how to research Business Content and understand why it is implemented the way it is, Business Content can be a powerful learning tool. The best sources of Business Content documentation is the SAP help portal and the SAP BW Meta Data Repository. To develop a deeper understanding of Business Content and its information models, you must thoroughly understand the SAP BW system, the source system, and the business scenario it supports.

The aim of this section is to highlight information modeling examples from the three subject areas of procurement, financials, and human resources. We chose these subject areas for their popularity and differences in the way Business Content was implemented. The code samples presume knowledge of ABAP, and non-technical readers can skip these. More details on how update rules are coded are covered in Chapter 6. Our objective in these chapters is for you to gain a feel for the different permutations of Business Content and to learn the information modeling options SAP chose in developing Business Content.

What follows is a discussion of Business Content information modeling examples organized by subject area and prefaced with a business scenario. First, the Business Content role and background is presented, followed by how Business Content supports the scenario. The design of Business Content information models are then related back to the concepts introduced in Chapter 4. By understanding how Business Content addresses basic information modeling questions, you will gain insight into any custom information modeling efforts.

The first role we present is a strategic buyer. The business scenario involves upgrading analytics for vendor evaluations from LIS to SAP BW, performing vendor consolidation using Dun & Bradstreet information and merging mySAP E-Procurement with traditional procurement processes. Information modeling questions addressed by Business Content in this scenario are:

- How does Business Content model business events?
- How does Business Content model its calculations?
- How does Business Content integrate master data?
- How does Business Content integrate transaction data?

The second role is that of consolidations accountant. After a reorganization, a restatement needs to be performed based on the organizational structure. In addition, the reporting scenario consists of reconciling consolidations with its feeder systems through comparison reporting at additional levels of detail. Information modeling questions posed in this scenario are:

- How does Business Content model different versions of truth in transaction data?
- How does Business Content model currencies?
- How does Business Content model non-cumulative key figures in financials?
- How does Business content model value types?

The last role is a human resources strategic analyst. The analytic scenario involves performing an age range evaluation of the employees leaving and entering the organization to identify trends. Business Content information modeling questions presented through this scenario are:

- How does Business Content model Infotypes?
- How does Business Content model evaluative ranges?

Strategic Buying

One of the SAP BW system's first example use of ODS objects was for a mySAP E-Procurement information model included in this example. The importance of ODS objects in Business Content has grown. The Business Content information models are adapting ODS objects, a step closer to a CIF-oriented architecture.

The business scenario is this: You are a strategic buyer who oversees the vendor selection process and must evaluate their performance. You negotiate and enter into agreement terms with suppliers and need to know how your vendors have been performing against their service-level agreements. You want to:

- Monitor the bidding process, making sure your purchasers actively solicit competing quotes from your vendors by measuring the number of quotes taken.
- Assess the quality of your vendor quotes by measuring the number of quotes that convert to purchase orders.
- Measure your vendor's performance for delivering the right quantities at the right time. On-time delivery performance is measured by delivery date

variances and delivery reliability is measured by delivery quantity variances. The variances are categorized into evaluative ranges for data selection in a query in order to stratify your vendors into varying performance and reliability levels.

- Consolidate your supplier base to reduce your expenses by identifying duplicate suppliers. You also want to analyze vendor spending from the top to bottom of a corporate structure. To do so, you've decided to complement your SAP BW investment with Dun & Bradstreet Business Content, which specifically supports such activities. This scenario assumes that purchasing Business Content has already been activated and loaded, before you decide to augment your system with Dun & Bradstreet Business Content.

Finally, you recently upgraded your procurement system to accept Internet orders with the SAP Markets Enterprise Buyer (Professional Edition) or SAPM EBP, but at the same time continue to run your traditional SAP R/3 procurement activities in parallel. Both processes need to be integrated into your SAP BW information model. You decide to take a decoupled approach of loading data into SAP BW from both the SAPM EBP and SAP R/3 for all of your procurement processes.

How Does Business Content Model Business Events?

To evaluate the quotation process, you need to measure the business events for quotations and orders, using quotation counts to validate that buyers are actively soliciting enough bids before placing orders. You also must compare purchase order counts to quotation counts by vendor to evaluate the quality of their quotes.

There are numerous criteria you can use to separate different business events in SAP R/3. Sometimes you separate business events by different tables, fields, or field values. For example, quotation and purchase order business events reside in different OLTP tables. Quotations and orders are also separate key figure fields in LIS dynamic summary tables. In LIS communication structures (which pass data between the OLTP tables and the dynamic summary tables) quotation and purchase orders are separated by LIS event values (which are how business events are represented in LIS).

The information modeling options can be divided along similar lines. Business events can be modeled as separate InfoCubes or as separate key figures or as separate characteristic values. The last two options are referred to as *specific key figure modeling* and *generic key figure modeling* approaches (concepts introduced in Chapter 4).

Business Content for procurement models InfoCubes using specific key figures, but the InfoSource uses a generic key figure model. Update rules convert the generic key figures into specific key figures. The characteristic used for differentiating business events in logistics applications is called a *process key*. An SAP BW concept, process keys are used to consistently model business events across different logistics applications. Process keys themselves may be derived differently per application.

For example, process keys in procurement are derived from a combination of LIS events and purchase order categories (which identify if the supplying plant is within the same company or from another SAP R/3 company or from outside SAP R/3). In inventory management, process keys are derived from material movement types (which represent business event types for inflows and outflows of materials such as a stock transfer, physical inventory, inventory correction, revaluations, and returns). Even within an application, the process key may be derived differently depending on the business event. For example, in sales and distribution the process key is defined differently for sales orders, deliveries, and invoices. Nevertheless, the process key consistently represents a business event.

The process key derivations themselves are performed via a technology called *business transaction events*. Business transaction events are business add-ins that allow external applications to capture SAP R/3 business event data. A more technical description is provided in Chapter 6.

To translate process keys into key figures, you use update rules to filter records passed to a specific key figure. In the Business Content example that follows, update rules are used to map the process key for quotations to the key figure count for number of quotation items. More specifically, the process key 009 (representing quotations) is checked in the update rules before passing the generic key figure for counts to the specific key figure for quotation counts. Additional checks performed by the Business Content update rule code example are if the application area is materials management and if the generic key figure for counts is not equal to zero:

```
     IF COMM_STRUCTURE-PROCESSKEY = '009'
      AND COMM_STRUCTURE-BWAPPLNM EQ 'MM'
      AND COMM_STRUCTURE-no_pos <> 0.
  * result value of the routine
        RESULT = COMM_STRUCTURE-no_pos.
```

Update rules are explained in more detail in Chapter 6.

Process keys are also used for filtering records in Business Content update rules. For example, the ODS objects for e-procurement use process keys to identify purchase orders, confirmations. and invoices. In this case, the logic around process keys is performed in the start routine of the update rules. The data package is scanned for all the relevant records with the correct process keys, while the rest of the records are deleted from the load. In the Business Content example sample code provided, the update rules for the purchase orders ODS object filters on the process keys for external transaction purchase orders, internal company purchase orders, and cross-company purchase orders (process keys 001, 011, and 021, respectively.

```
  LOOP AT DATA_PACKAGE.
     IF NOT ( DATA_PACKAGE-PO_STATUS <> 'K'
     AND ( DATA_PACKAGE-PROCESSKEY = '001' OR
           DATA_PACKAGE-PROCESSKEY = '011' OR
           DATA_PACKAGE-PROCESSKEY = '021' )
     AND DATA_PACKAGE-BWAPPLNM EQ 'MM' ) .
       DELETE DATA_PACKAGE.
     ENDIF.
 ENDLOOP.
```

How Does Business Content Model Calculations?

Business Content delivers most calculations as key performance indicators in queries. However, Business Content can also deliver calculations via the extractors (such as delivery reliability variances, percentages, points score, smoothing factors, and counts). Business Content extractors not only read data from the underlying SAP technical tables and manage their relationships but also perform business logic. Business Content extractors are designed to extract business-meaningful information for staging in the SAP BW. By transforming SAP source system data into meaningful business information, Business Content insulates the SAP BW designer from the technical complexities of the underlying tables. Not uncommonly, key figure calculations are performed in the extractor—particularly when the configuration settings that drive the business logic reside in the source system.

For instance, the evaluative ranges for on-time delivery performance and delivery reliability are configured in the SAP R/3 system. No more than five evaluative ranges can be configured for the delivery variances and can be set differently per purchasing organization. The variances themselves are either percentages (for the quantity variance) or days (for the date variance) and are used as the thresholds for the evaluation ranges. For example, on-time delivery variance is measured as the number of days a delivery arrives either prior to or after the delivery date on the purchase order. Similarly, the delivery quantity variance is the percentage difference between the purchase order quantity and the quantity actually delivered. An example of how the variance conditions might be configured is provided in the Table 5.1.

These intervals create five evaluative ranges, because the last interval is split into two ranges (in this case, the first range is between 5 and 10 and the last range is greater than 10). The evaluative ranges are passed through to the extractor as well as the values from the configuration table (such as the interval number, the quantity variance as a percentage, and the date variance as days, as in Table 5.1).

The Business Content extractor counts all purchase orders and scheduling agreement items that fall within each interval for performance and reliability. Business content key performance indicators then calculate another percentage: the share each evaluative range has of all the purchase orders and scheduling agreement items.

Before SAP BW, LIS referenced the configuration settings for delivery variances in the LIS update rule. The delivery variances were split into evaluative ranges based on conditions in SAP R/3 tables. This conditional logic neither migrated to SAP BW update rules nor BEx queries, but stayed in SAP R/3 system by moving the calculation to the Business Content extractors.

Table 5.1 Delivery On-Time Performance and Reliability Configuration Example

INTERVAL	QUANTITY VARIANCE	DATE VARIANCE
1	-10%	-10 days
2	-5%	-5 days
3	+5%	+5 days
4	+10%	+10 days

However, the SAP BW update rules do perform logic to transform the variances from generic key figures to specific key figures. Put differently, the evaluative ranges are modeled as separate records in the InfoSource but as separate key figures in the InfoCube. More specifically, the extracted data from SAP R/3 can have up to five separate records for each evaluation range. Each record maps to one of the five specific key figures depending on the evaluation range (represented by either a time interval or quantity interval key figure). Following is the BW update rule for the fifth evaluation range for on-time delivery performance:

```
IF ( COMM_STRUCTURE-PROCESSKEY = '002' OR      "WE
   COMM_STRUCTURE-PROCESSKEY = '012' OR
   COMM_STRUCTURE-PROCESSKEY = '022' )
 AND COMM_STRUCTURE-BWAPPLNM EQ 'MM'
 AND COMM_STRUCTURE-NO_TIME <> 0
 AND COMM_STRUCTURE-TIME_INT EQ '5'.
* result value of the routine
 RESULT = COMM_STRUCTURE-NO_TIME.
```

Records are mapped to the fifth delivery date variance only if the record is a good receipt (process keys 002, 012, and 022 for different purchase order categories), the application is material management, the variance is not zero, and the record represents the fifth on-time delivery interval (key figure 0TIME_INT). If the record represents another interval, the record is skipped (and is mapped to the correct corresponding variance key figure in another update rule).

How Does Business Content Integrate Master Data?

Integrating data is one of the largest challenges of a data warehouse. In many environments, developing an integration and transformation layer of a CIF can take as much as three-fourths the cost of implementing a data warehouse. Even when a perfectly integrated SAP BW system has been implemented, integrating new companies is not facilitated unless they share the same applications for the same processes as in an ERP solution.

As Business Content incorporates more third-party content into its domain, integration, and transformation complexities will increasingly have to be addressed. For master data, one approach is to outsource the function of integration to a third-party data provider such as Dun & Bradstreet.

From an information modeling perspective, the integration technique is to map the data to a unifying attribute or structure. If there are overlapping values from disparate source systems, you can easily keep and distinguish local values by extending Business Content with a source system identifier as a compound InfoObject (this involves merely flagging a check box indicator in the InfoObject definition). The advantage of storing both local and unified views of master data is that both consolidated and localized reporting needs can be met at the same time.

To consolidate a vendor master list, the master data can be integrated using the same approach. The process of integration identifies, duplicates, and cleanses master data of erroneous records. One advantage of outsourcing this function is that the task for formulating a universal numbering scheme is eliminated. In addition, third-party data providers can further enhance master data with external information such as industry and market categorizations for benchmarking.

Business Content supports vendor integration by adding the attribute D-U-N-S (Data Universal Numbering Scheme) number to the vendor InfoObject. The D-U-N-S number is a global attribute defined by third-party data provider Dun & Bradstreet.

The need for conformity and consistent values is increasingly important as data warehouse environments become more distributed (enabled by hub-and-spoke technologies) or pull from heterogeneous sources. Business benefits come in the form of greater visibility and comparability of analytical data and the potential to reduce expenses or increase sales through economies of scale opportunities. In the scenario presented, the D-U-N-S number is used to consolidate vendors in an effort to reduce procurement costs through means such as increasing economic order quantities.

In addition to the D-U-N-S number, Dun & Bradstreet Business Content introduces many more attributes, such as market statistics and information InfoObjects. Rather than model these InfoObjects as attributes of the D-U-N-S number, the attributes are part of the vendor InfoObject to facilitate reporting on them as navigational attributes. Dun & Bradstreet also provides information enhancement through hierarchies. The so-called family trees are represented in SAP BW as presentation hierarchies on the InfoObject for D-U-N-S number. The hierarchy shows all the associations in a corporate family (such as parents, subsidiaries, and branches) to allow navigation through a vendor's corporate structure.

As there are numerous InfoObjects introduced through Dun & Bradstreet Business Content, the additional meta data is handled in a specialized way through the use of Business Content components. To merge Dun & Bradstreet information into the vendor master, you must activate the Business Content component for the Dun & Bradstreet data provider. Otherwise, Dun & Bradstreet Business Content will remain hidden in the system (and hence not available for Business Content activation). You activate the component via a menu option in the Business Content tab of the Administrator Workbench. Figure 5.7 illustrates the maintenance view.

Once the Business Content component is activated, all Dun & Bradstreet meta data is available for installation. After Business Content has been properly maintained, the SAP BW is prepared to receive external market data from Dun & Bradstreet.

From an information flow modeling perspective, information is passed in and out of SAP BW through the use of flat files. For vendor consolidation, Dun & Bradstreet provides four files: two related to the vendor master data and two related to the D-U-N-S number master data. For eliminating duplicate records for the same company, the D-U-N-S number is essential. Dun & Bradstreet offers the service of matching all of your vendor records to their D-U-N-S numbers in order to eliminate duplicates and enhance the vendor record with vital statistics and information.

Maintenance View Business Content Components

Component	Descriptn	Activ
DP_DB	Data Provider: Dun & Bradstreet	☑
IS-OIL	Is Oil	☐

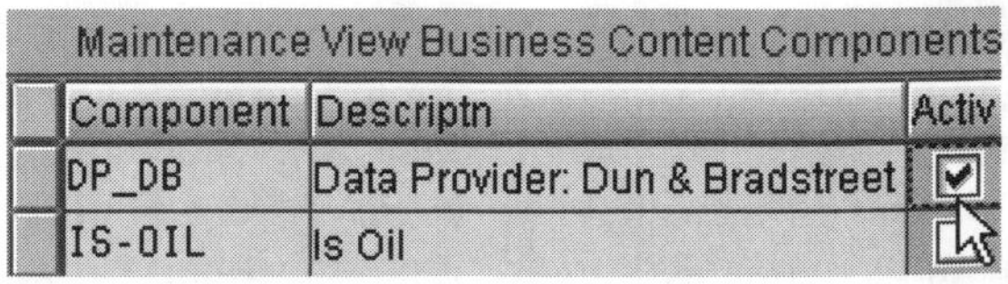

Figure 5.7 Activating a Business Content component.

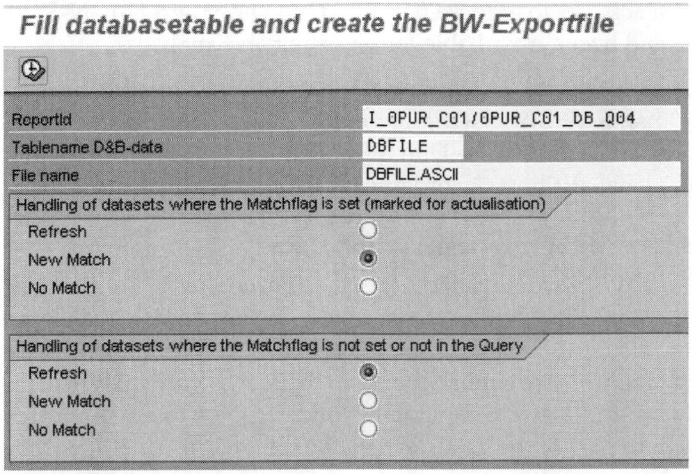

Fill databasetable and create the BW-Exportfile

ReportId	I_0PUR_C01/0PUR_C01_DB_Q04
Tablename D&B-data	DBFILE
File name	DBFILE.ASCII

Handling of datasets where the Matchflag is set (marked for actualisation)

- Refresh ○
- New Match ◉
- No Match ○

Handling of datasets where the Matchflag is not set or not in the Query

- Refresh ◉
- New Match ○
- No Match ○

Figure 5.8 Extractor for export to Dun & Bradstreet.

The files are in comma-separated values (CSV) format and come shipped on a CD consisting of a vendor analytics file, vendor contact details files, a D-U-N-S text file, and a D-U-N-S hierarchy (family trees) file, along with assorted files for all the codes.

Before Dun & Bradstreet can ship these files, extracts must be received of all the vendors needing to be matched to their database of D-U-N-S numbers. The extract file is created via a special extractor program (Figure 5.8).

The parameters for the extractors are the query name, table name, filename, and radio buttons controlling how a special indicator for matching should be handled. The ABAP program uses the BEx query specified as the first parameter to extract data from SAP BW. The standard-delivered Business Content query should be used in this case. The structure of this query has a specific format that must be followed. After extraction the data is loaded to both a generated table and a file as specified in the parameters of the special extract program. The table name specified is automatically generated and populated for validation and reporting from the Data Monitor. The file extracts to the default directory of the application server, which has to be sent to Dun & Bradstreet for matching and rationalization.

The match flags refer to a specific attribute on the vendor master for matching, which must be set via custom transfer rules in the update of the vendor master. How this flag is handled is then controlled by parameters in the extract program. In this scenario, custom transfer rules were written to flag all vendors without a D-U-N-S number so that new matches could be performed by Dun & Bradstreet, while all others left blank only have their information refreshed.

Figure 5.9 summarizes the information flow and the following steps:

1. You extract vendor data to a file via a special extract ABAP program and ship the results to Dun & Bradstreet.
2. Dun & Bradstreet performs matching and ships back a set of files that includes the D-U-N-S number matching to vendor, enhanced Dun & Bradstreet attribute information, and family trees.

3. Business ContentInfoPackages load these files into the Vendor and D-U-N-S number master data and become available for reporting and analysis.

The Dun & Bradstreet Business Content scenario demonstrates how data can be integrated with external data in an SAP BW system for vendor data that may be sourced from heterogeneous sources. In addition, the Dun & Bradstreet example shows how data can be enhanced with global attributes in order to enrich data for analysis.

How Does Business Content Integrate Transaction Data?

Merging transaction data across disparate subject areas and processes is an information modeling exercise that introduces another dimension to the integration challenge. In many cases, separate models must be built for separate transaction processes. However, in some scenarios the processes are similar enough to be merged for analysis. The underlying processes must be studied for comparability and common touch points for analysis. Care must be taken to ensure the data can truly be integrated.

Implementing a comprehensive ERP system is a better way to consolidate process flows, but there are other cases where disparate process are unavoidable, such as for standard procurement and e-procurement. In fact, SAP handles these two processes in separate systems: one in SAP R/3 and the other in SAP Markets Enterprise Buyer (Professional Edition), or SAPM EBP. How Business Content extracts and transforms data from the SAPM EBP is different than SAP R/3.

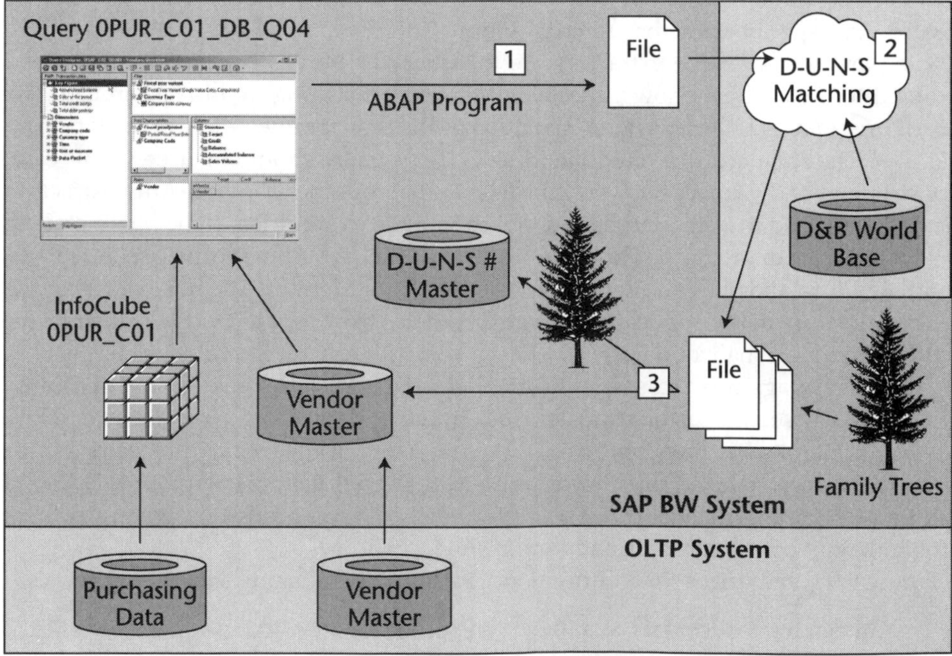

Figure 5.9 Dun & Bradstreet information flow.

The information models for SAPM EBP are organized by business event, while the models for SAP R/3 are organized by levels of granularity. More explicitly, the Business Content for e-procurement separate inbound ODS objects for orders, confirmations, and invoices, while the standard procurement information models separate inbound ODS objects for header, line-item, and schedule line details. Business Content integrates the standard procurement model InfoSources into the e-procurement ODS Objects and InfoCubes for reporting and analysis. As a result, the e-procurement DataSources map cleanly to the e-procurement ODS objects, since they are already modeled by business event. However, the SAP R/3 DataSources require transformations in order to map to the same e-procurement ODS objects. These transformations and mappings are provided by Business Content.

By modeling ODS objects by business event, e-procurement Business Content takes a de-normalized information modeling approach (versus the normalized ODS objects for standard procurement). For example, header, line-item, and schedule line details for purchase orders are denormalized into one ODS object for purchase orders. (The advantages and disadvantages for normalized versus denormalized ODS objects were detailed in Chapter 4.) The Business Content for this scenario provides comparable models for both design options by juxtaposing the normalized versus denormalized ODS objects in a common subject area.

The information from the e-procurement ODS objects are then further denormalized into an e-procurement InfoCube—an information modeling design that is more in line with the CIF approach than the data mart approach (as discussed earlier in the chapter). In other words, you summarize detailed data in the data warehouse into InfoMarts rather than directly loading InfoMarts.

Before we can discuss the information flow model for integrated procurement, we need to compare and contrast the process flows for e-procurement and standard procurement. The first consideration is that there are several landscape approaches to the way SAPM EBP can be set up vis-à-vis SAP R/3. For the scenario presented, we'll demonstrate the decoupled approach. Figure 5.10 illustrates the process flows for the decoupled approach to implementing SAPM EBP alongside SAP R/3.

In this landscape approach, all the locally processed product categories are passed through SAPM EBP and on to SAP BW. All back-end processed product categories are passed through SAP R/3 and onto SAP BW, and all follow-on documents to the purchase order post to the same system as the originating purchase order. The common touch point for analysis is the creation of the purchase order. SAPM EBP business events for confirmations and invoice approvals map to SAP R/3 business events goods receipts and invoice receipts, respectively.

Figure 5.11 illustrates how the information flows are modeled. The information flow model demonstrates how information is merged from separate SAP SAPM EBP and SAP R/3 procurement processes into ODS objects and onto the strategic reporting InfoCube for e-procurement. Note that not all integration issues are solved by Business Content. For example, Business Content does not provide mappings to the e-procurement accounting InfoCube for SAP R/3 data or mappings to the standard procurement InfoCube for SAPM EBP data.

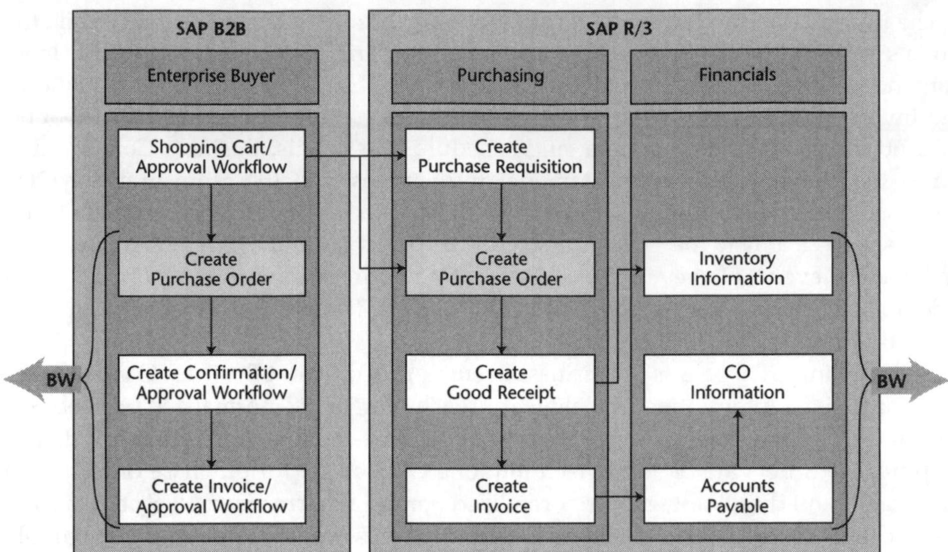

Figure 5.10 SAPM EBP and SAP R/3 process flows.

Additional complexities are produced by the integration effort. Information used in one application may have no equivalent in the other application. For example, the requester or accounting details in SAPM EBP is missing in SAP R/3, while certain delivery details available in SAP R/3 simply do not apply to confirmations in SAPM EBP. In addition, care must be taken not to duplicate data by redundantly posting the same events through both systems. In this case, support is provided through a special flag that can be used in update rules to prevent duplicate postings from both SAPM EBP and SAP R/3. The flag indicates whether or not a transaction in SAPM EBP has passed on to R/3.

For the scenario presented, the missing integration is not relevant, since the accounting InfoCube is outside its scope and the purchasing InfoCube is not being used for analysis pertinent to business-to-business scenarios.

Consolidation Reporting

The Business Content information models in accounting are consistent with characteristics used in dimensions. However, there are differences in the Business Content in how the key figures are defined, particularly in how currencies and noncumulative key figures are modeled.

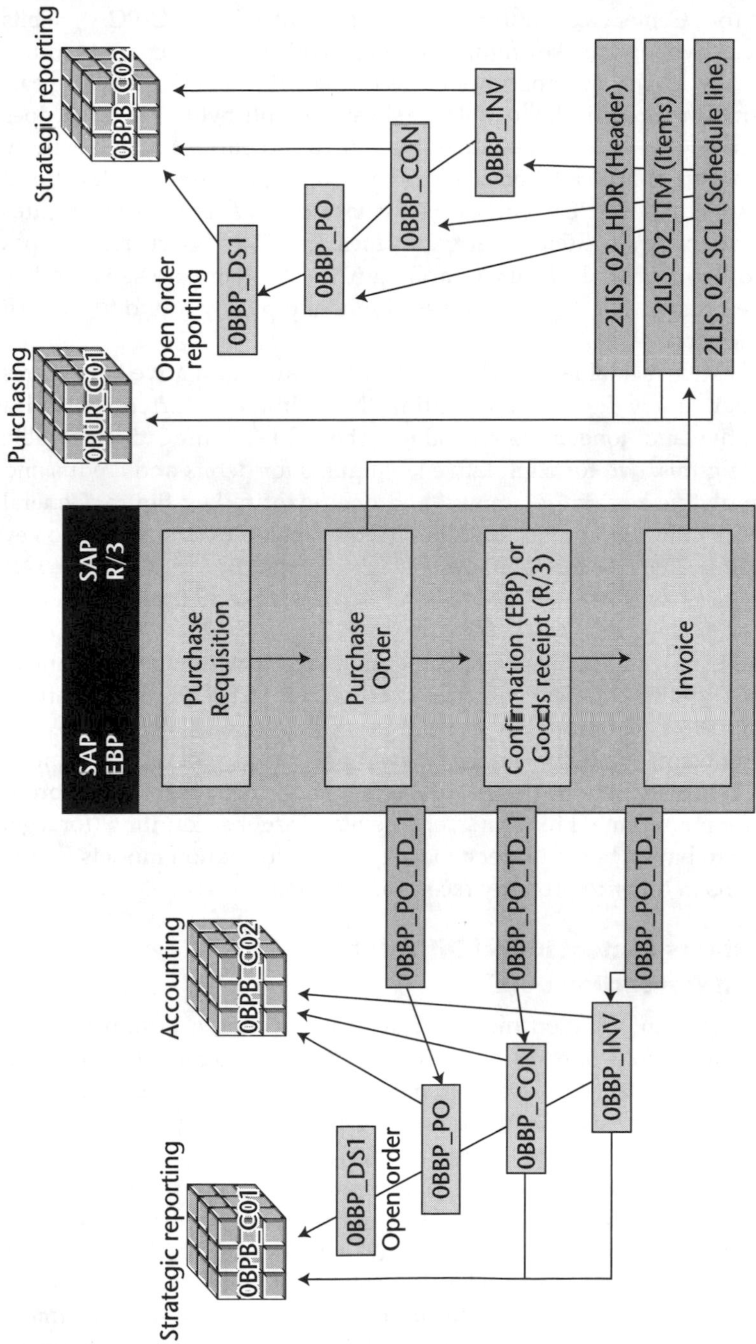

Figure 5.11 SAP EBP and SAP R/3 information flows.

For example, in Profit Center Accounting of Enterprise Controlling (EC-PCA), debits and credits are split as two separate key figure amounts, while in Cost Center Accounting of Controlling (CO-CCA) shows the amounts as one key figure. EC-PCA has year-to-date key figure amounts specifically for balance sheet amounts, while CO-CCA does not. The SEM BCS InfoCube stores year-to-date key figures and current period activity as separate key figures but specifically for each currency (one for transaction, local, and group). In both CO-CCA and EC-PCA, currencies are not stored as separate key figures but are modeled generically as different currency types. In SEM BCS, currency types are not used. In Profitability Analysis of Controlling (CO-PA), there are separate key figures per value field instead of the account-based model typically found in mySAP Financials information models.

The SEM BCS InfoCube fact table has eight key figures: four cumulative key figures and four noncumulative key figures representing three different currencies and a quantity for cumulative and noncumulative values. The EC-PCA InfoCube fact table consists of four key figures: two for cumulative key figures for debits and credits and one for the noncumulative key figure amount and one quantity key figure. General Ledger is like EC-PCA minus quantities. In CO-CCA, the fact table consists of two key figures: one for amounts and one for quantities.

When integrating or reconciling the information, you must take all these differences into account.

For our business scenario, say you are a consolidations accountant whose organization has a new parent holding company who has just divested and acquired operations as part of a reorganization. Not only do you want to restate your financials based on the new management hierarchy, but you need a new reporting currency. Furthermore, you want to reconcile consolidations data with the feeder applications such as profit center accounting (for management reporting) and general ledger accounting (for legal reporting). You want to have a better understanding of the information models for the respective applications in order to properly reconcile the data.

How Does the Business Content Model Different Versions of Truth in Transaction Data?

One of the more difficult information modeling tasks is building a design that can accommodate different versions of truth, as we discussed in Chapter 4, which focused on time-dependent master data as a solution. In most cases, time-dependent characteristics (represented as navigational attributes or as hierarchies) are enough for presenting different versions of truth, such as restatement based on a new management hierarchy versus the historical truth. However, in more sophisticated scenarios, time-dependent master data is not enough to model different version of truth or avoid realignments.

For example, reorganizations in SEM Business Consolidations (SEM BCS) must be handled differently because of the posting level concept (described in more detail in Chapter 8) built into its information model. In summary, consolidation-of-investment postings for each consolidation group within a consolidation group hierarchy must be realigned based on organizational structure changes (because of differing ownership impacts). A simple change in a time-dependent hierarchy is not enough; transactional records assigned to certain organizational elements must also change to reflect new calculations.

Another similar example is realignment of sales commission splits based on reorganized sales territories. Here it is not enough to restate what territory a sales representative belongs to, but any commission splits (i.e., transaction data) may have to be realigned to the new territories as well. Or perhaps the commission calculation itself changes because of new management rules, and transaction data must be replicated with the new calculation formula so that comparisons can be made to measure the effects of the new commission calculation.

In all these cases, transaction data must be duplicated and stored with the new hierarchy assignments to support reporting for both versions of truth. In addition, a means for avoiding data duplication in queries must then be designed. Either the old data must be deleted (which then no longer supports multiple versions of truth) or some sort of datestamp method must be developed. Fortunately, Business Content has an example of one approach for handling this tough information modeling issue.

Whenever the organization structure changes in SEM BCS a new data stream is posted to SAP BW InfoCubes. The number of data streams that SEM BCS keeps in its InfoCube (before deleting them) is configured in the data stream parameter settings. The setting is an important configuration for performance.

To avoid duplication of data in queries, you must use specialized variables that filter on only one version of truth at a time. Versions of truth are stored as date ranges in the InfoCube. The date ranges represent the time-varying hierarchical relationships of consolidation units to consolidation groups as well as associated postings. The assignment of consolidation units to consolidation groups is time-variant and subject to reorganizations. Also assigned to consolidation groups are consolidation-of-investment postings that are time-variant and sensitive to reorganizations. These assignments are stored in the transaction data rather than modeled as master data. More explicitly, reorganizations are handled in the InfoCube rather than as time-dependent characteristics.

When reorganizations occur, a new set of data is created and posted to the InfoCube, effectively doubling data in the InfoCube. One set of data represents the old version of truth, and the other set represents the new version. The data is separated by validity date ranges. Two InfoObjects dictate the date range: one InfoObject representing the start of the date range (or *source hierarchy*) and the other representing the end of the date range (or *target hierarchy*).

To select a specific version of truth, you use a set of variables on the date ranges. Three Business Content variables are used for selection: The first variable selects on the date-from characteristic, the second variable selects on date-to characteristic, and the third specifies the date within a date range. The first two variables must be included in every query as filters. The third variable is specified in the query properties as the key date of the query. The variable can be either the system default for system date or it can be a Business Content variable that can be entered in manually during query runtime.

NOTE The key date of a query, the key date of a hierarchy, and a time characteristic filter are all different things. The key date of the query is used in special scenarios such as in SEM BCS. The key date of a hierarchy is for time-dependent presentation hierarchies. The time characteristic is for OLAP navigation within a query.

Figure 5.12 shows how a representative query is configured. Note that the fourth variable used to filter on the time dimension is different from the time variables for hierarchy selection and the variable for the key date of the query (used to select which interval).

There is SAP exit code behind the two variables used for beginning and end dates for hierarchy selection.

The SAP exit variable for the date-from variable for SEM BCS hierarchy selection checks for the variable used in the key date of the query. The only variables allowed are either a default variable for the system date or an explicitly defined Business Content variable that allows for manual entry of the date. The date-from variable is then set less than or equal to the key date of the query. Similarly, if we were to analyze the code for the date-to variable, the logic would be exactly the same except the value it would be set to would be greater than or equal to the key date of the query.

TIP The logic for Business Content variables with SAP exits is stored in function modules. For many time characteristic variables, the logic is in function module `RREX_VARIABLE_EXIT`. Otherwise, the function module starts with `RSVAREXIT_` concatenated with the variable name. This is how the default variable for key date of the query and the SEM BCS date range variables for hierarchy selection are handled, respectively.

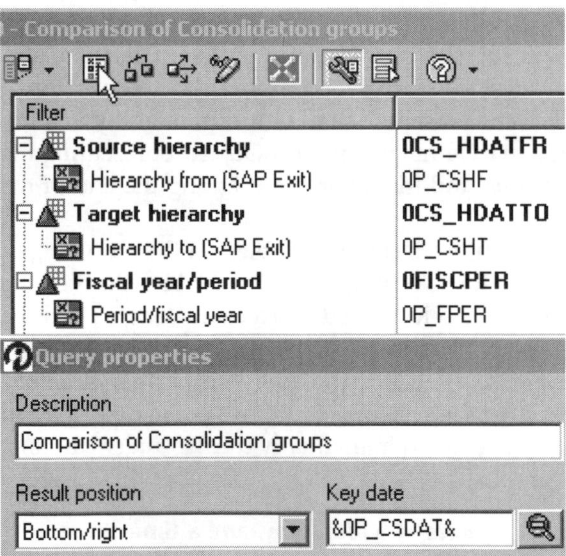

Figure 5.12 Hierarchy variables for consolidations.

How Does Business Content Model Currencies?

Currencies can be modeled either as generic key figures or as specific key figures. (Again, the difference between what is generic versus specific was discussed in Chapter 4.) Business Content models currencies both ways.

In the overhead- and enterprise-controlling information models, currencies are modeled generically. In the SEM BCS information model, currencies are specific key figures. When reconciling data from these different information models, you should understand how these currencies are modeled. To maintain consistency and comparability, perhaps the best currency to use is the group or client currency, which by definition can only be one currency key value.

The advantage of the generic key figure approach is that it is easier to add more currencies without changing the structure. In addition, more design options are available in query design when currencies can be modeled either as characteristics or as restricted key figures. The disadvantage is that should the Business Content model need to be extended, the standard translation functions in the update rules cannot be used to populate new currencies (since currency translation cannot be performed on one record and its results passed to a new subsequent record). In other words, the currency translation functions work only with specific key models for currencies. In addition, in generic key figure models for currencies, queries must constrain on a currency type to avoid data duplication. Lastly, there is a performance impact as more records are generated in the InfoCube per currency. The characteristic used to differentiate the currencies is currency type, and typically there are three values represented in the Business Content DataSources.

The advantage of the second approach is that the standard translation functions are supported and performance is improved with the reduction in the number of records. In addition, the information model is simplified without forcing users to include the currency type in their queries to avoid trebling values.

In SAP financial applications, there are only three currencies for each ledger. This restriction is because of the data model of the dynamic summary tables. When more than three currencies need to be tracked, an additional ledger needs to be configured. Essentially, this is what occurs at a technical level when parallel currencies are added to the General Ledger. In applications like Special Ledger, additional ledgers translate to additional DataSources.

The first currency in every ledger is typically the transaction currency. The currency key for the first currency is stored with the transaction (denoted as currency 1 in Figure 5.13). The second and third currencies are typically derived, and hence, are not stored with the transaction. Typically, these fields are derived based on configuration. For example, in Controlling, typically the second and third currency keys are the cost object currency and controlling area currency, respectively. The former is derived from the cost object master data (such as cost center currency), while the latter is derived from the configuration of the controlling area. In General Ledger, the second currency and third currency keys are company code and group currency. The company code currency key is derived from the company code master, while the group currency key is derived from the client.

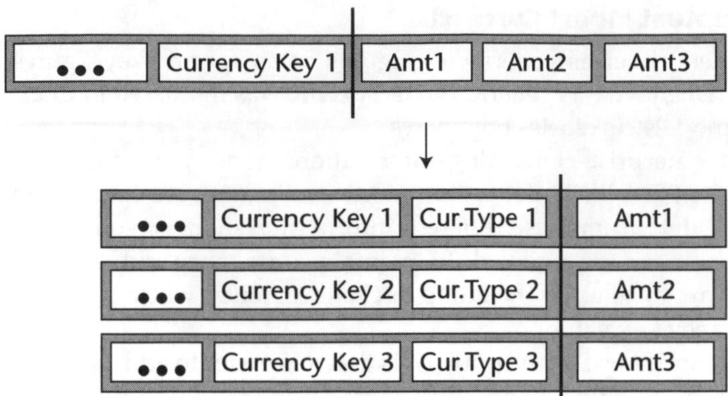

Figure 5.13 Generic key figures for currencies.

When currencies are modeled as generic key figures, the different currencies (such as transaction, cost object, and controlling area) translate to different currency types on separate records. Figure 5.13 demonstrates how one extracted record with three currencies becomes three records, each containing only one currency amount. The model translation is performed within the Business Content extractors. Figure 5.13 starts with a table record with three currency key figures and only one currency key. The currency keys for the second and third currency amounts are derived during extraction. During extraction derivation, the three specific key figures are transformed into one key figure with three different records. Each record is separated by a currency type value.

The alternative is to model currencies as specific key figures, as shown in Figure 5.14. The transformation for this scenario is minimal, as the specific key figure model of the DataSource is almost the same as the specific key figure model of the table being extracted. The transformation requires adding the currency keys for the second and third currencies into the records of the extraction structure.

NOTE In reality, there are more than three specific key figures per record in the dynamic summary table representing currencies. Each specific key figure also represents a period. As a result, there are actually many more key figures that map to three currency key figures.

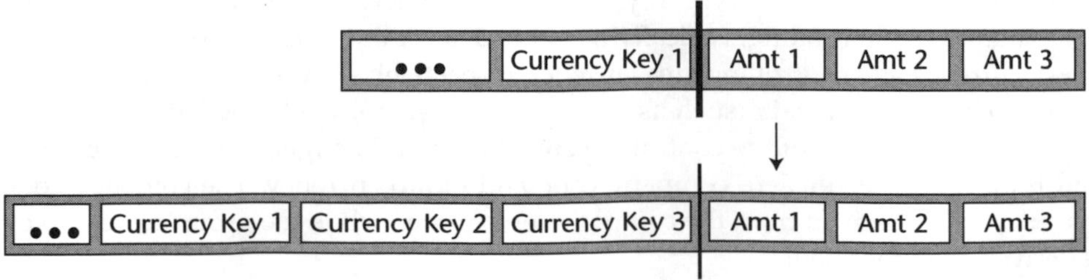

Figure 5.14 Specific key figures for currencies.

If additional currencies are to be custom-added to Business Content, you can more easily extend a specific key figure model using standard translation functions either in BEx queries or in update rules. In this manner, you can also translate new currency key figures from one of the existing key figures. Unit routines in the update rules can be used to derive new target currency keys.

How Should Noncumulative Key Figures Be Modeled in Financials?

The term *noncumulative key figure* has a specific meaning in SAP BW. It is a type of exception aggregation that calculates snapshot amounts based on the inflows and outflows in a referenced cumulative key figure. Noncumulative key figures were defined in Chapter 4. Primarily, they are used for inventory management reporting scenarios when inventory snapshots are needed at any given point in time or for comparison purposes.

Financial Business Content has a different method for calculating noncumulative (or snapshot) values without using noncumulative key figures. Snapshot amounts are needed for year-to-date balance sheet amounts. Year-to-date balance sheet amounts in financials are calculated differently than for year-to-date inventory amounts in materials management. First, balance sheet amounts are physically stored in cumulative key figures with either no exception aggregation or an exception aggregation of last value, depending on the financial information model. In contrast, snapshot amounts are calculated via exception aggregation through the use of noncumulative key figures.

The calculation to arrive at snapshot amounts in financials is performed in the Business Content extractors. The calculation of balance sheet amounts in R/3 financial applications is based on a process known as *balance carry-forward*. To better understand how noncumulative amounts are calculated in Business Content, let's briefly review the balance carry-forward concept and the SAP R/3 data models.

In the financial dynamic summary tables, fiscal periods are stored as specific key figures for each fiscal period. There are 17 period key figures per record, consisting of a balance carry-forward period, 12 fiscal periods, and up to 4 adjustment periods. The dynamic summary database tables do not separate records for each period. Often the technical field for period is confused with the time dimension for fiscal period in the dynamic summary table. This field is actually a technical field used to represent whether the periods stored on each record relate to 12 periods, 52 weeks, 365 days, or some other specially defined fiscal year variant.

The SAP R/3 Financials data model is important for understanding the business logic behind the extractors. The extractor transforms each specific key figure representing a fiscal period into a generic key figure separated by fiscal period values. As a result, even when an extraction is restricted by period, full table reads are still necessary, since period is not part of the key in the underlying table. For every new period, the number of records in the dynamic summary table does not necessarily increase. From an extraction perspective, the same records are potentially read, but each time, a new time dimension value gets populated. Figure 5.15 illustrates how period key figures are converted into time dimension values.

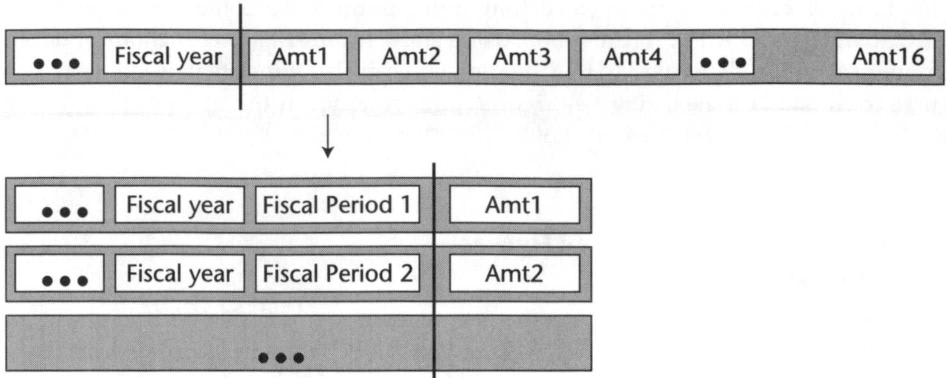

Figure 5.15 Period transformation.

In SAP R/3 reporting, year-to-date balance sheet amounts are calculated using a balance carry-forward period. Every year's activity is summarized into the balance carry-forward period in the following year via a year-end closing program. As a result, balance sheet accounts can accumulate year-to-year. Technically, the balance carry-forward period is stored as period 0. As a result, when you wants a year-to-date amount for balance sheet accounts in an SAP R/3 report, you must select all the periods in the current year, including the balance carry-forward period, up to the current period. Because all periods are stored as specific key figures on each record of the dynamic summary table, the calculation of year-to-date amounts is optimized. Technically, the specific key figures representing the balance carry-forward period through to the current period are summed.

SAP BW has no process or information models that support the execution of a balance carry-forward program against ODS objects or InfoCubes. The Business Content extractors, however, do support the balance carry-forward period, but only for dynamic summary tables. In other words, delta line-item extractors lack support of balance carry-forward amounts, since this value is only found in the dynamic summary tables in SAP R/3 and not in the OLTP tables (note that there are exceptions, such as Funds Management where balance carry-forward amounts are stored in the line-item tables).

Financial Business Content extractors deliver two sets of key figures: one for cumulative key figures and another for snapshot (or noncumulative) amounts. However, the ways the year-to-date balance sheet amounts are modeled differ by financial application. In Business Content, year-to-date balance amounts may be modeled either as: a separate key figure from profit-and-loss amounts with a last-value exception aggregation or as shared key figure with profit-and-loss amounts with no exception aggregation. Profit center accounting and General Ledger uses the first approach, while SEM BCS uses the second.

The two different approaches have different information modeling impacts. In profit center accounting, the debit and credit key figures are used to provide the cumulative amounts, while a balance sheet key figure is used for the year-to-date snapshot amounts for balance sheet accounts. In SEM BCS, two separate sets of key figures for cumulative and snapshot amounts are shared by both balance sheet and profit-and-loss accounts.

In both information models, the advantage of having two separate key figures for cumulative and snapshots amounts is that both can be reported simultaneously per fiscal period in queries. The difference is that in the first information model the key figures can be summarized across periods, while in the second they cannot (without adding snapshot amounts on top of each other, which the last-value exception aggregation avoids).

The way the extractors work for year-to-date balance sheet amounts is that each period gets rolled forward into all subsequent periods for the year in order to keep a running total. In the first information model, this calculation occurs on the same records. In the second information model, when the balance carry-forward amount is rolled into all the subsequent fiscal periods, up to 12 records are created for each subsequent period. For example, if an extraction is executed in period six, seven records are created (the current period plus all the subsequent periods for the year). As a result, there is a greater performance impact on loading data for the second information model than for the first. In addition, because of how the extractors work, queries will show data in the year-to-date key figures for future periods even though business activity in those periods is yet to occur. The cumulative key figures in those future periods show zero values but nevertheless are picked up in reporting if the query is not constrained by the current period.

TIP **Expect longer load times when loading the first period (where records are created for every subsequent period) than for the last period for the SEM BCS extractors.**

For year-to-date key figure reporting in financials, the Business Content extractors play an important role in the information model.

How Does Business Content Model Value Types?

While logistics performance metrics are business-event-oriented, financial information models focus on measuring different types of values. The different values that flow through financials may not only be actual data but can be commitments, budgeted amounts, forecasts, or plan versions.

Whereas Business Content for logistic applications uses process keys to differentiate business events, financials differentiates its records through value types. In addition, logistics Business Content models process keys as specific key figures, while financial Business Content models value types as generic key figures.

Value types actually consist of up to three InfoObjects: value type, key figure type, and detailing of the value type. Typically, these characteristics are used to create restricted key figures in queries, constraining amounts or quantities by the value types.

The first characteristic is the value type itself. Value types can differentiate between the different financial values that flow through the system such as planned versus actual. The second characteristic (if applicable) is the key figure type. The key figure type makes further accounting-relevant distinctions, such as whether the amount is sales revenue or stock, debit or credit, activity quantities or overhead cost rates, statistical key figures or activities, and variances or work-in-progress. The last characteristic is the detailing of the value type (used if applicable). The detailing of the value type is compounded by the value type and key figure type. It either more closely models specific financial business events, such as allocations versus reposting versus settlement (for CO transactions), or breaks down value types into more detailed categorizations, such as production variances into price, quantity, lot size, resource usage, or scrap variances.

By modeling key performance indicators as restricted key figures using value types you can quickly change and customize the measures more flexibly. The disadvantage is that these technical InfoObjects must be well understood if custom restricted key figures or queries are to be defined. These characteristics need to be actively used in order to define meaningful queries.

Value types in reporting is not unique to SAP BW. SAP R/3 reporting also uses value types, but the values are not consistent across applications. Because the SAP BW value types are consistent and integrated, mappings between SAP R/3 and SAP BW value types are defined in Business Content. The mappings are performed in the Business Content extractors and are either hard-coded or read from mapping tables in SAP R/3.

Human Resources Strategic Analysis

As more information modeling options become available in SAP BW, specific areas of Business Content may be impacted. For example, human resources (HR) Business Content maps many details of master data into its InfoCubes. Additional information modeling options include using InfoObjects as InfoProviders or, if an ODS Object is used to stage master data, using the ODS object as an InfoProvider.

HR Business Content also uses hierarchies or characteristics within a dimension of an InfoCube to create evaluative ranges. Alternatively, conditions can be configured in queries to segregate data based on thresholds. These evaluation ranges are not available for data selection, however. If evaluation ranges are configured as part of ABC Analysis (A, B, and C represent different evaluation ranges), the results of the ABC analysis in a query can be written back to the master data as a navigational attribute. In this case, the evaluation range can be used for data selection. The write-back-to-master-data functionality is part of analytical CRM but comes with SAP BW and is generic enough for use in other areas.

HR Business Content has its own distinct information models similar to the distinct design of its SAP R/3 application. For our business scenario, let's say you are an HR analyst assisting management in assessing the overall composition of the workforce to find any patterns or trends in the inflows and outflows of personnel. You want to perform an analysis on the percentage breakdown on the total number of employees, the number of entrants, and the number of leavers. You suspect a trend toward hiring more experienced personnel and want to find if there is a rising pattern with the average age of new entrants into your corporation. You decide to perform analysis on the rate of entry for various age ranges.

How Does Business Content Model Infotypes?

Human resources Business Content is fundamentally different than logistics and accounting Business Content. First, in place of transaction data and master data tables in SAP R/3, there are *Infotypes*. This then raises the issue of how the data should be modeled in SAP BW. The distinction of master data and transaction data becomes blurred where both can be staged via ODS objects. How Infotypes are modeled by Business Content can lend some insights.

First, you must understand the nature of Infotypes. Most Infotypes are time-variant with validity date ranges. SAP BW automatically recognizes these fields as beginning and end dates for time-dependent master data. HR applications also make heavy use of cluster tables, especially in payroll. As a result, one advantage of bringing HR reporting to SAP BW is greater information accessibility.

Business Content models Infotypes both as master data and transaction data. One expense of the approach is data redundancy in both the InfoObjects and the InfoCubes. The InfoSources that feed the InfoCubes are typically much smaller than other applications, containing only independent characteristics and key figures. As a result, the HR Business Content makes heavy use of update rules that look up master data attributes. Figure 5.16 depicts the difference between typical Business Content versus HR Business Content.

Although update rules can perform master data derivations to pull InfoObject attributes into an InfoCube, HR Business Content uses ABAP code. The main difference between the standard functionality and specialized ABAP in the update rules is that the former can only do simple master data lookups while the later can do more complicated lookups (such as finding an attribute of an attribute). The HR Business

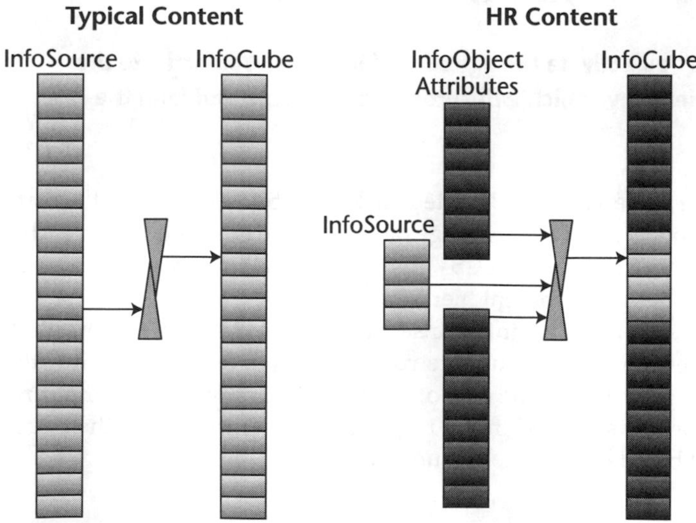

Figure 5.16 Typical versus HR Business Content.

Content update rules perform several consecutive lookups (i.e., find the age attribute from the person attribute of the employee ID InfoObject). The logic in Business Content routines can be found in the subroutines of general programs for HR Business Content. Example code for master data derivation will be given in a more comprehensive scenario pertaining to age range analysis.

How Should Evaluation Ranges Be Modeled?

Evaluation ranges can be modeled numerous ways. The two options presented as part of HR Business Content is the use of hierarchies and characteristics within the dimension of an InfoCube (saved as part of the transaction data). The advantage of using hierarchies over saving evaluative ranges with transaction data is that definition of evaluation ranges in a hierarchy is flexible; it can be quickly re-defined and changed. However, if transaction data in an InfoCube is constantly refreshed, the point is less relevant.

Age range is modeled as a hierarchy by grouping the age in years (InfoObject 0AGE) into hierarchy nodes to represent the evaluative age ranges. Age ranges modeled into the transaction data is stored as a separate InfoObject in the dimension of an InfoCube. Age is also represented as a key figure in HR Business Content so that age-based calculations in BEx queries can be performed.

The hierarchy does not have to be manually defined but comes as Business Content. There is a predelivered comma-delimited file for upload of the hierarchy. When you activate the InfoPackage for this file, it automatically uploads the hierarchy data into the SAP BW system. The InfoObject for age itself is a derived characteristic that contains the employee's or applicant's age at the end of a period. When you define age ranges, current age versus age at a certain historical date is an important distinction. Current age is constantly changing, while age at a certain point in time is frozen in the past. It is the latter calculation that gets stored into the InfoCube.

TIP Where in BW do you activate the age range hierarchy? You activate the InfoPackage for the hierarchy, which will automatically create and load the hierarchy.

The ranges in the age hierarchy are depicted in Figure 5.17 (note that they are defined similarly in the update rules to derive age range into the transaction data). This hierarchy comes as Business Content via a CSV file for upload, but a manual, custom one can easily replace the Business Content hierarchy.

When evaluation ranges are modeled into transaction data, update rules are needed. Business Content supplies the requisite update rules. The update rules perform the calculation for the age range by taking the date of birth of an employee and comparing it to the last day of the period specified in the respective InfoSource. Once the age is derived, it is categorized based on hard-coded update rules.

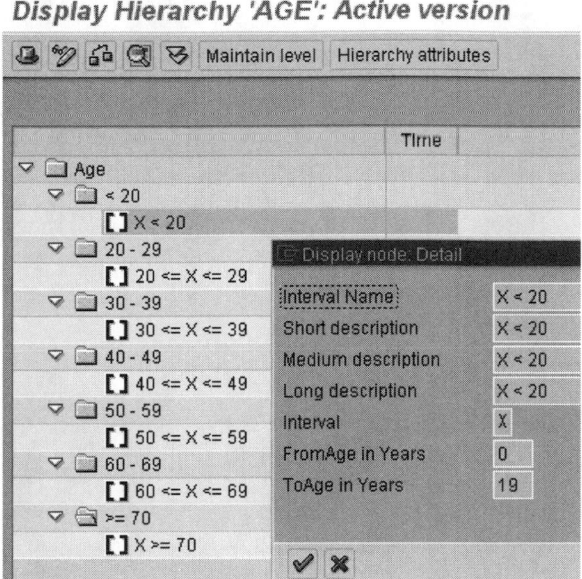

Figure 5.17 Age range hierarchy.

Following is a code sample from the Business Content update rules for the derivation of age ranges. The update rule for age range is for the HR InfoCube that stores head count and personnel actions (for analysis on such criteria as number of people in the organization, the number joining, and number of leaving). The update rules start by calling a subroutine to derive the first day of the next month, followed by a subroutine to look up the time-dependent records for employee and person. This routine selects all the attributes in the employee master data and person master data, but only the date of birth from the person master data is used. The date of birth is used to calculate age. After age is calculated, the age ranges are determined. The logic is as follows:

```
PERFORM CALCULATE_ULTIMO
        using COMM_STRUCTURE-calmonth
               RECORD_NO
               RECORD_ALL
               SOURCE_SYSTEM
        CHANGING ULTIMO
                 RETURNCODE.
PERFORM READ_MD_PERSON
        using    COMM_STRUCTURE-employee
                 COMM_STRUCTURE-calmonth
```

```
                  RECORD_NO
                  RECORD_ALL
                  SOURCE_SYSTEM
         CHANGING EMPLOYEE_WA
                  PERSON_WA
                  RETURNCODE.
EMPLOYEE_MD = EMPLOYEE_WA.
PERSON_MD   = PERSON_WA.
IF NOT PERSON_MD-DATEBIRTH IS INITIAL.
  AGE = ULTIMO+0(4) - PERSON_MD-DATEBIRTH+0(4).
  IF ULTIMO+4(4) LT PERSON_MD-DATEBIRTH+4(4).
    AGE = AGE - 1.
  ENDIF.
  IF AGE LT 20.
    RESULT = 1.
  ELSEIF AGE LT 30.
    RESULT = 2.
  ELSEIF AGE LT 40.
    RESULT = 3.
  ELSEIF AGE LT 50.
    RESULT = 4.
  ELSEIF AGE LT 60.
    RESULT = 5.
  ELSEIF AGE LT 70.
    RESULT = 6.
  ELSE.
    RESULT = 7.
 ELSE.
   CLEAR RESULT.
 ENDIF.
```

In summary, after the subroutine for calculating the last day of the month (CALCULATE_ULTIMO) is performed, the person master data is read for the date of birth (READ_MD_PERSON). The years are compared between the last day of the month to the year of birth. The age is calculated as the year of the calendar month minus the year of birth. The update rules then categorize ages into 7 ranges scaled by 10-year increments, starting at age 20 or below through age 70 or higher.

Because age ranges can be defined in both hierarchies and in update rules, inconsistencies in analysis may emerge if changes are made to one without corresponding changes to the other. Understanding how this Business Content is set up is important to avoid inconsistent reporting.

The Future of Business Content

Business Content is both improving and expanding. Improvements bring versioning considerations as better business practices and technological innovations spur the need for Business Content upgrades. Expansion brings opportunities for disintermediation as the product and market diversify. Analytic applications and complementary third-party solutions drive product segmentation, while industry sectors drive market segmentation.

The future outlook of Business Content and SAP BW is constantly shifting. As a result, we will provide updates on this ever-changing topic via our companion Web site for the book.

Technological Innovations

Technological innovations spur the growth of Business Content by adding new types of building blocks. Each SAP BW release has seen new types of Business Content objects introduced.

For example, when SAP BW was first introduced, the only information providers were basic InfoCubes. Now there are ODS objects, remote InfoCubes, MultiProviders InfoObjects, and InfoSets. The BEx Analyzer used to be the only analysis tool provided (with the option to use third-party tools). Now there are data mining models, Crystal Reports, InfoSet queries, mobile reporting tools, and Web reporting tools. In addition to extractors and the data mart interface, there are now InfoSpokes. The next innovations will most likely be in turning information into knowledge. Specifically, content management—or more broadly, knowledge management—will contain the next building blocks.

New building blocks create opportunities for better information models and best business practices. As a result, version management will become an increasingly important issue, especially when multiple SAP BW environments interacting with multiple SAP applications like mySAP SCM, mySAP CRM, and mySAP SEM are involved. Other technological improvements such as XML export and import of meta data promise to help keep systems synchronized.

Innovations in Business Content strengthen SAP BW as a platform for developing specialized applications more quickly and cost-efficiently.

Disintermediation

As Business Content becomes more flexible in supporting the increasingly segmented needs of industry and analytic applications, the possibility of disintermediation becomes more likely. Opening up Business Content creation to third parties would give the run in Business Content growth new legs. Technologies are already in place to facilitate such a development (such as partner namespaces and support for XML meta data interchange).

Some sort of content clearinghouse would have to be effected to prevent meta data chaos. A content clearing house would serve as a means of ensuring consistency and maintenance of best business practices. Conceivably, the role of SAP would change from Business Content development to Business Content management. Or perhaps this role will be assumed by one of the standards group.

The trend toward industry standards has had and will continue to have an impact on Business Content. Not only have technical standards emerged like Common Warehouse

Metamodel (CWM) and XML Metadata Interchange (XMI)[3] to facilitate the interchange of meta data, but business standards such as the SCOR model for supply chain processes have also emerged to facilitate the integration of information for activities like benchmarking.

Perhaps the day will come when meta data can be so flexibly and dynamically employed that the need for Business Content is diminished or takes another form. For example, if standardized meta data could be flexibly employed at query run time and then custom-mapped to information in the data warehouse, Business Content will take on a whole new meaning. Imagine pulling a newly defined SCOR metric and its associated meta data from the Web via XMI and then relating it to existing information models for on-the-fly analysis.

In the end, such speculation is risky and should be read with caution. However, the business needs will not go away, and technology has a way of continually improving how those needs get fulfilled.

Summary

Business Content is a roles-based, predelivered set of SAP BW information models. The roles-based nature of Business Content influences the design of its information models by driving what KPIs are needed to measure which processes.

The need for processes outside the SAP R/3 domain to feed roles-based information models has pushed Business Content growth horizontally across applications and systems. In addition, the need for industry-tailored information has pushed Business Content vertically. Also, because Business Content is the foundational building blocks for analytic applications, the increasing popularity of analytic applications will be another source of its growth.

With growth come challenges. Business Content must combat old notions or misplaced myths of its usability. Nevertheless, not all Business Content is usable, and in these cases, it is more helpful as a template. There is a general relationship between where a Business Content meta data object fits on the information flow scale and how usable it is. In addition, some subject areas are more standardized than others, and this standardization facilitates Business Content support. The two main challenges of growth are maintaining meta data consistency and managing meta data versioning. Despite the challenges, Business Content delivers value by way of faster implementations and helpful Business Content information model templates.

Business Content information models can help the SAP BW designer answer information modeling questions. In this chapter, we used scenarios for procurement, financials, and human resources as background and context to relate how Business Content implements the information modeling concepts presented in Chapter 4.

The future of Business Content and its information models will continually be impacted by improvements in SAP BW. New tools and techniques will translate into improved Business Content information models. As the market segments, so too will

[3] These standards are set by the Object Management Group. More can be found at www.omg.org.

Business Content, which will create an opportunity for disintermediation in order to meet the increased demand for specialized Business Content. How disintermediation might look is an exercise in speculation.

The next chapter delves deeper into the topic of extraction, transformation, and loading, one of the highest-value information model components of Business Content.

ETL Services

Identifying the right sources of data, extracting data from those source appropriately, applying the transformations required, and storing the transformed data in a way that best supports reporting and analysis is usually the most time-consuming part of building a data warehouse solution. In the corporate information factory framework, this is referred to as sourcing and manufacturing of data and information. More specifically, it involves extracting, moving, transforming, loading, and indexing data and information and is a significant component of information logistics modeling. All functionality required for the extraction, transfer, and loading (ETL) process is provided by the ETL services layer of the SAP BW architecture.

From an SAP BW point of view, the ETL services layer (Figure 6.1) is composed of:

- A Staging Engine
- A DataSource Manager supporting a number of interfaces to different types of source systems
- The persistent staging area (PSA)

The extraction interfaces break further down into the BW Service API used for extracting data from mySAP.com applications, including SAP BW systems, an XML interface, the DB Connect interface, a file interface, and the Staging BAPI. The *BW Service API* supports a large number of extractors: generic extractors, generated extractors, or extraction programs specifically implemented by SAP. The BW Service API is the standard extraction interface of SAP BW for all mySAP.com applications. The SAP Application Link Enabling (ALE) technology is used as a platform for handling all communications between source systems and SAP BW systems—although in a different way for the different types of source systems addressed through different kinds of interfaces.

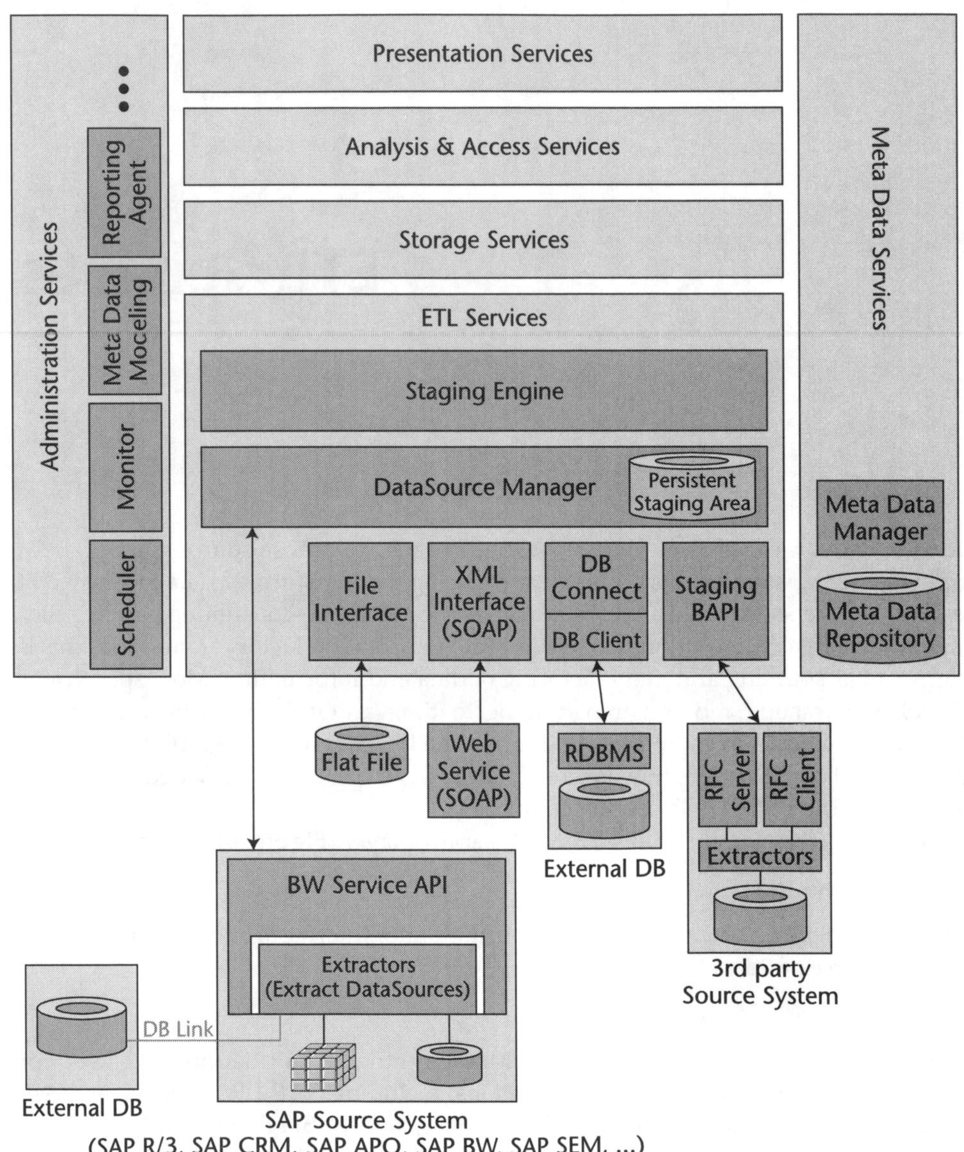

Figure 6.1 ETL services.

Staging in SAP BW encompasses the flow of information from the originating systems through the various stages of the BW system landscape in the information supply chain. As information moves up the information supply chain, it becomes more integrated and usually more aggregated. Information becomes more granular and disparate moving down the information supply chain.

Before information can actually flow into and through SAP BW, the information supply chain needs to be configured. The first step in doing so is creating a DataSource, which essentially describes the extraction side of things from an SAP BW point of view. The DataSource consists of a number of data fields, a transfer structure, and the optional PSA, as shown in Figure 6.2.

NOTE The DataSource fields and the transfer structure are used to formally describe the data format used to exchange data between a source and a target system. There is no physical storage assigned to either of these structures. However, the persistent staging area provides the option to store data in the transfer structure for error handling and other purposes.

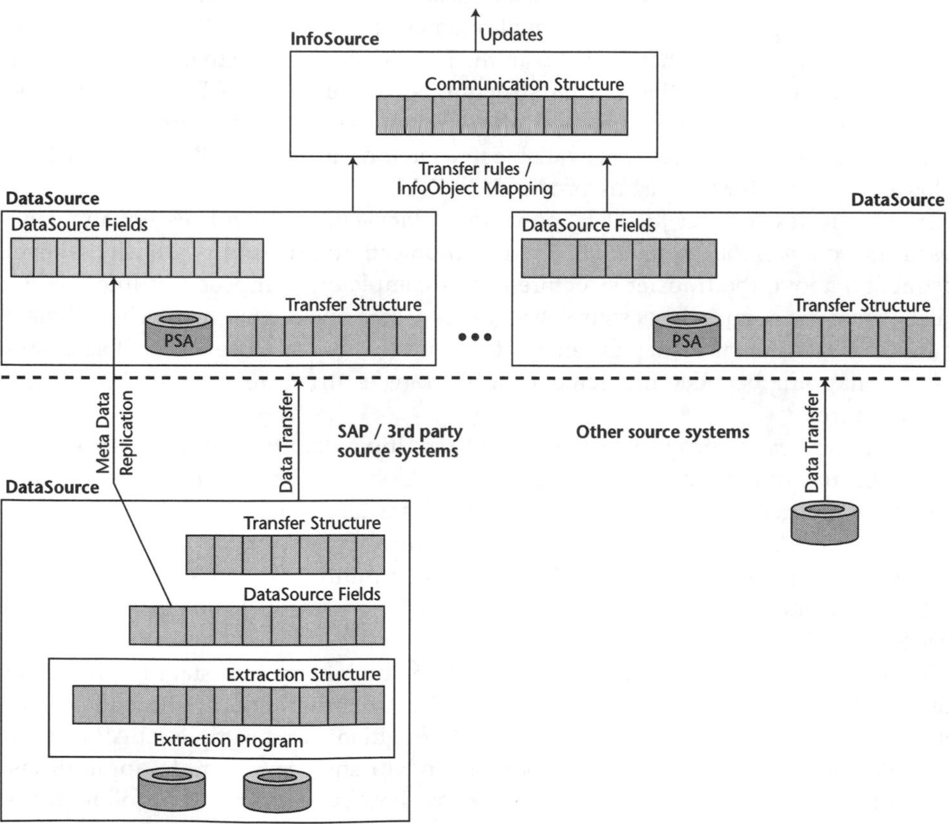

Figure 6.2 InfoSources and DataSources.

From an SAP source system point of view, first of all there is the extraction program—the generic extractor (as used for many master data extractors), an extraction program generated based on SAP customizing (such as for CO-PA transaction data extractors), or a specifically implemented extraction program (as for many hierarchy- and application-specific extractors). The data structure used by the extraction program to extract data is called the *extraction structure*. The fields of this extraction structure are mapped to the fields of the DataSource.

The fields of the DataSource are maintained in the source system using the DataSource definition transactions described later (see Figure 6.4) and is replicated to SAP BW systems connecting to the SAP source system. As an SAP system might provide data for several SAP BW instances, there is one transfer structure per SAP BW system extracting data for that DataSource. The transfer structure basically is an agreement between a specific SAP BW system and a specific SAP or non-SAP source system on how to actually transfer data and what data to transfer for a specific DataSource. The transfer structure usually is composed of a subset of the fields of the DataSource.

For non-SAP source systems, the fields of the DataSource may be replicated from a database catalog (as for the DB Connect interface), may have been uploaded using the Staging BAPI, or may have been entered manually, as with the file interface. All structures are stored in the SAP BW Meta Data Repository. The file interface, the XML interface, and the Staging BAPI allow manual maintenance of the DataSource fields. It is important to understand that the fields of the DataSource are effectively controlled by the source system, while the transfer structure is controlled by SAP BW. Even if the DataSource fields may be maintained manually in SAP BW, the source system still effectively defines what fields are available in what format, and SAP BW defines which fields are required for the staging process.

Transfer Rules connect the DataSource to an *InfoSource*, which is essentially composed of a *communication structure*. The communication structure is a business level abstraction above the transfer structure and is completely composed of InfoObjects. DataSources are composed of source system meta data and represent a technical view of the data. Transfer rules map the elements of the transfer structure to InfoObjects and define a mapping between the elements of the transfer structure and the communication structure.

The InfoSource in turn can be connected to multiple data targets (InfoCubes, ODS objects, or master data) by defining *update rules*. Update rules map InfoObjects available in InfoSources to InfoObjects used in the data target definition. While a DataSource can only be connected to one single InfoSource in a specific SAP BW system, an InfoSource can be fed from multiple DataSources on multiple source systems and may update different data targets, effectively establishing a many to many relationship between InfoSources and data targets.

In the remainder of this chapter, we'll discuss the information staging process in greater conceptual and technical detail, dividing it into three sections: extraction, transformation, and loading. We'll use pseudocode fragments and sample ABAP code to illustrate the transfer and update processes and to showcase sample applications. However, these are kept high-level; ABAP know-how is not required to follow those discussions.

Extraction

Since release 1.2, SAP BW supported loading external data through its file interface and the Staging BAPI without actually making a difference between SAP data and non-SAP data from a data transformation and storage point of view. Many ETL tool vendors, including Ascential Software, ETI. and Informatica have adopted the Staging BAPI to allow SAP BW users to load data and meta data from many different databases and file formats. Nevertheless, SAP BW had a reputation of not being open or open enough. SAP successfully addressed this reputation by adding interfaces (like the XML and DB Connect interface) and by entering a strategic partnership with Ascential Software and bundling their DataStage ETL software package with SAP BW.

Regardless of the actual technological specifics of the data extraction process, it is important in any data warehouse implementation to have skilled staff understanding the specifics of the source systems involved—from both a business process and a technology point of view. Without a sound understanding of details of the underlying business processes, it is neither possible to define a proper information model (see Table 4.1) nor to populate an existing information model with consistent data.

Once a first pass is made at information modeling, the core question is "We can build it, but can we fill it?" The conceptual part of this work especially in a heterogeneous system environment is definitely taking more time and effort than the actual technical implementation. This is why we start this chapter on extraction with a discussion of the basic principles of data extraction and with a discussion of the specifics of typical operational systems. Related to that is a discussion of the meta data exchange between the source system and the SAP BW system, including a translation from the source system semantics to the unified semantics of the SAP BW environment. In heterogeneous system landscapes this is usually the biggest challenge of integration; issues of differing data quality and completeness levels, system availability, granularity, and business semantics have to be solved. Besides being an information model for SAP BW implementations fed from mySAP.com applications, SAP BW Business Content has proven to be very helpful as a basis for this kind of integration work as well.

While this discussion very much focuses on SAP R/3, many of the principles and problems discussed here also apply for other ERP systems such as PeopleSoft, Baan, and Oracle, CRM systems like Siebel or legacy systems. We chose SAP R/3 for three main reasons: (1) SAP R/3 showcases all the basic principles and problems discussed here, (2) many (not all) SAP BW customers use SAP R/3 as one of their source systems, and (3) a large amount of predefined extraction programs is available for SAP R/3 as part of the SAP BW Business Content. Other types of source systems introduced in Chapter 3 are covered from an integration and interfacing point of view. Extracting data from these systems requires intimate know-how about these systems and cannot be covered in this book.

Basic Principles

Generically discussing data extraction for data warehouse applications is not an easy task, considering the many different ways data is physically stored in database systems or elsewhere, the many different data models used for storing the same data, and the many ways data may be used for data warehousing purposes. However, before going into the details of the extraction process itself, we discuss some basic principles related to different classes of data, to the data flow and integration in an ERP system, to the different dimensions of data extraction and finally, to data management technology.

Classes of Data

There are three basic classes of data in a typical ERP system like SAP R/3: master data, transaction data, and configuration data.

Master data represents any business entity in an ERP system. Many times it is organizational entities such as the company, a plant, a sales area, a cost center, or an account. Other times it represents external entities such as customers and vendors. Or it may represent things such as materials. Master data is an important concept to data warehousing, as it constitutes the dimensions or dimensional attributes of the data warehouse.

Master data itself can take on various forms. SAP BW categorizes master data into three forms: attributes, hierarchies, and texts. *Attributes* are any fields that describe a master data entity. *Hierarchies* are mostly separate tables that store parent-child relationships between master data entities such as a cost center hierarchy or a product hierarchy. *Text tables* simply contain the textual descriptions of master data and are usually stored in separate tables because they are language-dependent.

The primary keys of master data tables, of course, differ by application. SAP BW usually handles multiple field keys through the use of compound InfoObjects (effectively defining compound keys), as explained in Chapter 4. Universal extended key concepts like version and time dependency are handled by SAP BW through generated key fields like *0DATETO* and *0DATEFROM* for time dependency. What is different in each application is how this is reflected in the extraction tables. For example, in HR-PA, master data records for personnel are stored with start and end dates in the primary key. In CO-CCA, cost center date dependencies are stored with only the valid-to date in the primary key. In EC-CS, consolidation units are period- and year-dependent, but no date is stored; rather, the period and year make up the primary key.

Hierarchy tables tend to be more difficult to understand than master data attribute tables. First, the relationships of master data within hierarchies can be complicated. Second, the techniques for storing these hierarchical relationships can be different application by application. Many applications have unique tables and techniques for storing hierarchies. For example, the product hierarchy on the material master in SAP R/3 is a specific one. It stores the hierarchy as a string in an attribute field on the material master. Configuration settings allow parsing the string into user-defined categories and levels. In SAP R/3 accounting, general ledger accounts are organized hierarchically as financial statement versions that are stored in unique tables. In SAP R/3 HR, the employees are created within personnel development organization hierarchy, which is yet again technically stored in HR-specific tables. There are hierarchy technologies that cross applications, however; two of the most pervasive technologies in SAP R/3 are sets (commonly used in the Report Writer or for configuration data) and drill-down hierarchies (used exclusively for drill-down reporting).

Transaction data describes a business event (such as a sales order) or the result of business processes (e.g., current in-stock quantity of a specific product). Transaction data contain the preponderant share of the key figures that will become your fact table in BW InfoCubes.

There are two levels of transaction data: the document level and summary levels. The document level may consist of several tables; most commonly there are up to three levels of detail for the document level, such as headers, line items, and schedule lines. The header information normally contains information about the document itself—for instance, the document type and the date it was posted. The line items consist of the details of the document, such as materials ordered on a purchase order or general ledger accounts on a financial transaction. Schedule line details usually revolve around the delivery schedule, where a given quantity of a specific product ordered has to be broken into several scheduled deliveries. Because it provides the largest amount of information, usually the lowest level of granularity is the ideal source for extractions. Dynamic summary tables are redundant summarizations of line-item data and primarily exist in the ERP system for reporting purposes. SAP R/3's special ledger and logistics information systems are common examples. SAP BW steadily makes the summary level of SAP R/3 obsolete.

In SAP R/3 HR, the distinction between master data and transaction data is blurred. HR Infotypes—a hybrid between master data and transaction data—store details such as personal data and payroll results as Infotype data.

Configuration data drives the ERP application logic. Typically, many configuration data tables can be found in an ERP system. That so much application logic has been pushed to configuration tables created the reality of a highly customizable enterprisewide software solution.

Although primarily used for defining the details of business processes, configuration data often is required for data warehousing purposes. For example, configuration data assigned to the type of a schedule line of a sales order defines whether that schedule line is relevant for production planning purposes. This information is stored in the SAP R/3 schedule line type configuration table. Filtering this information on the extraction side would hide information from the data warehouse. Selecting sales orders according to this information in the analysis or reporting process allows analyzing information relevant for production planning.

NOTE In SAP BW configuration data is modeled as characteristics and may have master data attributes, texts, and hierarchies. SAP BW does not distinguish between configuration data and master data.

Configuration data, master data, and transaction data records all may contain fields that are relevant for reporting and fields that are not relevant for reporting. Often there are many fields of a very technical nature (used for controlling business processes or for tracking who actually changed a specific record at what time) that are not relevant to BW and can be ignored. To be understandable to the data warehouse, some of the reporting-relevant fields may need conversion even prior to going through the transformation process in SAP BW. This is the case when operational or configuration information required to perform this conversion is only available in the operational system and cannot, or for some reason, should not be made easily available to SAP BW. Common examples include the order type in SAP R/3 SD, which changes depending on the language, and cost objects in CO depending on the application. The order type OR (English version) for instance gets stored in the database as TA. In CO, cost center, internal orders, WBS elements, and production orders are all saved in the same field name of the same tables and are in a technical format that must undergo conversion before it is recognizable to the user. Although most of the transformation will be done by SAP BW, there still may be important transformations to be performed during data extraction.

NOTE Other than changes to master data, changes to configuration data reflect changes to business processes and may also require a substantial redesign of the SAP BW information model.

Data Flow and Integration

SAP R/3 persists as a complex system with many applications using their own data model idiosyncrasies. As SAP R/3 grew, it experienced cycles of divergence and convergence until SAP recently split its SAP R/3 solution into four major application areas: mySAP Financials, mySAP Human Capital Management, mySAP Logistics, and mySAP Product Lifecycle Management. Each of these application areas has its own distinguishing characteristics, especially from an information systems perspective. However, if we look at the bigger picture, we see they are still integrated with each other; business processes or events in one application can cause other business processes or events in another. In addition, by looking at the components of each of these applications, we see this is even more evident.

Understanding the process flows is important for cross-application information models and identifying where key figures should be sourced. For example, accounting postings often originate outside of the accounting application, for example, in logistics, where more and different details are stored with the originating document. Decisions must be made where to extract the information from. Many SAP BW clients debate whether to use the logistic extractors or CO-PA extractors for sourcing sales documents from SAP R/3. The bottom line is that one of the biggest achievements of SAP BW-compared to SAP R/3-based reporting is the comparable ease of cross-application analysis and reporting.

In the following paragraphs, we present two common SAP R/3 processes to demonstrate how data is spread in the SAP R/3 system and to highlight the difficulties in extracting from these sources: *Order-to-cash* and *purchase-to-pay*. Each is briefly described and the corresponding relevant tables highlighted. While this discussion very much focuses on SAP R/3, its business model, and even physical database tables, the same fundamental principal of a business event kicking off different business processes implemented in different application areas apply in other ERP packages and in legacy systems.

Order-to-Cash Business Process

Examples of analytics that require an understanding of the order-to-cash include:

Bookings, billings, and backlog analysis. This report evaluates sales orders (bookings) and invoices (billings), as well as the difference between quantities ordered and quantities delivered (backlog).

Sales commission calculations. In some business environments sales commissions are paid not only on sales but also on timeliness of customer payments. This requires a merge of sales order data and aged accounts receivable data and the availability of a sales representative reference in both types of documents.

Royalty payment analysis. Obligations for paying royalties have to be tracked from sales orders until money is received on the bank account, at which time a royalty calculation prompts payments to royalty recipients.

Days sales outstanding (DSO) and days sales inventory (DSI). This analysis requires sales information as well as receivables and inventory amounts. DSO calculation involves amounts from accounts receivable, while DSI involves quantities from inventory management.

Following is a simplified order-to-cash process in SAP R/3:

1. When a sales representative enters a sales order in the SAP R/3 system, it stores the transaction into three SD tables: VBAK (header), VBAP (line-item), and VBEP (schedule line). This transaction has no direct financial impact, so no accounting documents are created.
2. A delivery due list is executed for all sales orders, and deliveries are created in tables LIKP (header) and LIPS (line-item). A goods issue is subsequently made updating tables MKPF (header) and MSEG (line-item). This document does have an accounting impact, and the corresponding financial transaction tables BKPF (header) and BSEG (line-item) are updated.
3. An invoice due list is then executed for all deliveries. After an invoice is created (updating tables VBRK and VBRP), it is released to accounting, which creates an accounting document (BKPF and BSEG) and sets up the receivable in table BSID (line-item).
4. The receivable is cleared when a payment check is received. Another accounting document is created (BKPF and BSEG), the open receivable is cleared, and table BSAD (line-item) is updated.

Procure-to-Pay Business Process

Some examples of analytics for the procure-to-pay process are:

Vendor evaluations. This analysis involves assessing how well vendors are performing by measuring, for example, on-time delivery by comparing the requested delivery date of a certain purchase order with the actual time goods are delivered. The first event is generated in the purchasing application, while the second event is generated in the inventory management.

Commitments, obligations, cost, and disbursements analysis. This analysis evaluates how budget is committed (purchase requisitions), obligated (purchase orders), costed (goods receipt), and disbursed (invoice payment). This analysis sources its data from purchasing, inventory management, and accounts payable.

Payment analysis. This analysis involves making sure that discounts and promotions are being taken advantage of and late fees and penalties are being avoided. The pricing conditions on a purchase order or contract dictate the terms of the agreement, and the accounts payable holds the information of whether payment was made optimally.

Following is a simplified procure-to-pay process in SAP R/3:

1. A purchase requisition is created, and table EBAN (line item) is updated.
2. The requisition is converted into a purchase order and tables EKKO (header) and EKPO (line item) are updated.
3. A goods receipt on the purchase order is made that updates tables MKPF and MSEG.
4. The invoice is then received, updating financial tables BKPF and BSEG, as well as setting up the payable in table BSIK (line item).
5. The invoice is paid via a payment run, the payable is cleared, and table BSAK is updated (line item).

Dimensions of Data Extraction

Four dimensions are generally used to describe the different methods and properties of extraction processes:

Extraction mode. The extraction mode refers to the range of data extracted from the source system. There are two basic extraction modes: full extraction and delta extraction. The *full extraction mode* extracts all data records available in the source tables (based on the extraction scope defined, see the text that follows for more details). The *delta extraction mode* only reads updated or inserted records (*delta* refers to the set of updated or inserted records). From an SAP BW point of view, the extraction mode is referred to as the *update mode.*

Extraction scenario. Data can either be *pushed* into a data warehouse or *pulled* from an operational system. In a push scenario, the initiator of the extraction and data transfer process is the operational system. In a pull scenario, the initiator is the data warehouse.

The push-versus-pull concept has a connotation of directorship, while in reality, information logistics deals more with initiators and receivers of information flows.

A more meaningful way to convey the push concept is to connect it with the term *publish and subscribe.* Similarly, the pull concept could be ascribed to *request and response.*

Data latency. Data latency refers to the timeliness of data extraction. Whether or not an extraction is *synchronous* (real-time), *asynchronous* (stored and forwarded), or *asynchronous batch* (on-demand or event-driven or scheduled) determines the latency of the data.

Extraction scope. Extraction scope refers to the specification of how data must be extracted from a projection (which fields), a selection (which records are required), and an aggregation (at what level of granularity) perspective.

Every extraction process can be viewed along these four dimensions. The first SAP BW extractors available for SAP R/3 data mainly supported the full extraction mode in an asynchronous batch pull scenario. Some extractors, like the Logistics Information System (LIS) extractors, did already support delta loads. This was the beginning of an evolutionary development toward supporting today's analytical applications, such as planning with SAP SEM and SAP APO or customer analytics with SAP CRM that require delta extractions, push scenarios, and close-to-real-time updates in the data warehouse. Such applications involve a lot of development work on both sides. SAP R/3 and SAP BW were required and still are required to support as many delta extractions as possible, in order to support synchronous updates of data targets in SAP BW and to support push scenarios. As a general trend in SAP R/3, extractions have steadily moved from dynamic summary tables to transaction tables, and delta change capture mechanisms have become more sophisticated.

The main problem in implementing *delta extraction* lies in identifying the deltas. There are two basic approaches to delta loading: The use of delta queues and the use of timestamps. In many cases the timestamp approach is used, simply because it is easier to implement; often the timestamp is not stored in the transaction itself but is logged in some external table. Using timestamps usually leaves a gap in time between the timestamp being logged and the transaction being updated, however. Hence, some documents may be missed if they have not yet been committed to the database. To mitigate this risk, SAP often uses a "safety delta" concept, setting back a user's timestamp selection for a few hours to avoid missing late updates.

A more expensive but guaranteed delta mechanism is the use of delta queues, as used in the SAP R/3 logistics extractors. A delta queue is similar to logs written by database management systems in their attempt to ensure consistent data even after serious system failures. Delta queues essentially are tables capturing the key values of changed or inserted records or the entire transaction records. The SAP implementation of delta queues actually tracks before and after images of changed data records, allowing you to identify and to track every single change of a field value.

Other than the timestamp approach, the delta queue technology does not require any safety delta regardless of the extraction frequency. Another difference between the delta queue and the timestamp techniques is that the timestamp technique only captures the version actually stored in the database at extraction time. For low-frequency extraction (e.g., once a month), intermediate versions of the document are missed and cannot be made available in SAP BW.

NOTE ALE change pointers also use a delta queue approach. ALE tracks the keys of all changed data records in a separate table. While avoiding the safety delta problem, ALE change pointers are only designed to deliver the latest version of a data record and do not allow you to identify changes on a field level. The ALE pointer approach is used for some master data extractors in SAP R/3.

Another complexity in delta extraction, common to both techniques, is capturing changes in interdependent database tables. For example, you might want to indicate a change to a customer master data record when only the address details stored in a different database table have changed. Or perhaps a set of line-item-level documents must be reextracted because of changes applied to the header document. An additional challenge for managing delta extractions is when multiple systems extract data at different times using different selection criteria. Each of these systems expects a different delta data set depending on when the last delta data set has been extracted and on the selection criteria used. Many extraction programs available for the BW Service API support those individual deltas for multiple target systems.

Examples of both push and pull extraction scenarios with various data latencies can be found in today's SAP applications:

- A real-time extractor for SEM Business Consolidation (SEM BCS) that synchronously pushes data into an InfoCube. Inter-unit eliminations are performed on the fly.
- A business transaction event in SAP R/3 calls an SAP Advanced Planner and Optimizer (SAP APO) process interface to synchronously update SAP APO (push scenario).
- The sales order extractor of the SAP R/3 logistics extraction cockpit is available for periodically pulling sales orders.
- List reports downloading data to flat files, which in turn are pulled into SAP BW.

Currently synchronous push scenarios are not fully supported by SAP BW. While it is possible to synchronously update data into a transactional InfoCube or ODS object (see SEM BCS and SAP APO examples in the preceding list), this update is always performed as a direct update and bypasses the regular staging process. These updates neither apply transfer rules and update rules, nor do they run under the control of the SAP BW monitor.

Push technology usually goes hand in hand with delta updates, while pull is used for full and delta extraction mode. Currently, the most pervasive technique in BW for real-time reporting is via the use of remote InfoCubes utilizing extraction technology. The single biggest issue with this approach is performance, which can be mitigated through the use of MultiProviders. However, when real-time line-item data is needed; asynchronous extraction still is the way to go. The need for real-time data in, for example, web log analysis has increased the demand for push scenarios, so we can expect to see more push-type extractors in future versions of SAP BW and the Business Content.

While the available extractors for SAP R/3 allow dynamic specification of selection (defined in the InfoPackage used to schedule the load process) and projection criteria (defined by the transfer structure) criteria, only a few are suitable for a dynamic specification of the aggregation level. For asynchronous extractions, you can usually compensate for this by actually aggregating data in SAP BW instead of doing so in the source system. For synchronous extraction through remote InfoCubes, however, this is not possible.

OLTP Technology Considerations

The technology used to capture and read data independent of the application poses its own challenges to the data warehouse developer, since the data models and the storage technology chosen are optimized for use in OTLP environments typically with short read and write transactions, pulling the database performance requirements into two diametrically opposite directions. In this section, we'll take a closer look at how data is inserted and updated in an OLTP system, how the data is read, and what the important technical implications are. Again, this section showcases approaches used in SAP R/3 to illustrate basic principles of modern ERP and legacy systems.

Physical Updates

Data is updated in SAP R/3 in two different ways: synchronously and asynchronously. Synchronous updates are performed by the application itself, while the user is waiting for his or her transaction to come back. Asynchronous transactions usually are committed near-real-time, without the user having to wait for the update to complete; these updates are termed V1 or V2 updates in SAP R/3. V1 denotes time-critical updates used for updating the actual transaction tables. V2 denotes non-time-critical updates used for updating statistics tables related to the transaction tables. For instance, after a sales order entry transaction is completed, the corresponding sales order tables would be updated in V1 mode, and the corresponding statistics tables would be updated in V2 mode. The longer the task queues, the longer the updates will take. Depending on system load, the physical update may take anywhere from a more or less immediate update to a couple of minutes.

From a data warehousing perspective, there are two fundamental ways data is written to database tables in operational systems: with a delta change capture mechanism and without. As discussed, the coverage of delta change capture mechanisms in SAP R/3 is growing. Both basic delta capturing mechanisms have been implemented in SAP R/3 updates in several variants: timestamps and delta queues.

Before SAP BW was introduced, there was already a growing need to split R/3 into several instances while still having data flowing between these instances. The business framework concept was developed where the original vision was to decouple all the applications and have them talk via ALE (we'll discuss ALE in detail coming up in this chapter). Workflow also worked off of this technology to allow for alerts or notifications or to pass onto another link in the transactional supply chain. Even before ALE was introduced, a change log technology existed for audit purposes. BW leveraged this technology, and some of the early master data delta extractors used ALE change pointers to determine the delta. This wasn't enough, so other BW-specific techniques were developed. The first delta extraction technique in LIS involved two additional tables that toggled each other for the extraction of delta records. This was replaced by the delta queue technology supplemented by an additional V3 update mode that is similar to the V2 update mode. The main difference is that V2 updates are always triggered by applications, while V3 updates may be scheduled independently. Many extraction programs available for mySAP.com applications today use the delta queue technology to identify deltas.

Another option of capturing deltas is provided by the Business Add-in (BADI) technology. Essentially, BADIs are an evolution of the familiar customer exits, allowing you to hook customer-specific code into the standard application. BADIs can be used in various ways; often they are used for application-specific updating. More explicitly, business transaction events (BTE) allow hijacking the process and having it perform custom logic synchronously or asynchronously. BADIs technologically pave the road for real-time updates of SAP BW systems. However, as discussed, there are some restrictions for real-time updates of an SAP BW system as of release 3.0. A more complete support for real-time data warehousing is planned for the next release of SAP BW.

Volatile Documents

Every business transaction in SAP R/3 goes through a life cycle; it has an active phase and an inactive phase. During the active phase, a document can be continually updated with new or changed information, and any of these changes may have to be promoted to SAP BW. One of the more common examples of volatile business documents is status management; some SAP R/3 transactions (e.g., sales orders) track document statuses during its life cycle. Examples include but are not limited to *CREATED, OPEN, RELEASED, COSTED, CLOSED, BLOCKED*, and *TECHNICALLY COMPLETE*. These statuses in turn control what actions can be performed on a document, actions that may be relevant for reporting and analysis, such as the settling of costs to an internal order.

Similarly, subsequent data flows may be tied to a business document. For example, in the procure-to-pay business process flow, you might need to check the cycle time between order and delivery for evaluating a vendor. An active purchase order schedule line document is usually updated with the goods receipt date. In accounts receivable a clerk might extend the grace period for a good customer on a specific payment who requests it. This change in payment date recalibrates all the dates and affects aging analysis.

Understanding the volatility of data is important for developing the SAP BW information model (e.g., in an ODS object that supports overwrites) and when to archive the data in SAP R/3. After a business document becomes inactive it goes stale. Data about inactive documents only needs to be loaded once into SAP BW and is typically used for historical trend analysis. In some applications, the active and inactive thresholds are clearly defined. For example, when a document clears in accounts receivable and accounts payable, the information is deleted from one table and inserted into another (BSID to BSAD and BSIK to BSAK, respectively). In documents with status management there are statuses (like TECO, for technically complete) indicating that the document can no longer be changed.

Other documents in the system have a long life cycle, such as contracts in purchasing or outline agreements in sales. Some documents may have an indeterminate life, like a long-standing internal order for specialty requests and its corresponding costs.

Reading Data

There have been third-party attempts to connect to SAP's database directly without going through the application layer. Although it's true that many of the database tables SAP R/3 uses for storing data are directly available, there still are a couple of intricacies involved. First of all, just reading those tables completely ignores business logic that may have to be applied as part of the extraction process to provide meaningful data. Then there are some technical intricacies, such as the application server buffering data and locking data records above the database level. Handling these problems requires an intimate understanding of the technical details of the business processes involved and requires the functionality of the SAP Web Application Server.

Even when data is committed to the database, it may not actually be stored in an easily accessible database table. SAP uses a number of table concepts that you should be aware of. Some of these concepts deal with how data is technically stored (*transparent tables, database clusters, pooled tables*), while others deal with how information is presented (*logical databases, database views*).

Transparent tables. Transparent tables are ABAP dictionary tables that have a one-to-one relationship with database tables stored in the underlying database management system.

Database views. These are views in the ABAP dictionary that joins tables for data selection purposes.

Pooled tables. In earlier days, SAP R/3 needed more tables than the underlying database management systems would allow and had to group tables together in pooled tables. In other words, table definitions are in SAP that act and behave as transparent tables, but on the database no single corresponding physical table exists. Technically, these pooled tables had the table name as its key, and the data would be saved as a long raw string in a field in the database. When a pooled table is read, the data is parsed back into the data structure of the SAP table it is supposed to represent.

Cluster tables. SAP uses cluster tables, which are similar to pooled tables. The main difference is that in cluster tables, complex data objects in program memory can be saved to a cluster without any flattening operations (as would be necessary if this data had to be committed to a transparent table). Technically, data in clusters is saved as raw strings. Because of the requisite parsing and flattening transformations needed to read these tables, performance can be an issue. Many HR payroll tables are defined as cluster tables.

Logical databases. This is a hierarchy of reporting structures that are populated with values via an ABAP program. The structures in the hierarchy may or may not represent actual tables. Logical databases are popular for reporting because developers who program against its structures do not have to invest any development time into designing the data retrieval to the actual tables. In R/3, logical databases are a popular reporting structure for classic InfoSets (classic InfoSets are similar to SAP BW InfoSets introduced in Chapter 3, but differ in that they are not specifically designed for use with the SAP BW Meta Data Repository).

SAP Source Systems

Starting with the type of source system most frequently used for loading data into an SAP BW system, the SAP type source systems, in the next several paragraphs, we'll discuss the specific details of all available types of source systems and interfaces. We'll begin with a generic architectural overview of the three different subtypes of SAP source systems (R/3 up to 3.0d, R/3 after 3.0d, and SAP BW), as there are no serious technological distinctions between those.

Architecture

Figure 6.3 provides a detailed view of the extraction architecture. The BW Service API handles both meta data exchange and data extraction for SAP systems. It is composed of numerous smaller components not described here in full detail; the most relevant are meta data maintenance and transfer, data extraction and transfer, and the request dispatcher. Meta data maintenance and transfer is called by SAP BW to return a selected set of meta data mainly consisting of the DataSource fields and to propagate the transfer structure as defined in SAP BW to the source system, where appropriate dictionary structures and data transfer programs are generated automatically. The request dispatcher is built on top of ALE technology and is called by the ALE layer when a data load request arrives at the source system. It checks the request for consistency and correctness before passing it on to data extraction and transfer. This component in turn calls the appropriate extraction program, which extracts data from the corresponding database tables and sends both data packages and status information back to the calling SAP BW system.

The BW Service API lets you extract data from mySAP.com application components like SAP R/3, SAP CRM, SAP BW, and SAP SEM systems. While it is already integrated into some components, it needs to be installed separately on SAP R/3 systems as part of a plug-in that already includes all predefined extraction programs. Please note that the BW Service API also allows you to connect an SAP BW system to itself, allowing you to extract data from its own InfoCubes, ODS objects, and master data tables. This feature is sometimes used to set up multilevel staging scenarios within one single SAP BW system.

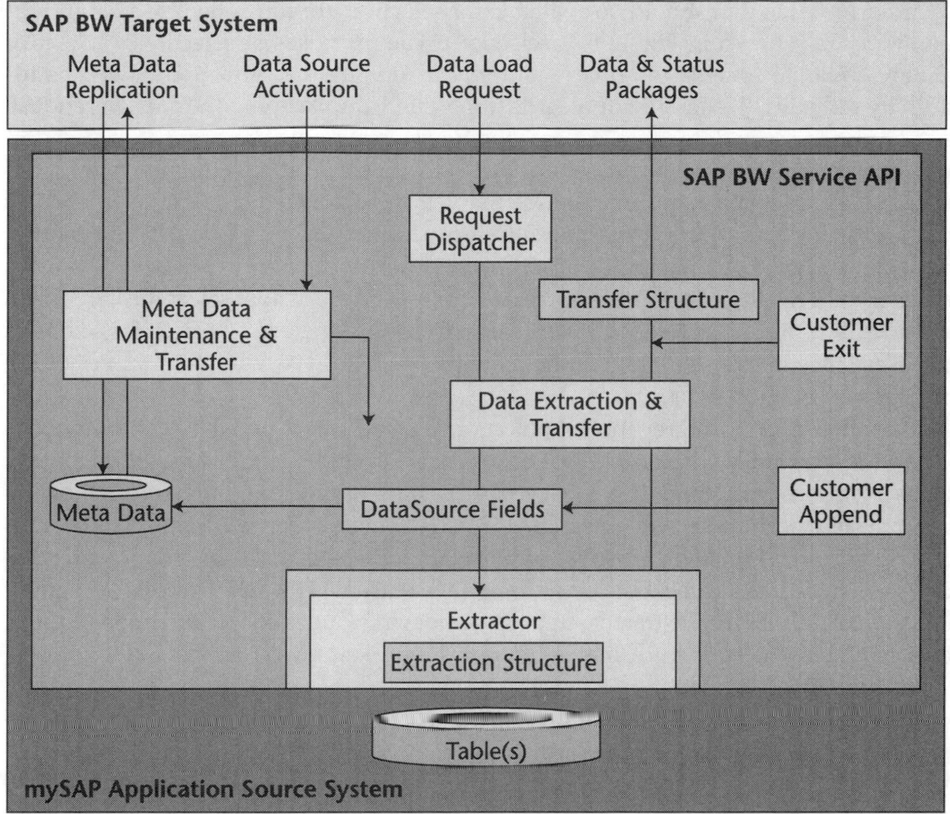

Figure 6.3 SAP R/3 extraction architecture.

Meta Data Flow

The extraction structures used by extraction programs, and eventually customer extensions to those extraction structures, basically determine the SAP R/3 source system meta data. They describe fields in which technical format are available through the extraction programs. This information is used as a basis for defining the fields of the DataSources in the DataSource maintenance dialog. Fields available in the extraction structure can be hidden as shown in Figure 6.4, effectively defining a projection of the extraction structure to the fields of the DataSources. An application example for such a projection can be found in the public sector Business Content, which extends CO DataSources by *grant*, *functional area*, and *fund*. These fields are not projected unless explicitly defined.

Similarly, fields that should be available for selection are controlled by a configuration switch, as shown in Figure 6.4 (selection). The purposes of selecting a subset of data are obviously saving resources required for running the extraction, saving bandwidth by reducing the amount of records transferred, and keeping the data warehouse clear of unnecessary data. Business reasons for selecting data are again showcased in the Business Content. In many cases an SAP BW implementation is run in waves, with increasing functionality and scope implemented in each wave. For example, the CO DataSource for actual line items partially replaced the CCA DataSource for loading actual data. The CCA DataSource is still needed for other value types (such as plan), however. As a result, if both DataSources are to be used, you must select the value type for the CCA totals extractor. The main reason to control the use of a field for selection purposes is technical; selections on fields without any index may result in very long run times for extraction programs.

As a rule of thumb, aggregation should normally be performed in SAP BW at query execution time, not by the source system at extraction time, since aggregation always means losing information. The most granular data should be extracted out of the source system and made available in SAP BW. However, whenever remote InfoCubes are defined directly using an SAP source system extractor, this extractor should support extraction time aggregation for performance reasons. The direct access flag shown in Figure 6.4 defines if an extractor supports remote InfoCubes and aggregation (2), supports remote InfoCubes but does not support aggregation (1), or does not support remote InfoCubes at all (0).

Most Business Content? DataSources (in particular, line-item delta extractors) do not support aggregation for remote InfoCubes (although many support remote InfoCubes). DataSources typically are defined with a fixed level of aggregation as implemented in the extraction program; this may be a very granular level, as in the CO *Actual Costs* DataSource, or at an aggregated level, as in CO *Costs and allocations*.

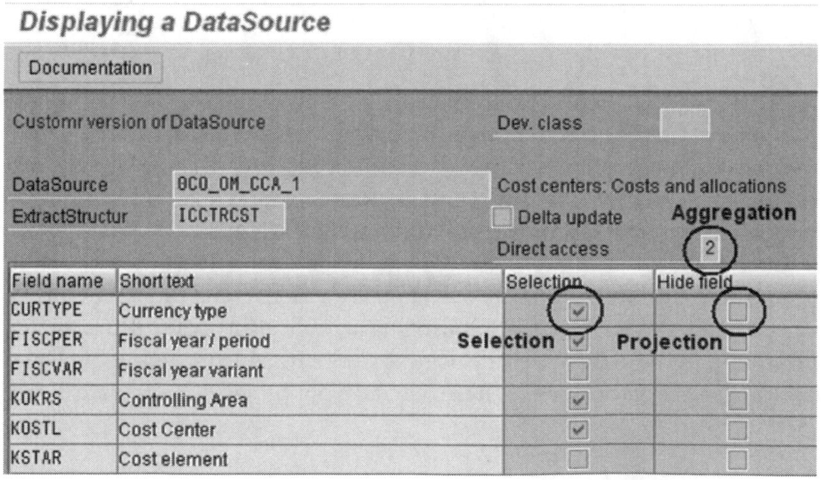

Field name	Short text	Selection	Hide field
CURTYPE	Currency type	✓	
FISCPER	Fiscal year / period	✓	
FISCVAR	Fiscal year variant		
KOKRS	Controlling Area	✓	
KOSTL	Cost Center	✓	
KSTAR	Cost element		

Figure 6.4 DataSource maintenance in SAP source systems.

Most of the extraction programs available in the Business Content have been developed by the same development team that originally developed the application itself, since the members of those teams are the most familiar not only with the typical business requirements but also with the technical details of the specific implementation of each application area. As a result, different extractors use different implementation approaches, sometimes even incorporating complex transformation rules. However, they all adhere to the same technical standards set by the BW Service API.

Once the required DataSources have been identified (if available in the Business Content), enhanced from the Business Content, or specifically implemented by the client, the next step is to make these meta data available to SAP BW. As shown in Figure 6.3, SAP BW calls the BW Service API of the SAP source system to retrieve either the complete set of meta data available or to update meta data for a specific DataSource—a procedure called *meta data replication*. Based on the DataSource definition, transformation rules are defined (discussed later in the chapter), and a resulting transfer structure containing all fields required to perform the transformation is propagated to the SAP source system by calling the BW Service API. The transfer structure is composed of a subset of fields available in the DataSource and is used as the technical structure for transferring data from the source system to SAP BW. Definition and propagation of the transfer structure complete the setup of a DataSource for a specific source system and allow for actually extracting data.

Data and Control Flow

To support fail-safe extraction and data transfer and to support detailed monitoring, SAP BW uses the *Application Link Enabling* (ALE) technology originally designed to support exchanging data between distributed but integrated SAP R/3 systems. ALE is composed of communication, distribution, and application services and provides all seven networking layers specified in the ISO-OSI reference model (ISO Basic Reference Model for Open Systems Interconnection, www.iso.org): physical layer, data link layer, network layer, transport layer, session layer, presentation layer, and application layer. It is the last, topmost layer, the application layer, which we will discuss further in this section, where SAP BW will be the application.

ALE exchanges messages or data between two systems by way of *Intermediate Documents* (or IDocs). An IDoc is a container for passing data between systems via ALE. The different types of messages and the related types of IDoc basically define the language spoken between two different systems using the ALE technology. SAP BW automatically performs all necessary customizing required for setting up the IDoc infrastructure on the SAP BW side and—by calling the BW Service API—on the SAP source system side. Three types of message are used in the communication protocol between SAP BW and an SAP source system:

Request IDocs. When an InfoPackage is executed, a data load request is created and sent to an SAP source system as an outbound IDoc (see Figure 6.5). This IDoc is processed by ALE and passed on to the IDoc dispatcher, where it is checked for consistency and correctness. The request IDoc is tied to message type *RSRQST* and contains the following information:

- Technical details about the request such as a unique request identifier, DataSource, type of DataSource (transaction data, master data attributes, texts, or hierarchies), who scheduled it, and when (date and time).
- Data selection criteria as defined in the InfoPackage.
- The data transfer mode; ALE/IDoc or transactional remote function calls (tRFC).
- The update mode (or extraction mode); possible modes include transfer of all requested data, transfer of the deltas since the last request, transfer of an opening balance for noncumulative values, repetition of the transfer of a data packet, or initialization of the delta transfer.

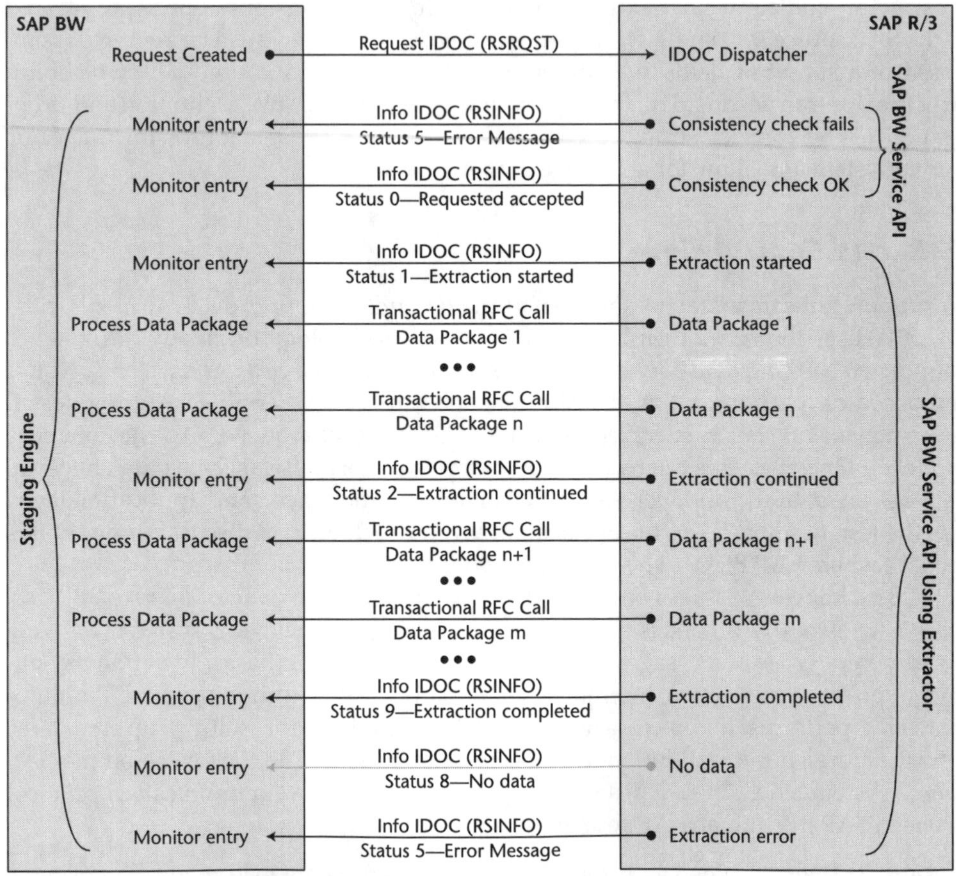

Figure 6.5 Data and control flow for SAP source systems.
Based on copyrighted material from SAP AG

Status IDocs. The status of every step in the extraction and data transfer process is logged by the source system by sending status IDocs to SAP BW. The status communicated in the status IDocs is used to update the SAP BW monitor. Figure 6.5 shows the different status IDocs an SAP source system may send. Status IDocs are tied to message type *RSINFO* and contain the following information:

- Technical details about the extraction such as the unique request identifier, extraction date, and extraction time.
- The current status (informational, warning, error) as depicted in the following, including a more detailed error message describing the error (only if available).

Data IDocs. Data IDocs are used to pass extracted data in the transfer structure format back to SAP BW. Depending on the size of the extracted set of data, the data set may be split into several data packages (and usually will be for transaction data and larger master data extractions). Status IDocs are sent after a certain customizable number of data packages to keep the monitor up-to-date when extracting large sets of data. Data IDocs are tied to message type *RSSEND* and contain the following information:

- Technical details about the request such as a unique request identifier, the data packet identifier, the DataSource, type of DataSource (transaction data, master data attributes, texts, or hierarchies) who scheduled it and when (date and time).
- All the data records in the data package in the format of the transfer structure.

Transactional remote function calls. SAP BW supports two load options, based on different layers of the ALE technology. Data can be transferred using Data IDocs as described in the preceding text or using tRFCs, effectively replacing the Data IDoc transfer (and only the Data IDoc transfer) by a function call but still adhering to the same communication protocol. Which alternative to use is controlled in the transfer rules definition dialog of the SAP BW system. Both options warrant safe asynchronous data transfer on a single data package level. Because only the tRFC method allows storing data in the PSA and provides a better performance, it is the method of choice for most applications.

Understanding how SAP BW communicates with SAP source systems is relevant for gaining a better understanding of the Data Monitor, and troubleshooting within the monitor is covered in more detail in Chapter 9. Following is a sample step-by-step extraction data and control flow for a successful data extraction:

1. An InfoPackage is scheduled for execution at a specific point of time or for a certain system- or user-defined event.
2. Once the defined point of time is reached, the SAP BW system starts a batch job that sends a request IDoc to the SAP source system.

3. The request IDoc arrives in the source system and is processed by the IDoc dispatcher, which calls the BW Service API to process the request.
4. The BW Service API checks the request for technical consistency. Possible error conditions include specification of DataSources unavailable in the source system and changes in the DataSource setup or the extraction process that have not yet been replicated to the SAP BW system.
5. The BW Service API calls the extractor in initialization mode to allow for extractor-specific initializations before actually starting the extraction process. The generic extractor, for example, opens an SQL cursor based on the specified DataSource and selection criteria.
6. The BW Service API calls the extractor in extraction mode. One data package per call is returned to the BW Service API, and customer exits are called for possible enhancements. Finally the data package is sent back to the requesting SAP BW system according to the transfer mode selected (IDoc or tRFC). The extractor takes care of splitting the complete result set into data packages according to the IDoc control parameters. The BW Service API continues to call the extractor until no more data can be fetched.
7. The BW Service API finally sends a final status IDoc notifying the SAP BW system that request processing has finished (successfully or with errors specified in the status IDoc).

NOTE Control parameters specify the frequency of intermediate status IDocs, the maximum size (either in kilobytes or number of lines) of each individual data package, the maximum number of parallel processes for data transfer, and the name of the application server to run the extraction process on.

Example of an Application Specific Extractor

Many of the extractors found in mySAP.com application components are complex, application-specific programs implicitly taking the underlying business logic into account. An example is the new logistics extractor, which is shown in Figure 6.6 extracting transaction data from SAP logistics applications. Note that this is just one example of a real SAP extractor. Extractors for other business areas may and do use a different approach in extracting full and delta data sets.

Sales orders entered in the SAP R/3 SD application are not only stored in the VBAK and VBAP tables, but also propagated to statistical tables in a separate step, if configured. These tables are used by the logistics extractor to provide delta initializations or full uploads. On the other hand, any changes are written to a delta queue utilizing the V3 update process discussed earlier in the chapter. The delta queue is used by the extractor to provide delta loads. For more details about logistics extraction and the logistics extraction cockpit, refer to the SAP BW area of the SAP Service Marketplace (http://service.sap.com/bw).

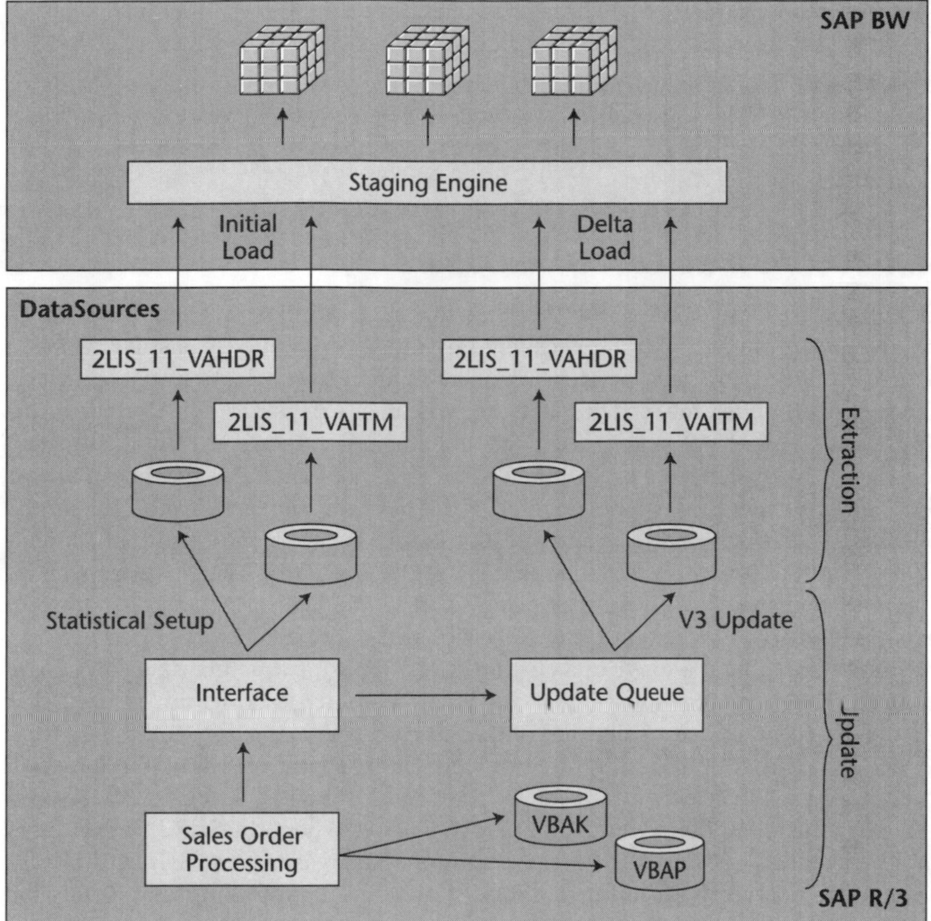

Figure 6.6 Logistics extractions.

Generic Extraction

In many cases DataSources are based on simple database table or view definitions and do nothing else but extract data from this specific table or view using the generic extraction technology. Three types of generic extractors are used by SAP:

Generic database extractors. These programs extract data from database tables and database views. Available for use by customers, generic database extractors are now able to handle delta extraction using the timestamp approach provided there is a timestamp available in the source table or view.

Generic InfoSet extractors. These programs extract data from functional areas (classic InfoSets). This type of generic extraction is available for use by clients.

ABAP Dictionary Domain Value Extractor. Some master data values are built into the ABAP definition of the underlying field instead of being stored in separate database tables. This type of extractor reads the ABAP dictionary to extract those values.

Client-Specific Data Extraction Options

Although the Business Content and the extractors supporting it have reached a significant coverage of the business areas covered by mySAP.com, there are still reasons to enhance existing extractors or develop custom extractors. Such reasons include enhancements for customer-specific data, for customer extensions to SAP data, or for the Business Content not supporting specific information required by the customer. Many client SAP systems are modified in some areas; custom fields have been added to SAP tables, or clients may have developed their own custom applications using the SAP ABAP Workbench. The resulting question is this: What are the options on extracting data from SAP source systems such as SAP R/3 and SAP BW? Depending on availability and coverage of the Business Content and on the kind of data to be extracted, there are several options, laid out in the decision tree in Figure 6.7.

Although it is possible to write a custom ABAP report, extracting data from some dictionary tables and downloading those to a file, which then could be uploaded using the flat-file interface, this is kind of the last resort for extraction technology from an integration and administration point of view. The first and best option to look into is utilizing the SAP extraction technology provided by the BW Service API. We only recommend using the file download approach in cases where the SAP BW extractors cannot be installed on the SAP source system for some reason (e.g., SAP R/3 release out of maintenance, SAP system freeze, lack of resources for installing, and testing the plug-in).

The first thing to check with the SAP BW extractors installed is Business Content availability. In many cases the exact required extraction programs are already available; in other cases, the extractors might provide even more information than required. The first place to go for this check is the Business Content documentation shipped with SAP BW or the SAP Service Marketplace (http://service.sap.com/bw). All Business Content DataSources are viewable via transaction SBIW. Extractors can also be tested and traced with the ABAP debugger from within transaction RSA3. Once a matching extractor is identified, it can be activated and used without further development work.

If not, there may be an extractor available in the Business Content that delivers a subset of the information required and is expandable. Extending an extractor basically means to add additional fields to the DataSource and fill those fields with some custom ABAP code in a customer exit customized in a transaction named CMOD. This custom ABAP code can be anything from some simple calculations or table lookups to complex business logic requiring access to multiple database tables.

Some R/3 applications do not use fixed data structures for extraction but generated ones. These typically require a specific program to be run to generate the DataSource. Some examples are CO-PA operating concerns, classifications master data, Special Ledger, and LIS.

Whenever there's a need to extract data from a single table or from a database view with only inner joins (see Date, 1999) or from a classic InfoSet, generic extraction is the way to go. The generic extraction technology does not distinguish between tables and views; however, Figure 6.7 illustrates all three different options. Before opting for classic InfoSets-based generic extractors, you should evaluate using tables or views. Both provide higher performance and are usually easier to define. The advantages of classic InfoSets are that a classic InfoSet can read logical databases and handle complex and flexible joins (including outer joins and joins on nonkey fields), as well as complex selection logic. Classic InfoSets allow you to use ABAP code for enhancing the results without going through the customer exit. Generic extractors can be defined in the SBIW transaction. Please note that in some cases self-defined extractors based on the generic extraction technology need to be extended in the way described previously and that generic data extraction does not support extracting hierarchies.

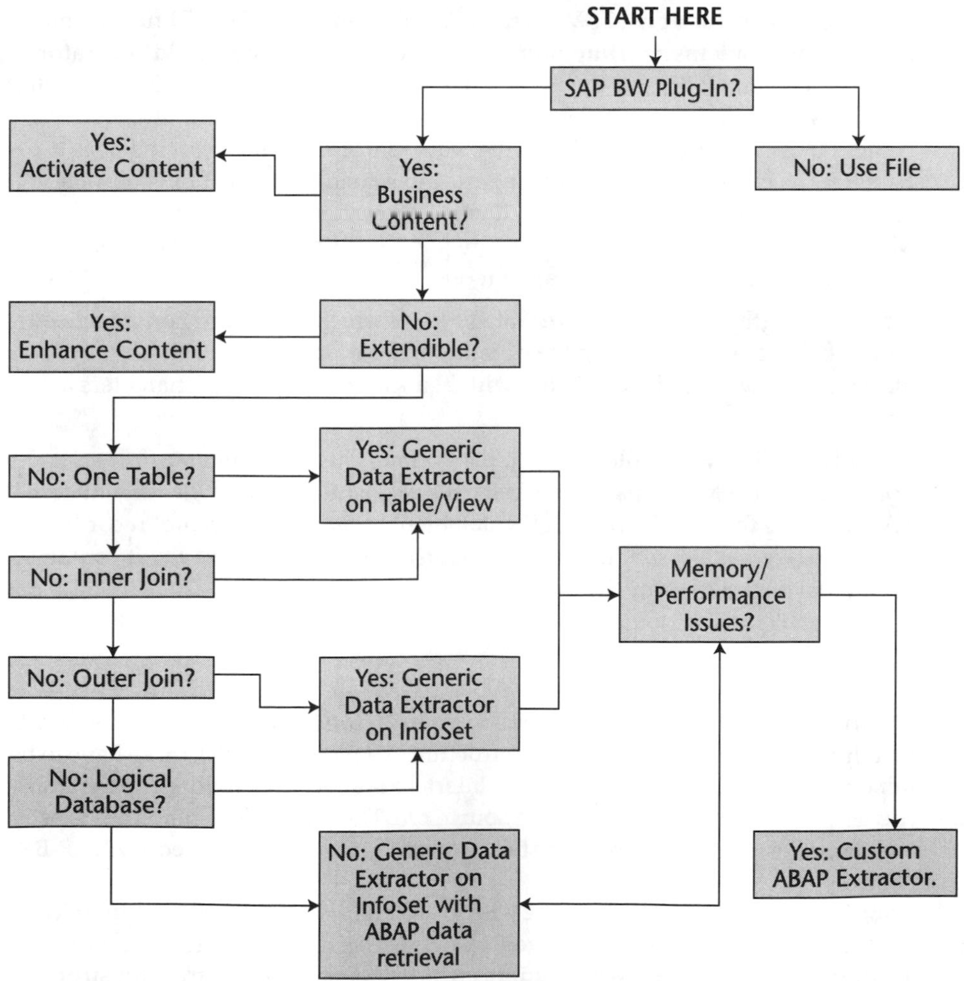

Figure 6.7 Decision tree for extraction methods.

For a detailed discussion of different types of join operations (inner and outer joins), refer to *An Introduction to Database Systems* by C. J. Date, 7th edition, Addison Wesley Longman, 1999.

Recent versions of the SAP R/3 plug-in extend the BW Service API to support custom extraction programs to be implemented. For a detailed description of the interface and the steps required to implement a custom extractor, refer to the SAP Service Marketplace (http://service.sap.com/bw).

The BW Service API and the generic extraction technology are also available in SAP BW systems. SAP BW adds generators generating export DataSources and corresponding extraction programs for a data target (InfoCube, ODS object, or master data table).

Flat-File Interface

The flat-file interface allows loading three different types of flat files into an SAP BW system:

Comma-separated variable (CSV) files. CSV files are simple ASCII files where every record contains a certain number of fields separated by a field separator (usually a comma). Files of this type can be generated by many PC-based applications, such as Microsoft Excel, Microsoft Access, and so forth. In the SAP BW context these files are—in a misleading way—sometimes also referred to as *Excel files* or *Excel CSV files*. The sequence and semantics of the fields of each record must match the definition of the DataSource in the SAP BW system. Missing trailing fields and characters are padded with blanks, and excess characters fields and characters are cut off.

Fixed field length files. These are ASCII files where every record contains fixed-length fields exactly matching the definition of the DataSource. Missing fields at the end of the record are padded with blanks; excess fields or characters are cut off.

Binary files. Binary files allow you to pass numerical data in binary format. For the technical format used for binary files, consult the ABAP documentation. SAP BW uses the ABAP TRANSFER statement to read and interpret records from a binary file. For loading binary files, a *control file* is required that contains additional parameters for the upload.

Architecture

The architecture of the flat-file interface is shown in Figure 6.8. Because there usually is no system providing meta data about the structure of a file to SAP BW, these have to be maintained manually. Meta data for the file interface is effectively reduced to the transfer structure, describing the layout of the source file. The DataSource fields are exactly the same fields as defined in the transfer structure and are maintained by SAP BW internally.

When a data load request is issued by SAP BW, the flat-file interface dynamically generates and executes a flat-file load program, which reads the flat file from the application server or from the client workstation, creates data packages in transfer structure format, and passes these data packages on to the Staging Engine.

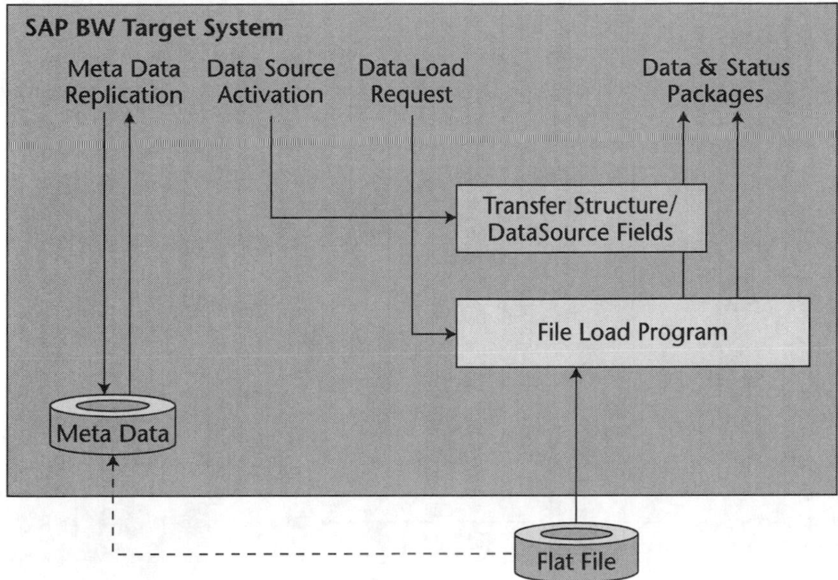

Figure 6.8 Flat-file interface architecture.

Data and Control Flow

The data and control flow protocol for the flat-file interface is essentially the same as for the BW Service API. However, SAP BW does not send any data IDocs; instead, it directly calls a generated transfer program. Figure 6.9 provides an overview of the data and control flow for the flat-file interface. Note that SAP BW does send status IDocs to itself for monitoring purposes.

DB Connect

The DB Connect interface succeeds the DB Link tool as the SAP offering to interface with database systems supported by the SAP application server. The DB Link tool was based on database capabilities to connect to a remote database and has never been a staging interface in its own right but has been hooked into the BW Service API, utilizing the generic extraction technology. While DB Link is still supported for upward-compatibility reasons, the new DB Connect interface provides increased flexibility and access to more diverse database management systems.

Architecture

The basic idea behind the DB Connect interface is to install the client software of the database management system that needs to be accessed (such as Oracle or SQL Server) on the SAP BW application server accessing it, thus making the database visible to the application server and to SAP BW. You would then use it in the same way other SAP

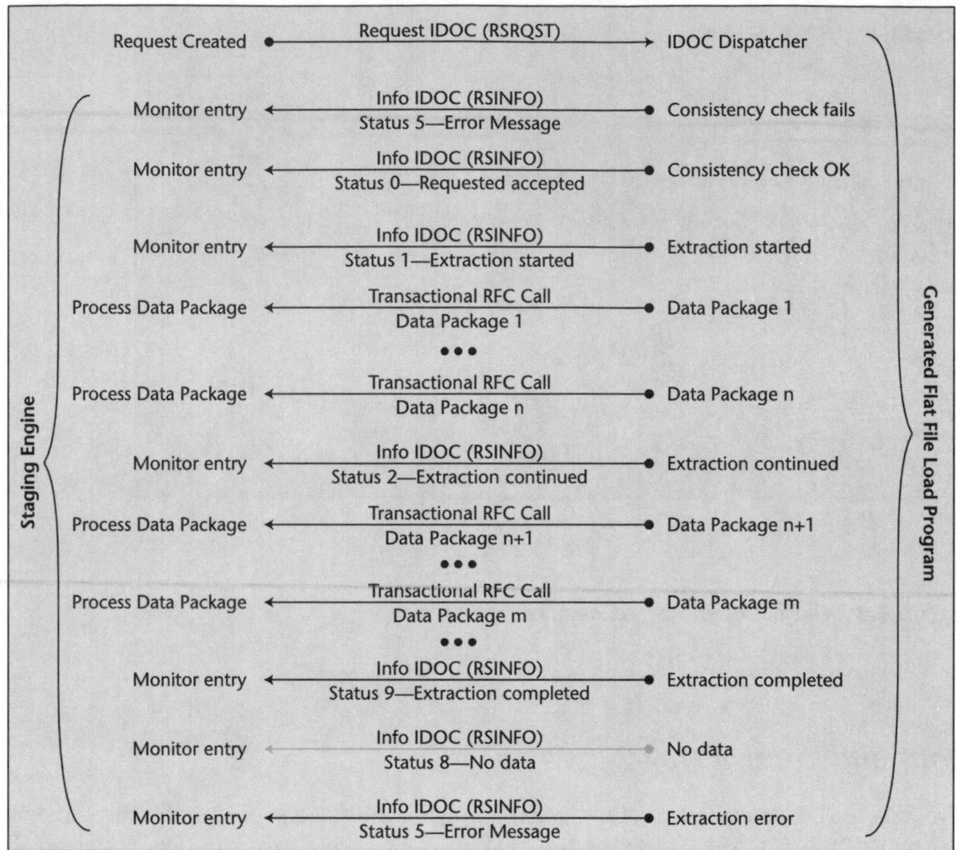

Figure 6.9 Data and control flow for the flat-file interface.
Based on copyrighted material from SAP AG

systems use it—as a bridge between SAP and the database management system. The DB Connect interface supports all databases that are supported by mySAP.com technology. Access to external databases is not restricted to the database management system that is used for running SAP BW. An SAP BW system running on Oracle would still be able to use the DB Connect interface to access a Microsoft SQL Server database on a Microsoft Windows server. Figure 6.10 shows the DB Connect Interface architecture.

Defining a DataSource for a DB Connect source system follows similar steps as defining a DataSource for the BW Service API. First, the DB Connect interface retrieves a list of tables and views available from the remote database. After an entry is selected from this list field, information for the selected table or view is retrieved from the database catalog; the selected fields are then used as a basis for generating the DataSource definition, which is stored in the Meta Data Repository. After that you can assign the generated DataSource to an InfoSource, create a transfer structure, and defined transfer rules just as you would do for any other DataSource. The fields of the transfer structure are then used to actually extract data from the remote database table or view.

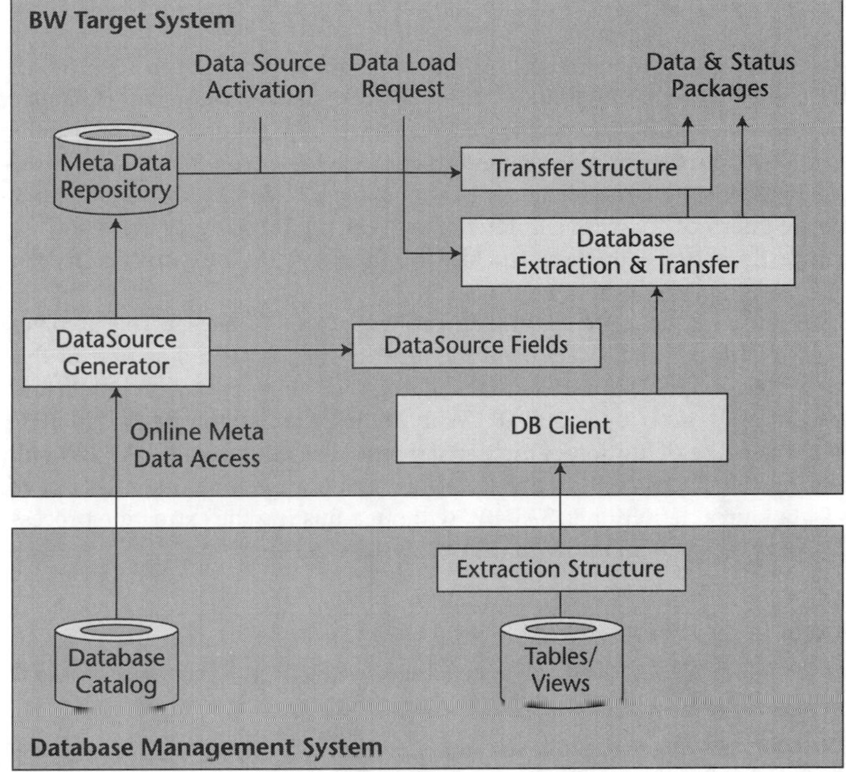

Figure 6.10 DB Connect interface architecture.

Data and Control Flow

The data and control flow of the DB Connect Interface is very similar to the data and control flow for the flat-file interface.

Staging BAPI

The Staging Business Application Programming Interface, or Staging BAPI, is an open interface for meta data and data exchange between SAP BW and third-party systems. The Staging BAPI has mainly been used by ETL tool vendors to provide SAP BW clients access to a wide range of database management systems, file formats, and applications. Some customers are using the Staging BAPI to connect their own custom data extraction programs to SAP BW.

Architecture

The Staging BAPI utilizes the BAPI framework that comes with the Web Application Server to provide an official, stable API for data and meta data exchange. For detailed information about this API and a sample application implemented in Visual Basic, refer to the SAP Service Marketplace.

A high-level overview of the Staging BAPI architecture is provided in Figure 6.11. Since release 2.0 the Staging BAPI provides complete meta data exchange functionality, allowing not only to read InfoSource meta data (as in SAP BW release 1.2) but also the ability to create DataSources, InfoObjects, and InfoCubes. However, the transfer structure and the transfer rules still remain under control of the SAP BW system. In the same way as for the file interface, there is no difference between the DataSource fields and the transfer structure; the actual extraction structure is only known to the extraction tool or program.

Staging BAPI source systems are required to implement an RFC server. This involves waiting for SAP BW to remotely call a specific function implemented as part of this RFC server to initiate a data load request, as well as an RFC client extracting data and sending the resulting data set back to SAP BW by calling the Staging BAPI. The RFC client should check if the definition of the transfer structure as stored in SAP BW still matches the technical details of the extraction process, because someone might have changed the DataSource definition in SAP BW without adjusting the extraction process or vice versa. This check is mandatory for ETL tools to be certified.

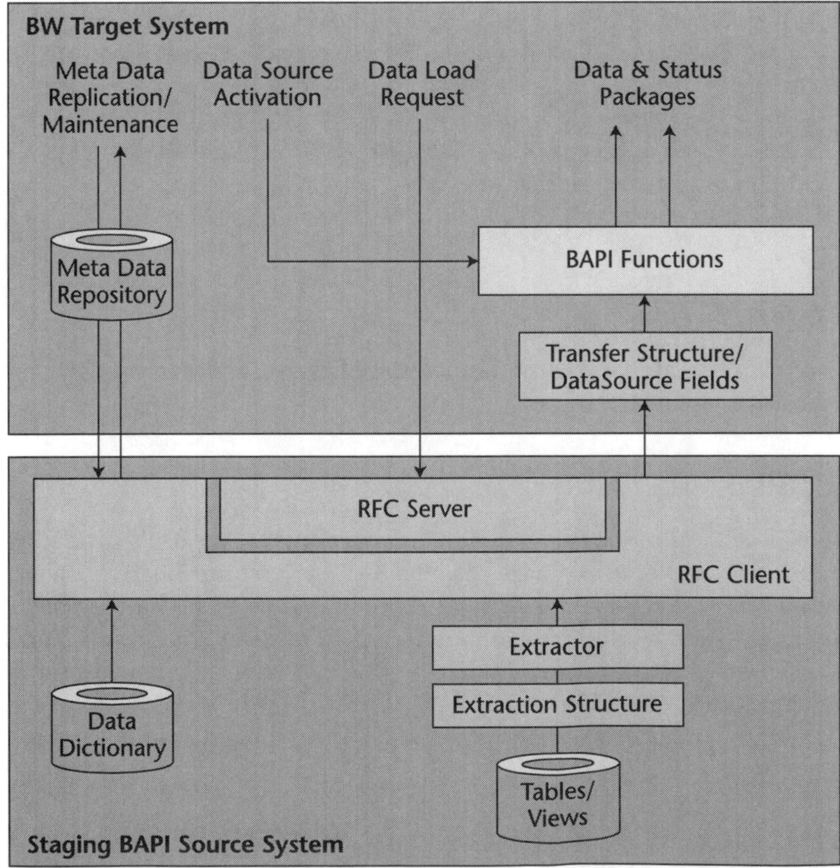

Figure 6.11 Staging BAPI architecture.

Data and Control Flow

Again, the data and control flow of the Staging BAPI is essentially the same as for all interfaces. However, the RFC client software does not need to know about the details of sending IDocs or calling the transfer program. All it needs to know is how to call the BAPI in order to send data and the definition of the transfer structure. The Staging BAPI takes care of all the communication protocol details and ensures monitoring support for data loaded through the Staging BAPI. Figure 6.12 shows the details of the data and control flow when you are using the Staging BAPI.

The SAP BW administrator needs to make sure that the transfer structure defined in SAP BW has the same format as the one provided by the extraction program. Most of the third-party clients do not allow automatically adapting their extraction programs to changes in the SAP BW transfer structure. However, some of the third-party clients do allow to dynamically check if the SAP BW structure still matches the one provided by the extraction process.

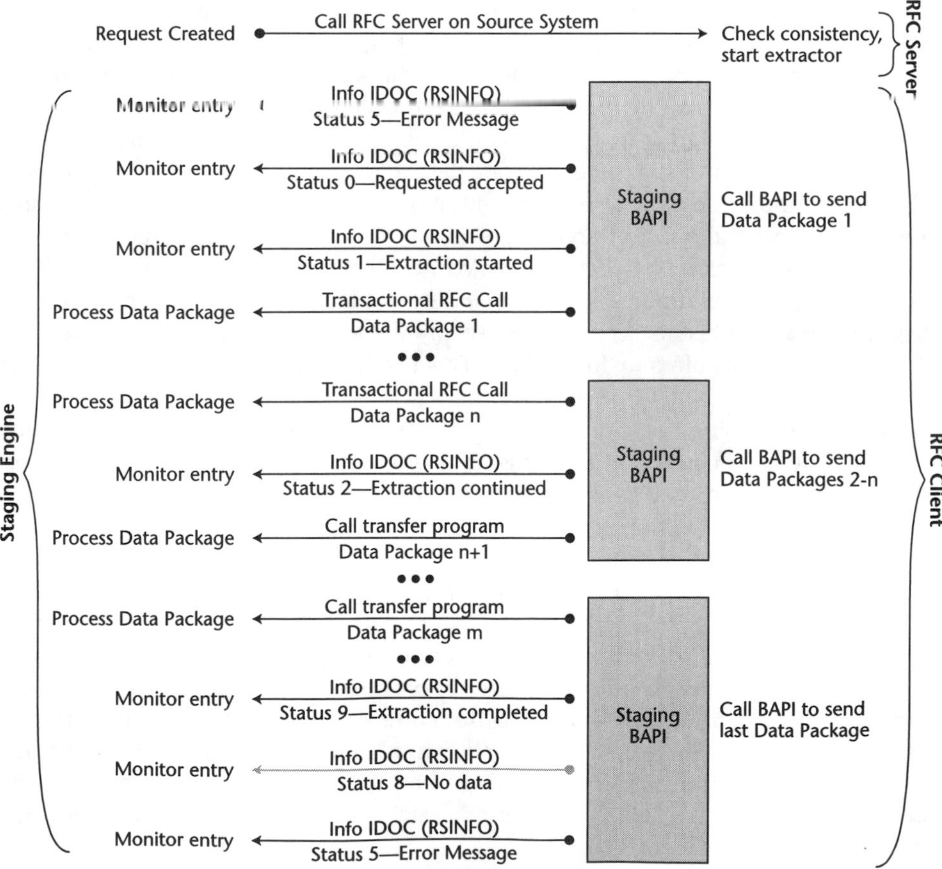

Figure 6.12 Staging BAPI data and control flow.

Ascential DataStage

As mentioned, many of the major ETL tool vendors support the Staging BAPI and allow you to exchange meta data with and transfer data to an SAP BW system. One of these vendors, Ascential Software, stands out, since SAP has signed a strategic partnership agreement with the company to closely integrate their ETL software package named DataStage into the SAP BW offering. The benefit for SAP not only lies in extending its offering by ETL technology but also in extending the reach of the Business Content by jointly providing integrated solutions for ERP and CRM solutions provided by other vendors, such as PeopleSoft, Siebel, and Oracle. This section briefly showcases the use of Ascential DataStage from an extraction technology point of view. More information is available at www.ascentialsoftware.com and in the SAP Service Marketplace.

From a technology point of view, the main advantage of ETL tools such DataStage is that they not only provide access to disparate systems and technologies including mainframe databases and merge their data, they also provide powerful and flexible transformation logic and sometimes even data quality maintenance functionality, all easily defined using graphical user interface designer software.

The need for a robust transformation engine is greater when disparate source systems data must be merged. When you are loading from SAP systems only, this is less of a necessity, since the system is integrated and shares common meta data. For example, for all the applications in SAP R/3, the same checklist is used for plants. In another system there may be an entirely different list of codes for plants. A tool must transform those records in a foreign system into a conformed set of plant codes. Further exacerbating matters, there may be more than one field that has to be considered in the mapping. For example, source systems might have one coding block structure that represents the natural account and responsibility center. SAP would require you to split that coding block into G/L accounts, cost centers, or profit centers, where there may not always be a mapping for each or at different levels of aggregations. For those with experience, the task is daunting, especially without a tool with flexibly defined, easy-to-use, and reusable transformations. This is where Ascential DataStage can add value.

An example of using Ascential DataStage is shown in Figure 6.13. Siebel data and data from an ODBC-connected database are loaded into SAP BW; both DataSources pass through a transformer stage, which performs the actual transformations.

Double-clicking on the transformer stage brings up the transformer stage definition screen. A transformer stage connects inputs (named *Siebel_EIM0* and *CODBCStage5* in our example) to outputs (in this case, *Load_PACK_forBW2* and *Load_PACK_forBW8*) via macros, functions, constants, routines, and transformations. DataStage, of course, allows much more complex transformation scenarios involving multiple inputs, multilevel staging, and multiple outputs; this example only illustrates the core principles.

Single transformations can be selected from a repository of predefined or custom-defined macros, functions, constants, or transformations. Reusing components already implemented makes transforming raw data from disparate sources into high-quality data for data warehousing purposes much easier and reduces the need to actually implement code.

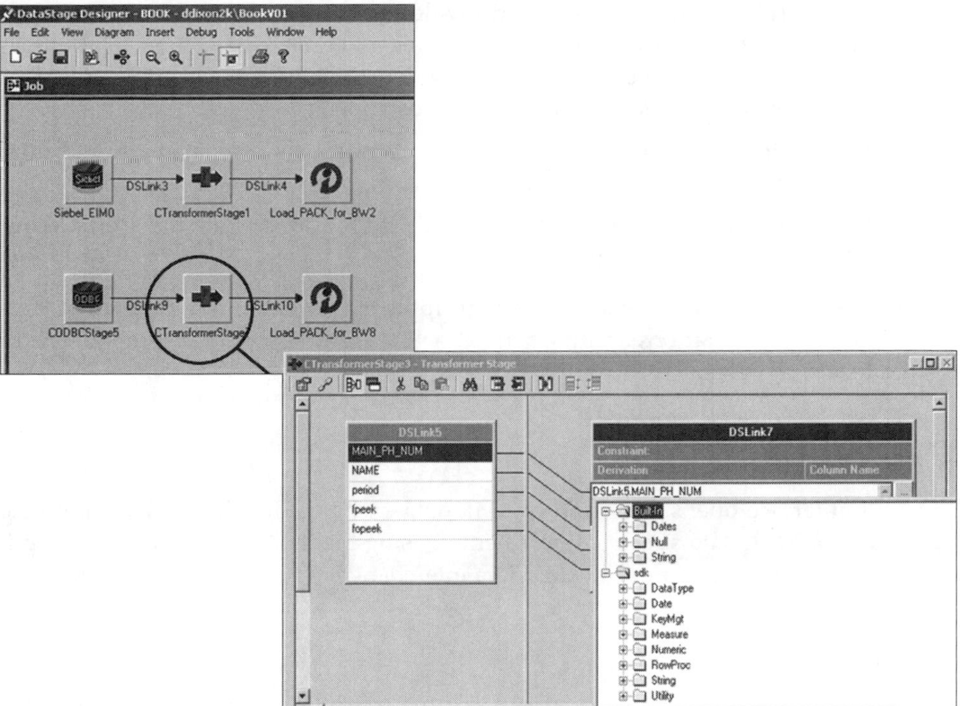

Figure 6.13 Ascential DataStage Designer example.

Ascential DataStage and other third-party ETL tools do not fully replace SAP BW transformations, however. There still is a need for BW transfer rules and update rules. As a rule of thumb, all enterprisewide, business-level transformations, and data cleansing activities should to be defined in SAP BW. All transformations and data cleansing activities specific to a DataSource should be implemented in the ETL tool.

More specifically, five data quality levels have been defined for transformation processes, and a dividing line between levels Q1 and Q2 has been drawn by SAP and Ascential for when to use DataStage and when to use SAP BW for transformations. These data quality levels are defined as follows:

Q0—Source system valid domain analysis. This check is performed by DataStage to validate that existing values in data records correspond to correct values in its domain (or check tables). For example, the gender value for male in the legacy system should have a value of either M or W. In the cases where it is X, DataStage converts the value to an M.

Q1—Completeness and validity. This check is also performed by DataStage to ensure that data is complete and accurate from the local source system perspective. For example, if any values are missing in any fields, DataStage would handle them. If the gender status field is left empty and must be derived, a value of G may be derived in order to ensure completeness of the data.

Q2—Structural integrity. All enterprisewide cleansing and transformations are done by BW transfer rules. For example, male and female have indicators of M and W, which does not conform to the BW domain values of M and F. An SAP BW transfer rule is needed to make this translation.

Q3—Referential integrity. All referential integrity checks and data harmonization are performed in the SAP BW transfer rules.

Q4—Business rules. All business logic routines for application-related InfoMarts are done via SAP BW update rules.

Note that these data quality levels not only apply for Ascential DataStage. In principle, the same considerations apply when extracting from SAP R/3 source systems or custom legacy systems.

XML Interface

The XML interface opens the world of XML data exchange for SAP BW by allowing you to accept XML data streams. Implemented using the SOAP protocol, it is compliant to current open standards for XML data interchange.

Architecture

Shown in Figure 6.14, the XML interface is actually not an interface of the Staging Engine; instead, it utilizes the delta queue technology to accept XML data from external Web services or applications and stores data received in the delta queue associated with the DataSource. The process of transforming the data and updating the associated data targets is performed by having the BW Service API read the delta queue and pass the data to the transformation programs in the same manner as it does for any other SAP source system. Note that while XML data is *pushed* into the delta queue, the actual update process still *pulls* data out of the delta queue. The XML interface is based on the SOAP services integrated into the SAP Web Application Server.

Meta data for XML DataSources need to be maintained manually. The Staging Engine checks incoming XML data records for consistency with the transfer structure defined. The DataSource fields and the transfer structure are identical for XML DataSources; the extraction structure is only known to the Web services or the external application and not relevant to SAP BW.

The XML interface is currently not able to interpret meta data incorporated into the XML data stream and propagate this information to the Meta Data Repository. The DataSource for the XML interface has to be generated based on a DataSource for the file interface. The XML interface is designed for use with relatively small data volume sent online by a Web service. An accompanying file interface DataSource is used for large-volume (full) updates. The XML data streams need to comply with the meta data definition stored in the Meta Data Repository in order to be accepted by SAP BW. A how-to guide for loading XML data is available from the SAP Service Marketplace (http://service.sap.com/bw).

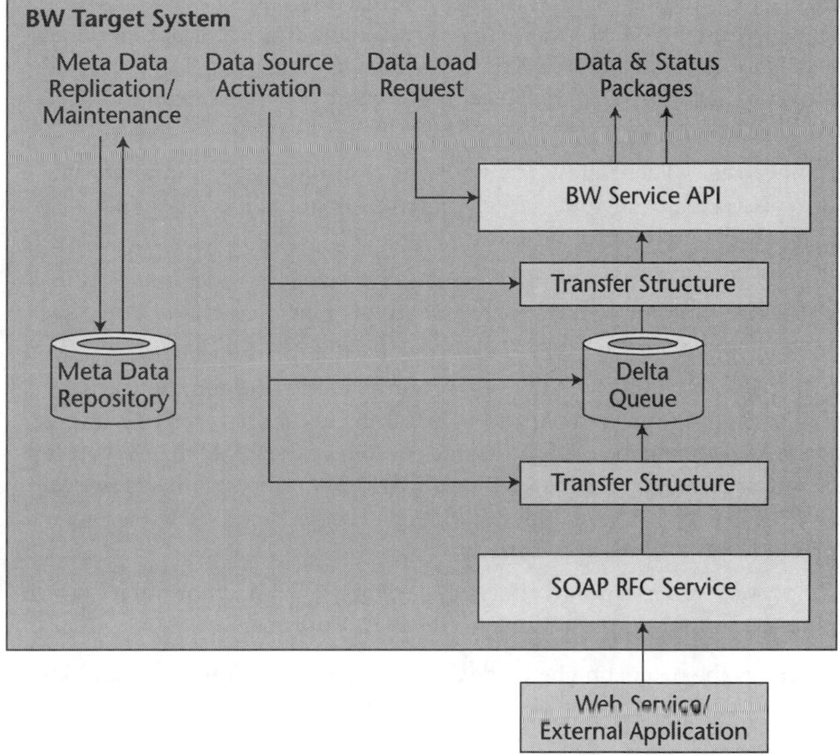

Figure 6.14 XML Interface architecture.

Data and Control Flow

The data and control flow for the XML interface is basically the same as for SAP source systems, as both are using the exact same technology. The data and control flow for pushing data into the delta queue is compliant with the SOAP protocol.

Because easy-to-use SOAP-compliant controls are available for many PC-based development environments such as Microsoft Visual Basic, using the XML interface is also an appropriate way to implement custom solutions for uploading smaller data sets into an SAP BW system.

Closing the Loop

SAP BW provides additional options for extracting data for use in interface programs feeding data streams into operational or analytical applications:

Data Mart interface. From a technical point of view, the data mart interface is nothing more than the BW Service API discussed previously. The Data Mart interface allows building complex SAP BW information logistics models by cascading multiple SAP BW systems, as shown in the functional and regional InfoMart example in Chapter 4. All data targets available in an SAP BW system are at the data mart interface's disposal. However, use of the data mart interface is restricted to SAP BW systems.

Open Hub Services. These allow you to define controlled and monitored data export processes, exporting data target contents into a flat file, a flat data base table, or an application for further processing.

Retractors. These are dedicated ABAP programs *reextracting* data from SAP BW into an SAP R/3 system. Retractors are a relatively new concept and are currently only available for a few applications including SAP CRM.

OLAP BAPI. This is an official API for executing queries and retrieving query results. Custom programs can use the OLAP BAPI to retrieve query results for any purposes. By using the ODBO interface on top of the OLAP BAPI, you can implement front-end applications, accessing SAP BW query results. However, the OLAP BAPI is not recommended for use with large result data sets, since it is optimized for interactive applications.

XML for Analysis. This standard allows generating an XML data stream, which can be hijacked by other applications for their own purposes.

Figure 6.15 shows the distinction between data mart, retraction, and hub-and-spoke information flows and their relationship to the BW architecture.

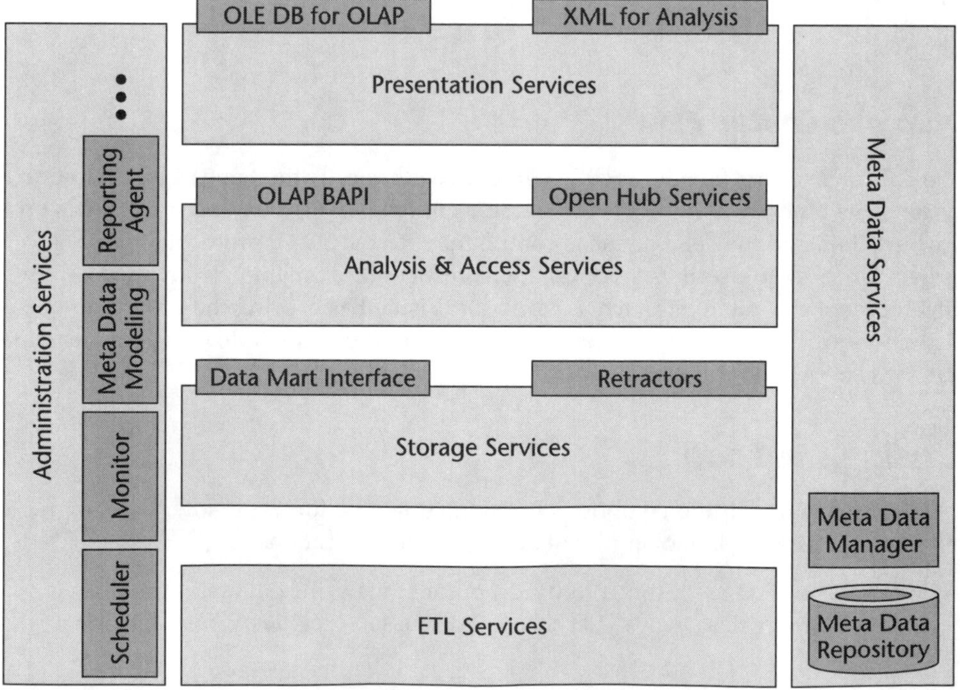

Figure 6.15 Closing the loop with SAP BW.

Transformation

Modern ETL tools and data warehouse solutions have reduced the effort needed to actually implement and test transformations by providing intuitive graphical user interfaces and libraries of predefined transformations. However, most of the time is actually spent designing the transformations from a concept point of view.

How does SAP BW support data warehouse developers when implementing and testing the transformations identified? We begin this section with a short discussion of commonly used transformations in data warehouse applications. Then we dive into the details of the SAP BW staging architecture and the SAP BW transfer and update rules.

Common Transformation Operations

There are two main drivers for implementing transformations on the data warehouse side: data integration and application logic. While *data integration* transformations aim at eliminating technical and semantic differences between data from disparate source systems, *application logic* transformations transform integrated data into an application-specific format optimized for a specific purpose.

Of course, categorizing commonly used transformation operations as we do in the following does not mean that those operations cannot be applied in a meaningful way in other stages of the information supply chain. All of the transformation operations discussed are principally usable at any stage. And there are additional transformations not discussed here in detail that are typically used at other stages, such as low-level technical transformations performed at extraction time (handling different database systems, operating systems, or hardware), as well as the calculation of high-level key performance indicators upon information retrieval or presentation. Transformations in the loading process include generation of surrogate keys—luckily, SAP BW takes care of this task automatically, as we will see later.

The common transformation operations discussed in the following text will be showcased as part of the detailed discussion of transfer and update rules later in this section.

Data Integration Transformations

The most important transformations involved in technical data integration are:

Straight mapping. Although a trivial transformation, straight mapping of two semantically and technically identical source and target fields is listed here for completeness.

Type conversions. Data types used in the operational environment are converted to those used in the data warehouse environment. SAP BW automatically performs compatible type conversions without further notice, while incompatible type conversions usually require the more complex transformations to be applied.

Character set conversions. Character sets used in the operational environment may include Extended Binary Coded Decimal Interchange Code (EBCDIC) character sets used in mainframe systems and different local ASCII character sets (such as LATIN or KANJI) need to be integrated into one single representation in the data warehouse (e.g., Unicode character set).

SAP BW now supports using Unicode character sets and automatically converts incoming data from the source character set to the Unicode character set. Some character set conversions, however, such as EBCDIC to Unicode, still have to be implemented explicitly.

Reformatting. The technical representation of values may need to be reformatted on the way from the source to the target system.

Dates represented as 01/31/2002 or 31.01.2002 may need to be converted to 20020131. Material numbers represented externally as 010-XYZ-9000 need to be reformatted to an internal format like 010XYZ9000. Customer key values may need to be converted from mixed-case "Duck Brothers" to uppercase "DUCK BROTHERS."

Missing values. Sometimes not all source systems are able to provide meaningful data for all required fields. In these cases constant *default values* or values retrieved from *lookup tables* have to be determined.

It is common, for example, for non-SAP source systems to send date information without information about fiscal year variants, since fiscal year variants tend to be an SAP-specific data element.

Unit and currency conversions. Unit and currency conversions are required wherever amount and quantity values need to be stored with a specific unified unit of measure or currency.

Semantic integration. Semantic integration involves converting values to a common standard notation as defined for the data warehouse environment.

The gender of a customer may be represented as M and F in one system and as 0 and 1 in another. SAP R/3 CO uses a value type of 4 for actual values, while LIS uses 10. Many times a single field is mapped to multiple target fields or vice versa. In the purchasing Business Content, for example, the process key 001 is derived from a combination of the LIS event MA and the purchase order category of 1.

Cleansing. More or less complex transformations may be required to make sure data stored in the data warehouse is correct. Cleansing transformations are most important in the data warehouse environment to ensure correctness and completeness of data. Cleansing transformations can range from simple value range checks on a field level to complex sanity checks referring to data packages or the whole extracted data set and may involve extensive table lookups.

Examples of cleansing include checking that the gender of a customer in the input record is always represented as M or F. Invalid values need to be flagged or replaced by meaningful defaults (e.g., determining the most probable gender by analyzing the first name of the customer). A more complex example would be to check consumer sales records reported by mobile devices for plausibility by comparing the reported revenue for every customer with the average revenue and the standard deviation and to flag "suspicious" records.

Referential integrity. Ensuring referential integrity requires checking the existence of referenced data (such as a customer master data record for a customer referenced in a sales order) and eventually creating such a data record using appropriate default values.

Application Logic Transformations

Application logic transformations are driven by business requirements. The most important operations used for this type of transformation are:

Calculations. More complex, high-level key figures may be calculated on the fly during the transformation process. Calculations may or may not require table lookups for reading additional information. In the staging process, calculations are frequently used in combination with aggregations or with other data read on the fly to achieve more comprehensive key figures. Of course, calculations are also daily business in the information retrieval and presentation processes.

Selections. Selections play an important role where only parts of the data available are desired for a certain analytical application, for example, in cases where an InfoMart is set up to serve a specific part of the sales organization.

Projections. Projections (effectively hiding fields) serve the same purpose as selections in that they hide away information that would technically be available.

Aggregation. Aggregation reduces the level of granularity, again reducing the amount of information available. Performance improvements through aggregations, of course, still are one of the most important reasons to aggregate data. However, SAP BW-persistent aggregates could be used for improving performance without losing the possibility to analyze data on the lowest-possible level of granularity.

De-aggregation. De-aggregation distributes aggregated values to a certain range of characteristics values. Yearly sales forecasts, for example, may be distributed to 12 months according to historic seasonal sales patterns to provide monthly forecast values.

Normalization. Normalization is a process where data is mapped from a denormalized into a normalized data model, usually reducing redundancy and sparsity but increasing the flexibility and complexity of the data model. Normalization is used for example, wherever a source system provides data using specific key figures, whereas the information model uses generic key figures. (For a review of specific versus generic key figures, refer to Chapter 4.) Normalization is also used wherever denormalized master or transaction data are provided by a source system and need to be populated into a normalized information model.

Planning applications, for instance, frequently use a record format where 12 key figures in a single record represent one plan value for each month of the planning year. Distribution would generate 12 data records with a year and month characteristic and one single plan key figure. For further information about normalization and various normal forms, refer to *An Introduction to Database Systems* by C. J. Date, 7th edition, Addison Wesley Longman, 1999.

Denormalization. Denormalization is the reverse process of normalization, usually merging several input data records into one output record. This usually increases redundancy and sparsity and decreases complexity but also flexibility of the data model.

Denormalization is used where a small, fixed set of values, for example different versions of costs—say, *actual*, *plan*, and *budget*—are required for reporting. A denormalized information model would use three different key figures to model this.

Reference Objects for Transformations

Another useful classification of transformations is based on the referenced object. Four different categories of transformations can be identified in SAP BW using this approach:

Field-level transformations. These use single fields of single data records as their input; examples are straight mapping, type conversions, or reformatting.

Record level transformations. These use multiple fields of single data records to determine or calculate values. A simple example is price calculation based on revenue and quantity. Other examples of record-level transformations include table lookups and more complex calculations.

Logical unit-level transformations. These use multiple records belonging to a single logical unit, such as multiple line items belonging to a single sales transaction. Logical unit-level transformations are difficult to implement in SAP BW, because extracted data is split into several packages by the extraction programs; data records belonging to a single logical unit may be distributed to several data packages. Aggregation transformations with nontrivial aggregation functions (such as Maximum, Minimum, or counting of different material numbers) are examples of logical unit-level transformations.

Data package level transformations. These use a complete data package. Because data packages have a random content—at least from an SAP BW point of view—these kinds of transformations are rarely useful and are mostly used to optimize the performance of transfer or update rules.

Extraction data set level transformations. These use the complete extracted data set comprising multiple data packages. SAP BW supports extraction data set-level transformations through the persistent staging area API, where programs may read and modify data sets identified by request identifiers.

Full data set level transformations. Rarely used for performance reasons, these transformations may be required for complex sanity checks, for instance, in CRM applications where customer sales transactions may be checked against historic transactions of the same customer or customer group.

Data Transformation in SAP BW

The following sections provide an overview of the data transformation process in SAP BW, including multilevel staging and persistency considerations.

Architecture and Data Flow

SAP BW implements the same distinction between data integration and application logic transformations in its data transformation process: *Transfer rules* connecting multiple source system specific DataSources to a single InfoSource take care of technically integrating data from different source systems in different formats. Transfer rules in SAP BW involve mapping the fields of the DataSource to adequate InfoObjects, applying transformations specifically tied to InfoObjects, and applying transformation rules tied to the InfoSource.

At the other end of the transformation process, *update rules* connect an InfoSource to one or multiple data targets (InfoCubes, ODS objects, and master data tables) and take care of transforming technically integrated data into application-specific formats as defined in the information model. Table 6.1 shows a side-by-side comparison of transfer and update rules.

All transformations in single-staged SAP BW data transformation scenarios are in-memory transformations, as Figure 6.17 illustrates. A data package is passed from one of the staging interfaces discussed previously to the Staging Engine as an in-memory data package stored in an internal table. Up to this point no transformations have been applied; the data still is in transfer structure format. The transfer rules program applies the transfer rules defined, effectively converting the data records into the InfoSource format and passes them on to another generated program, the update rules program.

Table 6.1 Transfer and Update Rules

CHARACTERISTIC	TRANSFER RULE	UPDATE RULE
Focus	Data integration and harmonization	Application Logic
Source	DataSource/Persistent Staging Area	InfoSource
Target	InfoSource	InfoCube/ODS object/master data table

Multiple update rules programs may be called sequentially, one for each data target, with activated update rules selected in the InfoPackage. The update rules program applies the update rules defined for this specific combination of an InfoSource and a data target and converts the resulting data records into a flattened data target format implicitly defined through the data target definition.

A third generated program receives these data records, converts them into the physical data model used for the data target, and loads them into the data target accordingly. More details on this loading process are provided in the next section.

Persistency Considerations

SAP BW allows persistently storing data along the information supply chain in the *persistent staging area* (PSA), also shown in Figure 6.17, without compromising the in-memory transformations by transformations based on persistent data. The persistent staging area stores data in exactly the format of the transfer structure before any of the transformation rules have been applied. Possible applications of the PSA include:

Error handling. Transfer rules allow flagging single data records as being incorrect and logging the cause of this error in the SAP BW monitor. Records flagged as incorrect are separately stored in the PSA for later manual or automated correction and reloading. More details on error handling are provided later in this section and in Chapter 9.

Repeated transformation of raw data. The PSA allows repeatedly performing transformations based on data stored in the PSA without having to re-extract from the source system. Repeated execution of transformation is most useful for tracing and debugging user-defined transformation rules and, in some cases, for populating data targets from scratch. However, we generally recommend using the data warehouse layer for this purpose.

Decoupling extraction and transformation. Some application scenarios involving multiple disparate systems require scheduling multiple extractions at different times, whereas transformations and updates into the data targets have to be performed at one single point of time because of, for instance, system availability or resource availability restrictions in different time zones. Again, we recommend using the data warehouse layer for this purpose whenever possible.

Extraction data set-level transformations. This is a special application of decoupling extraction and transformation, allowing you to perform extraction data set-level transformation of the data stored in the PSA using the PSA API.

Taking into account that the PSA stores operational data in an operational data format, why not use the PSA for modeling the operational data store? First of all, one of the requirements of the ODS is that it allows reporting. The PSA does not directly support reporting; instead, an InfoSet would have to be defined, joining the PSA database tables into one single InfoSet that would be available for reporting purposes in the Business Explorer. However, the names of the PSA database tables are not stable in that they are different on the development, test, and production systems, and every time the transfer structure needs to be changed for some reason, SAP BW will add another table with the new structure to the PSA, causing the InfoSet to be invalid or at least incomplete. Second, the PSA does not *allow* any transformations to be applied, whereas ODS objects do allow transformations.

While the use of error handling and debugging custom transformations is restricted to the PSA, the other two scenarios might as well be implemented using the operational data store built with ODS objects. The main advantage of using ODS objects is the reporting functionality available.

Multilevel Staging Considerations

So far our staging and transformation considerations focused on single-level staging scenarios, where all staging processes end with updating a certain number of data targets. SAP BW, however, allows implementing multilevel staging in the transformation process, as shown in Figure 6.16.

The most important reason for implementing multilevel staging is the implementation of a *data warehouse* layer, as shown in Figure 6.16. The data warehouse layer stores integrated consistent data. Populating the data warehouse layer usually requires complex transfer rules handling all kinds of transformations to harmonize data from different sources and only a little application logic in the update rules, whereas the focus in populating the InfoMart layer off of a harmonized data warehouse layer lies on application logic implemented in the update rules. We discussed the role of the data warehouse layer in SAP BW in more detail in Chapter 4.

A general drawback of multilevel staging in SAP BW is losing the efficiency of in-memory transformations, as Figure 6.17 shows. Every additional level in a multilevel staging scenario requires persistently storing data in a data target and subsequently extracting data from the data target before going to the next staging level.

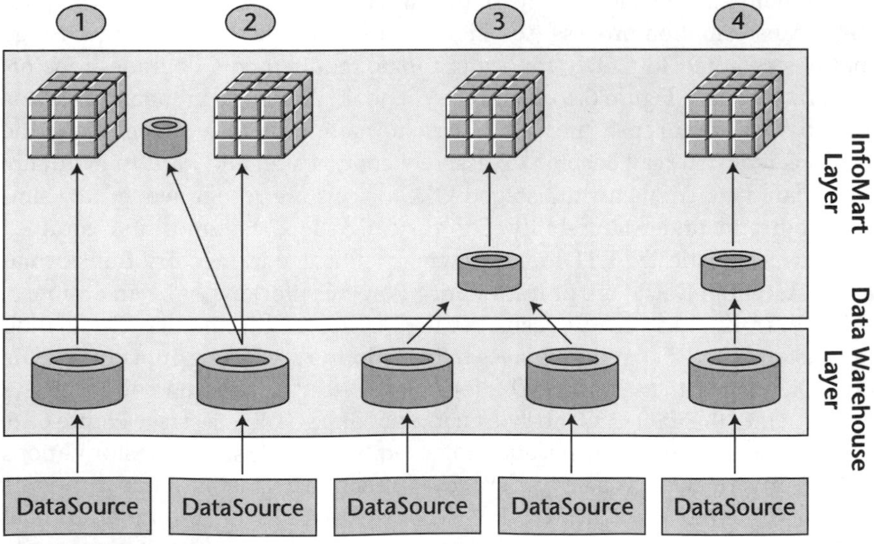

Figure 6.16 Multilevel staging.

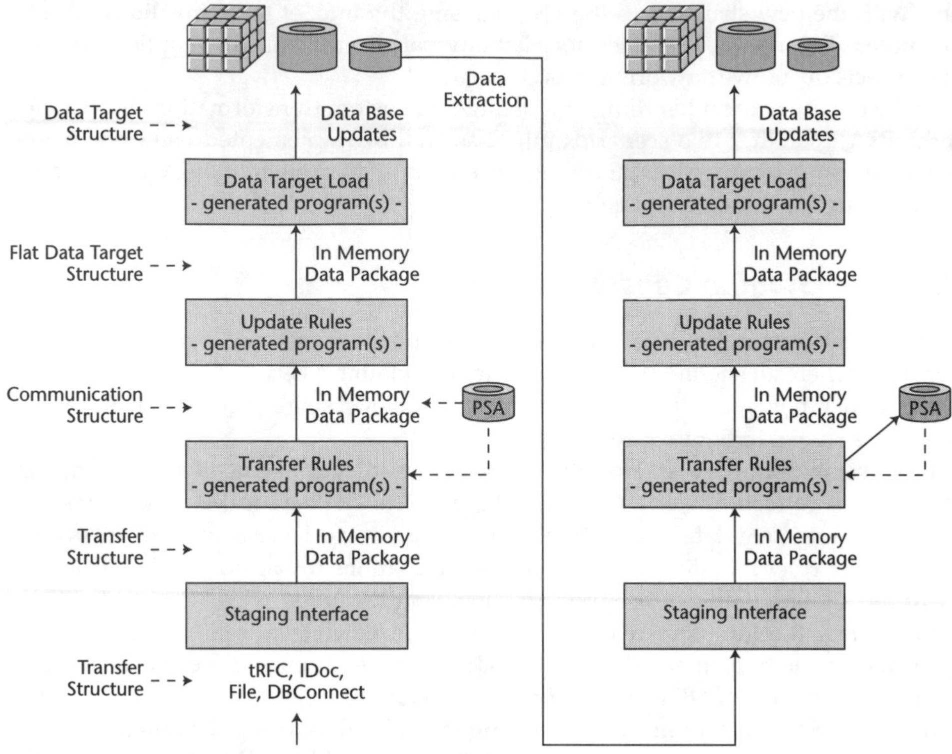

Figure 6.17 Transformation process details.

While it is a deliberate decision to pay for the data warehouse layer with developing a multistage transformation process (see Figure 6.16, examples 1 and 2), multistage transformations required to match application logic requirements degrade transformation performance (see Figure 6.16, examples 3 and 4). Although in many cases it is technically possible to collapse multistage transformations into a single stage, the transformations required may become excessively complicated and hard to maintain. If more levels are needed, then multistaged ODS objects are recommended for simplicity of design and understandability. For very high load volumes and complex transformations, sophisticated ETL tools allowing multistage in-memory transformations (such as Ascential DataStage or Informatica PowerCenter) might be an option.

A practical example has already been sketched earlier in this chapter. Calculating days sales outstanding (DSO) requires sales information as well as accounts receivable information. One option to model a DSO InfoCube is to feed sales and accounts receivable information into the DSO InfoCube via an intermediate ODS object (see Figure 6.16, example 3). Another example of application logic requiring multistage transformations is sales order status tracking. A sales order record keeps changing its status during its life cycle from *CREATED* to *COMPLETED* in several steps, each adding additional information. As InfoCubes do not allow updates of characteristic values, it is not easily possible to adjust the InfoCube to changes of sales order statuses. Adding an ODS object as an intermediary stage (see Figure 6.16, example 4) allows utilizing the ODS object change log functionality to automatically adjust the InfoCube.

There are no technical limits to the number of stages in an end-to-end transformation. However, the more stages there are, the more time is required to finally update the ultimate data target. Note that since release 3.0 there is no longer a significant difference between staging transaction data and staging master data, except that SAP BW still supports special master data DataSources for compatibility reasons.

Transfer Rules

Having discussed the transformation process from a concept perspective, we will now take a closer look at the options provided to implement transfer rules in SAP BW. Two types of transfer rules are available in SAP BW: InfoSource transfer rules and InfoObject transfer rules. *InfoSource transfer rules* (shown in Figure 6.18) define transformations specific to a combination of a DataSource and an InfoSource, while *InfoObject transfer rules* (shown in Figure 6.21) define transformations applied every time an InfoObject is used in the transfer rules. InfoObject transfer rules are defined as part of the InfoObject definition; they are covered as part of the section on the routine option that follows.

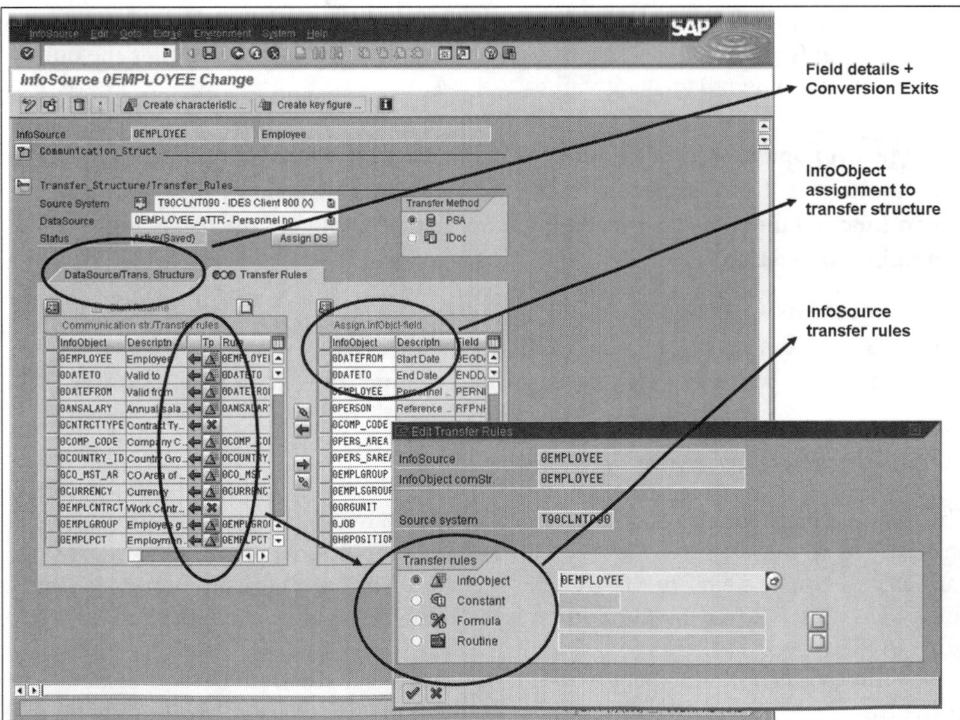

Figure 6.18 InfoSource specific transformations.

As part of the transfer rules, conversion exits are applied to convert from an external data representation to an internal representation before applying the actual transfer rules. There are four options available for defining InfoSource transfer rules: InfoObject assignment, constant value assignment, formulas, and routines, as shown in Figure 6.18.

Conversion Exits

In general, conversion exits apply reformatting rules on input and output operations, converting internal representations to external representations on output and external to internal representations on input operations. SAP BW data loads from non-SAP source systems are considered input operations. Data loads from SAP source systems already provide the internal format; therefore, no conversion exits are applied in this case. Conversion exits can be assigned to either an InfoObject (as part of the InfoObject definition) or explicitly for the transfer structure of non-SAP DataSources in the transfer rules maintenance dialog (by selecting the *DataSource/Transfer Structure* tab shown in Figure 6.18). Readers familiar with SAP R/3 might already have come across conversion exits there. Examples of conversion exits are "ALPHA," adding leading zeros on input and removing leading zeros on output and "SDATE," converting external date formats into internal data formats and back based on date formats defined in the current user's user profile.

Conversion exits should not be confused with InfoObject transfer rules, explained later in the chapter, which also operate on the InfoObject itself. If a conversion exit is defined on an InfoObject level, the Business Explorer automatically applies the output conversion exit when displaying values.

NOTE A number of predefined conversion exits are available in the systems. In addition to those, it is possible to create custom conversion exits. To do so, two function modules have to be implemented according to the following naming convention:

For input exits—`CONVERSION_EXIT_XXXXX_INPUT`
For output exits—`CONVERSION_EXIT_XXXXX_OUTPUT`
where `XXXXX` **is the five-digit name of your custom conversion exit identifier.**

InfoObject Assignment Option

The *InfoObject* assignment option performs a straight mapping of a field of the transfer structure to an InfoObject of the InfoSource. To use this option, you first need to assign InfoObjects to the fields of the transfer structure so that you can connect a source InfoObject to a field of the InfoSource (see "InfoObject assignment to transfer structure" in Figure 6.18).

The InfoObject option implicitly defines a type conversion from the source data type of the transfer structure to the target data type of the InfoObject definition. Note that the generated type conversions may fail at run time, since SAP BW is not able to check the correctness of type conversion at definition time (e.g., whether a character field is convertible into a numeric field depends on the field content). An example of a mismatching type conversion includes a 13-character material number from a non-SAP source system being mapped to the chosen data warehouse standard of 18 characters. In this case you must define how to fill the remaining five characters (for example, keep blank or add leading zeros). Even worse, if the input field is actually longer than the output field, a situation may arise that causes the transformation to lose information. Handling these kinds of situations either requires using one of the options listed in the text that follows or adapting the information model. More complex type conversions would have to be implemented using either the function or the routine option.

Constant Value Assignment Option

Missing information may sometimes be replaced by meaningful default values. It is common, for example, for non-SAP source systems to send date information without information about fiscal year variants, because fiscal year variants tend to be an SAP-specific data element. A constant value defining the fiscal year variant to use would typically be assigned in InfoSource transfer rules, since this is the place to ensure technically integrated data.

To reduce the maintenance effort in case of changing business rules (and subsequently changing default values), you may also choose to implement constant value assignments in the InfoObject transfer rules.

Formula Option

Release 3.0 added the Formula Editor to the options available for defining transfer rules. The formula option provides access to the transformation library, where several types of elements can be used to create complex formulas:

- Over 50 predefined functions from different categories, such as string functions, mathematical functions, date functions, and logical functions
- Standard arithmetic and logical operators
- Important system variables, such as current date and time, factory calendar day, and username
- Constant values of different data types
- Fields of the transfer structure
- Custom functions

All of this could, of course, be implemented as an ABAP routine as described a bit later in the chapter. However, using routines does not require programming skills and makes life easier by saving programming and, more importantly, testing effort. Routines are still available for more complex or performance-critical applications. Figure 6.19 shows a screenshot of the transformation library. The formula option is also available for defining update rules.

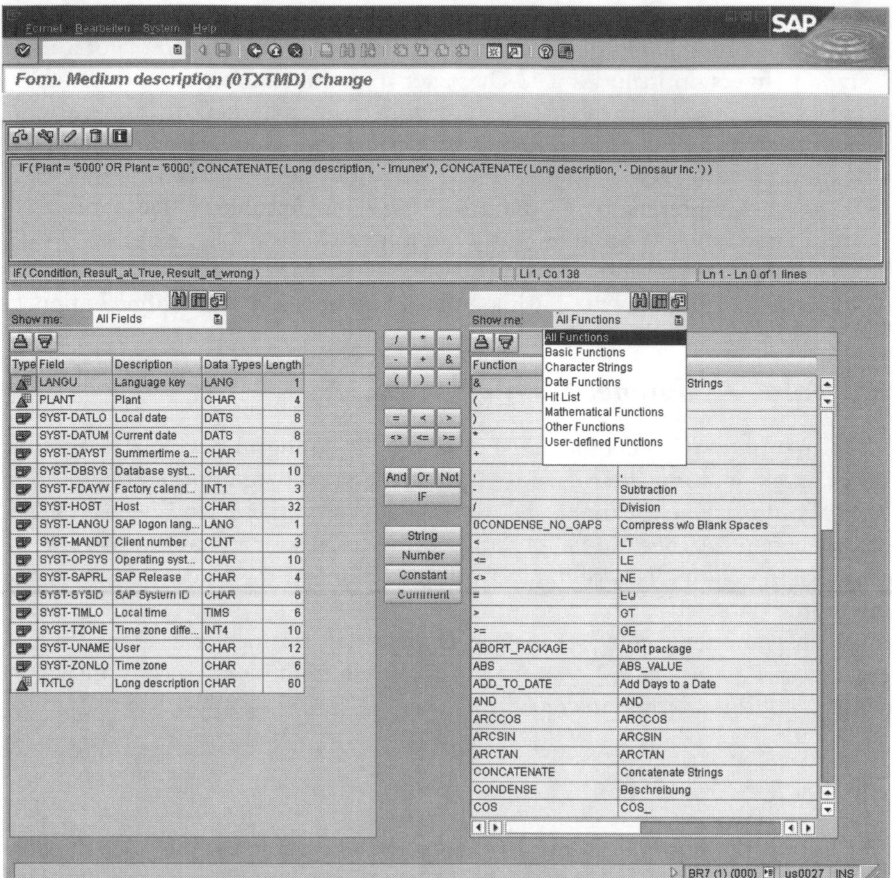

Figure 6.19 The transformation library.

NOTE Formulas are not a novel concept in SAP. The SAP Report Painter has been pursuing a similar concept with the calculator function; SEM BPS offers something called *formula extension* (also known as FOX). The transformation library used by SAP BW is part of the SAP Web Application Server software and might help to unify the different approaches used by mySAP.com applications so far.

The greatest strength of the transformation library is not so much the existing repository of functions but its extendibility. Customers can use the BAPI technology to implement their own custom functions that can be used anywhere in the transfer and update rules. The transformation library also is the starting point for a growing set of reusable custom functions commonly used by SAP BW customers. SAP development performed a survey of what type of custom routines customers are using and found a preponderant share of those routines redundant and eligible for standard delivery in the transformation library.

Routine Option

Routines allow you to implement any kind of transformation that can be coded in the ABAP programming language and cannot be defined using the Formula Editor, such as nontrivial database lookups, calculations, and unit conversions. The importance of routines will decrease over time now that the transformation library and its repository of reusable transformations are available.

Routines are similar to user exits in that they are called from within the generated transfer rule program as part of the transfer rule execution process. To illustrate the use of routines, let's assume we want to enhance the Business Content InfoSource *0EMPLOYEE* by an additional InfoObject *0PERSON*, as shown in Figure 6.20.

Creating a routine requires a name and a selection of fields of the transfer structure available for the DataSource to be used in the routine. The list of fields used in a routine is mainly required for a cross-reference on a transfer structure field level. Once you have selected all required fields, it's time to code the transfer routine. SAP BW automatically generates a framework for the transformation routine broken into the following sections:

- Type pools and transfer structure definition
- Global custom code (includes, global types, variables, form routines or constants)
- Transfer routine interface
- Local custom code (the actual transfer routine)
- Inverted transfer routine including interface

Although some of this is release-dependent, it helps to illustrate the transformation process and to lay out the options in defining transfer routines. Note that the following discussion is intended to showcase the structure of transfer routines rather than explaining the details of ABAP code. Further information about the details of writing transfer routines is available as online help.

NOTE Complex calculations in leading ETL tools always require custom coding. While some tools allow coding to be created in Java or C, many tools have proprietary scripting languages. The effort in creating a script is not much different compared to creating ABAP code.

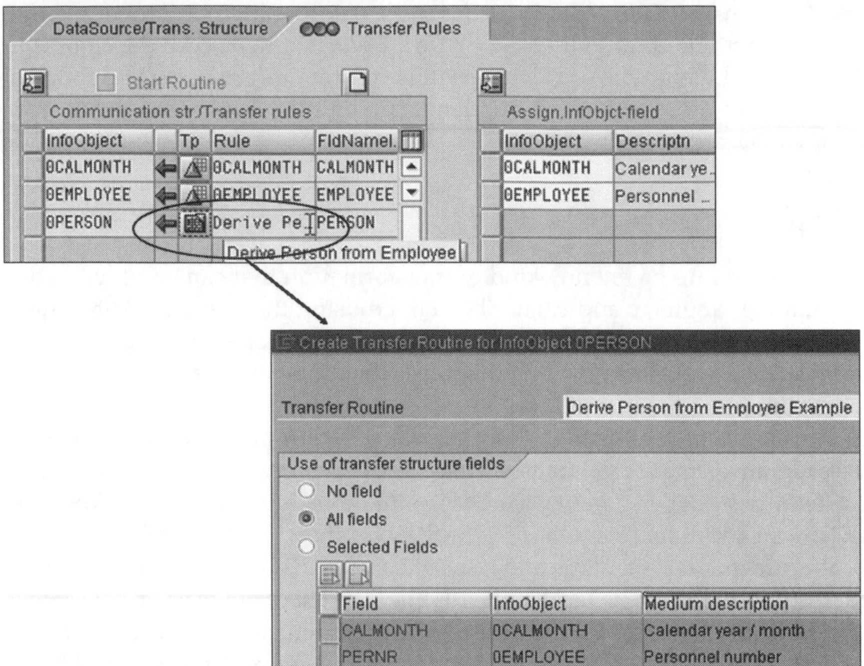

Figure 6.20 Routine transfer rules.

Type Pools and Transfer Structure Definition

Type pools and transfer structure definition set the stage for the custom transfer routine, by declaring all SAP BW standard data types required and the transfer structure. Following is the type pools and transfer structure definition for our example:

```
PROGRAM CONVERSION_ROUTINE.

* Type pools used by conversion program
TYPE-POOLS: RS, RSARC, RSARR, SBIWA, RSSM.

* Declaration of transfer structure (selected fields only)
TYPES: BEGIN OF TRANSFER_STRUCTURE ,
* InfoObject 0CALMONTH: NUMC - 000006
 CALMONTH(000006) TYPE N,
* InfoObject 0EMPLOYEE: NUMC - 000008
 PERNR(000008) TYPE N,
END OF TRANSFER_STRUCTURE.
```

The field selection shown in Figure 6.20 comment or uncomment the fields in the transfer structure in the BW-generated data declarations section. Notice that the lines with CALMONTH and PERNR are not commented out. Also note that the

0EMPLOYEE is referred to as PERNR and not referred to as EMPLOYEE, because the transfer structure is based on meta data from the source system and not from the SAP BW system. In this case PERNR is the fieldname for employee in R/3.

Global Custom Code

The next section of the generated code framework allows specifying includes, global type declarations, variables, constants, macros, and form routines between the two delimiter lines:

```
* Global code used by conversion rules
*$*$ begin of global - insert your declaration only below this line *-*
DATA: EMPLOYEE_WA   LIKE /BI0/MEMPLOYEE,
      PERSON_WA     LIKE /BI0/MPERSON,
      ULTIMO        LIKE SY-DATUM.

INCLUDE RS_BCT_HR_UPDATE_RULES_GENERAL.
INCLUDE RS_BCT_HR_PAPA_UPDATE_RULES.

*$*$ end of global - insert your declaration only before this line *-*
```

These are custom data declarations for our example. Besides data declarations, there are two INCLUDE statements, referencing two ABAP sources, containing reusable custom code used in the actual transfer routine.

Transfer Routine Interface

The interface definition of the transfer routine contains all information and fields required to implement the actual transfer routine. Our example routine header looks like the following:

```
*----------------------------------------------------------------------*
* FORM COMPUTE_PERSON
*----------------------------------------------------------------------*
* Compute value of InfoObject 0PERSON
* in communication structure /BIC/CS0HR_PA_0
*
* Technical properties:
* field name = PERSON
* data element = /BI0/OIPERSON
* data type = NUMC
* length = 000008
* decimals = 000000
* ABAP type = N
* ABAP length = 000008
* reference field =
*----------------------------------------------------------------------*
* Parameters:
* --> RECORD_NO Record number
* --> TRAN_STRUCTURE Transfer structure
* --> G_S_MINFO Request details
```

```
* <-- RESULT Return value of InfoObject
* <-> G_T_ERRORLOG Error log
* <-- RETURNCODE Return code (to skip one record)
* <-- ABORT Abort code (to skip whole data package)
*----------------------------------------------------------------------*
FORM COMPUTE_PERSON
  USING RECORD_NO LIKE SY-TABIX
        TRAN_STRUCTURE TYPE TRANSFER_STRUCTURE
        G_S_MINFO TYPE RSSM_S_MINFO
  CHANGING RESULT TYPE /BI0/OIPERSON
        G_T_ERRORLOG TYPE rssm_t_errorlog_int
        RETURNCODE LIKE SY-SUBRC
        ABORT LIKE SY-SUBRC. "set ABORT <> 0 to cancel datapackage
```

Most of the lines here are comments describing the meta data being passed through the interface. The actual parameters are as follows:

RECORD_NO. This provides the current record number.

TRAN_STRUCTURE. This defines the actual data record in reduced transfer structure format (as declared in the preceding declaration) being passed to the transfer rule.

G_S_MINFO. This passes technical information about the data load request, such as requesting user, request date and time, update mode, the handling of duplicate records, error handling flags, parallel processing flags, and what data targets to update.

RESULT. A changeable parameter; this is intended to contain the resulting value of the transfer routine after its execution.

G_T_ERRORLOG. This indicates an internal table (a table that resides only in main memory) returning information, warning, or error messages generated by the transfer routing back to the calling program.

RETURNCODE. This return code—unequal to zero—flags the current data record as incorrect. Depending on the error handling procedure defined in the InfoPackage, the transformation will either abort, abort after a certain number of incorrect records, or just track all incorrect records in a separate request in the persistent staging area.

ABORT. A value unequal to 0 aborts the transformation process of the currently processed data package.

Transfer Routine

The actual transfer routine is implemented between the delimiter lines as part of the transfer routine body:

```
*$*$ begin of routine - insert your code only below this line *-*
* DATA: l_s_errorlog TYPE rssm_s_errorlog_int.
 PERFORM CALCULATE_ULTIMO
```

```
    USING     TRAN_STRUCTURE-CALMONTH RECORD_NO RECORD_ALL SOURCE_SYSTEM
    CHANGING ULTIMO RETURNCODE.

  PERFORM READ_MD_PERSON
    USING     TRAN_STRUCTURE-PERNR TRAN_STRUCTURE-CALMONTH RECORD_NO
              RECORD_ALL SOURCE_SYSTEM
    CHANGING EMPLOYEE_WA PERSON_WA RETURNCODE.

  RESULT = EMPLOYEE_WA-PERSON.
 RETURNCODE = 0.
 ABORT = 0.
 *$*$ end of routine - insert your code only before this line *-*
 ENDFORM.
```

We recommend implementing nontrivial, reusable transformations as form routines and storing those form routines in separate include files, as shown in this example. This eases maintenance tasks and allows easier testing of these form routines using separate test programs.

The first routine CALCULATE_ULTIMO here determines the last day of the current calendar month into the ULTIMO field, a field which is then used to perform time-dependent master data lookups from employee and person master data in the second routine READ_MD_PERSON.

Inversion Routine

At this point the transformation routine is effectively complete. However, you should be aware of another routine in the transfer rules: the *inversion routine*. Inversion routines are optional and used for drill-down to SAP R/3 either using the Report-to-Report Interface (see Chapter 7) or the remote InfoCube functionality (see Chapter 3). The idea here is that an inverse transformation must be applied to transform the data warehouse representation of a value of a characteristic back into its source system representation:

```
*----------------------------------------------------------------------*
* FORM INVERT_PERSON
*----------------------------------------------------------------------*
* Inversion of selection criteria for InfoObject 0PERSON
*
* This subroutine needs to be implemented only for SAP RemoteCubes
* (for better performance) and for the Report/Report Interface
* (drill through).
*
*----------------------------------------------------------------------*
* --> I_RT_CHAVL_CS Ranges table for current InfoObject
* --> I_THX_SELECTION_CS Selection criteria for all other InfoObjects
* <-- C_T_SELECTION Selection criteria for fields of
* transfer structure
* <-- E_EXACT Flag: Inversion was exact
*----------------------------------------------------------------------*
```

```
FORM INVERT_PERSON
  USING     I_RT_CHAVL_CS TYPE RSARC_RT_CHAVL
            I_THX_SELECTION_CS TYPE RSARC_THX_SELCS
  CHANGING C_T_SELECTION TYPE SBIWA_T_SELECT
            E_EXACT TYPE RS_BOOL.
*$*$ begin of inverse routine - insert your code only below this line*-*

 DATA:
 L_S_SELECTION LIKE LINE OF C_T_SELECTION.

* An empty selection means all values
 CLEAR C_T_SELECTION.

* Selection of all values may be not exact
 E_EXACT = RS_C_FALSE.

*$*$ end of inverse routine - insert your code only before this line *-*
ENDFORM.
```

The inversion routine interface has a number of parameters. Three out of the four parameters deal with selections. The first two deal with what is coming from a query, and the last one deals with what will be asked from the DataSource. In more detail, the parameters are:

I_RT_CHAVL. This parameter provides the selection passed from the query for the InfoObject to be transformed.

I_THX_SELECTION. This parameter provides the remaining selection ranges for all other InfoObjects.

C_T_SELECTION. This parameter returns the selection based on inversed characteristics values to the calling program, where they are used as selections for the DataSource used for the Report-to-Report Interface or the remote InfoCube.

E_EXACT. This flag specifies whether or not the DataSource selections were exact so that results can be passed straight back without having to go through the transfer rules first. If this is not flagged, the transfer rules will be called twice for a query. The first time it will be called for the inverse transfer rules for the data selection; the second time it will filter out and transform what had been selected from the source system.

Start Routine

Start routines are executed prior to applying the other transfer rules. They have access to all the records in the data package (not the extracted data set!). The most practical use of start routines is to preload tables into memory for efficient nontrivial table lookups or to apply complex record filters to the data package. However, you must take care not break the memory limits of the application server, especially having in mind that multiple data packages executed at the same time will each require the same amount of memory.

Another example might be loading all the pay grade-level maximum and minimum amounts in memory and checking non-SAP payroll amounts against them:

```
FORM STARTROUTINE
 USING    G_S_MINFO TYPE RSSM_S_MINFO
 CHANGING DATAPAK type TAB_TRANSTRU
          G_T_ERRORLOG TYPE rssm_t_errorlog_int
          ABORT LIKE SY-SUBRC. "set ABORT <> 0 to cancel datapackage
*$*$ begin of routine - insert your code only below this line *-*
* DATA: l_s_datapak_line type TRANSFER_STRUCTURE,
* l_s_errorlog TYPE rssm_s_errorlog_int.

* abort <> 0 means skip whole data package !!!
 ABORT = 0.
*$*$ end of routine - insert your code only before this line *-*

ENDFORM.
```

SAP BW passes the complete data package into the start routine, where it is available for arbitrary transformations.

InfoObject Transfer Routines

InfoObject transfer routines are transfer routines directly tied to an InfoObject. In whatever set of transfer rules this InfoObject is used, the specified routine will be executed. InfoObject transfer routines are used to warrant consistent systemwide transformations for a specific InfoObject. They are maintained in the InfoObject maintenance transaction (see Figure 6.21).

The following sample routine changes the format of the material number by adding hyphens (e.g., material number 123Abc456789 is converted into the representation 123-ABC-456789):

```
PROGRAM CONVERSION_ROUTINE.

* Type pools used by conversion program
TYPE-POOLS: RSD, RSARC, RSARR.

TYPES: DE_0MATERIAL(000018) TYPE C.

* Conversion rule for InfoObject 0MATERIAL
* Data type = CHAR
* ABAP type = C
* ABAP length = 000018
FORM CONVERT_0MATERIAL
  USING RECORD_NO LIKE SY-TABIX
        SOURCE_SYSTEM TYPE RSA_LOGSYS
        IOBJ_NAME TYPE RSIOBJNM
  CHANGING RESULT TYPE DE_0MATERIAL " InfoObject value
           RETURNCODE LIKE SY-SUBRC.
*$*$ begin of routine - insert your code only below this line *-*
```

```
  CONCATENATE RESULT(3) '-' RESULT+3(3) '-' RESULT+6 INTO RESULT.
  TRANSLATE RESULT TO UPPER CASE.
  RETURNCODE = 0.
*$*$ end of routine - insert your code only before this line *-*
ENDFORM.
```

The interface imports the record number, the source system, the InfoObject name, the original characteristic value to the routine and exports the new value for the characteristic and the return code. The source system parameter allows implementing source-system-dependent transformations on an InfoObject level:

RECORD_NO. This provides the current record number.

SOURCE_SYSTEM. The name of the source system allows you to code source-system-dependent transformations.

IOBJ_NAME. This provides the name of the InfoObject this routine is defined for (may be used for referencing InfoObjects).

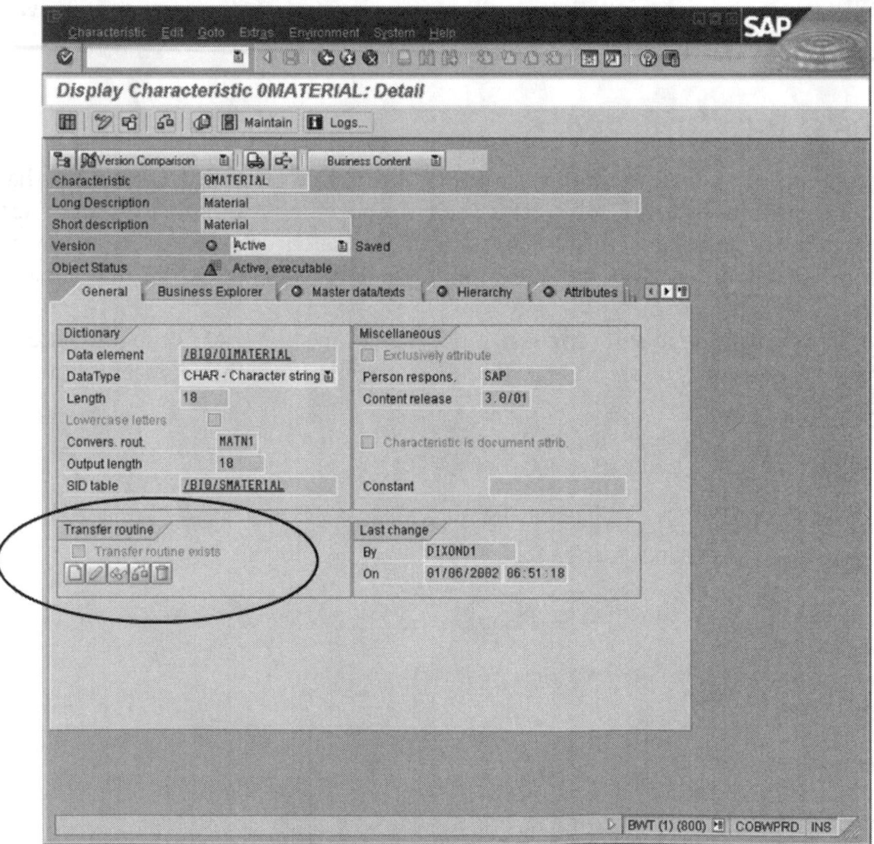

Figure 6.21 InfoObject transfer routines.

RESULT. A changeable parameter, this is intended to contain the resulting value of the transfer routine after its execution.

RETURNCODE. A return code unequal to zero flags the current data record as incorrect. Depending on the error handling procedure defined in the InfoPackage, the transformation will either abort, abort after a certain number of incorrect records, or just track all incorrect records in a separate request in the persistent staging area.

InfoObject transfer routines are executed whenever the corresponding InfoObject is used in an InfoSource, right after data records have passed through the traditional transfer routines. The classic business examples are formatting transformation methods such as converting to uppercase or inserting dashes to a product number.

Rules of the Game

All of the transformations discussed in the preceding text are executed in a certain order before the whole transformed data package is passed on to the update rules. The following pseudocode shows the highly simplified algorithm for executing the transfer rules:

```
*** STEP 1 - Data Package contains records in transfer structure format
Execute start routine with data_package.
*** STEP 2 - Record by record processing of the data package
Loop at data_package.

*** STEP 3 - Apply conversion exits field by field
  Process fields of transfer structure.
    If conversion exit available and applicable.
      Execute conversion exit on current field.
    End.
  End.

*** STEP 4 - Apply transfer rules field by field
  Process fields of communication structure.
    If InfoObject assigned to current field.
      Assign InfoObject value to current field converting data types.
    End.
    If constant value assigned to current field.
      Assign constant value to current field.
    End.
    If formula assigned to current field.
      Execute formula.
      Assign result to current field.
    End.
    If routine assigned to current field.
      Execute routine.
      Assign result to current field.
    End.
```

```
    If InfoObject routine assigned to current field.
      Execute InfoObject routine.
      Assign result to current field.
    End.
  End.
End.

*** STEP 5 - Call update rules passing data package in memory
call update rules with data package in communication structure format
```

The first step in applying the transfer rules is executing the specified start routine (if any). The resulting data package is processed record by record, field by field, applying the different transformations defined in the preceding sequence. Neither records nor fields are processed in a documented, warranted sequence. If a specific order of records is required, the start routine may be used to sort the records of the current data package (and only the data package). Forcing a specific order for processing the fields of the communication structure is not possible. Therefore, any custom transformation defined has to be independent of the field sequence.

Update Rules

Having applied the transformation rules, SAP BW is now ready to apply application-specific transformations in the update rules that are independent of the source system. The logic behind the update rules is more complex than the one behind the transfer rules: Data integration transformations are still supported, but the main focus is on application logic transformations such as normalization, denormalization, and aggregation. Analogous to the transfer rules, we present a highly simplified update rules algorithm at the end of this section. To understand the following discussion you just need to know that the update rules handle key figures (data fields) and characteristics (key fields) differently when updating InfoCubes (ODS objects, master data tables): Every characteristic (key field) update rule is executed for each of the key figures (data fields) of the InfoCube (ODS object, master data table). Each of the key figure (data field) update rules generates an in-memory result record with all characteristics (key fields) values and the key figure (data field) value filled. A sample update process is also described in more detail at the end of this section.

Before diving into the details of update rules for key figures (data fields), we'll begin by describing the options available for characteristics (key fields) update rules.

Characteristics/Key Field Update Rules

There are six standard methods for defining characteristics update rules: assigning a source characteristic, setting a constant value, executing a formula, looking up a master data attribute, executing a routine, and assigning an initial value. Assigning a source characteristic is essentially the same as the InfoObject transfer rule discussed previously, including an implicit data type conversion where necessary. Assigning constant values again is the same as for the transfer rules; in addition to assigning an arbitrary constant value, another option allows you to assign the (constant) initial value to the data target characteristic. Also, formulas are using the same transformation library and technology as in the transfer rules. The only difference is that instead of offering a list of the transfer structure fields, the transformation library here provides a list of InfoSource fields. Figure 6.22 shows the options available for characteristics update rules.

Master Data Lookup Option

Aside from straight mapping, the most common transformation is master data lookup. SAP BW allows this option for target InfoObjects that are used as an attribute in one of the InfoObjects used in the InfoSource.

For time-dependent attributes a reference date for the master data lookup has to be specified. Options available for reference dates are using the current system date, a constant date, or a date derived from an InfoObject of the communication structure (using either the start or end date of the period specified by that InfoObject). If, for example, the POSITION of an employee needs to be derived using the 0EMPLOYEE characteristic of the InfoSource, the calendar month can be used as the reference time period (see Figure 6.22).

NOTE It is not yet possible to perform master data derivation of a master data derivation. If, for example, the date of birth of an employee (InfoObject 0EMPLOYEE) is required, the person identifier must first be looked up on the employee master data table before being able to look up the date of birth in the person master data table. A routine would have to be coded in order to perform such a transformation.

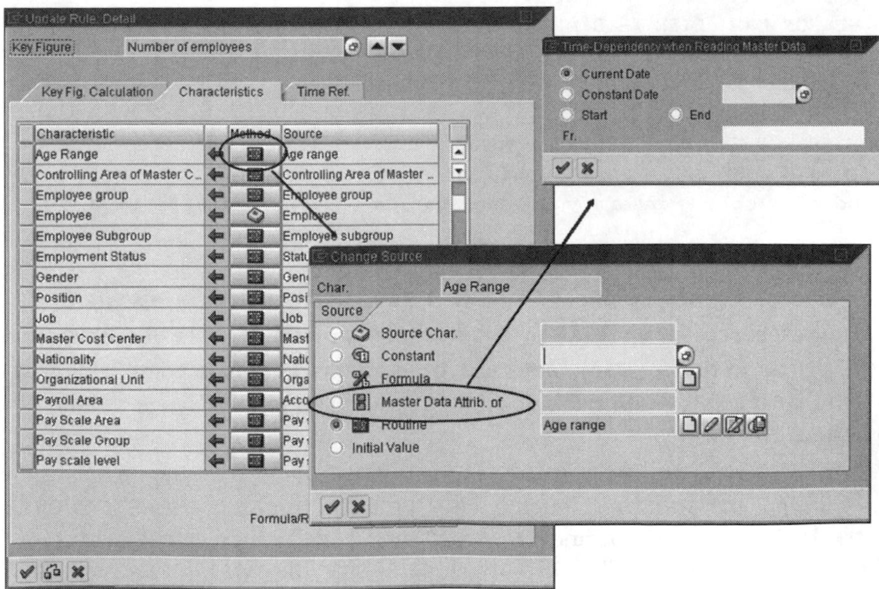

Figure 6.22 Options for characteristics update rules.

Routine Option

Routines used for characteristics (key field) update rules are similar to those used for transfer rules in that they return the value of a single characteristic (key field) of the InfoCube (ODS object, master data table) derived from the information available from the InfoSource. Update routines are divided into three sections:

1. Global custom code
2. Update routine interface
3. Custom update routine code

The first section contains all global custom declarations of includes, data types, variables, constants, and form routines. Global declarations are available anywhere in the update rules of a specific InfoSource and data target combination. Notice that it is possible to include other ABAP programs into the update rules via INCLUDE statements. This is good design, especially if there are reusable declarations and subroutines across different update rules. By creating include programs and coding all the routines there, you can centralize maintenance of business logic. The following sample code shows global declarations similar to ones used in the transfer rules example (please note that the following discussion is intended to showcase the structure of update routines rather than explain the details of ABAP code; information about the details of writing update routines is also available as online help):

```
PROGRAM UPDATE_ROUTINE.
*$*$ begin of global - insert your declaration only below this line *-*
DATA: EMPLOYEE_MD LIKE /BI0/MEMPLOYEE,
      EMPLOYEE_WA LIKE /BI0/MEMPLOYEE,
      person_md   LIKE /BI0/MPERSON,
      PERSON_WA   LIKE /BI0/MPERSON.

DATA: G_RECORD_NO LIKE SY-TABIX.

INCLUDE RS_BCT_HR_UPDATE_RULES_GENERAL.
INCLUDE RS_BCT_HR_PAPA_UPDATE_RULES.
*$*$ end of global - insert your declaration only before this line *-*
```

TIP To view all the SAP Business Content `INCLUDE` statements for update rules routines, search for all ABAP programs that start with `RS_BCT` and have `UPDATE_RULES` in the program name. Use transactions SE38 to accomplish this. Note that this information is release-dependent and might change at any point of time.

In this example the INCLUDE statement RS_BCT_HR_UPDATE_RULES_GENERAL contains the logic for the subroutine CALCULATE_ULTIMO, which calculates the last day of the month, while the INCLUDE statement RS_BCT_HR_PAPA_UPDATE_RULES contains the subroutine for READ_MD_PERSON, which reads the master data for the person.

The next code fragment shows a sample update routine interface, generated based on the resulting data target InfoObject and the communication structure layout:

```
FORM compute_key_field
  TABLES    MONITOR STRUCTURE RSMONITOR "user defined monitoring
  USING     COMM_STRUCTURE LIKE /BIC/CS0HR_PA_0
            RECORD_NO LIKE SY-TABIX
            RECORD_ALL LIKE SY-TABIX
            SOURCE_SYSTEM LIKE RSUPDSIMULH-LOGSYS
  CHANGING RESULT LIKE /BI0/V0PA_C01T-AGE_RANGE
            RETURNCODE LIKE SY-SUBRC
            ABORT LIKE SY-SUBRC. "set ABORT <> 0 to cancel update
```

The parameters specified in the update routine interface are as follows:

MONITOR. This passes an internal table (a table that resides only in main memory) returning information, warning, or error messages generated by the transfer routing back to the calling program.

COMM_STRUCTURE. This passes the values of the communication structure on to the update routine. The communication structure values cannot be changed by a routine.

RECORD_NO. This passes the current record number of the extraction data set on to the update routine. This value is not changeable.

RECORD_ALL. This passes the total number of records in the extraction data set on to the update routine. This value is not changeable.

SOURCE_SYSTEM. This passes the technical name of the source system on to the update routine. This parameter allows you to perform source-system-specific transformations. Note that source-system-specific transformations should generally be performed in the transfer rules.

RESULT. The value returned by this parameter will be assigned to the corresponding field of the data target. In this example, the result field refers to the AGE_RANGE InfoObject. Age categories are frequently used to compare customer behavior across different age groups.

RETURNCODE. This is a changeable parameter controlling whether a record should be updated (value equals zero) or skipped (value other than zero).

ABORT. This is a changeable parameter controlling whether the whole update process has to be continued (values equals zero) or aborted (values other than zero).

The last part of the update routine is dedicated to the actual transformation specified in ABAP. The routine is very similar to the one described for the transfer rules so we skip the details here:

Update Rules Example

```
*$*$ begin of routine - insert your code only below this line *-*
DATA: ULTIMO LIKE SY-DATUM,
```

```
        AGE    TYPE I.

  IF G_RECORD_NO <> RECORD_NO.
    G_RECORD_NO = RECORD_NO.
    CLEAR: EMPLOYEE_MD, PERSON_MD.
    CLEAR: EMPLOYEE_WA, PERSON_WA.
  ENDIF.

  PERFORM CALCULATE_ULTIMO
    USING     COMM_STRUCTURE-CALMONTH RECORD_NO RECORD_ALL SOURCE_SYSTEM
    CHANGING ULTIMO RETURNCODE.

  PERFORM READ_MD_PERSON
    USING     COMM_STRUCTURE-EMPLOYEE COMM_STRUCTURE-CALMONTH RECORD_NO
              RECORD_ALL SOURCE_SYSTEM
    CHANGING EMPLOYEE_WA PERSON_WA RETURNCODE.

  EMPLOYEE_MD = EMPLOYEE_WA.
  PERSON_MD = PERSON_WA.

  IF NOT PERSON_MD-DATEBIRTH IS INITIAL.
    AGE = ULTIMO+0(4) - PERSON_MD-DATEBIRTH+0(4).
    IF ULTIMO+4(4) LT PERSON_MD-DATEBIRTH+4(4).
      AGE = AGE - 1.
    ENDIF.

    IF AGE LT 20.
      RESULT = 1.
    ELSEIF AGE LT 30.
      RESULT = 2.
    ELSEIF AGE LT 40.
      RESULT = 3.
    ELSEIF AGE LT 50.
      RESULT = 4.
    ELSEIF AGE LT 60.
      RESULT = 5.
    ELSEIF AGE LT 70.
      RESULT = 6.
    ELSE.
      RESULT = 7.
    ENDIF.
  ELSE.
    CLEAR RESULT.
  ENDIF.

  RETURNCODE = 0.
  *$*$ end of routine - insert your code only before this line *-*
  *
  ENDFORM.
```

Time Reference Option

Time characteristics have the same transformation options as regular characteristics plus an additional option for time distributions. The time distribution option is a de-aggregation method allowing distribution of values from a lower granularity source time dimension (such as calendar month) to a higher granularity target time dimension (such as the calendar day) based on the calendar or a factory calendar. (Factory calendars are calendars carrying additional factory-specific information about local bank holidays, factory holidays, and so on.)

Assume for example that the value of 0CALMONTH is "200112" in a communication structure record. That record will be broken into six records, each record representing a week. The first record will contain 1/31th of the original key figure amount. That is because December 1, 2001, is a Sunday and the week starts on a Monday. That means the first week (0CALWEEK = '200147') only has one day in it (December 1, 2001). The weeks that follow are full weeks (each of the weeks "200148" through "200251" receive 7/31st of the original key figure amount) except for the last week (0CALWEEK = "200152"), which receives the remainder of 2/31st of the original key figure amount.

Simple time conversions are generated automatically wherever possible. In Figure 6.23 the calendar day is set to end of the month using a routine. Calendar month is derived from the InfoSource and is automatically converted to fill the quarter (QYYYY format), year (YYYY format), month (MM format), and quarter (Q format).

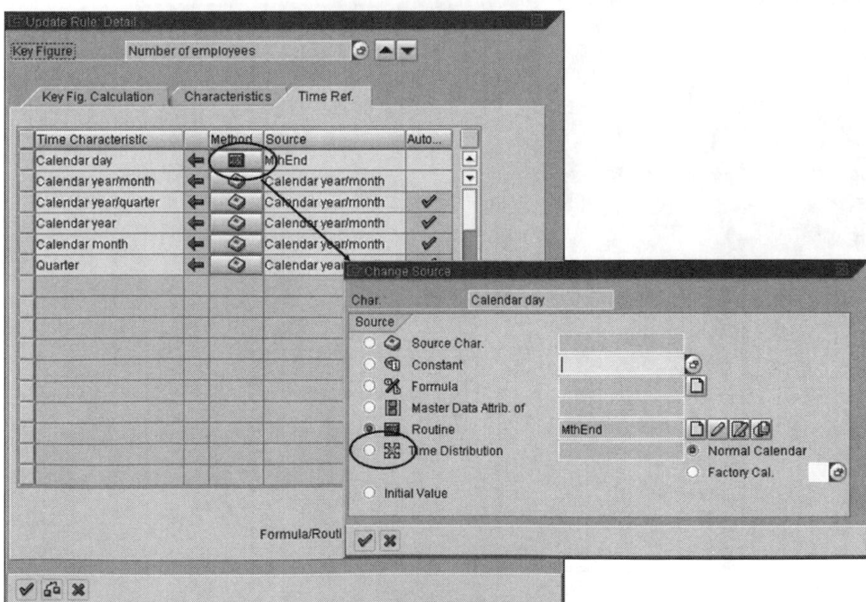

Figure 6.23 Options for time characteristics update rules.

Key Figure/Data Field Update Rules

The options for defining update rules for key figures/data fields are shown in Figure 6.24. The options offered there include source key figures, formulas, and routines. While source key figures and formulas work in the same way as already described, key figure routines add additional options we'll discuss in this section.

The *update* type allows you to specify if a key figure/data field should be updated at all. For InfoCube updates, there are two options: aggregate into the InfoCube using the standard aggregation function specified for that key figure in the InfoObject maintenance or do not update. For ODS objects and master data tables there are three options: aggregate the value, overwrite the old value, or do not update. Not updating a key figure/data field is required to avoid overwriting existing values in cases where multiple InfoSources each provide only a subset of the key figures/data fields required by the data target.

Finally, there are options for selecting automatic currency conversions to be performed wherever applicable. These are explained later in this section.

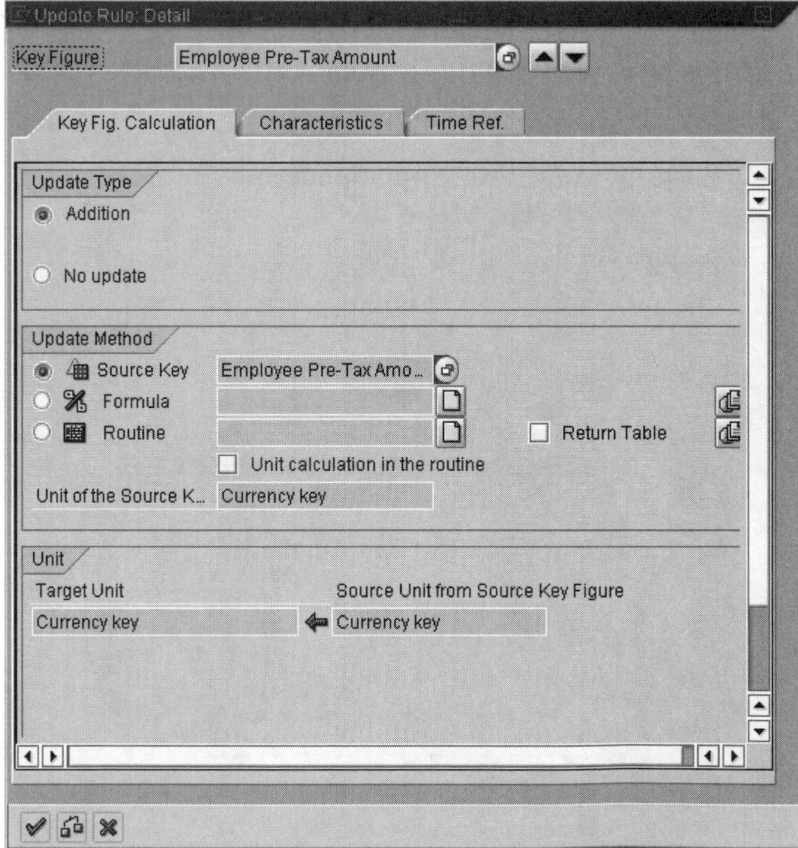

Figure 6.24 Options for key figure/data fields update rules.

Routine Option

Three types of key figure update routines are available: *basic*, *unit*, and *return tables*. Basic routines are exactly the same as characteristics update routines. The return table and unit routines, however, use different routine interfaces. Following is an example of the interface of a return table routine:

```
FORM compute_data_field
  TABLES    MONITOR STRUCTURE RSMONITOR "user defined monitoring
            RESULT_TABLE STRUCTURE /BI0/V0PA_C01T
  USING     COMM_STRUCTURE LIKE /BIC/CS0HR_PA_0
            RECORD_NO LIKE SY-TABIX
            RECORD_ALL LIKE SY-TABIX
            SOURCE_SYSTEM LIKE RSUPDSIMULH-LOGSYS
            ICUBE_VALUES LIKE /BI0/V0PA_C01T
  CHANGING RETURNCODE LIKE SY-SUBRC
            ABORT LIKE SY-SUBRC. "set ABORT <> 0 to cancel update
```

Notice that there are two changes in the interface. First the parameter for RESULT has changed into the parameter RESULT_TABLE. In other words, instead of passing back an individual target InfoObject value, this routine passes back an arbitrary number of entire records. This type of routine enables de-aggregation and normalization—that is, one input record from a communication structure can be transformed into multiple output records. Practical examples of result table routines are normalizing a plan value record with 12 plan values (one for each month of the year) into an generic key figure-based model with 12 records—each record specifying the year, the month, and the accordant plan value. (We provided details on generic key figure information models in Chapter 4.)

The second change to the interface is the parameter ICUBE_VALUES. Notice it references the same structure that the result table references. This parameter represents the flattened structure of the InfoCube. This parameter provides all characteristics/key field values already determined. Normally, the first thing to do in a return table routine is map this parameter to the result table in a statement like:

```
MOVE-CORRESPONDING ICUBE_VALUES TO RESULT_TABLE.
```

Unit routines are exactly the same as basic routines, except that one additional parameter is introduced: the UNIT parameter represents currency or unit codes. Routines of this kind are explicitly designed for currency translations and unit transformations where the target currency or unit is determined dynamically, based on other information available in the InfoSource or from the system. Following is a code example of a unit routine:

```
Example of a Unit Routine Interface
FORM compute_data_field
  TABLES    MONITOR STRUCTURE RSMONITOR "user defined monitoring
  USING     COMM_STRUCTURE LIKE /BIC/CS0HR_PY_1
            RECORD_NO LIKE SY-TABIX
```

```
            RECORD_ALL LIKE SY-TABIX
            SOURCE_SYSTEM LIKE RSUPDSIMULH-LOGSYS
   CHANGING RESULT LIKE /BI0/V0PY_C02T-AMOUNT
            UNIT LIKE /BI0/V0PY_C02T-CURRENCY
            RETURNCODE LIKE SY-SUBRC
            ABORT LIKE SY-SUBRC. "set ABORT <> 0 to cancel update
```

If the source unit or currency is available from the InfoSource there is no additional code required. Both can be mapped from the InfoSource to the InfoCube. For currency conversions a currency translation type has to be specified as shown in Figure 6.25.

Currency translation types provide a powerful means of specifying highly flexible currency translations. SAP BW inherited the currency conversion framework from SAP R/3 and is able to use currency translation types available and upload currency conversion rates there.

Copy Rule Option

In early releases of SAP BW, before the introduction of the return table key figure routine, the only way to convert one incoming communication structure record into multiple InfoCube records was to copy the update rules. For each copy of the update rules, a new record is created—provided at least one of the characteristic or time characteristic values of the InfoCube is different in each copy; otherwise, key figure amounts simply get duplicated. The limitation of this technique is that the designer has to know up front how many duplicated records will be needed. Often this is unknown, should be dynamic, or is too maintenance-intensive; therefore, copy rules have become redundant. We generally recommend using result table routines instead.

Start Routine

Start routines, shown in Figure 6.26, in update rules are essentially the same as in transfer rules. The following code fragment shows the interface of a sample start routine:

```
FORM startup
 TABLES MONITOR STRUCTURE RSMONITOR "user defined monitoring
 DATA_PACKAGE STRUCTURE /BIC/CS0HR_PY_1
 USING RECORD_ALL LIKE SY-TABIX
 SOURCE_SYSTEM LIKE RSUPDSIMULH-LOGSYS
 CHANGING ABORT LIKE SY-SUBRC. "set ABORT <> 0 to cancel update
```

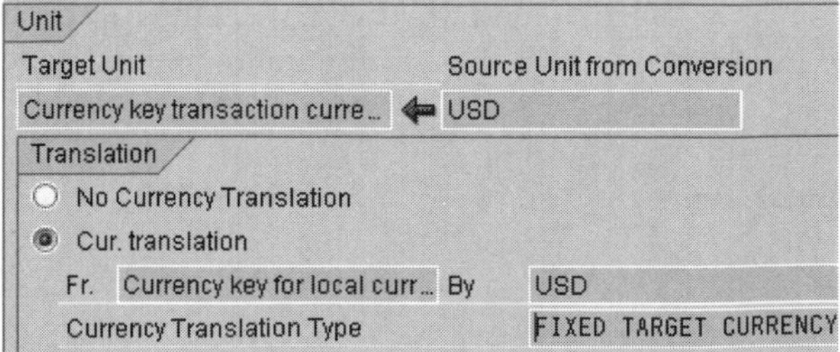

Figure 6.25 Currency translation in update rules.

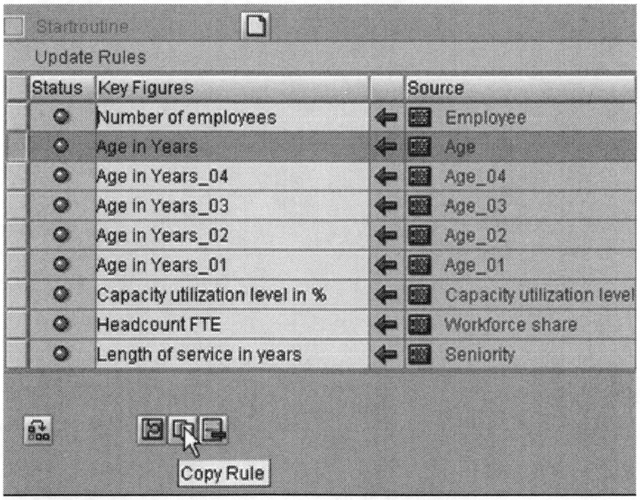

Figure 6.26 Start routines and copy rules.

Rules of the Game

Having discussed all the different options of defining update rules, we will now time to take a step back and look at whole picture from a higher-level point of view. The following pseudocode illustrates a highly simplified algorithm for executing the update rules:

```
Update Rules Execution Algorithm
*** STEP 1 - Data Package in communication structure format
Execute start routine with data_package.

*** STEP 2 - Record by record processing of the data package
Loop at data_package.

*** STEP 3 - Common characteristics/key fields
    Determine common characteristic/key field values (as shown below)

*** STEP 4 - Apply update rules for key figures/data fields
  Process key figures/data fields of data target.

*** STEP 5 - Apply update rules for remaining characteristics/key fields
    Process characteristics/key fields of data target.
      If InfoObject assigned to current field.
        Assign InfoObject value to current field converting data types.
      End.
      If constant value assigned to current field.
        Assign constant value to current field.
      End.
      If formula assigned to current field.
        Execute formula.
```

```
          Assign result to current field.
        End.
        If routine assigned to current field.
         Execute routine.
          Assign result to current field.
        End.
        If master data attribute assigned to current field.
          Retrieve master data attribute.
          Assign result to current field.
        End.
      End.

*** STEP 6 - Apply update rules for key figures/data fields
      If InfoObject assigned to current field.
        Assign InfoObject value to current field converting data types.
      End.
      If formula assigned to current field.
        Execute formula.
        Assign result to current field.
      End.
      If routine assigned to current field.
        Execute routine.
        If routine does not return a table.
          Assign result to current field.
        End.
      End.
      Convert unit / currency.

*** STEP 7 - Insert data record with current key figure into result
table
      Insert data record(s).

*** STEP 8 - Aggregate data package
      Aggregate data package.
    End.
End.

*** STEP 9 - Call data target update with data package in data
***          target format passing data package in memory.
Call data target physical update program.
```

As for the update rules, the first step is to call the start routine before processing the data package record by record. Table 6.2 shows a sample data package in communication structure format, containing 12 different plan values for sales revenue and discounts (in percent) for a specific material in 2002.

Table 6.2 Data Package in Communication Structure Format

MATERIAL-DISNCT 3	YEAR	PLAN 1	PLAN 2	PLAN 3	...	DISCNT 1	DISCNT 2	...
M01	2002	12	14	15	...	10	9	8
M02	2002	50	60	70	...	6	6	6
M03	2002	60	50	40	...	9	10	10

The plan in our example is to update an InfoCube with the *material*, *year*, and *month* as characteristics and *plan*, *discount* as key figures—effectively normalizing the communication structure record. Steps 2 initiates the record-by-record processing of the data package. Step 3 determines all characteristics with exactly the same update rules specified for all key figures, following the same procedure as in Step 5. This is an optimization avoiding multiple determinations of the same values.

Step 4 initiates the key figure by key figure determination of characteristics values where there are different update rules for each key figure (none in our example). Step 5 sequentially executes all characteristics update rules in the sequence specified. Note that the order in which data records, key figure update rules, and characteristic update rules are executed is not defined.

In Step 6 the value of the key figure itself is determined by applying the update rules, as well as unit or currency conversions. Our example requires a result table key figure update routine in order to be able to normalize the data record. The result table of our routine for the plan revenues looks like Table 6.3.

Table 6.3 Result Table Data Target Format

MATERIAL	YEAR	MONTH	PLAN	DISCNT
M01	2002	01	12	0
M01	2002	01	0	10
M01	2002	02	14	0
M01	2002	02	0	9
M01	2002	03	15	0
M01	2002	03	0	8

(continues)

Table 6.3 Result Table Data Target Format *(Continued)*

MATERIAL	YEAR	MONTH	PLAN	DISCNT
...				
M02	2002	01	50	0
M02	2002	01	0	6
M02	2002	02	60	0
M02	2002	02	0	6
M02	2002	03	70	0
M02	2002	03	0	6
...				
M03	2002	01	60	0
M03	2002	01	0	9
M03	2002	02	50	0
M03	2002	02	0	10
M03	2002	03	40	0
M03	2002	03	0	10
...				

Note that the discount key figure is always set to 0, as this is the update routine for the plan revenue key figure. The update routine for the discount key figure produces a similar table, where the plan revenue is set to 0 and the discount contains a discount value. Every key figure update rule (routine or not, return table or not) finally produces at least one data record where the results of all characteristic update rules have been assigned to the characteristics, the result value of the related key figure update has been assigned to the key figure, and all other key figures have been set to a value of 0. This intermediate result record (or records, in case of return tables) is inserted into an internal result table in Step 7.

Step 8 finally aggregates this internal result table, so that the final result looks like that shown in Table 6.4

In many simple update scenarios, one single communication structure record generates one single entry in the data target. This is the case when all characteristic values are the same for all key figures, so that aggregation is able to aggregate those multiple records of the nonaggregated table into one single record of the final aggregated table. Specifying different characteristics update rules per key figure provides another option for normalizing data records, because different characteristic values prohibit aggregation of the internal result table. This way, multiple data entries are written to the data target.

Table 6.4 Aggregated Result Table in Data Target Format

MATERIAL	YEAR	MONTH	PLAN	DISCNT
M01	2002	01	12	10
M01	2002	02	14	9
M01	2002	03	15	8
...				
M02	2002	01	50	6
M02	2002	02	60	6
M02	2002	03	70	6
...				
M03	2002	01	60	9
M03	2002	02	50	10
M03	2002	03	40	10
...				

Step 9 finally passes the internal result table in data target format to the generated data target update program that controls the loading process of SAP BW.

Loading

Loading data into a data target is the last step of the SAP BW staging process. So far all data have always been passed in some flat record format—transfer structure, communication structure, or flattened data target structure format. Loading data into a data target involves transforming this flat data structure into the data target specific format and generating or retrieving surrogate keys wherever necessary. Although SAP BW completely automates this process by generating and using data-target-specific data load programs, you should still understand what's going on behind the scenes when defining or optimizing an information model.

Additional topics related to data loading, like how to use request identifiers to maintain data consistency, are covered in more detail in Chapter 9 on administration and 10 on performance.

Master Data Loading

The three types of master data supported by SAP BW (attributes, texts, and hierarchies all are modeled slightly differently and require different loading procedures. Before going into the details of these different processes, you may want to have another look at our discussion of the master data data model in Chapter 4 and at Figure 4.3.

Generally, it does not make a difference in what order attributes, texts, and hierarchies are loaded. We recommend loading texts first, since this is usually the quickest load and will generate all required surrogate IDs, effectively speeding up subsequent load processes unless the master data check option is turned on when loading transaction data.

However, it does make a difference if master data or transaction data is loaded first. We strongly recommend loading master data first—not only for performance reasons. Loaded master data allows using the master data check functionality and ensuring that no transaction data records referring to unknown master data are updated into any data target.

Master Data Attributes

Loading flat master data attribute records affects several tables of the master data data model. First, surrogate IDs have to be retrieved from the SID table or generated, if not available. Second, the attributes have to be mapped to either the time-dependent or non-time-dependent attributes table. Finally, SAP BW has to retrieve or generate SIDs for navigational master data attributes and store those SIDs in the attribute SID tables. The following code fragment shows a highly simplified master data attributes update algorithm:

Master Data Attribute Update Algorithm

```
*** STEP 1 - Process data package record by record
Loop at data package.

*** STEP 2 - Surrogate key handling
  Retrieve/Generate surrogate key.
  Update SID table.

*** STEP 3 - Non time dependent master data.
  Retrieve existing non time dependent record.
  Insert/Update non time dependent attributes.
  Retrieve surrogate keys for attributes.
  If not all SIDs available.
    If master data check requested.
      Log error, start error handling.
    Else.
      Generate new SID.
    End.
  Insert/Update attribute SID table

*** STEP 4 - Time dependent master data.
  Retrieve existing time dependent records.
  Check for validity period overlaps.
  Adjust overlap records accordingly.
  Insert/Update time dependent attributes.
```

```
  Retrieve surrogate keys for attributes.
  If not all SIDs available.
    If master data check requested.
      Log error, start error handling.
    Else.
      Generate new SID.
    End.
  Insert/Update attribute SID table
End.
```

Several items are important to note:

- SAP BW automatically maintains all surrogate keys (see Steps 2, 3 and 4).
- SAP BW automatically handles overlapping periods of validity in master data updates (see Step 4).
- SAP BW allows you to update a subset of the attributes from one InfoSource without compromising existing values by updating only those fields that are available.
- Duplicate keys abort the load process, and SAP BW would not be able to tell which record to use for updating the data target. Using an incorrect sequence would result in inconsistent data. This feature can be turned off, though.

NOTE Automated SID maintenance also provides some protection from accidentally deleting SIDs. Before deleting master data, SAP BW always makes sure the corresponding SID is not used in any other data target.

Master Data Texts

Loading text records is similar to yet simpler than loading attribute records, as there are no additional SID tables to update:

```
Master Data Text Update Algorithm
*** STEP 1 - Process data package record by record
Loop at data package.

*** STEP 2 - Surrogate key handling
  Retrieve/Generate surrogate key.
  Update SID table.

*** STEP 3 - Non time dependent master data texts.
  Retrieve existing non time dependent record.
  Insert/Update non time dependent texts.

*** STEP 4 - Time dependent master data texts.
  Retrieve existing time dependent records.
  Check for validity period overlaps.
```

```
    Adjust overlap records accordingly.
    Insert/Update time dependent texts.
  End.
```

Master Data Hierarchies

Characteristic hierarchies all generate their own unique surrogate IDs to improve reporting performance. There are actually four different hierarchy tables that are generated if an InfoObject uses hierarchies as discussed in Chapter 4. Hierarchies are different from other data loads in that an extracted hierarchy is only valid in its entirety; it is not possible to update just a selection of the records of the hierarchy without compromising the hierarchy structure. It is, however, possible to load consistent hierarchy subtrees, as the following pseudocode fragment illustrates:

```
Master Data Hierarchy Update Algorithm
*** STEP 1 - Check hierarchy consistency
If hierarchy subtree loaded.
  Merge subtree into existing hierarchy.
Endif.

*** STEP 2 - Check hierarchy consistency
Check for duplicate nodes.
Check for loops.
Check for orphans.

*** STEP 3 - Update hierarchy
Write hierarchy into hierarchy table
Write hierarchy intervals into hierarchy interval table

*** STEP 4 - Create SIDs
Write hierarchy SID tables
```

Recently added options in hierarchy loading include:

- Loading hierarchy sub trees.
- Loading hierarchies into the PSA.
- Additional attributes can be assigned to hierarchy nodes.
- A sign can be assigned to a hierarchy node, allowing for applications like net profit calculations in an account hierarchy in the Business Explorer.

InfoCube Loading

Understanding the details of the InfoCube load process requires understanding the InfoCube data model, which is explained in detail in Chapter 4 and illustrated in Figure 4.4.

The fact tables and dimension tables primarily consist of surrogate keys. The fact tables contain the key figures plus all the dimension identifiers to link it to the dimension table. The dimension tables use SIDs to link characteristic values to the dimension table. All of these surrogate IDs are automatically retrieved or generated during data loads. The following pseudocode fragment shows the basics of the InfoCube update algorithm:

```
*** STEP 1 - Process data package record by record
Loop at data package.

*** STEP 2 - Surrogate key handling
  Retrieve SIDs.
  If not all SIDs available.
    If master data check requested.
      Log error, start error handling.
    Else.
      Generate new SID.
    End.
  End.
  Insert/Update SID tables

*** STEP 3 - Dimension key handling.
  Retrieve/Generate DIMIDs.
  Insert/Update DIMID tables.
  Assign DIMIDs to related fields of the fact table.

*** STEP 4 - Key figure handling.
  Assign key figure values to related fields of the fact table.
  Insert/Update fact table.
End.
```

Loading ODS Objects

Loading ODS objects is a two-step process. The first step is to load data into an activation queue. The second step is activating that data. Upon activation the contents of the activation queue are compared to the active data records, changes are tracked in the change log, and current records are written to the active data table of the ODS object. Both processes are illustrated in Figure 6.27. As of release 3.0, ODS object load and activation processes can be parallelized.

The following two pseudocode fragments show the basic procedure for loading data into an ODS object and subsequently activating the data from the activation queue:

```
*** STEP 1 - Process data package record by record
Loop at data package.

*** STEP 2 - Surrogate key handling
```

```
    If ODS object is BEx enabled.
      Generate SIDs.
    End.

*** STEP 4 - Key and data field handling.
    Assign key and data field values to output fields.
    Insert into ODS object activation queue.
End.

*** STEP 1 - Process activation queue record by record
Loop at activation queue.

*** STEP 2 - Handle new records
    Read active ODS record with same key.
    If record does not exist.
      Insert into active data records.
      Insert into delta queue.

*** STEP 3 - Handle updated records
    Else.
      Invert existing record.
      Insert inverted record into change log.
      Insert new record into change log.
      Update active data records with new record.
    End.
```

For a more detailed technical description of the ODS object load process, refer to the SAP Service Marketplace (http://service.sap.com/bw).

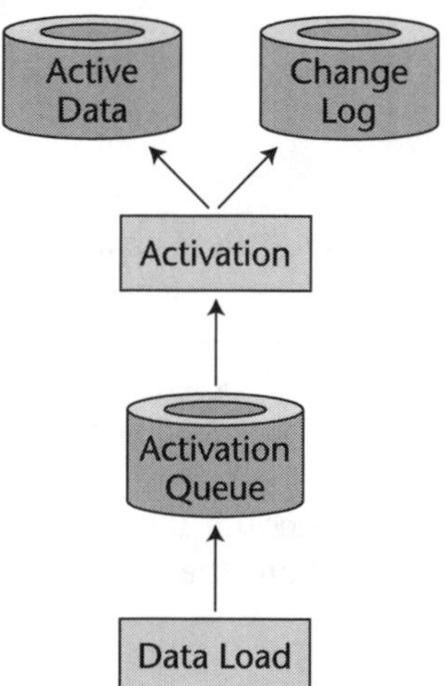

Figure 6.27 ODS object loading and activation.

NOTE The data load process for ODS objects has been reimplemented with SAP BW release 3.0 and changed fundamentally compared to previous releases.

Summary

Extracting, transforming, and loading data not only remains the most time- and resource-consuming part of a data warehouse project; it also remains the most critical part of a data warehouse project, as accurate, integrated, and comprehensive information is one of the key success factors for every information system. This chapter not only lays the foundation for understanding the extraction processes in SAP R/3; it also provides valuable insight for implementing extraction processes in other operational system environments, whether another ERP system or a custom legacy system.

SAP BW supports different interfaces providing access to data stored in SAP systems, in flat files, and in external database systems and accepts XML data streams. SAP BW data extraction and transformation is complemented by an open interface for standard ETL tools, such as Ascential DataStage, Informatica PowerCenter, and others to populate SAP BW with data.

SAP BW nearly eliminates the need to think about how data is actually loaded into the different data targets. All the details of the load processes, such as mapping flat data records to a complex data model and handling surrogate keys, are automatically handled by update programs that are generated according the meta data definitions of the data target.

Information Access, Analysis, and Presentation

The old saying that you can lead a horse to water but you can't make it drink is particularly apropos when discussing business intelligence tools. Information access and presentation is a topic that is often the center of great debate and controversy. Even if a tool delivers the right information to the right user at the right time, there is no guarantee that the user will use the tool. No single information access tool can satisfy an organization's or even an individual's requirements. It is not uncommon for each department to insist on using a particular tool because of its unique requirements. SAP BW has and supports a broad range of presentation and access tools that turn data into information and deliver it to the desired consumer.

In Chapter 6 we described how to integrate and transform data so it may be stored in SAP BW storage constructs such as ODS objects, InfoCubes, and master data. This chapter picks up where Chapter 6 left off. Here we'll highlight the main services provided in SAP BW that retrieve data, turn it into meaningful business information, and deliver that information to an information consumer. The chapter has been organized into two main sections: SAP BW information access and analysis services and SAP BW presentation services.

Architecture

SAP BW presentation services layer includes all the components required to present information available on the SAP BW server in the traditional Microsoft Excel-based Business Explorer Analyzer, in the Business Explorer Web Environment, or in third-party applications. Figure 7.1 illustrates the main architectural layers of SAP BW. In this chapter, we'll build on the previous chapters and start with the presentation services layer then. Then we'll move into the information access and analysis services layer. We will also highlight the interfaces that are exposed to third-party reporting and presentation tools.

Query Processing Overview

The query process in SAP BW is a series of requests and responses, including requests for information, database selections, application caching, number crunching, information formatting, and ultimately responding to the requester by presenting results sets. From an end user's perspective this process has been abstracted to the point that the end user's only concern is making a request for information that will lead him or her to solve the particular business problem at hand. However, behind the scenes, SAP BW is busy at work creating the optimal database access plan, locating aggregates, converting currency, applying hierarchies, filtering, and so on.

Let's look at the query request response process in the context of a typical business question. We will use the example of analyzing revenue and contribution margins across multiple geographies and customers to illustrate how the information request response process works in SAP BW. Figure 7.2 depicts the analysis process in SAP BW.

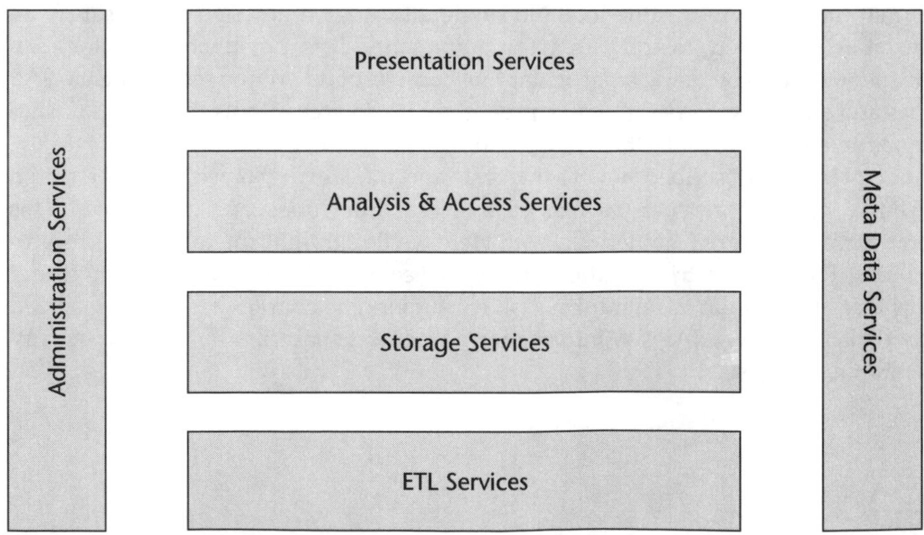

Figure 7.1 Main architectural levels of SAP BW.

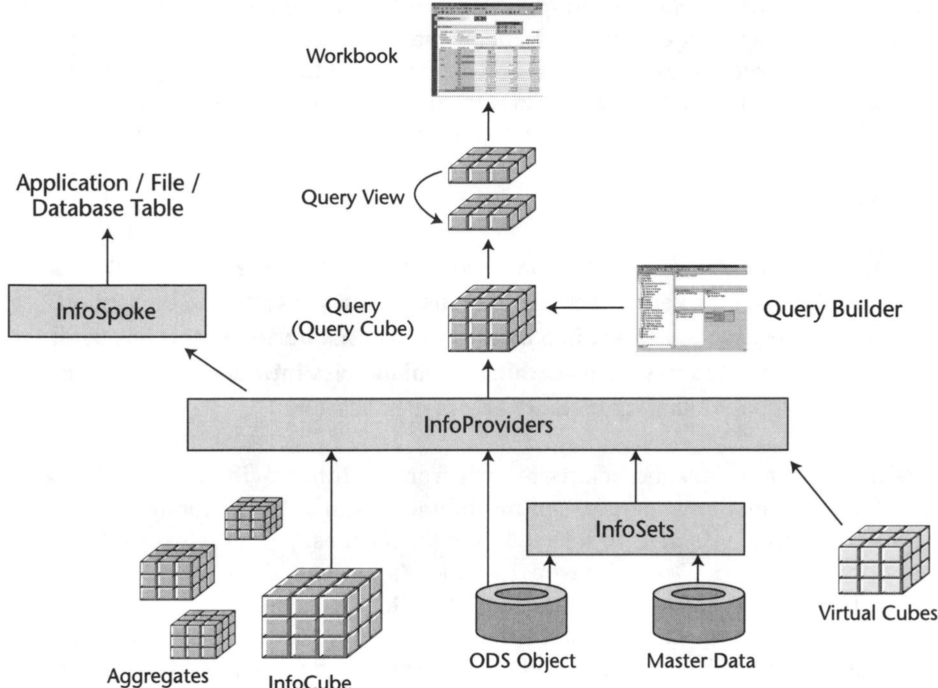

Figure 7.2 Analysis processing.

In our scenario, we'll assume that this is the first time the corporate controller has requested contribution margin and revenue to be analyzed by geography and customer. After launching her favorite Web browser and navigating to the SAP BW reporting homepage on the corporate intranet, the controller selects the *Create New Query* option. After selecting this option, she invokes the meta data services of SAP BW to return a list of potential information providers that may be queried. The controller selects the appropriate InfoProvider, and again invokes the meta data services in SAP BW. The services return a list of dimensions that contain characteristic InfoObjects as well as a list of key figures. The controller selects the *Revenue and Contribution* key figure, as well as the *Geography* and *Customer* characteristics, and assigns them to the rows or columns of the query result sets based on her preference. She then executes the query.

At the center of the information access, analysis, and presentation services in SAP BW is the OLAP engine. An information consumer application requests information from the OLAP engine in the form of a multidimensional expression or similar selection request. In our example the controller requests revenue and contribution margin for the current period and fiscal year for all customers and all geographies. Leading business intelligence tools generate selection expressions so the end users do not need to know the specific syntax. The request is sent from the browser to the SAP BW server. Consumers may be a browser, mobile device, Excel spreadsheet, or as in our example, a third-party client application. The SAP BW server takes the request through one of a number of standard interface techniques and hands it to the OLAP engine for fulfillment. (We will describe the interfaces in detail later in this chapter.)

The SAP BW server takes the request and determines if there is an aggregate cube in existence that may satisfy the request. In our example an aggregate cube that summarizes customer or geographies may be a candidate for optimal retrieval. If no such aggregate cubes exist for the query, the application server makes a request to the database server.

NOTE SAP BW attempts to limit the number of round trips from presentation server to database server by caching and reusing query results and navigation steps on the application server in a cross-transactional buffer after it has been selected from the database. This caching technique was introduced in version 3.0b with the goal of sharing memory across user sessions.

The database requests and selects records from an InfoProvider, or an aggregate, that is stored in a relational database or multidimensional database for aggregates as a star schema. The records that are selected from the database server may be returned to the application server. Depending on the query's read mode settings, records are cached for the OLAP engine to process and, ultimately, to calculate and return a query navigation state to the presentation server. The caching of the selected data on the application server is sometimes referred to as a *query cube* depending on the read mode that is set for the query. The OLAP engine will use the query cube to calculate and return result sets to the client for subsequent information requests, assuming the query cube contains the necessary data to respond to the request. We will discuss the options for setting a query's read mode and the impact on performance in Chapter 10.

The controller in our example would receive a listing of revenue and contribution margins for all customers in all geographies. She notices that revenue, which is displayed in U.S. dollars (USD), is higher than she had planned and proceeds to investigate which geography is exceeding her expectations. Her request is sent from the client to the application server, where it is once again handled by the OLAP engine. Once the appropriate storage service returns the records, the OLAP engine creates the query data and proceeds as previously described. The controller learns that the United Kingdom is exceeding her sales expectations.

Note that the OLAP engine will take care of any currency translations based on the meta data of the InfoObjects included in the query, as well as the meta data of the query itself. In this case the geographies are countries, and most countries have their own currency. The controller also may wish to analyze the revenue in the group currency of USD. Upon doing so, she notices that Argentina has failed to meet her sales expectation. Not satisfied she has found the cause of the shortfall, she investigates further and requests the currency be converted to local currency for all countries. A request is once again sent to the OLAP engine to be processed. The local currencies are either retrieved or calculated, depending on the modeling of the InfoMart, and the newly calculated query slice is returned to the client. Now the controller realizes that Argentina did in fact meet sales expectation but experienced a significant foreign exchange impact as a result of the rate dropping.

The process of requesting and responding to queries is the central concept of this chapter. We will first investigate the presentation services and then move to the information access and analysis services. It is not our intent here to re-create SAP documentation, nor is it possible for us to cover every reporting and analysis feature of SAP BW. However, we will look behind the scenes at the central services SAP BW performs and lay out the possible options for putting them to use to solve business problems.

Presentation Services

SAP BW presentation services layer includes all components required to present information available on the SAP BW server, including the traditional Microsoft Excel-based Business Explorer Analyzer, the Business Explorer Web applications, and Business Explorer Formatted Reporting. Mobile device and Enterprise Portal support are rendered from the same set of Business Explorer Web services as the Business Explorer Web applications. Figure 7.3 provides an overview of the components of the presentation services layer.

The line between the BEx Query Designer and BEx Analyzer is often blurred, as the tools are tightly integrated and users of the BEx Analyzer are often also query designers. There are numerous features that are often described as part of the BEx Analyzer when, in fact, they are part of the BEx Query Designer. Rather than split hairs, we have separated the Designer's functions and Analyzer's functions based on where the specific features are used in the process of creating and analyzing.

Business Explorer Components

The Business Explorer (BEx) is much more than an Excel add-in that allows access to the SAP BW server. There are several areas that the Business Explorer in SAP BW now covers—for example, support for formatted reporting, mobile devices, and pure HTML-based Web applications. The Business Explorer's integration with SAP Enterprise Portals enables a single point of entry for a wide spectrum of end-user roles and business-related information packs. This enables collaboration and integration with nonstructured information such as documents that capture users' comments on such things as the explanation of variances, justification for changes in forecast figures, graphics, syndicated information available via the Internet, and the ability to unify the analytics served by SAP BW with transaction processing applications. This functionality allows end users to dynamically create personalized analytic applications.

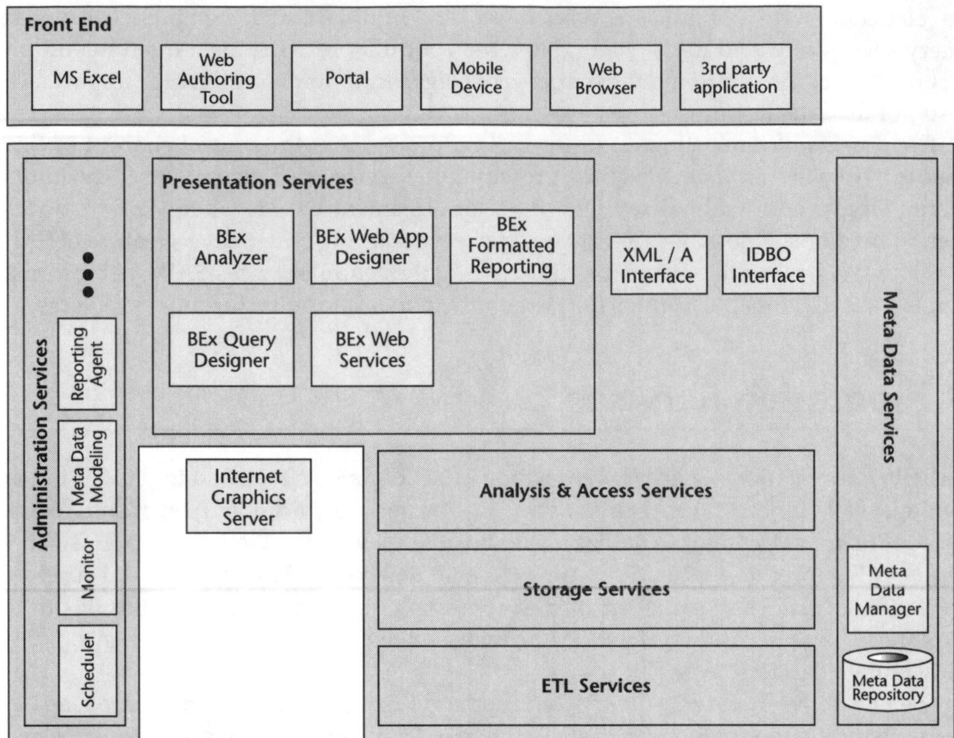

Figure 7.3 Presentation services.

In Figure 7.3 you will notice that the Business Explorer consists of several components: BEx Query Designer, BEx Analyzer, BEx Web Application Designer, BEx Formatted Reporting, and BEx Mobile Device Support. The BEx is designed to meet a vast range of business needs, from simple list reports (e.g., all the customers in a range of zip codes) to the complex (e.g., elimination of intrabusiness volume), while taking into account the local currencies and fiscal year variants of the business entities. The BEx is designed to appeal to a wide range of business users, from hunters and farmer to miners and explorers. Various end users will interact with the BEx tools. Farmers, for example, may request information via a Web browser by entering a URL. Explorers, on the other hand, may use the BEx Analyzer to create and re-create complex queries based on their findings. (For an explanation of the different group types, see Chapter 5.)

In this next section we describe BEx queries from design to execution, along with powerful OLAP functions that may not be obvious to the casual or first-time user. Throughout this chapter we refer to each of the five Business Explorer components by their specific names.

BEx Query Designer

All multidimensional reporting and analysis performed in SAP BW is based on a query definition stored in the Meta Data Repository. Queries provide access to multidimensional information providers (InfoCubes), as well as flat information providers (ODS objects, master data). The *Business Explorer Query Designer* allows you to define queries in an interactive standalone application by simply dragging and dropping the desired meta data objects into the query results area.

A *query* is a specification of a certain dynamic view on an InfoProvider used for multidimensional navigation. Queries are the basis for all kinds of analysis and reporting functionality available in SAP BW.

The BEx Query Designer is a standalone tool for defining queries. For some readers, *query* may conjure up the image of an SQL generator that creates a simple list of records. The BEx Query Designer is a graphical tool for defining both tabular queries and multidimensional queries that access powerful OLAP functions. The BEx Query Designer, while a standalone client program, interacts with the SAP BW server, more specifically the Meta Data Repository. Meta data about a query's InfoProvider is passed to the Query Designer so the form and function of a query may be defined and ready for ad hoc execution. Note that only one InfoProvider may be assigned to a query. If more than one InfoProvider is needed, a MultiProvider has to be used. We have covered this topic in Chapter 5.

All characteristics, navigational attributes, and key figures available through an InfoProvider are available for use in query definitions. Because queries are multidimensional objects, they effectively define subcubes called *query cubes* on top of the InfoProvider. Query cubes define the degree of freedom available for query navigation in the presentation layer.

To define a query, the Designer is launched in one of five ways:

- As a client application
- From the Web Application Designer
- Via the HTML Query Designer
- Via the traditional BEx Analyzer in Excel
- Via the Crystal Reports Designer

The first option the query designer has is selecting an existing query from a list of favorites or from a list of queries that have been assigned to the specific role the designer has in the organization. If the query does not exist, a new one may be created. Next, an InfoProvider for the new query is selected. The InfoProvider, as we will discuss further later in this chapter, is an abstraction layer that allows the query designer to define both tabular and multidimensional queries with the same tool without regard to how or where the physical data is stored. Upon selecting an InfoProvider, the query designer will see a list of meta data defining the following elements:

Structures. Predefined selection and layout criteria for a row or column that may be reused in all queries for a particular InfoProvider. Structures may contain a combination of key figures, characteristics, and formulas. A *reusable structure* is a particular, commonly used collection of key figures or characteristics stored in the Meta Data Repository for reuse in multiple queries (e.g., a plan/actual variance or a contribution margin schema).

Key figures. A type of InfoObject that is used to record quantitative facts or measures. All of the key figures for a particular InfoProvider are available for queries. A *calculated key figure* is a formula consisting of basic, restricted, or other calculated key figures available in the InfoProvider stored in the Meta Data Repository for reuse in multiple queries (e.g., an average discount rate). A *restricted key figure* is a key figure with an associated filter on certain characteristic values stored in the Meta Data Repository for reuse in multiple queries (e.g., year-to-date sales of previous year). A query consists of meta data elements arranged in rows, columns, and free characteristics.

Dimensions. The logical grouping of characteristic InfoObjects in InfoCubes.

The query elements assigned to the rows and columns are displayed in the initial query view. Free characteristics are not displayed in the initial query view. Free characteristics are available for navigation in the BEx Analyzer or in analytic Web applications. Each individual navigational step (drill down, drill across, add/remove filters, etc.) in the analysis process provides a different query view, and the steps are controlled by the BEx Analyzer, BEx Web applications, or third-party tools.

Query definitions are created and maintained in the BEx Query Designer by simply dragging the available query elements into the rows, columns, free characteristics, or filter areas and eventually defining additional properties. The Query Designer also integrates all functionality required to define the query elements. Query elements include characteristics, key figures, calculated key figures (formulas), restricted key figures, and reusable structures. Queries may have filters on characteristic values or filters on key figure values (conditions) assigned to select a certain slice of information from the InfoProvider, and they may be parameterized by query variables. Exceptions assigned to a query help identify key figure values regarded exceptional from a business point of view.

The simplest type of query is a tabular query. *Tabular queries* are often used to generate listings of master data, such as a listing of all customers in the state of Illinois. For instance, you could create such a query by locating the InfoObject for the characteristic *State* and dragging and dropping it to the column window. You could then right-click on the state to restrict the query to just the state of Illinois. You complete this simple tabular query by dragging and dropping the characteristic *Customer* to the column window.

NOTE Defining selection values that are valid for all the columns and rows of a query in the filter window will improve query performance.

Multidimensional queries provide more options but still are easy to define and use. Figure 7.4 illustrates the options a query designer is presented when working with multidimensional queries. Along with the rows definition window there is also a Free Characteristics window. In multidimensional mode, the query creator drags and drops key figures and the characteristics desired in the query from a dimension to the desired column or row. As the InfoObjects are placed in a row or column a preview of the query results is displayed. The designer may also place characteristics in the Free Characteristic or *Filter* window. Free characteristics are selected as part of the query's logic but are not displayed in the default view of the query. They may, however, be used for drill-down and drill-across functions by the user of the BEx Analyzer or Web application. You use filters to limit the selection of data to a particular characteristic value or set of values. For example, the query "analyze revenue generated across all product lines that were sold to customers in Illinois during the month of July in the year 2002" may have three filter values: the state of Illinois, the month of July, and the year 2002. If you are familiar with any of the leading OLAP tools, you will notice a great deal of parity in the basic functions of SAP BW multidimensional queries.

Several good sources of information on SAP Web sites are available that detail the basic steps for building queries, so we will not repeat that information here. The BEx Query Designer is simple enough to learn with a little practice. However, the key success factor is in understanding the information model. With this in mind, instead of the absolute basics, we will focus on the functions that may not be obvious to the novice query designer. We have recognized a plateau that self-taught BEx query designers and users reach in their learning. In this next section we'll help those readers reach the summit.

NOTE InfoCubes, ODS objects, InfoSets, and master data are available to the query designer for either tabular or multidimensional analysis.

Designing Queries with Hierarchies

SAP BW hierarchies were introduced in Chapter 3 and expanded on in Chapter 4 as we detailed the impact hierarchies have on information modeling. Hierarchies are used for data modeling, restricting data selection, navigation, and planning. For example, there are hierarchies for cost centers, profit centers, general ledger accounts, customers, and products, to name a few. In most reporting and analysis applications the concept of hierarchies exists. While it is not a new concept, it is an important one, and hierarchies are often the means of defining aggregation levels. SAP BW supports two kinds of hierarchies: internal and external. *Internal hierarchies* are modeled into a specific dimension. *External hierarchies* in SAP BW are called external because they are neither stored in InfoCube dimensions nor as navigational attributes; instead, they are stored in separate hierarchy tables associated to the base InfoObject (e.g., 0CUSTOMER for a customer hierarchy).

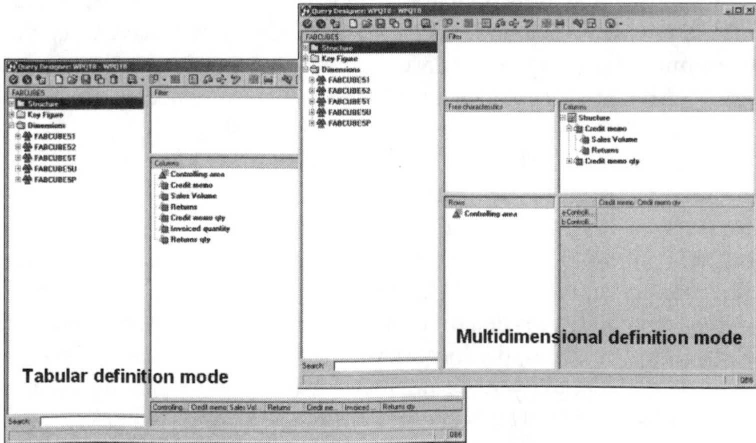

Figure 7.4 BEx Query Designer: tabular and multidimensional modes.

As mentioned in Chapter 4 there are several options for modeling hierarchies, including version and time dependency for the whole hierarchy tree, time dependency for the hierarchy structure, and the use of intervals instead of single values to assign a range of values to a specific hierarchy node. The hierarchy data model provides a means to store balanced and unbalanced hierarchies with different types of hierarchy nodes available at different levels or network structured hierarchies. These elements provide a tremendous amount of flexibility to the information modeler and query designer. Hierarchies may be explicitly assigned to a query at design time or may be entered by the query user at run time when a hierarchy variable is used.

A query designer may set the hierarchy as fixed for a given query, thereby eliminating the possibility that a user of the BEx Analyzer or a BEx Web application may switch to an alternative hierarchy. The query designer may go so far as to fix the query to a given node within a given hierarchy. If the hierarchy that is assigned to a characteristic is time- and/or version-dependent, the query designer may enable the query user to enter three variable properties for the hierarchy. The hierarchy name, version, and key date for data selection may all be prompted at query run time, providing the maximum amount of flexibility.

The query designer sets the display attributes for the hierarchy. When a query is executed in the BEx Analyzer the hierarchy is in either the rows or columns depending on the placement of the underlying characteristic. The hierarchy may be expanded and collapsed at its node levels. Each node level may contain an optionally displayed results line. The result line, if calculated, is defined by the query designer, but it may be changed in an ad hoc manner in the BEx Analyzer. The manner in which the result line is calculated may be set using the *Calculate* function on the right mouse context menu. The result line may be displayed as the min, max, first, last, variance, count, average, or standard deviation of the underlying data in the query cube. Values that are selected as part of the query view that do not have a corresponding external hierarchy node assignment will be displayed as *Not Assigned*. Note that each node level in a hierarchy can have its own settings for how aggregation should be performed, displayed, and used in calculating results rows. This allows for one node level in a hierarchy to be used as a negative value. For example, if a hierarchy is created for general ledger accounts, and all of the revenue accounts summarize to a node level, that node level may have a results line that is a negative number. This may be the case if your data model is tracking both debits and credits, since the revenue account is a credit in double-entry accounting. The hierarchy node may be set so the value is shown as a positive number.

A significant difference between SAP BW and other leading business intelligence tools is in the area of hierarchy handling. The Business Explorer toolset has a restriction that the hierarchy must already exist prior to the query being executed. Unlike many business intelligence tools on the market, the query user may not define hierarchies and nodes in an ad hoc manner on the fly while analyzing information. End users may, however, restrict the selection conditions of a predefined hierarchy at run time or select a new hierarchy for the query. Selecting the local query navigation window, selecting the characteristic that has the hierarchy assignment, and then right-clicking on the desired properties accomplishes this. The hierarchy properties window will appear and a new hierarchy may be selected by name, as illustrated in Figure 7.5. This is, of course, assuming the query designer has not set any restrictions on the hierarchy or node within a hierarchy that is to be used in a given query.

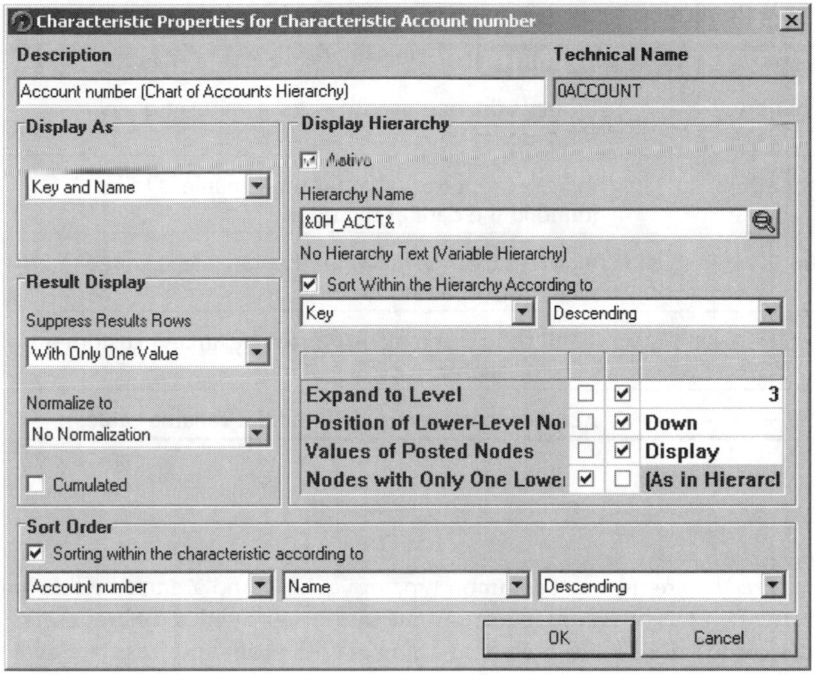

Figure 7.5 Hierarchy properties.

Variables

Variables are placeholders in a query definition that have their value defined at query run time, thus enabling the parameterization of queries. There are five types of variables: characteristic, text, formula, hierarchy, and hierarchy nodes. A classic example of the use of hierarchies is found in a common financial query to display a profit-and-loss statement. The variables enable the query designer to create the profit-and-loss statement once and allow the end user to determine at query run time the financial period for which the query should be run. In this example the characteristic fiscal period is entered by the end user or defaulted based on his or her personalization preferences.

Several processing types are available for the five variable types. The processing type sets the behavior of the variable. For example, if a variable has a processing type of "manual entry," a pop-up window will prompt the user to enter a value at the time of query execution. The five processing types are listed in Table 7.1. We will briefly describe the replacement path processing type, since it may not be self-evident. This will be done as we describe the five variable types, specifically the text variable. Note that variables need to be defined prior to being used in the BEx Query Designer and that the variables have a global scope. This means that once their properties are defined, those variable properties are inherited by every query that utilizes the variable and all variables are available for all queries. Once variables are input, personalization options may be set to prevent the user from entering the variable values more than one time.

Table 7.1 Variable Processing Types

PROCESSING TYPE	DESCRIPTION
Manual/default entry	Prompts the end user to enter a value at query run time.
Replacement path	Indicates that the value for the variable is to be found in the data of the query.
Authorization	Indicates that the value for the variable is stored with the user authorization.
Customer Exit	ABAP code that may be written by an SAP customer to fill a variable.
SAP Exit	ABAP code written by SAP to fill a variable value.

Characteristic variables are the most common type of variable and are used when an end user or group of end users would like to run the same query with a different set of parameter values, as described in the preceding example with profit-and-loss statement. The characteristic value is commonly defined with a processing type of manual/ default with the settings *ready for input* so at query run time the characteristic value may be selected. The entry for a characteristic variable is not necessarily limited to one value. For example, say an IT director is responsible for three cost centers. The director may run the same query definition for displaying direct costs as a sales manager that is responsible for one cost center. The sales manager will be prompted for her cost center numbers and the IT director for his. The processing type authorization is an alternative to the manual entry processing type. The authorization processing type looks to the end users' authorization settings as defined with transaction RSMM and uses the value found there as input for the variable.

Text variables are commonly used in conjunction with a characteristic variable. In our profit-and-loss example, imagine there are two columns on the report, one column for the base period and another column for a forecasted period. When the end user of the report is prompted to enter a number for the base period to be analyzed, the value entered will populate the characteristic variable for the query and the base period column on the report will be populated with the profit-and-loss values for that period. A text variable may be used in this situation to change the column header text for the base period, so when "0012002" is entered for the characteristic value, the column header may display the text "Period 1 2002". The text variable is commonly defined with a processing type of *replacement path data*, so at query run time the characteristic value in the text variable's replacement path is used for the column header. Text variables using a replacement path have the option to use the characteristic value or the accompanying text value for a characteristic value. In our example, if the characteristic value is defined the column header text would be set to "0012002". Text variables do not support the processing type authorization or exit. The replacement path is most frequently used for text variables.

Formula variables allow numbers to be passed to the query at run time. This is especially useful for entering exchange, inflationary, or growth rates in a query at run time. This may be used for simulations where the formula variable value is passed into the calculations of a column, row, or cell. For example, the forecasted period in the previous example may take the base period and multiply the revenue for the base period by a factor that the user enters at query run time to calculate the projected revenue in the forecasted period. In this scenario, the end user would enter a value (e.g., 5 percent), and the formula in the forecasted period column would select the values in the base period column and multiply the values in the base period column by 1.05 to determine the forecasted period. Formula variables do not support the processing type authorization.

Hierarchy variables and *hierarchy node variables* behave in the same manner as the characteristic variables. The hierarchy variable represents an entire hierarchy tree for a given characteristic. The hierarchy node represents a given substructure within a hierarchy. A difference between the hierarchy and hierarchy node variables is the support of the authorization processing type. The hierarchy node is able to look to the settings in transaction RSMM for the default value for a given user. The hierarchy variable allows the query user to select entirely new hierarchies versus simply selecting a different node within the same hierarchy.

With the release of SAP BW version 3.0 there is a wizard for creating variables that guides query designers through the process of defining variables of all four types.

Conditional Analysis

Conditional result set processing in the BEx allows the end user to limit the information that is returned to the query view to only the records that meet specific conditions—for example, a condition may be set to only display the top 10 customers from a revenue perspective or the bottom 15 percent of all employees based on their latest performance review. Conditions are an efficient way to zoom in on a specific subset of information.

A single query may have one or more conditions assigned to it, and a condition may have multiple preconditions assigned to it. There are six condition types that are applied to levels of navigational states:

Top N

Top percentage

Top sum

Bottom N

Bottom percentage

Bottom sum

When applied, the *top percentage* and *bottom percentage* and *absolute count* condition types act as their names imply. They reduce the list to display an absolute number, say the top 10 customers, from our revenue example and display the results line for the amount of revenue for all customers or a percentage. The percentage option works in a similar manner. In our performance review example, the scores would be looked at as a percentage of total, and those with scores in the bottom 15 percent would be listed individually.

The *top sum* and *bottom sum* are a bit different from the percentage and absolute count. The top sum, for example, has a threshold set for a particular key figure. If we use the example of revenue as we did for the top 10 customers, this time we would set the condition not to the number of customers we are looking to analyze but to the amount of revenue for which we are looking; let's assume 100,000EUR. All of the customers would be sorted according to their revenues, in descending order. Then moving down the list, customers would be selected and listed in the condition up until the point that the 100,000EUR total revenue threshold was broken. The customer that breaks the threshold is included in the list.

Along with the ability to create ranking lists, query designers and analyzers can create absolute lists that set thresholds that will either include or exclude individual rows of a query based on whether or not they meet the condition. For example, to support a physical inventory, a query may be set with a condition that displays all inventory positions that have negative stock quantities. Note that conditions may also be defined for combinations of characteristics—for instance, "show me the top 10 product/customer combinations."

Exception Analysis

Exception reporting is a bit different than conditional filtering. Exceptions allow for predefined or ad hoc rules to be applied to a query that indicate how the information should be highlighted to show that a threshold has been achieved. Up to nine different colors may be assigned to values that cross an exception threshold. These colors, in hues of red, yellow, and green, may be used to identify deviations.

There are three main areas of exception reporting that you should be aware of: the setting of exceptions, the online evaluation of exceptions, and the background processing of exceptions. The primary difference between the online exceptions and the background exception is that online exceptions highlight deviations within a query output, whether in the BEx Analyzer or in a Web application created with the BEx Web Applications Designer, but they do not allow for the automatic handling of notifications.

The background scheduling of exception reporting is done via the *reporting agent*. In the reporting agent the exception definitions that have been set in the BEx Query Designer are scheduled and follow-up actions are defined. Once the reporting agent performs the exception evaluation in the background, it updates a so-called exception log for the *Alert Monitor* to access. The Alert Monitor displays the exceptions collected in the log and provides a single place to evaluate all of the deviations that have been triggered by the background process run by the reporting agent. The Alert Monitor may be viewed in the BEx Analyzer, in Web applications, or in the Administrator's Workbench. The reporting agent allows settings to be set that indicate the follow-up action required to take corrective action. The follow-up actions may, for example, include sending an email to the responsible person. Background exception reporting—that is, the reporting agent settings—are organized by application component, InfoProvider, and query. We will discuss the administration options of the reporting agent in Chapter 9 and concentrate now on defining exceptions and online evaluations.

Exceptions are defined in the BEx Query Designer while defining the global query properties. The Alert Monitor icon allows for two menu selections: one for creating new exceptions and one for changing exceptions. Once the exception definition window is opened, the query designer must make three primary settings. The first setting is the key figure that the exception is to be applied to. The second setting is the threshold values and the alert level that should be used to highlight the exception should the threshold be reached. (As mentioned, nine unique alert levels may be set.) The third setting is the aggregation level and combination of characteristic values by which the threshold should be evaluated. Figure 7.6 depicts the characteristic combinations, or *cell restrictions*.

After the designer selects the appropriate characteristics, he or she must assign an operator for each characteristic. There are five options:

Totals Only. The exception is only evaluated when a characteristic is aggregated.

Everything. Exceptions are evaluated regardless of the level of aggregation for the characteristic.

Everything but Totals. Exceptions are evaluated for nonaggregated values for a characteristic.

Fixed Values. The exception is only evaluated for a preset characteristic value.

Hierarchy Level. Exceptions are only evaluated for specific levels of a hierarchy.

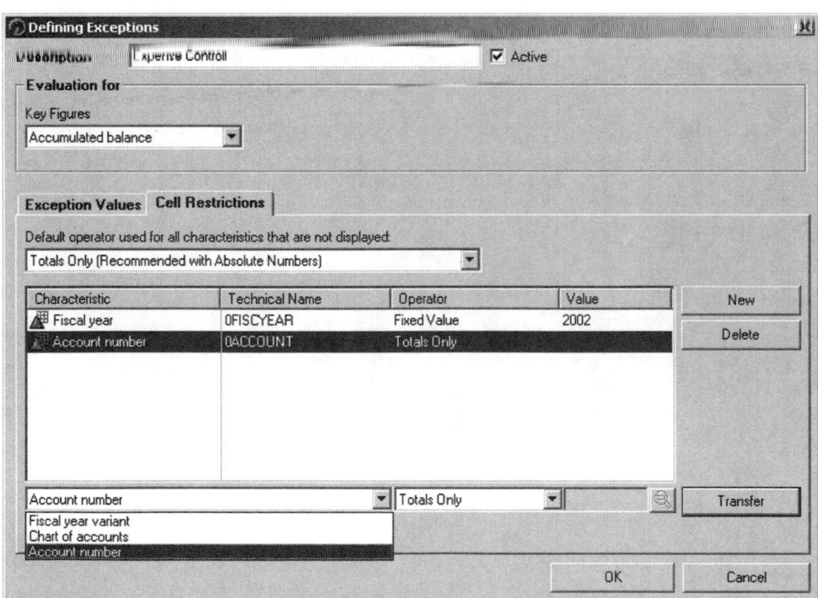

Figure 7.6 Exception definition.

A setting that query designers should be aware of is the default operator for all of the characteristics that do not have explicit cell restrictions defined. There are two options for characteristics that are not explicitly restricted: Totals Only or All. The *Totals Only* option is recommended for when the key figure for the exception is an absolute number. The *All* option is recommended when the key figure for the exception is a relative number. The *All* setting is typically used for key figures that are percentages or ratios. The default operator is applied regardless of the drill-down level of the characteristics that are not explicitly defined in the exception.

The ability to set the operators by characteristic and to combine multiple characteristics enables query designers to create a powerful set of business rules that may be evaluated and subsequently trigger alerts. Figure 7.7 illustrates online exception highlighting in the BEx Analyzer.

Restricting and Calculating Key Figures

Queries are designed for InfoProviders in the sense that only the characteristics and their attributes defined in the InfoProvider are available for analysis. Key figures are a bit different in that they may be used in one of three ways. In the first way, often referred to as *basic*, the key figure is dragged from the InfoProvider area of the BEx Designer to a column or row. The basic key figure is calculated by the OLAP engine based on the query's aggregation settings and the key figures attributes that were set when it was defined as an InfoObject in the Meta Data Repository. The other two options are restricted key figures and calculated key figures.

Microsoft Excel - Book3

BW207 Exceptions GR-00

Key Figures	Invoiced sales (cost)
Cal. year / month	
Sold-to party	

Cal. year / month	JUN 2002

Cal. year / month	Sold-to party		Invoiced sales (cost)
06/2002	1001	Lampen-Markt GmbH	342,683.03 DM
	1033	Karsson High Tech Markt	305,052.51 DM
	1172	CBD Computer Based Design	212,087.27 DM
	1174	Motomarkt Stuttgart GmbH	720,051.80 DM
	1175	Elektromarkt Bamby	276,483.05 DM
	1300	Christal Clear	582,521.16 DM
	1321	Becker Stuttgart	299,458.11 DM
	1360	Amadeus	182,407.43 DM
	1460	C.A.S. Computer Application Systems	84,436.39 DM
	1900	J & P	693,481.32 DM
	1901	Motor Sports	80,075.01 DM
	2004	SudaTech GmbH	276,796.61 DM
	2007	Software Systeme GmbH	233,885.66 DM
	2130	COMPU Tech. AG	244,955.93 DM
	2140	N.I.C. High Tech	128,170.53 DM
	2200	HTG Komponente GmbH	507,401.07 DM
	2300	Motomarkt Heidelberg GmbH	66,017.09 DM
	3000	Thomas Bush Inc.	8,452.43 DM
	3970	CCS Industrial	0.00 DM
	R110	SB Warenhaus R110	279,225.48 DM
	R310	GM Store R310	206,928.16 DM
	R311	GM Store R311	486,504.31 DM
	Result		6,217,074.35 DM

Figure 7.7 Displaying exception in the BEx Analyzer.

Restricted key figures are the combination of a key figure with a filter value for a characteristic or set of characteristics. For example, in a report, a query designer wants to display in one column the net sales revenue key figure for the northeast region and in the next column net sales for all regions. The designer drags and drops the net sales key figure to the column, then selects the *Edit* context menu option. Once done, a dialog box appears, enabling the query designer to select the characteristic value or variable to filter the key figure selection with.

Calculated key figures allow arithmetic formulas to be defined using one or more basic key figures or formula variables or calculated key figures. For example, a query designer wants to display in the column of a report the net sales revenue key figure and in the next column the cost of sales key figure. The reporting requirement is that the gross margin be calculated. If the gross margin were available in the InfoProvider, the designer can select it and drag it into a third column. If not, the designer can calculate it by using the basic key figures for net sales and cost of sales. To do this, after dragging and dropping the net sales key figure to the column and the cost of sales key figure, the designer selects the *New Formula* context menu option. A dialog box appears, and the query designer can set the formula to calculate gross margin—in this case by subtracting cost of sales from net sales using the Formula Editor. The Formula Editor contains a mathematically complete set of functions as well as data functions and boolean operators.

BEx Analyzer

The traditional SAP BW tool for actually performing multidimensional reporting and analysis in SAP BW is the *Business Explorer, or BEx, Analyzer*. It is implemented as an add-on to Microsoft Excel combining the power of SAP BW OLAP analysis with all the features (e.g., charting) and the VBA (Visual Basic for Applications) development environment of Microsoft Excel. Storing query results in Microsoft Excel workbooks, for example, allows you to use information in offline mode or to add comments and send information to other users.

The BEx Analyzer is the tool for the power users and analysts. It provides the typical functions of selecting a query, saving changes, refreshing data, formatting the query layout, and of course, navigating through the results of the OLAP engine. You can launch the BEx Analyzer from the Administrator Workbench, Microsoft Excel, or the BEx Browser.

The most common method for starting the BEx Analyzer is to open Excel, then select the BEx Analyzer add-in. This causes the Business Explorer toolbar and menu to appear. Four files may be found in the BW subdirectory of the SAPGUI installation on a client workstation. A typical path, although this is customizable, is C:\Program Files\SAPpc\BW. When installing the SAPGUI, you must select the SAP BW options in order to install the BEx front-end tools. Following is a list of the add-in files for Microsoft Excel and their usage:

sapbex.xla. Effectively the BEx Analyzer. This file is used as a Microsoft Excel add-in and is launched when the *Start | Programs | Business Explorer | Analyzer* menu path is selected in Windows environments.

sapbex0.xla. This file is used by SAP BW when the BEx Analyzer is launched via the BEx Browser or the Administrator Workbench.

sapbexc.xla. This file provides a front-end installation check. It should be used after the SAPGUI is installed on a client workstation or for troubleshooting errors. The utility performs a check on the workstation to make certain the correct DLL, OCX, and EXE files are installed to ensure the Business Explorer toolset, as well as OLE DB for OLAP tools, will be able to execute queries. Pressing the start button in this spreadsheet initiates the check and suggestions for corrective action are provided.

sapbexs.xla. This file is a sample style sheet that provides documentation for the query elements.

Once you have launched Excel with the BEx Analyzer add-in, you will see a Business Explorer menu has been added to the standard Microsoft menu, as well as a BEx toolbar. The toolbar consists of icons to open, save, refresh, format, change, and navigate queries. As we described earlier in this chapter, queries are defined in the BEx Query Designer; however, the toolbar has an option for launching the BEx Designer. Once a query is defined, it may be analyzed in Excel. You will need to select the folder icon in order to launch a query, a workbook, a query view, or to set exceptions conditions.

A *workbook* is a standard Microsoft Excel workbook with embedded references to query views and optional application elements built using Microsoft Excel functionality. For example, you can add charts, push buttons, and list boxes to a query workbook, alongside the result area and filter cell area of a query. You can also set the workbook template as a corporate standard so that all queries that are inserted into workbooks have the same look and feel. Remember that a query is independent of the workbook it is attached to and that a workbook may have several queries attached to it.

Workbooks allow query results and any applications built within Microsoft Excel to be saved and viewed offline and online. This is ideal for distributing the query workbooks to a larger audience, say, via email, while still requiring proper authorization to review the workbook. One of the nice features in the BEx Analyzer is the ability to protect the workbook from changes in addition to standard Excel sheet protection. Excel sheet protection limits the majority of the functions available to the end user. The SAP sheet protection password protects not only the query areas from changes but the entire active worksheet, yet it still allows for continued ad hoc navigation through the query cube.

The query designer determines the initial view of a query when the query is first defined. The properties of a query are considered global. That is, the designer of the query predetermines the rows, columns, filter values, variables, hierarchies, and free characteristics for all users who execute the query. This does not prohibit a specific user from customizing the query. The changes that are made to a query by an end user may be done in the local view or in the global definition, depending on authorization. Changes in the local view only impact the current user's session while analyzing a given query. A common example of a local change is to swap the rows or a query with the columns. The local view is also ideal for performing multiple navigation steps at one time. Hierarchies may also be added to a query in the local view, assuming the hierarchy definition exists for a characteristic in the query. Changes made to the global definition will impact all users of the query. The BEx Analyzer launches the BEx Query Designer for global definition changes.

Once a query is executed via the BEx Analyzer, the end user will see the initial view of the query. There are four parts to every query: title, filter, results, and text. The initial view of a newly created query will by default have the query name (title) and free characteristics (also known as dynamic filters) at the top left portion of the Excel spreadsheet. This is referred to as the *filter cell area*. Below the filter cell area is the query grid or results area. The query grid will be filled according to the selection criteria set forth by the query designer in the BEx Query Designer. The results area in the spreadsheet is under SAP BW's control. While an end user may type a value into a cell in the results area, a refresh or navigation step will cause the values to be overwritten by the newly created query view that is placed into the results area. The title, filter, results, and text may each be moved any place on a worksheet independent of each other.

The query is executed and the results area is filled. The BEx Analyzer toolbar, Business Explorer menu bar, or the context-sensitive right mouse button may be used to navigate through the query cube. The end user may easily filter, drill down and across, translate currencies, apply condition and exceptions, expand and collapse a hierarchy while navigating through the data. This navigation is often referred to as an *analysis path*.

The BEx Analyzer can display a variety of technical meta data as well as business meta data for a query. You display the technical meta data by selecting *Business Explorer | Settings | Display BW Server Information* from within Excel or by selecting the *Settings* icon in the BEx toolbar. In doing so, you will be presented with technical information pertaining to the system ID, host, database, hardware, and IP address. In addition, by switching the Trace option on, you can create a more powerful set of technical meta data. The trace option records all of the steps in an analysis path from connection to close. This utility is very helpful should you wish to extend workbooks by adding Visual Basic code to create custom pull-down lists, buttons, and the like. You can activate the trace log by selecting *Business Explorer | Settings | Trace*. To then view the trace log, you select *Business Explorer | Settings | Display Trace*. The SAP BW functions that are called from the Excel add-in are logged in the trace file. The log file helps programmers debug extensions to the front end that utilize the BEx Analyzer user exits.

NOTE Customer exits allow installation specific code to be added to an SAP software component without upgrade repercussions.

Visualizing Queries Results

There are two powerful visualization features in the BEx Analyzer. The features are relatively simple to use and apply to query results sets. Once a query is executed, you select the *Layout* button in the BEx toolbar. There you will find the *Attach Chart* and *Attach Map* options.

When the *Attach Chart* option is selected, a chart will appear in the current Excel worksheet. The chart may be moved to any place on the existing worksheet or to any worksheet in the current workbook. The chart is automatically attached to the query results area and updated as the query results area is updated. For example, if you attach a chart to a query that has a drill-down displaying countries and the revenue sold in those geographies and swap the country characteristic with the sold-to party, the chart would automatically adjust to the new characteristic. You may select any of the chart types available in standard Microsoft Excel to visualize the query results area. You simply select the chart, press the right mouse button, and select the chart type to display the charting options. A key point to remember here is that the navigation is conducted on the query results and then chart display is altered—not the other way around.

When the *Attach Map* option is selected, a map will appear in a new Excel worksheet named BEx Map. Unlike the chart, the map may not be moved any place on the existing worksheet or to another worksheet in the current workbook. The BEx Map is attached to the query results area in a similar manner as the chart is. However, the BEx map and its settings take precedence and control over the results area. The prerequisite is that the query consists of at least one geo-relevant characteristic. In the InfoObject definition of a characteristic, the geography-specific meta data is configured. There are two primary types of geographical settings for characteristics: static geo-types and dynamic geo-types. *Static geo-types* are used for characteristics that represent objects that do not change—for example, country or state borders. *Dynamic geo-types* are used to identify objects that may not be in the same locations—for example, vendors or store locations. Both the static and the dynamic types may derive their points from values stored as attributes for the characteristic.

The BEx Map may have up to three layers of data displayed visually for any query. Each layer may contain separate images or color shading. For example, for revenue sold to all customers in Europe, each country may be shaded according to the total sales value, with the darkest states representing the highest sales value. Then a second layer may be defined to show a pie chart with a breakdown of profit by product type, where the size of the pie chart indicates the amount of profit relative to profit in the other countries. See Figure 7.8.

NOTE The BEx Analyzer does not use the Internet Graphics Server (IGS) to render its images, while the BEx Web applications use the IGS.

BEx Formatted Reporting

Another component in the Business Explorer suite is *BEx Formatted Reporting*. SAP has partnered with Crystal Decisions to deliver a pixel based reporting tool to extend the Business Explorer and meet the formatted output requirements that many organizations have. Figure 7.9 is an example of the type of report that may be created with the BEx Formatted Reporting option. At this writing, SAP has entered into an original equipment manufacturing (OEM) and reseller agreement with Crystal Decisions, which may cause some confusion, since some of the options in BEx Formatted Reporting are included with the purchaser's SAP BW license and others may need to be purchased as an add-on to the SAP BW license. We will explain the functionality and options available to you, but advise that you contact SAP to determine the appropriate software licensing.

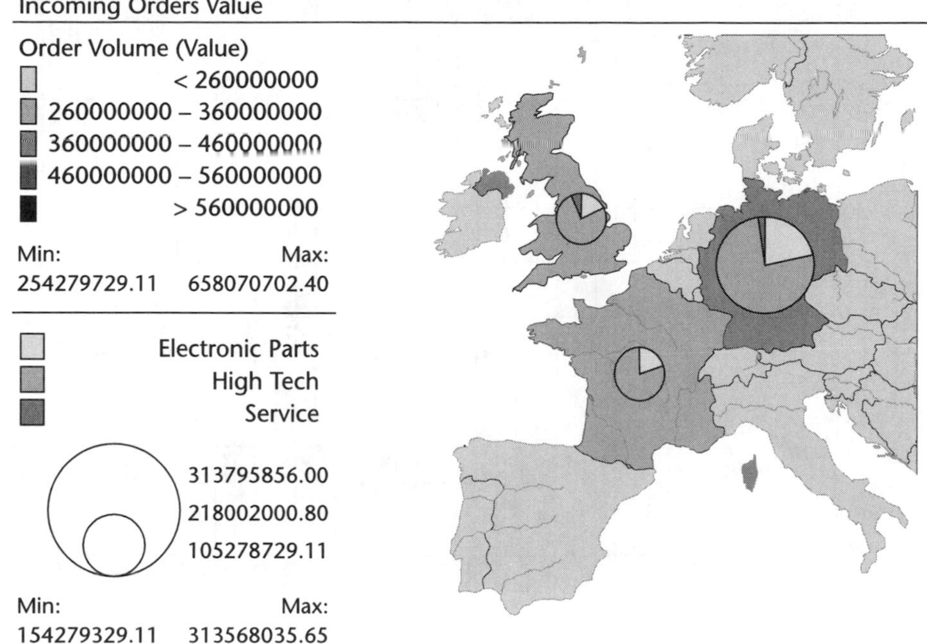

Figure 7.8 BEx Map.

There are many reports for the public sector, in particular, that must be into a specific format specified by different acts or amendments in government. These so-called legal reports need to conform to specific formatting requirements that are entered into law. Figure 7.9 shows an example from the Brazilian government called a *Mapa de Reintigrações*, or "Map of Reintegration." This report describes the reintegration of funds into a program. The data in the third column of this report is sourced from a BEx query that was created for an InfoProvider that is abstracting an ODS object. The data in the other columns is being sourced from another ODS object.

Of course, custom development using SAP BW interfaces, described later in this chapter, will accomplish the same results; however, the maintenance involved in supporting the solution would be too great. With the BEx Formatted Reporting option, the report designer does not require programming skills. The process of utilizing the Formatted Reporting option is reasonably straightforward once the additional software components are installed. There are five steps to creating, publishing and viewing a formatted report:

1. Create a tabular/single structure query in the BEx Query Designer.
2. Log in to the Crystal Reports Designer client software and select the tabular/ single structure query from SAP BW based on your SAP BW authorizations.

MAPA DE REINTEGRAÇOES

METODO DAS QUOTAS DEGRESSIVAS

Firma ____________________

(a) ____________________

Activade principal ____________________

(1)	(2)	(3)	(4)	(5)	(6)	(7)	(8)	(9)	(10)	(11)	(12)	(13)	(14)	(15)	(16)
01	300000000000	KRL3	001	2000	100.00	90.25	0.01		0.75	9.00	91.00				0.00
01	300000000000	KRL3	002	2000	100.00	89.50	0.01		0.75	9.75	90.25				0.00
01	300000000000	KRL3	003	2000	100.00	88.75	0.01		0.75	10.50	89.50				0.00
01	300000000000	KRL3	004	2000	100.00	88.00	0.01		0.75	11.25	88.75				0.00
01	300000000000	KRL3	005	2000	100.00	87.25	0.01		0.75	12.00	88.00				0.00
01	300000000000	KRL3	006	2000	100.00	86.50	0.01		0.75	12.75	87.25				0.00
01	300000000000	KRL3	007	2000	100.00	85.75	0.01		0.75	13.50	86.50				0.00
01	300000000000	KRL3	008	2000	100.00	85.00	0.01		0.75	14.25	85.75				0.00
01	300000000000	KRL3	009	2000	100.00	84.25	0.01		0.75	15.00	85.00				0.00
01	300000000000	KRL3	010	2000	100.00	83.50	0.01		0.75	15.75	84.25				0.00
01	300000000000	KRL3	011	2000	100.00	82.75	0.01		0.75	16.50	83.50				0.00
01	300000000000	KRL3	012	2000	100.00	82.00	0.01		0.75	17.25	82.75				0.00
02	300000000000	KRL5	001	2000	100.00	74.11	0.01		0.00	25.89	74.11				0.00
02	300000000000	KRL5	002	2000	100.00	74.11	0.01		0.00	25.89	74.11				0.00
02	300000000000	KRL5	003	2000	100.00	74.11	0.01		0.00	25.89	74.11				0.00
02	300000000000	KRL5	004	2000	100.00	74.11	0.01		0.00	25.89	74.11				0.00
02	300000000000	KRL5	005	2000	100.00	74.11	0.01		0.00	25.89	74.11				0.00
02	300000000000	KRL5	006	2000	100.00	74.11	0.01		0.00	25.89	74.11				0.00
02	300000000000	KRL5	007	2000	100.00	74.11	0.01		0.00	25.89	74.11				0.00
02	300000000000	KRL5	008	2000	100.00	74.11	0.01		0.00	25.89	74.11				0.00
02	300000000000	KRL5	009	2000	100.00	74.11	0.01		0.00	25.89	74.11				0.00
02	300000000000	KRL5	010	2000	100.00	74.11	0.01		0.00	25.89	74.11				0.00
02	300000000000	KRL5	011	2000	100.00	74.11	0.01		0.00	25.89	74.11				0.00
02	300000000000	KRL5	012	2000	100.00	74.11	0.01		0.00	25.89	74.11				0.00
03	300000000000	KRL4	001	2000	100.00	91.00	0.01		0.00	9.00	91.00				0.00
03	300000000000	KRL4	002	2000	100.00	91.00	0.01		0.00	9.00	91.00				0.00
03	300000000000	KRL4	003	2000	100.00	91.00	0.01		0.00	9.00	91.00				0.00
					2,700.00	2,286.82			9.00	504.18	2,295.82				0.00

Figure 7.9 BEx Formatted Reporting.

3. Design the report in Crystal Reports Designer and save the formatted report definition back to SAP BW.
4. Publish the report from SAP BW to the Crystal Enterprise Server.
5. View the report via an Internet browser.

First, you develop your reports by choosing your query, designing your report, and storing it within the SAP BW Meta Data Repository. You then publish this report to the Crystal Enterprise Server. The integration between SAP BW and the Crystal Reports Designer includes a so-called connector. This connector makes it possible to launch the BEx Query Designer from within the Crystal Reports Designer, assuming both software components are installed on the same client machine. Information is passed from SAP BW to Crystal Enterprise after SAP BW receives a multidimensional expression from the Crystal Enterprise Server.

One of the current limitations with the integration, although we anticipate it will be resolved in a future release, is the restriction to one structure in the SAP BW query. This reduces the opportunity to use complex structures and single cell calculations in the published formatted report. From a query and report design perspective, this may be its biggest limitation and at that it is not very big. Query designers should look to see if creating more than one query and having them populate the formatted report will work around the limitation.

From a publishing and viewing perspective, the integration of the components still leaves a bit to be desired as illustrated in Figure 7.10. A potentially large drawback is that the Crystal Enterprise Server is serving the formatted reports to a Web server that is not integrated with the SAP Web Application Server. This means organizations will need to administer multiple Web servers and Web security profiles in order to view formatted reports from SAP BW. While there is some security synchronization between SAP BW and the Enterprise server, this is a manual process that must be administered to keep in sync. Crystal Enterprise Server has its own security scheme that is quite different from the security scheme found in SAP BW.

Business Explorer Web Application Designer

In this section we will describe the components of a BEx Web application and how it is accessed, as well as integrated, in the SAP Enterprise Portal. BEx Web applications may be built in the *Business Explorer Web Application Designer* or in HTML editors like Macromedia's Dreamweaver or Microsoft's FrontPage. The BEx Web Application Designer is a visual development environment that allows Web designers to create tailored Web templates and cockpits that include traditional query elements like structures, calculated key figures, variables, filters, and free characteristics, as well as documents and Web content sources. Business charts, maps, and other graphical items may also be integrated into the Web applications. These graphical items and the traditional query elements are placed on a Web template that is the basis for BEx Web applications.

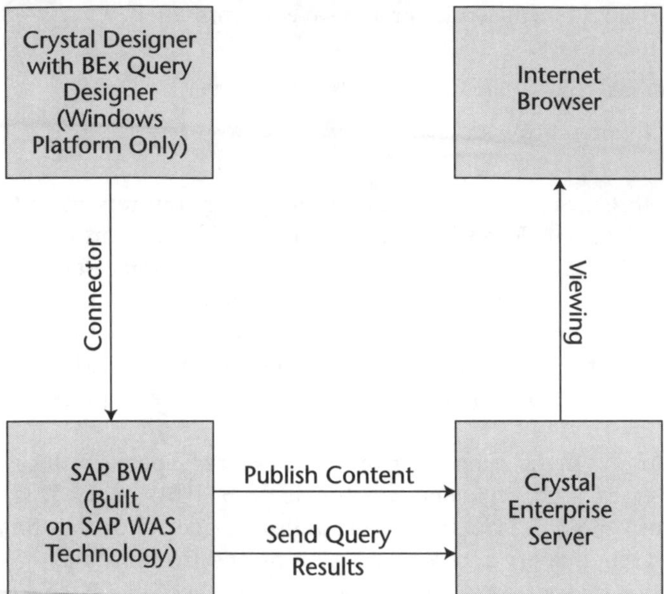

Figure 7.10 BEx Formatted Reporting components.

Figure 7.11 illustrates the Web Services object model supported by SAP BW. A Web template is composed of *data providers* and *Web items*. Data providers are objects, either BEx Queries, BEx Query view, or the entries in the Alert Monitor that Web items use to

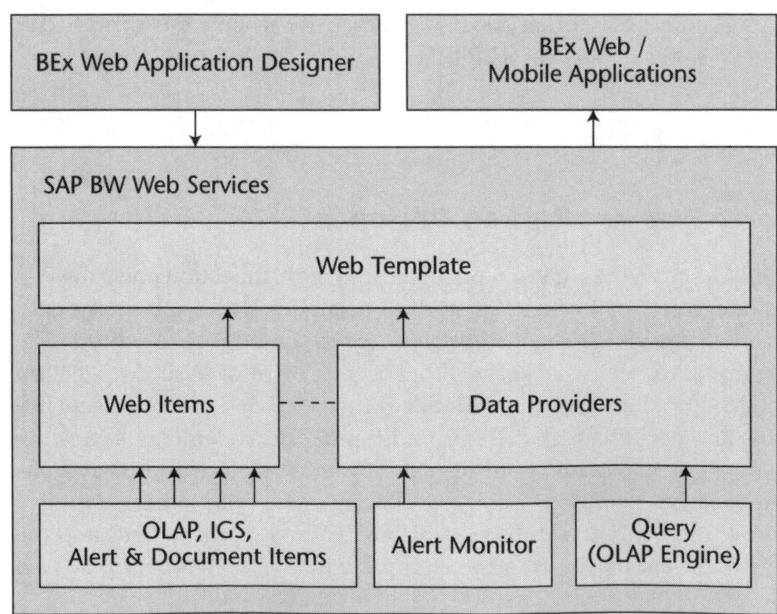

Figure 7.11 Web Services object model.

retrieve information. Web items are objects that make data available in HTML. It is the Web template that is invoked by a URL. When the template is filled with, or bound to, data, a Web application is instantiated. Prior to the binding it is simply a Web page with SAP BW-specific object tags—in other words, a Web template. The template's Web items are instantiated and are bound to a specific data provider.

Note that the query based data providers assigned to Web items and the data providers will eventually call an InfoProvider, since SAP BW Queries are defined for a given InfoProvider. The use of the terms *data* and *information* may cause confusion for some readers, since information is generally considered data within a useful or relevant context and data usually is thought of as facts that still need to be processed to be useful. To this we say, what is information to one service may be data to another.

Figure 7.12 illustrates the three main components of the BEx Web Application Designer. As shown from left to right, they are the Web items, template layout with overview and HTML tabs options, and the Properties windows. On the left side of the figure is a list of all of the SAP delivered Web items. Each of the standard Web items has a list of general and specific properties that control the behavior and appearance of the item. When a Web application designer drags the Web item to the template layout window, an icon representing a table appears in the layout window. At the same time the general Properties for the Table are displayed. The designer is asked to name the data provider and to select a Query or Query View for the newly created data provider. Each Web item has a list of general and specific properties, as shown for the Table Web item on the right side of Figure 7.12.

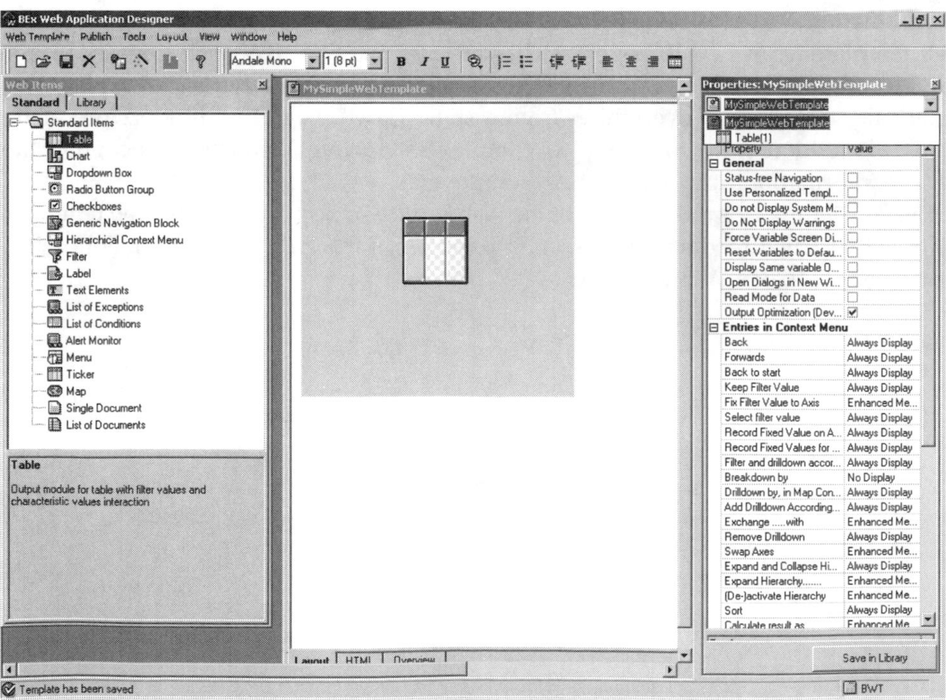

Figure 7.12 BEx Web Application Designer.

The general settings of a Web item control such things as whether or not the title is to be displayed for a Web item, whether or not a border should be displayed around the Web item, if the item should have links, should the Web item's initial view be closed or open, and what should the initial size of the Web item be set to. The general properties are the same for all Web items, with the exception of an additional sizing parameter for the Web items that represent graphical items.

There are four categories of Web items: OLAP, document, alert, and graphic. Every Web item is assigned to a data source, or, as is the case of the Alert Monitor item, the data source is implied. In Chapter 9 we will discuss the Alert Monitor in greater detail. Each of these Web items also has a set of specific properties. Again, there are exceptions, as the so-called list of exceptions and list of conditions Web items do not have specific object properties. The specific properties for all other Web items allow the Web designer to control how each item appears and the options each item represents to the end user. These properties may be set or replaced by the Web designer or at run time by the Web application user by setting or replacing the parameter in the URL or object tag.

The process of defining a new Web template starts when a Web application designer logs in to an SAP BW system from the BEx Web Application Designer. A Web item dragged to the template layout window in the BEx Web Application Designer HTML is created.

Before we dive into the Web Services object model, let's first make certain we are clear on what SAP means when it uses certain terms. BEx Web application is reasonably simple. A BEx Web application is an HTML page that contains one or more Web items and data providers that have rendered business information from SAP BW. The key words here are *have rendered*. It is with the BEx Web applications that the consumer of information interacts. SAP BW Web applications are based on Web templates. The Web template is an HTML page that has at least one SAP BW Web item and data provider defined as objects of the HTML page. SAP uses the term *Web applications* generically to represent everything from a static HTML page that renders precalculated information from SAP BW to complex interactive Web-based cockpits that retrieve information from various SAP components.

The Web template is the top level of the Web Services object model. The Web template controls the structure, data sources, and properties of the Web application. Following is sample HTML of a Web template:

```
<HTML>

!-- BW web template object tags -->
<object>
        <param name="OWNER" value="SAP_BW">
        <param name="CMD" value="SET_PROPERTIES">
        <param name="TEMPLATE_ID" value="MYSIMPLEWEBTEMPLATE">
        <param name="SUPPRESS_SYSTEM_MESSAGES" value="X">
        <param name="MENU_DISPLAY_DOCUMENTS" value="">

        TEMPLATE PROPERTIES
</object>
!-- BW data provider object tags -->
<object>
```

```
            <param name="OWNER" value="SAP_BW">
            <param name="CMD" value="SET_DATA_PROVIDER">
            <param name="NAME" value="DataProvider(1)">
            <param name="QUERY" value="0D_SD_C03_Q004">
            <param name="INFOCUBE" value="0D_SD_C03">
            DATA_PROVIDER:             DataProvider(1)
</object>
<HEAD>
<META NAME="GENERATOR" Content="Microsoft DHTML Editing Control">
<TITLE>MySimpleWebTemplate</TITLE>
        <link href= "MIME/BEx/StyleSheets/BWReports.css" type="text/css"
rel="stylesheet">
</HEAD>
<BODY>
<P>
!-- BW table web item object tags -->
<object>
            <param name="OWNER" value="SAP_BW">
            <param name="CMD" value="GET_ITEM">
            <param name="NAME" value="Table(1)">
            <param name="ITEM_CLASS" value="CL_RSR_WWW_ITEM_GRID">
            <param name="DATA_PROVIDER" value="DataProvider(1)">
            ITEM:             Table(1)
</object>
</P>
</BODY>
</HTML>
```

SAP BW Web Services

SAP BW version 3.0 has made significant advancements in its support of Internet protocols. SAP BW Web Services are the greatest example of this. They take care of requests from Web browsers or mobile devices that send requests via the Hypertext Transfer Protocol (HTTP). The services route the requests to the OLAP engine, along with the Internet Graphics Server (IGS) if necessary, and retrieves and assembles the requested Web components for delivery back to the requesting device (browsers, mobile phones, personal digital assistants, and so on).

SAP BW Web Services work with a request handler that receives requests from devices, validates those requests, and routes them to the SAP BW Web Services component. Once the SAP BW Web Services component receives a request, it disassembles it into its component parts, thereby separating content from format. The data requests are routed to the OLAP engine for processing. All requests for information from SAP BW are routed to the OLAP engine or the Alert Monitor. When the OLAP engine returns the result set to SAP BW Web Services, formatting and construction of the Web components are assembled. For example, say the OLAP engine retrieves a list of the top 10 customers for a given period. The requesting Web-based application asks for the results to be displayed as a bar chart. SAP BW Web Services takes care of rendering the results in this format.

Since SAP BW is built on top of the SAP Web Application Server (SAP WAS), SAP BW can take advantage of technology like the HTTP server, the Multipurpose Internet Mail Extensions (MIME) repositories, and version control. When a Web template is requested by a browser, the HTTP handler will identify the object tags within the template that is requested to find the objects in the template that are owned by SAP. The handler looks to the `OWNER` parameter, and if the value is set to `SAP_BW`, the object is routed to SAP BW Web Service. The other standard HTML tags are handled by the SAP WAS in the same manner a traditional Web server would.

Let's walk through a simple example of how a SAP BW Web application would access information from SAP BW, assuming the following URL was sent from a Web browser: http://yourcompany.com:1080/SAP/BW/BEx?CMD=LDOC&TEMPLATE_ID=MYSIMPLEWEBTEMPLATE. The URL starts off with the HTTP protocol and the domain and port number assigned to the SAP BW Web Application Server. /SAP/BW/BEx? represents the path and program for SAP BW Web Services. Next, you will find the command that is being sent to the Web service, in this case CMD=LDOC, which is requesting that a Web template be loaded. The & symbol marks the beginning of a parameter. The value assigned to the parameter follows the equal sign. In the example URL only one parameter, `TEMPLATE_ID`, is passed to SAP BW. The `TEMPLATE_ID` is set equal to `MYSIMPLEWEBTEMPLATE`.

Once the SAP WAS hands the request to the SAP BW Web Service, the template `MYSIMPLEWEBTEMPLATE` is retrieved and interpreted. The Web service looks for object tags that are owned by `SAP_BW` and determines if the objects are data provider objects or Web item objects. The data provider object in this case has set the parameter `CMD` with the value `SET_DATA_PROVIDER` and named the data provider, appropriately enough, `DataProvider(1)`. The `CMD` command must be sent to SAP BW in order to instantiate a query. The other parameters of the object prove more interesting, because they set the value for the InfoCube and query. In the code sample you will see that the query and InfoCube parameter values are set using the technical names for the desired query and InfoCube. In this example standard Business Content for a Sales and Distribution InfoCube and query have been assigned to the data provider object.

There are two types of data provider objects. The first type selects data from an SAP BW query, as defined in the preceding code. The second selects information for the Alert Monitor. You explicitly assign the data provider object for OLAP items in the BEx Web Application Designer by selecting a predefined query or query view. The behavior of a data provider may be changed by sending a URL to SAP BW containing the `CMD` parameter. For example, a Web template that has been designed and assigned to retrieve information about open sales orders from a query based on a sales and distribution query may reused to select data about sales deliveries from a different query and InfoCube. This is accomplished by calling the command `CMD=RESET_DATA_PROVIDER` and assigning the parameters `INFOCUBE` and `QUERY` with the values of a deliveries InfoCube and query.

The data provider is a parameter of the Web items and is assigned in our example to the Table Web item. This essentially binds the table presentation item to a query that is assigned to the Data Provider object. The Data Provider object will route its request for information to the OLAP request handler and subsequently the OLAP engine. The Table Web item object is instantiated and takes care of the presentation of the results returned from the OLAP engine and displays the results in a Table Web item.

Data providers may be manipulated by sending URLs that include commands and parameters. Web application designers may control such behavior as the filtering values, sorting, drill-down level, switching of characteristics, currency conversion, and exceptions. The lines between information access, analysis, and presentation are a bit challenging to separate. We will explain the topic of manipulating the behavior of data providers as we describe the presentation services later in the next section.

The second type of data provider selects data from the Alert Monitor. The data provider is automatically assigned when an Alert Monitor Web item is dragged onto the Web template layout. Like the Table object, the Alert Monitor is instantiated by setting the command CMD=GET_ITEM, assigning a name to the monitor and setting the ITEM_CLASS parameter as shown in the object code sample that follows. The difference between the Alert Monitor Web item and the Table Web item is that there is no explicit assignment of a data provider, since the data provider is the Alert Monitor and is controlled in the Administration Workbench with the reporting agent technology.

```
<object>
         <param name="OWNER" value="SAP_BW">
         <param name="CMD" value="GET_ITEM">
         <param name="NAME" value="Alert Monitor(1)">
         <param name="ITEM_CLASS" value="CL_RSR_WWW_ITEM_ALERT_MONITOR">
         ITEM:            Alert Monitor(1)
</object>
```

Web application designers may assign one or more data providers as well as multiple Web items to the same data provider. This enables the designer to create complex Web-based cockpits that source information from various SAP BW-based queries.

The data provider and associated Web items may be set in a Web template or they may be set and manipulated via an SAP BW URL. Together these objects create the so-called SAP BW Web API. The Web API is published and documented by SAP. The most comprehensive documentation is the Web API Reference (SAP AG SAP BW 3.0a Documentation 2001) that can be found on the SAP Web site

Enterprise Portal Integration

The BEx Web applications may be integrated into an Enterprise Portal environment, as the Web applications are accessible through a URL. The BEx Web Application Designer provides two options for easily integrating the BEx Web applications with the SAP Enterprise Portal: *Publish as iView* and *Save as iView File*. Both options accomplish the same result, which is to effectively place an iView wrapper around a BEx Web application so the iView Studio may manage the placement of and access to the BEx Web application as it would any information or application within its framework.

The Save as iView File option will create an IVU file. This may then be imported into the portal, which then creates an iView. The following code is an example of an IVU file:

```
<iView name=<![CDATA["BEx Web Template Name"]]> type="Java">
        <channel>BI Web applications</channel>
        <title><![CDATA[BEx Web Template Name]]></title>
        <params>
```

```
                <PhysicalService>
                <System  type="SimplePropertyType">
                        <Value><![CDATA[BWTCLNT800]]></Value>
                        ....
                </System>
                <SAP_BWReport  type="SimplePropertyType">

<Value><![CDATA[cmd=ldoc&TEMPLATE_ID=BWTIVUEXAMPLE]]></Value>
                        <PropertyAttribute  name="DispPropTitle"
final="false">
                        <Value>SAP_BWReport</Value>
                        </PropertyAttribute>
                        ....
                </SAP_BWReport>
                        <Description  type="SimplePropertyType">
                        <Value><![CDATA[BEx Web Template Name]]></Value>
                        ....
                        </Description>
                <MasterLink  type="SimplePropertyType">
                        .....
                </MasterLink>
                </PhysicalService>
        </params>
</iView>
```

For this to work, the portal must be set to recognize the SAP BW system. This is defined in the *Systems.xml* file within the portal. The XML in this document contains the information about the component systems that are integrated in the portal. It is located under the *System Landscape* tab inside the portal, which is assigned to all portal administrators. It may also be accessed directly in the filesystem. The administrator must enter the server name, client number, and system name into this document for each SAP BW system that the portal is to recognize. A unique name will need to be assigned for each SAP BW system. In the seventh line of code in our example, `BWTCLNT800` is the unique system name.

The iViews inside the portal are grouped into channels. Channels primarily make the job of the portal administrator easier. This does not have anything to do with the role concept, but rather it is a way to organize the copious amounts of iViews that will invariably be created. In our example, the iView is being assigned to the `BI Web applications` channel. If this channel does not exist in the portal, it will be created upon importation. If it does exist, the iView will be added to the existing channel. The iView will be given the name "BEx Web Template Name" as a reference in the portal and, in this case, will have the same as its title when rendered for the end user.

From within the portal framework an administrator may import the iView with a few clicks. First, the iView type must be set. In our example this is Java; however, this may be of .NET type. Next, the administrator navigates to the IVU file in the local filesystem and uploads it. Once the iView is inside the portal, it will appear under the appropriate channel. An iView may be created from within the portal with similar ease. When you are creating an iView for an SAP BW Web applications the two key elements are the component system and the query. The results are the same. The iView appears under the specified channel, regardless of the creation method. There is a preview button that may be used for testing the iView, but bear in mind that a valid SAP BW user-name will be needed unless the Single Sign-On or User Mapping has been configured.

For a user to access the iView within the portal, the iView should be assigned to an appropriate page in the portal. This page is assigned to a workset, which is in turn assigned to a role. The roles are then assigned to the users. This does not necessarily enable the user to enter the SAP BW system without a SAP BW username and password. If the user has a SAP BW username, the administrator can set up a mapping between the portal user and the corresponding BW user. This is quite easy to do, but it can be cumbersome if there are a lot of users. The portal addresses this issue by allowing users to set up their own mapping for the systems that appear in the Systems.xml. For more information on the Enterprise Portal, refer to SAP's Web site.

BEx Mobile Intelligence

One of the newest additions to the Business Explorer toolset is BEx Mobile Intelligence. The BEx Mobile Intelligence is less of a product than it is support for mobile data access protocols. There are no specific mobile devices that need to be purchased from SAP to use the mobile features. Any mobile phone or wireless PDA supporting the Wireless Access Protocol (WAP) or HTTP should be sufficient to access the Web applications from SAP BW. There is also support for Short Message Service (SMS) from the reporting agent.

There are two primary approaches to mobile access: online and offline. The offline approach involves prestaging a BEx Web application by scheduling the Web application page to precalculate the results of its Web items by selecting from the data providers in a background job. We will discuss the options for this in Chapter 9, as the settings in the reporting agent are abstracted from the presentation services. That is, the reporting agent doesn't care if the Web page is to be sent to a Web browser or a mobile device. The mobile device will then need to download the Web pages using Web Folders, WEBDAV, or other synchronization utilities.

WAP Device Support

Mobile phones that support the WAP send requests for information to a WAP gateway that is typically hosted by the mobile service provider. The request is translated by the gateway into an HTTP request and routed to the SAP BW server. The request from the gateway is little different than a request from a traditional Internet browser. The main difference is that the request is marked coming in from a specific WAP device type. The request uses the same SAP BW URL mechanism that the Internet browser would, and the data selection process in the SAP BW Web Application Server is the same regardless of the requesting device. SAP BW uses its so-called request handler to determine the appropriate output format for the Web application output. For a WAP device this would be the Wireless Markup Language (WML) instead of HTML for the Internet browser. The WML would be routed back to the gateway, where it would be translated into device-specific byte code and sent to the device for final rendering.

PDA Support

PDAs that support the HTTP send requests for information to an Internet service provider (ISP). Unlike the WAP request, there is no need to translate the request prior to routing to the SAP BW Web Application Server. The request uses the SAP BW URL mechanism the same as any Internet browser would. The data selection process in the SAP BW server is the same regardless of the requesting device. This time SAP BW uses its so-called request handler to determine the appropriate output format for the Web application and generates the appropriate HTML.

Design Restrictions

There are a few restrictions of which designers of mobile Web applications should be cognizant. They include but are not limited to the lack of support for HTML style sheets; limitations on the usage of Java Script; and the lack of support for the ticker, map, and hierarchy Web items. Otherwise, the Web application design process is the same regardless of the output device. There are also device display and color restrictions that should be considered prior to designing mobile Web applications.

Information Analysis and Access Services

In Chapter 3 we introduced the information analysis and access services aspect of the SAP BW architecture. In this section we will further explore these services. The information access services layer—as the name already says—provides access to structured and unstructured information stored in the SAP Business Information Warehouse. Structured information is retrieved through SAP BW InfoProviders, unstructured information is retrieved from a content management service. The integration of unstructured documents and structured documents has become an essential feature for business intelligence tools. Figure 7.13 highlights the components of the information access services layer.

The main services in this layer are the InfoProvider interface, the OLAP engine, the data mining engine, and the InfoSpoke Manager. We categorize these layers into request-handling services, processing services, and retrieval services. We will discuss each of these in detail with focused attention on the request-handling interfaces, since they are a primary integration point for third-party applications, specifically the interfaces that expose the service of the OLAP engine.

Information Provider Interface

SAP has isolated and abstracted functionality and complexity throughout the SAP BW product. Nowhere is this more evident than in the retrieval services and specifically the InfoProvider interface. The *Information Provider interface* has been introduced to standardize access to the structured data available to SAP BW. The Information Provider interface allows access to information that is stored in SAP BW, as well as data that is not stored in SAP BW. The interface enables the OLAP engine to treat all requests for information in the same manner regardless of where and how the data is physically stored. There are two generic types of InfoProviders: physical and virtual.

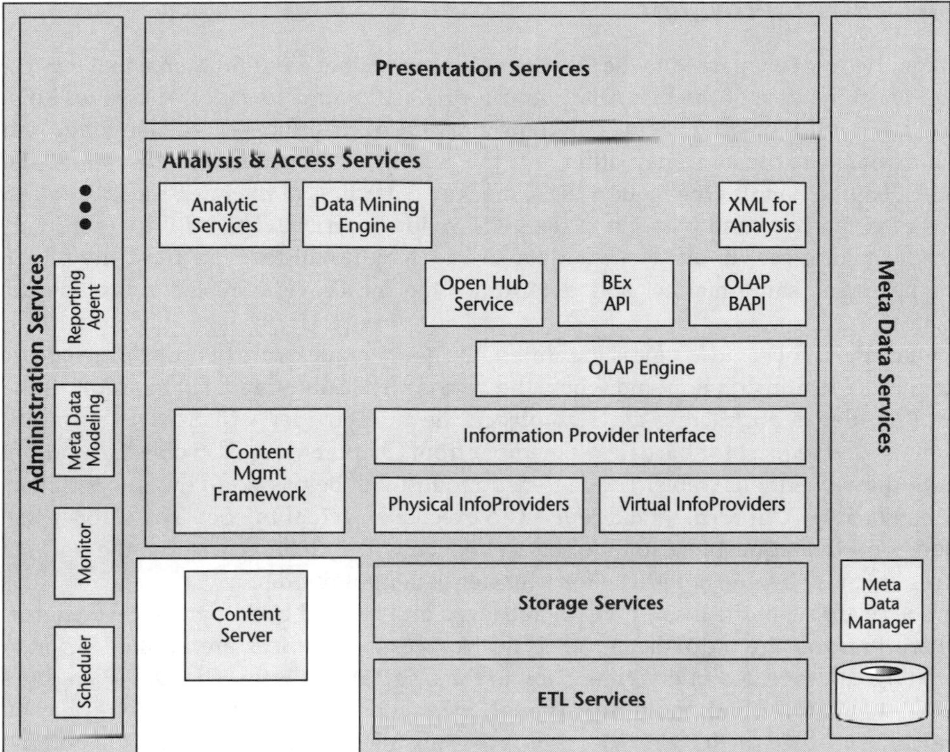

Figure 7.13 Information access services architecture.

Table 7.2 provides a list of the physical and virtual InfoProviders available in SAP BW. Both physical and virtual InfoProviders are accessed by the same set of OLAP services. The InfoProvider may be thought of as an abstraction layer for all data flowing through SAP BW either to end users, third-party business intelligence tools, other SAP components, or custom-built analytic applications. The ultimate consumer of the information requested from SAP BW need not be concerned about how or where the data is physically stored. While the OLAP engine accesses all different types of InfoProviders in the same way the InfoProvider in turn accesses the data storage services in very specific ways.

Table 7.2 The Foundation for InfoMarts: Types of InfoProviders

PHYSICAL INFOPROVIDERS	VIRTUAL INFOPROVIDERS
BasicCube (standard)	SAP remote cubes
BasicCube (transactional)	Generic remote Cubes
ODS objects	Virtual cube with services
Master data	MultiProviders

Physical InfoProviders

All queries that are passed to the OLAP engine send either a multidimensional expression or, in the case of the BEx Analyzer, proprietary command codes. As we will discuss later in this chapter, there are two primary OLAP interfaces, so the language and syntax of the expression may differ, but the essence of the requests is the same. The OLAP engine handles the request the same way regardless of the interface the request was received from and passes it to the InfoProvider interface. The InfoProvider interface, in taking care to abstract the data source, handles all requests from the OLAP engine in the same manner and determines the InfoProvider type for the specific request.

Once the InfoProvider type is identified, the query requests are handled in a specific manner depending on how and where the data is physically stored. For example, if the InfoProvider is abstracting an ODS object, the InfoProvider will flatten the multidimensional request for the data. Remember from Chapter 4, the ODS object is nothing more than a relational table. The flattened request will be passed to the InfoSet interface, which will, in turn, send a request to execute an actual InfoSet. The InfoSet will then hand the request to a storage service, which will, in turn, determine the optimal access plan. The same holds true for a master data InfoProvider.

The result set of the InfoSet will be retrieved and handed back to the OLAP engine, where (pardon the redundancy) analytical processing services are applied prior to handing the specified query view back to the original requester. The OLAP engine's ability to generate both multidimensional query cubes and tabular result sets has by and large enabled the InfoProvider interface to abstract both multidimensional and flat data sources. Note that both transactional ODS objects and standard ODS objects are available as InfoProviders.

In the case of a physical InfoProvider for basic InfoCubes (transactional and standard), the requests are routed to the storage services. The so-called Data Manager uses its Aggregate Manager to identify aggregate cubes and ultimately find the optimal database access path. The InfoProvider abstracts the storage and access details from the OLAP engine.

Virtual InfoProviders

The information requests flow into the InfoProvider layer in similar ways for both physical and virtual InfoProviders. The InfoProvider layer abstracts OLAP access from the Data Managers, and the Data Manager takes care to access the physical data storage if indeed the data is stored in SAP BW; if it isn't the Data Manager hands off the request to a remote system. The differences occur in how the requests are routed, and how/where the actual data access takes place. It is important to understand that the end user requesting information from SAP BW need not know or care where or how the information is physically stored.

We categorize virtual InfoProviders into two categories: remote and local. Remote InfoProviders are useful whenever data residing on a remote system cannot or should not be copied to the local database. Sometimes external data may not be copied to a local system for licensing reasons, and other times there are functional or nonfunctional requirements that prohibit data from being copied from an operational system into SAP BW. This may be the case when real-time data from an operational system is needed but access to the data must be tightly controlled. Virtual InfoProviders may be local if, for example, the InfoProvider does not directly interface with the SAP BW Data Manager. Such is the case when MultiProviders are used as InfoProviders.

Local Virtual InfoProviders

MultiProviders are typically used whenever there is information from different business processes or parts of a business process that needs to be displayed and available for navigation within a single query. MultiProviders are an alternative to modeling overly complex InfoCubes or ODS objects. It is important to keep in mind that MultiProviders are unions of InfoProviders and do not allow defining joins. The MultiProvider takes the retrieval request it receives from the OLAP engine and determines, based on the meta data for the MultiProvider, the number of physical or virtual InfoProviders that comprise the MultiProvider. For more information on InfoProviders, refer to Chapter 4.

Remote InfoProviders

Remote InfoProviders are easily defined for data sources available on SAP R/3 and other SAP BW systems. In the SAP BW system requesting the data, an SAP remote InfoCube is defined with an InfoSource that points to another SAP system. The BW Service API is used to access the remote data on the SAP systems. For non-SAP systems there is a generic remote InfoCube that may be defined. This generic interface enables custom-developed programs to act like an SAP remote InfoCube and provide information to the requesting SAP BW system.

NOTE The only outbound SAP BW interface that does not utilize the InfoProvider layer is the ODS BAPI.

Virtual InfoProviders are a powerful way to satisfy reporting and analysis requirements without the need to physically reconstruct InfoCubes or create new application-layer ODS objects. Virtual InfoProviders are InfoProviders that do not route data selection requests directly to the SAP BW Data Manager. For example, remote InfoCubes are physically stored on a remote system supporting the remote InfoCube interface definition; these can be flat database tables, R/3 DataSources, and actual InfoCubes stored in a remote SAP BW system. The virtual InfoProvider merely hands the request off to another retrieval service, which takes care of the data selection.

The SAP remote InfoCube interface allows direct access to data stored in SAP R/3 systems (through the BW Service API) and external systems supporting this interface like the ACNielsen workstation, providing access to market information. Using the Remote Cube interface, SAP BW users are able to define remote cubes for any type of data stored on any kind of system. There is also an option that allows for the master data to be selected locally from SAP BW while the data records are selected from a remote system.

Note that SAP BW does not currently support the Open Database Connectivity (ODBC) or OLE DB protocols for access to non-SAP data sources. It does not appear that SAP would need to apply very much engineering effort to accomplish such openness. This openness would enable SAP to effectively decouple the presentation services and the analysis and access services from the storage and ETL services and provide SAP with a standalone product for the business intelligence space.

OLAP Engine

Regardless of whether or not an organization decides to standardize on the Business Explorer front end that is delivered as part of the SAP BW product suite, the SAP BW OLAP engine provides all analysis and navigational functions. While there are several integration possibilities for third-party, so-called alternative front-end packages, the OLAP engine is the analysis brain for SAP BW. Later in this section we will discuss each option and the possibilities for certifying third-party software to the interfaces. For now, let's focus on functions supported by the engine itself.

The Meta Data Repository stores a list of all queries that have been defined in SAP BW regardless of the tool that will ultimately present the results delivered from the OLAP engine. When a query is requested by a presentation service, whether the Business Explorer or a third-party program, the query definition is retrieved from the Meta Data Repository. The OLAP engine takes the query definition and generates, updates, and executes the queries by running the generated program. Once the selection request is handed to the InfoProvider interface, the InfoProvider may determine the type and invoke the appropriate service be that a storage, analysis, or remote system service. The InfoProvider then returns the selected data records to the OLAP engine for runtime calculations, currency conversions, and authorization checks.

The OLAP engine checks the query definition of the so-called query read mode. There are three types of query read modes, each type controlling the behavior of the OLAP engine. The read modes are used to accelerate performance and are set based on a number of factors. We will cover the read mode and other performance optimization options in greater detail in Chapter 10.

Analytical Services

A handful of analytical services are delivered with SAP BW that are performed outside of the OLAP engine. It is a common misconception—most likely promoted by competing vendors—that SAP BW only supports OLAP. This is not the case. As we discussed, tabular reporting formatted reporting and what we categorize as generic analytical services are all supported. Examples of the so-call generic analytical services are customer lifetime value analysis (CLTV), recency, frequency, and monetary value (RFMV) analysis for campaign optimization, and ABC analysis for customer classification. SAP has delivered additional Business Content, including cubes, ODS, and queries, that utilize these services. In version 3.0, CLTV analysis may be accessed via the command code `RSAN_CLTV`. Entering this in the OK command box takes you to the CLTV Modeling functionality. Once logged into the SAP BW Administration Workbench, you'll find the `OK` command on the upper left-hand side of the GUI. A prerequisite for this functionality is the availability and activation of ODS objects 0CRM_OLVM and 0CRM_OLVF.

In the context of analytical business applications, we discuss the analytic services in greater detail throughout Chapter 8.

Data Mining Services

Data mining is the term commonly used to describe a class of database applications that uncover previously unknown patterns from data. The goal of data mining is to identify golden nuggets of information in large volumes of data. Many terms have been used somewhat synonymously with data mining, for example, knowledge discovery, data archeology, information harvesting, or predictive mining. Some of these terms represent types or components of data mining.Regardless of the terminology, data mining algorithms are finding their way out of university research papers and into enterprise software applications. Our goal here is not to provide a discourse on data mining but to sketch the methods that SAP delivers in SAP BW to support the data mining processes.

SAP has delivered data mining methods and Business Content to help organizations identify potentially significant patterns, association, and trends that otherwise would be too time-consuming to uncover through conventional human analysis or that was missed, since analysts tend to see the information they are expecting or hoping to discover and may miss valid information that lies outside their expectation zone. SAP BW also supports third-party data mining engines like IBM's Intelligent Miner and emerging interface standards for data mining like the data mining extensions to OLE-DB and the Predictive Markup Language (PMML) for exchanging data models and result sets between different data mining engines.

SAP BW is delivered with the following three types of data mining methods:

- Classification
- Association analysis
- Clustering

An important data mining transaction code to remember is `RSDMWB`. This transaction will take you to the data mining workbench. For those readers with investments in IBM's Intelligent Miner, transaction code `MINING_IBM` will take you to the customization options for the integration with SAP BW. As SAP BW evolves and more analytic applications are built on the platform, there is little doubt that new data mining functionality will be created or integrated by SAP. In Chapter 8 we will describe the SAP BW data mining methods and how they are applied, for example, to customer relationship analytics and other business applications delivered by SAP and we will investigate these services in greater detail as we discuss analytic applications that utilize the services.

Other Core Services

In this section we focus on two core aspects of SAP BW. The first is a unique feature that allows for an analysis path to jump to various receiver objects. These receiver objects may be other SAP BW queries, Web applications, SAP transactions, ABAP reports, or Web URLs. This functionality is called the Report-to-Report Interface. The second feature is the ability for an end user to personalize his or her experience. Personalization may be used to set commonly used variables, Web templates, and favorites lists.

Report-to-Report Interface

The *Report-to-Report Interface* (RRI) in SAP BW is a feature that enables information surfing. The RRI works in a similar way as Internet surfing, where the user jumps from one page to another following a path of predefined links from one Web page to the next. End users of queries may jump from one query in SAP BW to another query. The RRI enables linking together information based on the context of an end user's analysis path. For example, a sales manager may be analyzing her most profitable customers in a given year and from the profitability query jump to an accounts receivable query to analyze payment behavior. In doing so she may find that her most profitable customer is indeed not as profitable as first thought because of the drain on cash flow and increase in interest expense. The unique feature with the RRI is the ability to pass the context of the sending query—in this case, the specific customer number the sales manager analyzed the profitability of—to the receiving query as an input parameter. The RRI is configured in the Administration Workbench, which is not technically a part of the BEx Query Designer. The BEx Analyzer and the Web application's context menu use the *Go To* options in the context menu or toolbar to initiate the RRI.

The RRI is possible because of the common meta data definition in SAP BW. The meta data objects in the sending query will be matched to the meta data objects in the receiver. When a characteristic is common in both the sender and receiver, the value from the sender will be passed into the receiver if the receiver has a variable or input parameter. The RRI may help to avoid the problem of having particularly large or long-running reports, since information modelers may use a summarized report and still provide drill-down functionality into a more detailed query SAP BW or transaction in R/3. For example, you may have modeled your master data attributes in SAP BW in such a way that they are not necessarily representing the current value (refer to Chapter 4 for information modeling options), but the query users want to view or even maintain the master data for a certain characteristic. This may be accomplished by defining a receiver object for a query or InfoProvider that calls the appropriate maintenance transaction in R/3.

SAP BW's RRI allows you to call from a query (Sender) to another object (Receiver) by maintaining a Sender/Receiver Link. The Receiver may be any one or several of the follow objects:

- SAP BW query
- SAP BW Web application
- SAP BW formatted report
- InfoSet
- Transaction
- ABAP report
- Web address

The receiver objects may be located on remote systems or in the same logical system as the sending object. The technical settings on the remote system must be established with transaction SM59 so that the RRI will recognize the system as one with potential receiver objects. This functionality helps to support the InfoMart scenario we discussed in Chapter 4, where, for example, you have an InfoMart for the finance department that contains highly summarized data and a central data warehouse layer with detailed transactional level data. A query built on an InfoCube in the finance InfoMart may contain data at the month/period level of detail. The central data warehouse layer may contain the daily detail data. The receiver object in this case may be called when a specific analysis path requires details of the transactions that occurred within a month. This type of drill-through to the daily records (query built on ODS object) from a summarized report (query built on InfoCube) is not uncommon.

We mentioned that SAP R/3 transactions and ABAP reports are valid receiver objects. However, jumping back to R/3 from SAP BW might cause a few challenges. As we discussed in Chapter 5, the meta data and Business Content in SAP BW has been transformed from the meta data that exists in R/3. This poses a bit of a challenge for drilling through to R/3, but in most cases, it is achievable without coding a customer exit or routine. One of the preconditions for jumping back to an R/3 receiver object is that the data that was loaded into SAP BW was loaded through an InfoSource. The process of drilling back through to the R/3 system uses a kind of reverse meta data and data transformation in order to determine the appropriate field mapping to pass into and the appropriate characteristic values. Only trivial data transformations can automatically be reversed. Complex transformation rules may have to be reversed by implementing customer exits. There are two customer exits that should be used in the case where SAP BW cannot by itself derive all the information from the InfoSource definition: EXIT_SAPLRSBBS_001 and EXIT_SAPLRSBBS_002. The first exit is for the meta data transformation and the second for the data transformation.

Personalization

Personalization is the customization of information based on previously known or real-time preferences set by the consumers of the information. Personalization may take on many forms but has the goal of efficiently serving or anticipating the consumers' needs. While the personalization features in SAP BW are not only used by the BEx Analyzer but also in the BEx Web applications and Administrator Workbench, we will explain the concept and its underlying components here.

Prior to BW release 3.0, there was no useful server-side personalization for the Business Explorer Analyzer and very limited personalization available for Web reporting. The personalization options were configured on the client within the BEx Analyzer plug-in for Microsoft Excel. The limitations have created a burden on the data warehouse administrator, since the best way to achieve personalization was to create permanent variable assignments and limited access to queries and views through the use of authorizations and workbooks that were saved on the client. In typical SAP fashion the 3.0 release has not only overcome the personalization shortcoming of the previous release but lays a foundation for extension and integration with analytic applications.

There are three main areas of personalization in SAP BW:

- The automatic recording of previously accessed objects. This *history* is accessible to users of the BEx Analyzer, BEx Query Designer, and Web Application Designer. This is referred to as "open dialog" personalization.
- *Variables* may be automatically filled with personalized default values.
- Web applications and their underlying queries and query views may be bookmarked or added to a favorites menu. This is referred to as *Web template* personalization. Web templates and their usage will be discussed further in the next section as we discuss the BEx Web Application Designer.

Personalization provides information consumers with an experience that is customized to their preferences. The ease of navigation to specific Web queries from a favorites list or a history list are not difficult to imagine and are analogous to bookmarking your favorite Web site via your Web browser or adding a buddy to your buddy list in an instant messaging application. However, behind-the-scene personalization also impacts data warehouse administrators' jobs. The bad news is they have another data set to monitor and manage. The good news is the impact activating the personalization data is stored in specific ODS objects and may be monitored and managed via the Administrator's Workbench like any other ODS object.

Before using the three areas of personalization in SAP BW (variables, open dialog, and Web template), you must activate them. The activation process is straightforward and can be found in the implementation guide (IMG). Enter the transaction code SPRO and in the reference IMG under *SAP BW reporting relevant settings*. The process of activating a personalization option creates an underlying ODS objects that may be found in the Administrator's Workbench as part of the technical Business Content.

Personalizing History (Open Dialog)

When designing a query in the BEx Query Designer, the end user is prompted with a dialog window where he or she may select the InfoArea an existing query is stored in or create a new query. There are now selection buttons for history and favorites. These two options are similar in that they provide a customized list of queries to a query designer. They are different in that the history is automatically recorded based on the query user's most recent interaction with the Business Explorer, whereas the favorites list contains queries that the user has explicitly designated as his or her favorite. The history is stored in the ODS object 0PERS_BOD. The ODS object contains the history of all accessed queries, workbooks, and views for all users in the system. A user's favorites are associated with the role concept in SAP BW and not stored in the ODS object.

Personalizing Web Templates

When Web queries are accessed, a shortcut is automatically created in the user's favorites menu. This shortcut stores not only information about the Web query but also the information about specific viewing parameters selected by the end user. For example, say a user is conducting a drill-down analysis path while analyzing global sales revenue. The analysis ends with a detailed drill-down of the Americas region and the country of Argentina. This information is stored in the bookmark. The bookmark is an SAP BW URL that contains the parameters and values to re-create the ending place of an analysis path. The ODS object 0PERS_WTE contains the data for Web template personalization.

Variable Personalization

Variable personalization occurs automatically after the feature has been activated in the IMG. Once a query is executed and a value for a variable is entered, the value is stored in the ODS object for the user/query/variable combination. When the query is subsequently executed, the values for the variables are retrieved from the ODS object and automatically entered as the default values for the query. The ODS object 0PERS_VAR contains the variable information. Since it also contains the variable history from cost and profit center planning, update rules automatically update the ODS object with this new information.

Currency Conversion

Support for foreign currency translation has always been one of the strengths of SAP and SAP BW is no exception. There are two primary places where currency translation is possible in SAP BW: during the update of a data target via the update rules as described in Chapter 6 and during reporting. Currency translation during reporting also has two options: during query definition and ad hoc while analyzing a query. Readers familiar with the currency translation options and configuration found in SAP R/3 will recognize the terminology, configuration tables, and functionality.

Currency translation is the seemingly simple process of taking a specific value that is represented in a specified source currency, retrieving an exchange rate, and calculating the new value in a target currency. For example, revenue recorded in EUR may be translated into USD by looking up the exchange rate for the two currencies at a given point in time and multiplying the source currency by the exchange rate to determine the target currency. Figure 7.14 shows the four parameters that must be defined or derived in order to perform a currency conversion: source currency, target currency, translation date, and exchange rate type.

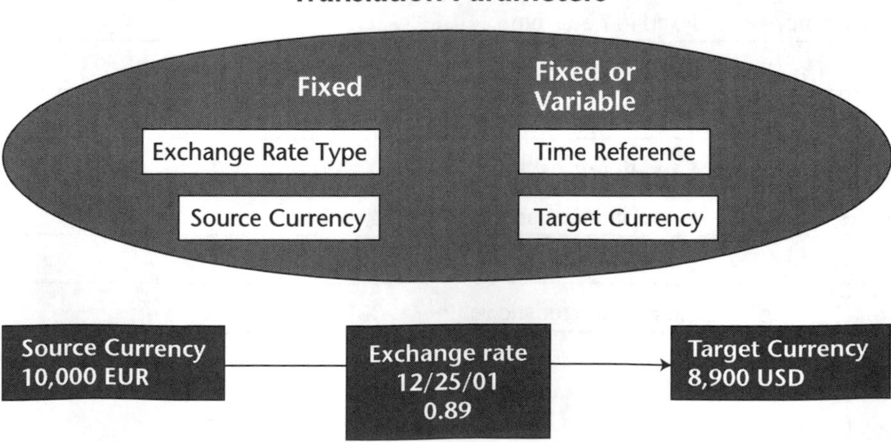

Figure 7.14 Currency translation.

Several currency translations may be defined or applied to the same query. During query design time a translation may be defined for each structure or key figure (restricted or calculated). During query execution a business analyst may right-click and from the context menu select the currency translation option. From there the analyst can select the currency translation type and target currency.

As is the case with SAP R/3, SAP BW has a configuration table where exchange rates from one currency to another are stored with an effective date. This is referred to as an *exchange rate type*. Exchange rate types are fixed values. The next parameter is the source currency. The *source currency* is the currency that is assigned to a specific key figure InfoObject in an InfoProvider. The currency of a key figure InfoObject may be fixed or assigned for each unique data record that is loaded into a data target, depending on the InfoObject definition in the Meta Data Repository. Regardless of the key figure InfoObject definition, the InfoProvider will send records to the OLAP engine for each key figure of type Amount. Query users will see this referred to as the database currency in the BEx Analyzer.

Currency translation may be established explicitly during query design time or ad hoc during query analysis. The next two parameters may have their values dynamically set. The time reference and target currency may vary depending on the values present in the context of a query navigation state. Table 7.3 highlights the options available for defining or deriving all four of the parameters.

While the currency conversion functionality is quite powerful because of its flexibility, we have seen that many organizations opt to design currency translation into the information model. In other words, they chose to store the data pretranslated as of a given time in a specific key figure.

Table 7.3 BEx Currency Translation Options

TRANSLATION PARAMETERS	PLACE DEFINED OR DERIVED	QUERY DESIGN OPTION	AD HOC OPTION
Source currency	Key figure in data record	X	X
Target currency	Fixed in trans. type	X	X
	InfoObject attribute	X	
	Variable entry	X	X
Exchange rate	Fixed in rate tables	X	X
Time reference	Fixed date in trans. type	X	X
	Current date	X	X
	Time characteristic value	X	

Content Management Framework

Integrating unstructured data with the so-called traditional data found in a data warehouse enables powerful collaborative business intelligence scenarios. SAP BW supports this requirement, since it includes a *content management framework* (CMF). The CMF is a collection of services that are the cornerstone for collaborative business intelligence and the knowledge management component of the Enterprise Portal. The SAP BW product uses these services to retrieve documents that are context-sensitive to an analysis path.

The CMF enables you to link documents stored in the SAP DB, or an HTTP content server, with the SAP BW meta data, transaction data, and master data objects. The documents may be used to provide administration advice or to supplement the documentation of the objects or to relate unstructured information to structured information. Common meta data objects that documents may be attached to include queries, InfoCubes, InfoObjects, and InfoProviders. Access to the documents is possible from the Administrator Workbench, from the BEx Analyzer, and from the BEx Web applications.

There are three main objects in SAP BW that may have documents attached to them: the meta data objects, master data values, and navigation state objects. Documents may be attached to enhance the documentation, to provide explanation of the data genealogy, or in the case of the documents linked to a query state, to explain variances from plan or assumptions used when forecasting. A *navigation state* is the set of attributes and measures that are being displayed to the end user at a specific stage in an analysis path. For example, a query may enable the analysis of the profitability of customers that purchased PopTarts, in February across all geographies. The combination of customer, profit, month, and geography and their specific values would be a query state. Documents may be linked to this state, as well as to the specific master data for the listed customers and to the geography meta data object, without regard to any specific geography.

Attaching Documents

You may attach documents to the objects two ways. The first way is by entering the Administrator Workbench and selecting a meta data object or master data value. The second way is to attach documents to a query state at analysis time either in the BEx Analyzer or in a BEx Web application.

Once in the Administrator Workbench, the documents for master data InfoObjects and meta data may be maintained. In the manual maintenance transaction there is an option for adding documents to a master data value. More than one document may be attached to a specific master data value. This allows for several file types to be attached. For example, you may wish to attach to a master data value for the InfoObject Personnel ID both a bitmap picture of the employee as well as a Microsoft Word document of their original resumé. During query analysis the type of document that is displayed may be controlled. More specifically, you need to set a parameter for the document

Web item to indicate which document type should be displayed. You may set the parameter at design time or analysis time. In both the BEx Analyzer and the BEx Web applications, you can view documents by selecting the context menu and the *Go to | Documents* or *Go to | Document Navigation State* option.

NOTE InfoObjects must be defined as a characteristic that supports document attributes before documents may be attached.

Attaching documents to a query state is a powerful way to capture in context comments from business analysts and use them to collaboratively solve business problems. Documents may be added at the time of analysis via a Web browser. This is a common method for both the BEx Analyzer and the BEx Web applications. A separate window in the Internet browser will be opened and the so-called document browser will be launched. In the document browser the characteristics and key figure will be listed for the query that launched the document browser. In the document browser window will be a listing of all the documents with their specific navigation state attributes.

Only documents with attributes that match the filter values for the selected navigation state are displayed. Characteristics that are aggregated (that is not implicitly selected) will not be displayed. By selecting the *More Functions* button, as shown in Figure 7.15, you will find the function for adding documents via the Web browser.

Internet Graphics Server

The Internet Graphics Server (IGS) represents the SAP attempt to standardize all graphics rendering for all their software components. The IGS takes data from SAP BW and other SAP components, as well as non-SAP components such as those from software vendor ESRI, and generates graphical output. The server is flexible enough to create graphics in many different formats to suit the application requiring the graphics processing. Available formats include BMP, JPEG, GIF, PNG, VML, and SVG. The SAP Web Application Server (WAS) is tightly integrated with the IGS even though the IGS is installed as a separate server. The two work together and communicate via an RFC connection that is configured both in the WAS system and in the IGS. When the IGS is being used with SAP BW, the server may be installed on the same physical machine as an SAP BW application server. The IGS is constructed in such a way that it will function in a heterogeneous environment, although in early 3.0 versions of SAP BW, the IGS must run on a Windows platform. The IGS is the foundation for Web items that are rendered in BEx Web applications as charts, graphics, and maps.

Information Access Interfaces

SAP has come a long way in overcoming criticism that its software is only extensible by programming with its proprietary ABAP language and that it has closed or inaccessible APIs. Figure 7.16 depicts the interfaces currently exposed for presentation services to invoke. We will examine the interfaces that are available to third-party independent software vendors and Web application developers, as well as the interfaces used by the Business Explorer.

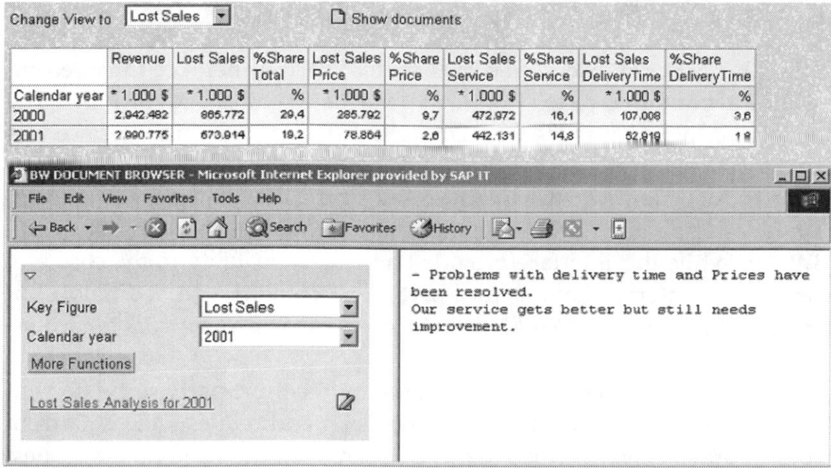

Figure 7.15 Documents for a query navigation state.

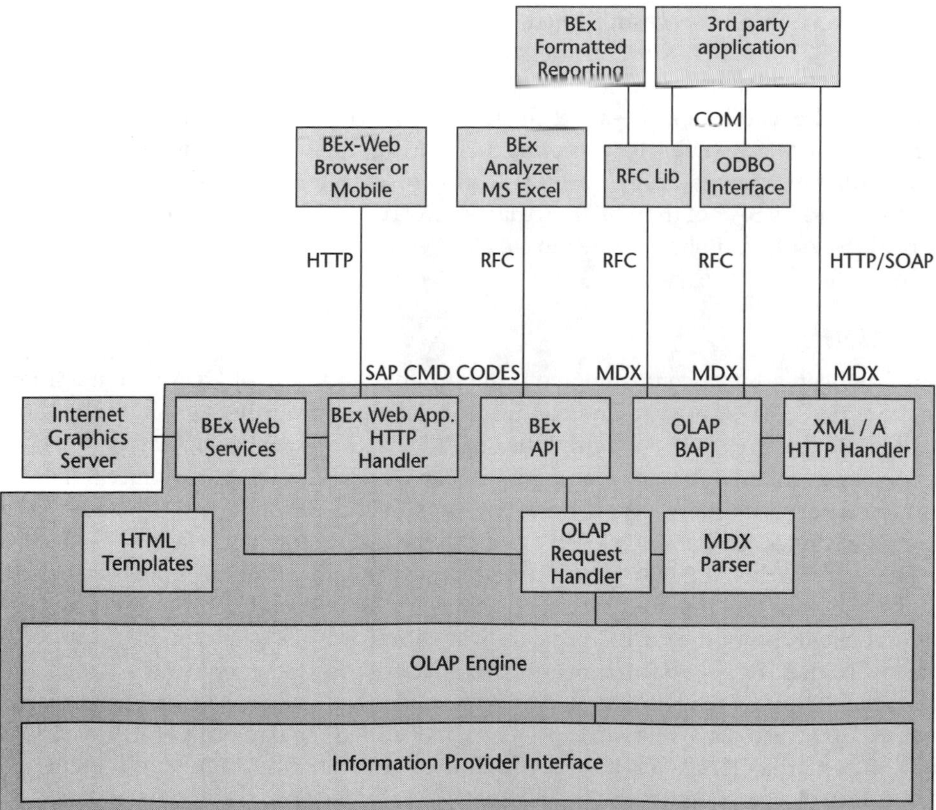

Figure 7.16 Interfaces for presentation services.

Interface Options for Third-Party Presentation Tools

In addition to the BEx Web API discussed earlier in this chapter, there are three recommend methods for integrating so-called front-end presentation tools with SAP BW. The first method supported by SAP was the OLE DB for OLAP interface. This interface was published with the 1.2 release of SAP BW and gained wide acceptance by the business intelligence tools vendors. However, this interface has several drawbacks, so a platform-independent business application programming interface (BAPI) was published with release SAP BW 2.0. While this interface provided a greater flexibility in the choice of operating systems and platforms that the third-party tools could run on, it did not support access through HTTP. The BEx Web API provides a command framework for accessing SAP BW information from a URL.

Note that regardless of the interface option chosen by the third-party software vendor, the OLAP engine performs the analytical processing and requests the data from the data provider as previously described in this chapter. The actual path that a request for data takes prior to arriving at the OLAP engine, however, is quite different.

NOTE ODBO is the acronym for the acronym OLE DB for OLAP or Object Link Embedding for Databases extended for Online Analytical Processing.

The connection protocols supported by SAP for third-party vendors to select from are COM, RFC, or HTTP. Most business intelligence tool vendors have chosen to support at least one of the protocols in order to meet the evolving demands of their customers. The leading business intelligence tool vendors support one or more of the interface protocols available for accessing SAP BW. For an up-to-date listing of certified vendors refer to www.sap.com/partners/software/directory. Because of the relatively recent support by SAP of the XML for Analysis (XML/A) and the Simple Object Access Protocol (SOAP), you should refer to SAP's Web site for the most up-to-date list of vendors.

OLAP BAPI

There has been a bit of confusion about the number and type of OLAP engine interfaces that SAP BW supports. The confusion has been primarily caused by the term *OLAP BAPI.* When SAP first exposed the analytic functions of the OLAP engine, there was a recommended approach to integration: the OLE DB for OLAP interface (ODBO). Application programmers would write to SAP's ODBO driver, and SAP would take care of the connection back to SAP BW and call the proper function via the OLAP API. The criticisms of the OLE DB of OLAP interfaces were varied, but the main issues were that the driver only supported Microsoft platforms and SAP's interpretation and that eventual extension of the ODBO protocol was different from other vendors' interpretations. To alleviate platform concern, SAP decided to document and publish the OLAP API, thus turning it into a BAPI that would be supported through release changes. Up until SAP BW version 2.0 (when SAP added the B in front of API) vendors could write to the OLAP API, but they had no guarantee that SAP would not change the interface in subsequent releases. In Figure 7.16 we have not distinguished between the OLAP API and OLAP BAPI, as the latter is the more current terminology.

You may notice that all three supported connection protocols eventually access the OLAP BAPI. There are two main groups of functions that are supported by the OLAP BAPI. The first group is the browsing of meta data and master data. The second group is the fetching of data and execution of multidimensional expressions. The naming of the interfaces may be the cause of the confusion, since the ODBO, OLAP BAPI, and XML/A interfaces all access the OLAP BAPI. While we believe that XML for Analysis will become the interface of choice, ODBO is the most common method for third-party tools to integrate with SAP BW. Nearly all of the leading business intelligence tools on the market today have integrated their products with SAP BW via the ODBO interface.

Note that the ODBO interface calls the same underlying BAPIs that application programmers may call via the RFC libraries delivered by SAP. The primary difference is the amount of knowledge a programmer needs to know about the connectivity calls. With ODBO the SAP BW-supplied driver abstracts many of the details, whereas the RFC library approach does not. While the interfaces have changed, the use of multidimensional expression has remained constant.

OLE DB for OLAP

To understand ODBO you must first understand its foundation. OLE DB is a set of interfaces that Common Object Model (COM) objects expose to provide applications with uniform access to data regardless of the data's type or location (www.microsoft.com/data/oledb/olap/faq.htm 2001). The OLE DB protocol has consumers that request information and providers that provide information. The providers do so by exposing the interfaces of their objects to consumers. OLE DB for OLAP is the addition of two interfaces to the OLE DB protocol. These interfaces provide access to multidimensional data sources. The SAP BW ODBO driver is a provider in this protocol.

ODBO PROVIDER

There are two types of providers: data providers and provider services. The data provider owns data and exposes it to the consumer as a row set or table. The provider services make certain the data exposed by the BW server is returned to the third-party consumer, somewhat like a router sitting between a consumer and the ultimate data provider. The provider service in the case of BW is the mdrmsap.dll.

There are actually several libraries and files that are needed to support calls back to the SAP BW application server and to invoke an OLAP BAPI:

- **mdrmsap.dll—The SAP BW OLE DB for OLAP Provider**
- **librfc32.dll—SAP's main RFC library**
- **wdtlog.ocx—Dialog box for login parameters**
- **mdrmdlg.dll—Manager for the connection to an SAP system**
- **mdxpars.dll—Parser for multidimensional expressions so they may be sent to BW**
- **scerrlklp.dll—Error-handling routines**

***Source:* SAP AG ASAP for BW**

This major drawback in using OLE DB, or its predecessor the Open Database Connectivity Protocol (ODBC), is that they require a client component to be programmed to interface with a specific provider component. The provider component for SAP BW is delivered and installed on the client machine with the SAPGUI and SAP BW front-end add-on. The installation is necessary in order for the consumer application to access an SAP BW provider. This causes a number of client and server dependencies, such as version, platform, and in some cases, programming languages.

Many of the third-party BI tools certified to this interface ran into significant challenges that prevent enterprises from fully deploying an alternative the BEx front end. The challenges vary widely based on the architecture of the BI tool. The protocol definition left consumers and provider to interpret how certain functions should be supported. There were a few common areas where consumers and SAP, as the provider, had differing interpretations. For example, the support variable intervals, hierarchies, and calculated members were all different enough that either SAP or the BI vendors would need to rework their products or isolated portions of their products. These challenges limited the rollout of alternative front ends to SAP BW.

Recent enhancements to the level of protocol support by SAP are encouraging signs that third-party BI vendors will be able to satisfy their clients and large installed bases with meaningful integration to SAP BW. However, this tight coupling of client and server is not suitable for Web applications that are inherently stateless—not to mention that the protocol is dependent on the Microsoft Windows platform.

XML for Analysis

One of the newer developments in the BI community's adoption of XML-based standards. *XML for Analysis* (XML/A) was defined by Microsoft and Hyperion Solutions and is said to advance the concepts of OLE DB that utilizes SOAP, XML, and HTTP. Since OLE DB is based on the Common Object Model and XML/A is based on the Simple Object Access Protocol, programmers will need to adapt their existing ODBO application to support XML/A. The communication API is designed to standardize access to an analytical data provider (OLAP and data mining) over the Web. It attempts to overcome the shortfalls of ODBO by decoupling the consumer and the provider. While ODBO was designed to standardize data access across data sources, and to some extent it did so, the technique required a client component to be deployed in order to expose COM or DCOM interfaces. XML/A is designed to eliminate this constraint.

The OLAP BAPI serves as a basis for the XML/A interface. The Web application that is requesting data from the SAP BW Application Server first passes through a so-called XML/A request handler. The request handler validates the inbound request, parses it, and passes the request to the OLAP BAPI.

In Figure 7.17 the provider Web service and data source represent SAP BW. Since SAP BW software components are built on top of the SAP Web Application Server, all necessary technology underpinnings are in place for organizations to expose SAP BW based Web services. Organizations would only need to describe the Web services they wish to expose to their trading partners by creating an XML document called a Web Services Description Language (WSDL) and register the document with a Universal Discovery Description and Integration (UDDI) directory. Loosely coupled, stateless applications may run across platforms in a language independent environment.

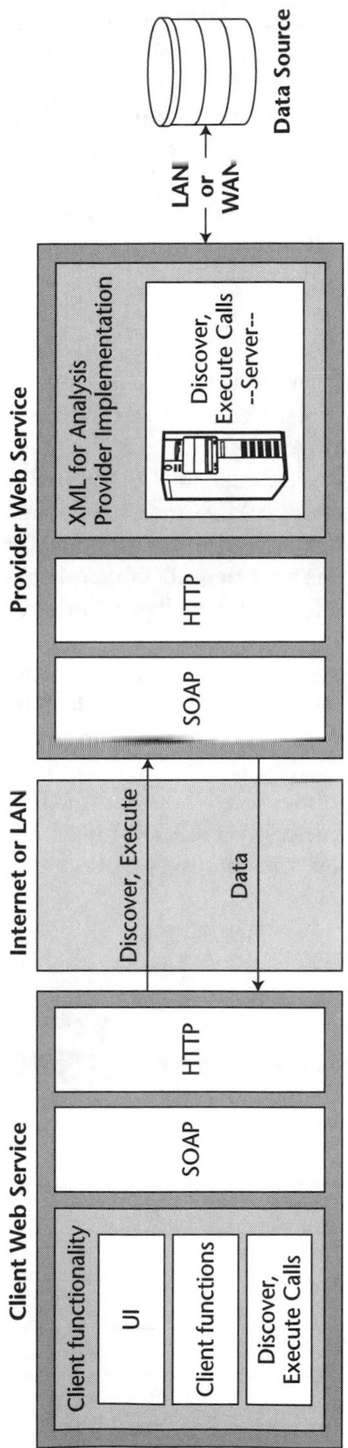

Figure 7.17 XML for Analysis.
Source: Microsoft Corporation

Both XML/A and ODBO send Multidimensional Expressions MDX commands to the OLAP BAPI and an MDX parser. The parser takes care to transform the expression into a format that the OLAP engine understands (i.e., ABAP). Once parsed, the request is sent to the OLAP request handler, which in turn invokes the OLAP engine. We find it somewhat ironic that the MDX is translated into ABAP prior to being passed to the Data Manager because if the MOLAP aggregate option is implemented, the request will be retranslated back into MDX for MOLAP aggregate selection. Nevertheless, the ABAP is generated and the appropriate InfoProvider is called.

Preparing for Third-Party Access

When a third-party application requests data from SAP BW, an MDX is used, unless data is being requested from an SAP BW Web template. If it is being requested from a Web template, an SAP BW URL is used. In this section we briefly discuss the steps taken to expose SAP BW queries to third-party applications that use the OLAP BAPI.

One of the challenges application programmers familiar with MDX may have when working with SAP BW is terminology. SAP is notorious for creating new names for terms that are generally accepted in the industry. SAP BW is no different. Table 7.4 contains a list of terminology differences between the Microsoft's OLE DB objects and SAP BW's objects.

SAP has included a tool to assist programmers in translating object definitions from one set paradigm to the next. Transaction code `MDXTEST` enables developers to test the result of their expression within the SAP BW Administration Workbench. This transaction and other query related administrational tools are briefly discussed in Chapter 9. If you are interested in more detailed information about how to write programs that access the ODBO interface, refer to the ASAP for BW Accelerator OLE DB for OLAP, which may be found on SAP's public Web site at www.sap.com/partners/software in the Business Intelligence section.

Table 7.4 OLE DB Objects and SAP BW Objects

OLE DB	SAP BW
Catalogs	InfoCubes
Cubes	Query cubes
Dimensions	Characteristics
Hierarchies	Hierarchies
Levels	Hierarchy nodes
Members	Characteristics
Measures	Key Figures

If you would simply like to execute SAP BW queries from a certified third-party tool, you need keep the following in mind:

- Queries must first be defined in the BEx Query Designer. To date, it is not possible to create the query definition in the third party too.
- The BEx query must be made available for OLE DB for OLAP. This is done during query design time by selecting the *Query Properties* icon and checking the *ODBO* radio button, as shown in Figure 7.18.
- In SAP BW version 3.0 it is now possible to directly access the InfoProvider without first creating a query. A so-called virtual query that contains all characteristics and key figures of an InfoProvider is accessed in this case.

In the third-party tool the end user would typical start by creating a query and selecting a data source. Selecting the SAP BW data source results in a list of BEx Queries (after the user has to be authenticated via the SAP login dialog). In the third-party tool the end user will see the BEx Queries listed as cubes (the OLE DB terminology) with the naming convention *<InfoCube name>/<Query name>*. These cubes may

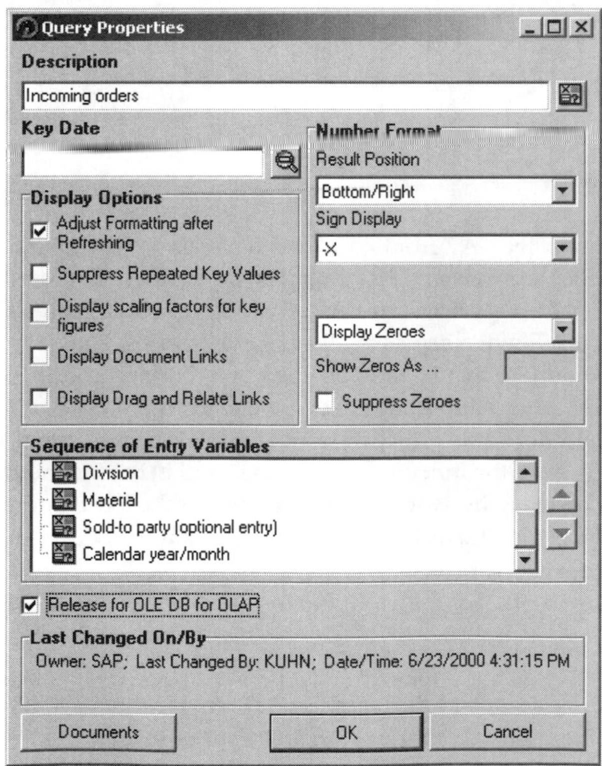

Figure 7.18 Activating OLE DB for OLAP.
Copyright © SAP AG

be customized in the third-party tool by the end user but only within the framework of the originally defined BEx Query—that is, members and measures in the underlying InfoCube may not be added to the query cube by the third-party tool. Note that not all of the OLAP functions that are available in the BEx Analyzer are available via the ODBO protocol and not all the ODBO functions are available in the BEx Analyzer.

NOTE If the BEx Query has not been released for OLE-DB for OLAP, it will not be accessible via the OLAP BAPI, XML/A, or ODBO interfaces.

Third-party Web application developers and independent software vendors (ISVs) are now confronted with an interesting option to use the BEx Web API or the OLAP BAPI to encapsulate the functionality of the SAP BW OLAP engine in their products without creating a maintenance and upgrade nightmare for themselves and their customers. At this writing, there was no statement from SAP on its intent to support the BEx Web API and its commands and parameters through release changes as it does with its BAPIs. Until such a statement is released, there is a risk that applications built to the API may need to be changed should SAP change the interface in a future release. We believe SAP will commit to not changing the specification in time. We also believe that SAP will not ask vendors to certify their products to the Web API. However, until an official statement of direction is made by SAP, ISVs that seek to certify their products with SAP BW will be making BAPI calls to the OLAP engine and sending multidimensional expressions.

The Business Explorer API

Like the third-party interface options, the SAP front-end tools have also evolved and undergone naming changes. The *Business Explorer API* connects the Business Explorer Analyzer and the Business Explorer Web Services (the SAP BW reporting and analysis front-end tools) to the OLAP engine, allowing access to all available queries. The Business Explorer API is not an open interface available to be used by other applications. As it is not a BAPI, the Business Explorer API, is subject to change from one SAP BW release to the next. SAP has come under some criticism from leading business intelligence tool vendors for not exposing all of the functionality that is found in the Business Explorer API in the OLAP BAPI; however, this was primarily a result of the loose interface definition by Microsoft. In fact, the OLAP BAPI only recently supports certain hierarchy, variable, and time functions. The BEx API, unlike the OLAP BAPI, supports a proprietary set of command codes in place of the multidimensional expressions used in the OLAP BAPI.

NOTE Business Application Programming Interfaces (BAPIs) are documented and supported methods of business objects that exist in SAP applications. BAPIs are the recommended method for integrating applications from independent software vendors with SAP applications.

There are two primary services that the Business Explore front-end components utilize: the BEx API and the BEx Web API. The BEx API is nearly analogous to the OLAP BAPI; however, the interface is closed and utilized only by the BEx Analyzer, running as a Microsoft Excel add-in, and the BEx Query Designer. We believe that over time SAP will work to standardize access to the OLAP engine through two methods: via the OLAP BAPI with its three options (native, ODBO, or XML/A) and via the Web component framework and its BEx Web API (see BEx Web Services in Figure 7.16). The development philosophy appears to be first developing additional functionality for the Business Explorer components and then expose those interfaces, if possible, through the OLAP BAPI.

The BEx API enables the BEx Query Designer to access meta data about InfoProviders and, as its name implies, the creation of queries. The BEx API also services the runtime requests generated by the BEx Analyzer as end users requests query views and analytical functions. The BEx API, like the OLAP BAPI, interacts with the OLAP request handler so it may send and receive commands to and from the OLAP engine. The most significant characteristic of the BEx API is that it enables the BEx Analyzer to expose functions that may not be exposed through the OLAP BAPI.

It is a much simpler process for SAP to extend a proprietary protocol than it is to extend and test an industry-standard protocol. For example, the use of variables is a powerful concept that has been pervasive across all SAP software components. The variable concept enables the filtering of a request by single values, a list of values, an interval, or list of intervals while allowing the variables to have default values set based on an individual's personalized settings. This concept has been a part of SAP BW since the 1.0 version; however, it was not until 2.0b that SAP enhanced the ODBO protocol to expose the feature to third party applications.

Summary

In this chapter we detailed the services for presenting, accessing, and analyzing information and touched on how these services interact with the storage services. We described the five main components to the Business Explorer. The BEx Analyzer, BEx Query Designer, BEx Formatted Reporting, BEx Mobile, and the BEx Web Application Designer together are the suite of tools to access, analyze, and present information from SAP BW. Information is retrieved from SAP BW via the InfoProvider interface and returned to the information consumer after it is processed either in the OLAP engine, analytic services, or data mining services. The information consumer will receive a view of the query cube for each step in the analysis navigation. The integration options for third-party software applications send multidimensional expressions to SAP BW. SAP BW interfaces take multidimensional expressions from the client application and process them accordingly. The adoption of the MDX and XML for Analytics standards has created an easily extensible platform for analytics. Furthermore,

SAP has published a BEx Web API that enables SAP BW Web applications to be incorporated in any HTML-based application by simply added a valid SAP BW URL and integrate it into the Enterprise Portal. SAP BW also supports the integration of unstructured documents to be attached to meta data objects and query navigational states.

Now that we have completed the core architecture of SAP BW, in Chapter 8 we will look into how it may be used as a platform to support analytic applications. The final two chapters will focus on the administration of the system and the performance optimization options.

Analytic Applications

SAP BW is the ideal BI platform for building analytic applications because it offers separation of function and time-oriented, integrated data (definition and an overview of analytic applications were provided in Chapter 5). As a result, SAP BW is at the heart of all SAP analytic applications. The construction of SAP analytic applications is expedited by the existence of predelivered meta data building blocks that Business Content offers. Not only can Business Content provide meta data components, it can also provide entire information models on which an analytic application can be built.

The architecture of an analytic application consists of more than Business Content and its information models. Analytic applications have their own builders, models, and engines. Builders are used to construct analytic models, and engines are then run against those models. For example, although data mining is closely integrated with SAP BW and typically uses Business Content queries to read information, it still has its own builder, model, and engine. As a more specific scenario, a customer behavior analysis may use a Business Content query to pass information to the data mining engine, which segments customers based on a decision tree model parameterized in the Data Mining Workbench.

The chapter gives three different examples of analytic applications in the areas of mySAP CRM, mySAP SCM, and mySAP Financials: the technology components SAP CRM, SAP APO, and SAP SEM, respectively.

mySAP CRM supports marketing, selling, and customer service. Customer Relationship Analytics (CRA) is the application that measures those processes. mySAP SCM supports sourcing, making, and delivering products. Likewise, the application that measures those processes is Supply Chain Analytics (SCA). Both mySAP CRM and mySAP SCM are composed of operational, collaborative, and analytical technologies that are tightly integrated and support closed-loop analytic scenarios. The technical component SAP SEM of mySAP Financials is used to tie all the enterprisewide pieces together for consolidation, financial analysis, planning and simulation, strategy management, corporate performance measurement, and stakeholder relationship management.

CRA comes integrated with SAP BW and consists of analytic engines such as data mining that can be used for customer behavior analytics, customer lifetime value analysis, and customer segmentation analytics such as recency, frequency, and monetary value (RFM) of purchases made by customers in marketing campaigns. Data mining methods in customer behavior analytics include decision trees, scoring, clustering, and association analysis.

SCA is heavily influenced by the Supply Chain Council's Supply Chain Operations Reference (SCOR) model, as introduced in Chapter 5. We therefore describe the SCOR model in more detail, explaining its significance to SCA before providing a summary of the SAP APO application and its architecture. We then explain the three ways that SAP BW interacts with SAP APO to deliver analytics. Namely:

- Through the supply chain cockpit
- Through interfacing with planning-book-based applications like demand planning
- Through Business Content, where SAP APO works to deliver analytics for more operationally based planning applications

In addition, we provide an SAP BW implementation case study for demand planning that details how data from SAP APO was loaded into SAP BW, what business logic was applied to the data in the update rules, and how analysis on the information is performed.

The three major subject areas of corporate performance management, enterprise planning, and consolidation fall under SAP SEM. Corporate performance management in SAP SEM is built on the principles of the balanced scorecard. The balanced scorecard is a strategy management system that strives to achieve two objectives: to change the way performance is measured and to change the way strategy is implemented. In the chapter, we highlight how SAP SEM achieves these two objectives. Then we explain enterprise planning, its architecture, and its predelivered planning applications, with the capital market interpreter separately highlighted as a sample planning application. Next, we cover business consolidation, detailing its history and migration path to the SAP BW platform. Finally, we detail the information modeling impacts for using the consolidation engine.

Analytic Application Architecture

SAP BW is at the heart of all analytic applications. Because it provides separation of function and time-oriented, integrated data, it is the ideal business intelligence platform for analytic applications. Figure 8.1 shows the various components of analytic applications. They include:

Builders. These are tools that allow you to build the analytic application environment. The Administrator Workbench, the Data Mining Workbench, and the SEM Planning Environment are examples of builders for analytic applications.

Models. These are designs that are either standard-delivered or custom-developed. Business Content and its information models play a major role here. Models such as data mining models or simulation models can also be outside Business Content.

Engines. These represent the application-specific logic that has to be applied during run time (such as specialized calculations). OLAP, data mining, and planning calculations are all performed by their respective engines.

The adjoining components in Figure 8.1 are:

ETL services. These can be provided by either SAP BW services or via third-party products like Ascential DataStage. Data can be loaded via SAP sources through the SAP BW Service API or via non-SAP sources through the flat-file interface, the DB Connect interface, the Staging BAPIs, or the XML interface. The transformation library offers predelivered transformation models to expedite the implementation of complicated information models. The SAP BW Staging Engine seamlessly handles the loading process behind the scenes.

Data warehouse. This is the enterprisewide SAP BW solution. The Administrator Workbench is the builder. The InfoCubes, ODS objects, and InfoObjects are the key components to the models that house the information in SAP BW.

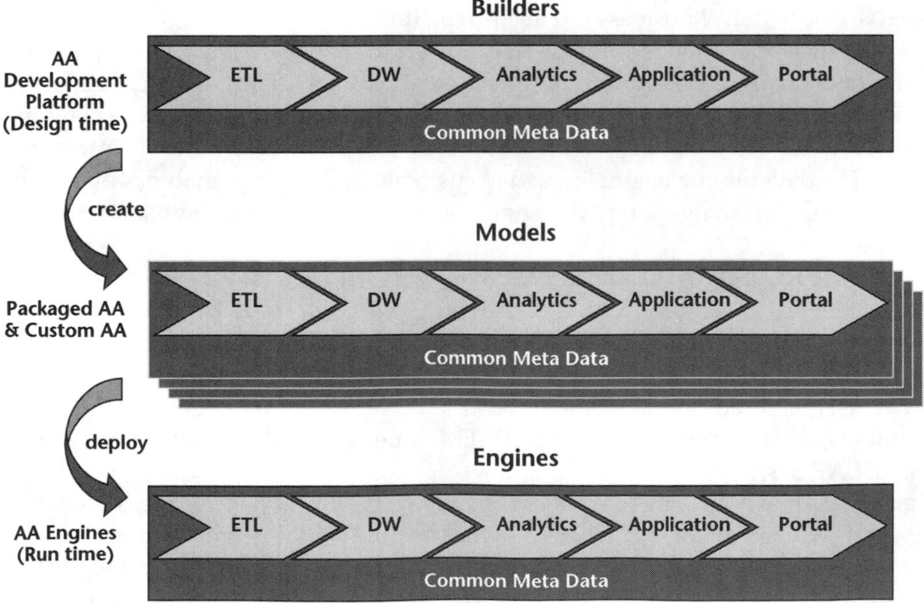

Figure 8.1 Analytic applications architecture.

Analytics. Queries can be built via the Business Explorer Analyzer and can include analytic calculations, exceptions, conditions, and currency conversion. The reporting agent can be used to trigger alerts. Planning functionality can be augmented to SAP BW via SEM BPS. Data mining engines score, cluster, and segment query data. Analytic models are either preconfigured or custom-built applications. The builders for analytics can fall in any one of the mySAP.com application components (SAP CRM, SAP APO, SAP SEM, or SAP BW).

Applications. These can be built via the Web application designer. Cockpits can be built out of Web components such as grids, charts, maps, alerts, and navigation blocks. Closed-loop functionality can be implemented via drill through to the source system either for reporting or executing a transaction.

Portals. These create a framework that analytic applications pass through. For instance, Web cockpits can be pushed through Enterprise Portals as a *workset* (or set of tasks). You can support complete roles by combining worksets from various analytic applications. The portal runtime environment handles services such as single sign-on, personalization, role-based menus, and authorization checks.

The glue that binds all the components together is common meta data. Common meta data enables tighter integration such as drill-through scenarios or passing data between applications. The consistent Business Content meta data jump-starts the building of new analytic applications.

In this chapter, we demonstrate how analytic applications can be built on the SAP BW business intelligence platform in SAP CRM, SAP APO, and SAP SEM, exploring specific builders, models, and engines in each application. For our purposes, how these builders, models, and engines are technically implemented in each of these applications is a less important lesson than learning how analytic applications can be built and evolved on the SAP BW business intelligence platform.

The analytic application technologies are subject to change themselves. Application subcomponents can roll in and out of the different packages. For example, CRM sales planning uses the SEM planning engine, while SAP APO has its own separate planning engine. CRM has a data mining engine that comes with SAP BW as a closely integrated solution. The data mining engine is used in customer relationship analytics purely for customer behavior analysis, but the engine is generic enough to be used for other applications.

How SAP CRM, SAP APO, and SAP SEM interact with SAP BW differs as well. The builders, models, and engines for CRM analytics come predelivered as part of Business Content with SAP BW. In contrast, the builders, models, and engines for SAP APO are not in SAP BW. Instead, they are built directly into the SAP APO application, while the SAP BW itself is directly embedded into SAP APO as part of a merged environment. The builders, models, and engines for SAP SEM come as an add-on application directly on top of SAP BW.

Figure 8.2 shows how these applications converge for certain business scenarios such as closed-loop planning, where all three applications interact with each other. (The process starts with SEM market analysis and simulation to gauge market growth feeding CRM sales planning. CRM sales planning then passes sales quantities to SAP APO demand planning which then drives supply networking planning to provide sales quantities to SEM profit planning.)

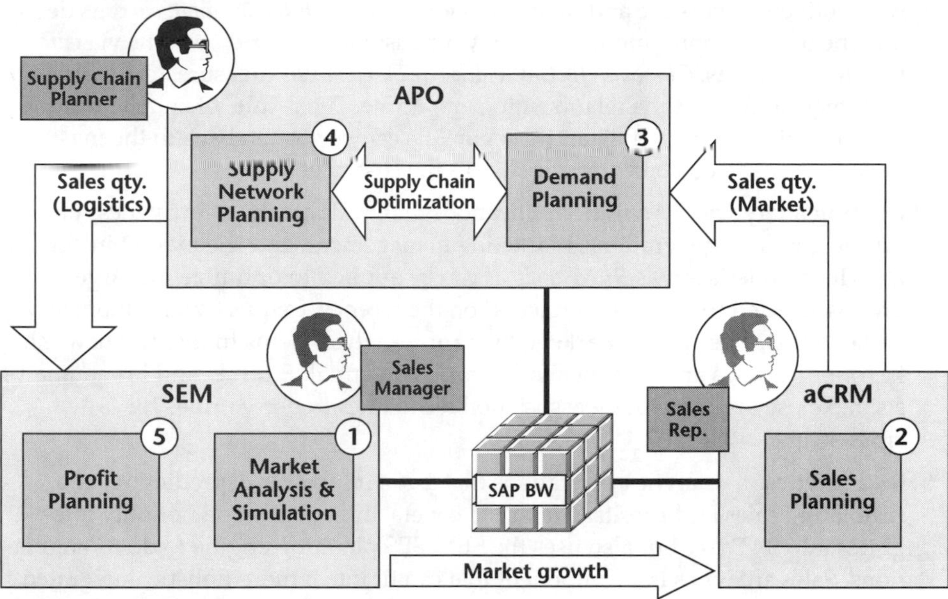

Figure 8.2 Integrated closed-loop planning.

Business concepts for analytics also converge. The SCOR model (employed in SAP APO) and the balanced scorecard (employed in SEM) share many of the same high-level concepts and complement each other.

Perhaps the forces for standardization and integration will merge the SAP technologies themselves. At the very least, how these applications interact with SAP BW is subject to change as fast as the underlying technologies themselves. Consequently, the most important thing to take away from this chapter is how analytic applications such as SAP CRM, SAP APO, and SAP SEM provide additional business process support over BW Business Content. These mySAP.com application components augment Business Content building blocks in order to deliver their business analytics. For each application, we provide an explanation of different technical approaches (in SAP BW, merged with SAP BW, or as an add-on to SAP BW for SAP CRM, SAP APO, and SAP SEM, respectively) toward the same goal (process support).

Customer Relationship Analytics

Customer relation analytics come delivered with SAP BW with specialized analysis techniques. These analysis techniques are typically targeted for specific scenarios but are reusable for custom designs. Briefly, the topic areas for analytical CRM are:

Customer analytics. Analytic applications that center around your customers and your customer knowledge base in order for you to gain greater understanding of who your customers are and their behavior. *Customer behavior analysis* digs deep into the buying habits and loyalties of your customers to find patterns via *data mining* techniques. *Customer lifetime value (CLTV) analysis* measures the worth of a customer from a lifetime relationship perspective. The results of an *ABC analysis* (which ranks data into A, B, and C segments) can be written back to the master data of an analyzed characteristic such as the customer.

Marketing analytics. Analytic applications that evaluate the effectiveness of campaigns, lead generations, marketing management, and the market in general. Techniques such as *RFM analysis* can be applied to optimize the target groups selected for a campaign based on the recency, frequency, and monetary value of their purchases. Market exploration analysis helps to identify new market opportunities and size the market for its potential. Product and brand analysis make use of data mining association techniques to derive rules for cross-selling.

Sales analytics. Analytic applications that assist in planning, predicting, and simulating sales and profits. Under the covers, this application not only integrates into SAP BW but also uses the SEM BPS planning engine to do its simulations. Sales analytics is a component that can fit into a more holistic, integrated sales planning process. Sales analytics involves not just planning but also quite a lot of reporting, such as pipeline analysis around objects available in operative processes (e.g., opportunities, contracts, orders, and quotations). These parts of sales analytics are covered by standard BW Business Content. Sales cycle analysis takes apart the sales cycle from lead to sales order processing to uncover any deficiencies.

Service analytics. Analytic applications that track service contracts, service processes, confirmations, and complaints to help ensure optimal levels of customer service. Customer satisfaction, product quality, and complaint patterns can be derived from such analysis.

Channel analytics. Analytic applications that track the effectiveness of varying sales channels such as the CRM Customer Interaction Center (CIC) or a Web site. Alerts can be provided to the CIC via a CRM alert monitor, for notifications such as cross-selling opportunities or particular promotions that match the customer profile. Web site analysis is part of e-analytics and allows for behavioral analysis of a customer based on his or her clickstream.

CRM-specific analytical techniques are highlighted and will be covered in more detail later.

Analytic Engines

SAP BW comes with specialized transactions to configure analytic engines for CRM calculations such as customer behavior analysis (data mining), RFM analysis, CLTV analysis, and ABC analysis. To use these techniques, you do not have to install SAP CRM, although some calculations would lose their relevancy outside the CRM context (note that CRM data can also be furnished by non-SAP systems). The transactions to configure these analytical CRM engines are accessible via roles-based user menus. RFM and CLTV analysis stores the results of its calculations to Business Content ODS objects. These ODS objects need to be activated before these specific analytic techniques can be configured. The techniques and their configuration are described in the chapter, as well as corresponding business scenarios.

Customer Behavior Analysis

Customer behavior analysis is based on data mining methods such as classification, clustering, and association analysis to find patterns and hidden relationships in a customer knowledge base. Customer behavior analytics centers on buying habits and churn (customer loyalty) behavior.

Data mining analysis is configured via a Data Mining Workbench and comes with a data mining wizard to guide the user through the setup. The setup is by data mining method (classification, clustering, and association analysis). Classification is further broken down into decision trees and scoring methods. The model parameters are different per data mining method and are covered in more detail later in the chapter. For each method, sources for training, evaluation, and prediction must be configured. These sources relate to ODBO-enabled queries.

Data mining is highly integrated into SAP BW. In addition, SAP CRM provides data mining interfaces to allow third-party data mining engines (such as IBM's Intelligent Miner) to integrate into the system when the standard methods are not sufficient.

From an SAP BW integration standpoint, SAP BW queries are used as sources for the training and mining processes. The data mining results can be stored back into the SAP BW system (as master data, for example) or forwarded to another system (such as cross-selling association rules to operational CRM).

Up to three sources of data are used in data mining: training data, evaluation data, and prediction data. Training data consists of small but representative subsets of data for the model to learn against before its learning is applied to historical data to make predictions. Historical data can be used for both evaluative and predictive purposes.

Historical data for evaluation and prediction should be separate sources. Evaluation is used to validate whether or not a model has been appropriately trained before it is turned loose against the historical data to make predictions. Note that model evaluation is not an explicit step in all mining processes. In some cases, the evaluation only means viewing the results of the training but not running the mining model with a separate mining source, because a classification only needs to be made and not a prediction.

All data mining methods share similar processes:

A data mining model is created. The configuration of the models differs depending on the data mining method (especially the model parameters). The model typically consists of two levels of configuration, one for the model itself and one for the modeling fields. The configuration settings for model fields and parameters differ per model.

The model is trained. Training allows the model to learn against small subsets of data. The query specified as the source for training should take this into account by selecting enough data to appropriately train the model but not too much that performance is adversely affected. Where predictions are not needed, such as association analysis, training is not needed. A model has a status indicator used to identify whether or not it has been trained.

The model is evaluated. After a model has been trained, it may be evaluated to determine if it was trained appropriately. You should use a sample of historic data to verify the results (but do not use the historic data that is to be used for predictions). A model has a status indicator used to identify whether or not it has been evaluated.

Predictions are made. Once a model is appropriately trained and evaluated, it is ready to make predictions. Predictions can be performed either online or as a batch process depending on the volume of data. Predictions should be made on yet another source for historic data separate to what was used in training and evaluation. The actual output of data mining depends on the method picked. Decision trees output probability trees, while clusters show percentage slices of an overall pie. A status indicator shows if a model has been predicted.

The results are stored or forwarded. Predicted values may be uploaded to SAP BW. For example, customer classifications generated by scoring models can be saved to customer master data. When loading the results back to SAP BW as a characteristic attribute, you must take care to match the meta data of the master data with meta data of the model fields. More explicitly, the keys of the model must match the keys of the master data. The master data load is triggered directly from the prediction and can be done online or in the background. When loading cross-selling rules determined via association analysis to a CRM system, you must specify the logical system name and target group to export the data. Predicted values can also be exported to file. Once these results are stored or forwarded, they can be used for operational use in order to drive decisions. For example, a bank may decide to offer or deny credit to a potential customer based on their attributes and behavior.

The following sections detail the different types of data mining methods available.

Decision Trees

Decision trees classify historical data into probability hierarchies (based on attributes for a specific characteristic like customer) for a specific key figure (like a count of all customers lost in a given period). Decision trees are used in scenarios such as identifying which customers are more likely to churn (in order to improve customer retention) or which customers keep good credit (in order to screen prospects better). For example, in a number of cellular phone markets, the struggle for market share is won through customer retention. Churn behavior decision trees can be produced by data mining historical data such as telephone usage, service, and payments coupled with customer attributes such as the brand or model used and the locale. The results of the decision tree can then be used to initiate a customer loyalty program.

The classifications of a decision tree are depicted hierarchically, which makes for good visual associations and linkages. Each hierarchy level of the decision tree represents a characteristic attribute (such as profession, age, membership status, marital status, and annual income of a customer) with associated probabilities for an outcome like churn. Based on the probabilities calculated for historical data, predictions can be made for other sets of data (such as the likelihood for churn on a different customer base or for a new customer). When a node of the decision tree is highlighted, the details behind the node percentage are given via a graph, such as the class distribution and node statistics showing the sample size (see Figure 8.3).

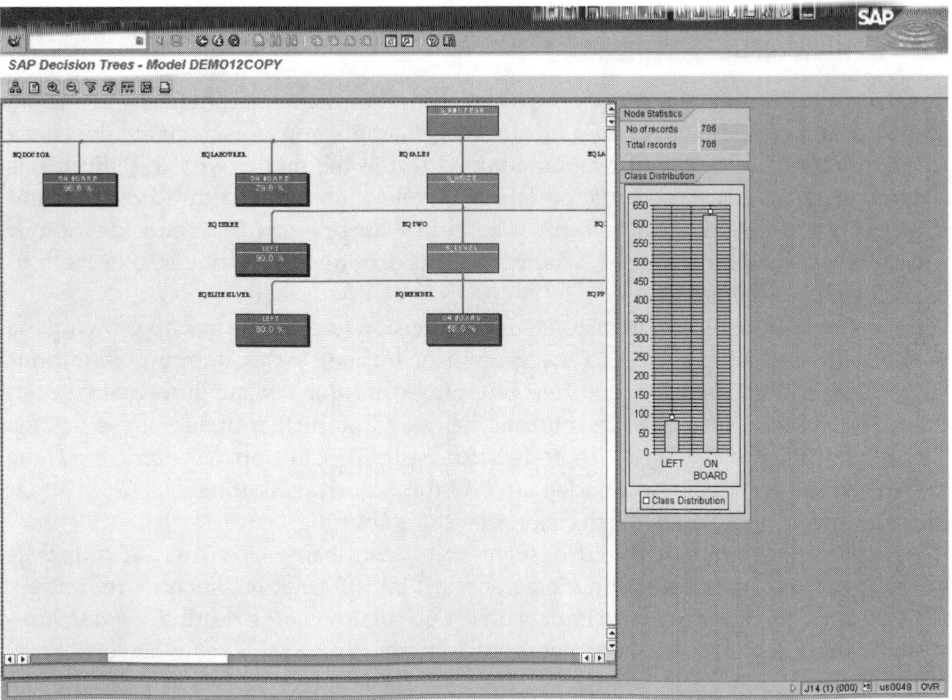

Figure 8.3 Decision trees.

The configuration for the decision tree consists of maintaining the parameters for the model and the fields of the model. The model parameters control the decision tree calculation, such as how much data to use for training, how to determine which records are relevant, when to stop the calculation, and how to prune the tree. Pruning cuts out the records that do not significantly impact the accuracy of the decision tree. The parameters for each of the model fields control how to handle missing or junk values within that field.

The training process can be controlled by what is called a *windowing technique*. Windowing is an iterative approach to growing the sample set of data used for training a decision tree model. If larger window sizes are specified, more data is used for training. Larger windows increase the accuracy of the trained model but have a greater impact on performance during training.

The settings for windowing are set in the parameters for the decision tree model. The settings dictate when windowing (or the growing of the sample set of data) should stop. Windowing settings consist of an initial window size, a maximum window size, and the number of trials to perform. The initial window size dictates the percentage of the sample data to use in the first iteration (or trial) of training. After the first trial of training, the decision tree is iteratively applied to the remaining data that is misclassified in the sample set until one of four things happens:

- The maximum window size is met.
- The number of trials is exceeded.
- There are no more misclassified records.
- The decision tree gets pruned.

Fields in a decision tree model can be excluded if they are irrelevant to classification. To perform the check for relevancy during classification, you must activate the check in the model and settings must be maintained to tell the model what constitutes as irrelevant. There are two methods for defining irrelevancy: either a threshold is maintained for how informative a field must be before dropping it from classification or top-N analysis can be performed, where a field is dropped if it is not among the topmost informative fields.

Stopping conditions define the criteria for the decision tree engine to stop growing the tree. While windowing relates to the growth of training data, stopping conditions relate to the growth of the decision tree. Stopping conditions dictate how many nodes to allow on a decision tree before splitting the node into further nodes, as well as the percentage of accuracy needed on a node before splitting can stop. *Node accuracy* is the percentage number of cases at a node that have the majority classification. When either of the minimums is reached, the decision tree stops splitting.

Pruning is a technique to avoid decision trees from being overfitted. It improves readability of the rules by eliminating nonessential information, such as redundant nodes, without having a negative impact on the calculation of the result. *Extended pruning* can be used, which checks whether more accuracy can be achieved when any given node can be replaced by its parent node. If this check is successful, the node and all its children are pruned. Extended pruning is a performance enhancement feature for large data sets.

For the model fields, parameters and field values must be set to dictate what is junk, what to include, and how to include it. For example, the field parameters control how initial values in the model field are to be treated. A flag sets whether null values in the model field are informative (meaning null is a valid value). If the flag is not set, all initial values are treated as missing. Alternatively, a default value can be specified to replace all initial or missing values.

For specific values within a specific field, there are even more specific settings. For example, a particular value or value ranges can be configured to be treated as a missing or ignored value. This level of detailed specification is helpful when you want to single out a particular field value as junk (like question marks, asterisks, or 9999).

Scoring

Although designed for CRM, the scoring technique has many general applications that can potentially run outside of CRM analytics (such as vendor scoring). In the context of CRM analytics, you might use scoring scenarios to identify customers of a particular market segment for a new product launch or to categorize customers most likely to cancel service to a subscription. One of three regression types must be picked to do scoring:

Linear regression. Scoring is trained by performing linear regression algorithms against historical data. This option is ideal for attributes that exhibit linear dependencies with a prediction key figure (such as discretionary income with sales).

The system creates a separate linear function for every combination of discrete values in the training source. For example, suppose a query is mapped to two discrete model fields in training source. If each discrete model field has five distinct characteristic values represented in the query, then 25 linear regression analyses are performed. This is also true of nonlinear regressions. Performance of the system must be taken into account when a scoring model generates a significantly sized Cartesian product.

Nonlinear regression. This is the same type of scoring as linear regression except the algorithm does not assume any direct linear relationship. More specifically (for the mathematicians), multilinear splines are applied to model the relationship. Multilinear splines are linear regression models glued end-to-end to explain nonlinear behavior.

Weighted score tables. Scoring is done without the need for any historic data (hence, training can be skipped). Weighting factors are given to specific attribute values to come up with a score.

The scoring parameters for model and model fields are different than the parameters for decision trees. The parameters of the scoring model consist of setting the regression type and default scores. The default scores are optionally set for any outliers or missing data records.

The configuration within each regression type is different. For linear and nonlinear options, outliers can be excluded by specifying minimum thresholds values. The threshold quantities exclude field values based on the number of records for that value.

These records can be excluded entirely out of a score value or a default score can be assigned, depending on a configuration flag. More explicitly, counts are determined for every combination of values, and when the number of records for each combination is exceeded, regression analysis skips over the combination.

For nonlinear regression, a smoothing factor can be specified additionally. The higher the smoothing factor, the closer the algorithm is to being linear, but overfitting to the training data where there are not enough records is prevented.

Additional field value parameters for linear and nonlinear regression types are:

Most frequent, all, or selected values. These options set whether all discrete values, specific discrete values, or the most frequent discrete values should be considered in the linear regression. If the most frequent values option is picked, a number up to 100 determines how many of the most frequent discrete values are to be included.

Full or specified data range. This option is similar to the preceding one but is for continuous values. Therefore, ranges have to be set or all values be permitted for use in regression analysis.

Automatic or manual intervals. Intervals within a continuous data range can be automatically generated or manually created. If the automatic option is picked, the number of intervals to generate must be specified. The data range limits are then calculated by automatically rounding off the maximum and minimum values of the training data. If data in the prediction source falls outside the limits, it is treated as an outlier.

Table 8.1 illustrates the field value parameters for both discrete and continuous content types per regression type.

Weighted score regression types are explained in more detail via calculation scenarios presented in Table 8.3. In the scenarios presented, the weighted score regression type scores customers in order to identify potential buyers for a new cocktail beverage based on two attributes: where they live and how old they are (or model fields "dwelling" and "age," respectively). Table 8.2 provides the model fields and their weights, as well as field values and their partial scores to be used in the calculation scenarios in Table 8.3. The definitions for weights and partial scores are:

Table 8.1 Scoring Field Value Parameters

REGRESSION	DISCRETE TYPE	CONTINUOUS
Linear	Most frequent, all, or selected values	Full or specified data range
Nonlinear	Most frequent, all, or selected values	Full or specified data range Automatic or manual intervals
Weighted Score	Weight of model field Partial scores	Weight of model field Threshold partial scores Function piecewise constant Left/right borders

Weight of model field. The calculation for weighted scores is calculated at two levels. Weightings are made at the field level (weight of model field) and at the field values level (partial scores). This parameter is for the first level.

Partial scores. Partial scores can be given per discrete value or by thresholds for continuous values. These entries are made per discrete value. All remainder values that are explicitly specified can be assigned a default partial score.

Threshold partial scores. For continuous values, thresholds can be maintained for partial scores that effectively work as intervals.

There are three discrete values for the dwelling model field: city, suburb, and town. All remaining values are treated as their own separate discrete value. For age, the continuous values are defined by the following intervals: 0 to 21, 22 to 31, 32 to 41, 42 to 65, and over 65. Partial scores are assigned to each of these values or intervals in the scoring model.

How a calculation is actually performed is dependent on the field value parameters (Table 8.1). The parameters influencing the calculation are:

Function piecewise constant. This setting is only for continuous values and if set partial scores are applied based on the ratchet values of the interval. Otherwise, partial scores are interpolated from the left and right borders of the interval.

Left/right borders. This setting is only for piecewise constant values (does not apply to discrete values) and specifies whether the left or right border is included into a numeric interval.

Outlier treatment. How the system handles outliers can be controlled. For discrete values, outliers are any values that are not explicitly addressed. For continuous values, outliers are any values that are outside the threshold limits. You configure how outliers are treated by picking one of these options: *Treat as separate instance, Cancel processing, Ignore record, Set default score, Constant extrapolation*, or *Extrapolation*. The first option is only for discrete values where all outliers are treated as one value. The last two extrapolation options are only available for continuous values.

Table 8.2 Example Customer Scores

MODEL FIELD	WEIGHT	CONTENT TYPE	VALUE/ THRESHOLD VALUE	PARTIAL SCORE
Dwelling	2	Discrete	City	25
Dwelling	2	Discrete	Suburb	15
Dwelling	2	Discrete	Town	10
Dwelling	2	Discrete	Remaining values	5
Age	5	Continuous	0	0
Age	5	Continuous	21	50

(continues)

Table 8.2 Example Customer Scores *(Continued)*

MODEL FIELD	WEIGHT	CONTENT TYPE	VALUE/ THRESHOLD VALUE	PARTIAL SCORE
Age	5	Continuous	31	35
Age	5	Continuous	41	15
Age	5	Continuous	65	5

Table 8.3 illustrates how weighted score calculations are influenced by the aforementioned field value parameters. The formula for the weighted score calculation is the sum of the weight of the model fields times their partial scores of their respective field values.

Table 8.3 Example Calculation Scenarios for Weighted Scores

CUSTOMER PROFILE	FIELD VALUE PARAMETER	CALCULATION	
35 year old, suburb dweller	Piecewise constant set (left border)	$(2 \times 15) + (5 \times 35) =$	205
21 year old, suburb dweller	Piecewise constant set (left border)	$(2 \times 15) + (5 \times 50) =$	280
35 year old, city dweller	Piecewise constant set (left border)	$(2 \times 25) + (5 \times 35) =$	225
35 year old, suburb dweller	Piecewise constant not set	$(2 \times 15) + (5 \times 25) =$	155
21 year old, suburb dweller	Piecewise constant not set	$(2 \times 15) + (5 \times 50) =$	280
35 year old, city dweller	Piecewise constant not set	$(2 \times 25) + (5 \times 25) =$	175
21 year old, rural dweller	Treat as separate instance is set	$(2 \times 5) + (5 \times 50) =$	135
70 year old, city dweller	Constant extrapolation (for outlier)	$(2 \times 25) + (5 \times 5) =$	75
70 year old, city dweller	Extrapolation (for outlier)	$(2 \times 25) + (5 \times 1) =$	55

All regression types support how missing values are treated. As a default, the system handles spaces or zeros as missing values. However, if there is an explicit value that represents a missing value (e.g., 9999), this value can be specified. For example, this might be useful when a distinction between null values and a zero values are needed for key figure values. If missing values are found, the system reaction is configured to either stop processing, ignore the record, set a default score, or replace the value. A replacement value must be given for the last option.

Clustering

The clustering method groups data into segments based on associations between different characteristics in the data. For example, an insurance company might want to identify the potential market for a new policy by segmenting their customer base according to attributes such as income, age, risk categories, policy types held and claims history. Clustering divides a set of data so that records with similar content are in the same group while records with dissimilar content are in different groups.

Clustering is also known as segmentation since the relationships it finds can be used to identify customer or market segments. For example, clustering might identify customers that are susceptible to specific marketing campaigns based on specific attributes or behaviors like a book club searching for a cluster of customers that may be interested in "home improvement" or "gardening" books. Clustering might have determined the different customer profiles presented in Table 8.2. Since the categories of clustering are unknown before clustering is performed, it has also been referred to as unsupervised learning or knowledge discovery. The results of its discovery (e.g., identified and validated customer segments) can then be stored to master data and can be passed on to other CRM analysis such as CLTV analysis.

The configuration of clusters is more simple and straightforward. Configuration controls how many clusters should be generated and specifies criteria for pruning the calculation for enhanced quality and performance.

For example, a numeric threshold can be set for a model field so that if the number of distinct values in that field is exceeded, the additional records are ignored in the calculation. This improves the trainability and performance of the model, because if a model field with high cardinality is included for clustering, the system has to use more data from more dimensions to find associations. Other performance savers are putting a cap on the number of iterations to be performed on the data set, as well as a defining a minimum threshold of change (expressed as fractions) required for clustering iterations to continue. If nothing much has changed, clustering stops.

For the model field parameters, weights can be assigned to skew the clustering in favor of a particular field, as well as default replacement values for missing or initial values. Weights and treatment of missing values can also be controlled for individual discrete field values or continuous field value ranges. For model fields that contain continuous field values, there is an additional setting that influences the graphical view. The graphical view of clustering can be controlled by specifying the number of binning intervals for visualization. This has no impact on training the model. The binning intervals are broken into equal intervals between the minimum and maximum amounts. Each binning interval contains the frequency of values within the range. Figure 8.4 shows sample output from clustering.

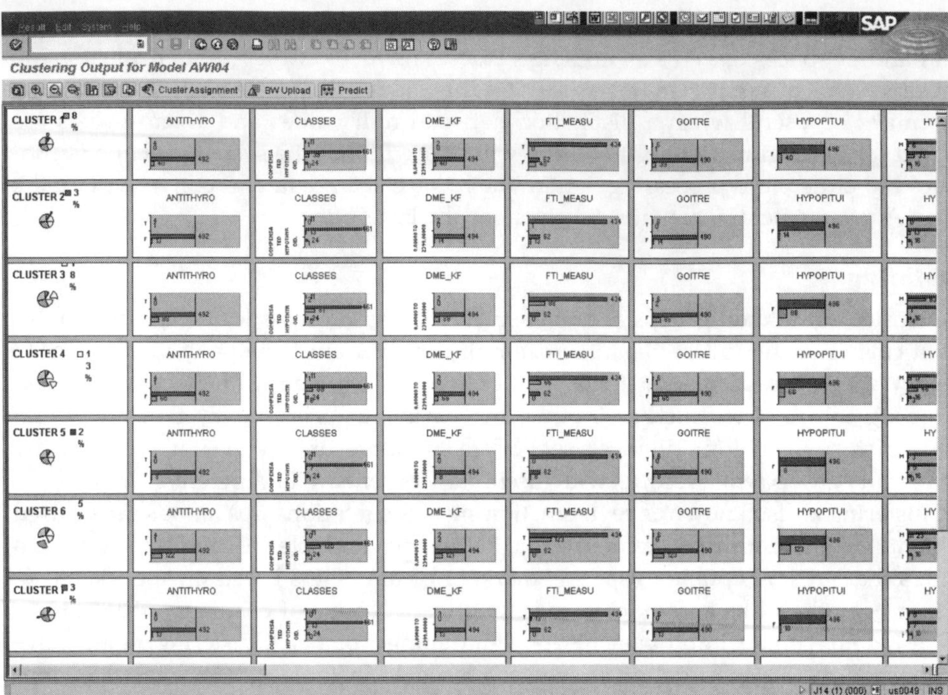

Figure 8.4 Clustering.

Association Analysis

Association analysis is a type of dependency analysis and is sometimes also referred to as market basket analysis because of its heavy use in retail. However, there are practical applications in other industries such as a telecom company offering additional services to customers who have already bought a specific set of services.

Association analysis is used to develop rules for cross-selling opportunities. As a result, this data mining model has the unique output option of exporting the association rules it calculates to operational CRM (to applications such as the customer interaction center). The association analysis generates boolean logic rules such as the famous association "If it is Friday, then male buyers of diapers also purchase beer."

To configure association analysis and understand its output, we must first define certain data mining terms:

Support. This is a percentage of how often a collection of items in an association appears. For example, 5 percent of the total purchases at an airport sundry shop support the sale of both toothbrush and toothpaste.

Confidence. From a statistical perspective, confidence has a close association with conditional probability. It is the percentage likelihood that a dependent item occurs in a data set when a lead item has occurred. For the diapers (lead item) and beer (dependent item) association, confidence could be expressed as a 50 percent probability of beer being purchased given a sale of diapers. This number is observational rather than predictive.

Lift. This is a measure of the effectiveness of an association analysis by taking the ratio of the results with and without the association rule. Lift can be used to eliminate records that do not have a true association but are picked up in the analysis because they appear frequently. More explicitly, lift is confidence divided by support for a given association. The actual mathematical formula the system applies is as follows: Lift is equal to the actual support of the lead and dependent items divided by the ratio of actual support for lead item to actual support of dependent item. Fractions are used in the equation rather than percentages.

The configuration curtails the association analysis by excluding records that fall below specified minimums for support, confidence, and lift or that fall above the maximums for the number of leading and dependent items used in any given association rule. These configuration settings improve performance and understandability of the association rules generated.

The model fields configuration for this analysis does not contain any parameters, although the content types are different consisting of items, transactions, and transaction weights (instead of key, discrete, and continuous values).

Figure 8.5 shows example output from an association analysis.

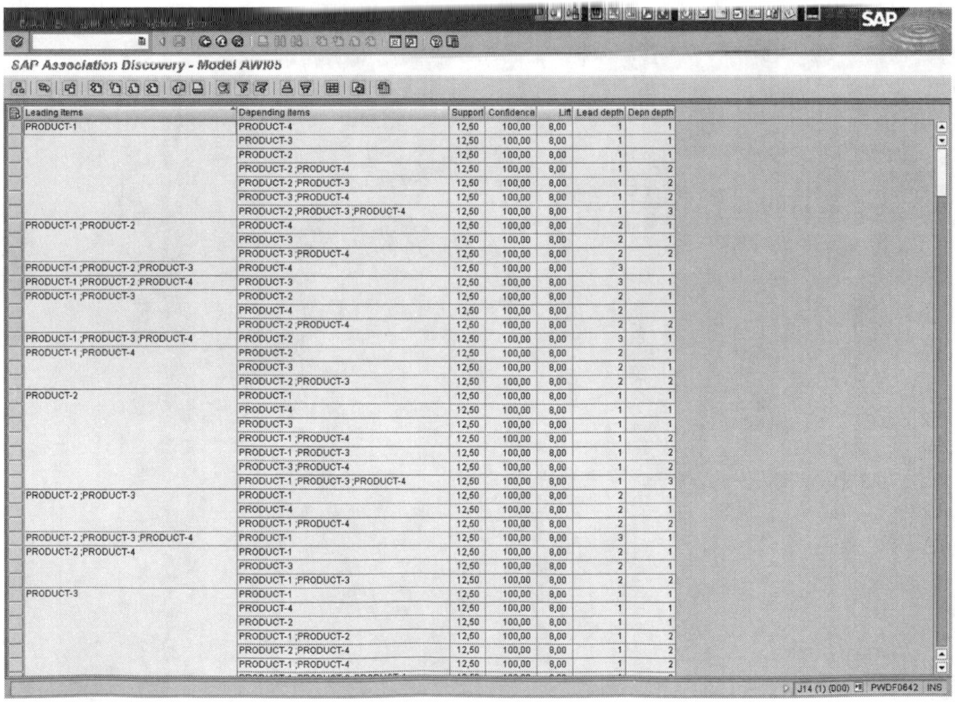

SAP Association Discovery - Model AW105

Leading items	Depending items	Support	Confidence	Lift	Lead depth	Depn depth
PRODUCT-1	PRODUCT-4	12,50	100,00	8,00	1	1
	PRODUCT-3	12,50	100,00	8,00	1	1
	PRODUCT-2	12,50	100,00	8,00	1	1
	PRODUCT-2 ;PRODUCT-4	12,50	100,00	8,00	1	2
	PRODUCT-2 ;PRODUCT-3	12,50	100,00	8,00	1	2
	PRODUCT-3 ;PRODUCT-4	12,50	100,00	8,00	1	2
	PRODUCT-2 ;PRODUCT-3 ;PRODUCT-4	12,50	100,00	8,00	1	3
PRODUCT-1 ;PRODUCT-2	PRODUCT-4	12,50	100,00	8,00	2	1
	PRODUCT-3	12,50	100,00	8,00	2	1
	PRODUCT-3 ;PRODUCT-4	12,50	100,00	8,00	2	2
PRODUCT-1 ;PRODUCT-2 ;PRODUCT-3	PRODUCT-4	12,50	100,00	8,00	3	1
PRODUCT-1 ;PRODUCT-2 ;PRODUCT-4	PRODUCT-3	12,50	100,00	8,00	3	1
PRODUCT-1 ;PRODUCT-3	PRODUCT-2	12,50	100,00	8,00	2	1
	PRODUCT-4	12,50	100,00	8,00	2	1
	PRODUCT-2 ;PRODUCT-4	12,50	100,00	8,00	2	2
PRODUCT-1 ;PRODUCT-3 ;PRODUCT-4	PRODUCT-2	12,50	100,00	8,00	3	1
PRODUCT-1 ;PRODUCT-4	PRODUCT-2	12,50	100,00	8,00	2	1
	PRODUCT-3	12,50	100,00	8,00	2	1
	PRODUCT-2 ;PRODUCT-3	12,50	100,00	8,00	2	2
PRODUCT-2	PRODUCT-1	12,50	100,00	8,00	1	1
	PRODUCT-4	12,50	100,00	8,00	1	1
	PRODUCT-3	12,50	100,00	8,00	1	1
	PRODUCT-1 ;PRODUCT-4	12,50	100,00	8,00	1	2
	PRODUCT-1 ;PRODUCT-3	12,50	100,00	8,00	1	2
	PRODUCT-3 ;PRODUCT-4	12,50	100,00	8,00	1	2
	PRODUCT-1 ;PRODUCT-3 ;PRODUCT-4	12,50	100,00	8,00	1	3
PRODUCT-2 ;PRODUCT-3	PRODUCT-1	12,50	100,00	8,00	2	1
	PRODUCT-4	12,50	100,00	8,00	2	1
	PRODUCT-1 ;PRODUCT-4	12,50	100,00	8,00	2	2
PRODUCT-2 ;PRODUCT-3 ;PRODUCT-4	PRODUCT-1	12,50	100,00	8,00	3	1
PRODUCT-2 ;PRODUCT-4	PRODUCT-1	12,50	100,00	8,00	2	1
	PRODUCT-3	12,50	100,00	8,00	2	1
	PRODUCT-1 ;PRODUCT-3	12,50	100,00	8,00	2	2
PRODUCT-3	PRODUCT-1	12,50	100,00	8,00	1	1
	PRODUCT-4	12,50	100,00	8,00	1	1
	PRODUCT-2	12,50	100,00	8,00	1	1
	PRODUCT-1 ;PRODUCT-2	12,50	100,00	8,00	1	2
	PRODUCT-2 ;PRODUCT-4	12,50	100,00	8,00	1	2
	PRODUCT-1 ;PRODUCT-4	12,50	100,00	8,00	1	2

Figure 8.5 Association discovery.

Customer Lifetime Value Analysis

Customer lifetime value analysis goes a step beyond customer profitability analysis. It treats customers as investments and calculates their net present value depending on projections of the lifetime profitability of the customer. Predicted customer profitability and the predicted relationship life span of the customer are the primary factors for the analysis. Maximum lifetime profit for minimum investment is what is sought via CLTV analysis. The costs of acquiring and keeping a customer must be evaluated by the stream of profits the customer is expected to bring. The concepts applied here are similar in spirit to financial investment theory (albeit simplified). During the customer life cycle, four types of customer interaction take place:[1]

Engage. Finding prospects and turning them into customers.

Transact. Actually selling the customer products and/or services.

Fulfill. Delivering products and services.

Service. Keeping the customer happy through customer care.

These interactions take place in a circular pattern in multiple cycles during the different stages of the customer engagement life cycle that is being evaluated in CLTV analysis (depending on the industry). In a sense, CLTV integrates the costs and revenues from customer interactions over several Engage, transact, fulfill, and service (ETFS) cycles into a more or less homogeneous, time-variant profit curve.

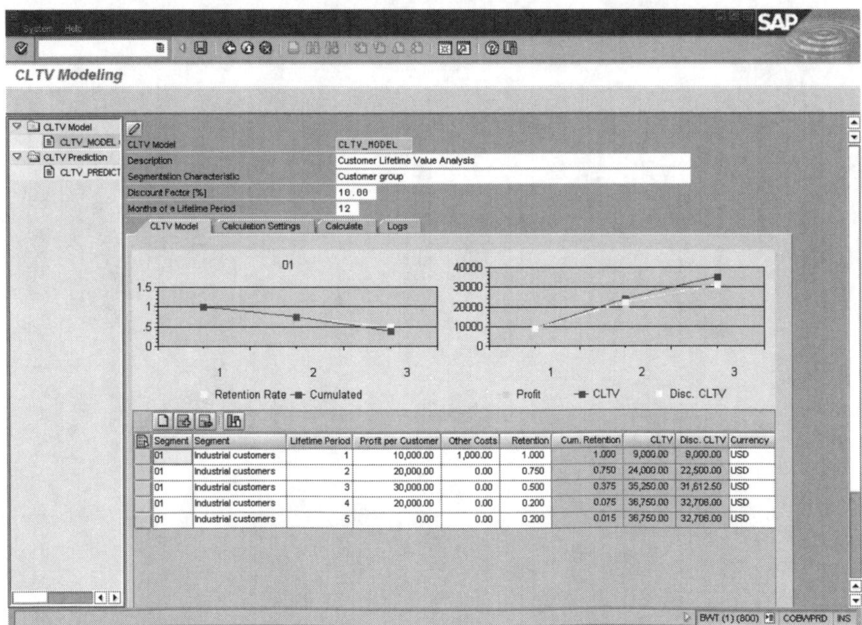

Segment	Segment	Lifetime Period	Profit per Customer	Other Costs	Retention	Cum. Retention	CLTV	Disc. CLTV	Currency
01	Industrial customers	1	10,000.00	1,000.00	1.000	1.000	9,000.00	9,000.00	USD
01	Industrial customers	2	20,000.00	0.00	0.750	0.750	24,000.00	22,500.00	USD
01	Industrial customers	3	30,000.00	0.00	0.500	0.375	35,250.00	31,612.50	USD
01	Industrial customers	4	20,000.00	0.00	0.200	0.075	36,750.00	32,706.00	USD
01	Industrial customers	5	0.00	0.00	0.200	0.015	36,750.00	32,706.00	USD

Figure 8.6 CLTV modeling.

[1]SAP AG. 2001. "Analytical CRM." p. 7. SAP white paper, www.sap.com

The CLTV analysis engine is configured via a menu transaction for a customer value analysis role. The transaction is composed of configuring the CLTV model, its calculation settings, and then its prediction settings. Figure 8.6 illustrates the transaction in question.

The CLTV calculation is centered on key figures for customer retention rates and customer profitability. Customer profitability can be sourced from CO-PA (R/3 profitability analysis). Retention rates are sourced from queries or from calculations. If rates are calculated, parameter settings must specify the number of periods for which data can be missing for a customer before that customer is deemed as lost. Then when the CLTV engine finds no data for a given customer for the specified number of periods, it factors the lost customer into its retention rate calculation.

CLTV calculations are done per customer segment (the segment is arbitrary but most typically comes from data mining clustering) per lifetime period. A lifetime period represents phases in a customer lifetime typically spanning years. Both the customer segment and the lifetime period are configured into the CLTV model. Figure 8.6 shows a CLTV model with the InfoObject customer group as the segmentation characteristic and a lifetime period of 12 months.

Consequently, the query specified as the source for CLTV analysis must contain characteristics representing the customer, the customer segment (attribute of customer), and the period. Key figures for profit and customer retention can be delivered in the same or separate queries. Additionally, a special InfoObject must be an attribute of customer representing a "customer since" date used as the starting point that marks the beginning of a customer relationship. These InfoObjects have to be explicitly configured into the calculation settings.

TIP Refer to InfoObject 0BPARTNER and corresponding attribute 0CRM_CUSSIN as templates for customer and customer since date, respectively.

Manual entries can be made for additional costs not picked up in the query sources as well as any other adjustments for the CLTV calculation. Furthermore, new entries can be manually entered into the CLTV calculation if data is missing. This can be an alternative to using queries for sourcing the data. The results of manual entries, data collection via queries, as well as the actual calculation are stored to Business Content ODS objects. Additionally, the results can be forwarded to the customer interaction center of operational CRM via a CRM alert modeler. Lastly, CLTV predictions can be performed based on the data stored to the CLTV ODS objects.

The CLTV calculation itself calculates two key figures: CLTV and discounted CLTV (the difference being a discount factor applied to the second key figure for its net present value). The discount factor is configured in the CLTV model. In this example, the discount was 10 percent (Figure 8.6). When used in conjunction with prediction, these key figures can then be compared to the estimated cost of acquisition to determine if a customer in a given segment is worth it. How the cumulated retention rate and CLTV is calculated is provided in Table 8.4. These calculations and values relate to the CLTV model depicted in Figure 8.6.

Table 8.4 CLTV Example Calculations

LIFETIME PERIOD PROFIT	RETENTION	CUM. RETENTION	CLTV	
1	9,000	1.000	1.000	9,000
2	20,000	0.750	0.750 = 1.000 × 0.750	24,000 = 9,000 + (0.750 × 20,000)
3	30,000	0.500	0.375 = 0.750 × 0.500	35,250 = 24,000 + (0.375 × 30,000)
4	20,000	0.200	0.075 = 0.375 × 0.200	36,750 = 35,250 + (0.075 × 20,000)
5	35,000	0.200	0.015 = 0.075 × 0.200	37,275 = 36,750 + (0.015 × 35,000)

The CLTV analysis starts its calculation on the execution date. If prior periods need to be picked up in the calculation, this can be configured in the calculation settings. The number of lifetime periods created depends on the time span of the source data and the length of the lifetime period. All customers in the query source can be considered or just the new customers. New customers are calculated by looking at the "customer since" attribute of the customer, determining the starting month of the calculation, and referencing a special configuration setting. The setting in question is the number of months from the start of a calculation that a customer can be considered as "new." Restricting a CLTV calculation to new customers simplifies the results of the calculation and gives a picture of the complete customer life cycle.

When you are executing CLTV prediction, the calculation determines how many customers are retained and the expected profit on the remaining customers. When configuring the CLTV prediction, you must specify the number of lifetime periods to predict as well as query source. The query source of the CLTV model can be used for prediction or a new query can be specified. The new query must have the same definition as the CLTV model query source, as well as contain the same segments. If data is missing, an option exists to reuse data from the last CLTV calculation.

RFM Analysis

RFM analysis evaluates the recency, frequency, and monetary value of customer purchases to determine the likelihood that a given customer will respond to a campaign. It is an empirical method that has long been applied to campaign planning and optimization as an alternative to segmenting a customer base by less effective demographic means. The results of RFM analysis provide marketing departments the financial justification for specific marketing campaigns. RFM analysis provides the measurements for success from both planned and actual perspectives. The RFM analytic engine performs two processes:

Segmentation. Similar to clustering, RFM analysis segments customers into different target groups. The main distinction is that RFM analysis is focused on specific aspects of customer behavior, namely:

Recency. When was the last purchase made? The most recent customers are sought based on the assumption that most-recent purchasers are more likely to purchase again than less-recent purchasers.

Frequency. How often were purchases made? The most frequent customers are sought based on the assumption that customers with more purchases are more likely to buy products than customers with fewer purchases.

Monetary value. What was the amount of the purchase? The biggest-spending customers are sought based on the assumption that purchasers who spent the most are more likely to purchase again than small spenders.

Response rate calculation. Once segments have been established, the response rates for each customer segment is calculated based on historical data of actual response rates of past campaigns. The results of the response rate are then saved to Business Content ODS objects and can then be passed on to the Segment Builder tool in SAP CRM. The Segment Builder models target groups by specifying attributes and building customer profiles for use in marketing activities such as running a campaign.

For the analysis to be effective, representative data must be used from prior campaigns. A campaign is considered sufficiently similar if the nature of the campaign and the customer target groups hold similar attributes. If historical data cannot be found for the representative target group, investments in learning must be made by launching new campaigns targeting the desired representative group so that RFM analysis can be applied. Using random, nonrepresentative data for RFM analysis can render it useless.

The process of RFM analysis is configurable, and the settings for the calculation are accessed via a transaction in the roles-based menu for a campaign manager. Figure 8.7 shows the configuration transaction for the RFM analytic engine.

To segment the customers, the system has to know which customers to segment, how many RFM segments to determine, and where to get the values for RFM analysis. This is controlled via the segmentation model settings. The customer values used for segmentation are represented by the InfoObject for business partner. The business partner determination is made either via a query source or directly from the business partner master data for all business partners identified as customers. If the source of the business partner is a query, the available characteristics in the query have to be assigned to the model field for customer.

The number of segments for recency, frequency, and monetary value has to be set separately. The system will segment each based on the value that is configured (the default is 5). The segmentation starts with recency, then frequency, and finally monetary value. First, customers are ranked into recency segments and given a score based on the number of segments. Within the recency segments, the frequency segments are then ranked and scored. Finally, within the frequency segments, monetary value scores are determined. Figure 8.8 illustrates the RFM segmentation process.

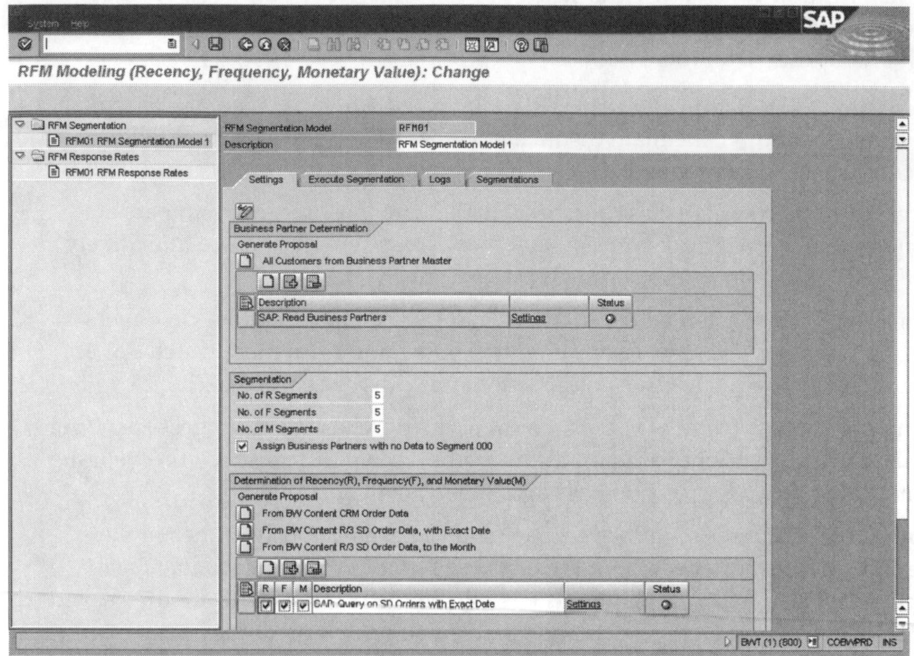

Figure 8.7 RFM modeling.

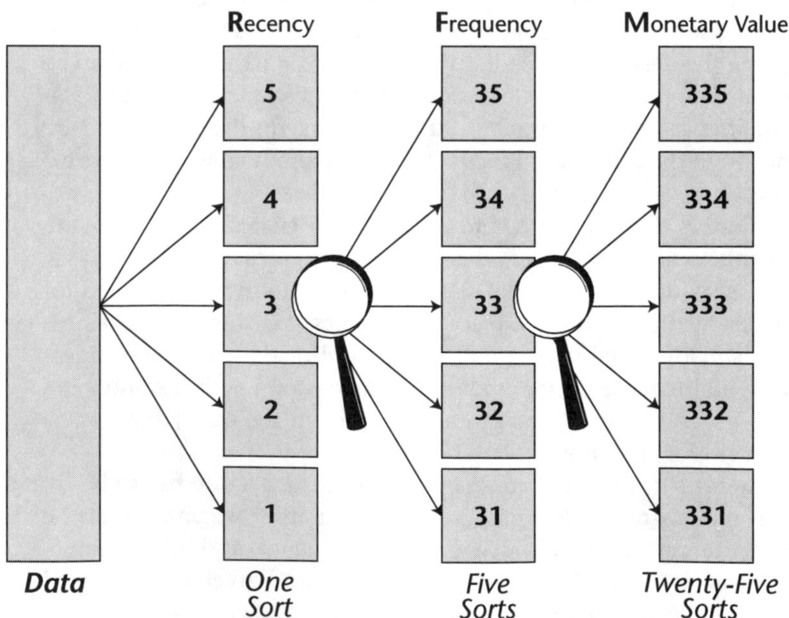

Figure 8.8 RFM segmentation process.

Another consideration is the number of segments that are created vis-à-vis the amount of records available and its impact on the response rate accuracy. For example, if the defaults of five segments per RFM were configured, then 125 segments would be calculated ($5 \times 5 \times 5 = 125$). Out of a customer base of 1,250,000 customers (10,000 customers per segment), one response would affect the response rate calculated by a hundredth of a percent (1/10,000). Out of a customer base of 1,250 customers (10 customers per segment), the difference of one response could swing the response rate by 10 percent. For smaller customer bases, the number of segments should be decreased. There are two options for handling customers that do not have data for the evaluation periods under consideration. The first option is the default, where all those customers fall to the bottom of the RFM analysis in the segment with the score of 111. The second option is to place these customers into a special segment with a score of 000, so that they fall out of the RFM analysis entirely (preventing any skewing of the segmentation results if there are enough customers missing data).

The queries that are used for the source of the RFM analysis must contain characteristic and key figures that map to the RFM segmentation model fields, namely business partner, RFM recency date, RFM frequency value, RFM monetary value, and currency key. A separate query can be mapped to each RFM key figure, or one query can cover all three. After these settings have been maintained in the RFM model, the segmentation can be executed and then response rates can be calculated.

For the response rate model, an RFM segmentation model must be assigned. Additional settings must be specified before you execute the calculations, such as whether or not the response rates should be viewable via the SAP CRM Segment Builder and the query sources for the representative target group and responding customers. During the response rate calculation, the first query is read to determine the campaign, the campaign start date and the target customers, which are then segmented based on the RFM segmentation model. The second query selects the responding customers to each campaign. The response rate calculation outputs the RFM segment codes (e.g., 335), the number of customers addressed (from the first query), the number of responses (from the second query), and the calculated response rates. This data is also written to a Business Content ODS object and is available via Business Content queries to check how effective the RFM analysis was in tying high response rates to the top-ranked RFM segments.

Supply Chain Analytics

One of the core technology components to mySAP SCM and supply chain analytics is SAP APO. Most of the SAP BW support for SAP APO comes through the BW system embedded into it directly or as standard Business Content on a remote SAP BW system. In contrast to CRM analytics, SAP APO does not provide SAP BW with separate analytic engines for its content.

We'll begin this section with an explanation of the SCOR model before briefly covering the applications and architecture of SAP APO. SCOR has modeling and analysis aspects that we'll topically cover with skewed emphasis on analysis. Finally, we'll explain how SAP APO uses the SAP BW platform. SAP APO integrates with SAP BW three basic ways: through the supply chain cockpit, through customizable planning book-based applications (such as demand planning), and through Business Content for fixed operational planning applications (such as production planning and detailed scheduling).

SCOR Model

Independent of SAP, a SCOR model has emerged as an industry standard. The SCOR model is largely the work of the Supply Chain Council (www.supply-chain.org), a nonprofit corporation founded in 1996 by Pittiglio Rabin Todd & McGrath and AMR Research. It has grown from its initial 69 volunteer members to over 500, testament to its importance to the industry. SAP now takes active involvement in the SCC.

The standardization movement facilitates the deliverance of Business Content for supply chain analytics. Because SCOR includes standardized key performance metrics for every detailed process in its model, SAP has a business model on which to build Business Content. For SAP, Business Content for SCOR metrics becomes more a matter of how to technically implement it than to devise useful business scenarios. Although there is some Business Content residing outside the SCOR model, much of the new development around Business Content is to deliver SCOR metrics. SCOR is not yet fully covered by Business Content, but the number of SCOR metrics supported grows. SAP furnishes a list of SCOR metrics that are supported by Business Content out on the SAP Service Marketplace.

A standardized operations reference model provides significant benefits. Standardized models provide companies' maps toward business process engineering establish benchmarking for performance comparison and uncover best business practices for gaining competitive advantage. By standardizing supply chain operations and metrics for managing such operations, companies can not only compare their results against others, but they are able to gain visibility of operations over a supply chain that may cross corporate borders. Partners in a supply chain can communicate more unambiguously and can collaboratively measure, manage, and control their processes. Greater visibility over complicated orchestration of supply chain activities lets you fine-tune targeted problem areas and identify the cause-and-effect relationships in a supply chain network.

SCOR and its corresponding performance metrics span supply chains from the supplier's supplier to the customer's customer. The process reference model contains:[2]

- Standard descriptions of management processes
- A framework of relationships among the standard processes
- Standard metrics to measure process performance
- Management practices that produce best-in-class performance
- Standard alignment to features and functionality

The SCOR model crosses all functions, incorporating business process reengineering (BPR), benchmarking, and best-practice analysis. (see Figure 8.9). The process model is the idealized "to be" model for any BPR project and can serve as industry benchmarks for practices and software solutions that embody best-in-class management principles.

[2]"Supply-Chain Operations Reference Model: Overview of SCORE Version 5.0." p. 2. SCOR, Supply Chain Council, Inc. www.supply-chain.org

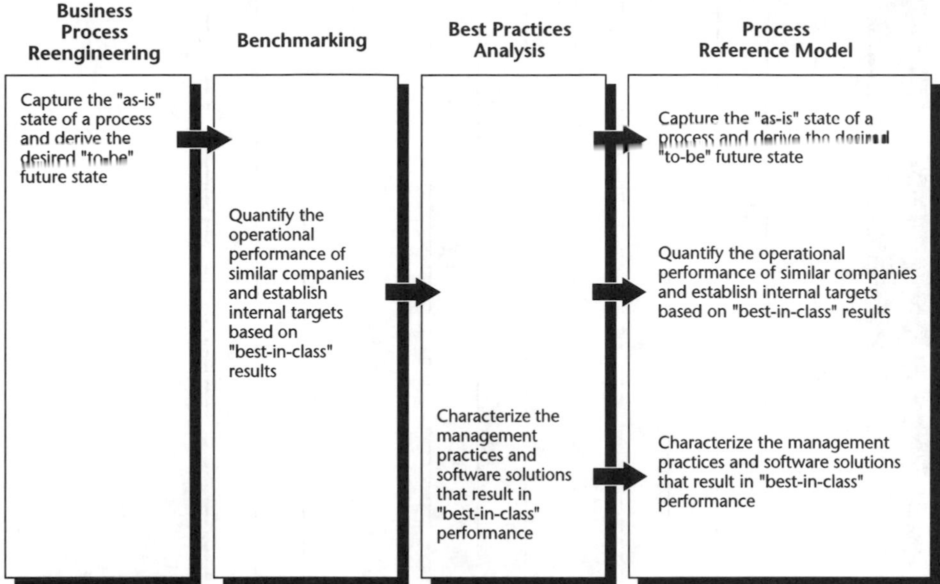
Business Process Reengineering
Benchmarking
Best Practices Analysis
Process Reference Model
Capture the "as-is" state of a process and derive the desired "to-be" future state
Quantify the operational performance of similar companies and establish internal targets based on "best-in-class" results
Characterize the management practices and software solutions that result in "best-in-class" performance
Capture the "as-is" state of a process and derive the desired "to-be" future state
Quantify the operational performance of similar companies and establish internal targets based on "best-in-class" results
Characterize the management practices and software solutions that result in "best-in-class" performance

Figure 8.9 Process reference model.

The SCOR model consists of five management processes:

Plan. This area encompasses demand-and-supply planning, which consists of balancing aggregate demand and supply to forge the optimization of sourcing, making, and delivering activities. Metrics on the actual planning process itself is not as robust as in the other areas.

Source. Analytics in this area revolve around performance attributes of the processes of procuring goods and services to meet planned or actual demand.

Make. Here analytics revolve around performance attributes of the production processes to develop finished goods to meet planned or actual demand. Production processes can be make-to-stock, make-to-order, and engineer-to-order.

Deliver. This area's analytics revolve around performance attributes of order, warehousing, transportation, and distribution management processes, providing goods and services to meet planned or actual demand.

Return. Analytics in this area revolve around performance attributes of the processes to return goods to suppliers or receive returned goods from customers for reasons such as defective products, maintenance, repair, and operating equipment (MRO) supplies, and excess, including post-delivery customer support.

Table 8.5 SCOR Performance Attributes

PERFORMANCE ATTRIBUTE	CUSTOMER FACING			INTERNAL FACING	
	RELIABILITY	RESPONSIVENESS	FLEXIBILITY	COSTS	ASSETS
Delivery performance	x				
Fill rate	x				
Perfect order fulfillment		x			
Order fulfillment lead time		x			
Supply chain response time			x		
Production flexibility			x		
Supply chain management cost				x	
Cost of goods sold				x	
Value-added productivity				x	
Warranty cost or returns processing cost	x				
Cash-to-cash cycle time					x
Inventory days of supply					x
Asset turns					x

The SCOR model processes are stratified into three levels of detail. The top level consists of the aforementioned processes (plan, source, make, deliver, and return) further subdivided into process types of *planning*, *execution*, and *enable*. Enable is the process of managing the information on which planning and execution rely and are categorized into performance attributes. All process metrics are an aspect of a performance attribute. The performance attributes for any given process are characterized as either customer-facing (reliability, responsiveness and flexibility) or internal-facing (cost and assets) metrics. A listing of all the top-level attributes defined by the SCOR model is provided in Table 8.5. Typically, only one metric should be focused on within a performance attribute. For instance, for the reliability performance attribute delivery performance, fill rate or perfect order fulfillment should be picked as a metric but not all three.

At the second level the intersection of process and process types forms process categories. Not all process categories are represented in a company's supply chain. Only the relevant process categories are chosen before decomposing them into process elements at the bottom level. A company can pick and choose from a menu of process categories to configure its own SCOR model (such as make-to-order, engineer-to-order, or make-to-stock categories).

The bottom level consists of the actual process elements and their process flows. It is this bottom level of the SCOR model that is most significant to analytics. Process elements are the most granular detail of the SCOR model and serve as the first level of process decomposition. Each process element has its inflows and outflows, as well as its own definition, features, best practices, and most notably, performance metrics. Any further process decomposition into lower levels of detail is outside the domain of SCOR. How a company uniquely implements the SCOR model is reflected as lower levels to the model consisting of more detailed process decompositions. The process element "Schedule Product Deliveries" and its corresponding performance attributes and metrics are listed in Table 8.6 as an example. For instance, the process element has a performance metric that measures the percentage schedules generated or changed within the supplier's lead time. The performance metric is characterized as a reliability performance attribute in the process element.

Table 8.6 Schedule Product Deliveries Process Element[3]

PERFORMANCE ATTRIBUTE	METRIC
Reliability	% schedules generated within supplier's lead time % schedules changed within supplier's lead time
Responsiveness	Average release cycle of changes
Flexibility	Average days per schedule change Average days per engineering change
Cost	Product management and planning costs as a % of product Acquisitions costs
Assets	None identified

[3]"Supply-Chain Operations Reference Model: Overview of SCORE Version 5.0." p. 11. SCOR, Supply Chain Council, Inc. www.supply-chain.org

The performance metrics of process elements can equate to the SAP APO key performance indicators. SAP APO key performance indicators are integrated with Business Explorer workbooks in BW. It is at this level where the Business Content (in the form of queries or calculated key figures) can meet the SCOR model. More information about the SCC and the SCOR model can be found at www.supply-chain.org.

Architecture

Figure 8.10 gives an overview of the components that the SAP APO application comprises and how it interacts with SAP BW and OLTP systems. SAP APO comes with its own analytic environment and corresponding tools—the supply chain cockpit. Then there are the applications that support the planning hierarchy: demand planning, supply network planning, production scheduling/detailed scheduling, transportation planning, and available to promise. These applications can be logically split into two types of planning applications. The first type has a highly customizable data basis and is planning-book-based (such as demand planning), while the second type has a fixed data basis and is more tightly integrated with operations (such as SNP, PP/DS, TPS, and ATP).

The planning-book-based SAP APO applications are integrated with R/3 via SAP BW extractors. Data can be loaded into SAP APO directly from R/3 or indirectly from R/3 through SAP BW Business Content and data mart extraction. For instance, the demand planning application is dependent on Business Content extractors to deliver sales history from R/3. This content can come from BW, but SAP APO can draw it from any data source.

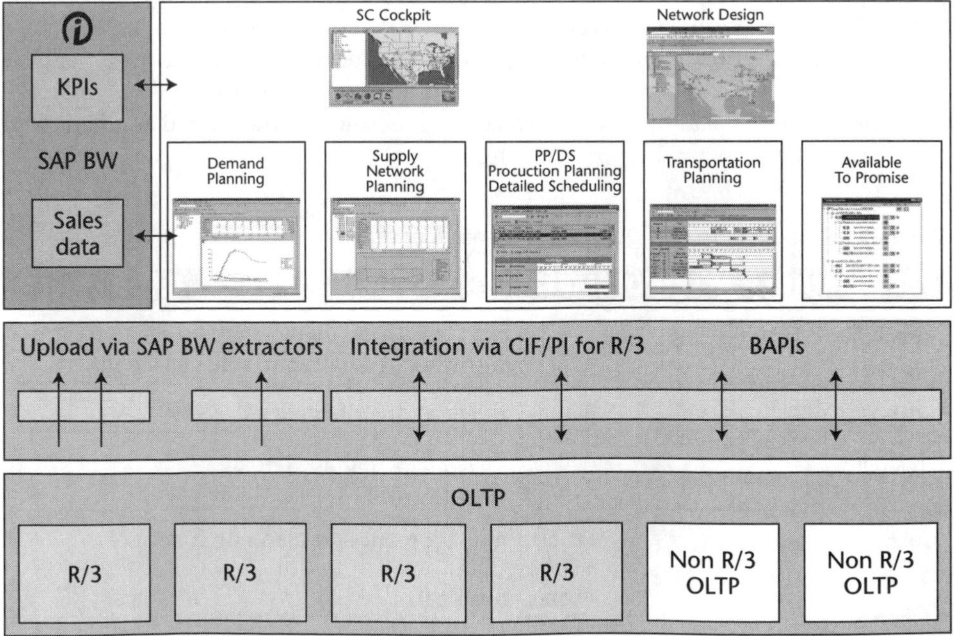

Figure 8.10 SAP APO application overview.

The SAP APO operational planning applications are integrated with R/3 via core interface (CIF) integration. This interface allows for the real-time exchange of data between R/3 and SAP APO systems. The core interface comes as part of the R/3 plug-in.

The SAP APO system contains an embedded BW system. As a result, all SAP BW functionality is available in SAP APO, such as the Administrator Workbench and Business Explorer Analyzer queries. Consequently, besides the core interface, data can pass data from R/3 to BW via standard Business Content extractors. Additionally, it is worth mentioning that all SAP APO Business Content predelivered with SAP BW systems are also available in SAP APO.

Consequently, the rationale behind why SAP recommends that reporting not be done out of SAP APO but out of a separate SAP BW system may be questioned. Technologically, nothing prevents SAP BW development work in the actual SAP APO system instead of a separate SAP BW system. The main motivation for setting up separate systems is performance. The SAP APO environment should be tuned for planning (primarily, "writes" to the database and complex computational tasks that impact performance and memory requirements), while the SAP BW environment should be tuned for reporting (primarily, "reads" from the database). With the Live Cache technology, performance is enhanced when planning and computations access memory rather than hard disk. The Live Cache database technology is an integral piece of SAP APO, kept on a server separate from the regular database server. Nevertheless, SAP APO still requires a regular database with regular I/O operations and still works with InfoCubes the same way SAP BW does.

Supply Chain Cockpit

The *supply chain cockpit* is a gateway monitoring tool that spans all the major SAP APO processes and allows access to the most granular details. The tool is graphical in nature, consisting of instrument panels to monitor and control different aspects of the overall supply chain, such as demand planning, manufacturing, distribution, and transportation. The supply chain cockpit is an analytic application in its own right and is integrated with SAP BW.

Via context menus, the supply chain cockpit can call both SAP APO queries and BW key performance indicators (KPIs). The context menu of the supply chain cockpit is the integration touch point between SAP BW and SAP APO. To configure the supply chain cockpit, you must configure the following items:

Context menus. Context menus allow user-defined menu items for queries and key performance indicators for any given SAP APO planning object (like locations, products, resources, etc.). A default context menu and default BW destination can be assigned to SAP APO planning objects if a context menu is not explicitly assigned. The context menu is configured via radio button selections determining if SAP APO queries or KPIs (sourced from SAP BW) will be assigned to the context menu. SAP BW queries are listed for drag-and-drop selection to the context menu for SAP APO key performance indicators. Note that KPIs link to specific SAP BW workbooks and not to a specific BW query. The implication is that the Excel Add-In for Business Explorer Analyzer must be installed on the SAP APO user's desktop.

Work areas. Work areas are ways to manage the view to the overall supply chain a section at a time. Two types of queries can be launched from a work area: SAP APO queries and SAP APO key performance indicators. The SAP APO queries are native to SAP APO, while the key performance indicators are actually BW queries. These queries are organized into query object pools that represent subsets of all the supply chain elements (or SAP APO meta data objects) composed of the following object types: locations, resources, products, production process models, and transportation lanes. Locations might be plants, customers, distribution centers, or suppliers. Resources might be for production, storage, handling, and transport. The queries or key performance indicators are called for these supply chain elements. The supply chain elements and their values or value ranges used in a work area are configured into the work area itself.

User profiles. The user profile controls how the navigation tree is displayed in the cockpit. This profile has settings such as the default context menu, if SAP APO hierarchies should be used in the navigation, how work areas should be displayed, how alerts should be displayed, and the planning calendar to use for time-dependent query data.

Control panel. The control panel is located at the bottom of the supply chain cockpit and contains individual context menus (see Figure 8.21 later in the chapter). These configurable monitoring options represent individual applications in SAP APO and are windows to alerts in the respective areas. Alerts can be monitored by products, resources, or locations. The configuration of the control panel is a matter of dragging and dropping the desired applications into the slots for the control panel.

If SAP APO has its own monitor and its own queries, an apparent question to ask is why SAP BW is needed or what additional functionality the supply chain cockpit offers. SAP APO queries can be displayed in the supply chain cockpit on the map, in graphics, in lists, or in tables. They are ABAP reports that select data by pointing to an object in the supply chain cockpit or through the data entry screen of a transaction.

Beyond SAP APO queries, BW queries have OLAP functions like drill-down to details, integration to R/3 data with drill-through, geographical information system (GIS) queries, Web reporting, and Web cockpits. The SAP BW queries are more flexibly maintained and configured. Example SAP BW queries for SAP APO demand planning for a consumer goods company will be detailed later in the chapter to provide a specific sample of the types of analysis that SAP BW can offer.

Finally, SAP APO does not keep a lot of history. As a result, SAP APO queries typically are executed for current data around the planning and execution situation. For example, a requirement/stock list displays the current availability of materials. A BW analysis would focus on historical trends rather than current data asking analytical questions such as "What was the average delay of our deliveries?"

Demand Planning

This component is used to develop a market forecast for the demand of the goods that a company provides. Many causal factors can be taken into consideration, as well as many forecast types generated (such as statistical, field, marketing, consensus, etc.). This application facilitates more accurate demand predictions.

Typically, sales history is loaded into SAP APO in order to extrapolate forecasts, and actuals are loaded to test forecast accuracy. No Business Content InfoCubes are delivered for demand planning because of the customized nature of the planning application. Because of its focus on historical data as input, demand planning is not immediately updated through the core interface. Demand planning is either directly loaded via Business Content extractors or indirectly loaded via the data mart interface from a sales history InfoCube. After demand planning data is performed, it is extracted out of SAP APO via the data mart interface back to an SAP BW InfoCube. Typically, the InfoCubes reside on a separate SAP BW instance.

Demand planning is done in Live Cache. To plan data (e.g., for statistical forecasts), you load sales history from SAP BW. Since data is only temporary in demand planning, data must be extracted back out to SAP BW InfoCubes where the data may more permanently reside. History can be matched with forecasts in order to do sales analysis. Business Content (InfoCube 0SD_C03) exists for such reporting. Figure 8.11 depicts the information logistics for such an information model. The sales analysis InfoCube can either be done as a single basic InfoCube or as a MultiProvider (splitting history and forecasts into separate InfoCubes, since these records typically are at different levels of granularity).

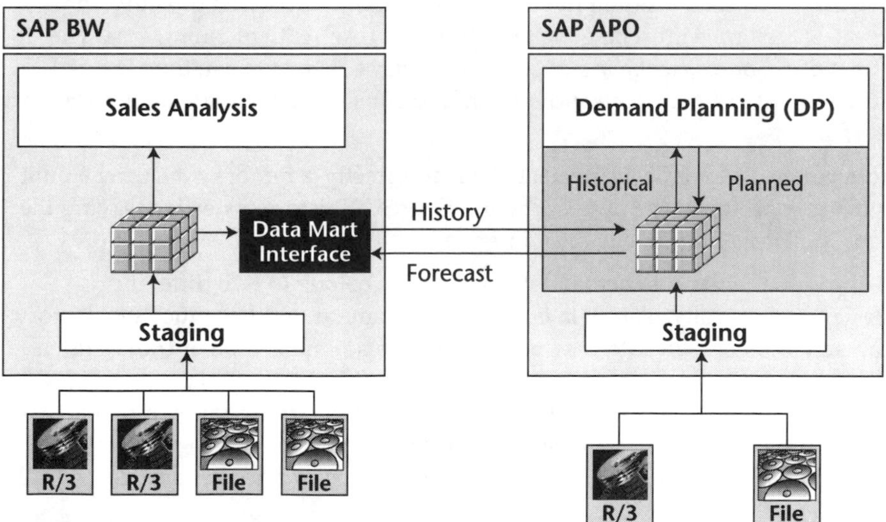

Figure 8.11 SAP APO demand planning information flow.

In the next section, we look at the design impacts such planning applications have on BW information modeling. We follow this with a case study of a SAP BW information model implementation for demand planning

Design Impacts

Analysis on data that is extracted from SAP APO Live Cache planning data has special design considerations. Irrespective if SAP APO or a separate SAP BW system is picked for reporting, there are still some SAP APO-specific information modeling considerations that must be made because of how its planning data is stored. Following is a list of these design considerations:

Noncumulative key figures. Only the most recent information is available in Live Cache. Live Cache does not store history. Its data can be backed up to hard disk for disaster recovery, but the data available is only a snapshot at the specific moment in time. As a result, transactional history or delta amounts are not available. This information must be extracted this way as well and cannot be cumulated over time. The key figures from planning are snapshots in nature. However, noncumulative key figures cannot be used to model this snapshot data, since it depends on delta increments to do its noncumulative calculation. Consequently, the snapshot quantities and amounts must be stored in a cumulative key figure with an exception aggregation (for example, a "last value" exception aggregation). This has a profound impact on how reporting InfoCubes should be modeled so as to avoid cumulating snapshot amounts over time.

Data Mart. The data residing in Live Cache cannot be accessed directly. An export DataSource must be generated from the SAP APO planning area. The export DataSource can be assigned an InfoSource. The data can then be extracted out of Live Cache and into an InfoCube for reporting via the data mart interface.

Remote cube. If Live Cache needs to be read directly, a remote cube can be built on directly on top of the Live Cache InfoSource. If history is needed, saving the plans to a basic InfoCube is recommended.

MultiProvider. Plan and actual data necessarily belong to two different InfoCubes. Typically, plan data is much less granular and has much less history than actual data. Plan data may be accessed via a remote cube or transactional InfoCube, while actual data resides in a basic InfoCube for which aggregates should be built. MultiProvider technology allows you to union plan and actual data together for variance analysis. Technically, it is possible to unite plan and actual data into a basic InfoCube, but there are performance advantages to MultiProviders that will be discussed in Chapter 10.

Master Data. SAP APO has its own master data. The planning model in SAP APO is separate from the information model in SAP BW. The planning model and associated meta data are created in the Supply Chain Engineer in SAP APO; in SAP

BW it is the Administrator Workbench. The master data may not only differ in values, but the meta data properties may differ as well. For example, SAP APO product is 40 characters long (identified by a generated ID), while materials in SAP BW are 18 characters long, since they are in SAP R/3. To reconcile the R/3 master data values loaded into SAP BW with SAP APO master data values, a crosswalk is needed between SAP APO and SAP BW for those values. This is done via navigational attributes on SAP APO master data. For example, the SAP APO product has material as a navigational attribute (technically, InfoObject 0APO_PROD has the navigational attribute 0MATERIAL). Similarly, SAP APO location number is cross-linked with plant (technically 0APO_LOCNO has the navigational attribute 0PLANT). Additionally, InfoObjects like SAP APO location number are predelivered with integration to the GIS.

Case Study

A consumer goods company has a rolling forecast cycle. Each forecast cycle plans demand for the next 12 periods on a rolling basis (i.e., a June forecast projects demand July through June of the following year). Within each forecast cycle, there are different forecast types planned at different points within the period. The forecast types are:

Statistical. This forecast uses sales history available in the first phase of the period to forecast demand based on forecasting algorithms such as regression analysis. This forecast is the first forecast made in the second phase of the forecast cycle.

Marketing. This forecast is made by the marketing department in the third phase of the forecast cycle.

Field. This forecast is the aggregated forecasts made by individual field sales representatives for their respective customers and products. This forecast is also made in the third phase of the forecast cycle.

Consensus. All the forecast types are evaluated, including the previous consensus forecasts, in order to come up with a new consensus forecast. This forecast is formulated in management team working sessions based on the analysis of specialized reports.

After the consensus forecast, the forecast cycle starts all over again in the next period when new history is available. The forecast cycle is shown in Figure 8.12.

History is then compared to the previous period forecasts to check for accuracy. Forecast accuracy is measured in four different lags (one through four period lags). Lag is calculated as the difference in periods between the forecast cycle (the period the forecast was made *in*) and the period forecasted (the period the forecast was made *for*). Forecast variances should decrease as the lag shortens. SAP APO and SAP BW were implemented in order to shorten the forecast cycle within the month and to enable better forecasting through improved reporting and analysis.

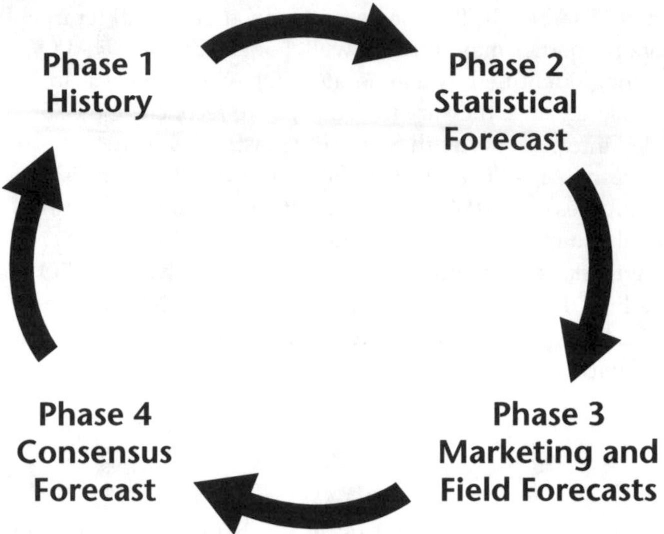

Figure 8.12 Forecast cycle breakdown.

Data Loads

Forecast accuracy cannot be calculated until history is available. As a result, some forecast accuracies cannot be computed until over a year has passed (i.e., a four-period lag for the last month forecasted in a forecast cycle). As history becomes available, forecast accuracies must be calculated for four different forecast cycles in order to determine the lags (one, two, three, and four periods) that have already been posted to InfoCubes.

For example, a forecast in May is made for the months of June through May of the following year. The next month, another forecast is made for the months of July through June of next year. With each new forecast cycle, the previous period's history becomes available for forecast accuracy variance calculations. Not only can the accuracy of a previous forecast (one period lag) be calculated, but variances can be determined for the accuracy of the forecast in two periods, three periods, and four periods.

Figure 8.13 shows the waterwheel schedule of the data flow for actuals and forecasts coming into the BW. The *x*-axis represents the forecast cycles, while the *y*-axis represents the forecasted periods. The value *F* in the cells represents the forecast data for that month. An asterisk represents the period that the forecast was made in. The value *H* represents the history as it becomes available. History is not shown in the figure until it coincides with a forecast to highlight when lags are available.

12 Period Rolling Forecast Generated In Period 1

	1	2	3	4	5	6	7	8	9	10	11	12	1	2	3	4	5	6
1	*	F	F	F	F	F	F	F	F	F	F	F	F					

12 Period Rolling Forecast Generated In Period 2 and History Loaded for Period 1

	1	2	3	4	5	6	7	8	9	10	11	12	1	2	3	4	5	6
1		F	F	F	F	F	F	F	F	F	F	F	F					
2		*	F	F	F	F	F	F	F	F	F	F	F	F				

12 Period Rolling Forecast Generated In Period 3 and History Loaded for Period 2
1 Period Lag Calculated for Period 1 Forecast

	1	2	3	4	5	6	7	8	9	10	11	12	1	2	3	4	5	6
1		F&H	F	F	F	F	F	F	F	F	F	F	F					
2			F	F	F	F	F	F	F	F	F	F	F	F				
3			*	F	F	F	F	F	F	F	F	F	F	F	F			

12 Period Rolling Forecast Generated In Period 3 and History Loaded for Period 4
1 and 2 Period Lags Calculated for Period 3 and Period 2 Forecasts, Respectively

	1	2	3	4	5	6	7	8	9	10	11	12	1	2	3	4	5	6
1		F&H	F&H	F	F	F	F	F	F	F	F	F	F					
2			F&H	F	F	F	F	F	F	F	F	F	F	F				
3				F	F	F	F	F	F	F	F	F	F	F	F			
4				*	F	F	F	F	F	F	F	F	F	F	F	F		

12 Period Rolling Forecast Generated In Period 3 and History Loaded for Period 4
1, 2, and 3 Period Lags Calculated for Period 4, Period 3, and Period 2 Forecasts, Respectively

	1	2	3	4	5	6	7	8	9	10	11	12	1	2	3	4	5	6
1		F&H	F&H	F&H	F	F	F	F	F	F	F	F	F					
2			F&H	F&H	F	F	F	F	F	F	F	F	F	F				
3				F&H	F	F	F	F	F	F	F	F	F	F	F			
4					F	F	F	F	F	F	F	F	F	F	F	F		
5					*	F	F	F	F	F	F	F	F	F	F	F	F	

12 Period Rolling Forecast Generated In Period 3 and History Loaded for Period 2
1, 2, 3, and 4 Period Lags Calculated for Period 5, Period 4, Period 3, and Period 2 Forecasts, Respectively

	1	2	3	4	5	6	7	8	9	10	11	12	1	2	3	4	5	6
1		F&H	F&H	F&H	F&H	F	F	F	F	F	F	F	F					
2			F&H	F&H	F&H	F	F	F	F	F	F	F	F	F				
3				F&H	F&H	F	F	F	F	F	F	F	F	F	F			
4					F&H	F	F	F	F	F	F	F	F	F	F	F		
5						F	F	F	F	F	F	F	F	F	F	F	F	
6						*	F	F	F	F	F	F	F	F	F	F	F	F

F = Forecast
H = History
* = Current Fiscal Period

Figure 8.13 Rolling forecast data loads.

Figure 8.13 starts the first forecast cycle in January of a new year. A one-period lag accuracy variance is not available until two forecast cycles later (in the month of March). Each subsequent forecast cycle, older lag accuracy becomes available (in period increments) until finally in June all lags are available for the month of May. Going forward, all lags (for the four periods) will be available for each previous month. The missing lags for the first five forecast cycles only occur when first starting the system.

Update Rules

The forecast accuracy variance calculation requires special programming in the update rules if the variance is to be stored with the detailed records of the InfoCube. Figure 8.14 illustrates how the variance records are generated (records in *italics)*. The first four request IDs represent records loaded for four different forecast cycles. Only the records that were forecasted for May are displayed. The lag is calculated as the difference between the period forecasted and the period of the forecast cycle. Forecast, history and variance are saved as separate key figures. When the forecasts are loaded, history and variance are left blank.

When history is loaded, the InfoCube is read for all the lags for the period in question. In this scenario, history is loaded for May, so the forecasts for forecast cycles 1, 2, 3, and 4 are read into the memory of the update rules so as to calculate variances on these same records. In this case, four new records are generated for each history record loaded.

This logic is repeated for each forecast and variance key figure pairs (one for each forecast type of statistical, field, marketing, and consensus).

Request ID	Product	Forecast Cycle	Period	Lag	Forecast	History	Variance
1	Chewing Gum	1	5	4 period	55		
2	Chewing Gum	2	5	3 period	85		
3	Chewing Gum	3	5	2 period	90		
4	Chewing Gum	4	5	1 period	105		

Request ID	Product	Forecast Cycle	Period	Lag	Forecast	History	Variance
5	Chewing Gum		5			110	
5	Chewing Gum	1	5	4 period			55
5	Chewing Gum	2	5	3 period			25
5	Chewing Gum	3	5	2 period			20
5	Chewing Gum	4	5	1 period			5

Figure 8.14 Lag and variance calculation.

Analysis

The purpose of the demand planning queries in SAP BW is to report on the forecasts generated in SAP APO. The queries give insight into forecast accuracy by comparing the different forecast types with the related actual and target data. Example SAP APO queries include:

Forecast accuracy. This query gauges the accuracy of forecasts by calculating the variance between forecast and actual data. Variances are shown for one-, two-, three-, and four-period lags to show any trends in accuracy over the forecast development stages. The query can be run for different forecasts, such as marketing, field sales, consensus, and statistical, and it can drilldown on different sales organization levels such as division, sales groups, and so on.

The query can also rank sales organizations by forecast accuracy. The rankings are based on a comparison between target and actual forecast accuracy per lag (one, two, three, or four). The target and actual forecast accuracy are measured as variance percentages.

Consensus. This is a query designed to assist with forecast consensus meetings every period. Several drill-downs are available in this report. The query provides previous history, previous consensus, statistical, field, and marketing forecasts. The query also provides the variance between the previous consensus and each of the current statistical, field, and marketing forecasts.

The query displays the consensus forecasts generated in the specified previous period (the forecast cycle minus a period) and all other forecast types generated in the current forecast cycle. History up to the forecast cycle is displayed as well. Furthermore, the query displays the variance of forecasts relative to the previous period consensus forecasts.

Consolidated demand. This query provides a list of all products forecasted in a specific forecast cycle. It reports each product's forecast by period, by sales organization, and in total. The results of the query are shared with the production planning department, deployment managers, and other operational individuals as a reference.

The query looks at the consensus forecasts generated for a specific forecast cycle. The query can filter the data by the period of the forecast cycle and specified products so as to gain an overview of the 12 periods (of consensus) forecasts.

Business Content

Although no Business Content is delivered for the highly customizable planning applications such as demand planning, there is Business Content for the fixed planning applications in the planning hierarchy. Two examples of fixed applications are network design and PP/DS (production planning/detailed scheduling). Both operational planning applications are explained in more detail later in this section. Although there are SAP APO reports to access the data within these applications, SAP BW Business Content delivers queries that are more analytical in nature.

Network design assists the strategic decision-making process around the design of a supply chain network, maximizing the utilization of a network's assets. In an environment with many products, many facilities, and many trading partners, strategic questions arise such as:

- What is the most effective way to set up manufacturing, transportation, and distribution networks?
- What changes can be made to the network design with the best cost impact?
- How can the network be expanded or contracted?
- What is the best sourcing strategy?

This component also interfaces with SAP BW via Business Content. The Business Content for network design is broken into three InfoCubes for location, shipment and transportation, and production analysis. The queries for these InfoCubes can be GIS-enabled for geographic reporting output.

The first InfoCube breaks down location-specific information for products, delivering key figures such as cost and quantities for procurement, production, goods issue handling, goods receipt handling, and so on. The second InfoCube breaks down product-specific information surrounding shipments such as transportation durations, shipment quantities, and shipment costs. The last InfoCube is for analyzing production planning delivering key figures around production capacity such as percentage utilization, availability, expected costs, and consumption.

Production planning and detailed scheduling supports order-to-shop-floor planning and scheduling for multisite manufacturing operations. Collaboration between multiple production plants and outsourced manufacturing sites are optimized to maximize the return on manufacturing assets. Example strategic questions addressed are:

- What happens if an unexpected event occurs such as a production-down scenario?
- How can production throughput be maximized?

This component interfaces with SAP BW via Business Content. The Business Content InfoCubes delivered for this component are for resource and operations data, order data, and order/customer assignment.

The first InfoCube differs from the others because its data comes from two InfoSources: one for resource data and one for operations data. The resource InfoSource delivers to the InfoCube key performance indicators such as total resource capacity, resource availability, and capacity loads. The operations InfoSource delivers key performance indicators such as operation durations (gross and net) and quantities for original, open, operational yields, scrap, and so on. The merged view of resource and operations in this InfoCube provides meaningful information around the resource situation and how it got there.

The second InfoCube holds all of the order data in the SAP APO system, providing status information and key performance indicators such as order lead time, setup time, delay time, work-in-process time, open orders, late orders, yield, and scrap. The last InfoCube provides pegging data. One is provided with picking and packing data per order per customer. Analysis can be done on which orders are late, their percentage of total orders, and quantities produced for specific customer, and so on.

Strategic Enterprise Management

SAP Strategic Enterprise Management (SAP SEM) is another example of an analytic application built on top of the SAP BW platform. The SEM analytic application is installed as an add-on application of SAP BW. Contrast this to SAP CRM and SAP APO. Analytics for mySAP CRM comes prebundled with SAP BW. The analytic applications for SAP APO come from an embedded SAP BW system.

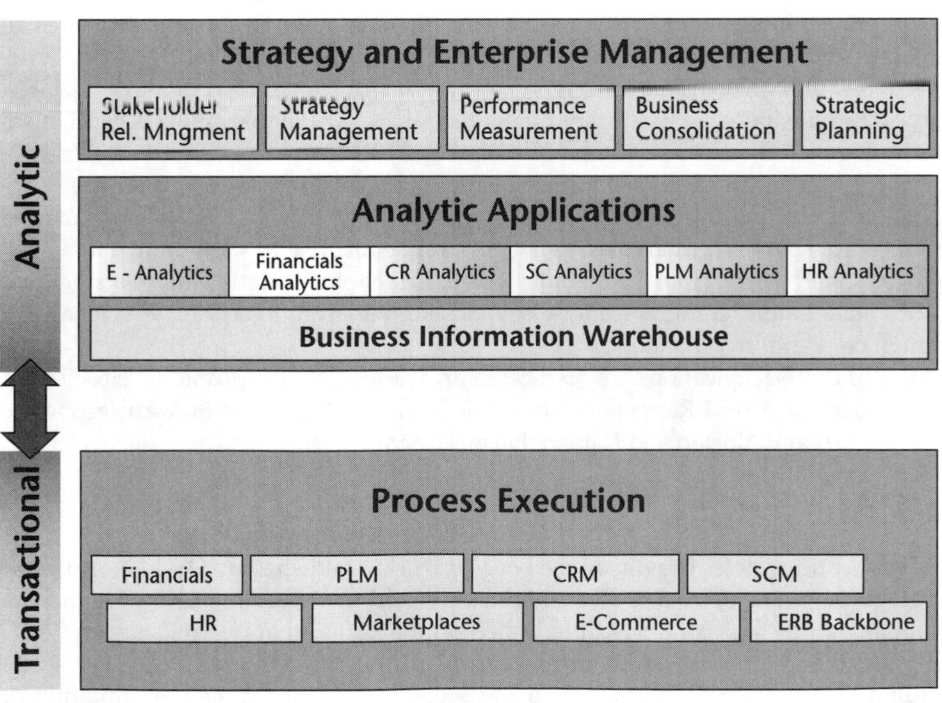

Figure 8.15 SEM overview.

In addition, SAP SEM comes with its own builders, models, and engines to extend the business intelligence platform for building analytic applications such as planning engines and performance measurement tools. SAP SEM comes with applications for stakeholder relationship management, strategy management, performance measurement, business consolidation, and strategic planning (depicted in Figure 8.15). All of these applications are aligned along the concepts of value-based management. The main SEM functions of corporate performance management, enterprise planning, and consolidation will be covered in this chapter.

Corporate Performance Management

Corporate performance management can be logically subdivided into three distinct areas: strategy management, performance measurement, and stakeholder relationship management. Strategy management consists of a suite of applications and tools that support the formulation of strategy and creating a framework for communicating it through an organization. Applications such as the balanced scorecard, capital market interpreter, risk management, and value-based management aid strategy formulation, implementation, and operationalization.

In contrast, performance measurement relates to applications that output the results of corporate performance. Performance measurement tools help link measures to strategies and present them visually for ease of understanding. Here the native functions of SAP BW offer the most value, but additional functionalities offered by the SEM suite extend business intelligence through tools such as the management cockpit, measure builders, and value driver trees.

Lastly, stakeholder relationship management controls how performance measurement gets communicated to the outside world, keeping stakeholders well informed of performance so that the market does not get caught surprised by anything that would have an adverse impact on shareholder value. Stakeholder relationship management pushes stakeholder communications beyond sharing traditional financial measures through conventional channels.

Most of these applications are predicated on academic theories and are closely tied to the works of Alfred Rappaport (shareholder value), Stern and Stewart (economic value added) and Norton and Kaplan (balanced scorecard).

Balanced Scorecard

This application relates heavily on the body of work established by David Norton and Robert Kaplan. The origins of the balanced scorecard traces back to 1990 when a multicompany study was conducted predicated on the notion that overreliance on financial performance measures was hurting more than helping value creation. The study revealed that some companies were using scorecards to overcome the limitation of financial performance metrics. These group discussions evolved into a more balanced approach by introducing the notion of adding four perspectives to scorecards. The new balanced scorecard then translates mission and strategy into objectives and measures organized into these perspectives.

The balanced scorecard addresses the needs for linking value creation to metrics other than financial, a more effective way to implement strategies, and more dynamic budgeting linked to strategy. Consider the following statistics:[4]

- Tangible book assets as a percentage of market value have been rapidly declining over the past three decades. For example, in industrial organizations it has dropped from 62 percent in 1982, to 38 percent in 1992, and then to 10 to 15 percent in 2000. In other words, 85 percent of the value of these companies is now intellectual. How do traditional financial measures capture the value of human capital?
- In the 1980s, a Fortune survey was conducted that revealed fewer than 10 percent of all strategies formulated were implemented successfully.
- Twenty percent of organizations spend more than 16 weeks to prepare the budget, 78 percent of organizations don't change their budget within the fiscal year, 85 percent of management teams spend less than 1 hour per month discussing strategy, and 60 percent of organization don't link their budget to the strategy.

The balanced scorecard has evolved even further. Not only is it a *performance measurement* system, but it is a central *strategy management* system used to accomplish critical management processes and enable effective strategy implementation. A common misconception is that a balanced scorecard is just another type of visualized report. The formulation of management strategy is a process just like any other process, such as sales, distribution, procurement, production, or accounting. The balanced scorecard not only supports strategy formulation but also the process of pushing strategies and objectives top-down in an organization. By translating strategies into measurable objectives, performance can be measured. When performance can be communicated and measured throughout an organization, the organization becomes more transparent and operations become more aligned with management objectives. Strategy management can be broken down into four main processes that feed into each other in a perpetual loop:[5]

Translating the corporate vision. This entails clarification of the vision and consensus building.

Feedback and learning. This is composed of vocalizing the consensus vision, receiving strategic feedback, and promoting strategy review and learning.

Business planning. Here targets are specified, strategic initiatives aligned, resources allocated, and milestones set.

Communication and linking. Here goals are set, rewards linked to performance, and communications and education takes place.

[4]Norton, D. P., R. S. Kaplan. 2000. *The Strategy Focused Organization: How Balanced Scorecard Companies Thrive in the New Business Environment*. Harvard Business School Press.

[5]Harvard Business Review. 1998. *Harvard Business Review on Measuring Corporate Performance*. Harvard Business School Press.

All these management processes revolve around the balanced scorecard framework. The balanced scorecard has two objectives:

- Change the way performance is measured and managed.
- Change the way strategy is implemented and how it is translated into actions.

Performance Management

To achieve the first objective, the balanced scorecard introduced two major distinctions to traditional financial performance measures: the addition of four perspectives to scorecards and the linking of performance measures to strategy. The four perspectives ask different strategic questions such as:

Financial. To succeed financially, how should we appear to our shareholders?

Customer. To achieve our vision, how should we appear to our customers?

Internal business processes. To satisfy our shareholders and customers, what business processes must we excel at?

Learning and growth. To achieve our vision, how will we sustain our ability to change and improve?

The balanced scorecard does not do away with financial performance metrics but augments it with different perspectives. These different perspectives add nonfinancial indicators and qualitative measures into the system of strategy formulation and evaluation. Nonfinancial measures may consist of measuring important but intangible assets such as employee motivation, customer satisfaction, operational efficiencies, and product or service quality levels. The balance scorecard marries the conventional accounting measures, which gives an enterprise a historical perspective with measures for intangible assets. This in turn gives an enterprise a future performance outlook. The perspectives do not have to be limited to the categories given or limited to only four. For example, a scorecard used in the public sector may consist of goal (mission goals of an agency), customer (citizens, taxpayers, and beneficiaries), and employee perspectives. Figure 8.16 illustrates the balanced scorecard and how it is translated into SAP SEM.

The SAP SEM balanced scorecard functionality allows for the formation of scorecard hierarchies and groups. These scorecards are assigned to organizational elements of your organizational structure, including integration to human resources, allowing for employee-specific scorecards. Higher-level scorecards can drilldown to lower-level scorecards, allowing for navigation throughout the organization. Scorecards can even be compared to each other. Scorecards are time-dependent, allowing for time-variant comparisons and creation of validity dates.

The linking of balance scorecard measures to strategy is done through cause-and-effect analysis. The different perspectives build on each other to influence financial key performance indicators. The perspectives can be viewed as a pyramid where learning and growth drive internal business process improvement, which in turn drives customer satisfaction. This ultimately improves the bottom line.

Cause-and-effect analysis links the outcomes and performance drivers of other perspectives to the financial perspective. Along the rows of cause-and-effect analysis are the perspectives. Along the columns are the strategies. In the bubbles are the strategic objectives. These objectives have measures associated with them (which can be displayed with an alternate view in SEM). Figure 8.17 illustrates cause-and-effect analysis in SEM.

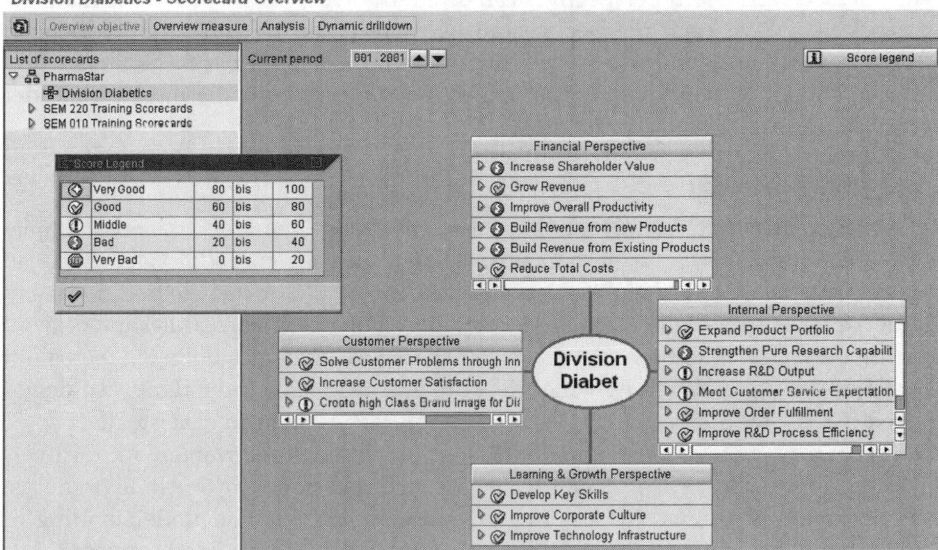

Figure 8.16 Balanced scorecard.

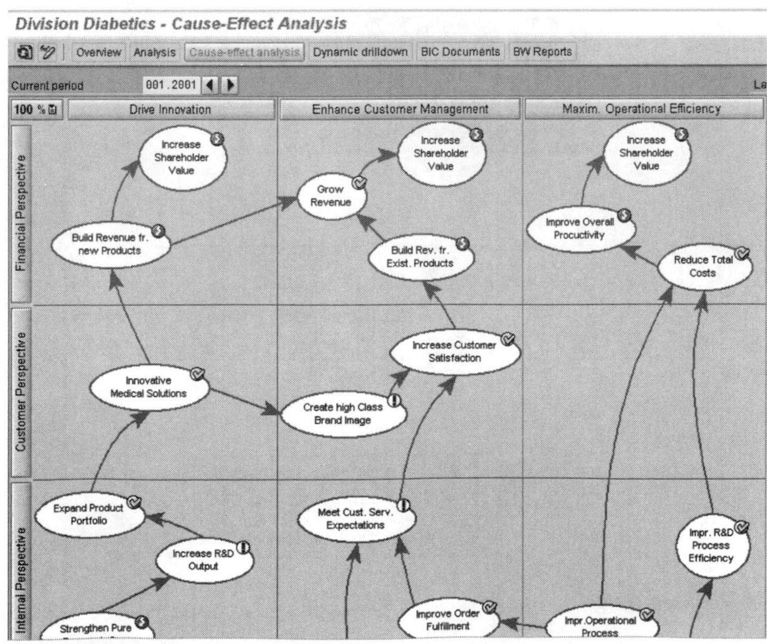

Figure 8.17 Cause-and-effect analysis.

The balanced scorecard perspectives can be alternatively displayed in the management cockpit, where each perspective can be represented by different color-coded walls (blue, black, red, and white) with different graphic types per measure (such as speedometer, tachometer, quadrant, chart, etc.) configurable in the measure builder (covered in more detail later in the chapter).

Strategy Implementation

The second objective of the balanced scorecard (to change the way strategy is implemented and how it is translated into actions) distinguishes it from traditional methods in two ways. The first way is that the balanced scorecard should bridge the traditional gap between strategy formulation and implementation. Balanced scorecards should avoid four main obstacles: nonactionable vision and strategies, strategies unlinked to goals at all levels of the organization (whether departments, teams, or individuals), strategies unlinked to resource allocation, and feedback that is tactical instead of strategic.

The second way is how the balanced scorecard provides the framework for overcoming these obstacles. The first and second obstacle is bridged by creating organizational alignment top-down by fostering shared commitment and understanding of corporate strategies among all employees. The third obstacle is avoided by incorporating the balanced scorecard into strategic planning and operational budget formulation processes. The last obstacle is overcome by a process known as *double-loop learning,* illustrated in Figure 8.18.

A company should not expect to implement a balanced scorecard by simply implementing the SAP SEM application. Before configuring this application, a corporation should already be well versed in balanced scorecard theory and know their strategies.

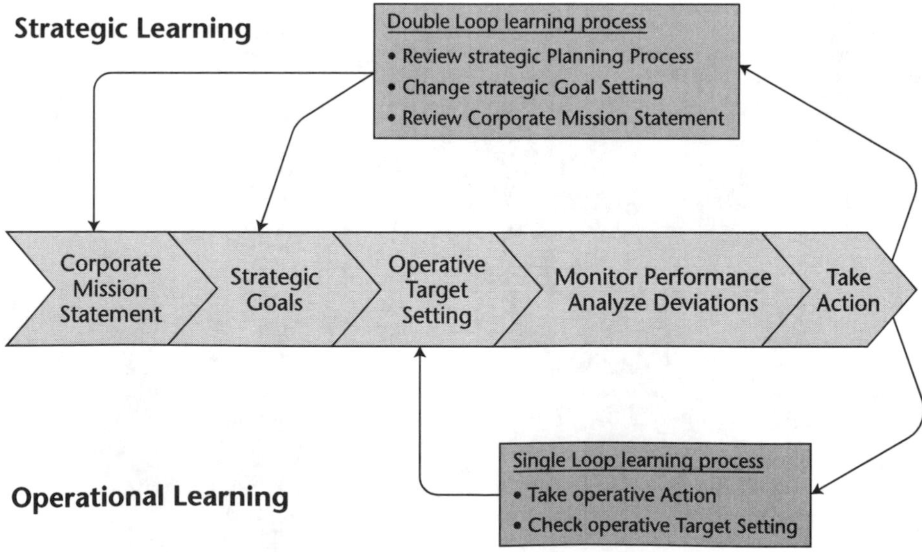

Figure 8.18 Double-loop learning.

The two main challenges to implementing a balanced scorecard solution is using the correct measures and measuring it correctly. The implementation process can take years and, hence, should be done incrementally.

The first challenge of using the correct measures relates to strategy formulation consisting of determination of what the strategies, objectives, initiatives, and measures are for an enterprise. This has to be accomplished before the SAP SEM application can be configured. From an SAP BW perspective, the second and more difficult challenge is capturing the measures correctly once they have been determined. Ironically, SEM CPM is typically the last application to be implemented after SAP R/3 and SAP BW have been implemented, when in an ideal world, it should be considered first. The balanced scorecard will have a potential impact on how OLTP source systems are configured and how information is modeled in SAP BW. For instance, one of our customers just finished implementing SAP R/3 only to discover a need to reimplement some areas to support the design of their SEM CPM application.

Once an enterprise is organizationally prepared for the balanced scorecard, the SAP SEM application can be configured. The advantage of building an electronic scorecard in SAP SEM is the integration capabilities to structured information (SAP BW queries), unstructured content (information gathered by SEM BIC), and planning (SEM BPS planning layouts).

The SAP SEM balanced scorecard has its own scoring engine to give data residing in SAP BW a qualitative context of whether a key performance indicator is bad or good. You can assign status symbols to a range of scores (which can be weighted) to measures based on performance levels, thereby giving a visual means for gauging performance.

Creating a scorecard in SAP SEM consists of building measures, creating a pool of balanced scorecard elements, maintaining general settings such as the creation of SEM-CPM variables, and then constructing the actual scorecard by assembling the balanced scorecard elements.

The configuration of measures via the measure builder is a central activity to SEM CPM. Measures are not only used for the SAP SEM balance scorecard but are also used in value driver trees, risk analysis, and the management cockpit. The measures are configured via the measure builder, which includes a measure catalog containing a large number of predefined measures with detailed descriptions. The definition of measures consists of settings such as the definition, a formula if relevant, assigning it benchmarks, and mapping technical key figures available via ODBO-enabled BW queries. The integration with SAP BW is achieved via value fields. Multiple value fields (such as plan and actuals) can either be assigned to objectives or measures that represent multiple query cubes.

Once measures have been configured, balanced scorecard elements can be configured. Balanced scorecard settings exist at two levels: balanced scorecard-independent settings and balanced scorecard-dependent settings. The independent settings must be maintained first.

The balanced scorecard (BSC) elements are centrally maintained and used as building blocks to balanced scorecards. When configuring BSC elements, the relationships between the elements have not been established. The basic elements consist of strategies, strategy categories, perspectives, objectives, and common objectives.

Then general settings such as SEM-CPM variables (which reduce the need for hard-coding values in the balanced scorecard), value fields (which link to BW queries), and technical settings for the integration to SAP BW (such as serial versus parallel processing of data requests) must be maintained. Status symbols and scoring methods are also configured at this point.

Finally, the balanced scorecard-dependent settings are maintained when scorecard elements are assigned to a specific scorecard as well as general scorecard parameterizations such as its time dimension, graphics, documents, and links. The configuration of the scorecard itself takes only a fraction of the time it takes to design it.

Enterprise Planning

Planning and simulation is an important business intelligence function. Performance measurement relies heavily on the variance analysis of plan versus actual. Planning is an essential activity to the forward-looking organization. Strategic enterprise planning closes the loop between strategic and operational planning.

The planning process typically covers multiple reporting areas on both a corporate and operational level. Corporate plans include capital investment plans, free cash flow plans, tax plans, profit and loss plans, and balance sheet plans. Operational plans include sales plan, expense plan, profitability plan, cost center plan, production plan, and so on.

The planning cycle typically involves the following methods:

Research and prognosis. Estimating future situations and assessing the impact on the enterprise.

Target setting. Setting goals and milestones.

Budgeting. Allocating resources for the achievement of targets.

The reality is that many corporations planning infrastructure is a fragmented environment consisting of heterogeneous data using different technologies supported by many interfaces. The reality of many planning cycles is that by the time the plan gets formulated, it is already obsolete. Enterprise planning addresses the need for timely, consistent planning data. Integration across all the reporting areas and methods is needed.

SAP SEM has its own planning engine that works quite differently compared to the current SAP APO planning engine. The SAP SEM planning engine works against what is known as transactional InfoCubes, while SAP APO planning works against Live Cache. Transactional InfoCubes are within the configuration domain of SAP BW, while Live Cache is not. InfoCubes are set transactional at time of creation, thereby changing the way data requests are updated. Planning and transactional InfoCubes have an impact on information modeling.

Architecture

SEM BPS can plan on InfoCubes in the same system or in a remote system. The advantage of keeping separate systems is that the SAP SEM environment can keep to a different release schedule than the SAP BW environment, and if heavy planning is done, then performance is better (as is the case with keeping SAP APO systems separate from

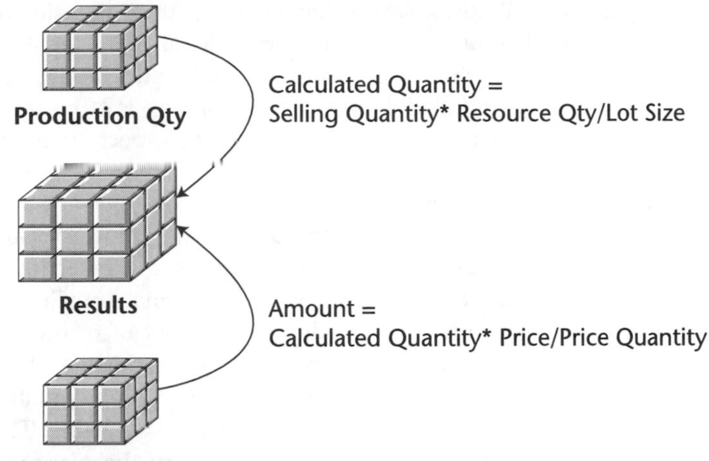

Figure 8.19 Multi-planning area.

SAP BW). By keeping the environments separate, read (querying) and write (business planning) contention is reduced. This would only be advantageous if the traffic in both applications was sufficiently high to drag down the environment. Even if SEM-BPS is installed on a separate instance, it is still possible to plan against InfoCubes on a remote SAP BW system. This approach also has a negative performance impact, particularly depending on the network connection to the remote SAP BW system.

Data can come into a planning area via multiple InfoCubes for a specific calculation as part of a multi-planning area. Sophisticated calculations that are linked and dependent on each other are thus possible. This is an example of how different reporting areas and methods can be integrated into each other, such as a profitability plan and expense plan integrating into a profit-and-loss plan. Figure 8.19 shows a simplified resource planning application that shows planned production costs by multiplying production quantities by resource prices.

When modeling a SEMBPS InfoCube, the designer must evaluate the account-based information model against the key figure-based information model. The advantages and disadvantages of both approaches are explained in Chapter 4. For SEM BPS, there are additional considerations that must be evaluated, such as the impact a particular information model has on record locking and update performance. For example, if accounts are modeled as key figures, there is more of a likelihood of record locking conflicts compared to planning across accounts (especially considering the fact that all data in a planning session gets locked until the session is over).

Navigational attributes and SAP BW hierarchies also must be modeled differently. Although navigational attributes are available in planning areas for reading of data, they cannot be written against. This is not a technical limitation but a logical one: Navigational attributes belong outside of the InfoCube and are not stored with the transactional data that is written with planning. If a navigational attribute is needed for planning, it should be included in the records written to the transactional InfoCube. This can be achieved by adding the navigational attribute as a characteristic within the dimension of an InfoCube. Similarly, hierarchy levels must be stored as dimensional characteristics. When you are planning on SAP BW hierarchies, the nodes must not be text nodes but characteristic nodes that belong inside the InfoCube on which planning is being performed. There are planning applications such as sales planning that support the mapping of hierarchy levels to characteristics within the planning InfoCube. Otherwise, this mapping must be done via SAP BW update rules.

SEM BPS uses transactional InfoCubes. The updates to transactional InfoCubes are different than to nontransactional InfoCubes. First, every update to a transactional InfoCube does not generate a request ID as it does in nontransactional InfoCubes. Instead, all updates collect in a request until a system-defined number of records is reached. Only then is the request formally registered and ready for reporting. As a result, until planning requests are closed out, data within that request is unavailable for reporting unless special techniques are employed. Two options are available: The first is to manually close out the request, and the second is to query the planning InfoCube with a "read most recent data" option via use of a special BEx variable.

The planning application architecture is modular and flexible. The architecture can be expanded to include new functionality in future releases without any change or modification to its core structure. The two main components to the planning architecture are structural and functional. The structural component consists of process-independent and separated planning objects such as planning areas, planning levels, and planning packages. The relationships between planning objects is hierarchical, with packages belonging to a level and a level to an area. The functional component consists of the business logic contained in the planning functions that are parameterized via parameter groups. There is a many-to-many relationship between planning objects and planning functions because of the decoupled nature of these components. Figure 8.20 illustrates the architecture.

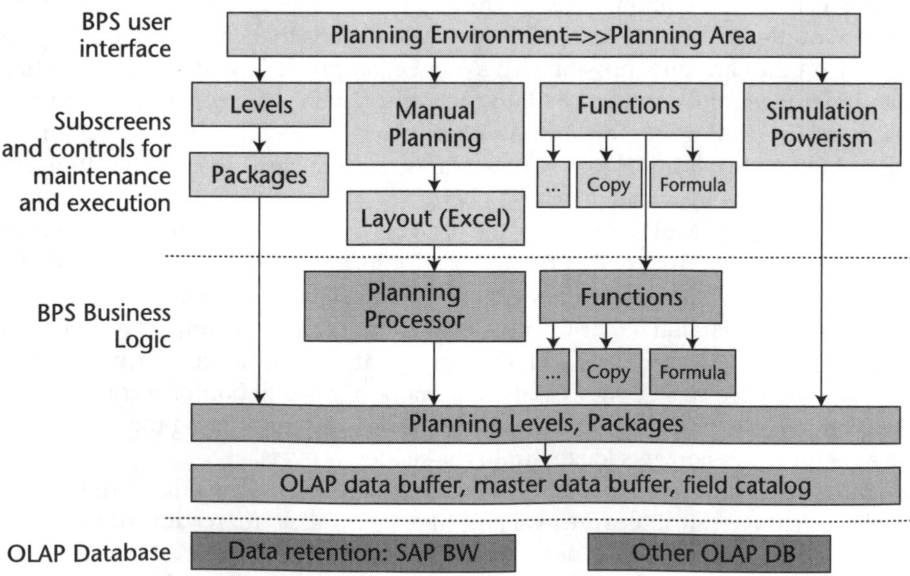

Figure 8.20 Planning architecture.

Planning objects control what data is available for planning. These planning objects are typically organized by the corporate or operational reporting areas (e.g., capital investment plan or sales plan) into the following categories:

Planning area. The planning area dictates what data basis to use for planning. More specifically, it controls which InfoCube to use in planning. This is the highest-level planning object. At this level variables are created, as well as data slices (which are a combination of characteristic values to which data can be locked against changes). Planning areas can be combined into multiplanning areas for cross-InfoCube calculations.

Planning level. The planning level is a projection of the planning area. The level controls which characteristics and key figures are available for planning. The data is then aggregated on the projected fields for better processing performance. Data selections can also be made at this level, but this is the primary purpose of the planning package, so only characteristics that always have the same fixed value should typically be specified (such as fiscal year variant). There can be multiple planning levels per planning area.

Planning package. Planning packages are used for data selections of the projected view of the planning level. Packages can only restrict on the available characteristics specified in the planning level. There can be multiple planning packages per planning level. Planning functions are executed per planning package.

These planning objects form a hierarchy but should not be used to represent the levels of an organizational hierarchy (although the planning packages themselves typically do represent different organizations such as departments or divisions). The design of these planning objects is contingent on the planning functions. Depending on what planning functions are needed (e.g., version copies dictate that the characteristic version must be in the planning level) should drive the configuration of the planning objects.

SEM-BPS offers two main services: direct manual data entry and a planning engine. Data entry is done via planning layouts or planning folders, which configure the format of the data entry interface. Additional services include documents attachment, status management, and tracking. The planning engine itself consists of planning functions. These planning functions typically support one of the planning methods mentioned earlier (i.e., forecasting, target setting, budgeting). Planning functions control what to do with the data; they manipulate the data. There are a wide variety of planning functions that can be categorized as follows:

Data management. Does not perform heavy business logic but is used for data handling such as copy, delete, repost (characteristic value changes), and revaluate (key figure value changes). Example uses of data management planning functions are rolling forecasts or realignments.

General planning. Involves sufficiently generic functions to be used by any planning applications. Functions include forecasting, formulas, currency translation, unit conversions, distributions (across characteristics), and allocations (within a characteristic). Example planning activities for such functions include seasonal or top-down distributions, demand forecasting, and cost driver rate calculations.

Specific planning. Serves a specific purpose and is usually designed for a particular planning application. Such functions include time lag calculations (e.g., order-to-cash cycle time), balance sheet carry-forward, double postings (i.e., debits equal to credits), simulations (PowerSim), and activity-based costing (Oros).

Each planning function has its own parameter group. Parameter groups are planning function-specific configuration settings, such as what characteristics and characteristic values to use within the planning function and what characteristic values can be changed. Planning profiles are roles-based collections of planning objects and planning functions.

SAP SEM also supports many different planning interfaces (even custom interfaces can be developed), such as Web interface, Excel interface, and SAPGUI.

Planning Applications

Planning applications can be custom-designed from scratch or predelivered. The predelivered planning applications are analytic applications in their own right. If used, the predelivered planning applications speed up the time of an implementation. These planning applications come with test data for master data and transactional data to jump-start familiarization with the applications. Planning objects (areas, levels, packages) come predelivered via a client copy, as well as the planning functions and corresponding parameters.

The planning applications are configurable and extensible. These planning applications also consist of specialized functions and logic built into the application. For example, the capital market interpreter has its own specialized logic and configuration settings, which will be explained in more detail later. In reality, all these planning applications can be integrated into one comprehensive planning application:

Balance sheet planning. This planning application actually is composed of income statement planning, balance sheet planning, and cash flow planning steps. Each step has an impact on the balance sheet amount, and all the interdependencies are demonstrated via an integrated planning folder with all the components. As a result, a cash flow change after data entry in balance sheet planning can be immediately assessed. The relationships between income statement, balance sheet, and cash flow are captured in this application. For example, receivables are calculated as a quotient of net sales (the quotient being calculated as the ratio of receivables to net sales in the prior year), so that when net sales are adjusted so are receivables. Special planning functions for accumulating balances, depreciating, and discounting are also included.

Investment planning. Investment planning allows for preinvestment analysis of planned investments or planned investment programs (a hierarchical structure of planned investments in investment management). There are two types of preinvestment analysis available: static and dynamic.

Static preinvestment analysis holds cash inflows and outflows static over the duration of the investment timeframe measured in years. Dynamic pre-investment analysis varies the cash inflows and outflows per period in the investment timeframe. Hence, dynamic pre-investment analysis involves more data entry but offers more precise pre-investment analysis. Furthermore, the cash flows in dynamic analysis can be discounted in order to calculate net present value. Additionally, a conventional interest rate can be specified or an internal rate of return can be calculated for the net present value formula. Static preinvestment analysis should be considered only for small investments with a short investment timeframe, such as relatively inexpensive replacement or expansion investment.

Since investment planning consists of adding assets to the balance sheet and an expected return on investment; this planning application is integrated with balance sheet planning and profit planning, respectively. The integration is achieved via multiplanning areas. For example, the profit planning application has unit prices such as the cost of good per unit, which can be read into investment planning. Investment planning may then drop the unit price, which in turn updates profit planning.

Sales planning. This planning application ties into analytical CRM. It has two versions: online and offline. The online version is performed in SEM BPS and is for top and middle management. The offline version is for the planning of key accounts by sales representatives in the field. The offline version is still Excel-based and is used to upload to the online version. This planning application starts with top sales management to establish performance targets that get distributed down the organization. Finally, once targets are set, the target plans are passed to operational sales planning. The operational sales plans are performed by sales employees who forecast expected sales orders based on current sales volumes and expected opportunities. This planning also has workflow aspects where planning tasks are arranged into worklists and at each level planning statuses can be set to specify whether or not a plan has been approved. Once complete, the consolidated sales plan can feed subsequent plans (potentially in other applications like SAP APO) like production and supply, and then come full circle to financial budgeting and profit planning.

Profit planning. Profit planning works against two InfoCubes: one for the planning results and one to read the values that will influence the profit planning results. The latter InfoCube contains key figures such as average prices like price per unit or cost of goods per unit (fixed and variable), percentages like direct sales costs or reductions, and quantities like sales units. By changing the key figure values in this second InfoCube, the profit planning results in the first InfoCube are influenced. Many scenarios and iterations can be performed to simulate different profit plans based on changes in prices or percentages in the second InfoCube. The calculations can be performed at various different levels of detail and can then be subsequently distributed either top-down or bottom-up.

Liquidity planning. This planning application allows planning of cash flows in multiple currencies. The data is posted by period to different organizational planning units and to account structures referred to as liquidity items. Plan and actual data can then be consolidated at a group level for analysis.

Simplified resource planning. This application is a standalone and simplified product-costing application to determine the overall cost of goods sold for given planned sales quantities. Product-costing InfoCubes are loaded as a basis for its calculations. One InfoCube has the itemization breakdown of a product and its quantities. The itemization represents a kit of materials, services, and overhead costs that compose a saleable good. The itemization is a much more simplified version of a bill of materials and routings in that it is nonhierarchical. A second InfoCube contains the resource prices for each of the itemizations. The overall cost of goods sold is then calculated by multiplying sales quantities by the price of goods (which in turn is calculated by multiplying the planned quantities of itemized resources by their respective planned resource prices). Because of its simple design, this planning application has numerous restrictions compared to other SAP planning applications; for instance, it doesn't take inventory levels into effect, resources are consumed at time of sales, and the itemization cannot change (although quantities can be adjusted). However, this application does illustrate that if some SAP planning applications are overengineered for a particular set of business requirements, a simplified version can be custom-built in SAP SEM.

Balance sheet, sales, and investment planning have similar configuration steps (while profit, liquidity, and resource planning do not have customizing). You set the planning area that points to a Business Content InfoCube, make settings in the planning environment, and configure the planning folder. The planning folder has specialized functions. For some planning applications such as sales planning, additional configuration is required—for instance, the mapping of hierarchy levels to dimensional characteristics.

Capital Market Interpreter

There are several competing theories on value-based management such as McKinsey's economic profit calculations and Stern and Stewart's economic value-added analysis. The capital market interpreter (CMI) incorporates the concepts of value-based management as set forth by Alfred Rappaport. CMI attempts to valuate the market impact of management decisions. CMI aids in maximizing shareholder value by evaluating the discounted cash flow effects of management decisions. CMI is one of the many tools available for analyzing the market value of an enterprise. The CMI has a number of different analyses available:

Shareholder value analysis. This is the primary function that the capital market interpreter performs. The calculations made here are reused in value gap and sensitivity analysis. This analytic engine calculates corporate value and shareholder value. The corporate value is a representation of the market value of the corporation by calculating the net present value of the discounted cash flows. The shareholder value is the corporate value minus debt. This calculation is made for a particular version of plan data representing the valuation (in Figure 8.21 the version is C01). The timeframe for shareholder value calculation is from the current start date to the competitive advantage period (CAP) specified in planning. The CAP can be up to 15 years. To perform the calculation, the following key figures (or value drivers) are necessary: sales, EBITDA (earnings before interest, tax, depreciation, and amortization), taxes, depreciation, asset investment, working capital, and the WACC (weighted average cost of capital). These values can be manually entered by planning layouts specified in CMI configuration.

The results of the calculation can be displayed in absolute amounts or as percentage comparisons to the previous year.

The analysis calculates two types of cash flows: free cash flow and discounted cash flow. The definition of the free cash flow calculation as well as the corporate value, debt, and shareholder value are all configured. After configuration, the value drivers within a shareholder value equation can be graphically charted (see Figure 8.21).

Value gap analysis. Different shareholder value calculations can be made for different versions and then compared. For example, if a broker's expectations for shareholder value needs to compared with an internal valuation, two versions of data can be created and then compared against each other to ascertain the value gap. Significant value gaps can assess exposure to hostile takeover risks, for example.

When executing the value gap analysis, you must specify the two different versions along with a simulation version called the *variation version*. The variation version is different than the comparison version in that its values can be overwritten and manipulated during analysis to do on-the-fly what-if scenarios. The version comparison is then performed for each of the value drivers in each version (first, second, and variation). An absolute and relative value gap for the shareholder value difference is calculated and outputted, then the second and variation versions are compared against the first version.

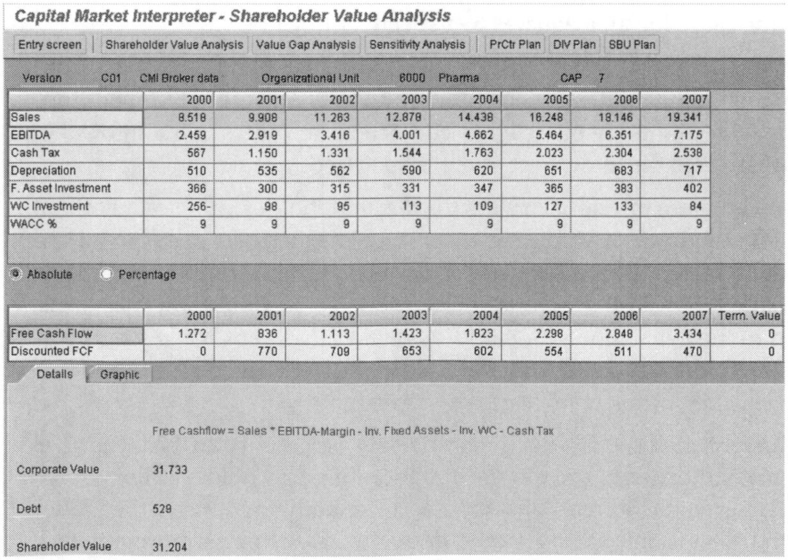

Capital Market Interpreter - Shareholder Value Analysis

Entry screen | Shareholder Value Analysis | Value Gap Analysis | Sensitivity Analysis | PrCtr Plan | DIV Plan | SBU Plan

Version C01 CMI Broker data Organizational Unit 6000 Pharma CAP 7

	2000	2001	2002	2003	2004	2005	2006	2007
Sales	8.518	9.908	11.263	12.878	14.438	16.248	18.146	19.341
EBITDA	2.459	2.919	3.416	4.001	4.662	5.464	6.351	7.175
Cash Tax	567	1.150	1.331	1.544	1.763	2.023	2.304	2.538
Depreciation	510	535	562	590	620	651	683	717
F. Asset Investment	366	300	315	331	347	365	383	402
WC Investment	256-	98	95	113	109	127	133	84
WACC %	9	9	9	9	9	9	9	9

Absolute Percentage

	2000	2001	2002	2003	2004	2005	2006	2007	Term. Value
Free Cash Flow	1.272	836	1.113	1.423	1.823	2.298	2.848	3.434	0
Discounted FCF	0	770	709	653	602	554	511	470	0

Details | Graphic

Free Cashflow = Sales * EBITDA-Margin - Inv. Fixed Assets - Inv. WC - Cash Tax

Corporate Value 31.733

Debt 529

Shareholder Value 31.204

Figure 8.21 Shareholder value analysis.

Sensitivity analysis. The shareholder value calculation is a complex one. All the component or value drivers that factor into the equation may have greater influence on shareholder value than others. This analysis tool facilitates identifying which value drivers have the most sensitive effect on the shareholder value calculation. Finding that shareholder value is particularly susceptible to a value driver such as WACC may lead to new strategies such as looking for lower-cost means of financing.

Sensitivity analysis is compared against the variation version for its analysis. During the initialization of the analysis, the variation version value is copied from the version specified for sensitivity analysis. The variation version values can then be manipulated for analysis either directly (by changing the value driver values in the variation version manually) or indirectly (by specifying a percentage change for a value driver in the comparison version). The indirect method multiplies the percentage amount entered against the comparison version in order to overwrite a new variation version value. After changes are made and the sensitivity calculation performed, the shareholder value percentage deviation is outputted and can also be visualized in a bar chart.

CMI comes with predelivered user-exit code (for the calculation functions and variables). The user-exits have to be configured because the CMI logic is not hard-coded to any Business Content. Consequently, the CMI engine can work against any information model. CMI consists of the following configuration items:

Data source. Any InfoCube can be used with the CMI. As a result, the planning objects to be used for CMI analysis must be specified here (planning area and planning level, as well as the initial data entry layout that is used strictly for data access). Planning layouts for data entry are a separate configuration item. Recall that the planning area equates to a specific InfoCube.

Evaluation groups. Three characteristics need to be specified for CMI calculation: an organizational unit, a version, and optionally an account (depending on whether or not accounts are modeled as characteristic values in the InfoCube or as key figures). Here the InfoObject name is specified.

Key figures. These are the value drivers for the shareholder value calculation. For each CMI key figure or value driver, a SAP BW key figure needs to be specified. If account values such as sales are not modeled as discrete key figures but rather as characteristics of an account dimension, the account InfoObject must be specified in the evaluation group and then restricted per CMI key figure. As there are a large number of value drivers, further details can be found in the SAP SEM measure catalog about each key figure.

Versions. Versions are used in sensitivity analysis. Sensitivity analysis involves changing each value driver used in the equation for shareholder value while holding all other value drivers constant, and ultimately identifying the value drivers with the most impact to shareholder value. Key figures represent each value driver (seven in total), and an additional key figure is needed for competitive advantage period (CAP). Each value driver key figure must be assigned a version so that its results can be saved separately. The sensitivity analysis can then be used to compare the different versions to evaluate which value driver was the most sensitive to changes. An InfoObject must be specified and characteristic values representing separate versions assigned to each value driver. The characteristic used to represent version is specified in the evaluation group.

Calculations. This tabstrip, shown in Figure 8.22, represents the configuration mapping of planning functions and their corresponding parameter groups to the different calculations for CMI. As a general rule, each planning function (except for the copy versions) must refer to user-exit functions that refer to user-exit function modules belonging to the specific function group for CMI calculations. These function modules can be used or replaced with custom user-exits if other calculations are desired. The user-exit function modules that are provided for the CMI calculations are based on Alfred Rappaport's definition of shareholder value.

Data entry layouts. This tabstrip is optional. It can be used to allow the entry of data such as sales, profit-and-loss, and balance sheet values that link to CMI calculations.

Consolidation

Consolidation is the most mature of all the SEM applications, because it has long been a part of SAP R/3. The first consolidation application was part of financial accounting and was designed to perform legal consolidation. It was an application that was originally based on the special ledger platform, taking advantage of the data transformation and reporting capabilities embedded in the platform.

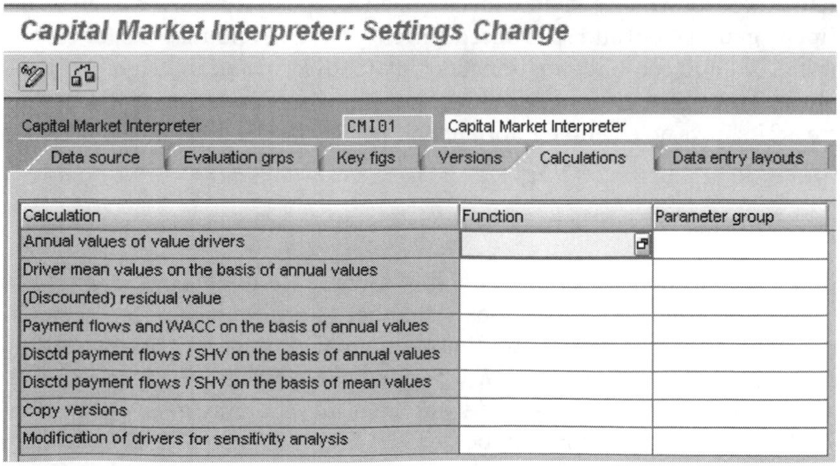

Capital Market Interpreter: Settings Change

Capital Market Interpreter CMI01 Capital Market Interpreter

Data source | Evaluation grps | Key figs | Versions | Calculations | Data entry layouts

Calculation	Function	Parameter group
Annual values of value drivers		
Driver mean values on the basis of annual values		
(Discounted) residual value		
Payment flows and WACC on the basis of annual values		
Disctd payment flows / SHV on the basis of annual values		
Disctd payment flows / SHV on the basis of mean values		
Copy versions		
Modification of drivers for sensitivity analysis		

Figure 8.22 CMI configuration.

The consolidation functionality was then expanded to include management consolidation. As opposed to legal consolidation where statutory requirements dictated the applications functionality, management consolidation had to be more dynamic, especially to accommodate management reporting. The most popular way to perform management consolidation was to eliminate inter-profit-center activities, such as profit in inventory transfers. However, the intent of the application design was that the application could source from anywhere, whether from an application such as profitability analysis or from non-SAP systems via flexible upload of flat files.

As the consolidation product matured, it has grown more extensible. At first the tables were fixed and could not be changed. Then three additional fixed fields were added to the table to allow for custom use. The application also changed its tables and moved under the enterprise controlling module, allowing rollups from applications such as profit center accounting. Currently, management consolidation has transformed into a generic consolidation engine that can sit on any platform, whether Special Ledgers in SAP R/3 or custom InfoCubes in SAP BW.

The first version of SEM BCS utilized the enterprise controlling architecture but added a real-time extractor to SAP BW. The consolidation application still resides in SAP R/3, but updates (such as intercompany eliminations or consolidation of investments) can be posted to SAP BW in real time to achieve a faster month-end closing of the financial books via the same interface business planning used to write to InfoCubes. Alternative, real-time reporting options were then added, such as a remote InfoCube that read the consolidation postings in SAP R/3 that have not yet been loaded to SAP BW. Then closed-loop integration was added, allowing retraction back from SAP BW to consolidation using its flexible upload technology, so that different versions of plan data from SEM BPS could be consolidated. Figure 8.23 illustrates and example of an integrated information logistics model for SEM BCS, SEM -BPS, and SAP BW for the current SEM-BCS architecture.

Now that the consolidation engine sits on top of SAP BW, real-time postings from SAP R/3 or remote InfoCubes or retractions are no longer necessary, since all data manipulations can be performed directly in SAP BW. The consolidation engine currently only supports management consolidation activities (such as standardizing entries, reclassification, and intercompany elimination) and specialized currency translation functions for consolidation reporting. The full consolidation functionality (both legal and management) will be the next phase, as well as new functionalities like value-based management adjusting entries. Figure 8.24 shows an example information logistics model for the new architecture (when the business consolidation engine can sit entirely on SAP BW).

Information Model

The consolidation application has a number of important master data components that are vital for its consolidation logic. As opposed to other typical consolidation systems, SAP performs eliminations on pairs of trading partners within a consolidation group versus eliminating specific accounts. A *trading partner* represents the entity in a consolidation group to which a transaction is made (and then subsequently needs to be eliminated). Typically the trading partner can be derived from the general ledger account the transaction posted to or from the customer or vendor on that transaction. These transformations are important to have already reflected in the records consolidations uses to make its eliminations.

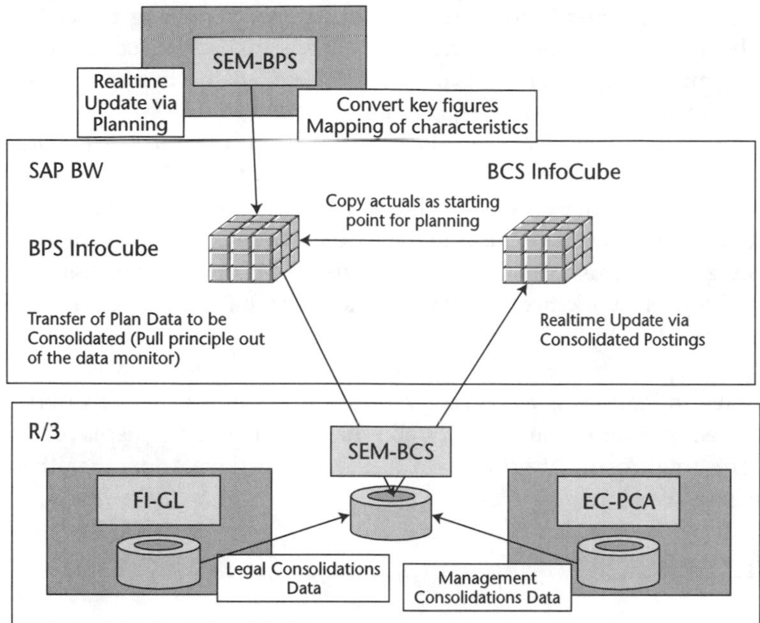

Figure 8.23 SEM-BPS, SEM-BCS, and SAP BW past integration.
Based on copyrighted material from SAP AG

Trading partners are essentially *consolidation units*. In legal consolidation, consolidation units are legal entities (companies) or lines of business (business areas). In management consolidation, consolidation units could be divisions, profit centers, or any other responsibility unit. Companies and profit centers or a combination of both must be mapped into consolidation units for the consolidation. Consolidation units can represent parents or subsidiaries. The collection of parent and subsidiary consolidation units that need to be consolidated is termed a *consolidation group*. Consolidation groups can belong in other consolidation groups, effectively forming hierarchies that can also often reflect complicated ownership structures and cross-holdings.

Another element that needs to be mapped into consolidations is the *financial statement item*. Financial statement items are what make up the consolidated profit-and-loss and balance sheet statements. It represents consolidated account structures. Potentially, each consolidation unit could have its own separate chart of accounts (especially when dealing with consolidation of entities in different countries). These different charts must be standardized. As a result, each account must be mapped to a financial statement item that represents the conformed and consolidated account structures of all the subsidiaries into the parent unit's books.

Management and legal consolidation are typically kept separate via different *dimensions* representing different data feeds. Different *versions* of data can also be kept for different planning and simulation scenarios in consolidation such as what-if reorganization analysis (like mergers, acquisitions, or divestitures). Reorganizations in consolidation typically present interesting restatement reporting scenarios where all data has to be realigned and reported as if a new organizational structure or hierarchy had always been in effect. Sometimes such restatements are simple to simulate via reporting tricks, but other times they can be much more complicated, forcing changes in the data set. Restatements in consolidation, much like realignments in SAP BW, have always been one of the more difficult areas to information model for reporting.

Adding to data complexities in consolidation is the *posting level* concept. The posting levels allow for the creation of a consolidation worksheet to view the different levels of consolidation postings that reconcile the consolidation statements with the simple summation of all the subsidiaries statements into the parent's financial books. The consolidation worksheet gives the user an overview of the consolidation process. For example, a four-posting-levels worksheet could show the user what the trial balance of all the reported data submitted by the subsidiary plus the parent unit trial balance for a given consolidation group. Posting levels for all standardizing entries (such as GAAP adjustments), interunit eliminations (such as receivables and payables), and consolidation of investments (i.e., investment and equity eliminations) could be displayed in separate columns. The final result of adding all these posting levels together then yields the consolidated trial balance.

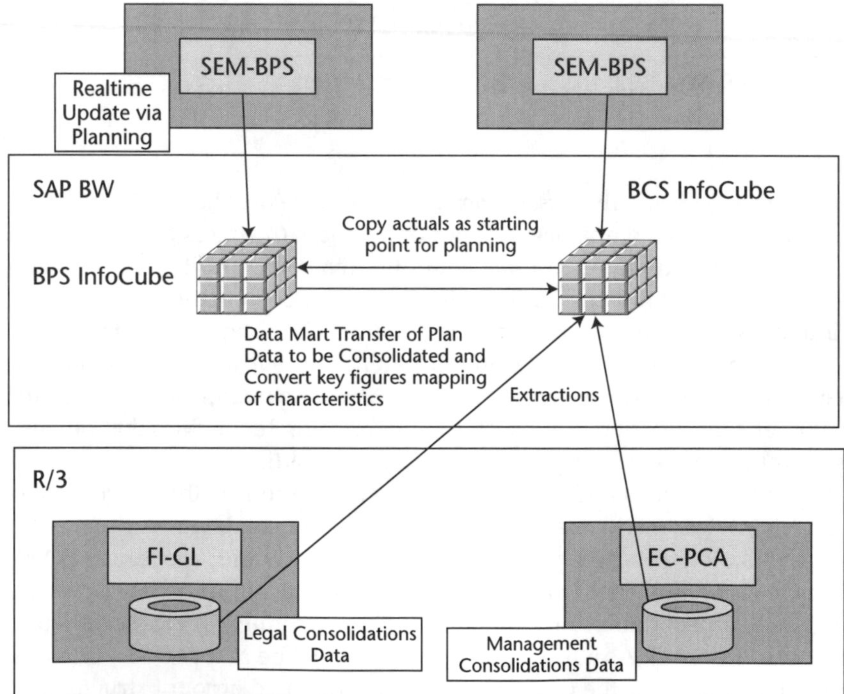

Figure 8.24 BPS, BCS, and BW future integration.
Based on copyrighted material from SAP AG

The posting level concept is very useful detail information for reporting, but it introduces data complexities in the consolidation information model. Each posting level has a different relationship to consolidation units, trading partner units, and consolidation groups. The first basic posting level represents data as it comes into consolidation (as reported by subsidiaries). No consolidation entries have been made at this point. This data is consolidation-unit-dependent. Any consolidation unit can belong to many consolidation groups. As a result, this data has to be repeated for every consolidation group it exists in. The same goes for consolidation-unit-dependent standardizing entries. In contrast, the posting levels representing interunit eliminations are consolidation-unit- and trading-partner-dependent. These data entries must repeat themselves in all consolidation groups that contain the consolidation unit pairs. Finally, consolidation-of-investment postings are consolidation-group-dependent. Since these data entries only pertain to one consolidation group, the data does not need to be repeated. Figure 8.25 illustrates the posting level impact on data redundancy.

The posting level's impact on data redundancy depends on how the consolidation group hierarchy is modeled. In this example, consolidation units are repeated in multiple consolidation groups. This might happen for any number of business scenarios, such as a consolidation unit belonging to more than one parent, multiple alternate hierarchies for management and legal consolidation, or modeling consolidation hierarchies as concentric consolidation groups.

Another important consolidation reporting topic is currency translations. Currency translations in consolidation are different than in SAP BW. The purpose of currency translation in consolidation is to report all subsidiary balance sheet and profit and loss activities in the parent currency so that they can be added into the parent's accounting books. Currency translations in consolidation typically must translate records differently based on the type of the financial statement item. Typically, the currency translation must be performed as follows (or some variant):

- If the financial statement item is a balance sheet account, its balances must be translated using a month-end spot rate.
- If the account is a profit-and-loss item, translation must be at an average rate.
- If the account is an investment or equity item, the translation must be at a historical rate.

More details on the reporting requirements for currency translations for consolidation can be found in Financial Accounting Standards Board Statement No. 52 and 95 (for cash flow reporting). The differences in the balance sheet and profit and loss must be then plugged to a currency translation adjustment item to keep debits equaling credits. SAP BW currency translations are not designed for this type scenario. The SAP BW is only meant to translate values straight from one currency into another.

For more details on the information modeling aspects of SEM BCS and how it is implemented in SAP BW Business Content refer to Chapter 5.

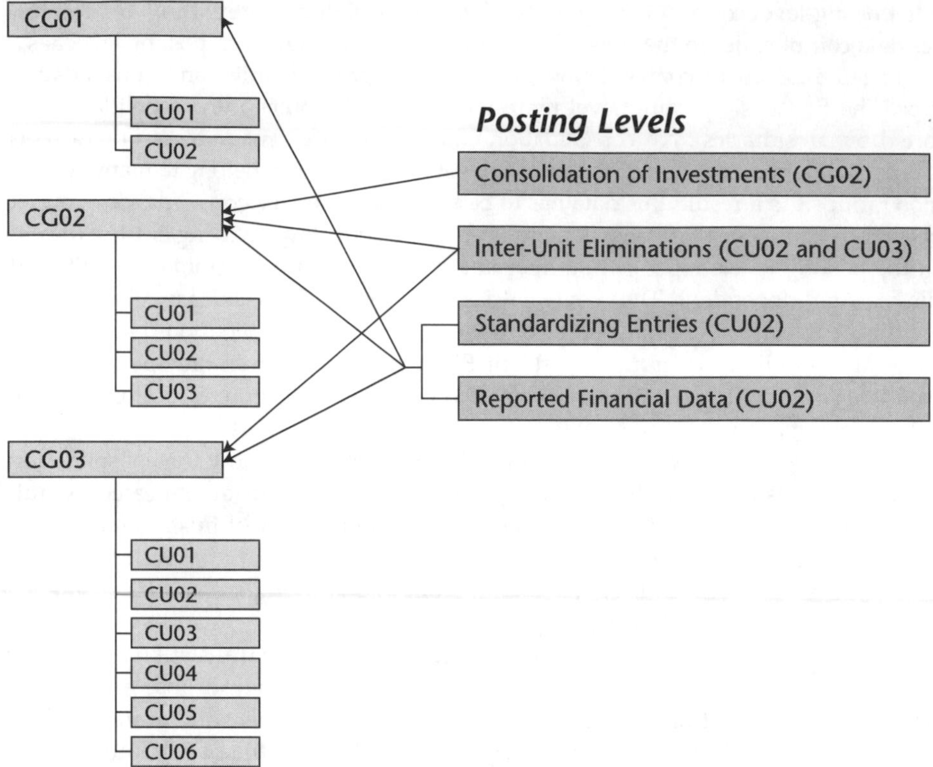

Figure 8.25 Data redundancy per posting level example.

Summary

Three examples of analytic applications built on the SAP BW platform were highlighted in this chapter:

Customer relationship analytics (CRA). CRA consists of customer behavior analysis, customer lifetime value (CLTV) analysis, and recency, frequency, monetary (RFM) analysis. Customer behavior analysis consists of the data mining techniques decision trees, scoring, clustering, and association analysis. RFM analysis is primarily used for campaign optimization.

Supply chain analytics (SCA). SCA is mainly influenced by the SCOR model. Analytics can be performed within SAP APO via the supply chain cockpit, which can be integrated with SAP BW or can be performed by a separate SAP BW environment using Business Content analysis. Some applications such as demand planning interact with SAP BW in order to get sales history and to return the demand plan for historical analysis.

Strategic Enterprise Management (SEM). SEM is primarily composed of corporate performance management, enterprise planning, and consolidation. Corporate performance management largely centers around the balanced scorecard framework. Enterprise planning extends the SAP BW BI platform to include a planning architecture with which planning applications can be built. Capital market interpreter was explained as an example of a prepackaged planning application. The consolidation application history and migration path to the SAP BW platform was then summarized, as well as design considerations for information modeling.

The next chapter covers SAP BW administration.

Administration in the SAP Business Information Warehouse

SAP BW administration tasks fall into two categories: process-oriented tasks and system-oriented tasks. While process-oriented administration tasks focus on scheduling and monitoring automated application processes, system-oriented tasks are more oriented to securing safe system operations.

There are many different application processes besides loading data, such as index maintenance, aggregate maintenance, data exports using the Open Hub Service or batch scheduling of reporting jobs—all these application processes can have complex dependencies. SAP BW 3.0 introduced a new technology termed *process chains* for handling the coordination of these processes. We cover configuring, monitoring, and troubleshooting process chains in the first section of this chapter.

System-oriented tasks are typically the same in any SAP system, but there are SAP BW-specific twists that need to be taken into consideration. For example, SAP BW provides additional functionality for both security and transports in addition to the standard ones. We explain SAP BW security from a design perspective, detailing the decisions to make when building authorizations, such as making them user-based versus role-based or object-centric versus data-centric. We then explain the SAP BW transport and its additional transport options, as well as special considerations that come with the transport of meta data. In addition, we consider the coordination of transports on SAP source systems. Finally, we highlight upgrade considerations for a multilayered application environment.

Process-Oriented Administration

Any activity in an IT system (SAP or non-SAP) that has a clear beginning and a clear end can be referred to as a *process*. Usually processes cannot be viewed in isolation; complex interdependent networks of processes need to be configured, scheduled, and monitored in order to accomplish a certain system task. While scheduling has always been a core part of the SAP Web Application Server (previously named the SAP Basis component), support for administering complex networks of processes has been poor until SAP BW release 3.0 became available. In particular, there was no centralized user interface for the administration of complex process chains.

The advent of the *process chain* technology and related extensions to the SAP BW Meta Data Repository enabled administrators to turn from a more technical job scheduling point of view and keep an application-centric focus in process administration, while still relying on the robustness of the time-tested functions of the SAP Web Application Server. Process chains replace the InfoPackage group and event chain technologies known from previous SAP BW releases, which are still supported for compatibility reasons. Open interfaces allow third-party job scheduling tools to interface with process chains and connect them to even more complex networks of processes that may span multiple heterogeneous systems.

Process Chains

The basic concept behind the process chain implementation is to have an additional abstraction layer on top of the basic scheduling functions with a more sophisticated functionality (called *general services*). Technically speaking, there are automatically generated *events* and automatically scheduled processes waiting for those events, gluing the application processes together. The process chain technology is completely modularized and built upon an object-oriented programming model where each process is an object, described by the following attributes:

Process category. All the processes are broadly grouped by process categories. These categories are *General services*, *Load process and subsequent processing*, *Data target administration*, and *Other BW processes*.

Process type. A process type is a specific type of application or system process such as data loading or index creation. A list of available process types is provided in the next list.

Variant. Each process has its own variant (a *variant* is a set of parameters passed to the process, such as the name of the InfoObject to perform a change run for, the name of the InfoPackage to use for loading, or the name of the InfoCube to drop the indexes for). While many variants may be available for a specific process, only one gets assigned.

Instance. The instance describes a specific execution of a process; it consists of all messages and information relevant to the process at run time, which are read and passed on to other processes.

While the currently available process types cover most applications in SAP BW, the list of process types is configurable via *Settings | Maintain Process Types* in the menu of the process chain administration transaction. The following is a list of available process types by process category (also see Figure 9.1):

General services. Includes process types for a *start process;* for logical *AND, OR,* and *XOR* operations; general ABAP programs; system commands; as well as local and remote process chains, which are referred to as *meta chains,* since they allow you to implement chains of process chains.

Load processes and subsequent processing. Includes application processes related to loading data, such as Execute InfoPackage, Update data target from PSA, Save hierarchy, Update data target from ODS object, Data export to external system, and Delete overlapping requests.

Data target administration. Includes data maintenance processes such as Delete/Generate indexes, Construct database statistics, Fill aggregates, Rollup aggregates, Compress InfoCube, Activate ODS object data, and Delete data target contents

Other SAP BW processes. Includes general SAP BW processes, such as Attribute change run, Adjustment of time-dependent aggregates, Deletion of requests from the PSA, and Reorganization of attributes and texts for master data.

When a specific process is executed, first its predecessors and their corresponding variants are determined, then the process object is instantiated, asking for additional information from the predecessor process if required before actually executing the process. After finishing the process it returns its status and instance to the process chain.

This new approach allows for greater flexibility in defining subsequent processing, which may be triggered based on three outcomes of a process: successful, failed, or always (ignoring the "failed or successful" state). The approach is more results-driven and object-oriented, and it makes use of complex criteria for starting the subsequent process. In addition to event handling, which was available earlier, boolean logic is available. From a usability point of view, process chains provide a higher degree of automation, centralized maintenance, and control, and much improved visualization where complex relationships and hierarchies of dependencies are maintained and depicted graphically. Three different maintenance views are available in the process chain maintenance transaction:

Planning view. How process chains are modeled.

Check view. How process chains are validated for the integrity of their design.

Log view. How the process chains are monitored. Monitoring process chains is now also integrated into the Computing Center Management System (CCMS).

An expert mode provides additional configuration flexibility in the planning view. Figure 9.1 shows the planning view of the process chain maintenance transaction for a simple process chain.

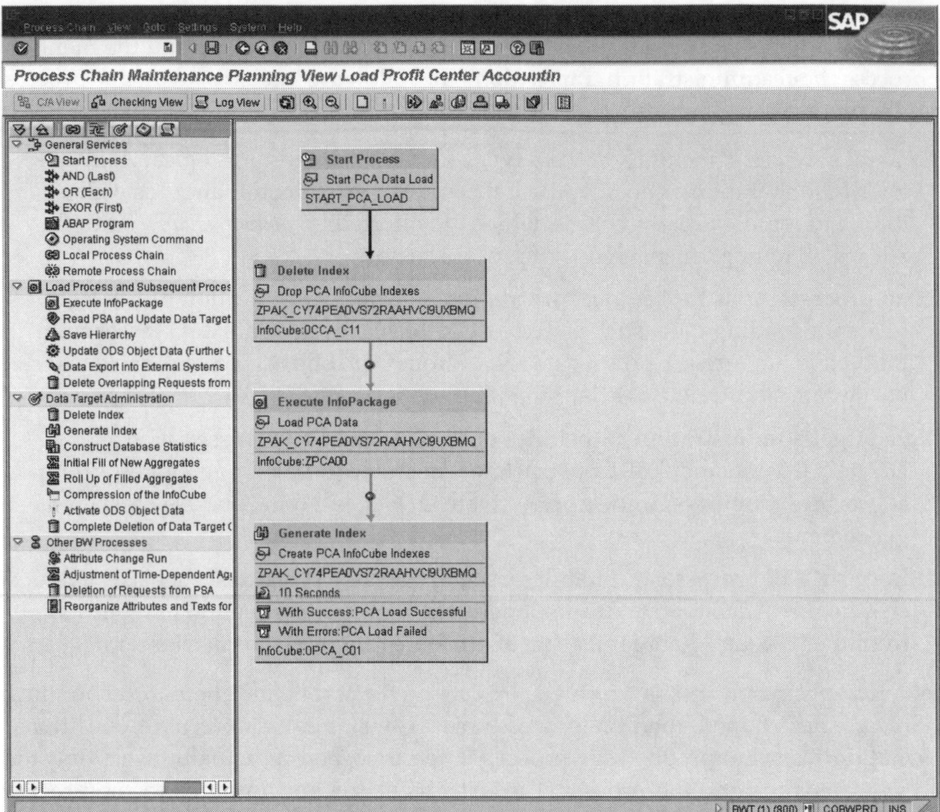

Figure 9.1 A simple process chain.

Dependencies

The need for process chains stems from the many dependencies of processes run in a productive data warehouse system. Defining a process chain requires careful planning and preparation, taking application logic, operational processes, availability of system resources, performance, and technical dependencies into account (many times these various factors work at odds against each other and must be balanced).

Types of Dependencies

This following lists several different types of dependencies. SAP BW is actually aware of some of these dependencies and provides corresponding consistency checks to make sure that process chains are defined appropriately.

SAP BW process dependencies. In SAP BW certain processes always need to be or should be executed in a specific sequence. Examples of these types of dependencies are attribute change runs after a master data load, or dropping and creating indexes before and after transaction data loading. The process chain maintenance transaction provides checks to make sure that all required processes are included and are defined in the correct order. When you are defining a simple process chain as the one shown in Figure 9.1, where a profit center accounting data load is dragged and dropped into the planning view, the system automatically inserts a process of process type *delete index* as a predecessor and one of type *create index* as an antecessor. Note that these automatically inserted processes are removable and configurable—that is, administrators are able to start the load process only if the delete index process was successful. Additional wait times (e.g., 10 seconds in the index creation process in Figure 9.1) can be added to honor timing or performance dependencies.

TIP All the process dependencies that the system enforces and checks against are stored in table RSPCTYPESDEP, which can be used as a reference when you are planning a process chain design.

Notification dependencies. If an individual needs notification on the completion status of a certain process within a process chain, you can easily configure a message by right-clicking the process and entering a message. For example, a notification message can be issued only if the index deletion fails. Another notification can be sent if the data load itself fails. Additionally, an alternative notification can be sent in the event of a success (e.g., a successful data load).

Referential integrity. Chapter 5 provided an example of an employee master data load where there was a hierarchy of master data loads (four levels) that had to be loaded before employee masters could be loaded. This was because the employee master had navigational attributes referring to other characteristics, which in turn had other navigational attributes, and so forth. If referential integrity checks for master data are activated, any compound characteristics or navigational attribute has to be preloaded. If referential integrity checks for transactional InfoSources are activated, all master data have to be preloaded. Another option for referential integrity checking for individual InfoObjects of an InfoSource can be configured in the InfoSource. Process chains need to be defined according to the dependencies imposed by referential integrity checks.

Transformation dependencies. These dependencies arise from transformation logic such as master data lookups in the update rules. If an attribute is to be derived from an attribute of a characteristic, then that characteristic must be loaded; otherwise, an old or blank value will be derived. This is different from referential integrity, which merely checks if the value already exists. Another example, for key figure derivations, is having the most recent exchange rates loaded before executing currency translation in the update rules. Typically, these transformation dependencies need to be taken into account to ensure data quality and correctness of custom business logic. Other examples might include proper unit conversions on the most recent conversion factors or derivations that read a preloaded hierarchy to determine an attribute, or an update rule that reads a custom table that must be loaded with the most recent and correct values before derivation.

Performance-enhancing sequences. Certain sequences may be better for performance, such as scheduling jobs after other jobs in order to avoid too many work processes contending with each other, causing bottlenecks or, worse, deadlocks. For example, if you have multiple transaction data loads for the same InfoCube, it may make sense to drop the indexes once, do all the loading, and then rebuilt the indexes once at the end rather than dropping and re-creating for each data load. Or some parallelization scenarios might be built to improve performance—for example, loading PSA and ODS objects at the same time or loading master data and transaction data simultaneously. Or perhaps parallelization is achieved by breaking up a data load job into various data selections (e.g., by company code for a large delta initialization). Finally, parallelization can be achieved by separating process-chain work processes onto separate servers (identified as part of scheduling).

Quality checks. There may be a need to insert manual intervention steps into the automated flow of process chains for quality checking. For example, before automatic loading of PSA to an InfoCube, administrators might want to execute data consistency checks on the PSA level to make sure the data loaded into the InfoCube is correct before changing the read pointer and making the data available for reporting.

Note that these process dependencies can span across multiple SAP and non-SAP systems. Within the SAP sphere are remote process chains that can integrate processes in other SAP systems into the current process chain, as well as processes that can call third-party external systems within a process chain (in the latter case, it is a matter of designing a custom process type by developing a class with the proper interface or using an appropriate third-party job scheduling tool).

It is good practice in process-oriented administration to document all processes, dependencies, and error-handling procedures in an operations guide. While process chains support the administrative processes by visualizing complex dependencies, they are not a replacement for documentation.

Process Chain Service Processes

Process chains provide special process types used for generically modeling the initiation of a process chain and boolean logic operators for collecting the results of multiple processes in a process chain. The process chain service processes are as follows:

Start process. Every process chain must have a start process that acts as the initial trigger to start the whole chain. Start processes never have predecessors (with the exception of other process chains within a meta chain or via an API), and only one exists per process chain. The variant for the start process simply contains scheduling parameters, like the time a process chain has to be executed or a specific event that causes the process chain to execute.

Collection processes. Collection processes collect the results of several parallel processes and merge those into one single result applying simple boolean operators:

- *AND (Last)*. The work process starts when all events in the predecessor process have finished.

- *OR (Each).* The work process starts each time an event in a predecessor process finishes.
- *XOR (First).* The work process starts when the first event from one of the predecessor processes finished.

Data Management Processes

Naturally, data management processes are the most common processes in a data warehouse environment. Different types of data management processes are available in SAP BW. Each requires a different set of parameters—for example, index maintenance processes require the name of an InfoCube; ODS object activation processes require the name of an ODS object. The required parameters are stored in so-called variants (readers familiar with SAP systems will already know the concept of variants used to store different sets of parameters for ABAP reports).

The configuration of variants in the SAP BW context either depends on specifying meta data objects, variants for other process types, or the actual configuration of the meta data object, as well as process-type-specific settings. Table 9.1 provides an overview of the data management processes in SAP BW and their parameters.

Table 9.1 Variants for Data Management Processes

DATA MANAGEMENT PROCESS	PARAMETERS
Data loading	InfoPackage
Data export	InfoSpoke
Initial fill of new aggregates	Aggregate InfoCube
Attribute change run	Hierarchy InfoObject Variant of an ABAP report
Compressing the InfoCube	InfoCube
Constructing database statistics	InfoCube
Deleting data target contents	InfoCube ODS object
Deleting index	InfoCube
Saving hierarchy	(None)
Generating index	InfoCube
Activating ODS object data	ODS object
Further processing of ODS object data	ODS object

(continues)

Table 9.1 Variants for Data Management Processes *(Continued)*

DATA MANAGEMENT PROCESS	PARAMETERS
Further processing of ODS object data	ODS object
Deleting requests from PSA	PSA table Data request
PSA update/reconstruction	Data request
Deleting overlapping requests	(None)
Rollup of filled aggregates	InfoCube
Adjusting time-dependent aggregates	(None)

The most complex set of parameters is required for loading data and is contained in a meta data object of itself: the InfoPackage. A whole section is dedicated to explaining the different configuration options available in InfoPackages. Similarly, the variant for data exports into external systems is hidden in the configuration of the InfoSpoke. Also, some processes do not require variants, such as adjusting time-dependent aggregates. A description of the variants of the remaining process types follows at the end of this section.

Data Load Process Variants

Data load process variants simply refer to an InfoPackage, which itself is a complex object providing a multitude of parameters for configuring data load processes. InfoPackages can be maintained outside the process chain maintenance transaction in the Administrator Workbench under *InfoSources* in the *Modeling* tab. Figure 9.2 shows an example of an InfoPackage for loading profit center accounting data used in the process chain flow in Figure 9.1.

InfoPackages can be run independent of process chains, as they include scheduling options and parameters that allow executing data loads immediately or as a batch schedule. For scheduling in batch mode, the same scheduling options as found in the standard SAP batch scheduling dialog are available, such as periodical execution of data load jobs, execution at a specific date and time, execution after a specific event, or execution after completion of a specific program. For compatibility reasons, subsequent processes executed after completion of the data load can still be specified. However, we recommend you use process chains instead. A Gantt diagram is available for display in the Infopackage to provide a simple graphical representation of scheduled processes.

Note that the process starting the data load normally only issues a data load request to the source systems (e.g., by sending a request IDoc to an SAP R/3 system) and terminates, thereby making the internal scheduler as well as external job scheduling tools believe that the process has terminated successfully while in fact it has just started the extraction process. Setting the *Request Batch Process Runs until All Data Has Been Updated in BW* flag can be used to keep the process active until all data have been uploaded completely.

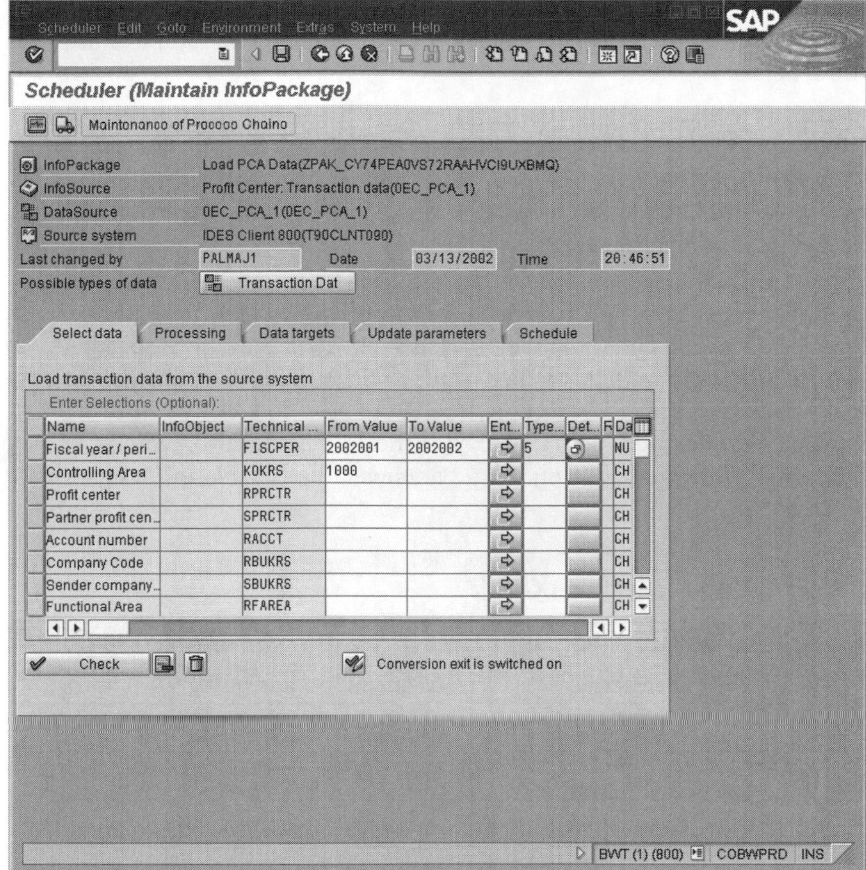

Figure 9.2 InfoPackage maintenance.

Additional configuration options for InfoPackages are listed and are detailed in the following sections:

- Data selection
- Processing options
- Data target options
- Update parameters
- External data specification
- External data parameters
- Third-party selections

Data Selection

Data selection criteria can be specified in the *Select Data* tab in the InfoPackage maintenance screen. The availability of fields for selection is controlled by the DataSource definition in the source system or in the SAP BW system for manually maintained source system types (e.g., for file source systems). Figure 9.2 shows a sample data selection in an InfoPackage.

NOTE If the InfoPackage is for a data mart export DataSource for an archived data target, then a button to the left of the conversion exit switch appears that allows you to alternatively select an archive file to load from. More on archiving can be found later in this chapter.

For dynamic or more complicated selections (especially for the time dimension), reporting variable selection criteria of the types listed in Table 9.2 can be specified.

The last three variable values require additional configuration. In the sample InfoPackage in Figure 9.2, type 5 selection criteria are used to specify a user-defined period of time for the fiscal year period characteristic. In this scenario, bimonthly plan data is loaded into profit center accounting. Parameters not visible in Figure 9.2 are detailed in Table 9.3:

Table 9.2 Types of Dynamic Selection Criteria

TYPE	DATA TYPE	SELECTION	DESCRIPTION
0	DATS	Yesterday	Midnight to midnight
1	DATS	Last week	Monday through Sunday
2	DATS	Last month	First to last day of previous month
3	DATS	Last quarter	First to last day of previous quarter
4	DATS	Last year	First to last day of previous year
5	NUMC	User defined	Recurring time series
6	ANY	ABAP routine	Custom-defined ABAP routine
7	ANY	BEx variable	SAP- or custom-defined OLAP variable

Table 9.3 Maintenance of Variable Selections

PARAMETER	VALUE
Fiscal year/period from	2003001
Fiscal year/period to	2003002
Next period from value	2003003
Period Indicator	1
Number of periods until repetition	12

Using this configuration, the first time the InfoPackage is executed, the first two periods in the fiscal year are loaded. The next time the InfoPackage is scheduled, the next two periods are loaded (i.e., 2003003 to 2003004). After 12 periods have repeated themselves, the period resets back to the first period. If the period indicator was set to zero, the cycle would restart itself in the same year. The period indicator of 1 was specially designed for rolling the year over into the next year so the new start would be 2004001. The period indicator 0 was designed for InfoObject time characteristics (like 0FISCPER3) that do not have a year in them.

For type 6 (ABAP routine) the detail push button generates an ABAP routine framework. The code figure that follows is an example where the current fiscal year and period is derived via the system date (assuming a fiscal year variant of K4):

```
*$*$ begin of routine - insert your code only below this line    *-*
 data: l_idx like sy-tabix.

* Find entry for fiscal period in selection criteria table
 read table l_t_range with key
   fieldname = 'FISCPER'.
 l_idx = sy-tabix.

* Initialize fiscal period selection criteria
 l_t_range-sign = 'I'.
 l_t_range-option = 'EQ'.

* Determine fiscal period for current date
 CALL FUNCTION 'DATE_TO_PERIOD_CONVERT'
  EXPORTING
   I_DATE = sy-datum
   I_PERIV = 'K4'
  IMPORTING
   E_BUPER = l_t_range-low+4(3)
   E_GJAHR = l_t_range-low(4).

* Update selection criteria table
 modify l_t_range index l_idx.
 p_subrc = 0.
*$*$ end of routine - insert your code only before this line    *-*
```

The same effect could be accomplished without code by using an OLAP or Business Explorer variable value. Table 9.4 illustrates the same selections described previously implemented with type 7 selection criteria using the BEx variable 0FPER.

Table 9.4 Use BEx Variable

PARAMETER	VALUE
BEx Variable of the OLAP	0FPER
Fiscal year variant	K4

The use of conversion exits for selections may be turned on or off. Conversion exits may be required to ensure correct formatting of the selection values passed to the source system. The extraction process first tries to apply the conversion exit in the source system, and if unavailable, it calls the conversion exit in SAP BW.

The data selection tab strip for hierarchies is different, as shown in Figure 9.3. A list of all hierarchies available in the source system can be retrieved by pressing the *Available Hierarchies from OLTP* button. Selecting a hierarchy simply means selecting the correct line in the table of hierarchies and specifying additional option such as automatically renaming the hierarchy or merge sub trees or insert sub trees. The ability to update subtrees rather than loading the complete hierarchy tree is a performance-enhancing feature, allowing targeted refreshes.

Processing Options

Processing options allow you to specify update processing options and whether or not additional consistency checks are performed in the transfer rules. If the flag for additional consistency checks is turned on, data will be verified for valid date and time values, permissible special characters, capitalized letters, and conversion routine compliance. Figure 9.4 shows the processing options screen, which is part of the InfoPackage maintenance transaction. A list of the available processing options is shown in Table 9.5.

Table 9.5 Update Data Processing Options

OPTION
PSA and then into data targets (packet by packet)
PSA and data targets in parallel (packet by packet)
Only PSA (and/or update subsequently in data targets)
Data targets only

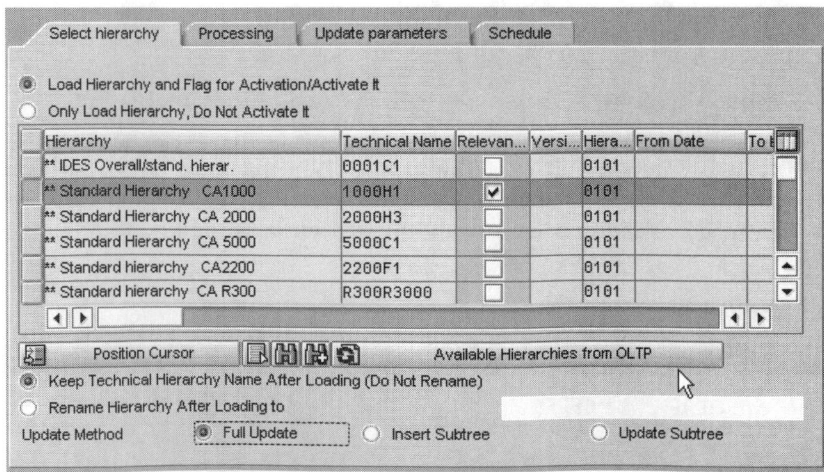

Figure 9.3 Hierarchy selection in InfoPackages.

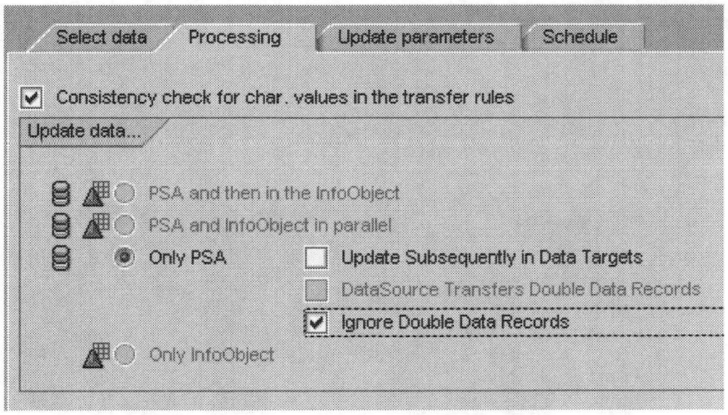

Figure 9.4 Processing options for master data.

In the first option in the table, data is loaded serially into the PSA and then within the same dialog work process is loaded into the data target. Each available work process processes exactly one data package. The number of work processes used is controlled by IDoc control parameters. The IDoc control parameters are maintained as part of SAP BW configuration in the SAP source system.

In contrast, in the second option, each data packet gets split into two work processes: one for the PSA and another one for loading the data target when the PSA is successfully updated. Here the IDoc control parameters are ignored and all dialog work processes are taken that are available (so make sure enough have been defined before using this option). The more data packages, the more work processes.

In the third option where data is loaded into the PSA only, all data packages in a request must be completely loaded before those data packages can be loaded to a data target. If the subsequently update in the data target flag is set for this option, this second job of loading the data target happens automatically.

The last option is the best for performance but worst for data integrity. Loading the data target only is not recommended unless it serves as an inbound ODS object and there is confidence in the extractor, or the source itself serves as an inbound staging area (such as a persistent file on the application server or archived data). This is important for data recovery but compromises the services that the PSA offers, which are the options to rebuild processes, repair invalid records, and simulate updates.

While Figure 9.4 shows an example of master data load, transaction data basically provides the same processing options. However, for master data—in this case, cost center master data—there are additional options for the *Update of PSA-only* option. The system is able to identify DataSources that potentially return duplicate records by identifying the primary key of the underlying DataSource and matching it up with the key of the transfer structure. If the DataSource potentially returns duplicates, the *DataSource Transfers Double Data Records* flag is set. This flag allows you to treat duplicate records as an error or ignore them by checking the *Ignore Double Data Records* indicator.

Data Target Options

Data target options, shown in Figure 9.5, primarily allow you to select the data targets that should be updated by a particular data load request, from those data targets that are connected to the InfoSource by active update rules. Additional options are available

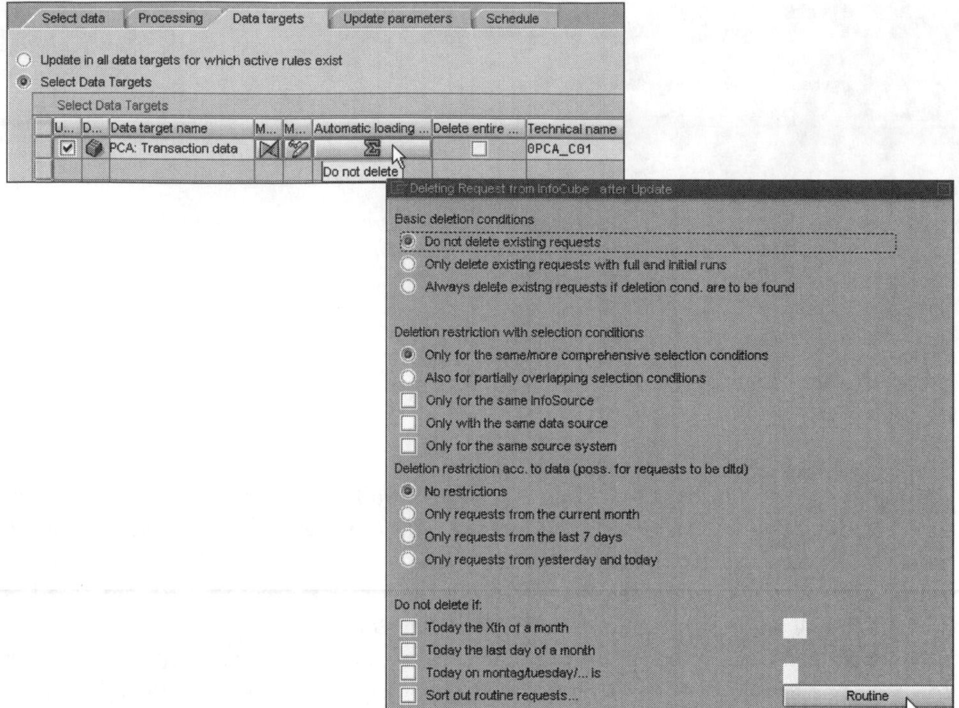

Figure 9.5 Data target options.

for selecting specific requests for deletion from the data target or deleting the complete data target content. Automated deletion of data, for example, is required where every upload into an InfoCube needs to be a full upload because the extractor is not capable of providing delta loads.

Deletion options can be specified based on:

- How the request was loaded—full or delta load.
- What selection conditions were used—InfoPackage selection conditions.
- When the request was loaded.
- When the deletion is being requested.

Finally, there are special criteria for preventing deletion depending on the day that the new request is loaded. Even more complex criteria can be implemented in an ABAP routine, returning a list of requests that have to be deleted from the InfoCube.

Update Parameters

Update parameters are used to control the update mode (full update, delta initialization, delta update—where available), referential integrity handling, and error handling. Figure 9.6 shows a sample update parameter screen for time-dependent cost center master data. Note that delta extraction needs to be initialized by either a delta initialization request or an initialization request (*Initialize without data transfer* flag). Once initialized, deltas can be loaded as required.

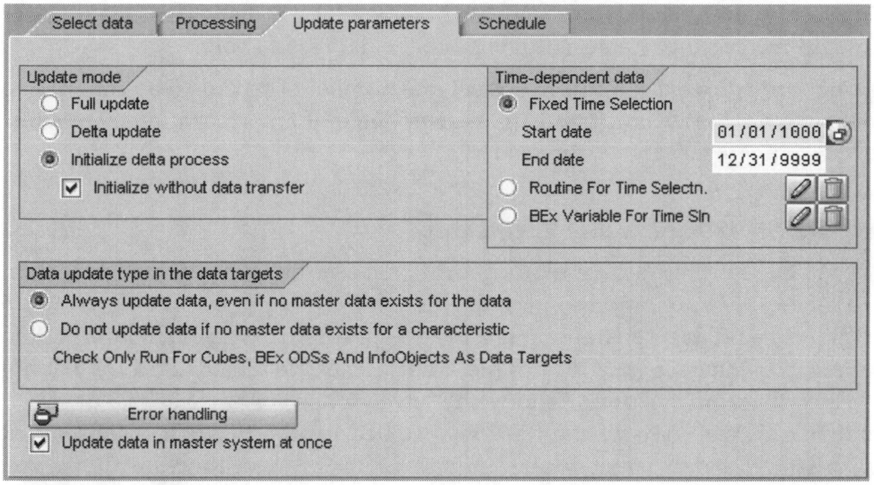

Figure 9.6 Update parameters.

For time-dependent data, additional options are available for selecting time windows for the extraction process. Just as for data selection options; the options for using ABAP routines or BEx variables are available here. These options work exactly the same as they do for data selection options.

Three different options for handling referential integrity are available:

- Update the data, regardless if corresponding master data has already been loaded.
- Do not update the data if the corresponding master data has not already been loaded.
- Simulate the update.

The error handling options define how incorrect data is handled:

No update, no reporting. This option means that if there is an error, no records are updated and, hence, will not be available for reporting. All incorrect records are highlighted in red in the Data Monitor and can be manually corrected and loaded individually.

Valid records updated, no reporting (request red). This option specifies that if an error occurs, all valid records will still be updated but will not be available for reporting. The request will stay in a red status, which will not update the reporting read pointer. All invalid records are physically separated from valid records in a new request that is written to the PSA for error handling and subsequent update.

Valid records updated, reporting possible (request green). This option specifies that even if errors occur, the data loaded in the request should update the reporting read pointer to make it immediately available for reporting. All invalid records are physically separated from valid records in a new request that is written to the PSA for error handling and subsequent update.

Termination by number of records. This parameter is a threshold for the number of invalid records that are permitted before the data load aborts.

No aggregation allowed. If this flag is set, the number of records read into BW must equal the number of records that are updated. If any records are generated, deleted, or aggregated, an error ensues.

External Data Specification and Parameters

Data loads via the flat-file interface require additional options, such as the file location (client workstation or application server), the filename and path, the file format (CSV, ASCII, or binary), and data separator and escape sign. Alternatively, such information can be passed in using a separate control file. Control files are mostly used for loading flat files in binary format. Figure 9.7 shows the screen for specifying external data.

The first five data records of the flat file specified can be viewed; a subsequent update of the selected data target can be simulated. This preview function allows you to check the integrity of the file before loading. Flat-file loads are more likely to have formatting issues than loads from other types of source systems. The simulation function is the same as that available through the Data Monitor.

Additional formatting options, such as the character used as the thousands separator and decimal points, can be specified in an additional screen not shown here. Also, the number of header lines in the file (which are then ignored for loading) and whether or not currency conversion needs to be applied can be specified.

Third-Party Selections

Third party selections are used for Staging BAPI source systems. The parameters here heavily depend on the third-party tool or custom program using the Staging BAPI. Ascential DataStage, for example, requires the name of a DataStage job to be entered here.

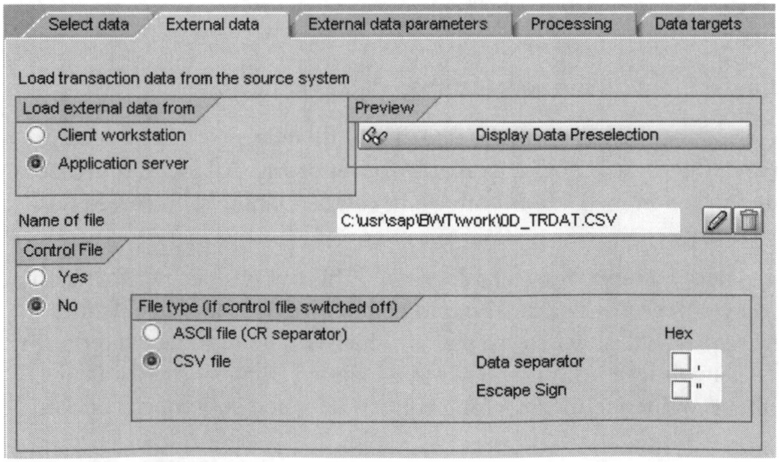

Figure 9.7 External data.

Miscellaneous Process Type Variants

For non-data load process types, there are different kinds of variants such as:

InfoCube compression. This variant has additional options controlling which requests are compressed (e.g., all requests of the last *n* days or all but *n* requests), how they are compressed (delete zero value records or not), and if the marker for noncumulative key figures should be updated. This marker stores the latest snapshot for noncumulative values and should be updated with latest snapshot for better performance. This should only be flagged for scenarios where past noncumulative value changes are being loaded.

Construct database statistics. This variant also requires a parameter that specifies the percentage of InfoCube data that should be used for compiling the database statistics.

Save hierarchy. A flag must be checked if the hierarchy load is to be activated after loading. If the hierarchy is used in an aggregate, it can only be marked for activation and the process type for attribute change run must be subsequently executed.

Activate ODS object data. This process type has two additional configuration settings in the variant for overriding performance enhancement defaults. The first flag prevents the compression of requests in the ODS object change log after activation so as to keep the details for additional data targets to be updated. The second flag loads requests in a serial rather than parallel manner to have stricter control over the work processes being used.

Deletion of requests from PSA. A date or the number of days as a threshold for PSA request deletion can be specified. In addition, you can specify that only successful requests, unsuccessful requests, or requests no longer available in a data target should be deleted.

Rollup of filled aggregates. As with other process types, cutoff points must be maintained for which requests are updated. The rollup will only update those requests that are older than a specified number of days, or the remainder requests after a specified number of requests.

Delete overlapping requests from an InfoCube. This process type is a piece of InfoPackage configuration and can be configured from a variant or from within an InfoPackage.

Reporting Agent Processes

Not all OLAP functions are online. There is an increasing need for functions to be done asynchronously in batch. Currently the reporting agent controls the following reporting related batch processes:

- Alert monitoring of query-based exceptions
- Batch printing of queries

- Prepublishing and posting of Web templates
- Pre-calculating value sets for use in characteristic variables

The configuration of the reporting agent is a two-step process. First, the reporting agent settings for either exception reporting, batch printing, precalculation of Web templates, or precalculation of variable values need to be specified. Once these specific settings have been configured, it is simply a matter of creating a scheduling package. The scheduling package basically is the reporting agent scheduler and is tied into the job scheduling function that is part of the core system. All reporting agent configuration functionality is integrated into the Administrator Workbench. However, reporting agent processes are currently not integrated into the process chain technology (although this is planned).

TIP To schedule reporting agent scheduling packages online (synchronously), call transaction RSRAJ and enter the scheduling package's technical name. This is helpful for scenarios such as troubleshooting.

Exception Reporting

The reporting agent settings for exception reporting are dependent on exceptions defined within queries. Exceptions and how they are created was covered in Chapter 7. Although online reporting can highlight exceptions within a query output, it cannot handle automated notifications.

By scheduling these queries and their corresponding exceptions, you can generate exception-based notifications and update the alert monitor. Figure 9.8 shows an example where the alert monitor is updated for billing disputes with a percentage greater than 4.20 percent, and an email is sent to the designated roles and users. The following options are available for configuring exception reporting:

Exceptions. Exceptions are broken down by their threshold categories, as well as by notification priorities.

Follow-up actions. This is either a notification or an update to the alert monitor.

Characteristics. These characteristics are used to define the alert monitor views where only one characteristic can be expanded at a time. As a result, there will be a different alert monitor report per characteristic combination.

You can access the alert monitor two ways: from the Administrator Workbench and from the BEx Analyzer.

In addition to workbooks, queries, and views, when you open the BEx Analyzer, it offers exceptions for selection. The exceptions available are based on the report agent settings and if a corresponding scheduling package was successfully executed. The advantages of viewing the alerts in the BEx Analyzer are a higher level of detail and the availability of additional drill-downs and a Web representation.

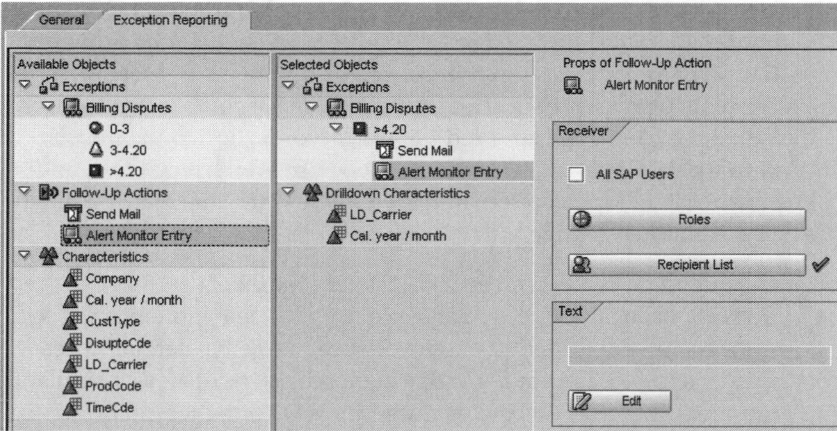

Figure 9.8 Exception reporting settings.

Printing

The Business Explorer supports batch printing through the reporting agent, spooling list output to the SAP spooler. This does not provide the same formatting options as other applications such as Microsoft Excel or Crystal Decisions. To print query results in batch mode, you must use key figures as part of a structure, and any variables that have manual data entry input must have an associated query variant to bypass online data entry.

The reporting agent settings for batch printing consist of two parts, as shown in Figure 9.9: one for print settings and one for print layout. The print settings contain general formatting and print control options such as suppression, positioning, paging, margining, and print direction:

- Repeated texts, zero values, colors, and print lines can all be suppressed via check boxes.
- Position placement options (selectable via drop boxes) can be set for currencies and units (left of amount, right of amount, or no display), minus indicators (before the value, after the value, or parenthesis), and totals results (bottom right or top left).
- Paging consists of specifying the number of rows and columns per page and a maximum number of pages (avoid killing too many trees).
- Page margins are set by specifying the width of the top and bottom of a page (constraining the number of rows), as well as the left and right of a page (constraining the number of characters).

- Print direction is either horizontal or vertical. This is only important if the number of columns spills over several pages. Print direction controls the order of the pages (i.e., if all the columns are printed first as separate pages before moving down the rows of the report or if all the rows of the report are printed first before the next set of columns is printed). In other words, horizontal means printing left to right then down, like reading a book in Western cultures, and vertical means printing top to bottom and then to the right, like reading a book in some Eastern cultures. Horizontal printing provides better performance.

The print layout settings are more involved. For instance, the display settings are very similar to the options available in the BEx Analyzer but with a few more print-specific options. First, print areas must be configured (cover sheet, page header, table header, table, page footer, and last page). The configuration behind these print areas is similar in concept to the print areas that need to be configured for any formatted reporting tool such as Crystal Decisions, and it contains standard options such as entering texts and dynamic variables (e.g., replacement values for characteristics, attributes, selection parameters print settings, and other technical details). InfoObject display options are also highlighted in Figure 9.9. The hierarchy tabstrip controls representation of hierarchies.

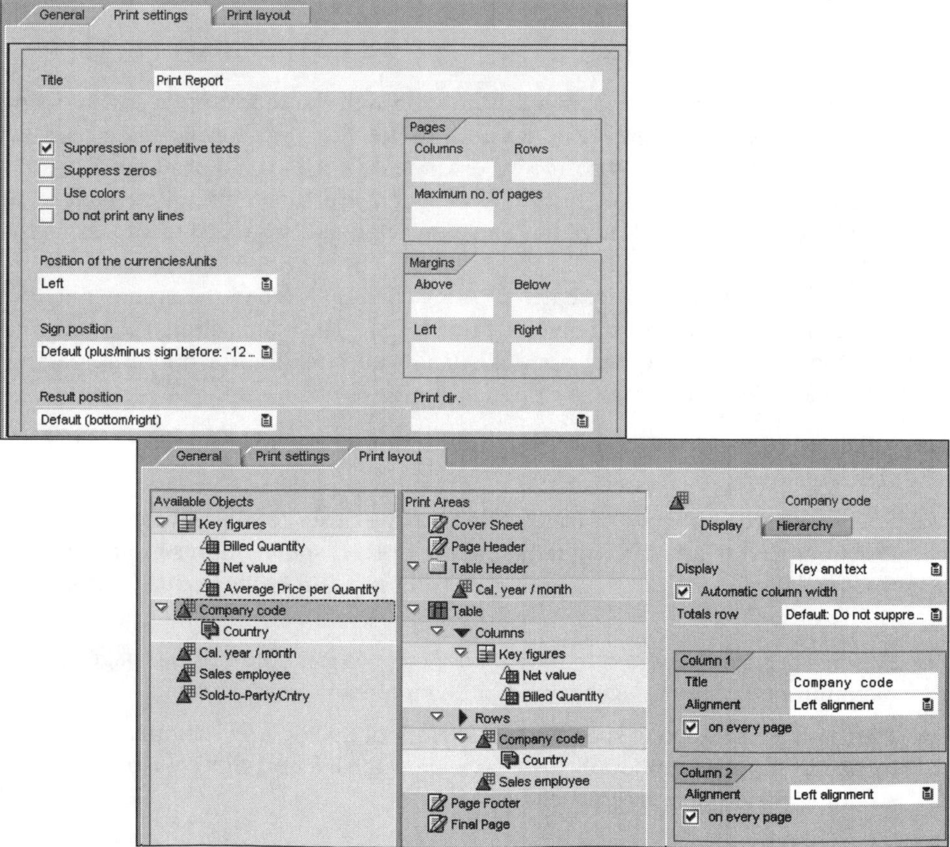

Figure 9.9 Reporting agent print settings.

Web Templates

The reporting agent allows for prepublishing and posting Web reports. Although such Web templates become static (no OLAP navigation) and frozen (no refresh of data until the scheduling package is executed again), this is a performance-enhancing option for those reporting requirements that do not need navigation or current information. Furthermore, precalculated HTML pages may be made available locally on the client workstation for offline reporting access via the webDAV service.

The reporting agent allows for two levels of precalculation. Web templates can either be precalculated one at a time as static HTML pages or many views of the same Web template can be generated and stored. As an example scenario, say a Web cockpit for cost center managers needs to be precalculated. The first option is to precalculate static HTML pages for each manager's cost center. This option would require maintaining reporting agent settings for each HTML page. The other option is to create one reporting agent setting and specify a control query that contains all the managers' cost centers. The latter option avoids maintenance. Additionally, it permits the generation of Web templates for more complex criteria, such as the generation of Web templates for the top hundred most commonly viewed cost centers. While the first option precalculates HTML pages for Web templates, the second option precalculates the data for Web templates. To access all the Web templates generated by the control query option, you can use Web Application Designer to generate the requisite selection lists needed to filter on the characteristic values (in this case, cost center). This selection list can be filled from the control query itself.

Technically, the control query is nothing more than a BEx Analyzer query without a key figure specified. In the reporting agent context, this query is specified as an optional setting for Web template precalculation. Every characteristic combination in the rows of the query serves to generate different views of data for the specified Web template.

Access to static, stored, or live data is controlled by a parameter setting in the URL for the Web template itself. The difference between a standard Web template (which accesses a data provider directly), a precalculated Web template, and Web template that accesses precalculated data is the value set for parameter DATA_MODE. The parameter DATA_MODE must be specified in the URL that accesses the Web template (refer to Chapter 7 for more information on using parameters in Web reporting). There are three basic parameter values for DATA_MODE:

NEW. This parameter value is optional, as it is the system default. The parameter value reads from the OLAP engine to get the most recent data.

STORED. This parameter value reads from precalculated data. The hybrid parameter value is HYBRID, which uses precalculated data as long as stored data is available. Otherwise, it uses the NEW mode.

STATIC. This parameter value reads from precalculated HTML pages. A hybrid parameter value is STATIC_HYBRID, which uses precalculated HTML pages as long as it available; otherwise, it uses the STORED mode. If stored data is not available, the NEW mode is used.

Regardless of whether the Web template is active, stored, or static, login is required, and hence, security is ensured. If there are mandatory manual entry variables in the query, a variant needs to be specified. Alternatively, the variable values can be preassigned via URL parameters. An example URL fragment specifying a variable value is *var_name_1=0COSTCNT&var_value_ext_1=10001000*, which sets variable *0COSTCNT* to the value *10001000*. A preview option allows you to preview either the Web template or the control query to give you an idea of what the precalculation results might be.

Value Sets

Value sets are a performance-enhancing alternative to pre-query variables. *Pre-query variables* are filled via the values from another query (also known as *bucket variables*). Pre-query variables are ideal for scenarios where sophisticated condition logic has to be applied for selection. For example, suppose you want to analyze if there is any correlation between the top 10 customers for sales for last year and any exposure to late receivables this year. Two queries are devised: a top 10 customers by sales query and an aged receivables query. The latter query uses a variable that uses the former query as the pre-query. In this case, the first query has to be executed before the second query has the customers to select its data against. As a result, if this analysis is popular (being run by multiple users, multiple times) performance may be compromised.

Value sets are an alternative solution. *Value set variables* are similar to pre-query variables except the values for the variable are precalculated and stored and then can be shared across multiple queries. In the BEx Variable Wizard, value set variables configure differently than pre-query variables. Pre-query variables are configured as characteristic values with a replacement path. Value set variables configure as characteristic values with a fixed value. The fixed value is the table that the reporting agent generates for the value set.

The reporting agent setting for value sets is similar to the replacement path configuration settings for a pre-query variable. A query must be specified, along with a variant if there are mandatory manual entry variables as well as a characteristic from the query. After this reporting agent setting is scheduled within a scheduling package, a table is generated with the surrogate ID keys of the top customers in the specified query.

Monitoring

The main monitoring tool of the Administrator Workbench is the Data Monitor, which allows tracking data loads and error handling. The Data Monitor is where all failed data loads can be investigated and where all the tools and mechanisms for identifying and investigating data load errors are available at a single point of access. A wizard supports walking through the process of error investigation. To maximize the error handling options available, we highly recommend using the PSA. This enables simulation of updates, direct manual corrections, and reprocessing of a request on a per data packet basis.

Data Monitor

The Data Monitor comprises three tabstrips: header, status, and details. To reduce the number of data load requests displayed in the monitor, various filters can be applied, such as time selections or meta data object selections like data target, InfoSource, and InfoPackage. Typically, when data loads fail, an express mail notifies the initiator of the data request. In Figure 9.10, a cost center's meta data changes and master data is reloaded. On the first attempt the data load fails. The initiator goes to the Data Monitor to investigate the cause of the error.

The request overview screen can be displayed as a tree, overview list, or planning table. The default is the tree display, illustrated in Figure 9.10. The tree display for the monitor is configurable and is organized by the details about the request.

From the status tabstrip, a wizard is available via the *Step-by-Step Analysis* button shown in Figure 9.11. The Step-by-Step Analysis Wizard walks through the steps of the data load process to pinpoint the error that has occurred. In the analysis in this example, we learn that the error occurs even before the data can be requested.

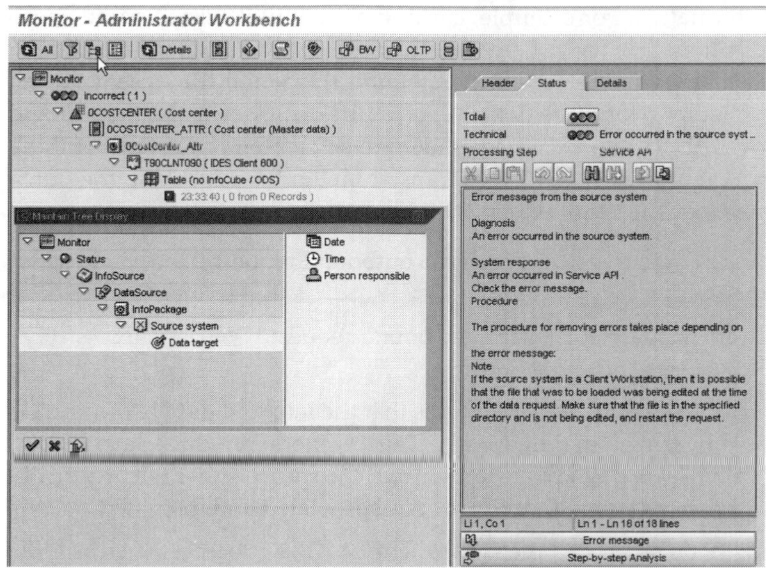

Figure 9.10 Data Monitor display.

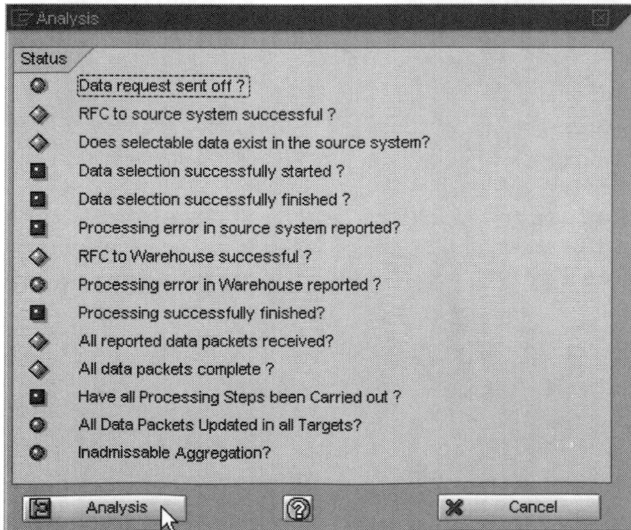

Figure 9.11 Step-by-Step Analysis Wizard.

Further analysis shows that the errors occur in the source system and leads the user to the error message. In this case, the transfer structure needs to be regenerated because of the meta data changes that have been applied to the cost center InfoObject. After regeneration, the data loads correctly. The header tabstrip in Figure 9.12 shows the successful load, providing information such as the request ID, dates and times, the technical names of the meta data objects involved, and InfoPackage settings (such as processing, update mode, and checking).

Underlined detail texts indicate navigation options to a transaction or screen providing additional information. For example, clicking on the InfoPackage name opens the InfoPackage definition.

The detail tabstrip shows all inbound and outbound IDocs and tRFCs sent during extraction (refer to Chapter 6 for more details). As Figure 9.13 shows, the request and all the subsequent info IDocs and tRFCs are shown in sequential order. Any of these IDocs or tRFCs can be reprocessed if the PSA transfer method is selected in the transfer structure maintenance. The detail screen is divided into four or more sections:

- The request node of the tree indicates if the outbound request IDoc has successfully been processed.
- The extraction tree node indicates if the inbound request IDoc has successfully initiated and processed the extraction.
- The transfer IDocs and tRFC node indicates that the info and data IDocs and tRFCs successfully arrived in the SAP BW. This tree node provides details about every data packet that is transferred from the source system. If any errors occur, the exact data packet with the error can be isolated and inspected.
- The processing node reflects all the subsequent SAP BW processes such as PSA update, transformation processing, and data target updates.

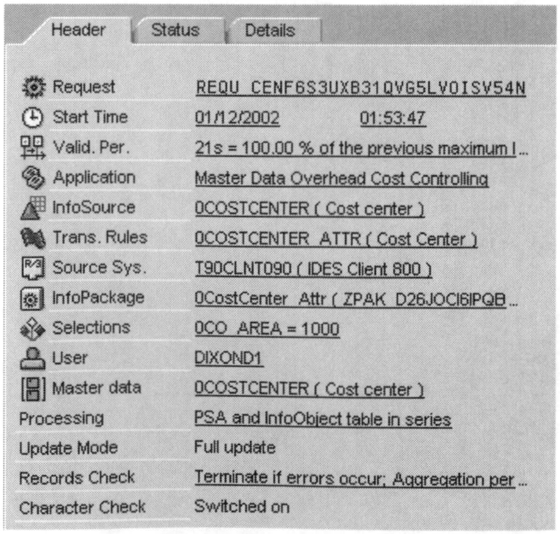

Header | Status | Details

Request	REQU_CENF6S3UXB31QVG5LVOISV54N
Start Time	01/12/2002 01:53:47
Valid. Per.	21s = 100.00 % of the previous maximum l...
Application	Master Data Overhead Cost Controlling
InfoSource	0COSTCENTER (Cost center)
Trans. Rules	0COSTCENTER_ATTR (Cost Center)
Source Sys.	T90CLNT090 (IDES Client 800)
InfoPackage	0CostCenter_Attr (ZPAK_D26JOCI6IPQB...
Selections	0CO_AREA = 1000
User	DIXOND1
Master data	0COSTCENTER (Cost center)
Processing	PSA and InfoObject table in series
Update Mode	Full update
Records Check	Terminate if errors occur; Aggregation per ...
Character Check	Switched on

Figure 9.12 Monitor header data.

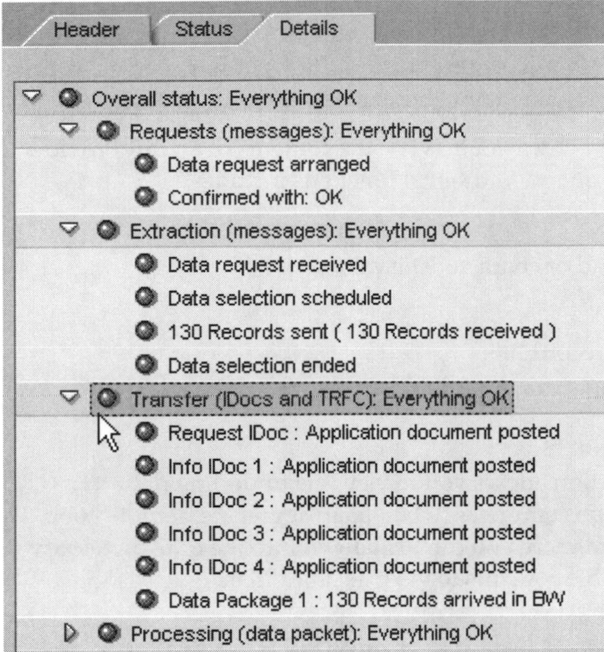

Figure 9.13 Monitor details data.

In case of unsuccessful data loads, data packages can be selected individually, single records can be selected for inspections, and the whole update procedure can be simulated and debugged, if the request was loaded into the PSA. Simulation shows how the data is passed from the transfer structure to the communication structure and to the data target; any incorrect values or transformations can be identified easily. During simulation you can use an analysis function to check for duplicate records or overlapping time intervals. If the debugging option is switched on, SAP BW generates breakpoints into the transformation programs that let you to step through the update rule logic, allowing you to debug custom code. Finally, any incorrect records identified can be maintained directly using the PSA maintenance transaction. Once the errors have been identified and fixed, the data package can be manually reprocessed to update the corrected record or records.

TIP You can develop custom ABAP programs to check and cleanse data records in the PSA before updating into the SAP BW using the following APIs: RSSM_API_REQUEST_GET to read the available requests, RSAR_ODS_API_GET to read the records of the corresponding requests, and RSAR_ODS_API_SET to modify and change the read records.

Troubleshooting

Besides the Data Monitor, other commonly used transactions are available for troubleshooting. Typically used after loading data, these transactions are as follows:

LISTCUBE. This transaction allows you to view the contents of an InfoProvider without having to design a query. Additional functions include:

- Viewing the SQL plan
- Viewing the SIDs instead of characteristic values
- Avoiding aggregation
- Output the number of record hits
- Storing the results to either a table or a file
- Turning off conversion exits

LISTSCHEMA. This transaction allows you to view the underling data dictionary tables an InfoCube comprises (whether an aggregate, remote cube, MultiCube, and so on). From there you can drill down into the data dictionary definitions or display the table contents to view technical data (such as the SID tables).

RSRV. This transaction contains a collection of reports to check the consistency of the meta data and data in the system and offers repair programs for most inconsistencies. These reports should be periodically run as a preventative maintenance measure to catch any data corruption, especially during stabilization exercises like a test phase. Figure 9.14 shows an example report where the dimension keys are compared with the surrogate keys for profit center in the profit center transaction data InfoCube. Instead of having to manually compare the dimension tables with the surrogate ID tables in transaction LISTSCHEMA, you can execute this reporting utility. All errors are logged and can be viewed in a separate session. Each report has its own parameters to conduct its tests.

RSRT. The BEx Analyzer is not the only way of viewing the output of a query. You can use transaction RSRT to view the results of a query instead. This transaction is normally used for troubleshooting purposes and for maintaining technical query properties. Transaction RSRT is discussed in more detail in Chapter 10 when we discuss performance optimization.

RSRT2. This is a Web version of the Query Monitor that allows you to troubleshoot Web queries. This transaction is similar to RSRT except the Web query URLs must be specified in this transaction. This transaction is particularly relevant for any enhancements to the Web table interface.

MDXTEST. If the ODBO interface or the OLAP BAPIs is being used to access SAP BW data, query statements have to be specified using a query language called MDX. This transaction allows testing the syntax of MDX statements. This transaction can also auto-generate MDX to jump-start familiarity with MDX syntax.

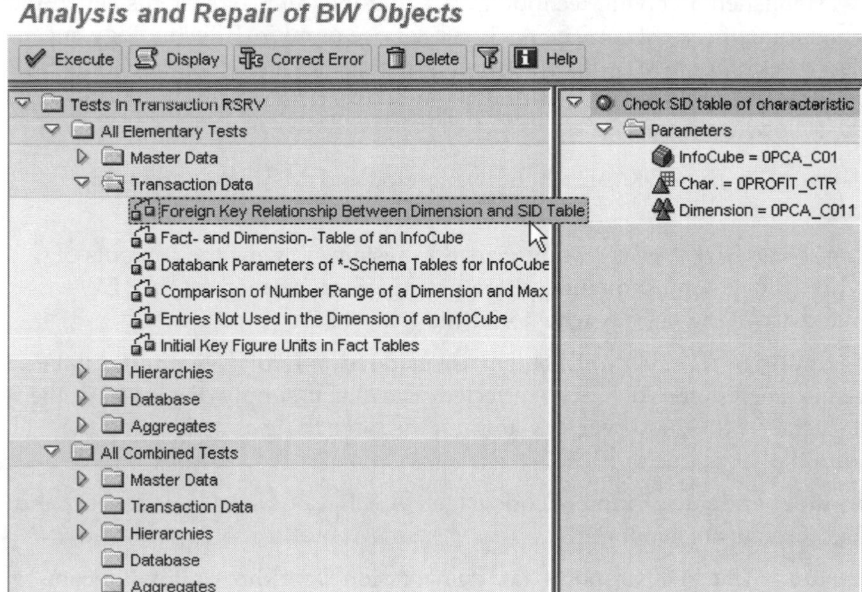

Figure 9.14 Analysis and repair of SAP BW objects.

System-Oriented Administration

System administration functions are part of every SAP system but SAP BW systems have unique design implications and specific functions to consider. Again, the intention of this chapter is not to review general concepts; in some instances knowledge is presumed in these areas so that the SAP BW-specific topics can be more readily addressed. Chapter 3 already introduced many of the high-level concepts. Here we will get into more detail. The system administration topics differ from the process topics in that no batch jobs need to be scheduled, and system administration is peripheral to operational functions such as data loads. More specifically, this section deals with archiving, security, transports, and upgrades.

Archiving

According to studies, business records decay at the rate of 2.5 to 3.5 percent per month. Combine that with the explosive growth in new data caused by all the data redundancies inherent in a corporate information factory (i.e., information marts and corresponding aggregates), and archiving quickly becomes an important post-implementation issue.

SAP BW archiving is not a new technology. Archiving was available in earlier releases for purging unnecessary IDocs out of the SAP BW environment. It is based on the already established archiving technology prebuilt into all SAP systems called the Archive Development Kit (ADK). The ADK is a service of mySAP Technology, meaning that it is a core component of all SAP systems. It provides an API that not only SAP but customers and partners can use to develop their own archiving solutions. The ADK provides the following features:

Administration. The ADK can schedule, monitor, and administer archiving sessions.

Reporting. The ADK has its own information system. To view the contents of an archive file, you must manually create an InfoStructure for the SAP BW–generated archiving object via customization.

Change handling. If structural changes are made to an InfoProvider after data has been archived, the ADK is not affected. The data is simply displayed in the new structure. Note, however, that this not the same thing as converting the data into the new structure.

Platform-independent. Different code pages (ASCII, EBCDIC, Unicode, etc.) and number formats are supported.

Compression. The ADK supports data compression algorithms, allowing compression down to one-fifth the original size.

What is new is archiving support for SAP BW data targets. As a result, this section will focus on the SAP BW-specific aspects of archiving. The more general topic of SAP archiving is beyond the scope of this book.

Because all the tables where transaction data is stored are generated and extensible, predelivered *archiving objects* do not exist as they do in other SAP systems (such as SAP R/3, where tables are usually fixed). An archiving object is a logical object. The archiving object consists of business data that can be grouped and treated together for reading, archiving, and deleting. The central piece of SAP BW–specific configuration for archiving entails creating the archiving object based on the data target definitions, as well as some design considerations. Currently, archiving only supports the InfoCube and ODS object data targets. Master data, PSA, and documents are not yet supported.

Once the archive object has been generated, archiving can be scheduled as a batch job. Although archiving is not yet integrated with process chains, it is an administrative process like any other. Batch schedules are created and have sequencing considerations. The process of archiving consists of first writing all the data out to a file and then deleting it from the data target. Once archived, the data file can be reloaded back into SAP BW if necessary. The export DataSource for the data targets archived has special archive features. As mentioned earlier, in the InfoPackage data selection for the export DataSource, archive selections can be enabled to read records from a file. SAP recommends that when reloading data back into SAP BW, you should update a new data target specifically for archived data and create a MultiProvider for marrying new data with archived data. Queries cannot yet directly access archived data in a near-line

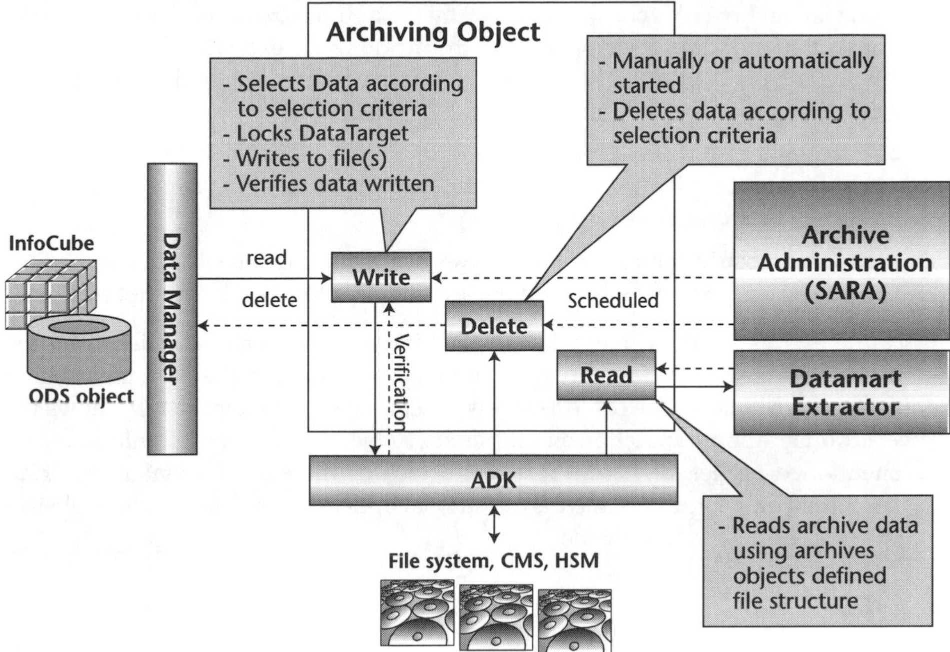

Figure 9.15 Archiving process.

storage. However, SAP has been working together with FileTek to provide solutions for online access to archived data. At this writing, online access to archived ODS object data is not available. Figure 9.15 illustrates the regular archiving process.

The archiving object is configured within the maintenance of the data target. It provides the following configuration options:

Select data. In this tabstrip the characteristics used for data selection is configured. In this example, when data is written to a file, only the calendar year can be specified. If the data target is partitioned, this characteristic must be the partitioning characteristic. Otherwise, a time characteristic must be used. ODS objects may be the exceptions where alternative characteristics may be used if a time characteristic is not available.

File structure. In this tabstrip, the *data object* is maintained. The data object is the most atomic unit of data in the archive. The data records read into the archive file are grouped and sorted by the characteristics specified here. If nothing is specified, all records will be written unsorted into the file. This tabstrip also controls the size of archive files one of two ways: by maximum size of the file or by maximum number of data objects per file. If the maximum is exceeded for a file, a new file is created until the same maximum is exceeded. If these fields are left blank, then all data is written to one file.

Folder. Here the storage settings are configured. If the archive storage is in SAP, a logical filename is given. Otherwise, third-party-specific settings must be maintained for the storage system.

Delete. This tabstrip controls how the subsequent data deletion job will be scheduled. The options are not scheduled but are started automatically or after an event.

Once the archive object is created, archive administration can be called from the Administrator Workbench (just a right-click menu option from the data target), and the process of archiving is the same as in any other SAP system. Figure 9.16 shows the archive administration transaction and the archive object for the payroll InfoCube.

As mentioned earlier, any InfoPackage created for the export DataSource of an archive-enabled data target will have an additional option in the data selection tabstrip to extract from a specific archive file.

Security

Fundamentally, security in SAP BW is handled the same way as security in any other SAP system—based on the standard SAP authorization concept. Before reading this section, readers should already be familiar with the standard SAP authorization concepts and terms such as users, roles, object classes, authorization objects, profiles, profile generator, and authorizations. This subsection deals with the SAP BW-specific authorization concepts and design issues.

SAP BW authorizations are fundamentally different from SAP R/3 authorizations and have to be designed and created separately. A large part can be attributed to the fundamental differences between a data entry (OLTP) system and a data access (OLAP) system. The roles, applications, and processes are all different as well. Consequently, the authorization objects and associated object classes are different (except for cross-application components and Basis).

There are fundamental differences OLAP and OLTP systems from a security perspective are highlighted in Table 9.6.

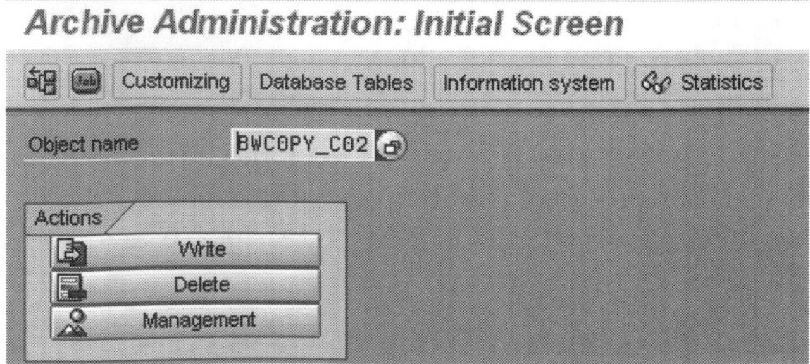

Figure 9.16 Archive administration.

Table 9.6 OLTP versus OLAP Security

CRITERIA	OLTP	OLAP
Application area	Within	Across
Transaction-oriented	Yes	No
Activities	Create, change, delete display,	Display,
Data focus	Master data	Transaction data

SAP BW authorization functionality also differs from SAP R/3 authorizations in another way. Not only can SAP BW authorizations be used for security, but they can also be used for personalization or data selection in reporting. For example, authorization variables can be used to automatically read a user's authorization profile and select data for the assigned query (without the need for user entry). Or authorization variables can be used as a value within an authorization itself. In the first case a query uses a variable to dynamically read the fixed values of an authorization. In the second, manually entered variable checks against a dynamically determined authorization value.

From a design perspective, security is designed along two dimensions: *who* and *what*. From the *who* dimension, security designers have the choice of assigning authorization profiles to either users or generating ones for roles. From the *what* dimension, security designers can authorize by SAP BW meta data *object* or by *data* sets.

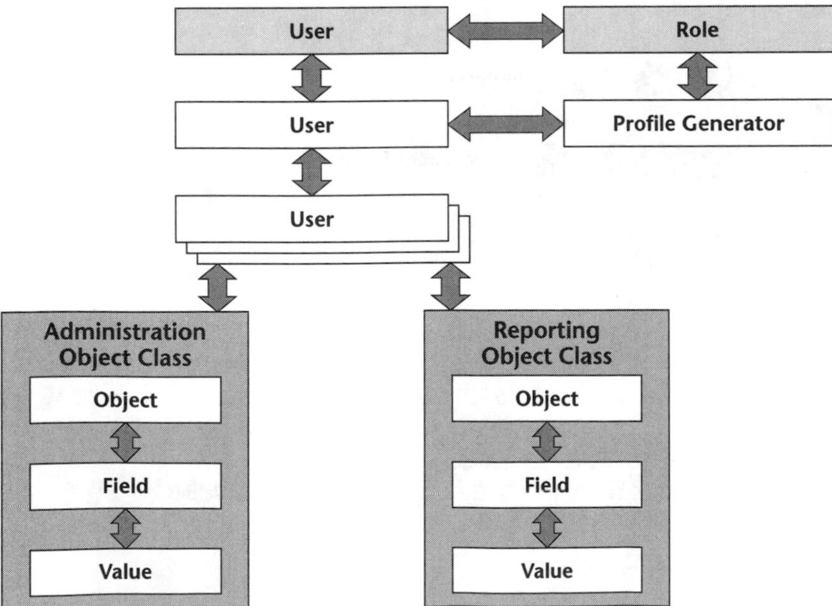

Figure 9.17 Authorization relationships.

The design decision between using SAP BW *objects* and reporting *data* (i.e., characteristic values) must be weighed before creating reporting authorizations. In contrast, administration tasks are handled by SAP BW meta data objects. There are fixed authorization objects predelivered that restrict activities to specific SAP BW meta data objects. These authorization objects belong to an object class for SAP BW administration.

For reporting authorizations, the same authorization objects for administration can be used to restrict user access to report output (e.g., by query). Alternatively, user access to report output can be controlled by specific characteristic values (e.g., by cost centers). The authorization objects for reporting values are not predelivered. Similar to archiving (where the archiving object must be configured and generated), reporting authorization objects must be custom-designed and implemented. Reporting authorization objects are assigned to a SAP BW reporting object class that is predelivered empty.

The relationship among users, roles, the administration object class, the reporting object class, profiles, and authorizations are depicted in Figure 9.17.

As security design goals move from user-centric to role-centric and from a focus on BW meta data objects to a focus on characteristic values in reporting, simplification is compromised for tighter and more targeted security control. Security design options are shown in Figure 9.18.

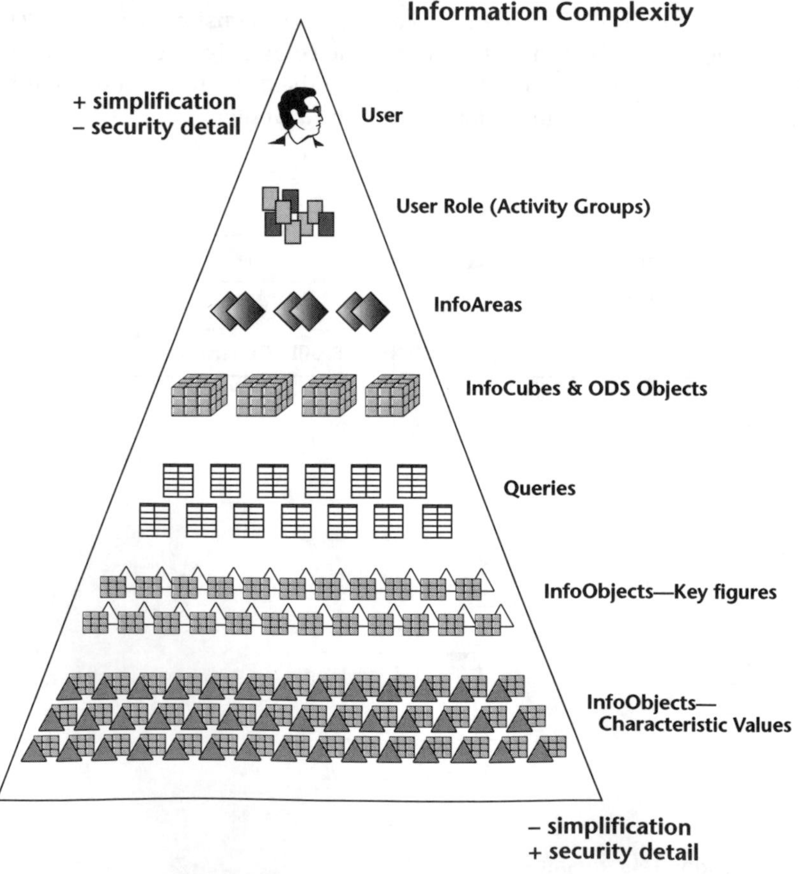

Figure 9.18 Security design considerations.

User versus Role

Authorization design should always start with designing roles. Where this approach breaks down in SAP BW is when reporting scenarios require the roles to be at the same level of detail as the individual users. For example, say an organization has 1,000+ cost centers (let's be conservative), with a manager assigned to each cost center. Should 1,000+ roles be created one-to-one with the users? Such a design is maintenance-intensive. If broad roles are created with many users assigned to those roles (say, to a specific cost center hierarchy node), maintenance is alleviated. Any changes to a role impacts many users. In many cases, this is desirable. But in such a design how does one handle exceptions (for example, one user needs access to a cost center outside the hierarchy node that no one else in the role should have access to)? If the roles were one-to-one with the user, individual user exceptions would be easier to handle. However, when many users share a role, an alternative is to assign the new authorization profile directly to the user rather than the role.

When broad reporting roles are defined, the standard SAP transaction for administering role authorizations (transaction PFCG) should be sufficient. When reporting authorizations need to be assigned to individual users, the SAP BW transaction for authorization administration should be used (transaction RSSM). This transaction will be covered in greater detail a bit later in the chapter.

Typically, authorizations are designed based on SAP BW meta data objects, roles can be defined broadly enough to restrict user access to a particular query or InfoCube. However, when authorizations are based on characteristic values in reporting authorization objects, they are typically more user-centric than role-centric. The difference between object and value definitions in authorizations will be covered in more detail in the next subsection.

The advantage of using roles over users for authorizations is that roles have additional features not available to user definitions, such as user menu configuration and portal integration. One simplistic way of providing security is restricting access to a query or a transaction via user menus. In other words, this design approach assumes that if a user cannot see it in the system, he or she is not sophisticated enough to find it and access it by other means. You should also design roles with portals in mind even if there are no immediate plans to implement them.

Table 9.7 User versus Role Authorizations

CRITERIA	USER	ROLE
Number of authorizations	Many	Few
Meta data object authorizations	Not typical	Typical
Reporting values authorizations	Typical	Not typical
Administration transaction	RSSM	PFCG
Restrict access by menu options	No	Yes

The user-centric over role-centric authorizations advantage is that there are SAP BW-specific features that can automate or expedite the use of detailed authorizations without the maintenance headache. You can accomplish this by either using specialized ODS objects to generate all requisite authorizations and assign them to users (sourcing the information from another system) or by using an InfoCube with all the assignments and restricting access by query design. These authorization design alternatives will be covered in the next subsection. Table 9.7 summarizes the design considerations for user-centric versus role-centric authorizations.

Object versus Data

As mentioned before, authorizations can be used to restrict each component of an information model, such as InfoSources, InfoCubes, InfoObjects, individual queries, and even their components (such as calculated or restricted key figures). If there are meta data objects that are shared within other meta data objects, restriction can be enforced at higher levels. For example, the InfoObject 0PERSON is used both in HR Business Content and CO Business Content. Access to the InfoObject can be centrally controlled by assigning the InfoObject to an InfoCatalog and restricting access to the InfoCatalog.

Another way to categorize SAP BW information modeling objects is by naming conventions. Authorization values can accept asterisks as wildcard values (such as 0CRM* for all CRM Business Content). If you are planning on using security by meta data object approach, you should design a naming convention at the beginning of a project before too many custom SAP BW objects are created!

SAP BW delivers role templates that contain a series of authorization objects and corresponding default values such as:

S_RS_RDEAD Role: Administrator (development system)

S_RS_RDEMO Role: Modeler (development system)

S_RS_ROPAD Role: Administrator (productive system)

S_RS_ROPOP Role: Operator (productive system)

S_RS_RREDE Role: Reporting developer (productive system)

S_RS_RREPU Role: Reporting user

Figure 9.19 depicts the types of activities and BW meta data objects assigned to such role templates.

The security designer has another option for restricting access to reporting data other than by SAP BW meta data object (such as query or query element). SAP BW reporting authorization objects can be custom-generated and used to restrict access by characteristic value. These reporting authorization objects consist of characteristics or hierarchy nodes of a characteristic (up to 10 values) and a key figure, which are then assigned to InfoCubes.

Key figures are handled differently than characteristics in the authorization object. A characteristic InfoObject by the technical name of 1KYFNM is used to represent the key figure. The actual key figure name is fixed in the authorization in the same way that characteristic values are fixed.

Role	Query	InfoCube	InfoSource	InfoObject
Reporting User	R E M			
Reporting Developer	R E M			
Reporting Power User	R E M D	R M		
Data Manager	R E M	R M		M R
Data Modeller	R E M	R E M D	R E M	R E M
System Administrator				

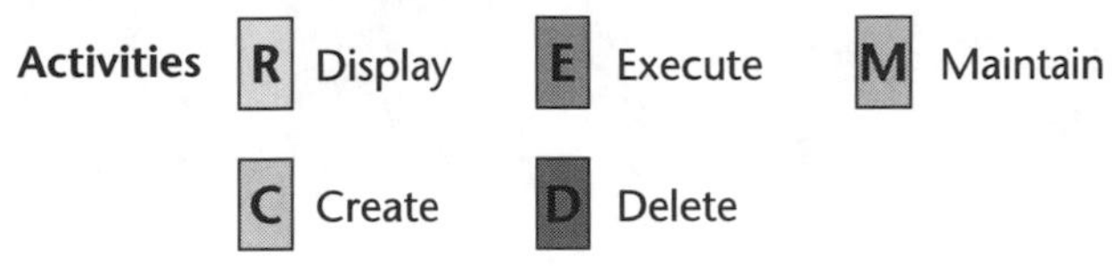

Figure 9.19 Example roles by object.

For hierarchy nodes, the InfoObject 0TCTAUTHH must be used in conjunction with a characteristic in the reporting authorization object. Additional configuration steps also are needed to specify the hierarchy or hierarchy node names (covered in more detail in the text that follows) in order to set the value for 0TCTAUTHH in an authorization.

Not all characteristics are available for use in reporting authorization objects. Only the characteristic InfoObjects that are flagged as authorization-relevant are available (in InfoObject maintenance, accessible via the *Business Explorer* tabstrip).

TIP There is another special characteristic available in the authorization object: the field ACTVT to represent authorization activity. This field is not necessary for SAP BW authorizations (which for reporting should always default to Display activity anyway), but it is used for applications such as SAP SEM where data is entered directly into an InfoCube for planning functions.

The authorizations maintained for the reporting authorization objects have additional values than what is found for nonreporting authorizations, such as #, :, and $ for "not assigned," "aggregated values," and "authorization variable," respectively.

The SAP BW authorizations can be centrally maintained (via transaction RSSM), as Figure 9.20 illustrates, or they can be maintained via the Profile Generator (transaction PFCG). The considerations for using one transaction over the other were explained in the previous subsection. Following is a more detailed explanation of transaction RSSM.

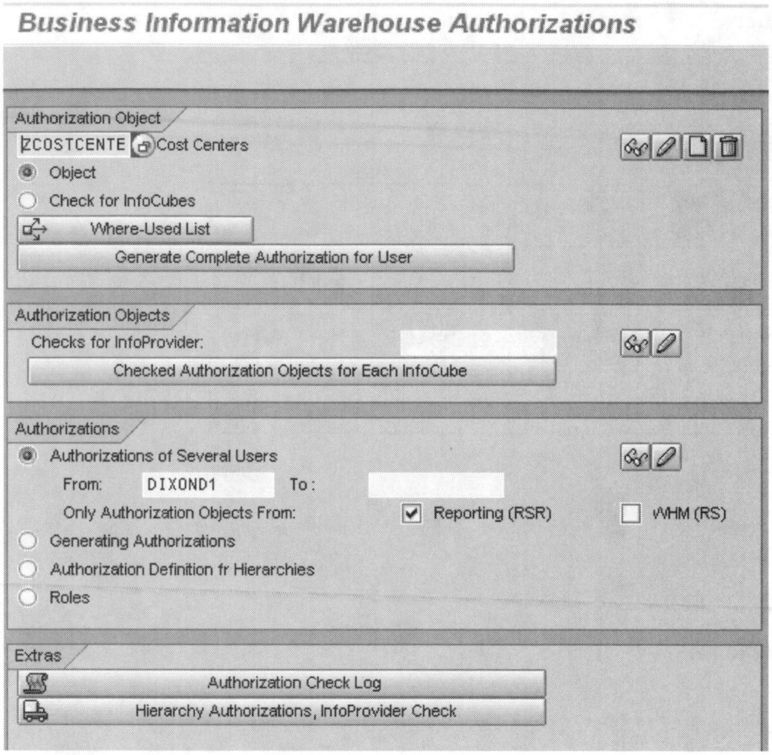

Figure 9.20 SAP BW authorization maintenance.

The central maintenance screen for authorizations is divided into the following sections:

Authorization object. For the *Object* radio button, a custom authorization object for the SAP BW reporting object class can be created. Characteristics and optionally key figures and hierarchy node InfoObjects must be included in the authorization object definition. A where-used report can be executed to provide a listing of which authorizations have been created for the authorization object and which users were assigned. An authorization can automatically generate and be assigned to the logged-on user by clicking on the *Generate Complete Authorization for User* button. For the *Check for InfoCubes* radio button, the reporting authorization object can be assigned to an InfoProvider.

Authorization objects. Here authorization objects can be assigned to InfoCubes per InfoCube. The *Checked Authorization Objects for Each InfoCube* option gives a report of the assignments for all InfoProviders.

Authorizations. Here the SAP BW authorizations can be manually created per user (in contrast to per role in transaction PFCG).

The *Generating Authorizations* radio button allows the authorizations to be automatically generated en masse via specialized ODS objects that contain the authorization values as transaction data. These ODS objects can be filled via extraction from the source system as long as the structural format of the ODS object is adhered to. There are several predelivered Business Content ODS objects that can be copied as templates.

The *Authorization Definition for Hierarchies* radio button is used to create technical description values for authorization objects containing hierarchies (InfoObject 0TCTAUTHH). These technical description values represent an InfoObject hierarchy and node value, as well as the authorization. In addition, hierarchy authorizations can be used to restrict navigation behavior (such as blocking access to information above or below a hierarchy node). These custom-defined technical description values must be used within the authorization for the authorization object in question. The *Roles* radio button allows you to jump to transaction PFCG.

Extras. The first button allows you to turn on a reporting authorization trace per user ID and check the authorization trace logs. The second button transports the authorization object.

Although maintaining authorizations is an administration task, the design of security is an important information modeling consideration that needs to be addressed at the beginning of a project and not saved until the end.

Transports

The end of Chapter 3 covered system landscape design consideration and mentioned the SAP Transport Management System (TMS). This section is dedicated to SAP BW-specific considerations. There are a number of features that make SAP BW transports different from traditional SAP R/3 transports:

- Most of the transported objects are meta data definitions as opposed to configuration data or programs. After import, methods are called to generate the meta data object environment (such as database tables, and ABAP programs) as part of meta data activation.
- SAP BW supplements the standard transport mechanism by the Transport Connection tool, which transparently handles dependencies between different SAP BW meta data objects. The Transport Connection tool is available as part of the Administrator Workbench.
- SAP BW object transports and related source system object transports need to be synchronized.
- As opposed to SAP R/3, SAP BW does allow changing certain types of objects (e.g., Infopackages) in the production environment.

Transport Connection Tool

The TMS distinguishes between local (assigned to a temporary package named $TMP) and transportable objects (assigned to a permanent package). As explained in Chapter 3, the TMS is used to record changes to all permanent objects. Changes recorded by the TMS include creation, modification, and deletion of objects. While most SAP applications—for instance, the ABAP Workbench—require explicit assignment of a package to a transport object (which may be $TMP), SAP BW meta data objects are always initially assigned to the temporary package $TMP. This keeps them out of reach of the TMS until they need to be transported to the quality assurance or production system. Once an SAP BW meta data object is transported for the first time using the Transport Connection tool, a package name has to be assigned explicitly and the meta data object is put under control of the TMS, which begins recording the changes.

The Transport Connection tool allows you to collect SAP BW meta data objects along two dimensions: meta data object cross-references (e.g., InfoObjects used in InfoCubes) and data flow (e.g., InfoSources feeding an InfoCube and queries defined for an InfoCube). Object collection ensures correctness and completeness of transport requests. The Transport Connection tool utilizes standard TMS functionality, thus enabling use of all standard TMS transactions in conjunction with SAP BW meta data transports. However, the Transport Connection tool is not able to identify and honor dependencies between SAP BW and non-SAP BW objects (such as ABAP programs, and dictionary structures).

BEx queries are similar to other SAP BW meta data objects in that newly created queries are initially assigned to the temporary package ($TMP) until ready to transport. However, BEx queries can be explicitly assigned to their own transports in the Transport Connection as an option for managing these transports separately. Once released, a new standard transport request must immediately be defined and assigned for BEx queries, or any additional changes will result in an error.

Table 9.8 illustrates the differences between the SAP BW Transport Connection tool and the standard TMS.

Transport Dependencies

The SAP BW Transport Connection tool does have a reputation of being complicated and error-prone. Part of this reputation surely stems from early releases of SAP BW transports, where this part of the software in fact had a couple of intricate bugs that took SAP some time to fix. However, much of this reputation also stems from using the Transport Connection tool without taking care of the following fundamental dependencies:

- Dependencies between different SAP BW meta data objects (e.g., the InfoObjects required by an InfoCube)
- Dependencies between SAP BW meta data objects and ABAP Workbench objects (e.g., includes, macros, or ABAP dictionary structures used in update rules)
- Dependencies between meta data stored in SAP BW and meta data stored in the source systems

Because of the nature of these dependencies, there is no easy technical solution. Instead, organizational solutions need to be defined that help to avoid transport problems with SAP BW meta data objects. An organizational solution approach for the first two problems is using collective transport requests, where all developers working on a specific part of the project use the same (therefore *collective*) transport request to record their changes.

Table 9.8 SAP BW Transport Connection Tool and the SAP TMS

CRITERIA	TRANSPORT CONNECTION	TMS
No tracking of changes until first transport	Yes	No
Meta data object authorization necessary	Yes	No
ABAP development or configuration	No	Yes

TIP **Custom ABAP code references to SAP BW-generated ABAP structures can be eliminated if sophisticated methods are used to make the code more dynamic and generic (such as the use of field symbols or runtime type identification). This makes custom code less maintenance intensive when changes are made to meta data, and it eliminates any dependencies in transport.**

Although the Transport Connection tool can handle dependencies between multiple meta data objects, it is still possible to define multiple transport requests and spread interdependent SAP BW meta data objects across these multiple transport requests. Centrally maintained collective transport requests help to avoid meta data spreading and allow for keeping control of non-SAP BW meta data objects required, although they do not offload the responsibility of taking care of such dependencies from the developers.

The most frequently ignored dependency, however, is the source system dependency. Figure 9.21 illustrates those dependencies and the sequence of steps that must be taken for a safe and reliable transport. The steps are as follows:

1. The first step is to transport the *information model*, consisting of InfoCubes, ODS objects, InfoSources, InfoObjects, update rules, queries, other SAP BW meta data objects not related to any source system, and non-SAP BW transport objects in an initial transport request. The Transport Connection tool can be used to collect all required SAP BW meta data objects.
2. While export DataSource for InfoCubes and ODS objects are generated automatically, SAP BW releases 2.0B and 2.1C did not automatically generate export DataSources for master data. These needed to be transported separately via maintenance of the DataSources (using the SBIW transaction).
3. The third step is to transport all required DataSources from the source system development landscape to the source system quality assurance landscape.
4. This step involves replicating all meta data for all source systems, including the SAP BW system itself to make sure all (export) DataSource definitions are up-to-date. Obviously, all relevant source systems need to be created at this time.
5. The last step is to transport all staging objects, such as DataSources (transfer structures), transfer rules, and InfoPackages.

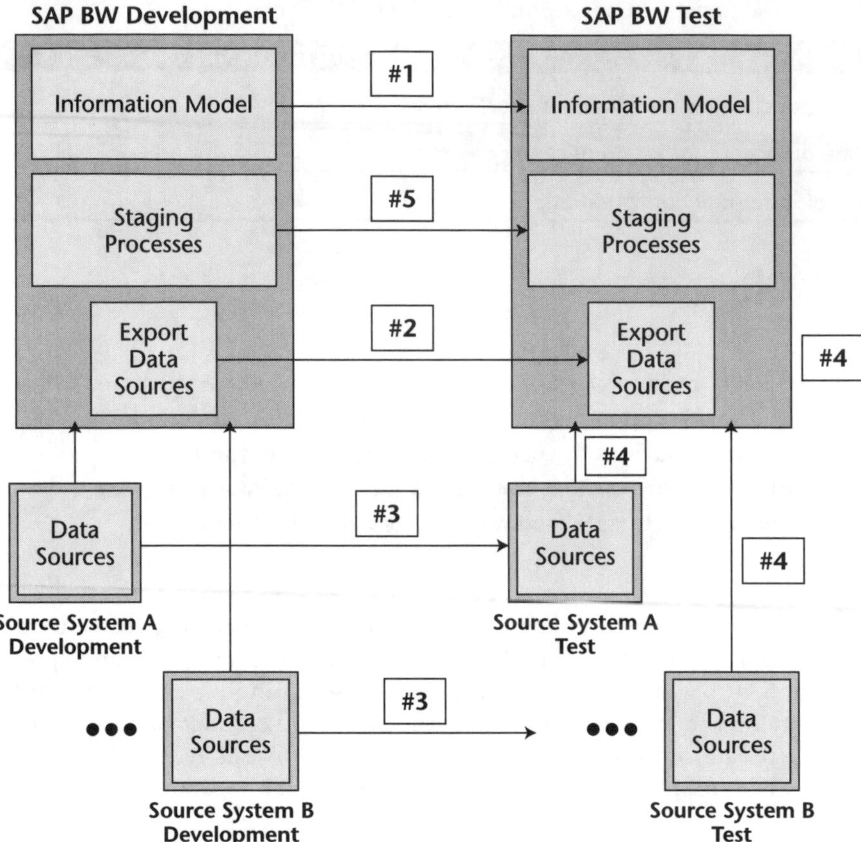

Figure 9.21 SAP BW transport dependencies.

In addition, two important configuration steps need to be completed prior to performing Step 5. The first configuration step is to select the source systems for which the Transport Connection tool should collect meta data. This avoids transporting meta data for source systems that are merely used in the development system for testing or sandbox purposes.

The second step is to make sure all source system mappings (mappings of different technical source system names in the development and quality assurance environments) are defined correctly in the target system. This second configuration step is much more important. As part of the import procedure the original source system name is mapped to the name specified in this mapping.

Activation

There are various object versions that typically belong to meta data: delivered, modified, and active. The only version that can be transported in customer systems using the TMS is the active version. SAP BW transports the active version of meta data definitions to downstream systems. The meta data environment (such as master data tables) is generated as part of the activation that is performed by so-called after-import methods, where applicable (e.g., currency types can be transported without a separate activation step).

TIP After-import methods can be called manually in a quality assurance system to debug the activation of a BW meta data object. The function module for the after-import method is RS_AFTER_IMPORT. Never transport the underlying generated ABAP dictionary objects directly.

Most SAP BW objects are not supposed to be changed in a productive environment. The TMS prevents such changes or records them in special "repair transport requests" depending on its configuration. However, some SAP BW objects must be changed in a productive environment, such as queries, workbooks, Web templates, InfoPackages, or process chains. The SAP BW TMS extensions allow changing the settings for these objects types to one of the following:

Not changeable. All BW object types with this setting must be changed in the development system and promoted to production using the TMS.

Changeable original. As a result, if an object (like a query) is transported from development to production, then that query cannot be maintained in production even if the *Changeable* option has been set. All changes to the object must be done in development and transported. Meanwhile, if the object is created directly in production, it can be changed freely.

Everything changeable. Regardless of whether or not an object type was transported, the object can be maintained. This option is not recommended, since changes made in production can be overwritten by changes transported from development. This option is accessible via the context menu of the *Object Changeability* pop-up.

Decisions have to be made whether or not these object types should be directly maintainable in production. Figure 9.22 shows how to configure object changeability.

Delete CTO Conversion BEx Object Changeability

Changeability of Object Types (if not changeable in system)

Object type		
AGGR	Aggregate	Not Changeable
CTRT	Currency Translation Type	Not Changeable
ELEM	Query Element	Changeable Original
EVEN	Event Processing Chain	Not Changeable
ISIG	InfoPackage Group	Not Changeable

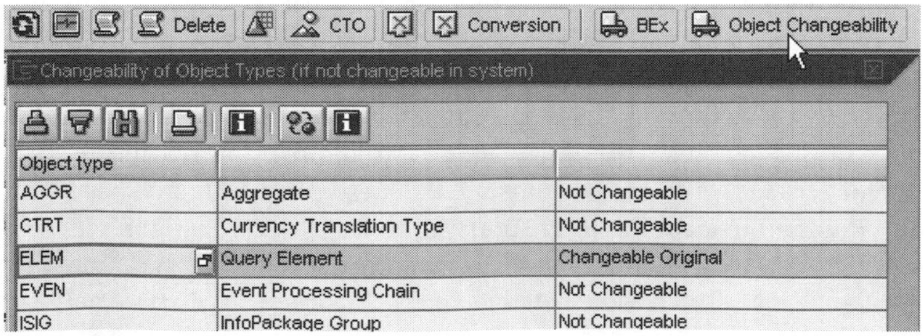

Figure 9.22 Object changeability.

Upgrades

Upgrades are changes to an SAP system that bring it to a new release or patch level. These upgrades typically introduce code, data changes, and new functionalities that must be applied in sequential fashion. Release upgrades are more involved then patch upgrades. To apply a release upgrade, typically a couple of days need to be scheduled to do the work.

In contrast, patch upgrades are much quicker and only require an hour or two of downtime. Patch upgrades typically consist of bug fixes (but can also introduce new functionality) that are packaged as independent units for application to a system. Technically, patches are nothing more than transport requests developed in SAP development systems and are applied much like how a transport is imported into a system, but via a special transaction (SPAM). Patches typically come out on a regular cycle of a month or two.

Upgrades are also similar to transports in that they must be applied following the same transport route of the system landscape. Any upgrade should first be performed on the development system, and after it has been tested, moved downstream to quality assurance and production. Upgrades to the SAP BW system and source system can be done in parallel, but you should study the release notes for the upgrade carefully before doing so.

There can be many independent levels to which an upgrade may be applied, and each level has dependencies on the other levels to be at a specified release and patch level. Figure 9.23 shows a sampling (not the inclusive list) of the different levels upgrades can apply to. With the exception of Business Content, all the different levels have separate release and patch cycles that must all be coordinated.

At the top of all levels we have the analytic applications such as supply chain analytics, customer relationship analytics, or SAP SEM, which interacts with Business Content, as covered in the previous chapter. Underlying Business Content is the SAP BW, which in turn sits on a core SAP system composed of a kernel and any cross-application components (such as the ADK, TMS, batch scheduling, etc.). A source system like SAP R/3 itself sits on the same core SAP system, but the application layer is different (and can actually be many different layers for different applications). To extract from this system, a plug-in must be added on to the source system (containing the BW Business Content DataSources).

There is another dimension to the coordination of different upgrade levels that are the front-end components. Deploying upgrades to front ends to a large, geographically dispersed organization is no small task. Matters are compounded when the front-end upgrades are add-ins to popular products like Excel, which may be different desktop-to-desktop (on different operating systems, on different releases, with different add-ins). Third-party solutions such as Citrix alleviate the problem by providing users a window to the server where the front end is installed. These products have been successful with deploying the Business Explorer Analyzer to large organizations.

However, the Web is changing all the rules. With the jump in reporting functionality, Web applications are a very attractive alternative to the Business Explorer Analyzer, especially from a deployment and upgrade perspective.

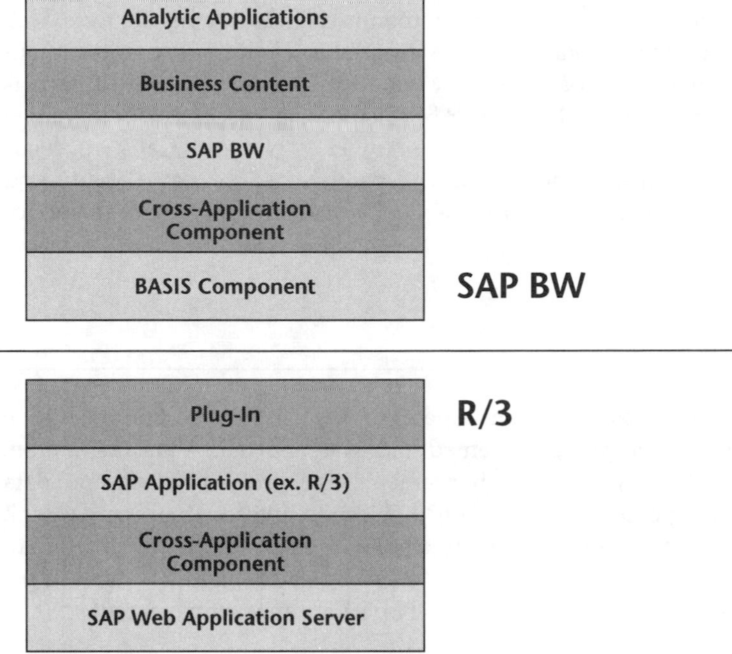

Figure 9.23 Different levels for upgrades.

Two types of patches can be applied to a system: a functionality patch and a stabilization patch. If the patch is a functionality patch, then our recommendation is to stay a patch behind. If the patch is a stabilization patch, then the patch only consists of notes to fix bugs and errors. These patches should be applied as the need warrants. SAP has an aggressive patch schedule, and your implementation should not fall too far behind in order to avoid the application of too many manual note corrections to the system and to avoid falling into the unfortunate circumstance of being on a patch level that is no longer supported.

In SAP BW, a conceptual distinction should be made between technical upgrades and functional upgrades. A technical upgrade of an SAP BW system does not change any of the preexisting information models in the system. A functional upgrade does so either by taking advantage of new functionalities or information modeling options or reactivating Business Content. Upgrading Business Content requires reactivation of the Business Content on the new BW release or patch level. When reactivating, you have the option of accepting changes per meta data object. More explicitly, you have the option to overwrite the existing objects with the new Business Content, keep the existing content, or merge the new changes to existing content (the last option is ideal when content has been custom-extended and you want to incorporate new Business Content). You should have a plan on how to adopt new Business Content and select options carefully in order to avoid losing work.

Information on new Business Content can be found in a variety of sources on the Web. If Business Content belongs to a vertical, then each industry has its own Web page where industry Business Content can be described. There is also application-specific Business Content that can be covered by application-specific Web sites, such as SAP SCM, SAP CRM, and SAP SEM. The SAP BW help portal has extensive coverage on Business Content, and occasionally SAP BW Know How Network Calls will focus on an area of Business Content. The release and patch schedules (availability and maintenance) as well as cross-compatibilities are well documented on the SAP Service Marketplace.

Summary

This chapter described the most important aspects of SAP BW-related administrative topics, categorizing them into process-oriented and system-oriented administration. SAP BW release 3.0 offers significant enhancements like process chains and data archiving (even including online-accessible ODS object archives in cooperation with FileTek), which extend the administration's functionality and ease the duties of SAP BW system administrators. Chapter 10 picks up on system administration with a specific focus on performance optimization, especially performance management.

Performance Planning and Management

Performance is one of the key success factors of every IT system. It requires careful planning and constant attention—even more so for data warehouse systems and reporting and analysis applications. In contrast to operational environments, data warehouse administrators are confronted with large or very large amounts of data that need to be handled, as well as a discontinuous, unpredictable user behavior.

For a data warehouse project to be successful, performance considerations have to be part of every single project phase from requirements analysis via design, implementation, and testing to deployment, and finally when administering and maintaining the deployed applications. This chapter looks at performance as a two-step process: planning and management.

Performance planning is part of the system development process and involves critical reviews of the information models chosen from a performance point of view; designing an appropriate information flow model and an appropriate system landscape; implementing efficient transformations; defining parallel, collision-free data load and data maintenance process chains; and, finally, managing user expectations. Performance planning lays the foundation for the overall system performance; correcting mistakes made in performance planning can be very expensive and may involve redesigning parts of the application. In particular, managing user expectations should not be underestimated; losing user acceptance because of insufficient performance—or performance just perceived as being insufficient—is easy. Winning the users back is a very cumbersome job.

Performance management is part of ongoing system administration and maintenance activities. Performance management involves constant monitoring of all processes and resources in the system and eventually tuning the system by defining aggregates; adjusting operating system, database management system, SAP Web application, or database server settings; adding or replacing SAP Web application servers; adding or replacing hardware; and so forth.

Much of performance planning and performance management centers on the trade-offs between space/flexibility/load time on the one hand and reporting time on the other (see Figure 10.1). The first trade-off is between time and space; spending more space on redundant storage of different aggregation levels of data, redundant storage of precalculated query sets, and additional indexes allows you to optimize reporting time by choosing the lowest-cost way to retrieve the desired result. Along with this trade-off is a second trade-off between load time and reporting time—the more redundant objects are created to optimize reporting performance, the more time is required to load data and maintain the redundant storage objects. A third-trade off is between flexibility (or functionality or user requirements) and reporting time, also shown in Figure 10.1, where functionality is sacrificed to improve reporting time.

Two types of performance optimizations are shown in Figure 10.1. The first one moves along the trade-off line, either sacrificing or saving space, load time, and flexibility for reporting time. The second one actually moves the trade-off itself closer to the optimum in the lower left corner of the diagram. Information modeling is the only performance optimization instrument that allows both types of optimizations: the first one by affecting flexibility and functionality, the second one by, for example, choosing an information model that allows for higher degrees of parallelization.

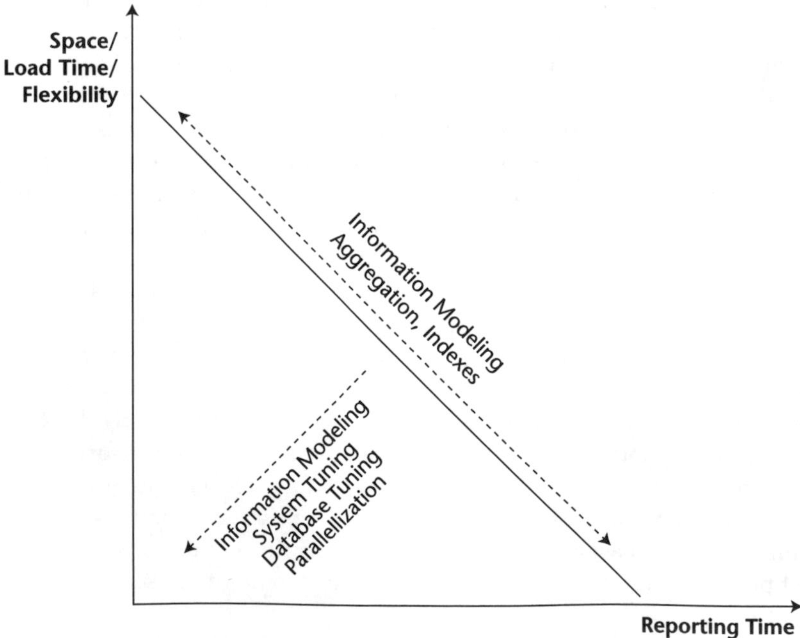

Figure 10.1 Performance trade-offs.

There is no silver bullet for performance optimization of data warehouse systems. Building a high-performance data warehouse application requires careful planning, monitoring, and optimization. Our goal here is to enable you to effectively plan for and manage performance. In the first half of this chapter, we lay out the options in planning for optimal performance, covering the impacts of information modeling and information flow modeling, as well as system landscape and process design. In the second half, we focus on the performance management process and the tools SAP BW offers in support of these processes.

Recommendations for configuring specific parts of your system are available from the SAP Service Marketplace (http://service.sap.com), from database vendors, and from hardware/system software vendors. These recommendations are highly dependent on your specific combination of hardware, operating system software, and database management software, and their respective versions or release levels, and therefore cannot be covered in this book.

Finally, we generally recommend having an experienced consultant support the performance planning and management activities.

Performance Planning

Planning for an optimal performance already starts in the early phases of a data warehouse project, the project planning and requirements analysis phases, where initial infrastructure decisions are prepared and user expectations and requirements are collected. Crucial project phases for performance planning are technical design and implementation, where an information model, transformation processes, and queries are designed and implemented. The testing and rollout phases finally yield valuable assumptions on user behavior and allow advance planning for redundant storage of aggregates.

The most important focus of performance planning is to make sure that all the things that are painful to change after going live with the system are designed properly, namely, the information model, the process design, and the system infrastructure. In addition, when conducting any performance planning, you should follow the following two general guidelines:

Only use what you need. Store everything you may need in the data warehouse layer; only store what you need for reporting now in the InfoMart layer.

Do as much as you can in parallel. Try to maximize the utilization of your system by planning for as high a degree of parallelization as possible.

Managing User Expectations

As a rule of thumb the user community of a data warehouse is composed of:

- Seventy-five percent occasional users who mainly execute queries customized to their needs
- Twenty-five percent frequent users who mainly execute existing parameterized queries and navigate through the query result set
- Five percent power users performing complex analysis tasks

While estimating the workload caused by occasional and frequent users is possible, it is much more difficult to estimate the workload caused by the power users who require more-advanced analysis functionality using a broader and more granular spectrum of data. Even worse, the 5 percent power users can easily produce much more than 50 percent of the overall system load.

To achieve a maximum of user acceptance for a data warehouse implementation, you should be sure to collect and assess user expectations about performance and identify gaps, then set expectations appropriately. Managing user expectations does not actually improve performance—it helps to close the potential gap between the user's performance expectations and what is achievable with a reasonable amount of money and time spent on the project.

Information Modeling

As in traditional software development, the biggest potential for performance improvement is buried in the early stages of the project: requirements analysis and design, ultimately resulting in an information model and an information flow model. The options of information modeling have already been discussed in detail in Chapter 4; this chapter picks up that discussion from a performance point of view. Information modeling involves modeling three layers of the corporate information factory using several types of InfoProviders. This section, however, focuses on the performance impacts of modeling options for the different types of InfoProviders: InfoCubes, ODS objects, master data, MultiProviders, and remote InfoCubes.

As with most standard software, there's not much to optimize in terms of the data model. There's no way to actually change the data model SAP BW uses to store InfoCubes, ODS objects, and master data. Using the right objects and techniques for your requirements from those available within SAP BW and setting these objects up correctly still has a huge impact on your system performance.

InfoCube Modeling

InfoCubes are still the most important InfoProviders in SAP BW for reporting and analysis. Much of this whole section is therefore dedicated to evaluating the different modeling options for InfoCubes from a reporting performance point of view, neglecting load performance considerations to some extent.

How Does SAP BW Execute Queries?

To fully understand the pros and cons of the different InfoCube modeling options available, we'll look more closely at how SAP BW actually executes queries. The following pseudocode illustrates this from a 10,000-feet perspective. Note that the purpose of this code is to illustrate the process rather than describing the actual programs, which obviously are much more sophisticated:

```
*** STEP 1 - Prepare query execution
Convert selections into surrogate key representation.
```

```
Generate optimized temporary hierarchy table.

*** STEP 2 - Prepare query execution
Generate query view
Open query cursor

*** STEP 3 - Execute query
Loop at cursor.
  Execute user exit for virtual characteristics / key figures.
  Apply dynamic filters.
Endloop.

*** STEP 4 - Complete query result
Read key values, texts, display attributes, hierarchies.
Format query results.
```

The first step of query execution converts selection criteria specified in the query definition into the surrogate key format. For restrictions on characteristic values, this basically means determining the surrogate keys for all key values used in the selection. In case of selections on hierarchies, SAP BW generates a temporary table containing the surrogate key values for all relevant nodes of the hierarchy.

Step 2 generates an SQL statement used to create a temporary database view, which is then used to open an SQL cursor for the required result set. In Figure 10.2, #1 shows the access path of such a generated SQL statement for a simple query not using any hierarchies or navigational attributes.

A standard SAP BW query execution effectively generates and executes a join of the dimension tables required (through characteristics used in the query definition) to a union of the two fact tables. Keep in mind that (1) no nonessential dimension table is used in the join and (2) no surrogate key table is used at this time, as illustrated in #1 of Figure 10.2. The generated SQL query returns surrogate key values for all characteristics and (usually) aggregated values for all key figures used in the query definition.

The third step reads the data set retrieved for the open cursor and applies user exits and dynamic filters (such as conditions and exceptions) to each data record.

Step 4 completes query execution by reading texts, display attributes, and hierarchies from the respective tables using the surrogate key values retrieved in Step 3 and formats the output accordingly.

Use of Line-Item Dimensions

The SAP BW concept of line-item dimensions corresponds to what is known to the data warehouse community as *degenerate dimensions*—dimensions with a cardinality that is close to the cardinality of the actual fact table. Data warehouse developers developed various ideas of how to effectively support line-item dimensions. The SAP BW implementation allows flagging dimensions with exactly one characteristic assigned as a line-item dimension. Instead of generating a dimension table holding the surrogate keys of the characteristics of that dimension, the surrogate key of the single characteristic is directly stored in the fact table.

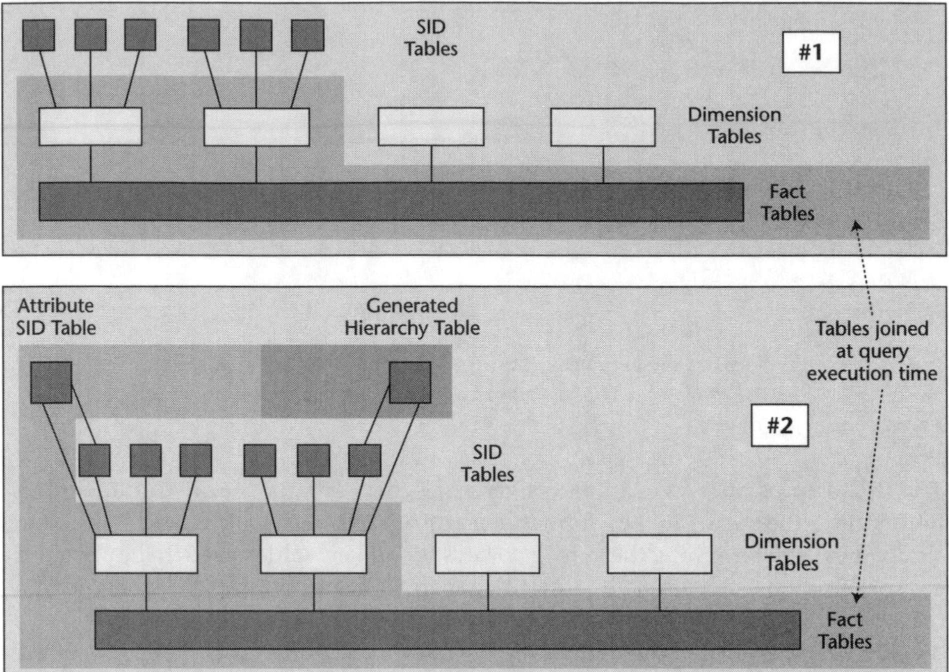

Figure 10.2 Query access paths.

Line-item dimensions are an effective means to speed up both loading data and executing queries. Data load performance is improved by saving the maintenance effort for an additional dimension table; on the query execution side, joining an additional dimension table to the fact tables is saved. SAP only recommends using line-item dimensions for very large dimensions (as typically found in line-item-level data, hence the name). However, we have successfully used line-item dimensions for applications with large numbers of customers and large numbers of products or product variants.

As we will see later, the same concept of storing surrogate keys in the fact table is used in maintaining special types of aggregates (flat aggregates). The only drawback of line-item dimensions is that a dimension that could potentially store more than 250 characteristics is effectively used for just one characteristic.

NOTE SAP BW 3.0 provides an additional option for large dimensions: Flagging a dimension as being a high-cardinality dimension allows for database-specific optimizations—for instance, of the index type used for the dimension key indexes on the fact tables by SAP BW.

Use of Navigational Attributes

Navigational attributes are special because they are not stored in the dimension tables but in the attribute tables of a characteristic used in the InfoCube definition (e.g., *material group* is an attribute of *material* and is stored in the material master data tables). These attributes have to be marked as navigational attributes in the InfoObject definition dialogs in order to make them available for reporting. Setting this flag for at least one attribute causes SAP BW to create one of the navigational attribute SID tables discussed in Chapter 4 and to store the surrogate key values for this attribute in this table. Note that SIDs of navigational attributes are not stored in any of the InfoCube tables. This is why changing the value of a navigational attribute does not require any realignment of the InfoCube. It may, however, require realignment of an aggregate containing the navigational attribute.

The access path of a generated SQL query for this scenario is shown in Figure 10.2, #2. The navigational attribute SID table is joined to the dimension table (e.g., *product* dimension) that contains the anchor characteristic (*material*), which itself is joined to the fact tables. Adding a navigational attribute to a query definition adds another dimension table to the join, if the dimension table is not already included.

The degradation of reporting performance corresponds to the cardinality of the master data attribute tables involved, the number of navigational attributes used in the query, and of course, the selectivity of the query. The smaller the cardinality, the lower the number of navigational attributes, and the higher the selectivity of the query, the better the performance will be. Although evaluating navigational attributes is more expensive than evaluating characteristics of an InfoCube, we do recommend using navigational attributes where required or where it makes sense (see Chapter 4 for a discussion of historical versus current truth). Possible performance problems can be addressed by defining appropriate aggregates (discussed later in the chapter—at the cost of having to maintain that extra aggregate.

NOTE **Defining additional indexes on the navigational attribute SID tables improves performance in cases where medium- to high-cardinality tables are read with high selectivity.**

While navigational attributes by no means affect data load performance for InfoCube data loads, they definitely add some overhead to the master data load process, which now needs to maintain one or two additional tables. This may significantly decrease data load and data maintenance performance in application scenarios like CRM, where many navigational attributes are required to perform complex analysis on millions of customer master data records.

Use of Hierarchies

The use of hierarchies leads to similar query access paths as using navigational attributes does. This is shown in Figure 10.2, #2, where an additional, generated hierarchy table is joined to the fact table. While the core query access plan is similar, two additional activities are required in the overall query execution process to retrieve the query results.

The first activity is listed in Step 1 of our high-level algorithm: On the fly it creates a temporary hierarchy table holding all hierarchy nodes selected by the filter associated to the query by reading the hierarchy, applying the selections to the hierarchy, and storing the remaining nodes in the temporary tables. The time required, of course, depends on the size of the hierarchy and on the complexity of the selection criteria defined. The second activity is part of Step 4 of our sample algorithm—the query results need to be rehashed according to the actual structure of the hierarchy.

From a performance point of view, everything depends on the number of nodes in the hierarchy and the number of levels of the hierarchy. The more nodes and levels, the more time it takes to compute the query results. In general, using hierarchies is more performance-critical than using navigational attributes.

Hierarchies do not affect load performance for InfoCubes or master data. Of course, it takes some time to load hierarchies into the system.

Use of Virtual Characteristics and Key Figures

Virtual characteristics and key figures allow you to replace stored values of characteristics and key figures with dynamically calculated values. Looking back at our query execution algorithm, we see that this functionality must be used with extreme care from a performance point of view, as the corresponding user exit is executed for every single line of data retrieved from the InfoCube. Using virtual characteristics and key figures may force the OLAP engine to implicitly add additional characteristics to the query, increasing the size of the result if these characteristics increase the granularity of the query.

ODS Object Modeling

There are not too many options in modeling ODS objects from a performance point of view. As already discussed in Chapter 4, ODS objects basically are collections of three similarly structured flat tables with key fields and data fields, allowing you to keep track of changes in a so-called change log, as shown in Figure 10.3.

The data model used to store ODS objects in SAP BW has experienced some internal changes in release 3.0, making life easier from a performance point of view. SAP BW now fully supports parallelized data loads and data activation steps. Change logs now are an effective means to determine changes in data sources not capable of providing delta extraction.

Apart from trivial discussions about the number of key and data fields affecting the performance of data loads and reporting and analysis, there's one option in modeling ODS objects that should be mentioned in a performance context: Enabling BEx Reporting for ODS objects causes the Staging Engine to compute and store surrogate keys for the fields of the ODS object and effectively slows down the data load process. This option should only be used where BEx reporting on ODS objects is required. Reporting on ODS objects using InfoSets will still be possible without enabling this option, although with slightly lower reporting performance.

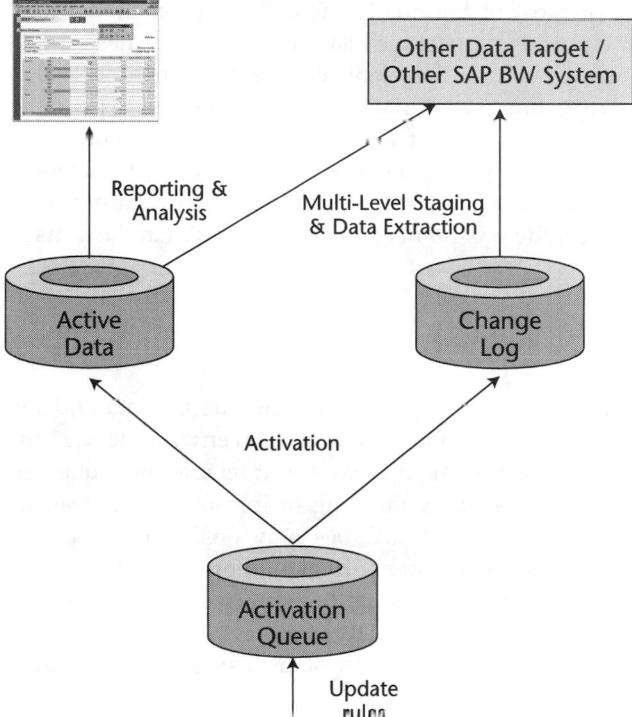

Figure 10.3 ODS object.

Master Data Modeling

The most important performance aspects of master data modeling are related to time dependency and the navigational status of attributes. The impact of navigational attributes has already been discussed in the section on InfoCubes. Time-dependent master data attributes, texts, and hierarchies should be used with care. Time-dependent master data tables can easily explode, as every change of a single time-dependent attribute creates another record in the time-dependent master data tables.

The introduction of time-dependent aggregates (see *Aggregates* coming up in this chapter) has eased the pain a bit. Still, you should make sure to estimate the expected number of changes in advance before deciding to flag a particular attribute, the texts, or a particular hierarchy as being time-dependent, and you should make certain it is required to be time-dependent. An average change rate of 10 changes per year brings a customer master data table from 1 million records to 10 million records per year. Also, consider bringing down the update frequency and the granularity required for validity periods down to minimum: If those average 10 changes per year all occur in, say, 3 months and the granularity of the validity period is 1 month, the system only needs to store 3 different records instead of 10.

For some applications, many or most of the queries actually request the current value of an attribute, while only a portion request the historical values. In these cases, including the same attribute twice—as a time-dependent and as a non-time-dependent attribute—may help speed up reporting performance of the non-time-dependent attributes. This approach avoids time-dependent aggregates and allows non-time-dependent queries to access the smaller non-time-dependent master data tables. However, all these considerations only apply to large master data tables and master data tables with a high update frequency; there is no need to worry about standard cases here.

Remote Cubes

Remote InfoCubes are used to avoid redundant storage of operational data and for providing real-time access to information stored in the operational environment. From a load performance point of view, there is not much to say about remote InfoCubes, as remote InfoCubes are virtual InfoCubes actually pointing to information instead of physically copying it. However, using remote InfoCubes may positively affect the overall system performance by reducing the number of data load processes required.

From a reporting performance point of view, remote InfoCubes usually can't provide the same performance as locally stored objects for two main reasons. First, queries against remote InfoCubes are executed on the source system, using data structures optimized for transaction processing instead of reporting.

Second, SAP remote InfoCubes are calling the data extraction programs available through the BW Service API. Most of these extractors are not capable of performing dynamic aggregations according to the query definition. Granular data is sent from the source system to the requesting SAP BW system, and aggregation is performed there as part of the query processing. Remote InfoCubes should be used with care wherever real-time access to operational data is required. Queries against remote InfoCubes should be highly selective to avoid long run times.

MultiProviders

MultiProviders define a dynamic union of InfoProviders such as InfoCubes, ODS objects, master data tables, or InfoSets. The first step in executing a query against a MultiProvider is to decompose the query into queries against the underlying InfoProviders. The second step executes the resulting queries in parallel. The final step computes the union of all query results. The beauty of MultiProviders is that parallel execution of the decomposed query helps to improve reporting performance by better utilizing available system resources—at the cost of additional overhead required for decomposing queries and computing the union of the query results. The ugliness is that this only works out if there actually are sufficient system resources for parallel execution. Executing queries against MultiProviders in highly utilized systems adds additional load.

NOTE **MultiProviders do not require additional storage; they just define a view across multiple InfoProviders.**

The impact of using MultiProviders on data load performance is negligible. However, performance of data maintenance functions such as aggregate rollups and InfoCube compression is improved by splitting the overall data volume into several manageable pieces. (These considerations, of course, are only relevant for very large data volumes.) Although it is not possible to define aggregates for MultiProviders directly, aggregates defined for the participating InfoCubes are utilized wherever possible.

There are two typical applications for MultiProviders in information modeling: partitioning and cross-application information models, shown in Figure 10.4. For the sake of our example, Figure 10.4 only shows MultiProviders defined using InfoCubes.

While SAP BW allows using database partitioning features for time characteristics, partitioning on other characteristics values, such as organizational characteristics, can only be achieved by defining several basic InfoCubes—one for each value or range of values defining a certain partition—and a MultiProvider combining the partitions. The left-hand side of Figure 10.4 shows an information model using regional partitioning. A side effect of characteristics-value-based partitioning is an increased degree of freedom regarding the local information models; InfoProviders participating in a MultiProvider don't need to be identical. The sales InfoCube for Europe might provide slightly different information compared to the U.S. sales InfoCube, as long as it provides all information required for the MultiProvider. A drawback of this approach is that there are multiple sets of update rules to be maintained, one for each participating InfoProvider.

The right-hand side of Figure 10.4 shows a cross-application information model using MultiProviders that can be used instead of defining a single large InfoCube storing the same information. Again, the same performance considerations discussed previously apply in addition to achieving an easier-to-understand and easier-to-use information model.

Database Partitioning

Database partitioning is not actually something that belongs to information modeling; it is transparent to the application. It does, however, belong to performance planning, as a decision for or against database partitioning cannot easily be revoked once large volumes of data have been loaded into an InfoCube. Changing this setting in a productive system requires deleting the contents of the InfoCube, adjusting the setting, reactivating the InfoCube, and finally reloading the InfoCube with data.

The basic idea behind database partitioning is to split a physical table and its indexes into several smaller physical tables and indexes. Database partitioning is handled by the database management systems and is completely transparent to the applications using the database.

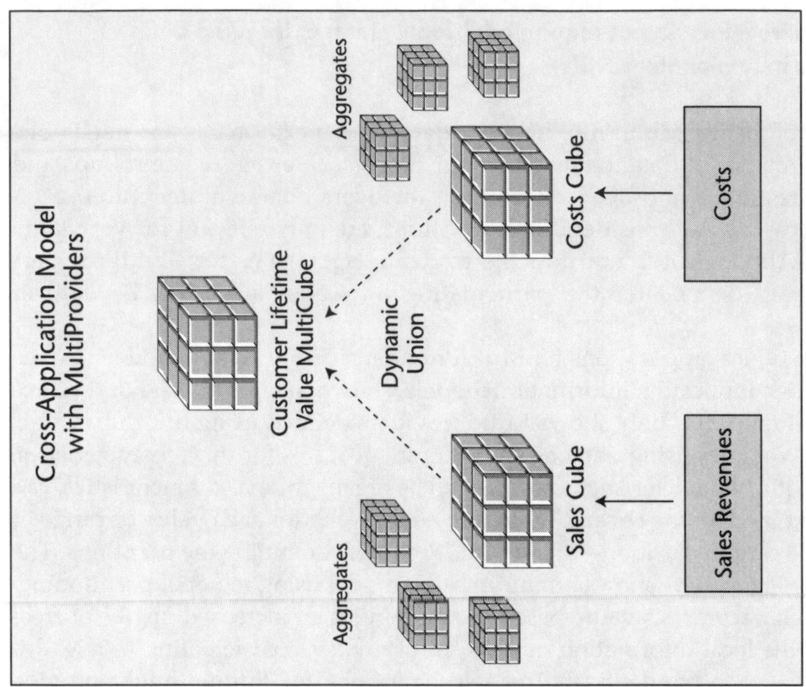

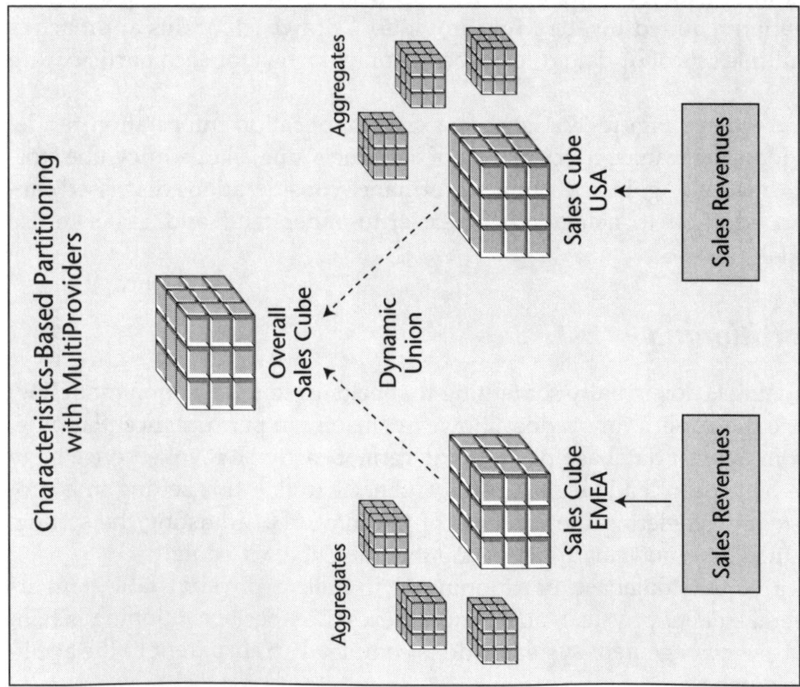

Figure 10.4 Use of MultiProviders.

Different partitioning techniques such as range partitioning and hash partitioning are offered by different database management systems. SAP BW supports partitioning techniques for InfoCubes, ODS objects, and the persistent staging area. Figure 10.5 shows a partitioned sales InfoCube. The main advantages of partitioning from an SAP point of view database partitioning are:

Faster updates. Mass updates on single or several smaller partitions run faster than updates on one single large table, mainly because of reduced effort for index maintenance. Another positive effect on performance can be achieved by parallelizing mass updates on partitioned tables.

Parallel query execution. Read access to partitioned tables can be executed in parallel in the same way as updates and similar to how SAP BW processes queries against MultiProviders.

Selective reads. Data warehouse queries commonly include some time characteristic in their selection criteria. Figure 10.5 shows an InfoCube range partitioned by calendar month and a query requesting information about the last 3 months of 2002 using range partitioning. Whenever the partitioning criterion is part of the filters of the query, the DBMS recognizes that it only has to read a subset of the partitions. In Figure 10.5 the DBMS only reads 3 out of 24 partitions. Depending on the application, selective reads may dramatically speed up query execution time. Note that this read strategy is only available for database management systems that support range partitioning.

Faster deletes. For deleting a contiguous range of data, tables partitioned using range partitioning allow using the `DROP PARTITION` statement whenever the partitioning criteria is contained in the selection criteria for the delete operation, instead of having to use the `DELETE FROM` statement. Again, this option is only available for database management systems that support range partitioning.

NOTE **There are cases where the query does not specify the actual partitioning criterion (e.g., month) but instead specifies a filter on some other time characteristic (e.g., quarter or day). Normally this would prevent the DBMS from performing selective reads. However, adding redundant filters on the partitioning criterion will allow the DBMS to perform selective reads. Partitioning criteria are also used for storing aggregate fact tables, if the partitioning criterion (e.g., calendar month or fiscal year period) is included in the aggregate definition.**

Database partitioning may already make sense for relatively low data volumes (e.g., a couple million records). However, the more partitions the database system creates, the higher the overhead for decomposing, executing, dispatching, and merging query results. We generally recommend using calendar month or fiscal year period as partitioning criteria.

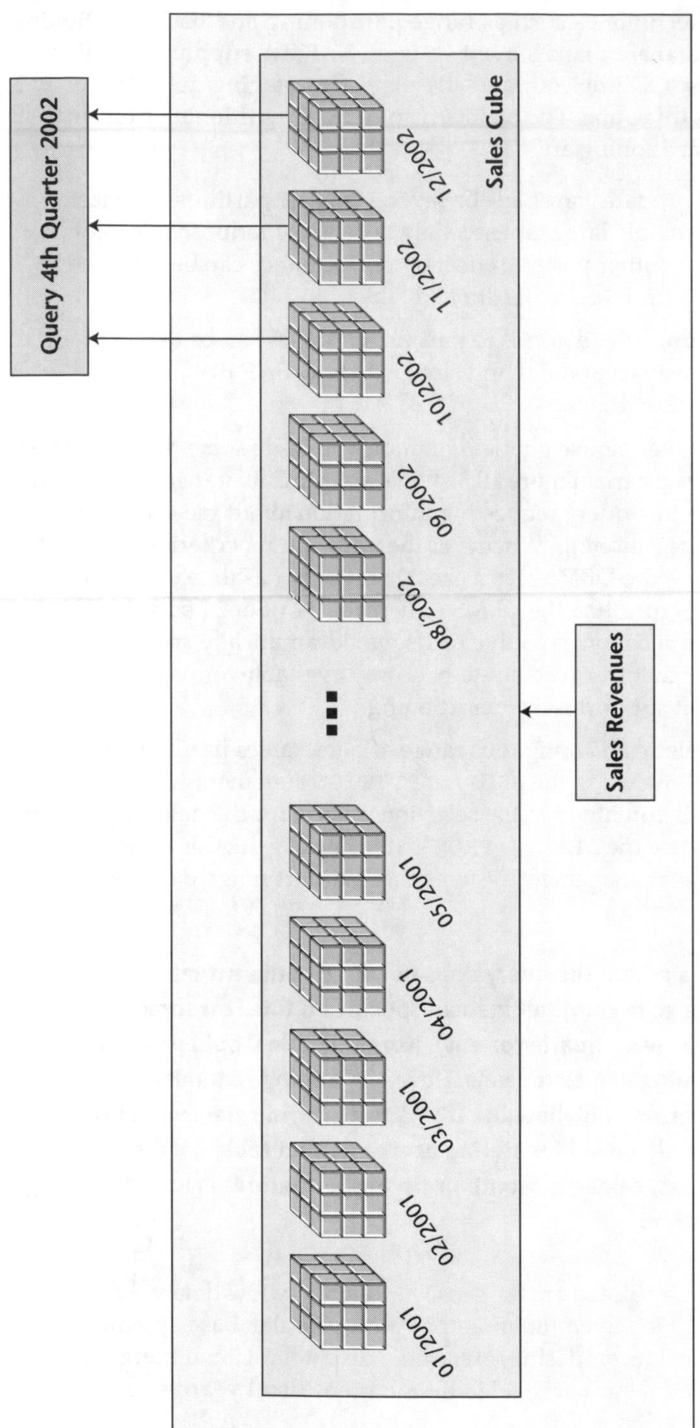

Figure 10.5 Database range partitioning.

Complex Aggregations

Where aggregates clearly provide the advantage of being completely transparent to the end user, the aggregation functions available are restricted to summation, maximum, and minimum. Additional aggregation functions (such as average, counting, deviation, and variance) are available under certain restrictions, but more complex aggregation functions are required in many applications, such as balanced scorecards. The definitions of high-level key performance indicators (KPIs) such as *customer lifetime value* and *return on investment* are based on multiple low-level key figures sourced from different applications using different aggregations paths.

High-level KPIs typically require cross-application information models like those shown in the text that follows. The dynamic aggregation variant stores data in two InfoProviders and merges those in a single MultiProvider, while the static aggregation variant stores precalculated values on a higher aggregation level in a single basic InfoCube. Figure 10.6 illustrates both variants of implementing aggregations.

Static aggregation allows more complex, aggregated key figures to be calculated at load time, reducing the time required for online calculations at query run time. Dynamic aggregation is more flexible because of a higher level of granularity in the basic InfoCubes, but it requires all (or most) calculations and aggregations to be executed online. Of course, all considerations of cross-application information models mentioned previously still apply here.

Multiple Staging Levels

Multiple staging levels are an integral part of today's data warehouse solutions. As our discussion of the corporate information factory in Chapters 3 and 4 showed, implementation of a data warehouse layer is highly recommended in large heterogeneous IT environments. An important reason for adding additional staging levels above the data warehouse layer are complex application-level transformations, requiring intermediate storage of data in a specific format.

At the first glance, an improvement of the data load performance is not expected after adding additional staging levels. However, if we take a step back and look at the whole picture, we see that adding additional staging layers may actually improve the performance of the overall load process, as the comparison of single- and multilevel staging approaches in Figure 10.7 shows.

Surprisingly, SAP BW transfer and update rules are very CPU-intensive processes. In fact, most of the time is spent processing the data rather than reading or writing it. The more complex the transformation rules are that must be applied for each of the data targets individually, the more effective a multilevel staging approach can be. The key here is applying complex or expensive transformation rules (such as database lookups) only once before writing into the first staging level and only leaving simple transformations for the second staging level. As a side effect, the multilevel staging approach easily allows more flexible scheduling of the individual transformation processes. Some InfoProviders may need to be updated daily or even more frequently, while others are updated on a monthly basis, although all are using the same data sources.

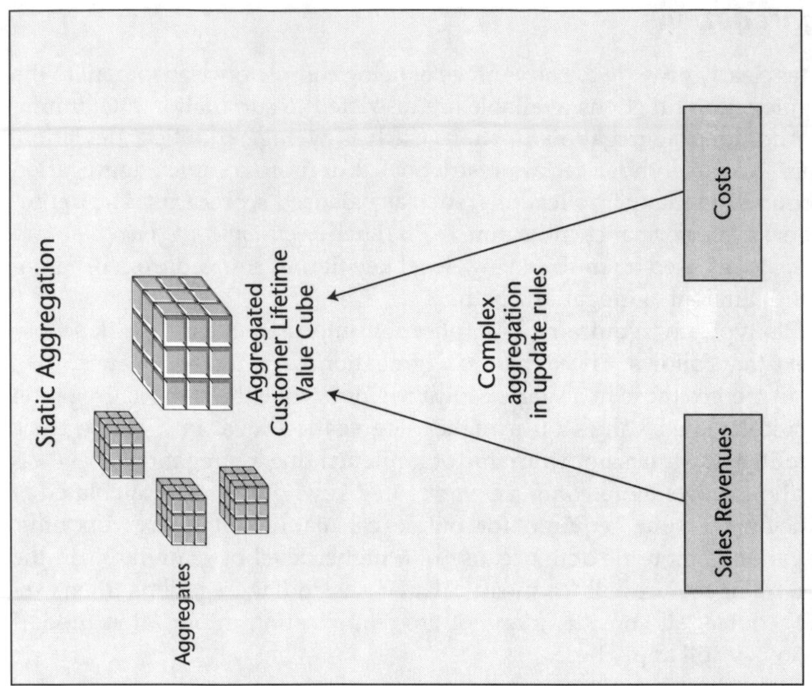

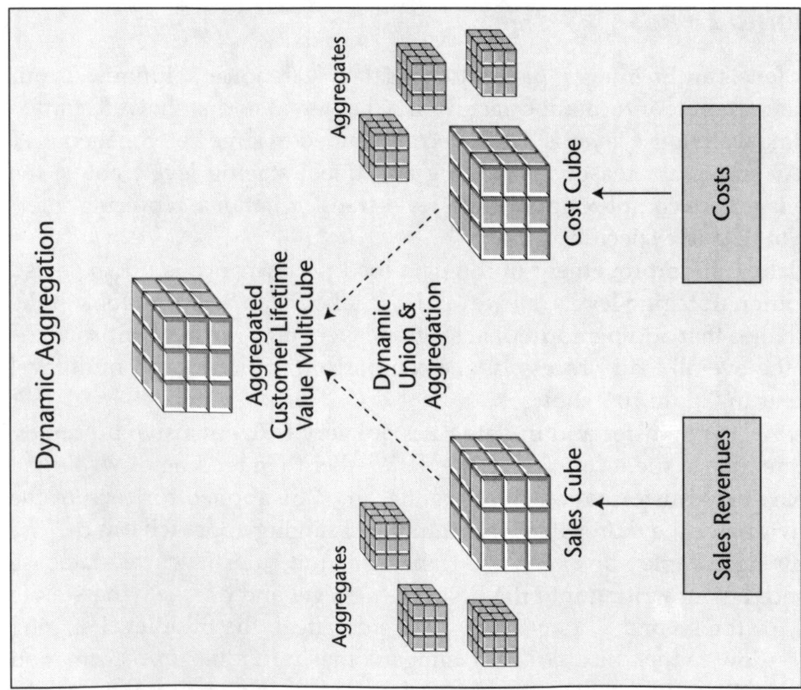

Figure 10.6 Dynamic versus static aggregation.

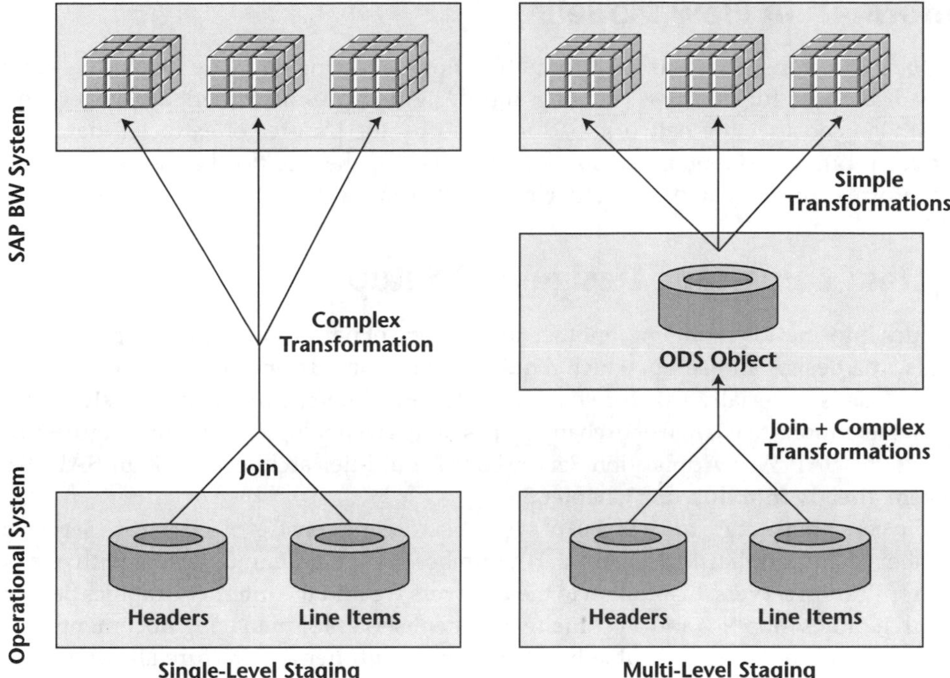

Figure 10.7 Multilevel staging performance.

Reporting performance is usually not affected by the number of staging levels. Reporting users and analysts usually just access the highest level. Multilevel staging may, however, enable you to choose a less granular information model, thereby reducing the size of the InfoProviders used for reporting purposes and letting the users access the data warehouse level for integrated, granular data where necessary. This way, multilevel staging may indirectly help improve reporting performance.

Staging data into the operational data store (ODS) layer is not discussed in this context, as the ODS layer is typically used for operational reporting purposes rather than as a source for the staging process. However, if used in such a way, the same considerations apply for the ODS layer as well.

In summary, there are situations where multiple staging levels actually help to improve both load and reporting performance. Overall, however, in most situations, single staging level approaches provide a better data load performance without affecting reporting performance.

Information Flow Modeling

Performance considerations for information flow modeling basically follow the same thread as those for multilevel staging and designing MultiProviders. However, you must also consider the network load imposed by the transfer of extracted data sets between source and target systems and, of course, by the workload of users accessing the information. We elaborate on this in the following section.

System Landscape Design and Setup

Besides information modeling, another cornerstone of performance planning is system landscape design and setup, which requires a basic understanding of the technology used. This is especially true for standard software, where, compared to custom systems, the options to change or exchange parts of this technology are limited. Figure 10.8 shows the SAP Web Application Server-based multi-tier architecture of an SAP BW system already introduced in Chapter 3.

The core architecture of an SAP BW system landscape consists of a database server, a number of Web application servers, and a number of clients communicating with one of the application servers. In addition to these servers we find the Internet Graphics Server, which handles graphics and, eventually, a content server for managing documents.

In addition to today's scalable hardware, this multi-tier architecture allows you to scale the system landscape flexibly by adding application servers, Internet graphics servers, and content servers. Nevertheless, starting an SAP BW implementation requires planning the system landscape; sizing the database, application, content, and Internet graphics servers; estimating network bandwidth requirements; and making sure the front-end systems match the system requirements.

SAP provides detailed information on how to size, install, configure, and monitor all these different systems in their service marketplace, updating this information on a regular basis. Rather than merely restate that material, in the next sections we'll instead provide a basic understanding of the performance-relevant aspects of the functionality of these different components of an SAP BW system landscape.

Database and Web Application Servers

The most performance-critical part of the multi-tier architecture obviously is the database server, which needs to be capable of handling all database requests from all application servers—and, in turn, all clients. At this writing, only the IBM DB2 UDB EEE database management software supported a (limited) distributed database server approach, where several physical servers are managed as one single logical database server, allowing you to physically distribute fact tables. The database server bottleneck is abridged to some extent by buffering frequently used data in main memory on the Web application server. However, most SAP BW requests for data from fact tables finally have to be executed on the database server.

Application server performance can easily be scaled up or down by adding or removing Web application servers from the system landscape. Dynamic load balancing features allow you to avoid bottlenecks with specific Web application servers by managing the distribution of the overall workload. Users log on to server groups instead of single Web application servers. Operation modes of application servers can automatically be switched between, for example, batch and user oriented setups, allowing you to reduce the number of online users (and thus the workload) while extraction and staging processes are running.

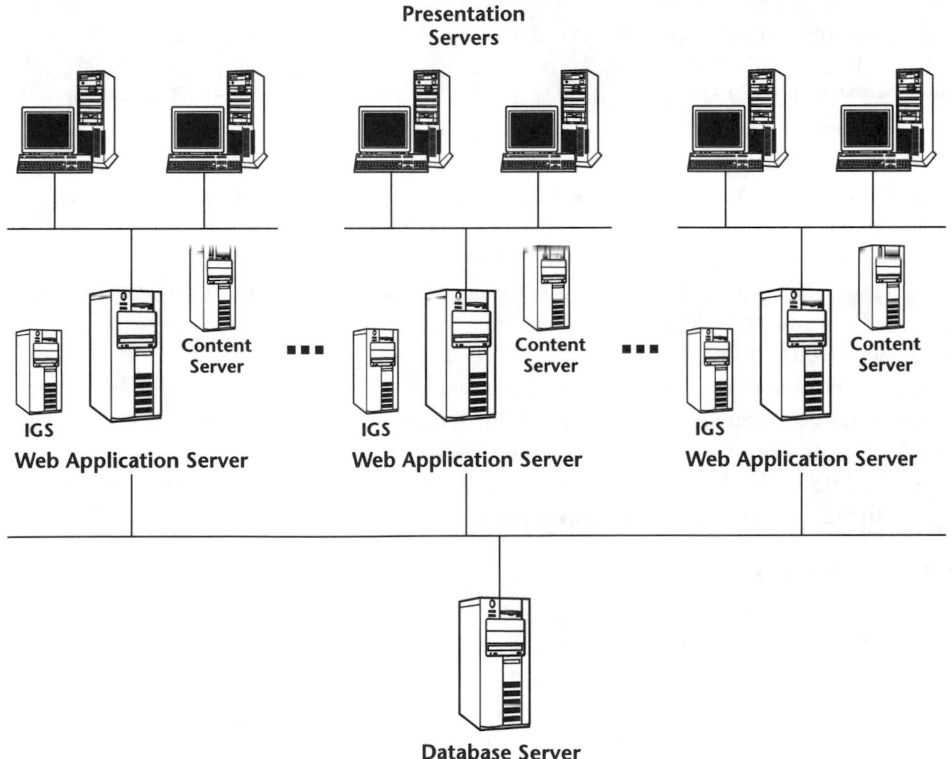

Figure 10.8 SAP multi-tier architecture.

Sizing the database server is the most critical part of the system landscape planning process. Experience shows that it is actually very difficult to precisely estimate the required configuration for an SAP BW system (or for any data warehouse system for that matter). A good estimate requires reliable information about a number of parameters, such as the number of users, the amount of disk space required, and a reliable forecast of the actual user behavior. While the user behavior may be relatively easy to predict for standard application scenarios (e.g., the sales controlling department checking the results of last month at the beginning of a new month), it is virtually unpredictable for ad hoc analysis that is typically initiated by some business issue needing to be resolved.

Another issue in sizing an SAP BW system is that a successful implementation drags a lot of interest of other business areas. A live system will most likely be extended to new applications very quickly, so scalability of the hardware and system architecture—especially for the database server—is crucial in system landscape planning. SAP BW actually scales fairly linearly with the amount of main memory used for buffering by both the database server and the application server, with the number and speed of the CPUs available in both types of servers, and finally with IO throughput.

A rough orientation of sizing can be gained using the t-shirt sizing approach published by SAP. A good starting point for a more accurate sizing of an SAP BW system is the QuickSizer tool for SAP BW. Both are available from the SAP Service Marketplace. As sizing also depends on the specifics of the hardware chosen, consulting your preferred hardware vendor to help with sizing large data warehouse applications is mandatory.

Concrete recommendations for a specific setup of the different components of an SAP BW system landscape are beyond the scope of this book. SAP supports many combinations of different hardware architectures, system software, and database management and continuously develops the configuration options of its own software. We recommend following the information offered in the SAP Service Marketplace (and, eventually, corresponding offerings of the vendors of hardware, system software, and database management software) when setting up the system. Periodically monitoring changes to this information and adjusting the systems accordingly helps ensure optimal performance. The next sections provide high-level, still useful information for setting up the database and application servers.

Operation Modes

As discussed previously, SAP BW systems are scaling very well with the number of CPUs. While determining the required number of CPUs is part of the sizing process, administrators must make sure that CPUs can actually be utilized by defining how many processes of what type are available at a specific point in time. The SAP Web Application Server distinguishes six types of processes:

Dialog processes (type *DIA*). These are used for processing dialog programs, such as the Administrator Workbench, the SAP BW Monitor, online analysis and reporting requests and data load processes submitted online.

Batch processes (type *BTC*). These are required for any kind of process submitted for batch processing. Typical batch processes are data load processes, aggregate rollups and InfoCube compression.

Update processes (type *UPD* and *UP2*). Used for asynchronous updates (V1 and V2 updates, as described in Chapter 6), this type of process is not used by SAP BW; still at least one process needs to be available for technical reasons.

Enqueue processes (type *ENQ*). These are used for locking and unlocking objects; one process of this type will usually be sufficient.

Spool processes (type *SPO*). These execute print requests. As most reports are usually printed from the client workstation SAP BW only requires a small number of spool processes (in many cases one single process will be enough).

The so-called operation mode of an SAP system defines how many processes of what type are available. Different operation modes can be defined by the administrator and can be selected at run time, allowing you to optimize the distribution of process types for specific needs.

Consider a scenario where 20 independent load processes must be executed on an 8 CPU machine every night. Assume the system provides 4 batch processes and 12 dialog processes in its dialog operation mode. While this setup allows 12 online queries to be run simultaneously, it only allows for 4 parallel load processes, effectively leaving 4 CPUs unused at night. Changing the operation mode to a distribution with at least 8 batch processes allows fully utilizing all 8 CPUs available in the system for running the data load jobs and will cut the total run time of all data loads in nearly half.

Buffers and Memory

Buffering data and programs is key to the performance of both database and the application servers. A general recommendation is to have as much main memory available as possible (and reasonable) and to use as much as possible for various buffers. Configuration recommendations for both types of servers are available in the SAP Service Marketplace.

The most important buffers on SAP Web Application Server are the table buffers used to reduce the number of database accesses by buffering data on an application level. Two types of table buffers are available: a single record buffer and a generic key buffer. Both types are used by SAP BW. The single record buffer is used to buffer all access operations to master data tables except for the hierarchy table (e.g., /BI0/HMATERIAL). The hierarchy table is buffered in the generic key buffer using the hierarchy identifier and the version as the generic key, effectively buffering a complete hierarchy. Buffering master data speeds up the retrieval of master data in reporting and analysis, as well as looking up surrogate keys during the loading process. SAP BW does not buffer any InfoCube, ODS object, or PSA tables. These are mostly used in complex database joins where the SAP Web Application buffers are not applicable.

Another buffer relevant for load performance is the number range buffer, which is used to identify available surrogate keys from the number range table NRIV. In addition, a couple of buffers are used by the application server. However, the effect of these buffers on the overall SAP BW performance is small compared to the table buffers. Monitoring the utilization of buffers is discussed later in this chapter.

General Database Setup

Having discussed buffering on the application server side, there's no need to discuss how buffering on the database management system side has a serious impact on the overall system performance. Additional configuration considerations include optimizer settings (such as star schema awareness), parallelization, and distributed data access.

Every SQL statement executed by the database management is optimized by a component usually referred to as the optimizer. To find the most efficient way of executing the statement, the optimizer needs statistical information about the actual field values of records stored in the database and about the structure of the database. Statistical information (the so-called database statistics) is used to estimate the cost of a specific database operation and the total cost of different possible ways of executing a specific SQL statement. Information about the database structure allows the database management system to take the specifics of the star schema data model into account.

Modern database management systems allow you to execute data retrieval and manipulation operations in parallel, fully utilizing as many CPUs and IO channels as possible. Some database management systems also allow you to distribute data to several physical servers, utilizing even more resources.

Physical Distribution of Data

A performance planning option frequently missed is the physical distribution of data on disk drives. Disk drives and IO channels have certain limits regarding access time and bandwidth. Simple automatic or manual distribution of data files in addition to RAID (redundant array of independent disks) techniques such as mirroring and striping allow you to get the most out of the disk storage subsystem. The main idea again is to parallelize data access as much as possible.

NOTE Depending on the operating system, database management system, and storage subsystem, some system configurations do not allow you to manually define the physical distribution of data.

Looking at the data models used by SAP BW and at how database management systems usually work, we can identify six different clusters of data:

- InfoCube and ODS object data, stored in fact tables, dimension tables, and ODS object tables
- InfoCube and ODS object indexes
- Master data, stored in attribute, text, and hierarchy tables
- Temporary data, internally used by the database management system for sorting purposes
- Database transaction logs, internally used by the database management to allow rolling back or reprocessing transactions
- System data, such as configuration data, customization data, SAP BW meta data, program source code, and application logs

The first step in performance planning is to make sure that clusters of data used simultaneously are not stored on the same physical device. Without going into detail, the most important thing to keep in mind is to keep clusters 1-2, 3, and 4 separate from each other. Executing a generated SQL query for reporting, analysis, or aggregation requires the database management system to read from InfoCube or ODS object tables and read or write temporary data for sorting purposes. Loading data, compressing InfoCubes, or creating indexes requires writing to InfoCube, ODS object, and master data tables and to the transaction log. As master data tables are relatively small compared to fact tables and mostly used separately (refer to the query execution algorithm described in the *InfoCube Modeling* section at the beginning of the chapter), keeping these separate does not have a major performance impact. The result of this first step is shown in Figure 10.9. Note that large and frequently accessed InfoCube and ODS object tables should also be kept separate. Figure 10.9 illustrates this with the first two clusters.

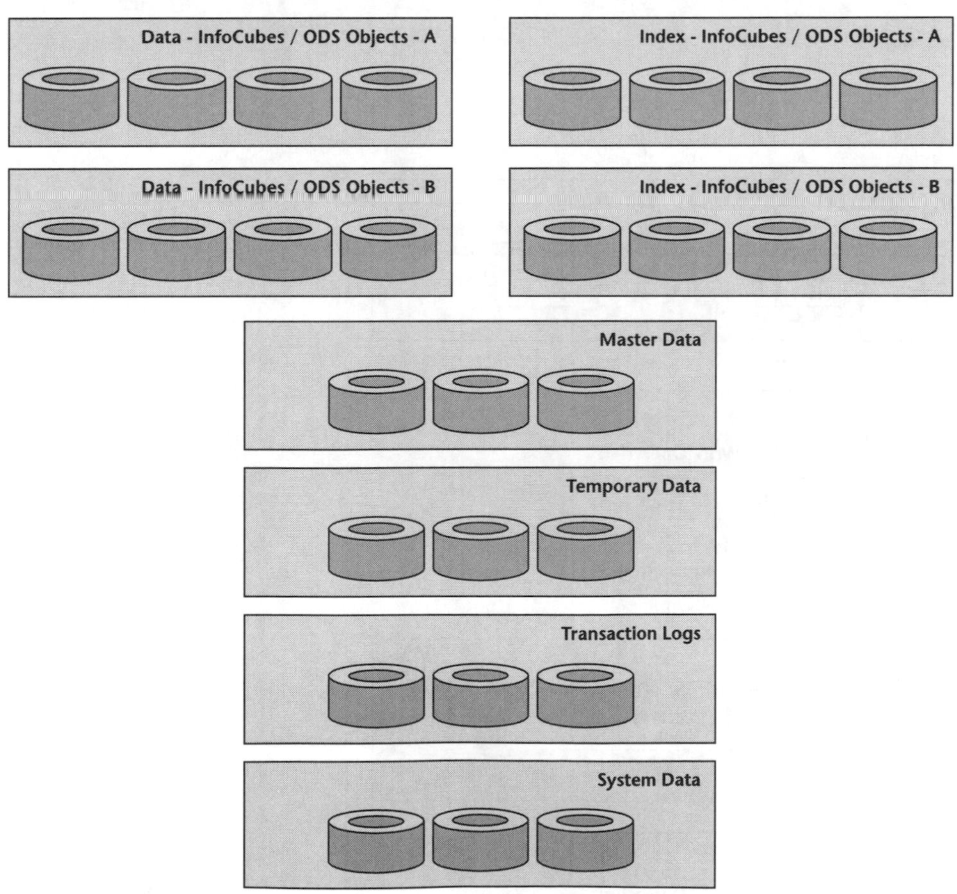

Figure 10.9 Clusters of data in SAP BW.

The second step in performance planning makes use of techniques like mirroring and striping. Mirroring automatically and redundantly stores data on several disks. It allows parallel read access but is most frequently used to provide increased availability by additional redundancy. Striping spreads single blocks of data to several disks, nearly dividing disk access time by the number of disks used for striping, and is used for read and write performance optimization. Figure 10.10 illustrates mirroring and striping. Striping (such as used in RAID level 5—see reference to the "RAB Guide" that follows) has proven to be more effective than mirroring in terms of performance optimization. Mirroring is used more from a reliability perspective.

A combined use of both techniques in conjunction with multiple and high-performance communication channels between storage subsystem and database server provides the best-possible performance and availability even in cases of disk failure.

More information about the techniques mentioned and other aspects of physical data access is available in "The RAB Guide to Non-Stop Data Access" by Joe Molina at www.raid-advisory.com/rabguide.html. Information on the configuration of specific storage subsystems is available through the vendors.

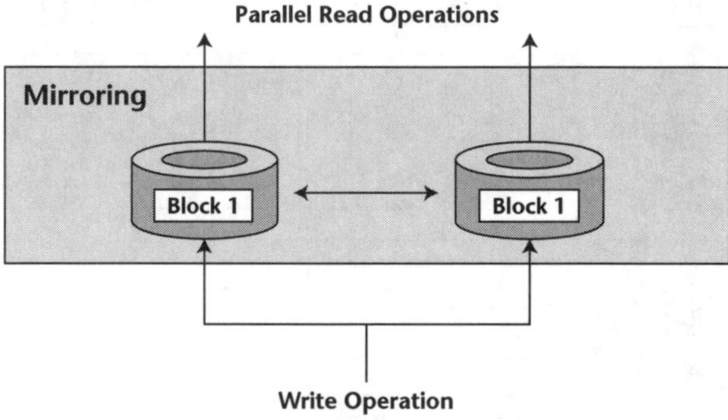

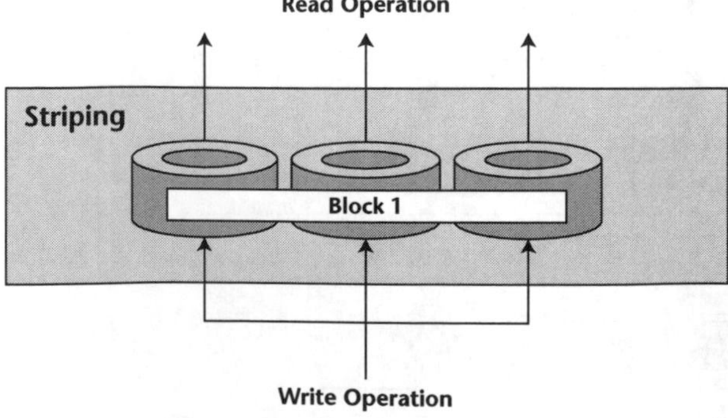

Figure 10.10 Mirroring and striping.

Client Systems

The requirements for client systems heavily depend on the choice of front-end solutions available to the end user and on the availability of terminal servers. Web reporting and SAP Enterprise Portals only require a thin client with minimal hardware requirements. Using the BEx Analyzer at least requires a workstation capable of running Microsoft Excel with a reasonable performance. Detailed hardware and software requirements are available in the SAP Service Marketplace.

Most users—between 70 percent and 90 percent—of the SAP BW user community can be classified as report consumers, accessing and navigating through standard reports. With the Web reporting and Enterprise Portal integration available in SAP BW release 3.0; this functionality will be available through Web browsers on thin clients in most of the SAP BW installations. Using thin clients reduces hardware and software requirements and keeps maintenance costs to a minimum.

The remaining users perform ad hoc analysis and reporting and require more sophisticated front-end solutions like the BEx Analyzer or a third-party front end. Hardware and software requirements for these users are significantly higher compared to the thin client requirements. The BEx Analyzer, for example, requires a certain amount of main memory for caching query results and a certain amount of processing time for formatting query results.

Low-performance client workstations can be enabled to use the Business Explorer and third-party tools by connecting to a terminal server (e.g., the Microsoft Windows Terminal Services).

Network Considerations

In times of increasing bandwidths in local, metropolitan, and wide area networks, network considerations have become less important. Still, it is worthwhile to keep an eye on the extra load that a data warehouse solution imposes on network traffic. Figure 10.8 not only shows the different systems participating in the SAP BW system landscape, but it also shows some of the different network connections between those systems. The different considerations for each of the different types of network connections are detailed in the following list:

Between database server and application server. This is the most critical network path in the SAP BW system landscape. Every database request that cannot be served out of the buffers of the application server is transferred to the database server, and the resulting data set is transferred back to the application server. Network performance can seriously degrade when queries that return large result sets or massively parallel data loads are executed. In most cases, however, these systems are located in the same computing center and are connected by high-bandwidth local area networks. Application servers connecting to the database server using a slow network connection should not be used for massive data loads. On the other hand client access to an application server through a slow network connection will not be able to return large query result sets with the same performance as local application servers.

Between application server and client workstation. Client workstations executing queries via the BEx Analyzer usually require 3 to 5 times the bandwidth of standard SAP GUI™ applications. Client workstations using the Web to access SAP BW queries are comparable to other typical Web applications. This type of connection is not critical, except for very large query results. Because the Web interface basically provides the same functionality as the BEx Analyzer, we recommend Web-based access to SAP BW queries. Smaller bandwidth requirements and a smaller number of roundtrips reduce the total latency.

Between application server and other servers. The SAP Web Application Server connects to several other servers, including the Internet Graphics Server and a content server. Many times these servers are actually installed on the same system as the Web application server. The network traffic caused by these servers being on separate systems is not critical.

Between application server and source system. Network traffic between the SAP BW application servers and the source systems is determined by the amount of data extracted on the source system and transferred to the SAP BW system. The total network load may be everything from very low to very high additional traffic for large data volume applications.

Between application server and target system. The data mart interface and the Open Hub Services allow you to create complex information flow scenarios between multiple operational and data warehouse systems. This additional information flow in turn adds traffic to the network. The impact of this additional traffic needs to be considered on a case-by-case basis.

Performance Impact on Source Systems

Although not shown in Figure 10.8 as part of the system landscape architecture, source systems must be considered as part of your performance considerations when you are setting up the SAP BW system landscape. Source systems need to run extraction programs on a regular basis, adding to the normal system load caused by transaction and batch processing. This may not be a problem from an overall system load perspective. A successful SAP BW implementation normally alleviates some of the load of the operational systems by taking over most of the system load caused by reporting and analysis.

On the other hand, timing of extractions may become a problem. Operational systems often are occupied with running batch processes during the typical extraction time windows. High peak loads during these time windows may have an impact on sizing there.

Finally, there is a transition period from starting live operation of the SAP BW implementation to finally shutting down reporting services in the operational system, where the operational system may have to deal with both the reporting load and the extraction load. Performance planning needs to cover both scenarios to warrant the source system's performance standards.

Process Design

Process design primarily involves scheduling the various different data load and data management processes, such as aggregate rollups, InfoCube compressions, index creation, and calculation of database statistics, in such a way that the total run time required to perform all tasks is minimized. (Process chains, used for complex scheduling tasks, were introduced in Chapter 3 and discussed in more detail in Chapter 9.)

The main guideline for process design is to utilize as many resources available on the SAP BW system as possible. Experience shows that SAP BW data load jobs scale pretty well with multiple CPUs, for instance, allowing you to schedule as many parallel data load jobs as there are CPUs available in the system. I/O-intensive jobs such as aggregate rollup, InfoCube compression, and index creations can be scheduled for parallel execution as long as there are no I/O bottlenecks and enough temporary disk space for simultaneous sort operations is provided.

Performance Management

Even if all performance planning efforts are successful and the application presents itself with great performance, managing performance is crucial. It is even more so for data warehouse applications, where user behavior tends to be more dynamic compared to operational environments, because their focus of analysis is constantly shifting, following the business issues that need to be solved. Finally, the more successful the data warehouse is, the more additional users from the same or other business areas it will attract.

Managing performance simply means to constantly monitor the performance of all system components, starting with the application (reporting, analysis, and data load performance) and including hardware, system software, database management, and database server software and the application server software. Then it's just a matter of waiting for the squeaky wheel and fixing it.

System administrators already running one of the mySAP.com components that come with the SAP Web Application Server—as the majority of SAP BW customers does—will immediately feel familiar with the multi-tier architecture and the Computing Center Management System (CCMS) tools available for monitoring and tuning.

SAP supports performance management efforts by offering Going Live Checks and periodical automated system checks called Early Watch Sessions. Parts of the Early Watch sessions can be scheduled for low utilization periods of time and evaluated by the administrator without the help of SAP.

This chapter is organized along the priorities of performance management: The higher the visibility of a potential performance problem from an end user's point of view, the more important it is to fix it quickly. We start with a discussion of analysis and reporting performance, continuing with data loading and management and ending with the more technical topics.

The Technical Business Content

The technical Business Content is composed of a set of InfoSources, InfoCubes, transfer and update rules, queries, and workbooks fully covering every detail of all performance-relevant processes in an SAP BW system:

- Query execution and navigation
- Data load processes
- Aggregate maintenance
- InfoCube compression
- Deletion of records from InfoCubes
- Meta data maintenance

The information available through the technical Business Content is used two ways. Time series queries allow you to identify performance trends, make increased use of queries or performance degradation over time visible, or prove that perceived performance degradation does not exist. Detail queries allow detailed analysis of the specific queries, data load, or data management processes. Meta data maintenance queries allow you to track changes made to the Meta Data Repository on various levels.

The next two sections provide an overview of performance-relevant information available. A complete documentation of the technical Business Content is available in the "System Administration Tasks" document, which is part of the SAP BW documentation. Please note that the technical Business Content (like all other Business Content) needs to be activated prior to using it for monitoring and analysis purposes.

Technical Content for Reporting and Analysis

The technical Business Content for reporting and analysis provides detailed information about what queries have been executed at what time by what user, what navigational steps the user executed, and what InfoObjects, hierarchies, and aggregates have been used in those navigational steps. The most important key figures available are shown in Table 10.1.

Additional key figures not shown here provide times and numbers about OLE DB for OLAP-related processes and information about other processing steps.

The key figures listed previously allow you to easily track how much time each of the steps in executing a query took and how many data records have been processed. Relating the times spent for different steps in executing a query to the number of records read, aggregated, processed, and finally transferred to the front end allows you to identify the cause of a performance issue, such as a potential need for database optimization or for aggregates, network bandwidth problems, and even performance bottlenecks on the front-end system. Although the technical Business Content already provides a couple of useful queries and workbooks that help you analyze performance issues, specifically tailored queries on top of the technical Business Content InfoCubes may assist in further analysis.

Table 10.1 Important Key Figures for Query Execution and Navigation

KEY FIGURE	DESCRIPTION
0TCTDBSCTR	Number of database selects executed
0TCTNAVCTR	Number of navigations performed
0TCTCHAVRD	Number of attribute values read
0TCTNCELLS	Number of cells transferred to the front end
0TCTNDBSEL	Number of records selected from the database
0TCTNDBTRA	Number of records transferred from the database to the server
0TCTNTEXTS	Number of texts read
0TCTTAUTH	Time spent for authorization checks
0TCTTDBRD	Time spent for reading from the database
0TCTTDMCACC	Time spent by Data Manager for InfoCube access
0TCTTDMDBB	Time spent by Data Manager for reading from basic InfoCube
0TCTTDMDBO	Time spent by Data Manager for reading from ODS
0TCTTFRONT	Time spent for front end operations
0TCTTNAVIG	Time spent between navigational steps
0TCTTOLAPAL	Total time spent for OLAP processing
0TCTTOLINI	Time spent for OLAP processor initialization
0TCTTRDMDA	Time spent for reading texts / master data
0TCTTREST	Time spent for what the system was unable to assign
0TCTTVARDP	Time spent for inputting variables
0TCTTOLAP	Time spent for OLAP processor

Technical Content for Data Loading and Data Management

The technical Business Content for data loading and data management provides information about the number of records processed and the time spent on loading data, maintaining aggregates, and compressing InfoCubes. The information provided here is not as detailed as for query execution. However, detailed information can be retrieved from the SAP BW monitor. Tables 10.2, 10.3, and 10.4 show the most important key figures available in this part of the Business Content.

Table 10.2 Important Key Figures for Loading Data

KEY FIGURE	DESCRIPTION
0TCTMNRECO	Records (WHM process) for a particular processing step when loading data
0TCTMTIME	Time (WHM process) for a particular processing step when loading data

Table 10.3 Important Key Figures for Aggregation

KEY FIGURE	DESCRIPTION
0TCTNAGGRRD	Number of records read for aggregation
0TCTNAGGRWR	Number of records written to the aggregate
0TCTTAGGIN	Time spent for aggregation during rollup
0TCTTAGGRD	Time spent for reading data during rollup process

Table 10.4 Important Key Figures for InfoCube Compression

KEY FIGURE	DESCRIPTION
0TCTNCNDDEL	Number of deleted records
0TCTNCNDINS	Number of added records
0TCTNCNDRAT	Summarization proportion
0TCTNCNDRPI	Number of added markers
0TCTNCNDRPU	Number of marker updates
0TCTNCNDSEL	Number of selected records
0TCTNCNDUPD	Number of update records
0TCTTCNDALL	Overall run time

The technical Business Content for data loading and maintenance helps to identify performance trends; it does not provide enough information for a detailed analysis of eventual performance issues. This kind of analysis can be done in the monitor (transaction RSMO).

Reporting and Analysis

Besides correctness of information, reporting and analysis performance is the most important prerequisite for users to accept a new data warehouse solution. Consequently, most of the performance management efforts are invested in this area. While constant monitoring using the technical Business Content allows you to manage performance proactively, there still are occasions where the reporting and analysis wheel starts squeaking. Action against reporting and analysis performance issues should follow a systematic approach like the one shown in Table 10.5.

Let's quickly discuss these performance optimization steps before diving into the very details in the next few sections. The first step is checking the query properties, which might already resolve the problem without any significant effort. The second step is checking if all—or at least all except a few—requests stored in the InfoCube have been compressed.

Another relatively simple performance optimization task is optimizing the query definition. This can be as easy as adding additional filter criteria but may also require a redesign of the whole query. In either case, it does not impact the overall system design or performance.

Table 10.5 Performance Optimization Steps for Query Execution

STEP #	DESCRIPTION	TOOL
1	Check query properties.	Query Monitor (Transaction RSRT)
2	Check if InfoCube is compressed.	Administrator Workbench
3	Optimize query definition.	BEx Query Designer
4	Analyze query execution.	Business Content, Query Monitor (Transaction RSRT)
5	Check for additional indexes.	Database Management System
6	Check system for bottlenecks.	CCMS
7	Check if dormant data can be archived.	Administrator Workbench
8	Check for partitioning options.	Administrator Workbench
9	Check for parallelization options.	CCMS, Database Management System
10	Check for additional aggregates.	Administrator Workbench
11	Revisit performance planning.	

If none of this helps, you'll need to further analyze query execution using the Query Monitor and eventually the technical Business Content. Both provide the same statistical information about query execution. The Query Monitor allows for additional analysis—for instance, regarding aggregates and database query execution plans and for debugging query execution. However, keep in mind that the query must be executed to perform any analysis. The Technical Business Content is restricted to statistical information but allows postmortem analysis, as statistical information has already been captured and promoted to the Business Content InfoCubes.

Defining additional indexes in Step 5 may help in cases where queries need to access navigational attributes in large master data tables.

Checking the system for bottlenecks in Step 6 requires CCMS functionality, which is discussed in more detail later in this chapter. Fixing bottlenecks may be possible by reconfiguring the system, the database server, or the application server. In cases where the system configuration has already been optimized, this step delivers valuable information for planning an eventual hardware upgrade (see Step 11).

Step 7 eventually allows you to reduce the amount of data stored in the InfoProvider by archiving data that is no longer required for querying.

Steps 8 and 9 go hand in hand, since partitioning usually is a prerequisite of extending the degree of parallelization that is possible. However, both steps are database-dependent. Increasing the degree of parallelization, of course, only makes sense if there are no bottlenecks left in the system after Step 5 and usually just requires changing the database configuration. Partitioning an InfoCube after having loaded data really hurts, as it requires deleting all data, defining partitioning criteria and reloading the InfoCube with data. Still, it only hurts once.

Checking for additional aggregates in Step 10, and not earlier, might appear a bit lazy, since aggregates still have the biggest impact on query performance. However, aggregates also may have a big impact on data maintenance performance because they require aggregate rollups every time transaction data is loaded and may require full or partial rebuilds after master data is changed.

The final resort for performance optimization is revisiting performance planning—reviewing the information model, reviewing the system landscape and eventually adding one or more application servers, upgrading hardware, reorganizing disk space, and, finally, reviewing your user's expectations.

Selecting Query Properties

SAP BW queries can be executed in different read and cache modes causing the OLAP engine to follow different strategies in retrieving data from the database and composing query result sets. The *query read mode* is defined as follows:

Mode 1—Read on navigation/hierarchy drill down. The OLAP engine retrieves all data required to create the result set for the initial query view or the current navigation step. Subsequent navigation steps or hierarchy drill-downs will require reading additional data or rereading the data read before.

Mode 2—Read on navigation. This is the same as mode 1, except for hierarchies. The OLAP engine reads and buffers all information required for hierarchy drill-downs in advance. Because the complete hierarchy must be read, providing the initial query view takes more time. Subsequent hierarchy drill-downs are performed faster, because they are read from the buffers instead of the database.

Mode 3—Read everything in one step. All data available through the query definition is read and buffered when creating the initial query view. All subsequent navigational steps are executed reading from the buffer instead of the database.

The query cache mode affects caching of query results and allows you to switch query result caching on and off and to define the query result cache as persistent (available across session boundary and system downtimes). Query properties can be defined on either an individual query basis or as a default value for new queries using the Query Monitor (transaction RSRT). Figure 10.11 shows a screenshot of the Query Monitor and how the query read mode can be set.

We usually recommend using query mode 1, except in cases where it does not really matter how long it takes to provide an initial query view but where navigation needs to be very fast. Mode 3 is required when user exits are applied during query execution. Choosing an inappropriate query mode can seriously degrade query performance.

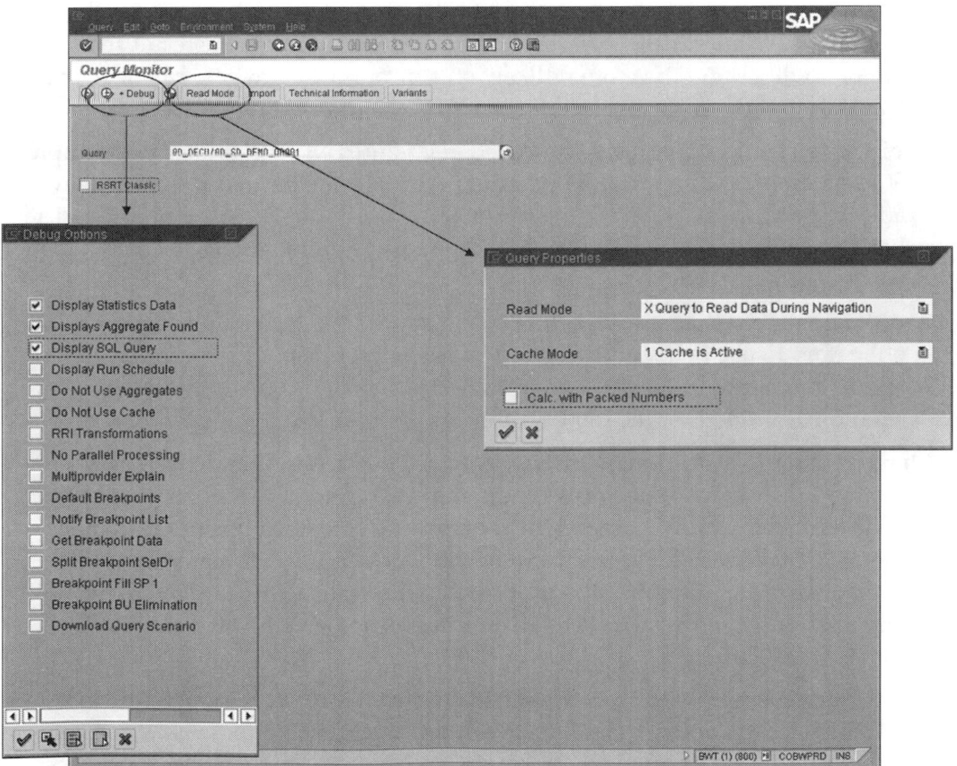

Figure 10.11 The Query Monitor.

Optimizing Query Design

The most common mistake in query design probably is using queries for list reporting, producing a large number of pages with detail information. This is not what SAP BW was made for. In fact, SAP BW was made for getting rid of list reporting by providing interactive, slice-and-dice analysis capabilities. Running list reports in SAP BW—even in batch using the reporting agent—is evidence of a not properly managed transition from operational batch reporting to modern data warehouse-based analysis.

The following is a checklist to keep in mind when optimizing query design:

Use filters. Filters found in the query definition are added to the SQL statement generated to retrieve the required data from the InfoProvider, reducing the amount of data that needs to be read at its very source. Using as many filters as possible can dramatically reduce query run times.

Avoid using conditions and exceptions. While filters are evaluated by the database, conditions and exceptions are usually evaluated by the application server, resulting in a much larger volume of data being transferred between both servers. Always try to use conditions and exceptions in conjunction with filters.

Use free characteristics. Use as few characteristics as possible in the rows and columns of the initial query view, or at least be careful about increasing the granularity of an initial query result set. The more granular the result set is, the larger it will be and the more unlikely an appropriate aggregate can be found. Use the characteristics required for navigation as free characteristics.

Avoid restricted key figures. Restricted key figures either require more complex SQL statements to be executed in order to retrieve the desired results or they add to the complexity of creating the query result in the OLAP engine. Restricted key figures specifically hurt when there are overlapping ranges of characteristic values used as restriction criteria.

Avoid using more than one structure. While one structure for all key figures is obligatory to use in query design, additional structures usually include some restrictions similar to those used in restricted key figures. Additional structures should be avoided for the same reason as restricted key figures.

Characteristics/Navigational attributes are more efficient than hierarchies. Evaluating hierarchies requires generating an additional temporary hierarchy table and increases the complexity of query evaluation. Consider replacing hierarchies with characteristics or navigational attributes. If hierarchies need to be used (as in many cases), make sure appropriate aggregates are defined and consider using a variable to select a number of specific hierarchy nodes for query execution.

Avoid complex queries. Don't define queries showing everything in the InfoProvider. Consider using the Report-Report-Interface to offer analysis paths rather than complex queries.

How far a query can be optimized using the preceding checklist, of course, heavily depends on the user requirements and on the information model in place. Not all of the optimizations discussed may be applicable in a specific scenario or application.

Analyzing Query Execution

Once a low-performance query has been identified, you have several options to analyze query execution: the Query Monitor (transaction RSRT), query tracing (transaction RSRTRACE), and of course, the CCMS, explained in more detail later this chapter. Figure 10.11 shows a screenshot of the query debugging options available in the Query Monitor.

The *Display Statistics Data* option essentially provides the same information as the technical Business Content and is helpful whenever the Business Content has not been activated for some reason. The *Display Aggregates Found* option shows a list of applicable aggregates (see text that follows for more details) for the query executed. *Display SQL Query* displays the generated SQL statement used to retrieve relevant data from the InfoProvider. Ultimately, query execution can be debugged using the breakpoints options available.

The query trace (transaction RSRTRACE) allows you to further analyze the query execution details. For experienced users, it is possible to analyze the aggregate determination process. The CCMS provides additional options for query analysis on a technical level. Finally, transaction RSRV provides a number of options for low-level analysis, including:

- Plausibility of database management system parameters
- Existence and consistency of SAP BW standard database indexes
- Existence and consistency of database statistics

Aggregates

The most effective means to improve query performance still is to reduce the amount of data to be retrieved from the database. Typical queries request a *selection* of *aggregated* data from the system. Selections are supported by database indexes where additional information is stored, allowing you to quickly retrieve the selected data set without having to read all data. Analogously aggregated data is supported by aggregates that redundantly store aggregated views on InfoCubes. Aggregates can be defined for InfoCubes at any point of time, are automatically maintained by SAP BW, and are transparent without the user having to include reference to a specific aggregate in his query definition.

From a technical point of view, it would be possible to support aggregates for ODS objects. However, the typical use of ODS objects for implementing an ODS, a data warehouse layer, or simply as an additional staging layer implementing some business logic does not justify the costs of implementing aggregate support for ODS objects. Local aggregates for remote InfoProviders are not supported, as this would require permanent synchronization of updates applied to the remote InfoProvider. Aggregates may be supported by the remote system, like a remote SAP BW does for basic InfoCubes accessed as a source for a remote cube. For similar reasons, direct aggregates for MultiProviders are not supported.

In general, SAP BW uses the same data model for storing aggregates as it does for storing InfoCubes. Common dimension tables are shared between InfoCubes and aggregates wherever possible. For aggregates with a maximum of 15 characteristics and without hierarchies included in the aggregate definition, SAP BW automatically uses a flat table instead of a multidimensional data model for storing the aggregates. This flat table is composed of the SIDs (surrogate keys) of all characteristics included in the aggregate definition and of aggregated values of all key figures available in the InfoCube. Flat aggregates speed up both aggregate maintenance (rollup and rebuild) and querying.

Aggregates are maintained in the Administrator Workbench by simply dragging and dropping the required characteristics and navigational attributes into the aggregate definition area. SAP BW automatically takes care of creating dimensions according to the original dimensions of the InfoCube. Figure 10.12 shows a screenshot of the aggregate definition dialog. Three options are available for including characteristics or navigational attributes values in the aggregate:

- Include all characteristics/navigational attribute values in the aggregate.
- Include all records with a specific value for a characteristic or navigational attribute value in the aggregate. This option allows you to create aggregates (e.g., for a specific part of an organization, for a specific region, or for a specific group of customers).
- Include all records on a specific level of a selected hierarchy of a characteristic or navigational attribute. This option increases the performance of queries that make use of external hierarchies.

From an aggregate maintenance perspective there are three types of SAP BW aggregates:

- Aggregates not including navigational attributes or hierarchies
- Aggregates including time-independent navigational attributes or hierarchies
- Aggregates including time-dependent navigational attributes or hierarchies

For all types of aggregates to be up-to-date, SAP BW aggregates all data records that have been added to the corresponding InfoCube since the last aggregate maintenance and updates the aggregate accordingly—a process called *aggregate rollup*. It is up to the system administrator to schedule aggregate rollups as part of the staging process or as a separate process.

In addition to the rollup, type 2 and 3 aggregates must be realigned every time the master data attributes or hierarchies used in the aggregate change. This task is performed during *master data activation*. Based on a threshold value defined by the system administrator, SAP BW dynamically decides if this realignment is performed by dropping the aggregate and re-creating it based on the new data or if it just realigns the aggregate based on the changed master data or hierarchy records. The default threshold value is 20 percent. If more than 20 percent of the master data or hierarchy records have changed, the aggregate is dropped; otherwise, the deltas are computed.

Type 3 aggregates require a reference date as part of their definition. All navigational attribute values and hierarchy nodes are retrieved using this reference date. In typical applications this reference date needs to be adjusted from time to time (e.g., a reference date referring to the last day of the previous month needs to be adjusted on a monthly basis), and with a changing reference date, the aggregate itself needs to be adjusted.

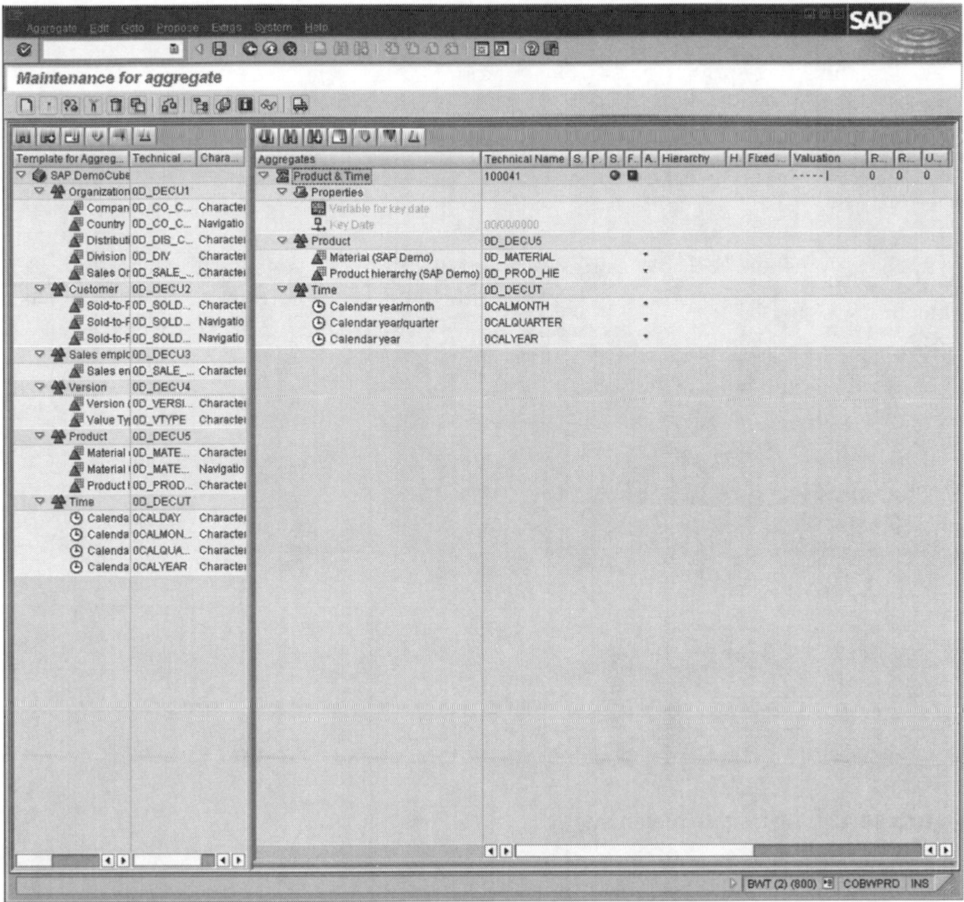

Figure 10.12 Defining aggregates.

You should recognize that SAP BW automatically identifies hierarchical relationships between the aggregates defined in the aggregate maintenance dialog. Figure 10.13 shows a simple aggregate hierarchy for four aggregates defined for an InfoCube: Aggregates 2 and 3 can be derived from aggregate 1, and aggregate 4 can be derived from aggregate 2 but needs additional hierarchy data. All aggregate maintenance (creation of aggregates, rollup, and realignment) is automatically organized along this hierarchy.

Optimizing the set of aggregates is a continuous process following the changes in user behavior and user requirements. An initial set of aggregates should be created before going live, based on user requirements, information about user behavior, and information about the actual distribution of data values collected up front. It is very important for gaining and retaining user acceptance to have the most important aggregates in place before going live. Aggregate adjustment is supported again by the technical Business Content. The following paragraphs provide some high-level guidelines and tips for aggregate design. Further information about aggregates can be found in a detailed how-to guide on aggregates, available in the SAP Service Marketplace (http://service.sap.com/bw).

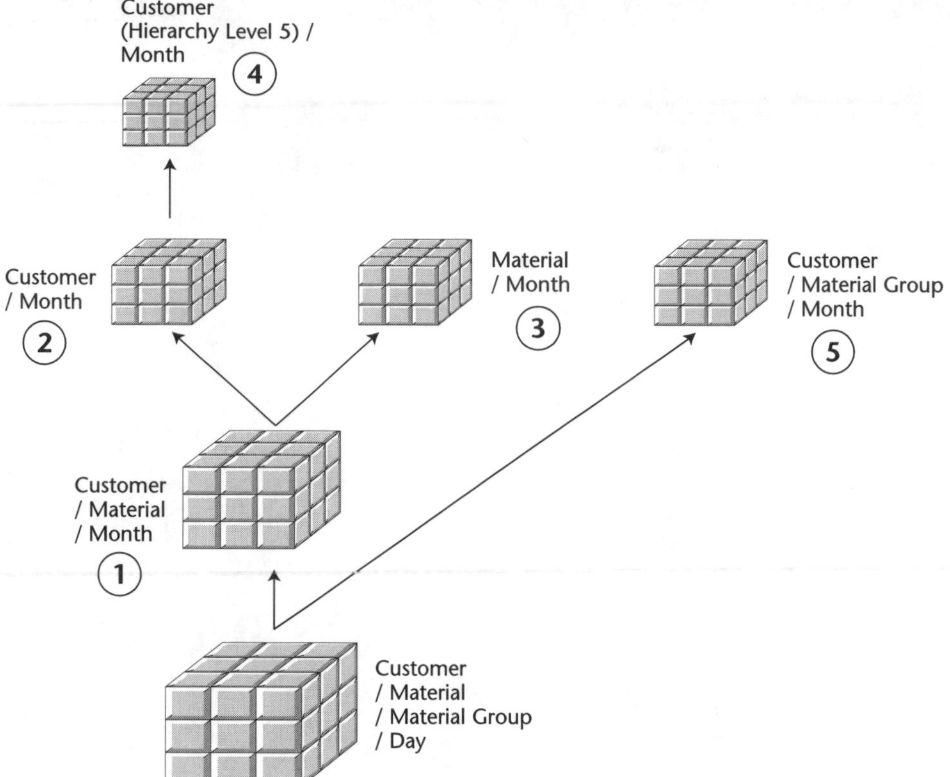

Figure 10.13 Aggregate hierarchy.

Upon request, SAP BW proposes a list of aggregates either based on static query definitions or based on actual user behavior. This proposal is usually too extensive and should be reviewed very critically according to the guidelines discussed here.

In principle, it is possible to build aggregates for all kinds of queries; however, loading data and maintaining the aggregates would become a nightmare. Optimizing the set of aggregates requires having the trade-off between reporting time versus space and load time in mind. The most important prerequisite for optimizing the set of aggregates is intimate know-how about the actual distribution of data values. Aggregate number 1 shown in Figure 10.13 is only useful for optimizing reporting performance, if there are multiple records per customer, material, and month (e.g., if a customer buys the same product more than once a month). While SAP recommends an aggregation factor of at least 10, we have seen applications where aggregates with smaller aggregation factors have proved to be useful—provided that the complete set of aggregates can be maintained in time. Even large aggregates may be useful, as aggregate 1 in Figure 10.13, with an aggregation factor of only 2, shows. Several other aggregates can be derived from this large aggregate; we call these kinds of large aggregates *base aggregates*.

As shown in Figure 10.12, the aggregate maintenance dialog provides statistical information about the aggregate, including the setup, maintenance, usage, and a rating of the aggregate's usefulness. The rating is based on the aggregation factors along the aggregate hierarchy and the actual usage of the aggregate. While this rating provides a first indicator on aggregate quality, it needs further consideration. Base aggregates will always be rated very low, because they are not frequently used for query execution.

A mistake frequently made in aggregate maintenance is to not include characteristics that depend on another characteristic already included in the aggregate. For instance, *quarter* and *year* are not included in an aggregate that includes *month*, and *material group* is not included in an aggregate that already includes *material*.

NOTE The *quarter* and *year* characteristics never change for a given *month*, as opposed to *material group* and *material*. However, as long as changes in the assignment of materials to certain material groups are rare, including *material group* in the aggregate will not significantly increase the number of records in the aggregate.

Including dependent characteristics is important for two reasons. First, as illustrated in Figure 10.13, aggregate 5, for example, could be derived from aggregate 1 instead of the underlying InfoCube, decreasing the time required for computing aggregate 5 roughly by the aggregation factor of aggregate 1. Second, InfoCubes and aggregates share common dimension tables, as long as they are composed of exactly the same fields, saving space and time for aggregate maintenance. If the material dimension of the InfoCube contained just *material* and *material group*, this dimension table could be shared between the InfoCube and aggregates 1 and 5.

Archiving

The problem of dormant data has been widely discussed in the data warehouse community already. Dormant data is data that is still available in the reporting structures of the data warehouse but is no longer used for reporting purposes. The most important reason for data to become dormant simply is time. Many reporting and analysis applications focus on a 2- to 3-year period; only few business areas (e.g., some marketing applications) require data for a longer period of time. Other reasons include organizational changes—for instance, if a part of the organization is sold to another organization.

The implementation of a data warehouse layer that is not used for reporting purposes and new database features like partitioning may already help to reduce the impact of dormant data on query performance. However, hierarchical storage management concepts and archiving are the ultimate means to remove dormant data from the system without actually losing it.

Data Loading and Data Management

Performance of data loads and data maintenance is crucial in order to provide information in a timely manner. The main entry point for performance analysis in data loading and data management is the SAP BW monitor available in the Administrator Workbench and through transaction code RSMO (a screenshot of the SAP BW monitor is featured in Figure 3.3). Six major steps are taken in processing a request, as shown in Table 10.6. The individual shares of time given refer to a typical upload of transaction data into an InfoCube and may largely vary depending on the complexity of the transfer and update rules and the information model. The time spent for data extraction adds at least 10 percent of the core staging process consisting of Steps 3 to 5 to the overall time spent. The time required for subsequent steps largely depends on what subsequent steps are scheduled for the data package.

The detail information provided by the monitor includes the time spent on executing each of these single steps. Relating this information to the typical values of Table 10.6 allows you to identify the performance bottlenecks of the upload process.

The options in optimizing the performance optimization of subsequent steps in the staging process, like ODS object and master data maintenance, aggregate rollups and realignments, and InfoCube compression are limited from an SAP BW point of view, as most of the run time required by these processes is consumed by the database management system. Refer to the discussion of database performance optimization later in this chapter.

Table 10.6 Data Staging Steps

STEP #	DESCRIPTION	TYPICAL SHARE OF TIME
1	Request a data package.	0%
2	Extract data from the source.	10% of the ETL process
3	Transformation rules/transfer to the PSA.	15% of the ETL process
4	Update rules.	40% of the ETL process
5	Surrogate key generation and database updates.	35% of the ETL process
6	Subsequent steps.	(varies)

Many performance problems in the extraction and staging process are actually caused by careless use of user exits, transfer rules, and update rules. Expensive database operations or calculations should either be avoided or carefully reviewed and optimized from a performance point of view.

Data Extraction

Data extraction performance obviously largely depends on the data model and data volume of the source system application. Table 10.7 provides an overview of the possible steps to improve data extraction performance.

Step 1 has already been discussed in the previous section. Step 2 basically defines the size of the data packages sent, the frequency for sending status IDocs, and the maximum number of parallel processes used to send extracted data. Provided there are sufficient system resources, you may want to increase the number of processes and the size of the individual data packages, and reduce the frequency of status IDocs in order to improve the performance of the extraction process (recommendations for parameter settings are available at the SAP Service Marketplace). However, the potential for improving extraction performance by manipulating these parameters is limited.

The next step is an application-specific one and cannot be discussed in further detail in this book. Experts of the specific application area should be consulted to identify and remove performance bottlenecks. Step 4 supports Step 3 in that it allows testing and even debugging the extractor locally without having an SAP BW system requesting data. Steps 5 and 6 are discussed in the *System Performance* section of this chapter. Adding indexes to extracted database tables and making sure the database statistics are up-to-date will in many situations help improving extraction performance.

Table 10.7 Performance Optimization Steps for Extracting Data

STEP #	DESCRIPTION	TOOL
1	Check performance of user exit for extraction.	Transaction CMOD
2	Check data transfer parameters.	Transaction SBIW
3	Check application specific setup.	Transaction SBIW
4	Check extractor.	Transaction RSA3
5	Analyze database performance.	See section on database performance
6	Analyze system performance.	See section on system performance

Data Staging

You have a couple of options to optimize the performance of the data staging process. Table 10.8 shows the different steps to be taken.

In the same way as for data extraction, data load and other parameters should be set according to the SAP recommendations. Checking the transactional RFC (tRFC) option instead of IDocs for sending data from the source system to SAP BW slightly decreases the time required for transferring the data packages between the source and the target system and the overhead required on the target system to access the data packages for further processing. If the PSA is used for intermediate storage, check if storing the data packages in the PSA is really required and turn it off eventually. If CSV files are used to load flat-file data, consider changing the file format to plain ASCII files with fixed field lengths. However, considering the overall share of 20 percent of the overall time spent before the update rules are executed, do not expect any dramatic performance improvements in Steps 1 through 4.

As stated above already, custom update and transfer rules implementing complex, data-driven business logic are a common cause of performance problems in transfer and update rules. Keep in mind that transfer and update rules are executed for every single record. Any logic that could be implemented as part of the start routines should be implemented there, eventually saving results in global variables for later use in the transfer or update rules. As always, common ABAP performance guidelines should be followed when implementing the code.

Steps 7 and 8 are related to the process of retrieving or creating surrogate keys for dimension table entries or master data records. Loading master data prior to transaction data reduces the need for creating new surrogate keys for master data and may significantly improve data load performance. Efficient number range buffering reduces the time required to create new dimension keys and SIDs.

Data staging processes in SAP BW scale very well with the number and speed of CPUs. While increasing the degree of parallelization does not speed up individual data staging processes, it does reduce the overall time required to load data.

Steps 10 through 12 are related to database performance. Typical causes for long database run times are degenerated indexes and out-of-date database statistics. SAP BW must read existing master and transaction data as part of the update process. Without up-to-date indexes and statistics, these operations can cause dramatic performance drops.

Finally, system bottlenecks may cause staging performance to degrade; check the system for bottlenecks as described in the text that follows.

System Performance

Having talked about monitoring and tuning an SAP BW system from the application point of view, let's finally take a quick look at the tools available for monitoring and tuning system behavior. The SAP Web Application Server component that bundles all activities of this kind is the Computing Center Management System (CCMS). This chapter briefly describes the most important functionality available (more information is provided in the SAP Service marketplace at http://service.sap.com/systemmanagement). All performance-relevant transactions are accessible by entering menu code STUN.

Table 10.8 Performance Optimization Steps for Loading Data

STEP #	DESCRIPTION	TOOL
1	Check data load and other parameters.	Transaction SPRO
2	Check if tRFC option can be used instead of IDocs.	Administrator Workbench
3	Check if PSA is required.	Administrator Workbench
4	Use plain ASCII files instead of CSV format.	Source System
5	Check performance of user defined transfer rules.	Administrator Workbench
6	Check performance of user defined update rules.	Administrator Workbench
7	Ensure availability of master data prior to loading.	Administrator Workbench
8	Check number range buffering.	Transaction NRIV
9	Parallelize multiple data loads.	Administrator Workbench
10	Analyze database performance.	See section on DB performance
11	Delete indexes prior to data load and re-create.	Administrator Workbench
12	Check database statistics.	Administrator Workbench
13	Analyze system performance.	See section on system performance

Application Server

On the application server level, buffering and user workload have the most significant impact on performance. This section provides a brief overview of the most important transactions available for monitoring the application server.

Buffers

Transaction ST02 is the entry point for information about all buffers maintained by the application server. Information available includes size of the buffer, available space, hit ratios, and the number of database accesses related to the buffer. Critical buffer parameters that may cause performance problems are highlighted in red. Figure 10.14

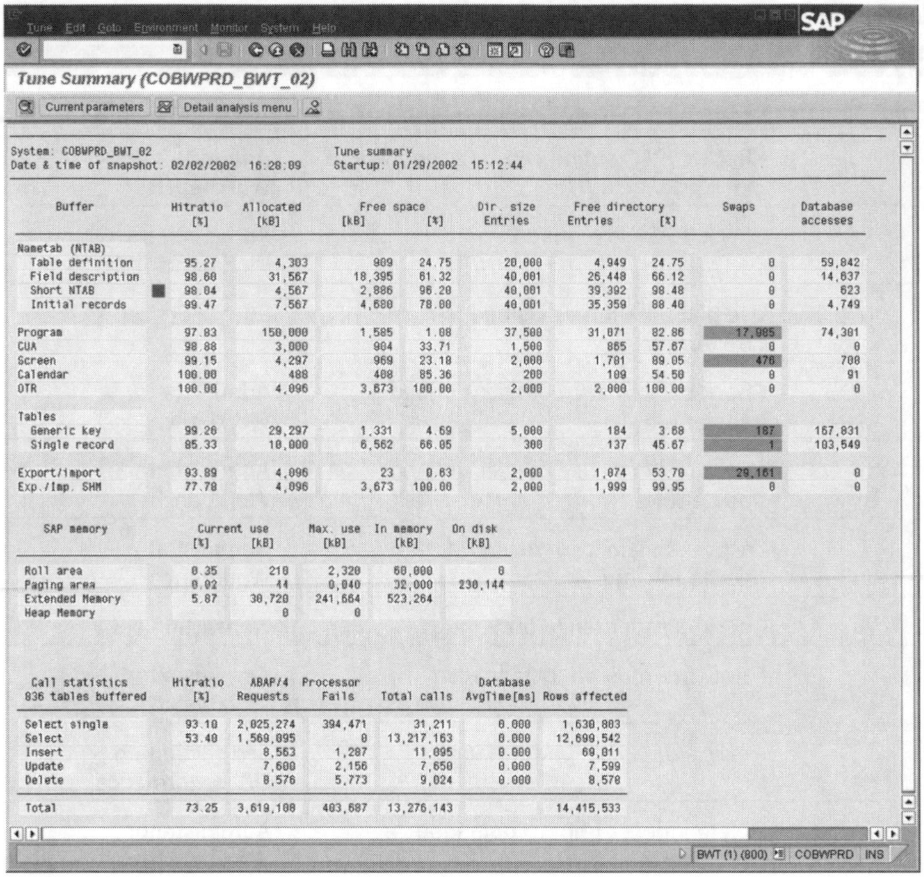

Tune Edit Goto Environment Monitor System Help

Tune Summary (COBWPRD_BWT_02)

Current parameters | Detail analysis menu

System: COBWPRD_BWT_02 Tune summary
Date & time of snapshot: 02/02/2002 16:28:09 Startup: 01/29/2002 15:12:44

Buffer	Hitratio [%]	Allocated [kB]	Free space [kB]	Free space [%]	Dir. size Entries	Free directory Entries	Free directory [%]	Swaps	Database accesses
Nametab (NTAB)									
Table definition	95.27	4,303	909	24.75	20,000	4,949	24.75	0	59,842
Field description	98.60	31,567	18,395	61.32	40,001	26,448	66.12	0	14,637
Short NTAB	98.04	4,567	2,886	96.20	40,001	39,392	98.48	0	623
Initial records	99.47	7,567	4,680	78.00	40,001	35,359	88.40	0	4,749
Program	97.83	150,000	1,585	1.08	37,500	31,071	82.86	17,985	74,301
CUA	98.88	3,000	904	33.71	1,500	865	57.67	0	0
Screen	99.15	4,297	969	23.10	2,000	1,781	89.05	476	708
Calendar	100.00	488	408	85.36	200	109	54.50	0	91
OTR	100.00	4,096	3,673	100.00	2,000	2,000	100.00	0	0
Tables									
Generic key	99.26	29,297	1,331	4.69	5,000	184	3.68	187	167,831
Single record	85.33	10,000	6,562	66.05	300	137	45.67	1	103,549
Export/import	93.89	4,096	23	0.63	2,000	1,074	53.70	29,161	0
Exp./Imp. SHM	77.78	4,096	3,673	100.00	2,000	1,999	99.95	0	0

SAP memory	Current use [%]	Current use [kB]	Max. use [kB]	In memory [kB]	On disk [kB]
Roll area	0.35	210	2,320	60,000	0
Paging area	0.02	44	8,040	32,000	230,144
Extended Memory	5.87	30,720	241,664	523,264	
Heap Memory		0	0		

Call statistics 836 tables buffered	Hitratio [%]	ABAP/4 Processor Requests	ABAP/4 Processor Fails	Database Total calls	Database AvgTime[ms]	Database Rows affected
Select single	93.10	2,025,274	394,471	31,211	0.000	1,630,803
Select	53.40	1,569,095	0	13,217,163	0.000	12,699,542
Insert		8,563	1,287	11,095	0.000	69,011
Update		7,600	2,156	7,650	0.000	7,599
Delete		8,576	5,773	9,024	0.000	8,578
Total	73.25	3,619,108	403,687	13,276,143		14,415,533

BWT (1) (800) COBWPRD INS

Figure 10.14 Application server buffers.

shows a screenshot of transaction ST02, where for example, the single record buffer and the generic key buffer are in a critical state. Administrators might consider increasing the size of these buffers in this situation. More detailed information is available by pressing the *Detailed Analysis* menu button.

Another buffer relevant for SAP BW load performance is the number range buffer. Information about this buffer is available via transaction SM56. The number range buffer is used for determining surrogate keys (SIDs and DIMIDs).

Workload

Several transactions are available for monitoring the application server workload from a user, process, and task type point of view. From a user point of view, transactions SM04 and AL08 list all active users on the local application server and all users on all application servers. Transactions SM50, SM51, and SM66 give information about the number and type of processes available on the local and global application servers and their current status. Current status information includes but is not restricted to the name of the active program, CPU time, elapsed time, number and type of database access operations, and the current database operation performed. More detailed information about the application server workload is available via transaction ST03 (or ST03N), shown in Figure 10.15.

Transaction SE30 finally allows analyzing the performance of an ABAP program. This transaction will normally not be used to analyze SAP programs but is helpful in improving the performance of custom ABAP programs.

Database Server

Much of the effort required to optimize the performance of the database management has already been done by SAP as part of the ongoing development and software maintenance activities. For example, different indexing schemes and parameter sets are used for different database management systems and their different versions. Because SAP BW is a generic data warehouse solution, however, there may still be some work left to do to further optimize the database. Adding indexes, maintenance of database statistics, and adjusting database buffers are the most prominent examples of these optimizations.

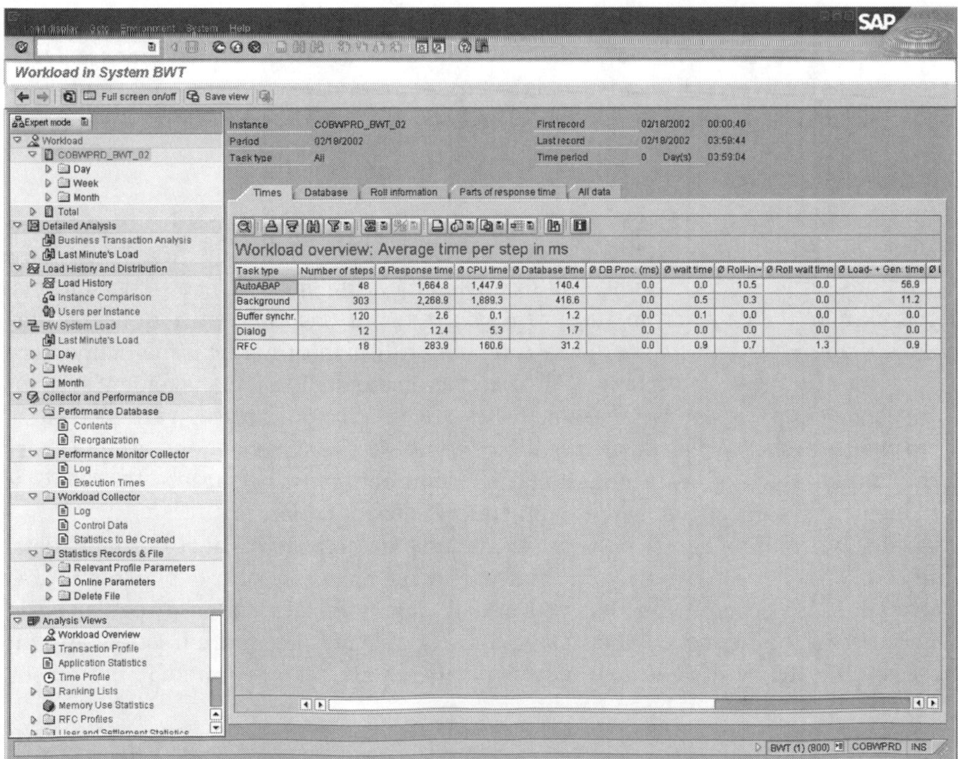

Figure 10.15 Workload analysis.

The next sections provide a generic discussion of the indexing scheme SAP BW uses, the implications of database statistics, and how the CCMS supports monitoring the database management system.

Database Indexes

The most important indexes for standard SAP BW operations are generated automatically when activating an InfoCube, ODS object, or InfoObject. As the exact layout and type of theses indexes varies with the database management system used and may change with later releases of the database management software or the SAP BW software, we recommend checking the SAP Service Marketplace under http://service.sap.com/notes for further information about indexing schemes (search for *indexing scheme*).

Common indexes for fact tables are one index per dimension key field in the fact table. Dimension tables use a composite index composed of all SIDs. Master data tables use a primary key index. Additional indexes on dimension tables or on the navigational attribute SID tables may help to increase performance in cases of dimension or navigational attribute SID tables with a high cardinality.

Missing indexes can usually be identified by looking at the query execution plan available in transaction ST04 (see text that follows). The time required by a full table access on a large dimension of navigational attribute table without indexes can be cut down dramatically by defining a corresponding index. On the other hand, the increased costs of update operations on this table have to be considered.

Other possible causes for performance degradation are degenerated indexes. Database systems try to optimize index maintenance operations, sacrificing space and index read performance. Indexes should be deleted and re-created periodically.

Database Statistics

Database statistics are statistical information about the data stored in a database table—for instance, the number of distinct values in a specific field, the distribution of these values, or simply the total number of records in the table or its indexes. This information is used by the database management system to find the most efficient way to execute a specific SQL request. If and what kind of statistical information is maintained and used in the optimization strategy again depends on the database management system.

In general, up-to-date database statistics are very important to warrant a high-performance system. We have seen outdated database statistics causing a simple query that could be executed in seconds to take several hours just because of the database management system choosing the wrong query execution plan.

Again, information about the query execution plan helps to identify outdated database statistics. Please consult your database management system expert for further information. We recommend that you update database statistics on a regular basis, depending on the frequency and data volume of uploads. The more frequent and the more volume, the more often an update of database statistics is required. In most cases, a monthly update should be sufficient.

SAP BW integrates functionality to maintain statistics in its Administrator Workbench transactions, supplementing the CCMS functionality available in transactions DB20 (Statistics Maintenance).

Monitoring

The CCMS includes a number of transactions for monitoring the database management system and identifying bottlenecks and other issues. The most important transactions are the database performance analysis transaction (ST04) and the database allocation transaction (DB02). Figure 10.16 shows a screenshot of transaction ST04 for a Microsoft SQL Server database. (Note that all the screenshots in this section may look different in your system, depending on the database management system you use.)

Transaction ST04 and subsequent functions available in the detail analysis menu allow you to track down database operations and their use of system resources even below the SQL request level. Figure 10.17 shows the information available at the SQL request level; the *Explain* button shows the query execution plan, which allows you to check if the optimizer of the underlying database management system has chosen an efficient execution plan. Inefficient execution plans are mostly caused by missing or out-of-date database statistics or missing indexes.

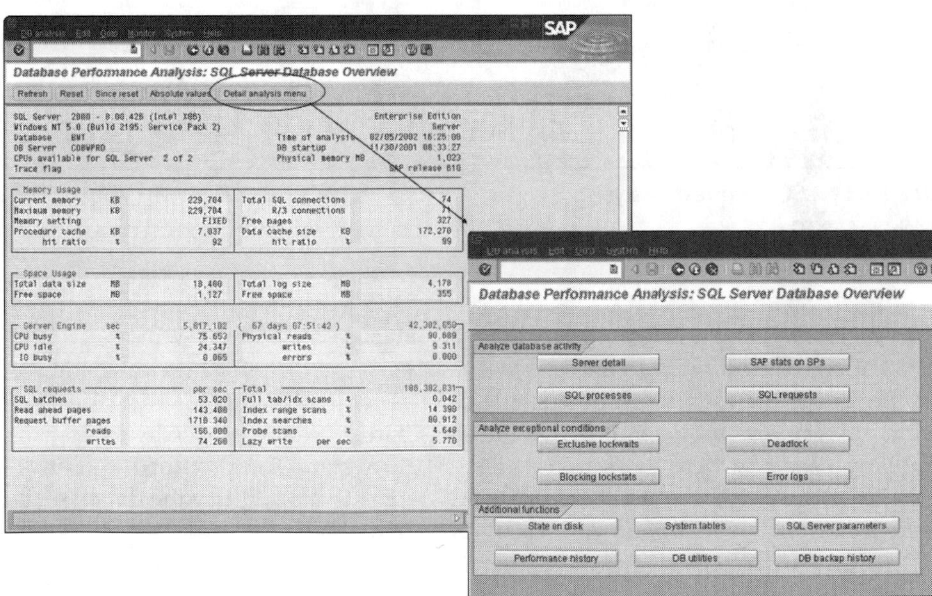

Figure 10.16 Database performance analysis.

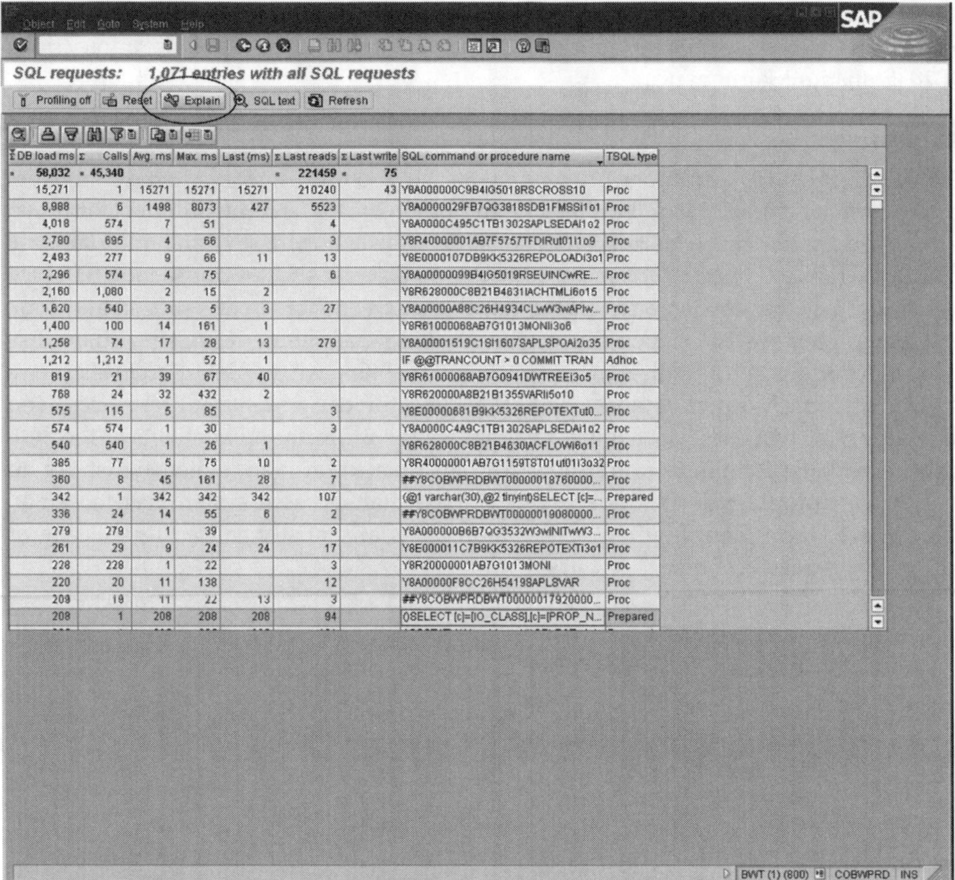

Figure 10.17 SQL request analysis.

Transaction DB02 provides an overview of database allocation—what data is at what location, at what rates do the database tables grow, and so forth. A detail view is available for more information about single database objects like tables and indexes.

Sometimes information about SQL requests is hard to catch, especially in systems with many users. In these cases transactions ST01 (System Trace) and ST05 (Performance Trace) are helpful to get ahold of the SQL requests executed by the database, its query execution plan, and other valuable information.

Hardware and Operating System

Finally, hardware bottlenecks may cause your SAP BW system performance to degrade. Again, the CCMS is the place to go for further analysis. (Note that layout and content of the screenshots in this section depend on the operating system used and may look different in your system. Transaction OS06 is the main entry point for operating system analysis.) Aggregated information about CPU, memory, and IO usage is available on one single screen; additional detailed information can be reached by selecting the *Detail analysis menu*. The same information is available for remote SAP servers using transaction OS07. Figure 10.18 shows a screenshot of transaction OS06.

Exceptions

Although not directly related to performance management, analysis of exception conditions sometimes provides helpful information. The main transactions available for exception analysis are RZ20 (Alert Monitor), SM21 (System Log), and ST22 (Dump Analysis).

The alert monitor is a one-stop-shopping solution for critical conditions in your SAP BW system. It allows for a quick high-level assessment of the overall system before you dive into the details of the analysis process. The system log available in transaction SM21 provides information about serious error conditions that cannot be handled or reported otherwise, including login failures, database error conditions, aborted transactions, and ABAP runtime errors. The latter can be examined in detail in transaction ST22, showing all information available in dumps of the aborted ABAP programs.

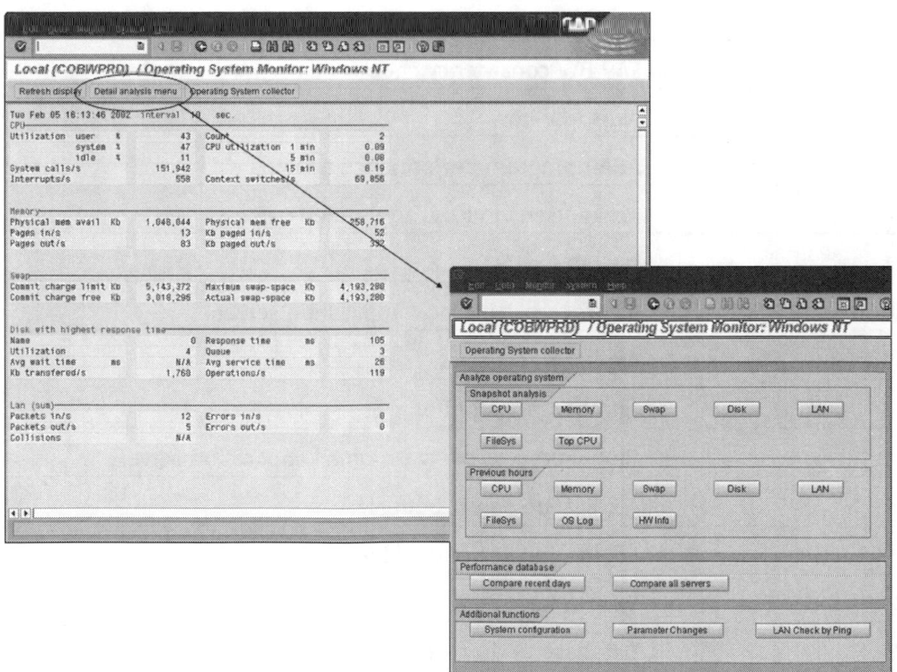

Figure 10.18 Operating system monitor.
Copyright © SAP AG

Transaction and Menu Summary

Table 10.9 provides an overview of the transactions discussed in the context of performance monitoring. Of course, a lot more transactions are available for analyzing and enhancing performance that have not been covered in this chapter, especially when actually changing the system setup is involved. Please consult your system documentation for additional information.

Table 10.9 Important Transactions for Performance Management

TRANSACTION	DESCRIPTION
AL08	Active users on all application servers
DB02	Database allocation
DB20	Statistics maintenance
OS06	Operating system monitor
OS07	Remote operating system monitor
RSMO	SAP BW monitor
RSRT	SAP BW query execution monitor
RSRTRACE	SAP BW query execution trace
RSRV	SAP BW consistency checks
RZ20	Alert monitor
SE30	ABAP program performance analysis
SM04	Active users on local application servers
SM21	System log
SM50	All processes on local application server
SM51	Application servers
SM56	Number range buffer
SM66	Global process overview on all application servers
ST02	Application server buffers
ST03	Application server workload analysis
ST01	System trace
ST04	Database performance analysis
ST05	Performance trace
ST22	Short dump analysis
STUN	Provides access to all performance relevant transactions

Summary

In this chapter, performance optimization was divided into two categories: performance planning and performance management. Performance planning accompanies the project team developing the SAP BW solution through all phases of the implementation project: From project definition via requirements analysis, information modeling, and implementation, to testing, where performance planning overlaps with performance management. The most important steps in performance planning are information modeling, system landscape definition and sizing, and finally management of user expectations. Although managing user expectations does not actually improve the performance of a system, it does help to set user expectations appropriately and avoid disappointment and consequently fading acceptance of the system.

Performance management is a continuous process and part of system administration and maintenance procedures. SAP BW offers a wealth of tools for system administrators to monitor performance and identify bottlenecks, starting with the SAP BW technical Business Content on an applications level and ending with various tools to identify database, operating system, and hardware bottlenecks.

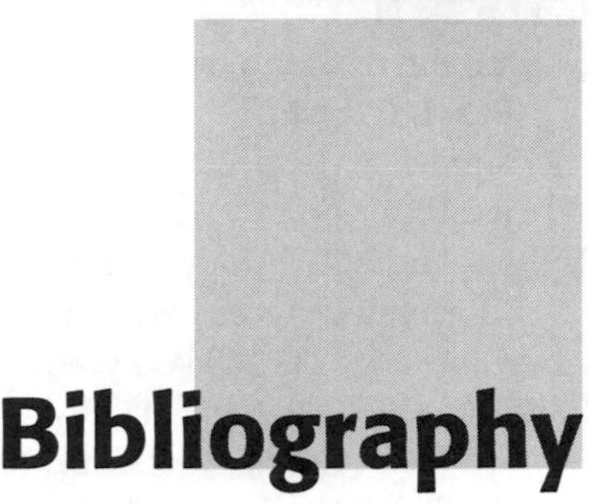

Bibliography

Books

Date, C. J. 1999. *An Introduction to Database Systems. 7th ed.* Addison Wesley Longman, Inc.

Harvard Business Review. 1998. *Harvard Business Review on Measuring Corporate Performance*. Harvard Business School Press.

Hashmi, N. 2000. *Business Information Warehouse for SAP.* PRIMA TECH.

Inmon, W. H. 1996. *Building the Data Warehouse. 2nd ed.* John Wiley & Sons.

Inmon, W. H. 1999. *Building the Operational Datastore. 2nd ed.* John Wiley & Sons.

Inmon, W. H. 2001. *Corporate Information Factory. 2nd ed.* John Wiley & Sons.

Kimball, R. 2002. *The Data Warehouse Toolkit. 2nd ed.: The Complete Guide to Dimensional Modeling*. John Wiley & Sons.

Kimball, R., L. Reeves, M. Ross, W. Thornthwaite. 1998. *The Data Warehouse Lifecycle Toolkit: Expert Methods for Designing, Developing, and Deploying Data Warehouses.* John Wiley & Sons.

Martin, W. 1998. *Data Warehousing—Data Mining—OLAP.* Bonn, Germany: MITP.

Norton, D. P., and R. S. Kaplan. 1996. *The Balanced Scorecard: Translating Strategy into Action.* Harvard Business School Press.

Norton, D. P. and R. S. Kaplan. 2000. *The Strategy Focused Organization: How Balanced Scorecard Companies Thrive in the New Business Environment.* Harvard Business School Press.

Rappaport, A. 1997. *Creating Shareholder Value: A Guide for Managers and Investors. Revised Edition*. Free Press.

Stern, J. M., J. S. Shiely, and I. Ross. 2001. *The EVA Challenge: Implementing Value Added Change in an Organization.* John Wiley & Sons.

Stewart, G. B., and J. M. Stern. 1991. *The Quest for Value: The EVA Management Guide.* HarperCollins.

Papers and Articles

Inmon, W. H. 2001. "SAP and the Corporate Information Factory." www.billinmon.com

McDonald, K. January/February/March 2002. "Understanding SAP's BI Strategy (Part I, II, and III)." *Flashpoint,* The Data Warehousing Institute.

McDonald, K. June 2001. "To BW or not to BW." *Flashpoint,* The Data Warehousing Institute.

Morris, H. 1997. "Analytical Applications and Market Forecast: Changing Structure of Information Access Markets." *Applications and Information Access Tools: Applications,* Volume 1, IDC 14064. /www.idcresearch.com

SAP AG 2001. "Analytical CRM." SAP white paper. SAP AG. www.sap.com

Supply Chain Council, Inc. 2001. "Supply-Chain Operations Reference-model: Overview of SCORE Version 5.0." SCOR, Supply Chain Council, Inc. www.supply-chain.org.

Wilmsmeier, A. 1999. "SAP BW in Action." *IntelligentERP.* www.intelligenterp.com/feature/archive/wilmsmeier.shtml

Standards and Internet Resources

Ascential Software Corporation. www.ascentialsoftware.com

COMPENDIT, Inc. www.compendit.com/offers/ka.htm

IEEE Meta Data. The Meta-Data and Data Management Information Page. www.llnl.gov/liv_comp/metadata/index.html

Informatica Corporation. www.informatica.com

Inmon, W. H. www.billinmon.com

Microsoft Corporation. www.microsoft.com

Molina, J. "The RAB Guide to Non-Stop Data Access." www.raid-advisory.com/rabguide.html

Object Management Group. www.omg.org

OLE DB for OLAP. Microsoft Corporation. www.microsoft.com/data/oledb/olap

OLE DB for OLAP. Frequently Asked Questions. Microsoft Corporation. www.microsoft.com/data/oledb/olap/faq.htm

OLE DB for OLAP. Business Information Warehouse. SAP AG. www.sap.com/partners/software

SAP-Certified Software Vendors. www.sap.com/partners/software/directory

SAP Help Portal. http://help.sap.com

SAP Service Marketplace. http://service.sap.com

SAP Service Marketplace, BW. http://service.sap.com/bw

SAP Service Marketplace, System Management.http://service.sap.com/system-management

SAP Service Marketplace, SAP Notes. http://service.sap.com/notes

Index

B

D

G

H

N

O

S

U